**The International Library of Essays in Terrorism**
*Series Editor: Alan O'Day*

# War on Terrorism

# War on Terrorism

*Edited by*

# Alan O'Day

*Greyfriars, University of Oxford, UK*

ASHGATE

Published by
Ashgate Publishing Limited
Gower House
Croft Road
Aldershot
Hants GU11 3HR
England

Ashgate Publishing Company
Suite 420
101 Cherry Street
Burlington, VT 05401-4405
USA

Ashgate website: http://www.ashgate.com

**British Library Cataloguing in Publication Data**
O'Day, Alan
  War on terrorism. – (The international library of essays in terrorism)
  1. Terrorism – Prevention 2. War on Terrorism, 2001– 3. World politics – 21st century 4. United States – Foreign relations – 2001–
  I. Title
  363.3'2

**Library of Congress Cataloging-in-Publication Data**
War on terrorism / [edited by] Alan O'Day.
        p. cm. — (The international library of essays in terrorism)
    Includes index.
    ISBN 0-7546-2424-2 (alk. paper)
      1. Terrorism. 2. War on Terrorism, 2001– I. O'Day, Alan. II. Series.

  HV6431.W36 2004
  973.931—dc22

                                                                              2004057428


ISBN 0 7546 2424 2

Printed in Great Britain by The Cromwell Press, Trowbridge, Wiltshire

# Contents

# Acknowledgements

The editor and publishers wish to thank the following for permission to use copyright material.

American Society for Public Administration for the essays: John Kincaid and Richard L. Cole (2002), 'Issues of Federalism in Response to Terrorism', *Public Administration Review*, **62**, Special Issue, pp. 181–92. Copyright © 2002 American Society for Public Administration (ASPA); William L. Waugh, jr and Richard T. Sylves (2002), 'Organizing the War on Terrorism', *Public Administration Review*, **62**, Special Issue, pp. 145–53. Copyright © American Society for Public Administration (ASPA).

Arnold Publishers for the essay: Colin Flint (2003), 'Political Geography II: Terrorism, Modernity, Governance and Governmentality', *Progress in Human Geography*, **27**, pp. 97–106.

Blackwell Publishing for the essays: Robert Warren (2002), 'Situating the City and September 11th: Military Urban Doctrine, "Pop-Up" Armies and Spatial Chess', *International Journal of Urban and Regional Research*, **26**, pp. 614–19; Dorothy Manning (2002), 'How Useful is the Economic Model of Crime in Assisting the War Against Terrorism?', *Institute of Economic Affairs*, pp. 21–28. Copyright © 2002 Institute of Economic Affairs; Peter Chalk (1998), 'The Response to Terrorism as a Threat to Liberal Democracy', *Australian Journal of Politics and History*, **44**, pp. 373–88. Copyright © 1998 Departments of Government and History, University of Queensland and Blackwell Publishers; Fernando Reinares (1998), 'Democratic Regimes, Internal Security Policy and the Threat of Terrorism', *Australian Journal of Politics and History*, **44**, pp. 351–71. Copyright © 1998 Departments of Government and History, University of Queensland and Blackwell Publishers; Ronald D. Crelinsten (1998), 'The Discourse and Practice of Counter-Terrorism in Liberal Democracies', *Australian Journal of Politics and History*, **44**, pp. 389–413. Copyright © 1998 Departments of Government and History, University of Queensland and Blackwell Publishers; Lawrence Freedman (2002), 'The Coming War on Terrorism', *Political Quarterly*, pp. 40–56. Copyright © 2002 Political Quarterly Publishing Co. Ltd; Martin S. Navias (2002), 'Finance Warfare as a Response to International Terrorism', *Political Quarterly*, pp. 57–79. Copyright © 2002 Political Quarterly Publishing Co. Ltd.

Cambridge University Press for the essay: Walter Enders and Todd Sandler (1993), 'The Effectiveness of Antiterrorism Policies: A Vector-Autoregression-Intervention Analysis', *American Political Science Review*, **87**, pp. 829–44. Copyright © 1993 American Political Science Association.

Chicago Journal of International Law for the essay: Walter Gary Sharp, sr. (2000), 'The Use of Armed Force Against Terrorism: American Hegemony or Impotence?', *Chicago Journal of International Law*, **1**, pp. 37–47.

Elsevier for the essay: Robert Gellman (2002), 'Perspectives on Privacy and Terrorism: All is not Lost – Yet', *Government Information Quarterly*, **19**, pp. 255–64. Copyright © 2002 Elsevier Science, Inc.

Guilford Publications, Inc. for the essay: Cathie J. Witty (2002), 'The Therapeutic Potential of Narrative Therapy in Conflict Transformation', *Journal of Systemic Therapies*, **21**, pp. 48–59.

MIT Press Journals for the essays: Barry R. Posen (2001–02), 'The Struggle against Terrorism: Grand Strategy, Strategy, and Tactics', *International Security*, **26**, pp. 39–55. Copyright © 2001 President and Fellows of Harvard College and the Massachusetts Institute of Technology; Ashton B. Carter (2001–02), 'The Architecture of Government in the Face of Terrorism', *International Security*, **26**, pp. 5–23. Copyright © 2001 President and Fellows of Harvard College and the Massachusetts Institute of Technology.

Sage Publications Ltd for the essays: Amitai Etzioni (2001), 'Implications of the American Anti-Terrorism Coalition for Global Architectures', *European Journal of Political Theory*, **1**, pp. 9–30; Yee-Kuang Heng (2002), 'Unravelling the "War" on Terrorism: A Risk-Management Exercise in War Clothing?', *Security Dialogue*, **33**, pp. 227–42. Copyright © 2002 PRIO; Nicholas J. Wheeler (2002), 'Dying for "Enduring Freedom": Accepting Responsibility for Civilian Casualties in the War against Terrorism', *International Relations*, **16**, pp. 205–25. Copyright © 2002 Sage Publications; Paul Kantor (2002), 'Terrorism and Governability in New York City: Old Problem, New Dilemma', *Urban Affairs Review*, **38**, pp. 120–27. Copyright © 2002 Sage Publications, Inc.

Oxford University Press for the essays: Sophia F. Dziegielewski and Kristy Sumner (2002), 'An Examination of the American Response to Terrorism: Handling the Aftermath Through Crisis Intervention', *Brief Treatment and Crisis Intervention*, **2**, pp. 287–300. Copyright © 2002 Oxford University Press; G. John Ikenberry (2001–02), 'American Grand Strategy in the Age of Terror', *Survival*, **43**, pp. 19–34. Copyright © 2001–2002 International Institute of Strategic Studies (IISS); Jonathan Stevenson (2001–02), Pragmatic Counter-terrorism', *Survival*, **43**, pp. 35–48.

Taylor & Francis Ltd for the essays: Saree Makdisi (2002), 'Spectres of "Terrorism"', *Interventions*, **4**, pp. 265–78. Copyright © 2002 Taylor & Francis Ltd; James J. Wirtz (2002), 'Counter-terrorism via Counter-proliferation', *Terrorism and Political Violence*, **14**, pp. 129–40. Copyright © 2002 Taylor & Francis http://www.tandf.co.uk/journals

The volume is made possible through the assistance of staff at the Harmsworth Library, University of Oxford and the aid of Miles L. Bradbury and Col. Helen E. O'Day.

# Series Preface

Acts of Terrorism have existed for centuries but since the late 1960s they have become more numerous and wide-ranging, giving terrorism fresh importance in the domestic affairs of countries afflicted and to the international community. Terrorism, or international terrorism, is not a constant but rather an evolving construct, manifesting itself in differing ways over time and in specific geographical contexts. Following the Cold War, terrorism has reared its head in places and in ways that were less common earlier. Presidents Reagan and Clinton in the 1980s and 90s stressed the importance of combating terrorism; President George W. Bush, too, recognised the threat. However, the attacks on the World Trade Center and the Pentagon on 11 September 2001, followed by incidents elsewhere, notably in Madrid on 11 March 2004, have given impetus to the study of terrorism in academic circles, among journalists and a heightened awareness by the general public.

A major problem for rigorous analysis of terrorism has been an absence of readily available, widely disseminated research and serious academic discussion. Many valuable articles have appeared in a range of academic and professional periodicals. Often these journals have limited circulations and even the great academic libraries of the western world, do not posses a full complement of articles. Thus the study of terrorism and the ability to offer university options in the field are frequently hampered by the absence of literature. This problem is vastly greater in the many small educational institutions. Even in libraries that do have a large number of the periodicals, the problem of searching out germane articles is demanding and time-consuming.

The series is directed, towards providing a partial remedy to this problem. It seeks to provide in a number of volumes, pertinent material for the study and understanding of terrorism, making these available to a wider audience. An important feature of the volumes is that the articles selected are intended to reflect various opinions and to afford a glimpse into the controversies about such matters as the very definition of terrorism, its various dimensions and future prospects.

ALAN O'DAY
*Series Editor*
*Greyfriars,*
*University of Oxford*

# Introduction

> Our war on terror begins with al-Qaeda, but it does not end there. It will not end until every terrorist group of global reach has been found, stopped and defeated . . . Americans are asking: How will we fight and win this war? We will direct every resource at our command – every means of diplomacy, every tool of intelligence, every instrument of law enforcement, every financial influence, and every necessary weapon of war – to the disruption and to the defeat of the global terror network. This war will not be like the war against Iraq a decade ago, with a decisive liberation of territory and a swift conclusion. It will not look like the air war above Kosovo two years ago, where no ground troops were used and not a single American was lost in combat. Our response involves far more than instant retaliation and isolated strikes. Americans should not expect one battle, but a lengthy campaign, unlike any other we have ever seen. It may include dramatic strikes, visible on TV, and covert operations, secret even in success. We will starve terrorists of funding, turn them one against another, drive them from place to place, until there is no refuge or no rest. And we will pursue nations that provide aid or safe haven to terrorism. Every nation, in every region, now has a decision to make. Either you are with us, or you are with the terrorists. From this day forward, any nation that continues to harbour or support terrorism will be regarded by the United States as a hostile regime. (President George W. Bush, 20 September 2001)

The 'war on terrorism' is a catchy – indeed catch-all – phrase to describe the determination of the United States and some allies to resist the terrorist onslaught. It differs from other issues emanating from terrorism by an American provenance and direction from the United States. This American focus is both a strength and weakness, giving it the impress of the most powerful nation but also making many others dubious about the ulterior motivations. The notion that the world was changed on 9/11, however, is in the view of Colin Flint (Chapter 11), US-centric. For many people outside America, 9/11 has had ephemeral significance.

In President George W. Bush's words, 'our enemy is a radical network of terrorism, and every government that supports them'. It was not concocted in the wake of 9/11. President Clinton's address to the nation on 20 August 1998 declared:

> Let our actions today send this message loud and clear: There are no expendable American targets; there will be no sanctuary for terrorists; we will defend our people, our interests and our values; we will help people of all faiths in all parts of the world who want to live free of fear and violence; we will persist and we will prevail.

Previously, Presidents Ronald Reagan and George Bush assailed terrorism against Americans. Yet, the attacks on the World Trade Center and Pentagon on 11 September 2001 certainly have given added thrust and universal pertinence to this war on terrorism. A problem of the war, though, is that its Americanized focus does not coincide neatly with the preoccupations of even its main European allies, excluding Britain. For many countries, commitment to the war on terrorism, at least as it is defined by the United States, has been less than wholehearted.

Unlike the Cold War, it is neither a battle against some ideology nor bounded by physical boundaries or conventional political units such as nation-states. The war on terrorism is the internationalization or, rather, globalization of previous wars. Terror is not a nation, and the enemies in such wars are not nations; any regime such as Libya simply by repudiating terrorism, can become an ally of the anti-terror coalition. It seems that regimes that continue to practise terrorism against domestic opponents qualify to participate in the wider war if they conform to certain norms in external affairs. The contours of the coming struggle are outlined in the United States Department of Defense document:

> The war against terrorism will be a protracted conflict. It is war in which there are no front lines and in which terrorism's practitioners have intentionally blurred the distinction between combatants and noncombatants. Terrorism differs from traditional combat because it specifically targets the innocent and, as a result, is particularly repugnant. Because each terrorist group and the challenge it represents are unique, [the] Department of Defense must work with the interagency counterterrorism community to develop a flexible response that is a mix of political, economic, military, and psycho-social capabilities, tailored to meet a broad range of challenges and threats. Terrorism is more than the bomb and the gun. It is a struggle that ultimately is fought in the political arena and, as such, is also a war of ideas and ideologies. Combating terrorism requires patience, courage, imagination, and restraint. Perspective is essential. Overreaction and bombast play into terrorist hands. Good intelligence, a professional security force, and a measured response are necessary. Most important for any democracy in its struggle against terrorism is a public that is informed and engaged, and understands the nature of the threat, its potential cost, and why the fight against terrorism is its fight too. It is how well the United States meets this challenge that will determine the winners, the losers, and the price paid by each. (US Department of Defense, 1997, ch. 9)

It is a prerequisite, Bush maintained in his address of 20 September 2001, that the successful prosecution of the war against terrorism will require the judicious use of 'every resource at our command – every means of diplomacy, every tool of intelligence, every instrument of law enforcement, every financial influence, and every necessary weapon of war . . .'.

As an observer puts it, following the military operations in Afghanistan that toppled the Taliban regime, new and projected phases in the war on terrorism raise the question of who are the proper targets of any military or police measures. Certainly, the US government met resistance in March 2002 when it attempted to persuade the United Nations and even the Western Alliance that enforced regime change in Iraq was part of the war on terrorism. Public opinion in the two leading members of the coalition has doubted Iraq's credentials as a suitable venue for the eradication of terrorism. Secretary of State Colin Powell's linkage of Iraq, al-Qaeda and 9/11 lacked credibility, even to the government of the United Kingdom. For many people within the Anglo-American sphere of influence and elsewhere, the test of clear and present danger remains firmly implanted. Whereas there was little contestation that Afghanistan harboured a lethal terrorist movement that had inflicted unacceptable damage on the United States and posed an evident danger to other nations, no similar consensus has been achieved on other nations such as Iraq, Iran or, until recently, Libya.

From another vantage-point Lawrence Freedman (Chapter 22) points out that it would have been possible to specify the enemy in terms of its ideology and objectives but instead the enemy is defined in terms of terrorism rather than just one group of terrorists. He observes that it is one thing to fight al-Qaeda as a particularly noxious form of terrorism but quite another then to feel obliged to take on all forms of terrorism, especially given the notorious problem of deciding what is to be included in this category. Freedman also warns that the war on terrorism may well continue to take the United States into the sort of operation it dislikes, without an enemy in the field to be annihilated or be obliged to surrender, into remote and inhospitable areas where struggles for local political power provide radical groups with the opportunity to define their identities and refine their tactics. The second Gulf War, part of the crusade against terrorism, exemplifies Freedman's hypothesis. The formal military campaign revealed the coalition in its most effective guise; the enemy was swiftly and decisively vanquished. But ensuing attempts to re-establish civil order exposed the limitations, in particular, of American capacity, while opponents of the occupation found an identity and purpose that did link local resentment to al-Qaeda. It has been the type of action that merits Freedman's warning.

Moreover, political rhetoric aside, it is evident that, though the great powers may enjoy longer-term assets in the war on terrorism, non-state terrorists hold an immediate advantage. They are difficult to discover, root out and disengage. Experience of the Taliban shows that toppling a regime can prove simple, but capturing or containing supporters is a much more complex task. As terrorism is a weapon of the relatively weak seeking to level the playing field, terrorists have the benefit of resourceful tactics, cunning, stealth and an impressive degree of operational flexibility. To date, the war on terrorism, rather than stemming the menace, has probably increased the recruitment, support and capability of Islamic terrorist groups. The call to battle has been a two-edged sword, with Muslim militants across the world becoming more responsive to the drums of war.

Another critical perspective is stated by Saree Makdisi (Chapter 18) who maintains that the war on terrorism names not a specific external enemy, a specific Other, but a general and omnipresent threat, of which Osama bin Laden happened to serve as a kind of focal point for a certain time. Unsurprisingly, American and European perspectives on the 'war' have not been identical. As Jonathan Stevenson (Chapter 14) explains, Americans have sometimes accused Europeans of being 'soft on terrorism', something that is true with respect to 'new' terrorism which he sees as groups not seeking to bargain but only to express their wrath and cripple their enemy. However, European nations have faced mainly ethno-nationalist, right and left-wing terrorism, and Europeans, particularly the British, have long suspected an absence of sincerity on the part of Americans and of US governments in supporting their efforts to limit and suppress ethno-nationalist threats. Not only has the United States been a source of finance for groups such as the Irish Republican Army (IRA) but there has frequently been a reluctance to extradite alleged terrorists for trial in the United Kingdom. In the new environment, targeting state sponsors of terrorism, as opposed to the terrorist groups themselves, poses a different set of policy challenges. On the whole, the United States is better prepared to face so-called rogue nations than to take on stateless groups in an undefined and nebulous conflict. Nation-states have assets that can be attacked, regimes can be replaced, but as al-Qaeda in Afghanistan demonstrates, a terrorist organization, even a relatively large and well-financed one, is elusive and able to hide and move operations to new locations at short notice.

The 28 essays reprinted in this volume consider aspects of that most amorphous of animals – the war on terrorism. They do not set out to provide all the answers, nor do they radiate a unified vision of what constitutes the war on terrorism; the essays begin from a range of political and intellectual outlooks. The essays as a group, however, pay significant attention to the difficulties of determining the limits and nature of the war on terrorism. The authors address several major themes within the war on terrorism: what falls within its perimeters, its shifting manifestations, implications, responses and future directions. Their analyses are not devoted exclusively to the war on terrorism and necessarily overlap with other topics – for example, defining terrorism, weapons of mass destruction and legal frameworks.

Several authors reflect on issues pertinent to the study of international relations, considering whether the 'war' is a new direction in American policy and global alignments. Ashton B. Carter (Chapter 26) notes that the challenge of catastrophic terrorism is destined to be a centrepiece of the field of international security studies. If security is understood to be the avoidance and control of mass threat, catastrophic terrorism must have a status that 'ordinary' non-mass terrorism never achieved. It is perhaps this element that distinguishes terrorism, particularly that experienced in Europe in the 1970s and 1980s, from the current war on terrorism. In Chapter 1 Amitai Etzioni argues that 'the 2001 anti-terrorism coalition presents a new architecture – the semi-empire – which is dominated by one nation (or a small group of nations) that pressures other nations to follow the course it sets, and has a limited number of missions' (p. 1). He speculates whether the coalition could expand to tackle other transnational problems also prophesying that an expanded alliance, or semi-empire, might gradually become more effective and legitimate over time. In light of the cracks already appearing in the coalition, there must be some scepticism about the prospects. At the very least, judgement must be suspended on the future of any new architecture arising out of the war on terrorism.

Etzioni's view receives affirmation from G. John Ikenberry's (Chapter 15) contention that, after a decade of drift, the United States has rediscovered its grand strategic purpose. The war on terrorism reinforces existing Western-centred international order and provides new sinews of cohesion among the great powers. He sees the campaign against terrorism changing the wider terms of great power cooperation. Again this early assessment merits the test of time. Furthermore, Saree Makdisi (Chapter 18) portrays the war on terrorism as a facet of American global dominance – the reassertion of political over an economic order that seems increasingly out of control. In this estimation the war is a calculated diversion from a greater, but unresolvable, dilemma. Viewing the war from a domestic standpoint, Robert Warren (Chapter 9) argues that, rather than a cause, the war on terrorism has served as a prism used to conflate and further legitimize dynamics that already were militarizing urban space. These include: the revision of long-standing military doctrine to accept and rationalize multiple missions within urban terrain; turning vast areas of cities into zones of video and electronic surveillance; and the prevention, repression and control of mass citizen political mobilization in cities. Thus, for him, the war is the crystallization of already existing trends.

## Location

The war on terror is seemingly global, and the USA and its allies have sought support everywhere, even in places that, to date, have posed little direct threat to European or American interests. Of course, the notion of national interest itself has also been developing; it no longer simply means the protection of territory or citizens alone but can include important assets such as oil or commercial interests. The major economies are so entwined in overseas commerce through the forces of globalization that any threat to these must have significant repercussions at home and for domestic economies. This is not an entirely new turn of events. There is an extensive literature on the motivations for nineteenth-century European expansion into Africa and Asia and informal control in South America in which comparisons are made between formal and informal imperialism. Trade and the flag have an extended legacy. However, it remains true that American determination to wipe out terrorism still largely excludes traditional ethno-nationalist forms that do not impinge on the international arena. Americans are more comfortable with confronting Islamic or left-wing terrorists than its other manifestations. Thus, Africa is particularly interesting for, apart from the northern flank, it has been marginal to the main theatres of terrorist action. No doubt with the benefit of some inducement, African countries overwhelmingly expressed their support for the American-led efforts on the war against terrorism shortly after the 9/11 attacks on New York and Washington, DC. Some African countries are reportedly sharing intelligence and coordinating their efforts with Washington to fight terrorism in Africa, and the Bush administration has actively been courting African governments to join the US-led anti-terror coalition. Bush administration officials note that Africa, with its large Muslim population, can play a pivotal role in solidifying support in Muslim and Arab countries. The frontline of the war, then, is potentially everywhere.

## Responding to the War on Terrorism

The war on terrorism is fundamentally a response to acts of violence but now has been assigned a proactive role as well. Threats alone would have not sufficed to unleash the counter-offensive. Several essays treat the implications of terrorism and the war against it, raising questions of preparedness, strategy and consequences. Barry R. Posen (Chapter 3) makes the germane observation that sound strategy requires priorities because resources are scarce. Even the United States, with its vast wealth, cannot engage in limitless and timeless actions. Sophia F. Dziegielewski and Kristy Sumner (Chapter 4) identify issues, such as impending threats of biological warfare, that can affect the previously open nature of the Western lifestyle. This turbulent environmental context has caused the Americans, in particular, unprecedented levels of stress. The authors maintain that the psychological effects of the terrorist threat are more intense and prolonged than reactions to natural types of disaster, giving them a higher degree of trauma. But, they do not ask why Americans should be more prone to trauma, if that is true, than the peoples of London, Madrid or Moscow – all cities that have had a more prolonged dose of terrorism over the past decades. Yee-Kuang Heng (Chapter 5) explores ways of dealing with a war that is rhetorical, urging that the experience of Afghanistan provides a means of understanding such a 'war' where enemies are elusive networks, where the aim is simply avoiding harm with no prospect of closure, and where success is defined more by non-events than by what can be seen.

Peter Chalk (Chapter 6), writing before 9/11, stresses that where the state fails to ensure that its response to terrorism is limited, well-defined and controlled, it is likely that institutionalized counter-terrorist policies will pose an even greater threat to the political and civil traditions that are central to the liberal democratic way of life. His theme is endorsed by Robert Gellman (Chapter 21) who assesses the Patriot Act's serious implications for privacy: many of the law's provisions expand the government's existing ability to intercept wire, oral and electronic communications. Chalk concludes that the effectiveness of the liberal democratic state's response to terrorism ultimately depends on its acceptability. It is therefore paramount that any solution implemented is made with due regard to the long-term impact that it will have on the wider process of liberal democratic life. Counter-terrorism typically falls into one of two categories – criminal justice and military models. In the former, he observes, terrorism is viewed as a crime with the onus of response placed squarely within the bounds of the state's criminal legal system.

In the latter, terrorism is viewed as an act of revolutionary warfare with the onus of response placed on the military and entailing the use of retaliatory strikes, campaigns of retribution and troop deployment.

The American Camp Delta at Guantonamo Bay illuminates the tension between the two modes. The detention/interrogation centre was created in order to place detainees from the war on terrorism outside the jurisdiction of the American or other national courts, so that justice could be implemented through unique military tribunals. It also explicitly rejected the claims of opposition participants that detainees should have prisoner of war status, thus disenfranchising their rights under the Geneva Convention. After an initial flush of enthusiasm, the procedure has predictably come under critical scrutiny from liberal democratic governments whose nationals are held (and potentially face punishment) in the hybrid mechanism. Many Americans, too, have doubted the legitimacy of the system, and recently the detainees have been declared to be within the jurisdiction of the federal courts. As Chalk observes, to be effective these measures must be acceptable both internally and internationally. It is not without significance that the vast reservoir of sympathy for the United States following 9/11 has increasingly dissipated into cynicism.

But where do the limits lay in the war on terrorism? In Chapter 8 Nicholas J. Wheeler argues that, while the Taliban and al-Qaeda are responsible for exposing Afghan civilians to US attacks, this does not absolve US political and military leaders of responsibility for their conduct of the war. While it may prove essential to develop fresh rules for a new form of warfare, it is clear that, to date, American attempts at formulating an innovative rubric have failed to meet with general acceptance.

Furthermore, as Ronald D. Crelinsten notices in Chapter 17, there is a post-Cold War tendency to broaden the counter-terrorism mandate to include other phenomena such as organized crime, drug-trafficking and illegal immigration. In the UK, Home Secretary David Blunkett uses the phrase 'internal terrorists' in reference to a widening theatre. This redefinition has important implications for democracy, both at the level of discourse and at the level of practice, Crelinsten observes. At the level of discourse, the plasticity of the word 'terrorism' and its application to a wide variety of phenomena is a form of claims-making activity by a variety of agencies fighting for budgetary allocations in an era of cost-cutting and deficit reduction. At the level of practice, the counter-terrorism mandate is being expanded to include the range of phenomena covered in the widening discourse and this, in turn, has led to a blurring of boundaries between internal and external security, police and military models of control, and public and private sectors. All this has an impact on the openness of government, the accountability of agencies of social control, the adherence to the rule of law in the fight against terrorism and related phenomena, and the possibility of informed consent by a public made fearful by the claims-making discourse as it is disseminated through the mass media. Similarly, M. Shamsul Haque (Chapter 20) turns a critical eye on the impact of new anti-terrorist initiatives on the fundamental rights and responsibilities of citizens and others, with special reference to public administration.

Terrorist attacks can have myriad effects. Paul Kantor (Chapter 7) places the destruction of the World Trade Center in the broader context of urban difficulties. He suggests that the problems of New York City are also found elsewhere: terrorism will pose similar challenges in other urban jurisdictions. Terrorism is combining with an older problem to change municipal politics. Yet, Jon Kincaid and Richard L. Cole (Chapter 10) anticipate little shift in distribution of powers; they foresee a highly federalized response to terrorism in the United States, but with intergovernmental cooperation. Colin Flint (Chapter 11) usefully notes that the research agenda on terrorism coincides with key themes of political geography – modernity, geopolitics, the state, representation and the public stance of geographers. There is much yet to be explored and learned through the various academic disciplines.

## Combating Terrorism

According to official US agencies, combating terrorism involves two sets of actions: anti-terrorism (defensive measures) and counter-terrorism (offensive measures). The latter necessitates principles of stability and support operations with an objective of neutralizing terrorist groups. Interagency action is required to combat terrorism. Intelligence is particularly important. International cooperation is increasing but, overall, it is easier to prescribe unity of effort than to achieve it. Identifying and capturing terrorists is difficult and entails tedious police and intelligence work. Martin S. Navias (Chapter 23) points to the wider context, observing that the money trail leading from the hijackers not only helped establish their political origins but also served to expose all too clearly the vulnerabilities of the international banking system to terrorist funding, money laundering and general financial logistics.

Counter-proliferation policies, James J. Wirtz maintains in Chapter 2, help to deter state-sponsored terrorism by bolstering the ability of US forces to retaliate with massive conventional force or with nuclear weapons. Counter-proliferation also probably helps to deter state-sponsored terrorism, although it has little effect on individual terrorists or independent terrorist networks. It reduces the prospects of terrorist incidents by helping to keep 'surplus' materials or weapons from entering black markets. But the downside is that, because counter-proliferation policies harden American or allied forces to terrorist attacks, efforts of this type channel terrorists toward softer (civilian) targets. Although it is often alleged that terrorism presents unusual obstacles, Fernando Reinares (Chapter 16) concludes that decline of terrorism in Western Europe, dating from the end of the 1970s onwards, coincided to a great extent with the development and implementation of sophisticated and comprehensive internal security mechanisms that, applied in conjunction with other measures of a political or juridical nature, have managed to narrow substantially the favourable opportunity structure available to these types of armed clandestine organization.

In a similarly upbeat tone Walter Gary Sharp, Sr (Chapter 13) contends that the United States is far from being impotent in its fight against terrorism – and it must continue to prevent and deter terrorism sponsored by non-state actors and states with the use of necessary and proportional armed force when states fail to cooperate and cause the law enforcement option to fail to protect Americans and US interests abroad. This, it might be supposed, offers a pattern for containing the present-day surge of terrorism, albeit one that necessarily implies a high-level continuous American, and possibility European, commitment. However, William L. Waugh, Jr and Richard T. Sylves (Chapter 19) speculate that a top-down, command-and-control approach to the war on terrorism, like that which the proposed Department of Homeland Security is intended to provide, may be counterproductive.

The debate about effective responses is continued by Henry W. Prunckun and Philip B. Mohr (Chapter 27), who believe that the level of activity of Libyan-associated terrorist groups declined after the US strike against Libya, and that this had a deterrent effect on international terrorism after 1986. In contrast, in a cautious assessment Walter Enders and Todd Sandler (Chapter 28) believe that the effectiveness of prevention of one sort of terrorism by defensive measures may lead to a rise in alternative risks. The raid on Libya in 1986, they point out, caused a number of different terrorist tactics to increase – a theme also developed by Wirtz in Chapter 2. A further aspect of the debate is opened by Charles T. Eppright (Chapter 12), who compares the US national security strategy's vision for counter-terrorism missions with the political realm in which conventional military forces and terrorists operate. Terrorist acts and state responses have differing political effects, which call into question the political utility of a conventional military counter-terrorist response. Eppright argues that terrorism's nebulous placement within the levels of war reveals another aspect of terrorism's different relationship to the political realm. Ultimately, this challenges the US national security strategy's conclusion that conventional military force used in 'punitive' or 'counter-terrorism' operations is an effective political response to terrorism. In addition, it reinforces the view that the United States and the West are better prepared for dealing with states that sponsor terrorism or situations where they can exercise direct military muscle than with the sort of terrorists targeted by Bush's 20 September 2001 war on terrorism.

**Conclusion**

Ultimately, the war on terrorism demands more than suppression; it demands the resolution of underlying causes. In Chapter 25 Cathie J. Witty writes that the transformation of the root causes of war, violence and hatred lies in integrating the analytical and transformational perspectives of conflict resolution and systemic therapy – particularly the narrative deconstruction of hate – with existing structural problem-solving models. From an arresting perspective Dorothy Manning (Chapter 24) applies the economic model of crime, concluding that it fits both secular and religiously motivated terrorism: policy-makers wishing to reduce terrorist activity should aim to devise policies which increase costs and/or decrease benefits to change terrorist incentives. The 'war' should continue as long as the probability costs to society incurred by terrorist activity are greater than the costs of abatement.

   The war on terrorism is a complex issue, demanding a range of techniques. In all probability the task of conducting the war on terrorism is rendered more difficult by the American insistence that it is global in nature. No doubt major states have long-term advantages in the contest, notably continuity of existence and preponderance of physical force, but, as al-Qaeda is showing, this is not a one-horse race. In a worldwide struggle, the terrorists are well placed to pick their targets and select their moments of opportunity. The recurrent major disruptions of international air flights provide sufficient evidence of what the mere whisper of an attack can do. Since 9/11, al-Qaeda has been adept at providing the Western world with sensational pieces of theatre. As Martha Crenshaw observes, the original conditions under which terrorism took place change as a result of the acts of terrorists. The jury is out – and perhaps has not even begun to sit – on the war on terrorism.

# [1]

# Implications of the American Anti-Terrorism Coalition for Global Architectures

Amitai Etzioni  *George Washington University, USA*

ABSTRACT: Given the rise in transnational problems and the inadequacy of the old, intergovernmental system, scholars are searching for a new, post-cold war global architecture. The 2001 anti-terrorism coalition presents a new architecture – the semi-empire – which is dominated by one nation (or a small group of nations) that pressures other nations to follow the course it sets, and has a limited number of missions. The article explores the possibility that the coalition could expand to tackle other transnational problems besides terrorism. Given the coalition's lack of scope and legitimacy, other options are explored that might be more effective and legitimate. The alternatives turn out to be either based on the old system (e.g. transgovernmental agencies), unrealistic except in the very long term (a global nation), or implausible (e.g. a global constitutional assembly). The article argues that an expanded coalition, or semi-empire, might gradually become more effective and legitimate over time.

KEY WORDS: *anti-terrorism coalition, global civil society, semi-empire, world government*

Ever since the end of the cold war there has been an intense interest in what new international architecture will follow it. This article asks whether the American anti-terrorism coalition formed in 2001 might be the beginning of (or a forerunner to) a permanent, new global architecture. In addition, can one learn from its limitations and defects which type of international architecture might provide a more effective yet legitimate treatment of transnational problems?

The discussion makes two assumptions that are not explored because their validity is taken to be well established and known. First, as the rise of transnational networks of terrorism highlights, the volume and severity of transnational problems are increasing. These problems include crime that is organized across national borders (above and beyond the already existing high volume of trade in narcotics);[1] trafficking in people, from illegal immigrants to sex slaves;[2] environ-

*European Journal of Political Theory* 1(1)

mental degradation;[3] the rapid infusion and withdrawal of short-term funds, which endangers the financial stability of even the largest economies; tax avoidance; the dissemination of weapons of mass destruction; genocide; cybercrime;[4] and the difficulty of regulating multinational corporations.

Second, the rise in transnational problems is prima-facie evidence that the existing system, which is centered around nation states and their representatives (either in intergovernmental endeavors or in international organizations), is not sufficiently effective. Indeed, nations' capacity to control their own affairs is declining, a point raised by the critics of globalization and recognized by its champions. To provide but one illustration: nations that object to material communicated over the Internet (e.g. violent material, pornography, and Nazi propaganda) have great difficulties in upholding policies that ban such material, which they previously were able to enforce.[5] When these nations seek to collaborate, they run into the problems the intergovernmental system (from here on, the 'old system') poses.

The old system is largely driven by intergovernmental agreements and projects (conducted by two or more governments) or international organizations governed by representatives of national governments, such as the World Health Organization and the International Labor Organization. The old system is unable to handle a high volume of significant activities because decision-makers must consult with their respective governments on most matters before they can proceed (or are instructed in great detail ahead of time, which greatly limits their maneuverability). Also, when it comes to global or even semi-global policies, so many different nations are involved, with divergent interests and values, that decisions are hard to reach. Exceptions include matters of relatively limited import and of clear value to all parties – postal arrangements, for instance, and arguably trade. However, on numerous other matters, progress is slow (compared to the pace of the increase in problems) and nations much more often agree upon declarations than they actually implement them.

Given the rise in transnational problems and the inadequacy of the old system, what post-2001 global architectures might prove to be more *effective* and yet *legitimate*? What implications does the anti-terrorism coalition have for such architectures? As the article deals with alternative futures, it is by necessity theoretical and somewhat speculative.

## The 2001 American Anti-Terrorism Coalition: A Characterization

It should be noted that the examination is limited to the first three months of the coalition's existence, as these lines are written in mid-December 2001. Usually such a short period would not justify an analysis. However, even if the coalition vanished immediately, its special nature would warrant consideration. Moreover, as will become clear, there are reasons to expect that similar coalitions might arise in the future.

The coalition is significantly *more global* than many if not all coalitions that preceded it, including those of the Korean War, the Gulf War, and peacekeeping missions in Bosnia and Kosovo (where NATO and Russia collaborated in SFOR and KFOR). It is, of course, more inclusive than the Allied Forces of the Second World War and much more global than the western alliance that was formed to counter communism during the cold war.

The scope of the coalition can be measured in two ways. One is fairly mechanical – simply comparing the number of nations that have agreed to participate or have actually made some contributions to its efforts to the number that have not. By this measure, almost all the nations of the world, including those that previously supported terrorists, such as Sudan, Iran and Yemen, have agreed to participate and have made actual contributions to the work of the coalition. For instance, Sudan has provided the United States with intelligence about terrorists.[6] Iran reportedly has recalled 700 intelligence agents and advisers from Lebanon, Sudan and Bosnia, where they were accused of aiding terrorist groups.[7] Yemen previously refused to cooperate with the United States in the investigation of the bombing of the *USS Cole*, but since 11 September has 'opened its files' to the United States, providing documents that shed new light on the bombing.[8] Fifty nations, including Egypt, Saudi Arabia, and Jordan, have arrested suspected terrorists at the behest of the United States, often working closely with the CIA.[9] Turkey has supplied troops for the fight against the Taliban, and Indonesia has offered to contribute troops.[10] Pakistan, once a major source of support for the Taliban, has provided much help to the coalition.

The scope of the coalition can also be assessed by its support among the most powerful countries; it has gained substantial and not merely nominal support from all the big powers, including Russia and China. Japan has committed non-combat troops and resources to assist the campaign. Although the campaign's military aspect is taking place outside NATO territory, NATO invoked very early on the article in its charter that stipulates that an attack against one member is an attack against all members.

One may argue that there have been numerous other situations in which global bodies such as the United Nations or conferences on issues such as the environment and human rights have reached unanimous resolutions. However, a major reason why such resolutions are so widely endorsed is that national governments know that the resolutions will be largely if not completely unenforced. When they have had the potential for more of a bite, it has been much more difficult to gain universal endorsement. For instance, only 46 countries have ratified the Rome Statute of the International Criminal Court.

Like all the other coalitions cited, the anti-terrorism coalition has been composed and *led* (fostered would also be an appropriate term) by the United States. As in all the others, it has used a mixture of diplomacy, normative appeals to the

11

*European Journal of Political Theory* 1(1)

peoples of the world's nations, covert operations, and the promise of economic aid and loans or the threat of withholding these, to form and sustain the coalition.[11] However, the anti-terrorism coalition has also engaged significant national interests of many nations, including key coalition members. (Reference is to national interests as perceived by the governments of these nations.) Russia has been seeking approval for its fight against Muslim insurgents in Chechnya whom it considers terrorists. China is concerned about Islamic radicals in its Xinjiang region. Egypt is among the score or more of nations that are struggling to keep radical Islamic groups that resort to means of violence – terrorists, to these regimes – under control. The Philippines consistently faces violence from two radical Islamic groups. Malaysian and Indonesian Islamic political groups are generally not militant, but there are some militant groups in these countries that aim to create Islamic governments.[12] India and Sri Lanka are also threatened by militant Islamic groups.

An unusual feature of the coalition is that it is composed of states fighting largely *non-state* actors (albeit supported by a few states) – terrorist networks with 'global reach',[13] said to be active in some 60 countries. This feature is of special interest for two reasons. First, previous coalitions were composed of some nations vying with other nations, which by definition makes it impossible for all of the world's governments to be on one side and thereby constitute a fully global coalition. Second, other pressing transnational problems also involve contests between national governments and non-state actors, such as drug cartels, traffickers in people, and polluting multinational corporations. As a result, some lessons might be gleaned from this coalition for dealing with these other transnational challenges. (It might be noted in passing that in numerous scholars' recent writings, non-state actors are treated almost exclusively positively, as actors who assist in the building of a global civil society. The discussion here focuses on non-state actors who are agents of disorder and conflict.)

Another distinct feature of the coalition has been the speed and scope of changes in *domestic* laws and policies it has engendered in several nations. There is a natural tendency to think about the treatment of transnational problems as involving international actions. Meetings at the United Nations, at NATO headquarters, in Geneva, and so on, although they occur within the space and jurisdiction of some nations, are, of course, meant to result in intergovernmental resolutions. Implementation then typically involves several national forces acting in another nation's space, such as Korea or Kosovo.

This has held true for the anti-terrorism coalition as well. However, members have made several significant and especially rapid and synchronized changes in domestic laws and policies in *their own countries*. These measures concern the balance between public safety and health (regarding protection from bioterrorism) and individual rights. Changes have been particularly drastic in the United States, where scores of new laws and regulations have been introduced.

Whether they are excessive or deficient, whether the government was already inclined to abuse its powers and violate rights or greater governmental powers have long been needed, is the subject of great differences of opinion. However, nobody questions that relevant American laws have been changed quickly and considerably. Significant changes have also been introduced in many other countries. The European Union introduced a community-wide arrest warrant.[14] Germany tightened its surveillance and immigration laws.[15] Britain expanded its anti-terrorism act.[16] France adopted a law that provides the police greater search powers.[17] The Indian government has placed before India's parliament an ordinance that would give the police sweeping new powers.[18] It is particularly relevant to the student of the ways nations may cope with rising transnational problems that these changes have occurred in a *semi-coordinated* fashion in several nations more or less simultaneously.

Finally, the coalition differs from several others in that, although it is an ad hoc and temporary one, it has set some relatively *longer range goals*. Unlike war-based coalitions, which are expected from the outset to disband once the war is won (e.g. in Korea, the Gulf, and Kosovo), the anti-terrorism coalition is built around the notion that the problem it tackles is complex and lasting and requires a longer run, global drive. There is no way to predict the future of the coalition; indeed, it may well have fallen apart by the time these lines are read, or may have greatly metamorphosed. It should be noted, though, that its stated aim was not to catch bin Laden or overthrow the Taliban, but to eradicate terrorist cells in some 60 countries. An approximate meeting of this goal will require some continuation of the coalition.

## What Kind of Architecture is the Coalition?

The discussion now turns to characterization of the coalition in analytical terms. If it were completely US-dominated, and most if not all the nations participated because they were pressured or threatened by the United States, and if it were lasting and broader in scope, it might be characterized as an empire, albeit a temporary one. Empires are defined as entities in which one member has a considerable amount of controlling power over the member-units.[19] Because membership in empires is not usually voluntary, and responsiveness to the needs of member-units is low, empires rely (by the definition followed here) relatively little on legitimation and draw much more on 'naked' power. Only a very few call for the United States to impose on its own a Pax Americana, the way Rome did on its world.[20]

Given that several big powers have a strong measure of self-interest in participating in the anti-terrorism coalition (granted that many actions, domestic and international, are driven by mixed motives), as do numerous smaller powers; given the coalition's limited scope and duration; and given that the United States has limited power over the many members of the coalition, one might refer to the coalition as a *semi-empire*.

*European Journal of Political Theory* 1(1)

Just as some may claim that 'semi' is too weak a term, others may argue that suggesting that the coalition has even an element of empire in it is too strong. However, the term seems justified because the United States is fostering a new world order, one in which terrorism will be actively suppressed in some 60 countries on four continents. It seeks the cooperation of numerous nations, but those who do not cooperate (e.g. Iraq) will be subject to pressure, including the means of warfare (as the Taliban have been in Afghanistan). Moreover, the coalition, but mainly the United States, is seeking to determine what kinds of national governments are to follow uncooperative regimes (e.g. in Afghanistan). Also, the United States actively promotes, through the CIA and other means, governments that support its policies and hold at bay their opposition (e.g. in Egypt, Jordan, and Pakistan). This is clearly a far cry from the global 'directorate' that some have suggested as a possible foundation for a new global order, which would be composed of a partnership of several big powers, more or less equal in their roles and power.[21] (Granted, some steps in this direction can be seen in recent plans to form a NATO of 20, or to include Russia in some of its decision-making – and not merely nominally – and in suggestions to restructure the UN Security Council to include Japan.)

One major attribute of the semi-empire at issue is that its scope (measured by the number of important transnational problems it tackles) is *thin*.[22] Although the anti-terrorism coalition is nearly global in its level of participation and the reach of its effects, it is narrowly crafted. At least, its stated missions are limited to stopping terrorism. Whatever legitimacy this semi-empire has acquired, which it needs in order not to rely only on its power base, is largely due to its narrowly constructed mission. Governments, opinion-makers, and citizens who strongly disagree about other matters and missions may recognize some merit in nations acting outside their borders, seeking to protect themselves from transnational terrorism. (This might be referred to as 'face legitimacy' which is based on the intrinsic merits of the action rather than on the ways the decisions to engage in it are reached.)

At the core of the semi-empire are *nation states*. No formation of a new kind of international body nor any formal surrender of sovereignty is involved. The difficulties involved in many governments making many joint decisions are here avoided by either the United States making most of them or by leaving them up to each nation – following pressure, encouragement, or other forms of inducement by the United States or other strong members of the coalition. This contrasts sharply with the procedures used in the first stages of the war in Kosovo, in which each bombing target had to be approved by a 19-nation committee – typical of the old system.[23]

International relations scholars compare unilateral and multilateral actions. It is often suggested that multilateral action is more cumbersome and in that sense less efficient than unilateral action, but at the same time more legitimate because the parties involved have been consulted and have concurred on the course of action to be followed. In these terms, the anti-terrorism coalition might be characterized as unilateralism-plus (the plus refers to limited consultation with coalition members and some attention to their considerations and sensibilities). In line with this analysis, one finds that, so far, the coalition has been rather effective but the legitimacy of its actions has been largely provided by its goals and has not by the ways decisions are made or the specific means that are being employed (e.g. extensive bombing, military tribunals, and targeted assassinations of leaders).

## Limited Futures

Given that the world is plagued by a large variety of transnational problems beyond terrorism, the question arises whether a global architecture might arise that is much broader (in terms of the problems addressed) and more legitimate than the American anti-terrorism coalition.

### 'Mission Creep'

A new global system might develop out of the American anti-terrorism coalition if it deliberately, or without full prior consideration, gradually expanded its missions. First steps in such a direction are evident in the movement toward 'nation building' in Afghanistan (that is, working to ensure that a country will not break into tribal war and that a united government will be formed, and generally helping it become a more integrated nation). This is taking hold even though, initially, the mission was to be limited to uprooting the Taliban and the terrorists and nation building was strongly opposed.[24] Coalition forces are being sent to Afghanistan, although both the Taliban and the terrorists have been largely banished, adding peacekeeping to the mission list. Also, some steps, albeit very small ones, are being taken to provide for economic and political development (some are even calling for a Marshall Plan[25]). A similar expansion of missions took place in the coalitions that acted in Kosovo and Bosnia, which were early and limited precursors to the 2001 coalition. Moreover, any expanded mission would likely propel further expansion because it is difficult to complete a mission without taking on additional tasks. As often noted, if a country such as Afghanistan is left in the same state of destruction and anarchy that led it to welcome the Taliban in the first place, it is likely soon to become a fertile ground for terrorists again – hence the call for at least some measure of nation building and economic reconstruction.

A much more significant candidate for mission expansion is for the coalition to act to limit the threat of the use of weapons of mass destruction by terrorists and by rogue states. This is an issue of particular interest to the United States, but other big powers and many small ones are also concerned that nuclear weapons and other weapons of mass destruction may fall into the wrong hands.[26] The 15

*European Journal of Political Theory* 1(1)

immediate concern is that terrorists might acquire such weapons, which would allow them to blackmail a big power or actually employ them, as bin Laden has openly threatened to do. Closely related is the fear that states may employ them against one another, such as India and Pakistan, or Iraq and Israel, or even one of these states against a superpower. Some of us have been warning about this danger for 40 years. However, the danger has become much more acute as the threat from terrorists has been added to that from rogue states, as the weapons have become miniaturized (to suitcase, vial, or envelope size), and as control over them has weakened following the collapse of the Soviet Union. Moreover, there seems to be specific evidence that the terrorists have been actively seeking, possibly even successfully, to acquire or build such weapons.

True, the big powers do not all have the same stake in this issue. The United States is much more concerned about being attacked than, say, China. However, other countries may be concerned that, if terrorists use such weapons to blackmail or attack another big power, they may be the next one under the gun as all major powers are vying with terrorists and terrorists have been shown to help one another. Also, these nations fear that if the United States made a major investment in an anti-ballistic missile defense, which they would be hard put to match, they could be subject to a unilateral attack by the United States.

Such a mission to curb the threat of weapons of mass destruction would entail numerous steps, including banning the sale of certain materials on the international market, which would be enforced by the coalition (somewhat in the way the United States has in the past pressured Russia and China not to sell missiles and plutonium to countries such as Iran and Iraq); paying laboratories and scientists trained in the production of weapons of mass destruction to engage in other activities;[27] and systematically pressuring nations to give up such weapons and allow inspection to verify that they do not possess or produce them. (Reference is to all but the big powers, although they, too, would scale back their production and stockpiles. They already allow some international inspection. The, at least initial, exclusion of big powers from the envisioned global requirements to destroy weapons of mass destruction is not based on a conception of justice or fairness, but on the fact that they are not currently considered the main threat and that it is impractical at this stage to expect them to submit to such a regime.)

The main difference between past efforts to the same effect and the ones the coalition may be drawn into is the much larger scale and scope of the endeavor and an increased willingness of the United States and some other nations to use military force to limit the spread of weapons of mass destruction, beginning with Iraq.

As control of weapons of mass destruction is a continuous rather than a temporary task, a major feature of the expanded coalition would be its lasting, standing rather than transient, nature. It would likely lead to further mission expansion. If the coalition were going to impose effectively a ban on the production of weapons

16

of mass destruction, it would have to field peacekeeping forces to guarantee the borders of small nations that face large conventional forces (such as Israel). To be effective, such forces could not be assembled ad hoc over the course of months (as was the case when Kuwait was invaded by Iraq) because small nations might be wiped out in short order. Hence, the mission expansion or creep would tend to favor positioning peacekeeping forces ahead of time in various parts of the world and storing there military assets for larger, backup forces.

Expansion to include still other missions related to order can also be envisioned. These could include tackling cybercrime, transnational drug smuggling (beginning with the opium smuggled out of Afghanistan), and trafficking in people, especially sex slaves. Another major direction in which the coalition might expand (as it metamorphoses) would be to add humanitarian interventions, the demand for which has been increasing in recent years.[28]

The United States has experienced a major change in its orientation toward international affairs, which needs to be mentioned here because, as the kingpin of the coalition, changes in its orientation are particularly significant. The 2001 campaign in Afghanistan has completed a process that started during the 1991 war in the Persian Gulf and continued in the subsequent campaign in Kosovo: it did not merely erase the Vietnam complex, but reversed it. Vietnam left the United States with many casualties, huge public dissent, and a failed mission, reinforcing strong, existing isolationist tendencies. The development of new technologies of war has allowed the United States to win the three recent campaigns, with next to no casualties, gaining wide public acclaim in the United States. These repeated successes have not only laid to rest the Vietnam complex but have greatly whetted the United States' appetite for international actions. The United States seems more inclined now to expand its overseas missions than it was previously, not merely in response to terrorism but also because of the changes in the technology of warfare and in its international orientation. It has moved again from semi-isolationism to interventionism.

With every expansion, the difficulties the coalition is most likely to face are those that would result from the inadequacy of its mechanisms for working out differences in the values and interests of the governments involved and of their citizens. The whole point of a semi-empire is that it makes short shrift of such consensus building because it relies to some extent on the face legitimacy of its mission – and on its ability to enforce its choices. However, the face legitimacy of several of the missions listed is much smaller than combating terrorism; the means used – say, in combating cyberpiracy or the illegal flow of people – are viewed very differently by different governments and peoples. Hence, it is safe to suggest that the more transnational problems the coalition took on, the more opposition it would evoke.

The difficulties would likely multiply if the coalition were somehow to turn to non-order-related issues, such as significantly increasing the enforcement of human rights or environmental protection, not to mention significant cross-

*European Journal of Political Theory* 1(1)

national reallocation of wealth. Given that the coalition has been composed and is largely controlled by the United States, it is difficult to envision it acting against what the United States' government and many of its citizens consider to be their interests and values. In addition, on such issues other members of the coalition have sharply conflicting values and interests, much more so than in matters concerning order, although here, too, the amount of conflicts is far from small. Regarding wealth, the difference between the 'have' nations (often, the power-wielders) and the 'have-nots' is particularly substantial. Also, in dealing with these non-order-related missions, the main objects of transnational policies would be nation states rather than non-state actors, which would, on the face of it, seem to undercut the possibility of a global coalition. (This does not mean that current operations under the United Nations, UNICEF, the World Bank, and many other international bodies such as the Red Cross, as well as national efforts such as peace corps, could not be continued or even expanded. These bodies, though, do not amount to a new world architecture and have not proven capable of coping on their own with the rising transnational problems.[29])

In summary, mission creep may occur, especially regarding select order-related issues. However, the more missions are added, the more exacerbated problems of legitimacy will become due to strongly divergent values and interests and the absence of mechanisms to work out disagreements, given the coalition's semi-empire nature. It is particularly difficult to imagine the coalition being expanded to deal with transnational problems not concerning order, especially social justice. The search hence turns to the possibility of architectures that could both deal effectively with a broad array of transnational problems, including non-order-related ones, and generate much more legitimacy than the semi-empire is able to marshal.

## Multiple Mono-Functional, Transnational Agencies

Another possible scenario, also grafted onto the old system, is that, in response to the pressure of increasing transnational problems, several thin transnational agencies could develop, each dedicated to one mission, that would each resemble the anti-terrorism coalition in the scope of its mission but be much less hierarchical. One transnational agency might seek to deal with the international environment, one with global public health issues, and so on.

Such an architecture has been called functionalist.[30] As described by Anne-Marie Slaughter,[31] each agency would be composed of networks of those national officials who work for the agencies dealing with the same missions in their countries. These officials would acquire or be granted considerable latitude so that they would not have to consult too closely with their national governments or be instructed by them about details. As a result, these agencies would be able to do much more than heretofore has been accomplished by typical intergovernmental bodies or international organizations.

Such functional transnational agencies would be an extension of informal networks that are said already to exist among government officials who serve in the same field and get to know each other personally, and reportedly seek to cooperate above and beyond their instructions.[32] Examples given by Slaughter include the Basle Committee of Central Bankers and cooperation between the Antitrust Division of the US Department of Justice and the EU's European Commission.[33]

In considering the possible effectiveness of such agencies, one notes that they face several serious difficulties. As long as nations maintain their sovereignty, they are likely to be disinclined to allow their representatives to work out transnational agreements and arrangements without elaborate prior instructions and continuous consultation. Otherwise, the results may well be outside the consensus worked out in domestic politics and in the institutions to which the executive branches of national governments are accountable, especially legislatures. As long as the license given to the officials involved is limited, there is not much that such transnational agencies can accomplish above and beyond garden variety intergovernmental endeavors.

Moreover, the less hierarchy there is among the nations involved (this being the main difference between the envisioned transnational agencies and the anti-terrorism coalition), the more difficult it will be for nations to follow a joint, coherent policy. In a thin semi-empire, the dominant nation (or nations) can set the course. Others either find it in line with their national goals or are offered incentives or pressured to fall in line. However, the more equal the participants become in their say over the decision-making concerning the shared course, the more national instruction and consultation is required, and the more difficult it is to set a course of action. (At issue is not merely that the process of instruction is slow and cumbersome and cannot bear much added traffic, but the values and interests of different nations are often incompatible. This may be true in a semi-empire as well, but in a semi-empire less powerful countries are pushed into acting partially against their values and interests.) The limits of the functional approach are reflected in the examples provided by Slaughter of transnational informal networks that might be seen as forerunners of the transnational agencies. These networks either involve few nations or deal with rather few and thin issues.

In short, although grafted onto the old system, either an expanded version of the anti-terrorism coalition or transnational agencies could provide more horsepower for coping with transnational problems. However, their capacity is expected to be limited by two factors: lack of legitimacy (especially in the case of the coalition) and the need to involve myriad national governments (particularly in the case of transnational agencies). The mind hence turns to examine whether there have been recent developments that point to types of architecture not based on the old system, and whether they might be more effective and command a higher level of legitimacy than the grafted-on designs explored so far. 19

*European Journal of Political Theory* 1(1)

# Steps Toward Global Crowning

## The 'Crowning' Issue

The term 'crowning' is used here to refer to two related issues: first, to the need for an institutional layer on top of nation states and inter*national* arrangements (because it is assumed that in any new world system nations would not disappear, but rather would become integrated into the new system); second, to the need for institutions in which value and interest differences can be worked out, in a way that is functionally equivalent to the way they are worked out in national legislative bodies and cabinets.

It ought to be noted that there are major differences of opinion among scholars about the way national polities work. Some see them as the coming together of special interest groups, which work out policies that serve them. The legislature – and more generally the government – serves as a sort of clearing house. The arrangements are voluntary and basically no sharing of values and affective bonds is required. This model suits well the existing old, intergovernmental system because, in principle, there is no reason that in this system the coalescing of interests needed to create a global policy cannot be worked out.

In contrast, the analysis conducted here relies on (but cannot justify within the limits of this article) the Durkheimian model that assumes that collective decision-making often entails imposing on various participants sacrifices for the common good (e.g. to protect the environment for future generations). If these sacrifices are not backed up by shared values and bonds, they will not be treated as legitimate and hence either will have to be effected through force (which moves back in the hierarchical, empire direction) or will not be effectively enforced. It follows that crowning entities, in order to encompass groups of nations, would have to possess some Durkheimian qualities: a measure of shared values and bonds. That is crowning presumes a measure of development of consensus within the public, which in turn entails some sharing of values and the development of an imagined community.

Because of the difficulty of envisioning a global society and government, especially one which commands such Durkheimian qualities, it has long been taken more or less for granted that these are impossible goals. Their implausibility has also been grounded in experience, as centuries of grand schemes to form world governments to ensure order, justice, or both have yielded only disappointments.[34] Hence, for the last several decades, most of the serious international relations literature has focused on other architectures than any form of global government.[35] However, over the same period, three major developments have occurred that suggest that the times invite a re-examination of the subject. First, nation states and the old system based on them have proven more and more inadequate for coping with transnational problems. Second, new developments have increased the potential for worldwide action and hence governance, including new communications and information technologies, a de facto lingua franca,[36] and greater economic links. Third, as has long been argued, the world might unite if it faced a worldwide threat that amounted to 'the moral equivalent of war';[37] the current threat of terrorism may qualify as such a threat. Thus, oddly, as international relations theory has increasingly taken it for granted that even thin forms of world government and society are utopian, conditions have arisen that may make moving in this direction possible. The discussion turns to examine developments that lay the foundations for architectures that would be more effective and legitimate than the old system, or the anti-terrorism coalition or thin transnational agencies grafted onto the old system.

## Supranational Decision-Making

Supranational decision-making provides a degree of crowning. Some supranational institutions have recently been developed on the regional and even the semi-global level, albeit to a much more limited extent.

One element of supranational decision-making is that decisions are reached by a governing body not composed of national representatives, a body that follows its own rules, policies, and values rather than being instructed by national governments. This often allows supranational bodies to move with more agility and speed and more broadly than decision-making bodies based on the old system.

Another element is that the nations encompassed by supranational entities – as well as their citizens and member-units, such as corporations and labor unions – are expected to follow the rulings of these bodies (rather than their requiring approval by the national governments whose people are affected, as is the case in the old system). In addition, supranational bodies may have some kind of effective enforcement capacity of their own, such as the ability to fine corporations within the member states directly or to order them to desist from some action rather than fining the governments or asking them to rein in the corporations. That is, supranational bodies have more power than traditional intergovernmental entities; indeed, supranationality presumes some surrender of sovereignty by the member nations.

The development of supranational decision-making in the European Union is well known and provides by far the strongest illustration of such an approach to date. Among the semi-global institutions that have some features of supranationality are two courts (the International Criminal Tribunal for the former Yugoslavia and the International Criminal Tribunal for Rwanda),[38] the Internet Corporation for Assigned Names and Numbers (ICANN),[39] the World Trade Organization (WTO),[40] and non-state bodies that provide transnational commercial arbitration, such as the International Chamber of Commerce International Court of Arbitration.[41]

Supranational decision-making, to the extent that it has been allowed to work, seems to have lived up to the expectation that it can handle a higher volume of

*European Journal of Political Theory* 1(1)

work than the old system (a point not documented here). However, it faces in all cases the same criticism: it is imposed, unaccountable, and undemocratic.[42] The reason is elementary: supranational bodies acquire some of the powers of national governments, but are not equally accountable to legislatures. ('Equal' is used because the EU Commission is accountable to the EU Parliament in some ways, but the EU Parliament is weaker than national parliaments.) Also, existing supranational bodies on the regional level, let alone on the global level, cannot draw on the Durkheimian qualities nations provide. The question then follows whether it is possible to transfer some national features (a community invested in a state, a common identity) to supranational bodies. Supranational decision-making per se is thus found to be an effective and potentially important building block of a new global architecture, but the rest of the building is missing.

## Regional Communities as Intermediary Steps and Organizational Levels

A direct transition from the old system – which contains some 200 nation states and an even larger number of communities – to a global state and society is hard to imagine, let alone bring about. For reasons spelled out elsewhere,[43] there is good reason to believe that if a global state and society ever did develop, they would be preceded by and based on regional groupings that would integrate several nations into a community and state (as some envision the European Union will do). Briefly, the reason for this is that consensus building becomes overloaded when large numbers of participants are involved, especially if there are significant differences in values and interests among them. Digesting some of the differences first within small groups, and then fashioning consensus among their representatives, is more workable. (One can even imagine three levels, the way local, state, and federal government works – having regional and inter-regional communities as stepping stones to a global one.)

Some have argued that the recent formation of regional communities such as the European Union may hinder the formation of a world government and society. It should be granted that this could be the case, especially if regional communities were formed on the basis of antagonism to other communities. However, there is no a priori reason that such antagonism must develop. (For instance, although the growth of the European Union has caused some minor tensions with NAFTA, it has caused no serious conflicts with the United States, Canada, and Mexico in international organizations such as the United Nations.) In effect, the opposite seems to be the case. Instead of having to negotiate with 15 (or 27) European countries, on numerous issues other countries and regional associations now can increasingly deal with one representative.

If more and more nations formed a number of regional bodies – a United States of Europe, a Union of Latin American States, of Southeast Asia, and so on – interactions among these communities would likely be significantly more productive than among 200 nations. This might open the road to the formation of a more encompassing community, a community of communities. (Note that the formation of the European Union itself benefited from the coming together of two blocs – the inner six and the outer seven – as well as from the pre-existent bonds among the Benelux countries.)

One can even imagine that the development of regional communities would be followed by supraregional blocs, as another intermediary step on the way to a global architecture. The Council of Europe acts to some extent in this way, encompassing both the European Union and eastern Europe (former members of the Warsaw bloc). Under this scenario, for example, a North American alliance might form a Western Hemispheric supraregional bloc with South America. These, then, might one day be incorporated into a global society and government. In contemplating such visions it is important to recall the obvious: as of now, there are only a few, with the exception of the European Union, very weak regional communities.

Regional communities are based on much more encompassing types of architecture than supranational decision-making, which is merely one feature of regional communities. To the extent that they develop legislative bodies, cabinets, and other accountability mechanisms, as well as values and bonds shared across national borders, they can both be more effective than the old system in dealing with transnational problems and gain in legitimacy. However, by definition, they deal with the problems of one region or another. Many rising problems, though, are global, and it is at this level that they will eventually have to be treated if they are to be dealt with effectively. The discussion hence turns to examine three alternative global rather than regional architectures that could develop in the world following the anti-terrorism coalition or as an outgrowth of it. The discussion proceeds by necessity in broad strokes because it focuses merely on a few select features of these designs. As the discussion deals with alternative futures, it is inevitably highly speculative and tests the extent of license the reader is willing to grant to the author.

## Alternative Future Global Architectures

### A Global Nation: The Whole Nine Yards

With time, measured in generations rather than years, one can envision a world of, say, 20 regional communities, further grouped into six supraregional ones, being crowned by a global government and civil society. It would have many of the features of a nation, which is often defined as a community ensconced in a state. That is, the evolving architecture would not merely have the powers of a state but also a core of shared values and would command a measure of loyalty from the world's citizens. These features are essential if what may be called a 'global nation' is to be able to contain conflict and legitimately impose burdens

*European Journal of Political Theory* 1(1)

on some parts of the citizenry for the benefit of others, as happens, for example, when wealth is reallocated. (The term 'global nation' is justified because it suggests that the global state would have to command some of the loyalty and possess some of the political legitimacy and value endorsement now commanded by nation states.)

Several scholars see some indication that the world has been moving in the direction of a global society, however long the journey. The development since 1989 of a very large number of international non-governmental organizations (I-NGOs), transnational networks, and transnational social movements[44] is widely considered to be laying the foundations for such a society.[45] The developing global society is said to be able to carry out some of the duties that would otherwise remain unmet, absent a world government (this notion is captured by the phrase 'governance without government').[46] A highly regarded scholar, Lawrence Lessig, believes that we are approaching the formation of a global society. He compares the development of American identity in the 19th century to the development of a world identity today, referring to Daniel Webster's pronouncement that he spoke not as a man from Massachusetts or the North, but as an American, which heralded the birth of a new, primary identity:

> We stand today just a few years before where Webster stood in 1850. We stand on the brink of being able to say, 'I speak as a citizen of the world,' without the ordinary person thinking, 'What a nut.'[47]

Others have pointed to the rise of transnational norms, laws, and courts to suggest that the rising global civil society is laying the foundations for a global state.[48] The growing worldwide respect for the UN Universal Declaration of Human Rights is also cited in this context.[49] Although all of these observations seem valid, few expect a global nation to develop in short order. This necessitates looking for other global architectures that might be put in place much more rapidly.

## A Constitutional Assembly: Jumping Forward

Just as some favored transitioning from Soviet socialism to capitalism and democracy in Russia over two years rather than waiting for a gradual transition, there are those who favor moving rapidly by first forming a global state (rather than waiting for the development of a global society) through a legislative feat. In this plan, a world government would gain legitimacy not from being the organic expression of an evolving world society, but from the process by which the government would be constituted and from its democratic procedures. The United World Federalists are among those who have taken this position.[50] Champions of a much transformed United Nations have developed similar models.[51] An often evoked image in this context is that of the American Constitutional Convention – that is, all the nations of the world would participate in forming the world government and would endorse the constitution formulated by a world assembly.

This architecture would include an executive branch that would be accountable to a world legislature (and, presumably, through it to the 'citizens of the world'),[52] which is an essential prerequisite for legitimacy, especially for a government engaged in a broad array of activities, including many non-order-related ones. A broad agenda would be likely because if the nations of the world were going to agree to be subject to a world government, various issues they consider important would have to be addressed. Because it is high on the list of concerns of many nations and people, topping the list of issues would likely be the reallocation of wealth between the haves and the have-nots – that is, issues of social justice. (Many specific issues now often discussed reflect this underlying matter, including loan forgiveness to poor nations, providing drugs either free or below market cost to developing nations, changing the terms of trade, and much else.)

If a world government could be constructed that dealt with a broad array of issues, in ways that at least the majority of the people (or nations) of the world found in line with their values and interests, and if it were the result of a voluntary coming together of nations (rather than being imposed by some superpower or directorate of big powers), it would likely be effective and might be considered legitimate. However, very few students of international affairs find such a development plausible, most certainly not in the short term. The Durkheimian assumptions mentioned suggest that a sense of community must precede a constitutional assembly. True, the European Union has recently agreed to call a constitutional convention in 2002, but only after two generations of community building, and it encompasses only 15 nations.

## A Gradualist Approach: Building on the Semi-Empire

Surely one can envision all kinds of still other global architectures; indeed, many have. However, these are typically either narrow in the scope of the transnational problems they aim to handle, or their requirements can only be met in the long term, leaving us with a high volume of pressing transnational problems largely untreated. Some envisioned courses of action are add-ons to the old, inter-governmental system and hence are constrained by its limitations – for example, formulating additional international agreements. Others require expansion of supranational decision-making and of organizations that could serve as building blocks for the construction of a global nation, but their development on the global level cannot be much accelerated as long as people's prime loyalties and sense of identity are centered around their respective nation states. I-NGOs are building blocks for a global civil society, but they are particularly unsuited for treating transnational order-related problems.[53]

The mind, then, turns back to the expanded semi-empire model – an out-

25

*European Journal of Political Theory* 1(1)

growth of the anti-terrorism coalition or some future one composed along similar lines. As we have seen, it could be formed in short order because it initially
would be limited to missions that many national governments have a serious
interest in, would deal largely with non-state actors, and would be based on a
model that, so far at least, has been effective. Whether such a coalition (despite
likely changes in composition) could be made to last, and its missions much
expanded, is far from a foregone conclusion, but as long as one superpower (in
conjunction with some other powers) is willing to undergird the coalition with
economic and military means, it might well have some staying power.

An expanded semi-empire might, gradually, grow less hierarchical and more
legitimate. This suggestion is more than merely an expression of optimism.
Historically, ever since the advent of mass education and the development of
popular media, it has become increasingly difficult to lock people out of politics.
Empires have been dismantled and there have been movements in numerous
parts of the world to move toward less authoritarian governments (in Russia,
China, etc.) and less hierarchical global systems (especially since the end of the
cold war). Indeed, even in previous eras, nations that were initially formed
through the power of one state (such as Prussia in the formation of Germany)
eventually democratized. The United States has granted non-property-holders
the right to run for office, women the right to vote, and has ensured that minorities have de jure and largely de facto the right to vote. All this is not to suggest
that democratization in any one country, and surely not in any global organization, is nearly ideal. The argument is merely that, whenever empires or semi-
empires with broad agendas have been formed, over time they have generated
pressures that have made them gradually less hierarchical and more accountable
than they were at their starting points.

I cannot stress enough that I do not advocate starting with a global semi-
empire and improving upon it; I merely point out that the more alarmed one is
about transnational order-related problems, the more one will be inclined to
consider it, despite its considerable normative failings. Moreover, there is little
reason to doubt that the broader the scope of the missions the coalition took on,
the more its lack of accountability and hence legitimacy would stand out, which
would create forces that would work to change it. Also, many of these missions
would entail not merely tackling non-state actors (backed by a very few nations,
such as those that earn a good part of their income from the drug trade), but
imposing order among nations or on nations to achieve goals such as preventing
genocide. Such missions would directly confront the cornerstone of the old system – national sovereignty – and hence would lead to an intensified quest for new
architectures that might provide greater legitimacy for some kind of a new world
order. That is, a semi-empire might generate forces that would – gradually – push
toward the global nation architecture. In the long run, an architecture like that
of the coalition could only continue to expand its scope (especially dealing with
important, non-order-related transnational problems) and enhance its stability if

simultaneously efforts were made to develop the kind of social and political foundations on which a global society and government could eventually rest. Although such developments could take a very long time to mature, progress in that direction – say, via changes in the membership of the UN Security Council and in the role of the UN General Assembly and via the creation of new world courts, paralleled by an increasing global normative consensus on the issues at hand[54] – could move the semi-empire toward a more accountable and legitimate architecture.

## Conclusion

The old, international system has been found to be inadequate for dealing with rising transnational problems. The 2001 American anti-terrorism coalition presents a new attempt to foster order in the post-cold war world. It may be characterized as a semi-empire, thin in mission, effective, but without account-ability to any global body. Its legitimacy is thus limited to that provided by the nature of its mission. The quest for global architectures that are able to deal with a much broader scope of transnational problems than terrorism and that are much more accountable leads one to consider architectures that are either expected to be very slow to develop (a global nation, building on the evolution of supranational institutions and communities) or next to impossible to bring about (a world constitutional assembly leading to a world government). The mind hence turns to the possibility that the coalition may gradually expand the scope of its missions (initially, mainly to order-related ones), which seems plausible. Such an expansion might engender forces that would gradually push toward con-version to a more accountable global architecture.

### Post Hoc

This article was written in December 2001. Looking at the same coalition in May 2002, it may appear that it is already waning given mounting criticism of the way in which the United States is conducting the war against terrorism and wide opposition to attacking Iraq. However, as discussed in the article, even if the coalition vanishes, it still will deserve attention, including, of course, examining why it did not stabilize and transform into a more legitimate architecture.

I should add, though, that most countries continue to collaborate with the United States in the war against terrorism, including in their own territory. In addition, it is not completely obvious that, if Iraq is liberated and its weapons of mass destruction are removed, those countries now opposed to such an intervention will not welcome it after the fact, which might lead to further expansion of the scope of the missions of the coalition.

### Acknowledgements

I am greatly indebted to Andrew Volmert for numerous suggestions.                         27

### Notes

1. National Intelligence Council (2000) 'Global Trends 2015: A Dialogue about the Future with Nongovernment Experts', December, available at: http://www.cia.gov/cia/publications/globaltrends2015/index.html (accessed 13 Dec. 2001); James H. Mittelman and Robert Johnston (1999) 'The Globalization of Organized Crime, the Courtesan State, and the Corruption of Civil Society', *Global Governance* 5(1): 103–26.

2. Joseph Kahn and Judith Miller (2000) 'Getting Tough on Gangsters, High Tech and Global', *New York Times* (15 Dec.).

3. Intergovernmental Panel on Climate Change (2001) 'Third Assessment Report–Climate Change 2001', available at: http://www.ipcc.ch/ (accessed 13 Dec. 2001).

4. John Schwartz (2001) 'Securing the Lines of a Wired Nation', *New York Times* (4 Oct., final edn).

5. See David R. Johnson and David Post (1996) 'Law and Borders: The Rise of Law in Cyberspace', *Stanford Law Review* 48 (May): 1367–1402; Lawrence Lessig (1999) *Code, and Other Laws of Cyberspace*. New York: Basic Books; on recent cooperative efforts to control Internet pornography, see Warren Hoge (2001) '19 Countries Join in Raids on Internet Pornography', *New York Times* (29 Nov.).

6. James Risen and Tim Weiner (2001) 'CIA is Said to have Sought Help from Syria', *New York Times* (30 Oct., final edn).

7. Bryan Bender (2001) 'US Welcomes Support from its Former Foes', *Boston Globe* (11 Nov.).

8. Bob Drogin and Josh Meyer (2001) 'Yemen Aiding Terror Inquiry', *Los Angeles Times* (17 Oct.).

9. Bob Woodward (2001) '50 Countries Detain 360 Suspects at CIA's Behest', *Washington Post* (22 Nov.); also, Alan Sipress (2001) '55 Nations Endorse Measures to Fight Terrorism', *Washington Post* (5 Dec.).

10. Patrick E. Tyler (2001) 'Rebels in Control in Kabul as Taliban Troops Retreat', *New York Times* (14 Nov.); Harry Sterling (2001) 'Turkey Takes Risk in Joining Allies', *The Gazette* (Montreal, 17 Nov.).

11. Paul Blustein (2001) 'Aid to Turkey Raising Issue of Motive', *Washington Post* (23 Nov.); Christopher Cooper (2001) 'Allies in War on Terror Get a Helping of U.S. Largess', *Wall Street Journal* (12 Dec.).

12. Shefali Rekhi (2001) 'Web of Terror', *Straits Times* (Singapore, 11 Nov.); Brendan Pereira (2001) 'KL Signals it's No More a Safe Haven', *Straits Times* (Singapore, 27 Nov.).

13. This term was used by President Bush to exclude groups that are fighting only for national liberation.

14. Alison O'Connor (2001) 'Leaders Expected to Agree on European Arrest Warrant', *Irish Times* (14 Dec.); (2001) 'Member States Agree Thirty Crimes for EU Arrest Warrant', *European Report* (17 Nov.).

15. Bertrand Benoit and Margaret Heckel (2001) 'Berlin Deal on Security Measures', *Financial Times* (29 Oct., London edn 2); Steven Erlanger (2001) 'German Cabinet Supports New Immigration Laws', *New York Times* (8 Nov., final edn).

16. Paul Waugh (2001) 'Terror Suspects to be Rounded Up under New Law', *Independent* (London, 15 Dec.).

17. Peter Ford (2001) 'European Nations Broaden Police Powers', *Christian Science Monitor* (15 Nov.).

18. Celia W. Dugger (2001) 'India, Too, Weighs Antiterror Measure against Liberties', *New York Times* (22 Nov.).

19. Amitai Etzioni (2001) *Political Unification Revisited: On Building Supranational Communities*, pp. 7–8. Lanham, MD: Lexington Books.

20. Max Boot (2001) 'The Case for American Empire', *Weekly Standard* (15 Oct.); Charles Krauthammer (2001) 'The Real New World Order: The American Empire and the Islamic Challenge', *Weekly Standard* (12 Nov.); cf. Charles Kupchan who argues that the Pax Americana is already over: (1999) 'Life after Pax Americana', *World Policy Journal* 16(3): 20–7.

21. For discussion, see Kupchan (n. 21), 26.

22. Robert O. Keohane (2001) 'Governance in a Partially Globalized World', *American Political Science Review* 95(1): 2–3.

23. Michael R. Gordon (1999) 'Allied Air Chief Stresses Hitting Belgrade Sites', *New York Times* (13 May, final edn); Blaine Harden (1999) 'A Long Struggle that Led Serb Leader to Back Down', *New York Times* (6 June, final edn).

24. During his campaign, then-Governor George W. Bush vigorously derided the idea of nation building.

25. Gordon Brown (2001) 'Marshall Plan for the Next 50 Years', *Washington Post* (17 Dec., final edn); Lee Walczak and Stan Crock (2001) 'Winning the Peace', *Business Week* (3 Dec.); Michael Hirsh (2001) 'Give More U.S. Aid . . .', *Newsweek* (8 Oct.).

26. Kai Bird and Martin Sherwin (2001) 'The First Line against Terrorism', *Washington Post* (12 Dec.); Daniel Schorr (2001) 'Dust Off Those Reports on Nuclear Threats', *Christian Science Monitor* (23 Nov.).

27. Dick Lugar (2001) 'Eye on a Worldwide Weapons Cache', *Washington Post* (6 Dec., final edn); David S. Broder (2001) 'Safeguard Russia's Nukes', *Washington Post* (25 Nov., final edn).

28. David Rieff (1999) 'A New Age of Liberal Imperialism', *World Policy Journal* 16(2): 1–10; Rieff (2000) 'The Crusaders: Moral Principles, Strategic Interests, and Military Force', *World Policy Journal* 17(2): 39–47.

29. Etzioni (n. 20), pp. viii–xvi.

30. See David Mitrany (1943) *A Working Peace System*, London: Royal Institute of International Affairs.

31. Anne-Marie Slaughter (1997) 'The Real New World Order', *Foreign Affairs* 76 (Sept./Oct.): 183–97.

32. Robert O. Keohane and Joseph S. Nye (1974) 'Transgovernmental Relations and International Organizations', *World Politics* 27(1): 39–62.

33. Slaughter (n. 31), 190.

34. *Encyclopedia of Government and Politics*, s.v. 'international relations'; *World Encyclopedia of Peace*, 2nd edn, s.v. 'world government'.

35. See e.g. James N. Rosenau and Ernst-Otto Czempiel (eds) (1992) *Governance without Government: Order and Change in World Politics*. Cambridge: Cambridge University Press; Keohane and Nye (n. 32); Jessica Mathews (1997) 'Power Shift', *Foreign Affairs* 76 (Jan./Feb.): 50–66.

36. Joshua A. Fishman (1998–9) 'The New Linguistic Order', *Foreign Policy* 113 (Winter): 26.

37. William James (1968) 'The Moral Equivalent of War', in Leon Bramson and George W. Goethals (eds) *War: Studies from Psychology, Sociology, Anthropology*, pp. 21–31. 2nd edn, New York: Basic Books.

38. On the nature of the tribunals, their powers and procedures, see Sean D. Murphy (1999) 'Progress and Jurisprudence of the International Criminal Tribunal for the Former Yugoslavia', *American Journal of International Law* 93 (Jan.): 75–9; Radmila May (1999) 'The Yugoslav War Crimes Tribunal: Part Two', *Contemporary Review* 275 (Oct.): 174–9.

39. A. Michael Froomkin (2000) 'Wrong Turn in Cyberspace: Using ICANN to Route
    Around the APA and the Constitution', *Duke Law Journal* 50 (Oct.): 17–86.
40. Alec Stone Sweet (1997) 'The New GATT: Dispute Resolution and Judicialization of the
    Trade Regime', in Mary L. Volcansek (ed.) *Law Above Nations: Supranational Courts and
    the Legalization of Politics*, p. 139. Gainesville, FL: University of Florida Press. Mary L.
    Volcansek (1997) 'Supranational Courts in a Political Context', ibid. pp. 1–19.
41. Karsten Ronit and Volker Schneider (1999) 'Global Governance through Private
    Organizations', *Governance: An International Journal of Policy and Administration* 12 (July):
    243–66; Christopher R. Drahozal (2000) 'Commercial Norms, Commercial Codes, and
    International Commercial Arbitration', *Vanderbilt Journal of Transnational Law* 33 (Jan.):
    79–146.
42. See e.g. Joseph S. Nye, Jr. (2001) 'Globalization's Democratic Deficit: How to Make
    International Institutions More Accountable', *Foreign Affairs* 80(4): 2–6.
43. Etzioni (n. 20), pp. xliv–xlix.
44. See Lester M. Salamon (1994) 'The Rise of the Nonprofit Sector', *Foreign Affairs* 73
    (July/Aug.): 109; Mathews (n. 35); Peter Spiro (1995) 'New Global Communities:
    Nongovernmental Organizations in International Decision-Making Institutions',
    *Washington Quarterly* 18 (Winter): 45–56; and James N. Rosenau (1995) 'Governance in
    the Twenty-first Century', *Global Governance* 1 (Winter): 13–43.
45. Ronnie D. Lipschutz (1992) 'Reconstructing World Politics: The Emergence of Global
    Civil Society', *Millennium* 21 (Winter): 389–420; Paul Wapner (1997) 'Governance in
    Global Civil Society', in Oran R. Young (ed.) *Global Governance: Drawing Insights from the
    Environmental Experience*, pp. 65–84. Cambridge, MA: MIT Press; cf. John Boli and
    George M. Thomas (1997) 'World Culture in the World Polity: A Century of
    International Non-Governmental Organization', *American Sociological Review* 62(2):
    171–90.
46. See Rosenau and Czempiel (n. 35).
47. Lessig (n. 5), p. 226.
48. Joseph H.H. Weiler (2000) 'The Democracy Deficit of Transnational Governance: What
    Role for Technology?' paper presented at the International Political Science Association
    congress in Quebec City, 1–5 Aug.; Paul B. Stephan (2000) 'International Governance
    and American Democracy', *Chicago Journal of International Law* 1 (Fall): 237–56;
    Laurence R. Helfer and Anne-Marie Slaughter (1997) 'Toward a Theory of Effective
    Supranational Adjudication', *Yale Law Journal* 107 (Nov.): 273–328; Slaughter (2000)
    '40th Anniversary Perspective: Judicial Globalization', *Virginia Journal of International
    Law* 40 (Summer): 1103–23.
49. Mary Ann Glendon (2001) *A World Made New: Eleanor Roosevelt and the Universal
    Declaration of Human Rights*. New York: Random House.
50. Ernest S. Lent (1955) 'The Development of United World Federalist Thought and
    Policy', *International Organization* 9(4): 486–501.
51. Grenville Clark and Louis B. Sohn (1958) *World Peace through World Law*. Cambridge,
    MA: Harvard University Press.
52. Ibid.
53. Amitai Etzioni (2001) 'Beyond Transnational Governance', *International Journal* 56(4):
    595–610.
54. On cross-national moral dialogues see Amitai Etzioni (1996) 'The Final Arbiters of
    Community's Values', ch. 8 in *The New Golden Rule: Community and Morality in a
    Democratic Society*, pp. 217–57. New York: Basic Books.

# [2]

# Counter-terrorism via Counter-proliferation

## JAMES J. WIRTZ

Do counter-proliferation policies help or hinder efforts at stopping terrorists from using chemical, biological, nuclear or radiological (CBNR) weapons? Counter-proliferation bounds the terrorist threat by reducing the vulnerability of US forces, allied military units and even civilian populations to terrorist attack. It helps to deter state-sponsored terrorism by bolstering the ability of US forces to retaliate with massive conventional force or with nuclear weapons. Counter-proliferation also probably helps to deter state-sponsored CBNR terrorism, although it has little effect on individual terrorists or independent terrorist networks. It reduces the prospects of terrorist incidents by helping to keep 'surplus' materials or weapons from entering black markets. Because counter-proliferation policies harden US or allied forces to terrorist attacks, however, counter-proliferation efforts might channel terrorists toward softer (civilian) targets.

Does US counter-proliferation policy or the concept of counter-proliferation help prevent terrorists from launching chemical, biological, nuclear or radiological attacks?[1] Is there a relationship between US counter-proliferation and counter-terrorism policies?

The answers to these questions are not at all obvious. Counter-proliferation and counter-terrorism cut across existing conceptual, policy and organizational boundaries. Identifying relationships between counter-terrorism and counter-proliferation thus represents a research question of immediate theoretical and policy significance, especially since some analysts believe that terrorists want to arm themselves with nuclear, chemical or biological weapons.[2]

Serious technical and operational obstacles will limit the ability of terrorists to employ radiological, chemical or biological weapons to generate mass casualties and a classic social science debate exists about whether preparing for the use of weapons of mass destruction (WMD) by terrorists is worth the opportunity costs involved.[3] But the destruction of the World Trade Center demonstrates that mass casualty terrorism has arrived. CBNR weapons might be increasingly attractive to terrorist groups, especially if they want to launch attacks that replicate or top the level of death and destruction that was achieved on September 11, 2001.

Both officials and theorists treat counter-proliferation and counter-terrorism as separate issues. Counter-proliferation largely deals with the struggle between those militaries or sovereign states that want to acquire, threaten to use or actually employ chemical, biological or nuclear weapons to achieve political or military objectives, and those that want to stop them. Counter-terrorism is a term generally used to describe the efforts of states against non-state actors (criminal organizations, separatist groups, fanatics, etc.) that intend or try to use violence against civilian targets to achieve political objectives or to create death and destruction for ideological or millenarian reasons.

This theoretical and policy compartmentalization is in turn reflected by the division of responsibility for counter-terrorism and counter-proliferation among competing organizations within the US government, although it is too early to tell if and how the new homeland defense organization and anti-terrorist initiatives launched in the aftermath of the September 2001 attacks will integrate these responsibilities.

The intelligence community, police agencies and special operations units are generally concerned with preventing or responding to terrorist attacks against US interests at home or abroad. By contrast, counter-proliferation is a Department of Defense (DoD) activity that is intended to eliminate or contain the threat posed by WMD primarily to US military forces.[4] Recent efforts to evaluate the WMD threat treat US counter-terrorism and counter-proliferation policy as separate topics, although the 2001 Quadrennial Defense Review (QDR), redrafted in the wake of the September 2001 terrorist attacks, highlights the relationship between DoD and the newly created Office of Homeland Security.[5]

Even though theoretical concepts and bureaucratic preferences can explain why no one has asked how counter-proliferation contributes to or detracts from counter-terrorism efforts, it is equally clear that no good logical or empirical reason emerges to dismiss the issue out of hand. In its December 1999 report to President Clinton, for example, the Advisory Panel to Assess Domestic Response Capabilities for Terrorism Involving Weapons of Mass Destruction, chaired by James Gilmore (hereafter referred to as the Gilmore report), offered judgments about the nature of the terrorist threat. These judgements were based on the presence of an effective US counter-proliferation capability, although Gilmore and his colleagues failed to note specifically the way counter-proliferation helped to constrain the terrorist threat.[6]

Theory, policy and organization have blinded us to the way that US counter-proliferation efforts help to deter or prevent chemical, biological and nuclear terrorism. Common cognitive biases also have slowed widespread recognition of the negative interaction between counter-proliferation and counter-terrorism policies and of the tradeoffs that might have to be made between these two policies. Individuals often find it difficult to recognize the opportunity costs and unintended consequences produced by the policies they advocate and adopt. They also find it difficult to see how well-intentioned policies can produce negative consequences.[7]

Counter-proliferation and counter-terrorism are related in at least four ways.[8] First, counter-proliferation policy has bounded the terrorist threat by cutting supplies to black markets and by reducing the incentives for state sponsorship of WMD terrorism. Second, superior US conventional military capabilities, which are bolstered in several ways by counter-proliferation policies, force determined US adversaries to seek asymmetric responses, including terrorism. To the extent that counter-proliferation policies harden US military units and installations to terrorist attack, counter-proliferation also might channel terrorists toward civilian targets.

Third, US counter-proliferation efforts address key allied vulnerabilities to terrorism involving weapons of mass destruction, further bounding the terrorist threat. Fourth, potential policy and budgetary tradeoffs are looming between counter-proliferation and a major component of counter-terrorism policy, consequence management (the protection of civilian populations from weapons effects following a successful terrorist attack).

The increase in homeland defense efforts following the terrorist attacks against the World Trade Center and Pentagon will only exacerbate the need for tradeoffs between counter-proliferation and consequence management. This article explores each of these claims and then concludes by offering some observations about the relationship between counter-proliferation and counter-terrorism.

## Counter-proliferation and the Limits of State-Sponsored Terrorism

Current US counter-proliferation policy reflects the guidance laid out in the May 1997 Quadrennial Defense Review (QDR), which estimated that chemical or biological weapons were likely to be used in future conflicts.[9] The 1997 QDR called upon the Defense Department to undertake two initiatives in response to this threat estimate. First, the Defense Department was to institutionalize counter-proliferation by using the concept as an organizing principle in every facet of military activity. US forces were to prepare to operate in a WMD environment. Second, Defense was instructed to 'internationalize' counter-proliferation to encourage allies and potential coalition partners to train, equip and prepare their forces to operate alongside US units in a nuclear, chemical, or biological warfare environment.[10] Counter-proliferation is a multifaceted enterprise that embodies DoD efforts to reduce and counter the threat posed by weapons of mass destruction.

Counter-proliferation addresses the 'supply-side' of the WMD issue by reducing the availability of nuclear, chemical and biological weapons that might find their way into the hands of terrorists. Arms control and nonproliferation efforts are an important part of counter-proliferation because they can be used to constrain, roll back, or even prevent states from acquiring unconventional weapons.

The Cooperative Threat Reduction program reduces the latent threat posed by Soviet 'legacy' systems. By properly disposing of weapons that are no longer needed, counter-proliferation helps keep obsolete munitions and materials from falling into hostile hands. Similarly, US export controls help to reduce the possibility that irresponsible or aggressive groups or states will acquire weapons of mass destruction and associated technologies. International norms against trafficking of dangerous materials or weapons help prevent dual-use technologies from reaching black markets and terrorists.

Counter-proliferation also embodies Defense Department efforts to counter existing WMD capabilities by: (1) deterring the use of WMD against US interests by denying adversaries their political or military objectives; (2) defending US and allied forces and populations from missile attack; (3) sustaining offensive and defensive military operations in a WMD environment; and (4) preparing for chemical, biological or nuclear use against US and allied civilians.

By making military forces a less vulnerable target and by guaranteeing that any use or prospective use of WMD will be preempted or met with prompt retaliation, US counter-proliferation policy reduces the threat of state-sponsored WMD terrorism. In other words, because counter-proliferation helps to insure that US forces can retaliate after military units or civilian targets suffer a WMD attack, American policy makers can make credible deterrent threats that discourage state-sponsored terrorism.

Counter-proliferation efforts 'bound' the terrorist threat by reducing the incentives for state-sponsored WMD terrorism and by limiting the opportunities for states to transfer materials and technologies to non-state actors to construct and use nuclear, chemical or biological weapons. Counter-proliferation is an *ex ante* and costly indicator (witness the financial and psychological costs of anthrax vaccination alone) of US resolve that bolsters general deterrence.[11]

The assumption that US deterrent threats are credible is a cornerstone of the Gilmore report, which dismisses the prospect of state-sponsored nuclear, chemical or biological terrorism as extremely unlikely. According to Gilmore, the threat of US conventional preemption – here the 1998 cruise missile attack on the Al-Shifa pharmaceutical plant in Khartoum, Sudan comes to mind – or nuclear retaliation in the aftermath of a mass casualty terrorist incident creates enormous disincentives for states to become involved in terrorism.[12]

These disincentives apparently are clear even to so-called 'rogue states': despite accesses to nuclear, chemical or biological weapons, no state has put its unconventional arsenal at the disposal of terrorists, although it is too early to tell if the anthrax attacks suffered in the United States in October 2001 has a link to a state sponsor.[13] The benefits of even a successful state-sponsored terrorist attack against US forces might be short-lived. US forces are preparing to operate effectively in the wake of a WMD attack; terrorism directed against US military units should only prove to be a limited setback on the battlefield. The price for this temporary setback, however, could be severe retaliation once the sponsor of a terrorist attack has been identified.

Deterrent threats strengthened by counter-proliferation, however, would be less effective if they were directed at terrorists that lack state sponsors. Independent terrorists probably would expect to avoid symmetrical retaliation. They also might hope to escape discovery. If discovered, they might pose an inappropriate target for retaliation. Indeed, if terrorists embraced a millenarian philosophy or objective, they might even welcome severe retaliation.[14] The objectives of the Heaven's Gate cult, for example, were literally suicidal.

**Terrorism as an Asymmetric Threat**

To the extent that counter-proliferation policies provide escalation dominance on the battlefield, they help limit conflict to the conventional level of combat, a level where US forces have repeatedly demonstrated their ability to overwhelm adversaries. This escalation dominance also enhances US deterrent threats, which reduce incentives for states to sponsor terrorist activities.

But counter-proliferation, combined with US dominance of the conventional battlefield, could produce an unwelcome paradox: counter-proliferation might increase the likelihood of WMD terrorism by forcing adversaries to find asymmetric responses to US conventional superiority.[15] As David Kay notes in his assessment of the terrorist challenge, 'nations will seek courses of action that will allow them operational freedom from US conventional attack or, at least, the ability to inflict significant losses on the United States if it does attempt to frustrate their ambitions and military actions'.[16] Terrorism supplies an asymmetric response to US dominance of conventional battle, although likely US adversaries would never want to take credit for a successful terrorist attack.

Because counter-proliferation also channels terrorist attacks away from relatively hard military targets, terrorists might find it easier to direct chemical or biological attacks against civilian, transportation or industrial targets that would have an impact on the course of conventional battle. In other words, counter-proliferation channels attacks away from well-prepared military units towards relatively unprepared civilian or logistical targets.

History, theory and recent events appear to undermine this claim about the effect of counter-proliferation policy. Ideology, technology and political objectives, not just vulnerabilities, have shaped the four distinct waves of terrorist activity that have emerged over the last century. Recent history also suggests that the ongoing fourth wave of 'sacred terrorism' focuses on military or government targets.[17] Attacks against the US Marines deployed in Lebanon in 1983, the 1996 Khobar Towers bombing, the 1998 US embassy bombings in Kenya and Tanzania, the October 2000 attack against the USS Cole, and the September 11 attack against the Pentagon demonstrate that US military and government installations and units are the terrorist targets.

Although they do not provide blanket protection from terrorism, US forces employ tactics and equipment that reduce their vulnerability to WMD terrorist attacks. US military personnel are equipped with personal and collective protective equipment (suits, masks and shelters). Units are also equipped with point and standoff chemical and biological agent detectors that can reduce exposure to these hazards by warning of their presence in the environment. Decontamination equipment and medical countermeasures (vaccines and antidotes) also reduce the potential damage that might be inflicted by chemical and biological agents on US forces.

US military forces are more accessible to terrorist attack because they are forward deployed and often operate in chaotic environments. But, because of extensive defensive preparations, forward-deployed forces are not a particularly lucrative target for terrorists armed with chemical or biological weapons. US military units have the equipment and training needed to mitigate the impact of a WMD terrorist incident, pushing terrorists to find more lucrative (vulnerable) targets.

## Counter-proliferation and Coalition Warfare

If American units find themselves in high-intensity conventional combat, they probably will be participating in an international coalition. Coalition warfare is important to the US because it demonstrates the overwhelming political commitment of the United States and the international community to stop aggression and egregious abuses of human rights. Coalitions, however, can be politically fragile. Opponents often attack an alliance by destroying its political cohesion, demonstrating to alliance members the unavoidable fact that the risks and benefits of warfare are not shared equally among the members of the coalition.

Indeed, this was Saddam Hussein's intent during the Gulf War when Iraq attacked Israeli cities using SCUD missiles. Unable to stop the Gulf War coalition militarily, Saddam sought to stop it politically by attempting to turn the war into an Arab-Israeli dispute, not a battle to end Iraqi aggression. If allied populations and militaries are vulnerable to state and non-state WMD terrorism, US-led coalitions might find themselves increasingly vulnerable to terrorist blackmail. Because counter-proliferation efforts have reduced the impact that WMD terrorism might have on forward-deployed US units, allied populations and militaries could be viewed as appropriate targets within easy reach of terrorist groups. By showing that allied governments are unable to protect their citizens, terrorism could undermine allied support for coalition operations by undermining popular support of allied governments themselves.[18] The possibility that asymmetric responses might occur to US conventional superiority and the logic of coalition warfare coincide to identify allied military forces and populations as a tempting target for terrorist attacks.

Counter-proliferation further bounds the terrorist threat by hardening allied military and civilian targets against terrorist attacks. International counter-proliferation and consequence management preparations are valuable counter-terrorism instruments. The United States has launched two major regional initiatives to improve the ability of forward-deployed US forces and local allies to respond to the threat posed by chemical, biological and nuclear terrorism.

On the Korean peninsula, for instance, the Office of the Secretary of Defense and the South Korean Ministry of Defense have undertaken a series of initiatives to improve the ability of South Korean and US forces to deter and defend against weapons of mass destruction. US and South Korean officials also have opened a dialogue to facilitate counter-proliferation planning. As a result, combined military exercises now include nuclear, chemical and biological warfare scenarios. Additionally, the Koreans established a new Nuclear, Biological and Chemical Weapons Defense Command in June 1999 and have included funding for improved protective and detection equipment in their 1999 defense budget.[19]

The Defense Department also has launched a Southwest Asia Cooperative Defense initiative. The initiative is intended not only to improve the ability of US and coalition forces to operate in a CBW environment, but also to improve the ability of host nations to protect their populations and industry from chemical and biological weapons attacks. Already, extensive cooperation is planned in four areas: (1) Command, Control, Communications, Computers, Intelligence (C⁴I) and shared early warning; (2) active air and missile defense; (3) passive defense (force protection and sustainment of military operations following chemical or biological attack); and (4) consequence management.[20]

As potential 'front-line' states, US friends and allies on the Korean peninsula and in Southwest Asia are particularly vulnerable to both state and non-state sponsored acts of terrorism. Although the initiatives currently underway do not completely eliminate the threat posed by WMD terrorism, especially to the civilian populations of America's allies, they are a logical first step in closing off a 'window of opportunity' for terrorists.

## Counter-proliferation vs. Consequence Management

Although US counter-proliferation policy has helped reduce the threat posed by state-sponsored WMD terrorism directed against US forces, allies and even civilians, it has done little to reduce the threat posed by non-state actors to the US population. According to the Gilmore report, this threat is real, although it has been mischaracterized. Gilmore and his colleagues believe that there is a high probability that a low-casualty event will occur in the United States involving some type of 'mass casualty' device.

Terrorists lacking state sponsors probably do not have the technical expertise, equipment and materials needed to construct or use nuclear, biological, chemical or radiological weapons to inflict casualties and destruction on a truly massive scale. Instead, Gilmore suggests that poisonings, agricultural sabotage or product tampering seem to be plausible activities for terrorist organizations, a prediction that may be coming to pass, especially if the October 2001 anthrax infections are linked to the Al-Qaeda network. Clearly, counter-proliferation can do little if anything to address this sort of activity.

If officials really do believe that non-state actors pose a serious WMD threat to the United States and that these individuals cannot be deterred, preempted or arrested before they strike, then significant material and personnel resources must be devoted to deal with the consequences of a WMD attack against civilians. 'First-responders' need to learn how to deal with chemical or biological weapons; without training and equipment, police, firefighters and paramedics actually can spread pathogens or toxins, thereby producing more casualties. Vaccines or antidotes need to be made available to contain disease outbreaks or to save the lives of people exposed to deadly agents. Military organizations, here the National Guard comes to mind, must equip, train and prepare to act rapidly to contain and reduce weapons effects in large urban areas. A whole new set of strategies, protocols, doctrines and tactics needs to be developed to counter the effects of terrorist attacks.

Viewed in isolation, consequence management is no small task. Further complicating matters is the fact that counter-proliferation and consequence management differ fundamentally. Counter-proliferation initiatives primarily involve military forces and are directed against threats located outside of the United States. Counter-proliferation is intended to deter or

COUNTER-TERRORISM VIA COUNTER-PROLIFERATION 137

prevent acts of state and even non-state sponsored terrorism before they occur. In contrast, consequence management is intended to limit the impact of a failure of counter-proliferation policy to prevent a WMD terrorist attack against civilians.

Counter-proliferation and consequence management policies will soon present policy makers with significant tradeoffs in terms of budgets, personnel, organizational structures and philosophies that govern the fight against WMD terrorism. So far, these tradeoffs have not received much attention from those involved in either counter-terrorism or counter-proliferation. But as the urgency to respond to the 2001 September terrorist attacks increases, lawmakers, government officials and military officers might confront several stark dilemmas.

First, throughout the twentieth century, US efforts to counter the effects of chemical or biological weapons have been undertaken with military units in mind. For example, troops likely to encounter biological weapons are vaccinated, but similar efforts to vaccinate entire populations would be enormously expensive and possibly counterproductive. Anti-toxins issued to soldiers are extraordinarily potent agents which could themselves create a public health hazard if issued in peacetime to American households. Military personnel are supplied with expensive equipment that requires extensive training for proper utilization.

It is unrealistic to believe, however, that average citizens can be equipped and trained in peacetime to the high standards needed to operate sophisticated chemical and biological weapons detection devices or to utilize protective equipment properly. In other words, equipment and techniques used to protect military formations and personnel cannot simply be given to fire departments to help protect a local population.

Second, although counter-proliferation initiatives can constrain non-state actors by drying up black markets in contraband materials and equipment or by deterring state support to terrorist groups, counter-proliferation policy is primarily directed against threats that can be identified in geographic terms, if not always by national origin. Counter-proliferation policy is intended to strengthen the capability of US forces to operate in a chemical, biological or nuclear environment, a setting which implies war between recognized national entities.

In this sense, counter-proliferation policy reflects the state-centric bias of America's armed forces, which prepare to fight roughly similar units in opposing military organizations. Counter-proliferation policy only addresses non-state threats in a tertiary manner because it supports a US military that views non-state threats as a minor concern. Increased emphasis on consequence management thus reflects a fundamental shift in American defense priorities.

Third, to combat WMD terrorism better, consequence management and counter-proliferation policies must be better coordinated. But this coordination would have to occur at the weakest point in US security: at the bureaucratic and legal nexus between foreign and domestic policy. Further complicating matters is the fact that even though counter-proliferation is organized by DoD, the domestic response to terrorism is loosely organized. The Gilmore report noted, for example, that today the scope or severity of an incident involving a chemical, biological or nuclear weapon would determine which (local, state, federal) agency would take the lead in responding to a terrorist incident.[21]

Terrorism cuts across national, bureaucratic and jurisdictional borders, but the American effort to stop terrorism has a long way to go before it too is a seamless enterprise. One can only hope that the new Homeland Defense Organization can respond effectively to this challenge.

## Conclusion

Counter-proliferation contributes to counter-terrorism in several significant ways. It bounds the terrorist threat by reducing the vulnerability of US forces, allied military units and even civilian populations to terrorist attack. It helps to deter state-sponsored terrorism by bolstering the ability of US forces to retaliate with massive conventional force or with nuclear weapons. Although leaders that possess chemical, biological or even nuclear devices might find common cause with some terrorist group, they apparently have no desire to have their state linked to a terrorist attack involving unconventional weapons. Counter-proliferation also reduces the prospects of terrorist incidents by helping to keep 'surplus' materials or weapons from entering black markets. Officials or analysts rarely mention these positive contributions because counter-proliferation is not intended to address the terrorist threat, although on occasion (for example, the Gilmore report) they are factored into intelligence assessments or strategic calculations.

Counter-proliferation and counter-terrorism also are linked in less desirable ways. The dominance of US conventional forces compels antagonists to seek asymmetric responses to American superiority on the battlefield. To the extent that counter-proliferation bolsters this conventional superiority by providing escalation dominance, it might channel an enemy's response to available targets (such as terrorist attacks against civilians). Similarly, counter-proliferation policies that harden US or allied forces to terrorist attack might channel terrorists toward softer (civilian) targets. Unlike the positive contributions made by counter-proliferation policy, officials and analysts are highly aware of the possibility that opponents might use asymmetric attacks to respond to US conventional superiority. Concern about asymmetric attacks helps to blind observers to the ways counter-proliferation bounds the terrorist threat.

The relationship between counter-proliferation and counter-terrorism, however, is based on more than cognitive biases – risk averse officials and analysts could be expected to be more aware of potential losses (domestic terrorism) than existing gains (reduced threats against forward-deployed military units). If fear of domestic terrorism continues to grow, significant budgetary tradeoffs between counter-terrorism and counter-proliferation might be looming on the horizon. These tradeoffs cannot be avoided because many counter-proliferation initiatives simply cannot be used to help in consequence management.

Counter-proliferation is intended to help military units in battle against relatively symmetrical state-sponsored military forces, while consequence management closely resembles disaster management. Military units can hope to defeat their opponents in battle, thereby avoiding the costs of defeat. But disaster managers cannot defeat hurricanes; they can only take steps to minimize the impact when disaster strikes. It is this difference in fundamental objective that ultimately limits the possibility of simply applying counter-proliferation capabilities in a counter-terrorism campaign, and that will force policy makers to make difficult organizational and budgetary choices in the years ahead.

### NOTES

1. This article is based on a paper entitled 'Antiterrorism via Counter-proliferation' presented at the USAF Institute of National Security Studies, 7th Annual Topical Conference, National Defense University, 27–28 July 1999. I would like to thank Peter Lavoy, James Smith and David C. Rapoport and an anonymous reviewer for their insights and advice.
2. Richard Betts, 'The New Threat of Mass Destruction,' *Foreign Affairs* Vol. 77, No. 1 (January/February 1998), pp.26–41. US officials have stated that members of the Al–Qaeda (bin Laden network) have experimented with chemical weapons and have attempted to buy nuclear ones. Kenneth Katzman, 'Terrorism: Near Eastern Groups and State Sponsors, 2001,' (CRS, The Library of Congress, 10 September 2001) pp.11–12.
3. For eloquent statements of each side in this debate see David C. Rapoport, 'Terrorism and Weapons of the Apocalypse,' *National Security Studies Quarterly*, Summer 1999, pp.49–67; and David Kay 'WMD Terrorism: Hype or Reality,' in James M. Smith and William C. Thomas (eds.), *The Terrorism Threat and US Government Response: Operational and Organizational Factors* (USAF Institute of National Security Studies, Colorado Springs, CO., 2001), pp.69–78.
4. In February 1994, the National Security Council defined counter-proliferation as 'the activities of the Department of Defense across the full range of US efforts to combat proliferation, including diplomacy, arms control, export controls, and intelligence collection and analysis with particular responsibility for assuring that US forces and interests can be protected should they confront an adversary armed with weapons of mass destruction'. See Office of the Undersecretary of Defense, Acquisition and Technology, Report on Nonproliferation and Counter-proliferation Activities and Programs (Washington, DC: Department of Defense, 1994), p.1.
5. For example, see David C. Rapoport, 'Terrorism and Weapons of the Apocalypse,' *National*

*Security Studies Quarterly* Vol. V. No. 3 (Summer 1999), pp.49–67; Ashton B. Carter and Celeste Johnson, 'Beyond the Counter-proliferation Initiative to a 'Revolution in Counter-proliferation Affairs',' *National Security Studies Quarterly* Vol. V. No. 3 (Summer 1999), pp.83–90; and Quadrennial Defense Review Report (Washington, DC Department of Defense, 30 September 2001), pp.18–20.

6. Advisory Panel to Assess Domestic Response Capabilities For Terrorism Involving Weapons of Mass Destruction, 'Assessing the Threat,' 15 December 1999.

7. Robert Jervis, *Perception and Misperception in International Politics* (Princeton: Princeton University Press, 1976); and Robert Jervis, *System Effects* (Princeton, Princeton University Press, 1997).

8. Similarly, analysts have claimed that the bureaucratic division of labor between US nonproliferation and counter-proliferation efforts protects organizational bailiwicks, but undermines policy coherence. See Brian Bates and Chris McHorney, *Counter-proliferation in the 21st Century* (Lewiston, NY: the Edwin Mellen Press, 2000).

9. The 2001 QDR simply notes that the proliferation of chemical, biological, radiological and nuclear weapons continues, see 2001 QDR, p.12.

10. William S. Cohen, *Report of the Quadrennial Defense Review*, May 1997. http://www.defenselink.mil/pubs/qdr/sec7.html.

11. James D. Fearon, 'Signaling Versus the Balance of Power and Interests,' *Journal of Conflict Resolution*, 38/2 (June 1994), pp.236–269.

12. 'Assessing the Threat,' pp.17–18.

13. Seth Carus, *Bioterrorism and Biocrimes: The Illicit Use of Biological Agents in the 20th Century* (Washington, DC: Center for Counterproliferation Research, National Defense University, March 1999), p.37.

14. William C. Martel, 'Deterrence and Alternative Images of Nuclear Possession,' in T.V. Paul, Richard Harknett and James J. Wirtz, (eds.), *The Absolute Weapon Revisited: Nuclear Arms and the Emerging International Order* (Ann Arbor: University of Michigan Press, 1998), pp.213–234; and Walter Laqueur, 'Postmodern Terrorism,' *Foreign Affairs* (September/October 1996), pp.24–36.

15. On this point see Jonathan Tucker, 'Asymmetric Warfare,' *Forum for Applied Research and Public Policy* 14/2 (Summer 1999), pp.32–38.

16. Kay, p.74.

17. David C. Rapoport, 'Terrorism' *Encyclopedia of Violence Peace and Conflict* Vol. 3 (London: Academic Press, 1999), pp.497–510.

18. Peter Chalk, *West European Terrorism and Counter-Terrorism, The Evolving Dynamic* (London: MacMillon, 1996), p.13; and Bruce Hoffmann, *Terrorism and Weapons of Mass Destruction: An Analysis of Trends and Motivations* (Santa Monica: RAND P–8039, 1999), pp.53–54.

19. Peter R. Lavoy, 'Antiterrorism via Counter-proliferation,' presentation delivered to USAF Institute of National Security Studies 7th Annual Topical Conference, 'Twenty–First Century Terrorism and US National Security,' National Defense University, Washington, D.C., 27–28 July 1999.

20. Peter R. Lavoy, 'Cooperative Defense Against Weapons of Mass Destruction in the Arabian Gulf,' in Jacquelyn K. Davis, Charles M. Perry, and Jamal S. Al–Suwaidi (eds.), *Air/Missile Defense, Counter-proliferation and Security Policy Planning* (Abu Dhabi, United Arab Emirates: The Emirates Center for Strategic Studies and Research, 1999), pp.51–57.

21. 'Assessing the Threat,' pp.61–62.

# [3]

# The Struggle against Terrorism

*Barry R. Posen*

## Grand Strategy, Strategy, and Tactics

$\mathbf{T}$hree to four thousand people, nearly all American citizens, perished in the aircraft hijackings and attacks on the World Trade Center and the Pentagon on September 11, 2001.[1] They were murdered for political reasons by a loosely integrated foreign terrorist political organization called al-Qaeda. Below I ask four questions related to these attacks: First, what is the nature of the threat posed by al-Qaeda? Second, what is an appropriate strategy for dealing with it? Third, how might the U.S. defense establishment have to change to fight this adversary? And fourth, what does the struggle against al-Qaeda mean for overall U.S. foreign policy?

## The Adversary

Al-Qaeda is a network of like-minded individuals, apparently all Muslim but of many different nationalities, that links together groups in as many as sixty countries. Osama bin Laden, a wealthy Saudi who took part in the Afghan rebellion against the Soviet occupation (1979–89), developed this network. He inspires, finances, organizes, and trains many of its members. He seems to be in direct command of some but not all of them. Bin Laden and his associates share a fundamentalist interpretation of Islam, which they have opportunistically twisted into a political ideology of violent struggle. He and his principles enjoy some popular support in the Islamic world, though it is difficult to gauge its depth and breadth. Al-Qaeda wants the United States, indeed the West more generally, out of the Persian Gulf and the Middle East. In bin Laden's view, the United States helps to keep Muslim peoples in poverty and imposes upon them a Western culture deeply offensive to traditional Islam. He blames the United States for the continued suffering of the people of Iraq and

*Barry R. Posen is Professor of Political Science in the Security Studies Program at the Massachusetts Institute of Technology.*

I would like to acknowledge the contributions of the faculty, research staff, and graduate students of the MIT Security Studies Program to the evolution of my thinking on the challenge posed by September 11. I alone am responsible for the views expressed here.

1. It is impossible at this time to offer a more precise figure. See Eric Lipton, "Numbers Vary in Tallies of the Victims," *New York Times*, October 25, 2001, pp. B1, B10.

for the Israeli occupation of the West Bank and the Gaza Strip. For him, Israel is a foreign element in the Middle East and should be destroyed. The U.S. military presence in Saudi Arabia is a desecration of the Islamic holy places and must end.[2] Once the United States exits the region, al-Qaeda hopes to overthrow the governments of Saudi Arabia and Egypt and replace them with fundamentalist, Taliban-like regimes. It is no wonder that the Saudi regime considered bin Laden so dangerous that it stripped him of his citizenship in 1994.

Al-Qaeda is an ambitious, ruthless, and technically proficient organization. The stark evidence is at hand. It has attacked the United States before, but not with such striking results.[3] For the September 11 attack, at least nineteen men, supported by perhaps a dozen others, plotted for years an action that at least some of them knew would result in their deaths. Each member of the conspiracy had numerous opportunities to defect. The terrorists piloting the four passenger jets understood the level of destruction they would exact. They carefully studied airport security and found the airports that seemed most vulnerable. Several of these men appear to have trained for years in U.S. flight schools to learn enough to pilot an aircraft into a building. The cockpits of the 757 and 767 are quite similar, which does not seem coincidental; a single experienced pilot could tutor all of the hijackers on the fine points of operating the aircraft. Between the two aircraft types, the conspirators could choose from a wide selection of flights. The 767s, the aircraft with the most fuel and hence the greatest destructive potential, were directed at the biggest target, the World Trade Center. The proximity of the departure airports to the targets permitted tactical "surprise." All four planes had small passenger complements relative to their capacity; this hardly seems coincidental given the hijackers' plan to take the aircraft with box-cutters. The hijackings of all four airliners were carefully synchronized. If this had been a Western commando raid, it would be considered nothing short of brilliant. Given the demonstrated motivation and organizational and technical skills of its members, al-Qaeda will likely attempt further large-scale attacks on the United States or its citizens and soldiers abroad, or both.

---

2. United Kingdom, Foreign and Commonwealth Office (FCO), *Responsibility for the Terrorist Atrocities in the United States, 11 September 2001*, pp. 4–5, http://www/fco.gov.uk/news/keytheme pages.asp. See also Kenneth Katzman, *Terrorism: Near Eastern Groups and State Sponsors, 2001*, Congressional Research Service, report for Congress, September 10, 2001, pp. 2, 9.
3. FCO, *Responsibility for the Terrorist Atrocities in the United States*, pp. 6–10, links al-Qaeda to the fight against U.S. special operations forces in Somalia in October 1993, to the bombing of the U.S. embassies in Kenya and Tanzania in August 1998, and to the attack on the USS *Cole* in October 2000, as well as to several thwarted operations. See also Katzman, *Terrorism*, pp. 10–11, which also links bin Ladin indirectly to the February 1993 World Trade Center bombing.

*The Struggle against Terrorism* | 41

Al-Qaeda benefited from the direct support of Afghanistan, which had been governed in recent years by the fundamentalist Taliban religio-political movement. The Taliban ruled Afghanistan as a kind of crude police state. Not only was bin Laden protected by the regime, but his money and his forces were a pillar of its power. The Taliban had been asked before by the United States to expel bin Laden but always demurred. This base proved to be of great utility to bin Laden and to al-Qaeda. Individuals came from around the world to receive training in terrorist techniques and tactics.[4] Afghanistan is a large country, with rugged terrain and long and lawless borders, far from any Western base; it is hard to monitor, let alone attack—in other words, a perfect hideout. Without this bastion, bin Laden would probably have been on the run much of the time. Al-Qaeda also seems to have benefited from the tacit support of some other governments; persistent reports suggest that wealthy individuals in several Gulf states have contributed to the organization, with the knowledge though not the active cooperation of their governments. Saudi Arabia is often mentioned by name.[5]

As has often been pointed out, the United States and most developed, democratic countries are extremely vulnerable to terrorist attacks. These are open societies that have not policed their borders successfully. Drugs and illegal immigrants move into the United States with ease; cash, guns, and stolen cars move out. Dangerous activities occur in modern society every day. Aircraft take off and land; hazardous materials—flammable, explosive, or poisonous—move by truck, train, and ship. And in the United States, those with money and some patience can obtain explosives, firearms, and quantities of ammunition. Prosaic means can be employed against everyday targets to produce catastrophic results. One must nevertheless also be concerned about chemical, biological, or nuclear attacks. The ability to make chemical agents and biological poisons is more widespread than ever, though turning the basic ingredients into useful weapons and delivering them effectively on a large scale has thus far not proven easy for small clandestine groups.[6] Nuclear weapons are more difficult to obtain, but fears remain that some of the very large number manufactured during the Cold War, or some of those built by new nuclear states, could fall into the wrong hands. Alternatively, primitive nuclear weapons de-

---

4. Ali A. Jalali, "Afghanistan: The Anatomy of an Ongoing Conflict," *Parameters*, Vol. 31, No. 1 (Spring 2001), p. 5, http://carlisle-www.army.mil/usawc/Parameters/01spring;jalali.htm.
5. "Saudi Arabia: The Double-Act Wears Thin," *Economist*, September 29, 2001, pp. 22–23.
6. As of this writing, the anthrax poisonings in the United States do not contradict this statement. Until we know more, all we can conclude is that small amounts of lethal anthrax can be obtained and, through the mail, can hurt or kill small numbers of people.

signs are widely available; getting the fissionable material to make a nuclear bomb is still difficult, but not all of this material is as secure as it should be. Thus the possibility of a major terrorist attack with biological, chemical, or nuclear weapons cannot be ruled out.

Most terrorists do not exploit the vulnerabilities of advanced industrial societies; law enforcement helps to make it difficult, though obviously not impossible. More important, most terrorist organizations do not wish to make the United States an implacable enemy. Many have limited political objectives, which the United States can hinder or help. Al-Qaeda clearly has more ambitious objectives than most terrorist organizations; it seeks to expel the most powerful state in history from a part of the world that has been central to U.S. foreign policy for more than half a century, and it intends to do so without a large standing military. Hence al-Qaeda has opted for large-scale murder to achieve its objectives, and it will seek to kill Americans so long as the United States does not give in to its demands.

## What Is To Be Done?

Like any war, or even any large civil project, the war against al-Qaeda and other terrorist groups bent on mass destruction requires a strategy. A strategy lays out an interlinked chain of problems that must be solved to address the ultimate problem, the defeat of the adversary. Although the United States and its allies may never fully destroy al-Qaeda, or aligned organizations, or new organizations that emulate them, the antiterror coalition that the United States has built can aspire to reduce the terrorists to desperate groups of exhausted stragglers, with few resources and little hope of success. A strategy sets priorities and focuses available resources—money, time, political capital, and military power—on the main effort. Strategies have both a military and a diplomatic dimension. Within the military dimension, states may choose among offensive, defensive, and punitive operations. In this war, diplomacy will loom larger than military operations, and within the military dimension, defensive activities will loom larger than offensive and punitive ones. That said, without a militarily offensive component, this war cannot be won. Finally, this is a war of attrition, not a blitzkrieg. Al-Qaeda cannot be rounded up in a night's work. If the United States wishes to pursue a major effort against al-Qaeda, its supporters, and any future imitators, it must be prepared to accept significant costs and risks over an extended period. There will likely be an exchange of blows, in the United States and abroad. This war is necessary because bin Laden and

The Struggle against Terrorism | 43

others like him will continue to attack the United States so long as it asserts its power and influence in other parts of the world.

Sound strategy requires the establishment of priorities because resources are scarce. Resources must be ruthlessly concentrated against the main threat. There are two primary adversaries in this fight against terrorism: the extended al-Qaeda organization and the states that support it. Al-Qaeda is the principal terrorist organization that has attempted to engage in mass destruction attacks on the United States.[7] It has shown itself to be more capable and more politically ambitious than most. It is the imminent threat. Other terrorist organizations, however, must be kept under surveillance and attacked preemptively if they seem ready to strike the United States or its allies in mass attacks, or if they appear intent on aligning themselves with al-Qaeda.

Allies are essential for success in the war on terrorism, which helps to explain the determination of President George W. Bush and his administration to build a broad coalition. Bin Laden had training camps and bases in Afghanistan, but in other countries al-Qaeda's presence has been more shadowy. Wherever this organization takes root, it must be fought. But it will not always be necessary or possible for the United States to do the fighting. Allied military and police forces are more appropriate instruments to apprehend terrorists operating within their national borders than are U.S. forces. They have information that the United States may not have, and they know the territory and people better. The odds of finding the adversary and avoiding collateral damage increase to the extent that the "host" nation-state does the hard work. Moreover, host states can deal better politically with any collateral damage— that is, accidental destruction of civilian life and property. Much of the war will look a lot like conventional law enforcement by the governments of cooperative countries. Efforts must also be made to weaken terrorist organizations by attacking their infrastructure; both cooperative and clandestine methods can be used to deny these groups access to funds and matériel.

As noted earlier, al-Qaeda has found tacit and active support from nation-states. In the case of partial or tacit support, it may be assumed that there is some disagreement within the political leadership of the country in question about the wisdom of such a policy. The objective is to induce these states to change their practices through persuasion, bribery, or nonviolent coercion.

---

7. The February 1993 bombing of the World Trade Center is not directly attributed to al-Qaeda, but Ramzi Yusef, convicted of masterminding that crime, reportedly collaborated with al-Qaeda to organize several unsuccessful terrorist efforts in Asia. Katzman, *Terrorism*, p. 10.

Again, diplomacy looms large in this struggle. Nevertheless, the United States must be prepared to bypass national governments should they fail to cooperate. Given the utter ruthlessness of al-Qaeda, the United States cannot afford to allow it a sanctuary anywhere. From time to time, U.S. forces may simply need to attack al-Qaeda cells directly. This may be a job for special operations forces who would try to avoid contact with national armed forces. In any case, to deter national armed forces from getting in the way, or to foil them if they try, the United States must maintain a strong conventional military capability. Occasionally, it may be necessary to engage in conventional wars with such countries.

Some regimes may choose to support bin Laden's cause, like the Taliban did in Afghanistan. Where a regime has close relations with the terrorists, it is reasonable to treat the host nation as an ally of al-Qaeda and an enemy of the United States. The United States must be prepared to wage war against such states to destroy terrorist groups themselves, to prevent their reconstitution by eliminating the regimes that support them, and to deter other nation-states from supporting terrorism. The United States must make it clear that direct support of terrorists who try to kill large numbers of Americans is tantamount to participation in the attack. If a nation-state had directed a conventional weapon of war at the World Trade Center, U.S. forces would have retaliated immediately. Particularly in the age of weapons of mass destruction, the United States cannot allow any state to participate in catastrophic attacks on its homeland with impunity. More intensive defensive precautions can reduce but not eliminate U.S. vulnerability to mass destruction attacks, so deterrence must be the first line of defense. For these reasons, the Taliban regime in Afghanistan had to be destroyed.

Initially, the Bush administration hesitated to embrace the objective of ousting the Taliban regime.[8] The administration was more interested in bin Laden and al-Qaeda than in their hosts, and in his speech of September 20, President Bush gave the Taliban an opportunity to "hand over the terrorists" *or* "share

---

8. Indeed, as of late October 2001, both the U.S. Department of State and the U.K. Foreign and Commonwealth Office used elliptical language to discuss coalition war aims in Afghanistan. Secretary of State Colin Powell could only bring himself to say, "There is, however, no place in a new Afghan government for the current leaders of the Taliban regime." See "Campaign against Terrorism," prepared statement for the House International Relations Committee, U.S. Department of State, October 24, 2001, p. 2, http://www.state.gov/secretary/rm/2001. The United Kingdom's statement of war aims suggests that "we require sufficient change in the leadership to ensure that Afghanistan's links to international terrorism are broken." Foreign and Commonwealth Office, "Defeating International Terrorism: Campaign Objectives," p. 1, http://www.fco.gov.uk/news/keythemehome. asp.

their fate."[9] Even after the first five days of air strikes, in his press conference of October 11, President Bush gave the Taliban a "second chance" to turn over bin Laden and evict his organization from Afghanistan.[10] Given the difficulty of finding these terrorists, as well as the political complexities of waging war in Afghanistan, this was a reasonable offer, though in my judgment a harmful one from the point of view of deterrence of future attacks. Once the Taliban declined the opportunity to cooperate, the United States had no choice but to wage war on them to the extent that was militarily and politically practical, with the objective of driving them from power.[11]

## Tactics: Forces and Methods

Any military campaign has defensive and offensive aspects. Because of its geographical position and great military potential, the United States is accustomed to being on the offensive, but in this campaign the defensive must assume equal or greater importance. Considerable time will be required to develop enough political and military pressure on al-Qaeda to suppress its ability to conduct operations. That organization will probably have the opportunity to attack the United States or its friends again. The United States must thus do all it can defensively to reduce the probability of additional attacks on the U.S. homeland, and to limit the damage should such attacks occur. The United States has been taught a costly but valuable lesson about the vulnerability of modern society to terrorism. Thus, even after al-Qaeda is destroyed, the United States will need to maintain its defenses. This means new vigilance in the most fragile corners of the transportation, energy, power, and communication systems and closer attention to the security of government buildings.

The mobilization of thousands of National Guardsmen and reservists after September 11 had the immediate purpose of enhancing U.S. territorial defenses—including more attentive airspace management, port surveillance, and airport security. This is only the beginning. A new or reoriented joint, multiservice command, staffed by active-duty regulars and reservists and dedicated exclusively to territorial defense, should be created to oversee this en-

---

9. See "The President's Address," *Washington Post*, September 21, 2001, p. A24.
10. Patrick E. Tyler and Elisabeth Bumiller, "'Just Bring Him In,' President Hints He Will Halt War If bin Laden Is Handed Over," *New York Times*, October 12, 2001, pp. A1, B5.
11. U.S. leaders wisely exercised some restraint; they did not put large ground forces into the country, who would have provided numerous targets for Afghan riflemen and the appearance of a mission of conquest. Nor did they use firepower indiscriminately, and by large-scale killing of Afghan civilians create the appearance of making war on all Muslims.

during mission.[12] Many additional military man-hours will likely be required on a sustained basis for territorial defense. Elements of the active armed forces, the Coast Guard, and the National Guard and Reserves may require redirection or expansion, or possibly both. The United States may need to ask its weekend warriors to serve more weekends, and indeed more weeks, each year.

Enhanced intelligence capabilities are necessary for both defense and offense. Students of terrorism and its close cousin, insurgency, invariably stress the critical importance of intelligence.[13] Intelligence must be gathered on terrorist groups overseas. Such intelligence will come not only from U.S. technical surveillance methods and spies but also from the daily hard work of national police forces abroad. The critical importance of intelligence is one of the main reasons why the United States needs the support of allies. U.S. law enforcement agencies will also have to redouble their efforts. Intelligence provides the data necessary for preventive and preemptive attacks by the national military or police forces of the countries in which the terrorist groups have taken refuge, or by U.S. forces. Even tardy warning of terrorist attacks as they get under way may provide a useful and life-saving margin of time. Intelligence from abroad must also be blended with intelligence gathered at home.

More sustained attention is necessary to the organization of the U.S. counterterrorism intelligence effort. Historically, the following has proven of great utility in all kinds of military endeavors: the staffing of a dedicated intelligence center with full-time, long-serving professionals with a deep knowledge of the adversary; the timely collection of intelligence from multiple sources in that center; the analysis of that data for specific information as well as patterns that reveal the adversary's presence or intentions; and the transmission of that data to those who can best use it for offensive or defensive pur-

---

12. U.S. Department of Defense, *Quadrennial Defense Review Report*, September 30, 2001, p. 19, states that "DOD will review the establishment of a new unified combatant commander to help address complex inter-agency issues and provide a single military commander to focus military support." This is too tentative.

13. "Nearly all of the threatened or their experts agree that the key to an effective response to terrorism is good intelligence and that such intelligence is difficult to acquire." J. Bowyer Bell, *A Time of Terror: How Democratic Societies Respond to Revolutionary Violence* (New York: Basic Books, 1978), p. 134. Douglas S. Blaufarb draws similar lessons from the U.S. counterinsurgency effort in Vietnam: "Small, lightly armed units, pinpointed operations assisted by 'hunter-killer' squads, imaginative psychological warfare operations—and all of this based upon coordinated collection and exploitation of intelligence—should be the main reliance of the military side of the effort. The police, if they have or can be brought to develop the capability, should play a major role in the intelligence effort and in other programs requiring frequent contact with the public." Blaufarb, *The Counterinsurgency Era: U.S. Doctrine and Performance, 1950 to the Present* (New York: Free Press, 1977), p. 308.

The Struggle against Terrorism | 47

poses.[14] Anecdotal information suggests that the United States suffered shortcomings in this regard; data may have been present that could have permitted the early detection of the September 11 plot, but it was not fully exploited.[15] Formally, the Central Intelligence Agency's Counterterrorist Center (CTC) is responsible for "coordinating the counterterrorist efforts of the Intelligence Community," including "exploiting all source intelligence."[16] Nevertheless, this intelligence effort has been the subject of persistent criticism, in particular for weaknesses in interagency cooperation; failure to concentrate all potentially useful information in one place, especially information gathered by law enforcement agencies in the United States; and untimely analysis.[17] The CTC's mandate needs to be strengthened so that all useful information gathered by any intelligence or law enforcement agency is concentrated for analysis. The CTC will also require more money and staff.

Offensive action and offensive military capabilities are necessary components of a successful counterterror strategy. Offensive action is required to destroy regimes that align with terrorists; offensive capabilities allow the United States to threaten credibly other regimes that might consider supporting terrorists. Offensive action against terrorists is needed to eliminate them as threats. But even unsuccessful offensive actions, which force terrorist units or terrorist cells to stay perpetually on the move to avoid destruction, will help to reduce their capability. Constant surveillance makes it difficult for them to plan and organize. Constant pursuit makes it dangerous for them to rest. The threat of offensive action is critical to exhausting the terrorists, whether they are with units in the field in Afghanistan or hiding out in cities and empty quarters across the world. This threat will be credible only if the United States launches

---

14. The clearest historically grounded exposition of this argument is to be found in Patrick Beesly, *Very Special Intelligence* (New York: Ballantine, 1977), pp. 1–24, which details the formation of the Royal Navy's Operational Intelligence Center, to exploit all source intelligence for the antisubmarine warfare campaign early in World War II.
15. James Risen, "In Hindsight, C.I.A. Sees Flaws That Hindered Efforts on Terror," *New York Times*, October 7, 2001, pp. A1, B2. "In hindsight, it is becoming clear that the C.I.A., F.B.I. and other agencies had significant fragments of information that, under ideal circumstances, could have provided some warning if they had all been pieced together and shared rapidly."
16. "The War on Terrorism, DCI Counterterrorist Center," http://www.cia.gov/terrorism.ctc. html.
17. The National Commission on Terrorism, Ambassador L. Paul Bremer III, Maurice Sonnenberg, Richard K. Betts, Wayne A. Downing, Jane Harman, Fred C. Iklé, Juliette N. Kayyem, John F. Lewis, Jr., Gardner Peckham, and R. James Woolsey, *Countering the Changing Threat of International Terrorism*, report of the National Commission on Terrorism (Washington, D.C., June 5, 2000), http://www.fas.org/irp/threat/commission.htm; and James Kitfield, "CIA, FBI, and Pentagon Team to Fight Terrorism," September 18, 2000, GOVEXEC.com, http://www.govexec.com/dailyfed/0900/091900nt.htm.

*International Security 26:3* | *48*

an offensive operation from time to time, large or small. Offensive action is also necessary to support U.S. diplomacy. Thus far, U.S. diplomats have stressed the concerns of existing and prospective allies that the United States might overreact with excessive and indiscriminate violence. It is disturbing that they believe that U.S. decisionmakers could be so stupid and brutal, but it is a good thing that they understand the deep emotion that drives U.S. purpose. The United States must threaten offensive war so that these allies understand the seriousness of U.S. intent. The more cooperation the United States gets from allies on the intelligence and policing front, the less necessary it becomes for the United States to behave unilaterally, militarily, and with the attendant risks of collateral damage and escalation. If the United States does not act militarily from time to time, this risk will lose its force as an incentive for U.S. allies. Periodically taking the offensive is also necessary to maintain morale at home. Given that al-Qaeda will continue to try to hit the United States and its friends, the public will probably want to see the United States "bring justice to our enemies."[18]

To take the offensive, the United States will need to exploit perishable intelligence on the existence and location of terrorist cells. Flexible, fast, and relatively discriminate forces are essential. The American people and the leaders of the American military must be prepared to accept the risk of significant U.S. casualties in small, hard-hitting raids. Even when other nations cooperate by providing intelligence, and would be willing to arrest or destroy terrorists in their midst, they may lack the capability and need augmentation from the United States. In any event, political decisionmakers in the United States and abroad who approve strikes on the basis of this information will have to come to terms with the risks to innocent civilians. Occasions will surely arise when there are trade-offs between effectiveness against the adversary and casualties to U.S. and allied forces, or to innocents caught in the crossfire. It will occasionally be necessary to err on the side of effectiveness. This is a tragic fact of war that will stress the persuasive skills of U.S. diplomats, as it did in the first weeks of the air campaign against Afghanistan.

The United States has large special operations forces well suited to the counterterror mission: small groups of highly trained individual fighters from all the services, supported by an array of specially designed and expertly pi-

---

18. This sentiment was expressed by President Bush in his address to a joint session of Congress on September 20, 2001: "Whether we bring our enemies to justice or bring justice to our enemies, justice will be done." See "The President's Address."

*The Struggle against Terrorism* | 49

loted helicopters, aircraft, and small watercraft. (They also include experts at training and advising foreign soldiers.) These forces may be more effective and cause less collateral damage than cruise missiles or precision guided bombs in certain situations. In the past, U.S. decisionmakers have been reluctant to employ these forces because their missions involve a significant risk to the troops. Given the seriousness of the new war and the apparent commitment of the American people, such concerns are likely to diminish. These forces may require additional mobility assets—planes, helicopters, and other more exotic equipment. It may also be reasonable to expand the special operations forces by reorienting some active units such as the 82d Airborne Division and the 101st Air Assault (Helicopter) Division to this mission. The U.S. Marine Corps also deploys many units that could prove useful to the counterterror mission. Three separate reinforced battalions of marines are generally deployed afloat, on special assault ships loaded with helicopters and hovercraft, around the world at any one time. Though the marines judge these forces to be "special operations capable," it would be sensible to stress even further their special operations mission. Moreover, given that most U.S. Navy carrier air wings do not currently fill the hangar space available on existing carriers, it is reasonable to put a company of army or marine special operations troops and their associated helicopters on each one.[19] To permit speedy action, emergency basing and overflight rights around the world must be obtained in advance—yet another task for diplomacy.

The military will also need to augment its ability to gather tactical intelligence to support operations under way. Often the United States will have only a rough idea of where terrorist training camps, quasi regular units, or clandestine units are hiding. An enhanced ability to focus intelligence assets on key objectives is of great importance. Insofar as the adversary operates in small groups without much heavy equipment, the task will be difficult. For the last decade, the United States has experimented with unmanned aircraft, "intelligence drones." It needs to buy more drones, and soon. These devices have been used profitably to police Bosnia and Kosovo. They also played a role in the Kosovo war. Unlike satellites, intelligence drones are extremely flexible; they can focus on a small piece of terrain and remain overhead for several hours at a time. They are just machines, and by current standards not very ex-

---

19. If U.S. Army special operations units are to be permanently deployed at sea, they will need to purchase new "marinized" versions of their current helicopters that are better able to fit below decks, communicate with navy vessels and aircraft, and withstand the corrosive effects of salt air.

pensive ones; the American people will not mind losing one every now and then to obtain critical information.[20]

Above all, the "war" against terrorism will require patience and sustained national will. It will take time for the United States and its allies build up a full intelligence picture of the adversary and enhance existing worldwide intelligence capabilities to better detect these elusive foes. As the United States pursues terrorist groups, they will fight back. They will resist locally when U.S. and other forces try to apprehend or destroy them. More important, the terrorists will try to mount additional attacks against the United States, against U.S. installations abroad, and against U.S. allies. Terrorists will attempt this anyway, but in seeking to destroy them, the United States may cause them to accelerate their attacks. The U.S. security establishment will need to be innovative and adaptive, just as the adversary has proven to be.[21] The American people cannot go into this fight without understanding that they may suffer more pain before the problem recedes.

Finally, American leaders will have to fight political and bureaucratic inertia at home and abroad. Prior to September 11, the United States had a counterterror "administered policy." Administered policies prevail in democracies, where the political leadership regularly trades off initiatives that might be highly effective in one policy area against their costs measured in terms of other agendas, values, and policies. Bureaucracies struggle to maintain their autonomy and often fail to cooperate to achieve stated purposes. Change, when it comes, is incremental. Before September 11 the counterterror effort was like any other administered policy; although it enjoyed higher priority and more resources than it once did, it still competed for political, financial, and human resources on a relatively level playing field with many other policies. That approach was entirely reasonable to me, but has been proven wrong. War is different; in war other policies assume significantly lower priority. Be-

---

20. The U.S. Air Force RQ-1A Predator costs about $8 million apiece. This is the price for a small production run; production on a larger scale would reduce the unit cost. The air force currently has only thirteen Predators. Ted Nicholas and Rita Rossi, *Military Cost Handbook*, 22d ed. (Fountain Valley, Calif.: Data Search Associates, 2001), p. 4-2. See also Craig Hoyle, "US Build-Up Highlights UAV shortage," *Jane's Defence Weekly*, October 10, 2001, p. 5.

21. For example, the Bush administration has appointed Governor Tom Ridge head of the new Office of Homeland Security to coordinate the activities of all the disparate governmental organizations that contribute to territorial defense; he controls nothing. It may instead prove necessary to organize a new Department of Territorial Security, to consolidate control over some or all of the following: air surveillance and defense units; the Coast Guard; the Border Patrol; counterterror elements of the FBI; and federal-level emergency medical response, humanitarian relief, and damage-repair capabilities.

cause terrorists are elusive, it will be difficult to sustain the kind of focus that war requires. Failure to sustain that focus will allow al-Qaeda to remain quiet, lick any wounds its sustains in the first flush of U.S. anger and coalition solidarity, rebuild its cadres, and then strike again—harder and more effectively than before. While life must go on, a return to treating counterterrorism as an administered policy must await significant evidence of real success in destroying the al-Qaeda organization.

## The Diplomacy of a Counterterror War and the Implications for U.S. Grand Strategy

Both enthusiastic allies and quiet back-channel assistance from around the world will be central to a successful counterterror campaign, but allies are not always easy to find. The United States has been spoiled by its Cold War success. Threatened neighbors of the Soviet Union quickly sought alignment with the United States. During Operation Desert Shield, Arab states in the way of Saddam Hussein's legions did not require much persuading to join the U.S. coalition; those farther away needed subsidies just to show up. The war against terrorism is more difficult. The major al-Qaeda terrorist action has been directed against the United States, though attacks both at home and abroad have caught many foreign nationals in the crossfire. States that have been the victims of tenuously related or unrelated terrorist groups have proven responsive to U.S. requests for help (e.g., Russia, India, and Israel). The United States also needs the assistance of states whose leaders believe that (1) they are not terrorist targets, (2) they can easily redirect terror toward others, or (3) their own citizens may sympathize with al-Qaeda.

The United States needs friends, and thus must prioritize among its many foreign policy and defense policy initiatives, because these initiatives have frequently antagonized other governments and peoples. All the governments whose help is required, whether they are democratic or not, must deal with their own publics. Therefore the United States must find ways to explain to their people why cooperation against these terrorists is in their interest. The United States clearly cannot afford to make every state in the world prosperous and happy. It cannot afford to end every conflict in favor of any ally the United States needs. Sometimes the United States will want the help of both parties to a regional conflict, and cannot reward one party at the expense of another. And it cannot afford to peremptorily abandon long-standing allies in a heartbeat. Such actions have their own costs and risks. But the United States

*International Security 26:3* | 52

must be much more disciplined in its choices, and much more attuned to the views of others, if it is to sustain this coalition over the long term.[22]

In the years since the Cold War ended, the United States has been immensely powerful, and relatively capricious. It has often acted against the interests of others in pursuit of modest gains, as it did in the case of NATO expansion, the Kosovo war, and the Bush administration's early insistence that national missile defenses would be built with or without Russian cooperation. All these policies had alternatives that could have achieved many of the goals of their U.S. advocates while leaving Russia and others less displeased. Similarly the United States has often failed to act out of fear of incurring modest costs: It has applied insufficient pressure on Israel to suppress its settlement policy in the West Bank and Gaza; has shown little creativity in trying to end the politically damaging low-grade war and leaky economic embargo of Iraq; and made no effort to help others inhibit the course of the Rwanda genocide. The American media have been content to cover international politics episodically and often superficially. The U.S. foreign and security policy record is not one of unalloyed failure.[23] It is, however, a record of indiscipline in which calculations of short-term domestic political gains or losses often dominated decision-making.

The post–Cold War world of easy preeminence, controlled low-cost wars, budgetary plenty, and choices avoided is over. In the past I argued that the United States failed to settle on a grand strategy to guide its international behavior after the demise of the Soviet Union.[24] Democrats and Republicans

---

22. Examples of the kinds of diplomatic choices that the United States faces abound. Russia can control its own nuclear materials and weapons and provide intelligence; Russia has been unhappy with NATO expansion and the Bush administration's national missile defense program. Saudi Arabia and the Gulf states have great air bases, all used by the United States during the Gulf War. These bases would prove useful if the counterterror campaign expands to Iraq. These countries find U.S. tolerance of Israeli settlement policies on the West Bank and Gaza to be a significant irritant. Though the UN oil-for-food program has enabled Iraq to feed and care for its people—and Saddam Hussein deserves the blame for their current misery—the continuation of Gulf War sanctions and the regular bombing of Iraq by U.S. and British warplanes help Saddam portray Iraq as the aggrieved party in the Arab world. Pakistan, a former close supporter of the Taliban, was alienated by the United States' cavalier treatment after the end of the Soviet occupation of Afghanistan. Pakistan was also, until recently, under economic sanctions enacted to show U.S. displeasure with its May 1998 nuclear weapons tests. Pakistan may have the most political influence over Pashtun tribes in Afghanistan whose cooperation will be needed to bring a stable government to that country.
23. Russia did not collapse; the nuclear weapons of the Soviet Union were gathered up and consolidated in Russia for safekeeping; the Balkan wars ended; and the great and middle powers of the world have not yet fallen into any new cold wars with one another. U.S. foreign policymakers get much of the credit.
24. Barry R. Posen and Andrew L. Ross, "Competing Visions for U.S. Grand Strategy," *International Security*, Vol. 21, No. 3 (Winter 1996/97), pp. 5–53.

*The Struggle against Terrorism* | 53

could agree on only one thing: The United States should remain the most powerful state in the world. Beyond that, a good many Democrats wanted to use this power to pursue liberal purposes: improving international organizations and institutions, strengthening international treaties, increasing the power of international law, and spreading democracy. Republicans seem to have wanted to use this power to consolidate U.S. superiority and to create still more power. Russia was viewed as perpetually on the verge of backsliding toward Soviet-style imperialism, and China was feared as a budding peer competitor; both needed containment. Neither political party energetically discussed its preferred policies with the American people. Neither was willing to ask the American people for serious sacrifices to pursue its preferred objectives, and neither had to do so. Sacrifice is now necessary if the United States is to sustain an activist foreign policy, and thus the reasons to pursue such a policy must be explained to and accepted by the American people. Otherwise, if the war on terrorism proves to be not only long but more costly than Americans hope, the temptation to retreat from the world stage will be strong.

Although the outlines are not clear, advocates of alternative U.S. grand strategies during the last decade now seem inclined to superimpose these strategies on the campaign against terror. Advocates of greater restraint in U.S. foreign policy, often unfairly dubbed "neo-isolationists," argue that the United States must retaliate strongly for the September 11 attacks if it is to deter future attacks. But they are uninterested in what comes after, because they believe that the United States should do less in the world. If the United States is less involved, it will be less of a target. If it is less often a target, it needs less assistance to defend itself and its interests. This approach to terror is internally consistent, but it definitely does not defend an active U.S. world role.

Liberal internationalists seem much more interested in the process by which the campaign against terrorism is conducted. The United Nations must be involved at every step. Resort to law must take precedence over tactical advantage. Terrorists must be treated like criminals, not enemies: Police should apprehend them; courts should try them. Military action should occur seldom if at all, and it should always be precise. A state that sponsors terrorism, such as Afghanistan, should be diplomatically isolated, condemned at the UN, subjected to an arms embargo, and economically sanctioned in any way that does not harm the general populace. The United States should join the international criminal court, and as a token of its good intentions sign most of the treaties it has eschewed. This approach preserves a world role for the United States but, given the determination of the adversary and the foibles of other countries, seems doomed to failure.

*International Security 26:3* | *54*

Primacists have also tried to direct this campaign. Perhaps the strangest advice is rumored to have come from Paul Wolfowitz, the U.S. deputy secretary of defense. He seems to believe that the time is ripe to deal with all of the United States' enemies and problems in the Middle East and Persian Gulf and further consolidate an already dominant U.S. power position. Wolfowitz is reported to have recommended action against Iraq, Syria, and Hezbollah bases in Lebanon.[25] Violent regimes and movements they are, and no strangers to terrorism, but none of them seems to be connected to al-Qaeda and its maximalist objectives and methods. Were this to change, Wolfowitz's inclinations would make more sense. But going after all of them now looks too much like a script written by al-Qaeda propagandists; such attacks would surely cause states whose cooperation the United States needs to see the campaign as anti-Arab and anti-Islam, and sit this war out. Such a multifront attack might produce the very rebellions in Saudi Arabia, the other Gulf states, and Egypt that the United States hopes to prevent. This proposed four-front war is especially odd given that the Bush administration campaigned on the proposition that the U.S. military was incapable of dealing with two nearly simultaneous major regional wars.

One grand strategy advocated over the last decade is broadly consistent with the requirements of an extended counterterror war. That strategy, termed "selective engagement," argues that the United States has an interest in stable, peaceful, and relatively open political and economic relations in the part of the world that contains important concentrations of economic and military resources: Eurasia. This is an interest that others share. In this strategy, U.S. power is meant to reassure the vulnerable and deter the ambitious. This is a big project that requires a careful setting of priorities. Yet its objectives are limited: The project seeks neither power for its own sake, nor the wholesale reform of other states' domestic constitutions, nor a transformation of international politics. The U.S. position in the Persian Gulf and the Middle East is a central element of this strategy. Al-Qaeda aims to challenge this position. Its leaders believe that if the United States left the region, they could take power in the Gulf and in Egypt. Were this to happen, one can easily imagine several possible dangers: a war between Iraq and Saudi Arabia as Saddam Hussein tries to strangle the fundamentalist Islamic baby in the cradle before

---

25. Steven Mufson and Thomas E. Ricks, "Debate over Targets Highlights Difficulty of War on Terrorism," *Washington Post*, September 21, 2001, p. A25. The article depicts a policy fight between Secretary of State Colin Powell, the principal advocate of a policy focused on al-Qaeda, and Deputy Secretary of Defense Wolfowitz, "pushing for a broader range of targets, including Iraq."

*The Struggle against Terrorism* | 55

its strangles him; war with Iran over security, religious, and nationalist issues; or war with Israel. Given the extreme destructiveness of the 1980–88 Iraq-Iran War (500,000 dead), which saw the use of chemical weapons and rocket attacks on cities—as well as the continued presence of chemical, biological, and nuclear weapons, and rocket delivery systems in the area—any of these possible wars could prove devastating for those in the region and harmful to those farther away. Moreover, any one of them would surely affect the production, distribution, and price of oil—still important to the global economy. Their political, military, and economic ripple effects would likely be felt globally, affecting other political relationships. The grand strategy of selective engagement does necessitate the campaign against al-Qaeda. The requirements of that campaign have already forced the Bush administration to act in ways that are more consistent with the strategy of selective engagement than they are with primacy.

The United States faces a long war against a small, elusive, and dangerous foe. That struggle must be pursued with discipline and determination if it is to be successful. The United States requires a strategy to guide its efforts, including the allocation of resources. That strategy must set priorities, because resources are scarce and this war will prove expensive. Significant changes in the U.S. national security establishment, including intelligence collection and analysis, military organization and equipment, and emergency preparedness, will prove essential. Finally, if the United States is to sustain both public and international support for the war on terrorism, it will need to resolve long-delayed questions about its future foreign and security policy through an extended discussion involving policymakers, policy analysts, and the American people.

# [4]

# An Examination of the American Response to Terrorism: Handling the Aftermath Through Crisis Intervention

Sophia F. Dziegielewski, PhD, LCSW

Kristy Sumner, MS

The United States has never seen terrorist attacks such as those experienced on September 11, 2001. Following the attacks, many individuals have struggled with how to best address the vulnerabilities of American society relating to terrorist activity. This article identifies several issues that can affect the previously open nature of the American lifestyle with impending threats of biological warfare. This turbulent environmental context has caused the American people to experience a level of stress never before experienced. The purpose of this article is to present a brief overview of America's policy on terrorism stressing the application of Roberts' seven-stage model of crisis intervention as one means to address the growing fears of the American public. All helping professionals, whether or not they're working directly with a crisis survivor, need to be aware of basic crisis intervention techniques. Application of this model is stressed as one way to provide education in this area while highlighting how to best help individuals cope when faced with the continual threat of a new and different type of war. Recommendations for therapeutic content are made within the current time-limited practice setting. [*Brief Treatment and Crisis Intervention* 2:287–300 (2002)]

KEY WORDS: crisis training, stress management, bioterrorism, terrorism, terrorist attacks, aftermath of September 11, crisis management.

The United States, along with the rest of the world, was shocked and stunned as the terrorist attacks of September 11, 2001, unfolded. Following the attacks, debates relating to terror-

From the School of Social Work (Dziegielewski) and the Department Health and Public Affairs (Sumner) at the University of Central Florida.

Contact author: Sophia F. Dziegielewski, PhD, Professor, School of Social Work, College of Health and Public Affairs, University of Central Florida, P.O. Box 163358, Orlando, FL 32816-3358. E-mail: sdziegie@mail.ucf.edu.

ist activity within the United States and the vulnerabilities inherent within American society began to emerge. The issues of extensive borders and the relative ease in which immigrants can disappear into American society, as well as the global and open nature of lifestyles Americans have come to depend upon, leave the society susceptible to terrorist threats and attacks. Furthermore, the threat of biological warfare and fears of a new type of war abound. This has caused the majority of American people to experience a newfound level of stress. The purpose of this article is to present a brief overview of America's policy on terrorism, and to reveal the need for a proactive joining of law enforcement, government agencies, and professional practitioners. These groups can collectively assess potential threats within the United States and address the growing fears of the American people in regard to safety and security for the American public.

## Terrorism and the United States

Terrorism is defined by the Department of Defense as "the calculated use of violence or the threat of violence to inoculate fear; intended to coerce or to intimidate governments or societies in the pursuit of goals that are generally political, religious or ideological" (Terrorism Research Center, 2000). Terrorism is a crime that targets innocent and unsuspecting victims, and its purpose is to heighten public anxiety. Also, while acts of terrorism may seem random, they are actually planned by the perpetrators whose main objective is to publicize their attacks. The growing threat of terrorism and terrorist activity is expanding across the United States, and success in combating it will require agencies to implement proactive approaches and strategies (Terrorism Research Center, 2000). "It is time to recognize certain events that are currently occurring in society as potential forewarning. Disregarding them may result in tragic consequences. History clearly shows that those law enforcement agencies caught behind the operational curve of [terrorist] campaigns have a harder time controlling them and reducing their societal disruption than those that are properly prepared" (McVey, 1997, p. 7).

## Terrorism Trends

It is the current trends in terrorism and terrorist activity that makes the need for a proactive ap-

proach critical. These trends include the following: (a) terrorism is becoming the war strategy of the future; (b) terrorists are becoming more sophisticated and proficient at using technology; (c) the targets of terrorist attacks will advance from buildings and airplanes to economic systems and countries; (d) traditional weapons will become obsolete against technically advanced terrorists; and (e) the United States will continue to be a target of terrorism (Badolata, 2001; Bowman, 1994).

Since the 1980s, the United States has had a policy relating to counterterrorism; however, it is largely reactive in nature and lacks preemptive capabilities. This four-pillar policy states: (a) the United States makes no concessions to terrorists and strikes no deals; (b) the United States uses a "full-court press" to isolate terrorists, and to apply pressure on state-terrorism sponsors in order to force them to change their behavior; (c) rules of law are followed to bring terrorists to justice; and (d) the United States seeks international support to increase counterterrorism capabilities (Badolata, 2001).

## United States Vulnerabilities

Examining the vulnerabilities inherent within the United States further supports the need for a preemptive approach to combating terrorists and terrorism. First, the United States has an extensive amount of borders that are extremely easy to penetrate. Millions of legal and illegal immigrants enter the country each year. Second, the security measures at airports and other ports of entry are poor, and resources are stretched thin. In most cases personnel that are undertrained and ill equipped are hired to secure ports of entry. Third, the structure of law enforcement in the United States can also be seen as a vulnerability because federal, state, and local agencies often lack communication between them and, in cases where jurisdictions and charters overlap, friction between the agencies often occurs. Finally, the infrastructure of the United States has been centralized, allowing for large concentrations of people to inhabit relatively small areas. These large population areas capture the attention of terrorists because they allow for a larger casualty rate and a more public arena for attacks (Terrorism Research Center, 2000).

Since the September 11 terrorist attacks, government and law enforcement agencies have begun to implement strategies to counter these vulnerabilities. However, the "openness" of American borders, which is the most critical area in need of change, is the most difficult vulnerability to effectively control. The current influx of immigrants into the United States highlights the necessity of an effective system that can scan and monitor those individuals entering the United States.

## Problems Contributing to Increased Terrorism

In the United States in 1991, there were 455 million entries made to the United States by immigrants and international travelers via air, land, and sea. By 1993, that number had increased to 483 million entries; in 1995 alone, at the ports of entry to the United States the 4,000 immigration inspectors intercepted almost 800,000 persons who were ineligible for admission into the United States. Furthermore, there is no estimate available as to the number of those who were able to escape detection (Badolata, 2001; Gibb, 2001; Hays, 1996; McDonald, 1997). This massive amount of entries is problematic in that there is no effective national system that screens those individuals coming into the United States. The infrastructure necessary to efficiently process this increasing movement has not kept pace with its growth resulting in an easing of the

barriers that formally kept out ineligible travelers such as criminals, terrorists, and economic migrants.

## Bioterrorism: Threats of Anthrax and Smallpox

Individuals, groups, or governments define bioterrorism as the expressed purpose of causing harm for ideological, political, or financial gain (Texas Department of Health, 2001). Further, biological weapons are defined as referring to as any infectious agent such as a bacteria or virus, which is used intentionally to inflict harm (Texas Department of Health, 2001). Since the September 11 attacks the threat and fear of bioterrorism has escalated within the United States. The recent cases of anthrax infections have exposed America's vulnerabilities to biological agents, and has highlighted the need for greater security measures to protect against bioterrorism attacks.

### Bioterrorism Possibilities

According to the Center for Disease Control and Prevention (CDC), biological agents can create a risk to national security because they are easily disseminated. Furthermore, bioterrorism can have high mortality and great impact on public health systems, causing panic and social disruption. This high cost of bioterrorism could lead to special action and funding to increase public preparedness (Scardaville & Spencer, 2001). Bioterrorism mirrors conventional terrorism because it is designed to affect a large number of people, can be implemented with little or no warning, and instills panic and fear in the population. However, there are several other aspects of bioterrorism that must also be examined. First, the vast number of methods that can be used to spread biological agents into an environment is a concern. Airborne dissem-

Dziegielewski and Sumner

ination, pharmaceutical contamination, food or drink contamination, injection or direct contact, and water contamination are all methods that can be used by terrorists attempting to unleash biological agents (Scardaville & Spencer, 2001). Other considerations that must be taken into account include the vast number of biological agents that could be used in a bioterrorism attack, the ability of terrorists to acquire such biological agents, and the massive casualties that could result if a bioterrorism attack occurs.

### Anthrax and Smallpox

The biological agent that has gained the primary attention since the September 11 attacks is anthrax. Anthrax, according to CDC, is an infectious disease that is caused by the spore-forming bacterium *Becillus anthracis* (CDC, 2001a). Although it is not contagious, humans can contract the disease through inhalation and breaks in the skin. If contracted through inhalation, the incubation period is generally 2 to 5 days, and the symptoms mirror those of the flu—fever, muscle aches, nausea, and coughing. More serious symptoms include difficulty breathing, high fever, and shock. Inhalation anthrax is almost always fatal once symptoms appear. If contracted through the skin, the incubation period is generally 1 to 2 days. Symptoms of skin exposure to anthrax begin as a small, itchy bump followed by a rash. Left untreated, the lesions fill with fluid and eventually turn black as the tissue begins to die. About 20% of untreated cases of infection through the skin result in death (Gibb, 2001, p. 44). Anthrax, although potentially fatal, can be treated effectively through antibiotics if initiated early (CDC, 2001a).

A second biological agent that has gained attention as a possible bioterrorism tool is smallpox. According to the American Medical Association (AMA), when used as a biological weapon, smallpox represents a serious threat because

of its fatality rate of 30% or more among unvaccinated persons. Although smallpox has long been feared as the most devastating of all infectious diseases, its potential for devastation today is far greater than at any previous time. Routine vaccination throughout the United States ceased more than 25 years ago. In a now highly susceptible, mobile population, smallpox would be able to spread widely and rapidly throughout this country and the world (AMA, 1999).

According to CDC, smallpox is a virus that has an incubation period of 12 days following exposure. Initial symptoms include high fever, fatigue, and head- and backaches that are then followed by a rash on the face, arms, and legs. The rash progresses into lesions that become pus-filled, turn into scabs, and eventually fall off. Smallpox is highly contagious and is spread by infected saliva droplets. While many patients with smallpox recover, death occurs in up to 30% of cases. There is no proven treatment for smallpox; however, a vaccine can lessen the severity of or prevent illness if given within 4 days of exposure (CDC, 2001b).

### Is the United States Prepared for a Bioterrorism Attack?

On June 22–23, 2001, the Johns Hopkins Center for Civilian Biodefense Studies, in conjunction with the Center for Strategic and International Studies, the ANSER Institute for Homeland Security, and the Oklahoma National Memorial Institute for the Prevention of Terrorism, held an exercise at Andrews Air Force Base in Washington, DC, titled "Dark Winter." The first such exercise of its kind, "Dark Winter" was constructed as a series of mock National Security Council (NSC) meetings in reaction to a fictional, covert smallpox attack in the United States (O'Toole & Inglesby, 2001).

The result of the drill highlighted several areas of concern with regard to governmental preparedness against bioterrorism attacks. First, there was a basic lack of understanding by leaders on the subject of bioterrorism. Second, early responses to the "attack" were slow to determine how many persons were "exposed," and how many trained medical personnel would be needed. Also, the drill highlighted that the American health care system lacks the ability to deal with mass casualties, and there is a shortage of necessary vaccines and medicines. Finally, the "Dark Winter" drill indicated that conflicts between different levels of federal and state government and uncertainty in authority hampered responses (*The Economist*, 2001, pp. 29–30).

Due to the results of the "Dark Winter" drill and the September 11 attacks, lawmakers are trying to increase funding for various agencies to counter bioterrorism and its effects. In an effort to increase support, the U.S. House of Representatives passed fiscal 2002 spending bill for the departments of Education, Labor, and Health and Human Services (HR 3061-H Rept 107-229). This bill includes $393 million for measures to defend against biological or chemical attacks, which is an increase of $100 million in this area Furthermore, the Senate bill (S 1536-S Rept 107-84) would allocate $338 million, and the House and Senate Armed Services committees have also greatly expanded biological defense and research efforts. The House's fiscal 2002 defense authorization bill (HR 2586-H Rept 107-194) would fund chemical and biological defense procurement at $361.7 million. While the House bill would cut the administration's request for chemical and biological weapons research and development by $5 million to $502.7 million, it would also increase spending for the Defense Advanced Research Projects Agency's (DARPA) biological warfare defense program by $10 million to $150 million. The Senate's defense authorization bill (S 1416-S Rept 107-62) would include similar increases for chemical and biological weapons programs as part of an overall boost of more than $600 million to deal with "nontraditional threats" such as terrorism and cyber attacks. The Senate bill would also direct the Defense Department to build a new facility to produce vaccines against anthrax and other biological agents (McCutcheon, 2001).

## Psychological Implications

A central aspect of terrorism that should be examined is the psychological effect on the American people caused by acts of terrorism. Research on natural and human-caused disasters suggest that psychological reactions to terrorism are more intense and more prolonged than psychological reactions following natural types of disaster (Myers, 2001). Terrorist attacks, by their very nature, are designed to instill fear, anxiety, and uncertainty within a population (Badolata, 2001).

There are several characteristics of terrorism that can increase the magnitude and severity of psychological effects. First, terrorist attacks occur with a lack of warning that produces a disruption to society and people's way of life. A lack of warning also prevents individuals from taking protective action, both physical and psychological. Terrorist attacks become more horrifying for individuals because there is usually a sudden change in reality and surroundings. For example, the New York City skyline changed in a matter of hours when the World Trade Center buildings collapsed and only a pile of smoking debris was left. Another psychological effect of terrorism is the threat to personal safety and security for both citizens and responders. Areas that were previously believed to be safe suddenly become unsafe. This feeling of insecurity can be instilled in an individual for an extended period of time. Acts of terrorism can also be traumatic because of the following elements: (a) the scope of their destruction, (b) the exposure by citizens, survivors, and responders

Dziegielewski and Sumner

to gruesome situations, (c) the emotional anger caused by the intentional human causalities, and (d) the degree of uncertainty, lack of control, and social disruption that a society is exposed to (Myers, 2001).

The September 11 attacks were different from other terrorist acts because of the magnitude and suddenness of the tragedy, the vast loss of life on American soil, the ability of citizens to follow the events of the attacks through extensive media coverage, and the use of airplanes, considered to be a common and "safe" mode of transportation, as a means of destruction (Dyer, 2001).

While every person who experiences a traumatic event responds to that event in different ways, there are many feelings and reactions that are common in the aftermath of a tragedy. These include sadness, anger, rage, fear, numbness, stress, feelings of helplessness, feeling jumpy or jittery, moodiness or irritability, change in appetite, difficulty sleeping, experiencing nightmares, avoidance of situations that are reminders of the trauma, problems concentrating, and guilt because of survival or lack of harm during the event (Dyer, 2001).

According to the National Center for Post Traumatic Stress Disorder, there are several steps that individuals can take in the wake of a disaster to reduce symptoms of stress and to readjust to some sense of normalcy. First, following a tragedy, an individual should find a quiet place to relax and attempt to sleep at least briefly. Next, there should be an evaluation of the situation where the survivor reaffirms priorities to establish hope and a sense of purpose. The survivor must also rely on the natural support of others such as friends, family, coworkers, and other survivors to establish a sense of togetherness and to help in the reduction of stress. Individuals should also try to engage in positive activities that can serve as a distraction from traumatic memories or reactions of the event. Finally, a person should seek out the advice of

a doctor and/or counselor for help in treating symptoms of depression and/or post-traumatic stress disorder (National Center for Post Traumatic Stress Disorder, 2001).

## Application of Roberts' Seven-Stage Crisis Intervention Model as an Acute Post-Traumatic Intervention

Effective intervention with survivors of trauma precipitated by a crisis of this nature requires a careful assessment of individual, family, and environmental factors (Lewis & Roberts, 2002). According to Roberts (1990, 1991, 2000), a crisis by definition is short term and overwhelming, and the response will involve an emotionally taxing change. In terrorism, the crisis event has caused a senseless disruption within the individual's normal and stable state. It makes sense that the individual's usual methods of coping will not work and a quiet place must be established, allowing the individual to think, ponder, and regroup.

Roberts (1991) has presented a seven-stage crisis intervention model that includes: (a) assessing lethality and safety needs, (b) establishing rapport and communication, (c) identifying the major problems, (d) dealing with feelings and providing support, (e) exploring possible alternatives, (f) formulating an action plan, and (g) providing follow-up. In the process, counselors need to remember that both pleasure and pain are a necessary part of growth and adaptation. Individuals who have experienced a crisis must realize that both emotions can coexist as well as fluctuate throughout the healing process. Early intervention for the individual in crisis can lead to a more rapid and effective adjustment.

When applying Roberts' model, the following assumptions are made: (a) all strategies will follow a "here and now" orientation, (b) most in-

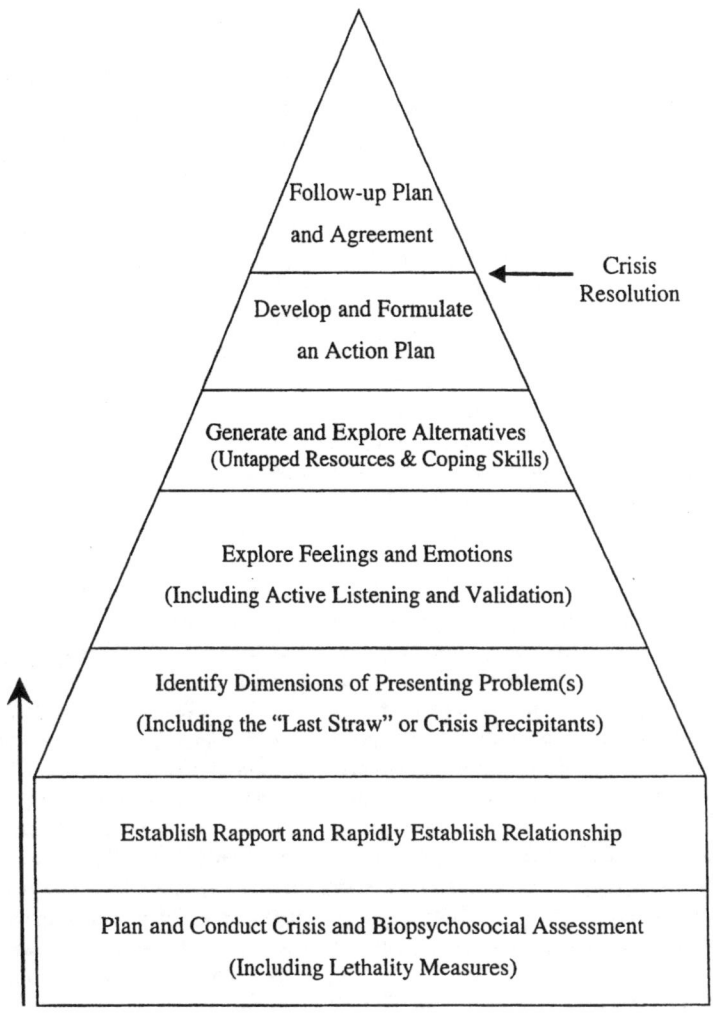

Crisis
Resolution

Follow-up Plan
and Agreement

Develop and Formulate
an Action Plan

Generate and Explore Alternatives
(Untapped Resources & Coping Skills)

Explore Feelings and Emotions
(Including Active Listening and Validation)

Identify Dimensions of Presenting Problem(s)
(Including the "Last Straw" or Crisis Precipitants)

Establish Rapport and Rapidly Establish Relationship

Plan and Conduct Crisis and Biopsychosocial Assessment
(Including Lethality Measures)

**FIGURE 1**
Roberts' Seven-Stage Crisis Intervention Model. © 1991 Albert R. Roberts. Reprinted by permission of the author.

terventions provided should be given as close to the actual crisis event as possible (Raphael & Dobson, 2001; Simon, 1999), (c) the intervention period will be both intensive and time limited, typically 6 to 12 meetings (Roberts, 1991, 2000), (d) the survivor's behavior in relation to stress is an understandable, rather than a pathological reaction (Roberts & Dziegielewski, 1995), (e) the crisis counselor will assume both an active and directive role assisting the survivor in the adjustment process, and (f) all intervention efforts are designed to increase the survivor's remobilization and return to the previous level of functioning (Dziegielewski, 1998; Dziegielewski &

Dziegielewski and Sumner

Resnick, 1996). These assumptions must be considered before applying Roberts' model during crisis intervention.

### Stage 1: Assessing Lethality

The unpredictability of terrorist attacks and the fear of further attacks make recovery from this type of acute trauma particularly problematic. Also, other events that happen in the environment are more likely to be perceived as terrorist activity, regardless of actual cause. This makes it more difficult for the survivor to progress past the active danger phase. Listed below are some of the hazardous events or circumstances that can be linked to the recognition or reliving of traumatic terrorist events. These events, while possibly unrelated to terrorist activity, can still trigger anxious responses from individuals. These events can include: (a) growing public awareness of the prevalence of the traumatic event or similar traumatic events (e.g., an accidental plane crash with subsequent loss of human life or incidents related to bioterrorism in the environment), (b) the acknowledgment by a loved one or someone that the client respects that he/she has also been a victim, (c) a seemingly unrelated act of violence being committed to them or someone they love such as rape and/or sexual assault, (d) the changing of family or relationship support issues, and (e) the sights, sounds, or smells that trigger events from the client's past (these can be highly specific to individuals and the trauma experienced). Thus, when dealing with trauma, the sensitivity thresholds and the memories as to cues associated with the individual's interpretation process can vary (Wilson, Freidman, & Lindy, 2001).

One of the immediate dangers in Stage 1 is the possibility of suicidal tendencies. With the seriousness and unpredictability related to terrorist acts, any intervention efforts will require care-

ful assessment of suicidal ideation. In addition, initial and subsequent hospitalization and/or medication may be required to help deal with serious episodes of anxiety and depression surrounding the event. Although no individual wants to experience pain, some professionals believe that a moderate degree of pain is needed to facilitate the healing process. Therefore, medications should be used with individuals in the most severe cases or as conjunct to intervention, rather than as a means to simply avoid dealing with uncomfortable feelings (Dziegielewski, 2002; Dziegielewski & Leon, 2001).

When addressing the potential for suicidal behavior, questions to elicit signs and symptoms of suicidal ideation or intent should be direct in nature. The client should be asked about feelings of depression, anxiety, difficulties in eating or sleeping, psychological numbing, self-mutilation, flashbacks, panic attacks or panic-like feelings, as well as increased incidences of substance use. After carefully identifying the degree of loss experienced by the individual, the individual's living situation needs to be assessed based on the age and the circumstances of the trauma experienced. Helping the client identify members of his or her support system will help to assure the client that he/she is out of danger, as well as remind the client of support that remains immediately accessible.

The initial contacts the crisis worker has with the client in crisis should be individualized, structured, and goal oriented to assist the individual to move past the traumatic event. It is critical for the crisis counselor to help the client understand that the traumatic terrorist event was beyond his or her personal control.

In these initial meetings (Meetings 1–3), the goal of the therapeutic intervention is to identify the hazardous event and help the client to acknowledge the event. In addition, when dealing specifically with terrorism, the client must be made aware that other seemingly unrelated events might also trigger a similar panic-like response. Once aware that panic symptoms may reoccur, specific preparation needs to be made as to how to handle these occurrences and subsequent feelings. Since the client is currently being subjected to periods of stress that disturb his or her sense of equilibrium, attempts to maintain or restore the homeostatic balance can be commonplace.

Crisis counselors should understand that the dynamics often following a crisis situation could be so overwhelming that the client may choose to focus on events other than the crisis event. If this happens, the crisis counselors must help the client focus on the problem (i.e., the event that precipitated the crisis or the reason for the visit). During these initial meetings, the client realizes and acknowledges that the crisis or trauma has occurred. Once this is realized, the client enters into a vulnerable state (Roberts & Dziegielewski, 1995). The impact of this traumatic can be so horrific that it disturbs the client, and his or her ability to utilize traditional problem-solving and coping methods. When these usual methods are found to be ineffective, tension and anxiety continue to rise, and the individual becomes unable to function effectively (Roberts, 2000).

In the initial meetings, the assessment of the client's past and present coping behaviors are important; however, the focus of intervention must remain in the "here and now." The crisis counselor must make every effort to stay away from past or unresolved issues unless they relate directly to the handling of the traumatic event.

## Stage 2: Establishing Rapport and Communication

Many times the devastating events that surround the immediate and unforeseeable loss of a loved one may leave the survivor feeling as though family and friends have abandoned him or her, or that they are being punished for something they did. Crisis counselors need to be aware that these types of unrealistic interpretations may cause the client to feel overwhelming guilt. Feelings of self-blame may limit the client's capacity for trust, which may be reflected in a negative self-image or poor self-esteem. Low self-image and poor self-esteem may increase the individual's fear of further victimization. Many times, survivors of trauma question their own vulnerability and realize that revictimization remains a possibility. This makes the rapport between counselor and client essential.

When possible, the crisis counselor should progress slowly and allow the client to set the pace of intervention attempts. Coercion and forced confrontation may not be helpful. Allowing the client to set the pace creates a trusting atmosphere that sends the message, "The event has ended; you have survived and you will not be hurt here." Clients often need to be reminded that their symptoms are a healthy response to an unhealthy environment (Dziegielewski & Resnick, 1996). They need to recognize that because they have survived heinous circumstances, they must continue to live and cope. The trauma victim may require a positive future orientation, with an understanding that he or she can overcome current problems and arrive at a happy, satisfactory tomorrow (Dolan, 1991). Restoring hope is crucial to the client's well-being.

Unconditional support and positive regard must be maintained throughout the crisis intervention process. This is especially crucial between the counselor and client in order to avoid lack of support, "blaming," and breach of loyalty, which are common within the working relationship between counselor and clients. The therapeutic relationship is seen as a vehicle for continued growth, development of coping skills, and the ability to move beyond the traumatic event (Briere, 1992).

Dziegielewski and Sumner

### Stage 3: Identify the Major Problems

Terrorist attacks can be multifaceted. Once the major problems relevant to the particular event are identified and addressed, the establishment of support mechanisms becomes essential. After a client has been given individual attention, he or she may be ready for group participation. In crisis work, emphasis should be placed on teaching relaxation techniques, encouraging physical exercise, and creating an atmosphere where the client gains an understanding that self-care is at the root of all healing. This provides the basis for future coping and stabilizing efforts.

In these next few meetings (Meetings 3–6), the crisis counselor needs to assume a very active role. First, the major problems must be identified. These problems must be directly related to the effects of responses and actions upon the present situation. Education in regards to the effects and consequences of terrorism should be discussed. Discussing the event can be very painful for the client, and simply reacknowledging the event can elevate the individual to a state of active crisis marked by disequilibrium, disorganization, and immobility (e.g., the last straw). Although the client's acknowledgment of the event may be painful, it will generate new energy for problem solving. This challenge stimulates a moderate degree of anxiety, in addition to hope and expectation. The actual state of disequilibrium can vary, but it is not uncommon for individuals who have suffered severe trauma to remain in that state for 4 to 8 weeks or until some type of adaptive or maladaptive solution is found.

### Stage 4: Dealing With Feelings and Providing Support

This process is steered by the energy generated from the client's personal feelings, experiences, and perceptions (Briere, 1992). It is critical that the crisis counselor demonstrate empathy and an understanding of the client's worldview. The symptoms the client is experiencing are to be viewed as functional and as a means of avoiding further abuse and pain. Even severe symptoms, such as dissociative reactions, should be viewed as a constructive method of removing oneself from a harmful situation and exploring alternative coping mechanisms. The experiences of the client should be normalized to facilitate the understanding that victimization is not their fault. Reframing symptoms are coping techniques that can be helpful. In this stage (Meetings 6–8), the client begins to reintegrate and gradually reaches a new state of equilibrium. Each particular crisis situation (i.e., type and duration of incest, rape, etc.) may follow a sequence of stages, which can generally be predicted and mapped out. One positive result from generating the crisis state in Stage 3 is that in treatment, after reaching active crisis, clients seem particularly amenable to help.

Once the crisis situation has been obtained, distorted ideas and perceptions regarding what has happened need to be corrected so that the client can better understand what he or she has experienced. Victims eventually need to confront their pain and anger so that they can develop better strategies for coping. Increased awareness helps the client face and experience contradicting emotions (e.g., anger/love, fear/rage, dampening emotion/intensifying emotion) without the conditioned response of escape (Briere, 1992). Throughout this process there must be recognition of the client's continued courage in working through these issues.

### Stage 5: Exploring Possible Alternatives

Moving forward requires experiencing a mourning process (generally in Meetings 8–10). Sadness and grief over the loss needs to be experienced. Expressions of grief regarding betrayal and lack of protection open to the client a spectrum of feelings that have been previously numbed. This stage allows the client to experience acceptance and letting go so that making peace with the past may begin.

## Stage 6: Formulating an Action Plan

In the sixth stage, the crisis worker must be very active in helping the client determine how the goals of the therapeutic intervention will be completed. Many techniques are used to address intervention planning such as practice, modeling, behavior rehearsal, role play, and the writing down of an action plan along with one's feelings. Often, the client has come to the realization that they are not at fault or to blame. The doubt and shame of what his or her role was and what part he or she played becomes more clear and self-blame less pronounced. The client begins to acknowledge that they did not have the power to help themselves or to change things related to the event. Oftentimes, however, these realizations are coupled with anger at the lack of control over what has happened. In this stage, the role of the mental health professional becomes essential in helping the client look at the long-range consequences of acting on their anger and to plan an appropriate course of action. The main goal of these last few sessions (Meetings 10–12) is to help the client reintegrate the information learned and processed into a homeostatic balance that allows him or her to return to a state of normalcy. Referrals for additional therapy should be considered and discussed at this time (e.g., additional individual therapy, group therapy, couples therapy, family therapy).

## Stage 7: Follow-Up Measures

While Stage 7 is often overlooked, it is very important to the process of intervention in general. In the successful therapeutic exchange, signifi-

cant changes have been made for the client in regard to his or her previous level of functioning and coping. Measures to determine whether these results have remained consistent are essential. Oftentimes follow-up can be as simple as a phone call to discuss how things are progressing. Follow-up within 1 month of termination of the sessions is important. It may also be helpful to suggest that debriefing or intervention be addressed to help the client reach a higher level of adjustment (Everly, Lating, & Mitchell, 2000; Raphael & Dobson, 2001). It is important not to push the client beyond the point that he or she is willing to go. In addition, the client may need the time to self-recover, which could lead to willingness for further intervention.

Other measures of follow-up are available but require more advanced planning. A pretest/posttest design can be added by simply using a standardized scale at the beginning of treatment and later at the end (Dziegielewski & Powers, 2000). Scales to measure the signs and symptoms of psychological trauma are readily available. See Corcoran and Fischer (1994) for a thorough listing of measurement scales that can be used in the behavioral sciences.

Finally, it is important to realize that when dealing with this type of stress reaction, the determination of the course and type of intervention will always rest with the client. At follow-up, many clients may need additional therapeutic help, yet may be unable to express the request for a debriefing session. Whereas others, after having initially adapted to the crisis and learned to function and cope, may find that they want to continue some type of intervention. Supporting the client as he or she progresses through the crisis period remains the ultimate goal of any crisis intervention. Whether the client requests additional services or not, the crisis counselor should be prepared to present available options for continued therapy and emotional growth. If additional intervention is requested, referrals for group therapy with

Dziegielewski and Sumner

other survivors of similar trauma, individual growth-directed therapy, couples therapy that is to include a significant other, and/or family therapy should be considered.

## Future Directions: Where Do We Go From Here?

The tragic events of September 11, 2001, changed America forever. Terrorism, in its various forms, has exposed, on a national scale, the need for tighter security at the nation's borders as well as continued efforts to ensure protection from biological warfare (Eisenburg, 2001). Questions arise, such as how can Americans once again feel safe after the September 11 attacks? Furthermore, whether directly exposed to terrorist activity or not, the fear of terrorism can affect everyone.

With so many people being directly affected by terrorism, and many more suffering the by-products of living in an unpredictable environment, the issue of crisis counseling to address stress and coping has gained significant attention. This increased attention has lead to a rapid increase in many theoretical, evidence-based measures, models of critical incident stress debriefing, and other related materials such as professional journals devoted to research in this field and books and related materials for the general public (Lewis & Roberts, 2002; Spitzer, 2002, Wilson et al., 2001). Recent events have lead some researchers to claim that coping with trauma and stress has become a socio-cultural phenomenon, which might result in higher self-reported stress levels due to the proliferation of information about stress in the popular culture (Moss & Lawrence, 1997).

The recent experiences of terrorism and the ways to cope with the resulting trauma and stress remain diverse. Levels of stress that these survivors experience, the sources of stress, stress related to self-esteem and self-perception, stress and coping skills, and how to best handle stressful situations are just a few of the many issues that need to be researched further. The violence caused by the recent turn of events starting with the incident on September 11, 2001, remains unprecedented in American history. The American people have traditionally been expected to adjust to new social environments, maintain good personal and occupational standing, and face pressures related to supporting friends and family. Survivors of trauma need to continue to develop new roles and modify old ones in response to the developmental tasks they face. More attention needs to be given to understanding crisis and the responses that will occur initially and those that will continue to resurface after the initial phase of the trauma has passed. The threats of terrorist attacks can have considerable psychological effects from immediate responses to those that are prolonged or delayed in nature (DiGiovanni, 1999). More information is needed as to when is the most effective time to address a stressful event (Raphael & Dobson, 2001). Coping and stress management techniques can help an individual return to a previous level of functioning, where healthy individuals who have been exposed to extreme trauma can receive the health and support needed.

## References

American Medical Association. (1999). Smallpox as a biological weapon: Medical and public health management. *Journal of American Medical Association, 281*(22), 2127–2137.

Badolata, E. (2001). How to combat terrorism: Review of United States terrorism policy. *World and I, 16*(8), 50–54.

Bowman, S. (1994). *When the eagle screams.* New York: Birch Lane Press Book.

Briere, J. N. (1992). *Child abuse trauma: Theory and*

*treatment of the lasting effects.* Newbury Park, CA: Sage.

Center for Disease Control and Prevention. (2001a). Anthrax fact sheet [On-line]. Available: www.cdc.gov/ncidod/dbmd/diseaseinfo/anthrax_g.htm#currissue.

Center for Disease Control and Prevention. (2001b). Facts about smallpox [On-line]. Available: www.bt.cdc.gov/DocumentsApp/FactSheet/Smallpox/About.asp.

Corcoran, K., & Fischer, J. (1994). *Measures for clinical practice: A source book* (2nd ed.). New York: Free Press.

DiGiovanni, C. J. (1999). Domestic terrorism with chemical or biological agents: Psychiatric aspects. *The American Journal of Psychiatry, 156*(10), 1500–1505.

Dolan, Y. M. (1991). *Resolving sexual abuse.* New York: W. Norton.

Dyer, K. (2001). What is different about this incident? [On-line]. Available: www.kirstimd.com/911_health.htm.

Dziegielewski, S. F. (1998). *The changing face of health care social work: Professional practice in the era of managed care.* New York: Springer.

Dziegielewski, S. F. (2002). DSM-IV-TR © *in action.* New York: Wiley and Sons.

Dziegielewski, S. F., & Leon, A. M. (2001). *Social work practice and psychopharmacology.* New York: Springer.

Dziegielewski, S. F., & Powers, G. T. (2000). Procedures for evaluating time-limited crisis intervention. In A. R. Roberts (Ed.), *Crisis intervention handbook* (2nd ed., pp. 487–506). New York: Oxford University Press.

Dziegielewski, S., & Resnick, C. (1996). Crisis assessment and intervention with adult survivors of incest. In A. R. Roberts (Ed.), *Crisis management & brief treatment: Theory, technique, and applications* (pp. 83–102). Chicago: Nelson Hall.

Eisenburg, D. (2001). How safe can we get? *Time, 158*(13), 85–91.

Everly, G. S., Lating, J. M., & Mitchell, J. T. (2000). Innovations in-group crisis intervention: Critical incident stress debriefing (CISD) and critical incident stress management (CISM). In A. R. Roberts (Ed.), *Crisis intervention handbook,*

(2nd ed., pp. 78–92). New York: Oxford University Press.

Gibb, N. (2001). Homeland insecurity. *Time, 158*(19), 40–54.

Hays, R. (1996). INS passenger accelerated service system [On-line]. Available: www.biometrics.org/REPORT/INSPASS.html.

Lewis, S. J., & Roberts, A. R. (2002). Crisis assessment tools. In A. R. Roberts & G. J. Greene (Eds.), *Social workers' desk reference* (pp. 208–212). New York: Oxford University Press.

McCutcheon, C. (2001). From "what-ifs" to reality. *Congressional Quarterly Weekly, 59*(40), 2463–2464.

McDonald, W. (1997). Crime and illegal immigration: Emerging, local, state, and federal partnerships. *National Institute of Justice Journal, 237,* 21–25.

McVey, P. (1997). *Terrorism and local law enforcement.* Springfield, IL: Charles C. Thomas.

Moss, S. E., & Lawrence, K. G. (1997). The effects of priming on the self-reporting of perceived stressors and strains. *Journal of Organizational Behavior, 18,* 393–403.

Myers, D. (2001). Weapons of mass destruction and terrorism: Mental health consequences and implications for planning and training. Presented at the Weapons of Mass Destruction/Terrorism Orientation Pilot Program, August 2001. [On-line]. Available: www.icisf.org/Acrobat%20Documents/TerrorismIncident/WMD_Myers.htm.

National Center for Post Traumatic Stress Disorder. (2001). Self-care and self-help following disaster [On-line]. Available: www.ncptsd.org/facts/disasters/fs_self_care_disaster.html.

O'Toole, T., & Inglesby, T. (2001). Shining a light on dark winter. *John Hopkins Center for Civilian Bio-defense Studies* [On-line]. Available: www.hopkins-biodefense.org/.

Raphael, B., & Dobson, M. (2001). Acute posttraumatic interventions. In J. P. Wilson, M. J. Friedman, and J. D. Lindy (Eds.), *Treating psychological trauma and stress* (pp. 139–157), New York: Guilford Press.

Roberts, A. (1990). *Crisis intervention handbook: Assessment, treatment and research.* Belmont, CA: Wadsworth.

Roberts, A. R. (1991). *Contemporary perspectives on*

Dziegielewski and Sumner

crisis intervention and prevention. Englewood
Cliffs, NJ: Prentice Hall.

Roberts, A. R. (2000). *Crisis intervention handbook:
Assessment, treatment and research* (2nd ed.). New
York: Oxford University Press.

Roberts, A. R., & Dziegielewski, S. F. (1995). Foundation skills and applications of crisis intervention and cognitive therapy. In A. R. Roberts (Ed.),
*Crisis intervention and time-limited cognitive treat-
ment* (pp. 3–27). Newbury Park, CA: Sage.

Scardaville, M., & Spencer, J. (2001). Understanding
the bioterrorist threat: Facts and figures. *The
Heritage Foundation Backgrounder,* No. 1488
[On-line]. Available: www.heritage.org/library/
backgrounder/pdf.bg_1488.pdf.

Simon, J. D. (1999). Nuclear, biological, and chemical terrorism: Understanding the threat and
designing responses. *International Journal of
Emergency Mental Health, 1*(2), 81–89.

Spitzer, W. J. (2002). Critical incident stress management. In A. R. Roberts & G. J. Greene (Eds.) *Social
workers' desk reference* (pp. 447–451). New York:
Oxford University Press.

Terrorism Research Center. (2000). *U.S. army field
manual* (ch. 8, combating terrorism) [On-line].
Available: www.terrorism.com.index.html.

Texas Department of Health. (2001). Bioterrorism
FAQ's [On-line]. Available: www.tdh.state.tx.us/
bioterrorism/default.htm.

*The Economist.* (2001). Avoiding dark winter.
*361*(8245), 29–30.

Wilson, J. P., Friedman, M. J., & Lindy, J. D.
(2001). Treatment goals for PTSD. In J. P. Wilson,
M. J. Friedman, and J. D. Lindy (Eds.), *Treating
psychological trauma & stress* (pp. 3–27).
New York: Guilford Press.

# [5]

# Unravelling the 'War' on Terrorism: A Risk-Management Exercise in War Clothing?

YEE-KUANG HENG*

*Department of International Relations, London School of Economics and Political Science, United Kingdom*

Since the 11 September terrorist outrages, policymakers have waxed lyrical about a 'war' on terrorism as the greatest challenge to international security. The word 'war' implies easily identifiable (normally state) adversaries, and dramatic military action producing decisive, highly visible results at the end. However, this 'war' is in fact more rhetorical than about interstate warfare. Like other rhetorical wars on drugs or crime, it has no visible end, and outcomes will be neither easily apparent nor decisive. This article addresses the conceptual difficulties of a rhetorical 'war' on terrorism from a perspective of risk management. Drawing on military issues in Afghanistan so far, it seeks to provide a more appropriate analytic prism for understanding such a 'war' where enemies are elusive networks, the aim is simply avoiding harm with no prospect of closure, and success is defined more by non-events than by what can be seen.

## Introduction

IN LATE SEPTEMBER 2001, US Defense Secretary Donald Rumsfeld observed that the 'war' on terrorism was something 'very, very different from what people think of when using the word "war" or "campaign". We need to fashion a new vocabulary and different constructs for what we are doing'.[1] This article argues that the language of risk management serves this purpose. To begin with, the use of 'war' terminology spawned inaccurate comparisons with war in its classical form rather than the more appropriate rhetorical variety. In the West, it fuelled what Sir Michael Howard termed a 'media-stoked frenzy' and unrealistic public expectations of visible, quick, decisive results. Classical war assumes a fixed set of identifiable physical (normally state) enemies, not amorphous terror networks. Furthermore, war

228                                          *Security Dialogue* vol. 33, no. 2, June 2002

implies *seeking* positive outcomes with a finite end. The rhetorical war on terror, on the other hand, *avoids* negative futures with no prospect of closure: officials recently indicated that it was more important to constantly disrupt Al-Qaeda than to nab bin Laden. Yet even after shifting gears from classical to rhetorical war, key questions lie unanswered: How does one gauge success, and when does the war end? These inadequacies of 'war' terminology serve as a springboard for broadening the present article's core argument that the rhetorical 'war' against terrorism is more about managing risks than war. First, the guiding philosophy of risk management is anticipatory action to forestall adverse outcomes: a utilitarian moral calculus rather than a focus on guilt or justice. The 'war' on terror also exhibits these features. Second, risk management constantly monitors risks, taking action if necessary. This cyclical, open-ended process also characterizes a protracted struggle where disrupted terror networks regroup and new ones constantly emerge. There is neither a fixed foe nor the finite end point often associated with 'war'. Third, non-events like simply avoiding harm are the criteria for successful risk management. Outcomes will neither be apparent, decisive nor positive, as would be suggested by 'war'. A successful blitz on terror is also defined by non-events like preventing terrorist attacks. Combating terrorism involves political, military, diplomatic, financial, intelligence and police tools of statecraft. However, this article is limited to aspects of the military campaign in Afghanistan, attempting to develop an analytic perspective of risk management for addressing the rhetorical 'war' on terrorism.

## 'Terrorism': The Phenomenon and Its Physical Manifestation

Two levels of analysis are relevant to the 'war' on terrorism. The first comprises the rhetorical war against 'terrorism' as a phenomenon, somewhat akin to the 'war' on crime. The second involves more concrete warfare against bin Laden's Al-Qaeda and the Taliban in Afghanistan: almost a classical war. Ostensibly, each level has different criteria for success. The former defines success in terms of non-events and less visible goals, like preventing further terrorism. The latter entails more measurable results, such as the removal of the Taliban regime. President Bush famously wanted bin Laden 'dead or alive'.

Yet, as this article will show, results like capturing bin Laden and destroying the Taliban regime have been sidelined in Afghanistan in favour of less visible results such as preventing further terrorism generally. The two levels of analysis are interlinked. This article attempts to combine these two levels by extrapolating aspects of risk management from military action in Afghanistan relevant to the broader campaign against international terrorism. By comparing this action with other rhetorical 'wars', such as those on drugs, it will argue that this rhetorical war on terror does not quite qualify as classical warfare but bears a far closer resemblance to risk management.[2]

A central feature of terrorism is the difficulty of defining its amorphous concept. Attempts to do so are often inconclusive – 'one person's terrorist is another's freedom fighter'. The US State Department report 'Patterns of Global Terrorism' defines terrorism as 'premeditated, politically motivated violence against non-combatant targets by subnational or clandestine agents, usually intended to influence an audience'.[3] Some additional elements would render this definition more complete and relevant to this article. Terrorism is not just what has happened, but also what might happen in the future – a risk, so to speak. The threat of terrorism is itself terrorism.[4] Britain previously saw terrorism as merely part of a range of asymmetrical threats. Since the 11 September attacks, it has been elevated to a 'strategic risk' by Britain, prompting a new chapter to its *Strategic Defence Review* (SDR).[5] Furthermore, Al-Qaeda's brand of terrorism deviates from the State Department's definition: it aims to destroy, not to influence an audience. This is discussed in further detail below. Terrorism is more a phenomenon or method of political violence than a clear set of adversaries. The USA's war on terror is open-ended and still ill-defined, further complicating analysis.

## The Consequences of Using 'War' Terminology

President Bush's use of the word 'war' normally implies spectacular military action against fixed, easily identifiable adversaries and a clearly defined end point, with quick, visible, decisive results in a media age shaped by images of smart bombs in the Gulf War.[6] As a result, the use of 'war', to describe the campaign against terrorism contains significant conceptual drawbacks. The context of modern war is traditionally violence between fixed enemies, particularly states. The current war on terror targets the Taliban, hardly an established state, and Al-Qaeda, a loosely organized, transnational network. Furthermore, fighting terrorism is more forward-looking and anticipatory than tackling state enemies. The nature of victory is fundamentally unclear. There will be no ceremonies of surrender on the battleship *Missouri* or Military-Technical Agreements, such as those that ended the Kosovo campaign. Instead, success will be defined by what does not happen rather than by what does. Notwithstanding, the classical 'war' terminology retains startling value because of its emotive, value-laden nature. It rallies the nation by emphasizing the scale of the threat.

*Security Dialogue* vol. 33, no. 2, June 2002

The understanding of war in the West has been shifting from classical inter-state 'war' to intrastate conflict and rhetorical wars on risk scenarios like drugs, crime and now terrorism. Indeed, James Lindsay remarked on the campaign against terror: 'this is more like the drug war'.[7] Instead of the dominant interstate connotations outlined above, it makes more sense to use the word 'war' in this context to mean mobilizing resources against a dangerous activity, which can never be eliminated but can be reduced to a tolerable level.[8] Still, terrorism is a more serious threat than other rhetorical threats like drugs and crime. So-called 'post-modern terrorism' involves all manner of organizations spouting causes from animal liberation to fundamentalist religious fanaticism.[9] Enemies in other rhetorical wars – drug runners, for example – do not aim to destroy a 'host state', such as the USA; they aim to milk it. Al-Qaeda is more interested in destroying its host state altogether, possibly even with weapons of mass destruction (WMD). Bin Laden has described obtaining such weapons as a religious duty. While 'old style' terrorism is normally inclined to negotiations, 'new' terrorism is now seen as part of a new 'war' paradigm that takes a strategic campaign-oriented view of protracted violence rather than episodic efforts in the past.[10] Unlike the 'coercive diplomacy' paradigm of terrorism, there is no proportionate relationship between levels of force employed and aims sought. Unrestrained by political concerns for public support or legitimacy, the aim is to inflict death and destruction, with no specific calls for concessions. The 11 September attacks were not followed by any such demands or by groups claiming responsibility. This 'war' paradigm, of course, is not completely new. Indeed, terrorists have often declared 'war' on the USA and considered themselves as 'armies'. President Clinton invoked the imagery and language of war by describing military retaliation after the 1998 US Embassy bombings as the 'first shot of protracted war',[11] suggesting that this 'war paradigm' is increasingly relevant. If terrorists are increasingly becoming a major security threat to democratic societies, those nations targeted should then consider terrorism more as a military problem than one for policemen and courtrooms,[12] especially since previous assumptions about deterrent measures like retaliation are now impotent against fanatics who welcome death. The focus is now on measures to reduce terror risks, and on applying force if necessary.

The rhetorical war on terrorism invokes the language of war as a semantic instrument for mobilizing public support but employs the vocabulary of risk management in explaining strategic options and outcomes. An *Atlanta Journal-Constitution* article usefully raised many interesting points of entry in what it called the 'quirky character of this new war'.[13] These included difficulties of knowing the enemy, no clear definition of victory with invisible successes, and virtually no prospect that the war will be finally over and conclusively won. Unfortunately, that article did not offer an alternative notion to 'war'. The present article merely suggests risk management as a possible conceptualization.

It does not pretend to offer a definitive interpretation, for many prominent commentators – from James Der Derian to Lawrence Freedman[14] – have offered their own convincing take on events.

## What Is Risk Management?

Risk is defined as the possibility that an adverse state of reality may occur owing to human action or natural events. In theory, addressing the initiating activity can alter this reality. Intuitively, risk means danger in the future. Risk management may be broadly defined as a 'field of activity seeking to monitor, eliminate, reduce and generally control pure risks'.[15] It is a set of ongoing activities including 'feedback mechanisms and continuing performance monitoring', with no finite point.[16] 'Pure' risk denotes only the prospect of harm; 'speculative' risk entails the possibility of gain in return for accepting some harm. It is useful to differentiate between managing 'pure' and 'speculative' risk. For the former, success means simply the avoidance of damage or loss; while the latter means that consequences may range from spectacular gain to great loss.[17] International security risks like terrorism clearly are 'pure' risk rather than 'speculative' risk. The latter is more commonly associated with the fields of investment banking and finance. For 'speculative' risks, objectives need to be clearly articulated in terms of risk and return involved. When managing 'pure' risk, the main aim is simply to avoid harm, making it difficult to establish a clear marker for this goal.

We are interested in addressing one of three levels identified for risk-management research: the global level dealing with international conflict.[18] Unfortunately, no common usage of risk management is discernible in international relations, although the notion has crept into policy documents. One whole chapter of the US Department of Defense's (DoD) *Quadrennial Defense Review* (QDR) published on 30 September 2001 is entitled 'Managing Risk', a central 'strategic tenet' in defence policy. The DoD's 'risk-management framework' balances and mitigates an array of present demands and future risks, from operational force management and institutional risks to future challenges.[19]

The DoD framework is thus too broad for our purposes, since we are concerned more with reducing particular risks than with balancing them against others. After all, there is no single generic model of risk management applicable in all contexts.[20] In order to operationalize risk-management principles into a viable framework for our purposes, the notions described below guide the present analysis.

First, the centre of risk consciousness lies in the future. The potential event is a stimulus to action. Risk management is bound up with attempts to control

232                                                          *Security Dialogue* vol. 33, no. 2, June 2002

and colonize the future. This explains the rationale behind preventing potential terrorist attacks associated with the continued operations of Al-Qaeda.

Second, risk management aims not to totally eliminate problems like terrorism (which is unrealistic anyway) but to minimize or reduce the factors which lead to risks occurring. The factors identified in the present case are Al-Qaeda and the Taliban, whose existence constitutes the risk that further terrorism will be inflicted on Western populations. There is no grand narrative lying behind risk management as there is with war. Its moral calculus is utilitarian: simply avoiding further human harm, not bringing about desirable historical change or processes, or including other moral considerations of guilt or fairness. Although President Bush has couched the struggle in grandiose terms of 'good' against 'evil', the Afghan campaign has in fact been more utilitarian than one of retribution against evil.

Third, the prevalent value system is negative, that is, it is based more on trying to prevent something 'bad', like another terrorist outrage, than on attaining something 'good', such as properly sorting out Afghanistan. Results will be more invisible than visible. Risk management is 'minimalist' in nature, an open commitment with no quick, quantifiable results. This has implications for how we gauge progress in the 'war' on terror.


## The Modes of Risk Management

### Controlling the Future Through Proactive Actions

Despite its bloody and cruel connotations, modern war normally also presumes to bring about a desired outcome, such as the expulsion of Saddam Hussein from Kuwait or Nazi Germany's unconditional surrender. In contrast, one feature of risk management glimpsed in the rhetorical war on terror is that it is specifically aimed at avoiding unwanted future outcomes like further terrorism. Risk management is thus more proactive than war, going beyond mere punitive actions and attempting to avert future adverse consequences. Terrorism involves a key factor of uncertainty about the future, much more than assumed in past wars, where the aim was relatively clear: defeating a present enemy. The centre of consciousness for combating terrorism lies in the future: reducing the risk of its occurrence. Preventing the recurrence of terrorist actions has always been accorded a central place in the anti-terrorist agenda: for example, according to the National Commission on Terrorism, 'priority one is to prevent terrorist attacks'.[21]

Proactive risk management is a standard part of the managing process.[22] It informs the military action against Al-Qaeda in Afghanistan. The 'precautionary principle' of acting even without definitive evidence prevails. Fighting terrorism refers to managing the risk of future terrorist outrages. UK Prime Minister Tony Blair's official statement on the commencement of Operation Enduring Freedom, while pointing out the 'dangers in acting', added that 'the dangers of inaction are much higher'.[23] US Defense Secretary Rumsfeld described pursuing terrorists as a 'proactive' policy, since it was impossible to defend against terrorists everywhere and at all times. He later stressed that recent actions such as Operation Anaconda were not 'retribution' or 'revenge' for 11 September, but rather were 'to protect our country and people from further attack': terrorists under fire in Afghanistan have less time to plan attacks on the USA.[24] Concern about averting adverse future outcomes is indicative of risk management. As Michael O'Hanlon mused, 'prevention rather than revenge should be the guiding principle for US military action' since the central objective is to 'reduce the probability and severity of future attacks'.[25]

A risk-management approach to pre-empt and anticipate future metamorphosis of the terrorist threat seen in Afghanistan informs the broader rhetorical war on terror too. Terrorism is unpredictable, dependent on the smallest whim of individuals and loosely strung groups, compared to the relatively static hierarchy of states and militaries that interstate warfare implies. Planning should be based on several possible images of the future, not just a single one.[26] Although sometimes sensationalistic, public discussion of possible terrorist scenarios has been generally helpful in conceptualizing alternative sets of possible risks. After the 9/11 attacks, risk engulfs seemingly everything we do: from anthrax spores coming through the post to hijacked planes crashing into nuclear plants. As Homeland Security chief Tom Ridge conceded, 'there is a universe of potentials we have to deal with'.[27] In Rumsfeld's words, 'prepare for the unknown, uncertain, the unseen and the unexpected'.[28] The UK Ministry of Defence (MoD) consultations on a new chapter of its SDR give an inkling of emerging future-oriented concepts in dealing with international terrorism. British Defence Secretary Geoff Hoon wanted 'more emphasis on being proactive, pre-empting problems than waiting for them to come to us'.[29] Since 9/11, the tolerance for terrorist risks has greatly diminished. The nexus through which regimes like Iraq might pass WMD to Al-Qaeda is certainly an intolerable risk, despite the lack of convincing evidence on the matter. (At the time of writing, the promised intelligence dossier linking Saddam to Al-Qaeda has yet to materialize. No evidence that resembles what Washington presented to its NATO allies to tie Al-Qaeda to the 11 September attacks has been forthcoming.)[30] Blair upped the ante further by warning that action was necessary now, otherwise 'we will find out too late the potential for destruction'.[31] Such warnings are serious because 'there is no margin for error and no chance to learn from any mistake', according to President Bush.[32] One has to be proactive, for there is no chance to react. Declaring that he 'will not wait on events, while dangers gather', the tone of Bush's 'axis of evil' speech was proactive and anticipatory, indicative of a risk-manager's mind-set.

### Not Focusing on Errant Individuals: No Right or Wrong

A risk-management approach to terrorism is based on a utilitarian moral calculus that replaces other moral criteria such as generosity, guilt or evil. It is managerial, not corrective or punitive. It does not focus on problems or causes, wrongdoing or the morality of erring individuals, but on reducing risks and avoiding harm to the population at large.

The Gulf War and the Kosovo campaign constantly dwelt on the evils of Saddam Hussein and Slobodan Milosevic. In contrast, while bin Laden presently remains at large, the focus in Washington thinking – at least in public – has shifted from an initial one on Osama the 'evil one' 'dead or alive' to one of simply managing the risks posed by Al-Qaeda. National Security Advisor Condleezza Rice stressed that 'the most important thing is to disrupt the capability of this network to operate'.[33] To President Bush, 'focusing on one person' misunderstands the 'scope of the mission': 'terror is bigger than one person'.[34] Admiral Robert Natter, commanding the Atlantic Fleet, felt that 'the answer to this war is not that we have captured bin Laden, but rather keeping them running'.[35] Furthermore, terror networks like Al-Qaeda can function without bin Laden. Al-Qaeda is a loose grouping of people all over the globe who use modern technology to coordinate. New networked terrorist groups are less affected by the loss of individuals. They cannot be decapitated in the traditional sense of 'personalized deterrence'; they can only be disrupted and have their effectiveness reduced. Eliminating bin Laden would only mean a stumble, not a pause in terrorist operations. He is only a 'cog, albeit a large one, in a system that will outlast his demise'.[36] For this reason, Secretary Rumsfeld recently suggested it was 'unwise' to personalize the conflict in the way in which the Gulf War was personalized through the focus on Saddam Hussein.[37]

A managerial approach to bin Laden has useful implications for the rhetorical war on terrorism. As with other rhetorical wars – such as the war on crime – networks are the predominant form, and singling out individuals will only divert scarce resources. The real focus should be on disruption, not decapitation.

### Militarily Reducing Risks of Future Terrorism

Terrorism spawned from foreign countries and committed within another state's borders stands the best chance of being called 'war'. But the practical aim of retaliatory military action remains the same: more effective suppression indicative of risk management, rather than the total elimination evoked by the term 'war'. Military force is probably a blunt instrument to use against terrorist organizations, and hierarchical military structure is unsuited for tackling networks. The use of military force might also be counterproductive, fuelling more hatred by killing civilians. Intelligence and police activities are needed to prevent further attacks, not just bombing. But CIA chief George Tenet's Congressional testimony in February emphasized that 'intelligence will never give you 100% predictive capability on terrorist events'.[38] Leaving terrorist infrastructure intact will still leave states vulnerable to further attacks. As a former State Department counter-terrorism czar put it, 'there's no point addressing root causes with bin Laden. He doesn't like America. We are the root cause'.[39] Where terrorists want to destroy, not bargain, and intelligence and diplomatic cooperation cannot be foolproof, what we *can* do is manage the risks we know of.

Risk management, in this case, reduces the currently known factors that lead to risks occurring, such as the terrorist infrastructure in Afghanistan. Secretary of State Colin Powell suggests that 'we can reduce the likelihood of ... [terrorist] incidents if we go after those terrorist organizations'.[40] This is a form of active military containment, not always assuming the shape of war.

A Congressional bill of April 1996 dictates that the president 'use all necessary means including ... military force, to disrupt, dismantle, and destroy international infrastructure used by international terrorists'.[41] The strategic military goal in Afghanistan is precisely this. As CIA chief Tenet recommended in his Congressional testimony, 'we have to minimize their ability' to commit further terrorist acts. By 'environment shaping', it is possible to 'shrink zones of chaos and terrorist sanctuary',[42] such as Afghanistan, by destroying terror infrastructure and conditions there that make them conducive to terrorists, and to prevent new zones from forming. The ability of networks like Al-Qaeda to make opportunistic use of weak states makes it more imperative to do this, although it is unclear what impact modern communication technologies have on the need for quasi-virtual organizations to secure a territorial refuge.[43]

Broadening the analysis beyond Afghanistan toward the rhetorical war on terror, adopting a military risk-management approach can make it more difficult for terrorists to organize and operate, but nothing will stop the most determined terrorists. This applies in the case of other rhetorical wars as well, especially the drugs war, where the temptation of huge profits will always draw new recruits. Certain physical manifestations of terror networks, such as training camps in Somalia or Yemen, can be destroyed, reducing the risk of terrorism, but not eliminating it. Furthermore, given the lack of anti-terror deterrence in the case of suicide bombers, the case for pre-emptive strikes grows.[44] Already, the UK MoD is hinting that its forces are to be given a new mission to find and destroy overseas terror networks threatening Britain. However, Afghanistan was a unique case, a militarily weak state isolated diplomatically and facing unprecedented international consensus. Other countries will not present the same set of relatively straightforward arguments for using force.

236 *Security Dialogue* vol. 33, no. 2, June 2002

# Defining Success

Success in 'war' is normally positively defined by desirable outcomes like defeating a fixed identifiable enemy or grand ideological causes. It has a visible finite point. However, most analyses of terrorism concur that it cannot be eliminated, only controlled and reduced; it is a problem that is not to be solved once and for all, but rather managed.[45] Success in risk management is negative in nature: it aims more at *avoiding* negative outcomes, rather than at *desiring* or *attaining* positively defined results. The key principle is that reduction of harmful actions is a gain, as this lessens the number of victims.[46] By focusing on avoidable harm, the risk-management approach fosters a negative, if not dystopian, outlook: understandably so, for the rhetorical war on terrorism is like the war on drugs, 'unwinnable'. The idea of 'winning' with 100% success in counter-terrorism is impossible given that there are so many possible points vulnerable to terrorist attack. Even positive results like the Taliban's demise provide no prospect of closure.

### Unseen Successes

As President Bush's address to the Joint Session of Congress made clear, in addition to dramatic strikes, possible actions include covert operations, 'secret even in success'. People aren't going to see 'exactly what's taking place on their TV screens'.[47]

Yet visible results on television have been assumed to be the context of modern war, especially since the Gulf War. The difficulty of measuring success in Afghanistan was exemplified recently by calls for Washington to produce numbers of enemy dead and hard evidence of success in Operation Anaconda. The stated aim of Operation Enduring Freedom has been to 'degrade and disrupt' terrorist networks, and to 'prevent further terrorism', not to produce body counts.[48] Disrupting and reducing the capability of terrorists has been central to current anti-terror strategies. The USA's 1997 National Security Strategy for a New Century declared its aim as being to 'prevent, disrupt and defeat terrorist operations before they occur'.[49] The key benchmark of successful risk management is simply avoiding harm. Success will be low-key, unpublicized, sometimes even unknown, involving the disrupting and quashing of networks here and there. There will be no grandiose victory parades. Disruption means targeting a terrorist organization and not only stopping one of its particular operations but rendering all of its activities more difficult. The ultimate goal is to make it more ineffective. Keeping bin Laden on the run helps keep him 'neutralized'. Senior US military officials feel that the recent Operation Anaconda impaired Al-Qaeda's ability to continue operations, with senior commanders on the run and mid-level commanders killed.[50] The USA's constantly chipping away at Al-Qaeda can at least curtail the latter's ability to strike at will or operate with impunity. Secretary Rumsfeld will allegedly continue in this way 'until Americans can go about their lives without fear' and in 'relative freedom'.[51] The criteria to be met in order to affirm that such a state has been attained remain unclear.

Events from Afghanistan suggest that a rhetorical war on terrorism is about managing risks, not aiming for absolutely zero terrorist attacks. Although FBI figures suggest that, by the end of December 2001, Al-Qaeda capabilities had diminished by no more than 30%, a triumph of risk management lies in the non-events, the number of days that go by without a terrorist outrage. In this sense, the campaign against terrorism mirrors rhetorical 'wars' waged on crime and drugs. Success must be defined in terms of 'reducing both the probability and consequences of further attack'.[52] The benchmark of success will not be quantifiable, and much of the success will not be visible to the public eye. According to Secretary of State Powell, 'success may never come in the form that there is never another terrorist incident'. It may well take the form that 'we bring this under control and make it far more difficult for such organizations to exist'.[53] This is typical risk-management language, not an expression of the relative certainties of war. It is about managing insecurity, rather than providing total security, which – especially in this context of terrorism – is impossible. Victory is hard to define, and even more so when there is no clear conclusion of the battle.

### *An Open-Ended Process: Tackling the Hydra Effect*

Such an end point has eluded operations in Afghanistan. The initial name of the military operation before it was changed to assuage Muslim sensitivities, 'Infinite Justice', suggests the type of operation it will be. Army Secretary Thomas White noted that it was difficult to 'draw a finite box' expecting things to be completed by certain dates.[54] Tony Blair urged 'patience' and digging in for the 'long haul'.[55] Despite the collapse of the Taliban, US-led forces have had to constantly attack regrouping Al-Qaeda and Taliban elements. In November and January, the Zawar Khili cave complex was struck repeatedly after attempts to reconstitute Al-Qaeda were observed in the area.

In March, Operation Anaconda reminded the world that the conflict was not yet over. British officials warned that Al-Qaeda remnants posed a continuing threat to Britain. Taliban and Al-Qaeda fighters are arguably adopting classic guerrilla tactics, though guerrillas normally do not pose international security risks. From a risk-management approach, managing the risks they pose entails constant monitoring, and taking repeated action if necessary. Such actions as we have seen – the toughest and bloodiest to date – even after the fall of the Taliban, suggest that the endgame is far from over. British Defence Secretary Hoon described the latest deployment of Royal Marine Commandos to

238                                              *Security Dialogue* vol. 33, no. 2, June 2002

Afghanistan as 'open-ended'.[56] If Al-Qaeda attempts to regroup and strike again, Bush has said that he wants the USA to respond with a 'sustained, tireless, relentless campaign' to keep the terrorists on the run, adding that 'we're going to stay at it for however long it takes'.[57] These vague criteria for measuring military progress in managing terror risks – disrupting terror networks and keeping the terrorists on the run – leave open the possibility that more action will follow assessments that terrorists once again are capable of causing harm.

The nature of the Afghan campaign offers risk-management lessons for the rhetorical war on terrorism. Encouraged by the terminology of 'war', the prevalent strand of thinking about counter-terrorism is an erroneous tendency towards absolute solutions and talk of quickly eradicating terrorism, rather than seeing the problem as something to be managed through a more long-term process.[58] President Bush's remarks that 'this is not an instant gratification war' aptly describe a process of risk-management, where the finishing line is not easily apparent.[59] In risk management, it is essential to constantly assess the effectiveness of measures taken. This is a cyclical and ongoing process rather than a linear progression toward definitive end goals. Such a process is never complete, as new risks are always emerging or old risks are reconstituted. In sum, the process does not establish a definitive conclusion.[60] Policy should not be gauged in terms of definitive end goals but rather in terms of this ongoing process of risk management.

Perhaps we should see the 'war' on terrorism in light of other interminable, unwinnable rhetorical wars, in which a similar lack of clarity of mission and the 'hydra effect' predominate.[61] With US forces deployed from Georgia to the Philippines and talk of action against Iraq in the terror war, demands are being made both in Congress and in the media for the Bush administration to better define new missions, to specify how long they will last and to clarify objectives.[62] However, counter-terrorism should not be too obsessed with flavours of the moment or specific time-frames, for there are always new threats ready to replace bin Laden – the so-called 'hydra effect'. Counter-terrorism is about constantly being on the lookout, managing known terrorist risks as well as newly materializing ones. As RAND's Ian Lesser reiterated, 'terrorism as a phenomenon is so diffuse with so many points of risk that 100 percent success in counter-terrorism is not realistic'.[63]

Terrorist networks are notoriously elusive and lack the hard physical infrastructure that states possess. They are also many and diffuse, and one easily springs up to replace another. President Bush's speeches emphasize that 'patience will be one of our strengths' in a 'task that does not end'.[64] Managing terror risks has no endgame because of the need to constantly disrupt and harass terrorist cells, reducing the risks they pose. Al-Qaeda will not be totally eliminated despite its Afghan setbacks; it will only be weakened. Attempts are already under way to reconstitute it elsewhere, using such tools of globalization as the Internet and e-mail encryption. Meanwhile, other terror networks can arise. Homeland Security Chief Tom Ridge further warned that coping with the threat from Al-Qaeda or other terrorist organizations would be a 'permanent condition'.[65]

# Conclusion

Employing 'war' terminology has had several consequences for the campaign against terror. It has focused attention on military actions against easily identifiable state enemies, with the aim of attaining clearcut, decisive, positive results. Two factors suggest why such implications have misled efforts to understand this war. First, this 'war' is more rhetorical than a classical interstate war: it has no defined end point and is unwinnable. Second, despite the high profile of military force in Afghanistan, this rhetorical war exhibits more features of risk management than of warfare: the philosophy of 'anticipationism' informs military action against Al-Qaeda, seen as a precautionary measure to prevent further terror attacks. The moral calculus is utilitarian, seeking to avoid harm rather than desiring positive outcomes or addressing questions of guilt or justice. Managing risks of terrorism is an open-ended endeavour against hydra-headed enemies, where results are neither quickly achieved nor readily apparent. In sum, a risk-management approach explains these aspects of the 'war' on terrorism better than the idea of 'war' itself.

## NOTES AND REFERENCES

\* Yee-Kuang Heng is a Doctoral Student at the LSE working on the concept of risk management and international security. He is grateful to anonymous referees and the editor for comments on an earlier draft of this article. E-mail: yeekuangheng@yahoo.com. The publication of the article was supported by the Berghof Foundation for Conflict Research, Berlin, as part of *Security Dialogue*'s series on 'Resolving Modern Conflicts'.

1 'DoD News Briefing – Secretary Rumsfeld', *US Department of Defense News Transcript*, 20 September 2001, available at http://www.defenselink.mil/news/Sep2001/t09202001_t920ruma.html.

2 I am grateful to anonymous reviewers for these suggestions.

3 See 'Introduction' to US Department of State, *Patterns of Global Terrorism 1999* (Washington, DC: Office of the Secretary of State, April 2000).

4 Paul Pillar, *Terrorism and US Foreign Policy* (Washington, DC: Brookings Institution, 2001), p. 14.

240                                                   *Security Dialogue* vol. 33, no. 2, June 2002

5  UK Ministry of Defence, 'Public Discussion on the New Chapter for the Strategic Defence Review', London, February 2002, available at http://www.mod.uk/issues/sdr/new_chapter/glance.htm.

6  Michael Howard, 'What's in a Name? How to Fight Terrorism', *Foreign Affairs*, vol. 81, no. 1, January/February 2002, pp. 22–35.

7  Don Melvin, 'Enemy, Victory Hard to Define', *Atlanta Journal-Constitution*, 18 September 2001.

8  Howard (note 6 above), p. 22

9  Walter Laquer, 'Post-Modern Terrorism', *Foreign Affairs*, vol. 75, no. 5, September/October 1996, pp. 24–36.

10  Ian O. Lesser, Bruce Hoffman, John Arquilla, David F. Ronfeldt, Michele Zanini & Brian Michael Jenkins, *Countering the New Terrorism* (Santa Monica, CA: RAND, 1999), Document No. MR-989-AF, p. 46.

11  Ibid., p. 70.

12  Daniel Pipes, 'War, Not Crime: Time for a Paradigm Shift', *National Review*, 1 October 2001; Caleb Carr, 'Terrorism as Warfare', *World Policy Journal*, vol. 13, no. 4, Winter 1996–97, pp. 1–13.

13  Melvin (note 7 above).

14  For example, James Der Derian, '9.11: Before, After, and In Between', *Social Science Research Council*, available at http://www.ssrc.org/sept11/essays/der_derian.htm; Lawrence Freedman, 'The Third World War?', *Survival*, vol. 43, no. 4, Winter 2001–02, pp. 61–88; Mary Kaldor, 'Terror in the US: Murky Road to War', *Fathom*, 13 September 2001, available at http://www.fathom.com/feature/122358.

15  Eve Coles, Denis Smith & Steve Tombs, *Risk Management and Society* (Dordrecht: Kluwer Academic, 2000), p. 24.

16  Alan Waring & A. Ian Glendon, *Managing Risk: Critical Issues for Survival and Success into the 21st Century* (London: Thomson Learning, 1998), p. 3.

17  Ibid., p. xxii.

18  The others are corporate organizational culture and individual perception and cognitive beliefs; ibid., p. 426.

19  US Department of Defense, *Quadrennial Defense Review* (Washington, DC: DoD), pp. 13, 57.

20  Christopher Hood & David K. C. Jones, *Accident and Design: Contemporary Debates in Risk Management* (London: UCL Press, 1996), p. 5.

21  Report of the National Commission on Terrorism, *Countering the Changing Threat of International Terrorism*, June 2000; available at http://www.fas.org/irp/threat/commission.html.

22  Coles, Smith & Tombs (note 15 above), p. 47.

23  Tony Blair, *Prime Minister's Statement on Military Action in Afghanistan*, 7 October 2001, available at http://www.number-10.gov.uk/news.asp?NewsId-2712&SectionId=32.

24  See 'Secretary Rumsfeld Interview with the Telegraph', *DoD News Transcripts*, 23 February 2002; and Kathleen T. Rhem, 'Coalition Turning Up the Pressure, but Battle Not Over', *American Forces Press Service*, 6 March 2002.

25 Michael O'Hanlon, 'The Case for a Careful Military Response', Brookings Institution Analysis Paper 1: Response to Terrorism, 25 September 2001; available at http://www.brook.edu/dybdocroot/views/articles/ohanlon/2001_militaryoptions.htm.

26 Pillar (note 4 above), p. 229.

27 Ridge cited in 'US Tries to Guess Next Terror Target', *Guardian Unlimited*, 3 November 2001, available at http://www.guardian.co.uk/uslatest/story/0,1282,1287584,00.html.

28 'Terror Prompts Huge US Military Revamp', *BBC News Online*, 1 February 2002.

29 Michael Evans, 'Forces Take On Anti-Terror Role', *The Times* (London), 15 February 2002.

30 Ivo Daalder & James Lindsay, 'Force Isn't Only Way to Confront Axis', *San Jose Mercury News*, 24 March 2002.

31 See Andrew Grice, 'Blair Defends Bush Plan for Attack on Saddam', *The Independent*, 4 March 2002.

32 Jim Garamone, 'Bush Pledges To Hunt Terrorists, Calls for Quick Budget Approval', *American Forces Press Service*, 15 March 2002.

33 Rice cited in 'Bin Laden Search Brings Frustration', *Guardian Unlimited*, 15 February 2002; available at http://www.guardian.co.uk/worldlatest/story/0,1280,-1521784,00.html.

34 President's comments in 'President Bush holds Press Conference', *Office of the White House Press Secretary*, 13 March 2002.

35 Admiral Natter quoted in 'USS Roosevelt Returns Home', *Washington Post*, 27 March 2002.

36 Walter Pincus, 'Al Qaeda to Survive Bin Laden, Panel Told', *Washington Post*, 19 December 2001.

37 For these arguments, see Lesser et al. (note 10 above), p. 132; Paul Dibb, 'The Future of International Coalitions: How Useful? How Manageable?', *Washington Quarterly*, vol. 25, no. 2, Spring 2002, pp. 131–144; and 'Secretary Rumsfeld Television Interview with MSNBC', *DoD News Transcripts*, 28 March 2002.

38 Tabassum Zakaria, 'CIA Tenet Defends Agency, Warns of New Plots', *Reuters*, 6 February 2002; available at http://dailynews.yahoo.com/h/nm/20020206/ts/attack_cia_dc.html.

39 Pillar (note 4 above), p. 29.

40 'Jeremy Paxman Interviews Colin Powell', *BBC Online*, accessed 21 September 2001.

41 Cited in Christopher Harmon, *Terrorism Today* (London: Frank Cass, 2000), p. 257

42 Lesser et al. (note 10 above), p. 134

43 Steven Simon & Daniel Benjamin, 'The Terror', *Survival*, vol. 43, no. 4, Winter 2001, pp. 5–18.

44 Ehud Sprinzak, 'Revisiting the Superterrorism Debate', *Foreign Policy*, September/October 2001; available at http://www.foreignpolicy.com/issue_SeptOct_2001/sprinzakrevisiting.html.

45 See Christopher Harmon, *Terrorism Today* (London: Frank Cass, 2000); Pillar (note 4 above); Philip B. Heymann, *Terrorism and America: A Commonsense Strategy for a Democratic Society* (Cambridge, MA: MIT Press, 1998), Jeane J. Kirkpatrick, 'The Case for Force', *Chronicle of Higher Education*, 28 September 2001, available at http://www.aei.org/ra/rakirk010928.htm.

242                                          *Security Dialogue* vol. 33, no. 2, June 2002

46  Hazel Kemshall, 'Risk Assessment and Management of Known Sexual and Violent Offenders: A Review of Current Issues', *Police Research Series Paper 140* (London: Home Office Police and Reducing Crime Unit, 2001), p. 39.

47  George W. Bush, 'Address to a Joint Session of Congress and the American People', *Office of the White House Press Secretary*, 20 September 2001.

48  Donald Rumsfeld, 'Message from the Secretary of Defense to DoD Personnel', *American Forces Information Service*, 7 October 2001; available at http://www.defenselink.mil/news/Oct2001/n10092001_200110091.html.

49  William J. Clinton, *A National Security Strategy for a New Century* (Washington D.C: The White House, May 1997); available at http://clinton2.nara.gov/WH/EOP/NSC/Strategy/#threats.

50  For an analysis of disruption, see David Tucker, *Skirmishes at the Edge of Empire* (Westport, CT: Praeger, 1997), pp. 103–104; Bob Stewart, 'Finding Bin Laden Is Not the Priority', *BBC Online*, accessed 27 September 2001; 'US Says Al Qaida Network Rendered Ineffective', *YahooNews*, accessed 23 March 2002.

51  Rudi Williams, 'War Will Continue Until Americans Live Without Fear', *American Forces Press Service*, 29 October 2001.

52  Kurt M. Campbell & Michele A. Flournoy, *To Prevail: An American Strategy for the Campaign Against Terrorism* (Washington, DC: CSIS Press, November 2001), p. 300.

53  'Jeremy Paxman Interviews Secretary Powell', *BBC Online*, accessed 21 September 2001.

54  Cited in Kim Burger, 'USA Embarks on 'Infinite Task', *Jane's Defence Weekly*, 21 September 2001.

55  Tony Blair, 'Prime Minister's Statement to the House of Commons', *10 Downing Street Newsroom*, 8 October 2001; available at http://www.number10.gov.uk/news.asp?NewsId=2707&SectionId=32.

56  Cited in Richard Norton-Taylor and Julian Borger, 'Commandos Going In as Confusion Reigns', *The Guardian*, 20 March 2002; available at http://www.guardian.co.uk/afghanistan/story/0,1284,670452,00.html.

57  Garamone (note 32 above).

58  Pillar (note 4 above), pp. 5–6.

59  George W. Bush cited in 'Nigerian President Offers Solidarity, Support to US', *Office of the White House Press Secretary*, 2 November 2001.

60  Ron E. Hester & R. M. Harrison, eds, *Risk Assessment and Risk Management* (Cambridge: Royal Society of Chemistry, 1998), p. 6; Coles, Smith & Tombs (note 15 above), p. 47.

61  Eva Bertram & Kenneth Sharpe, 'The Unwinnable Drug War: What Clausewitz Would Tell Us', *World Policy Journal*, vol. 13, no. 4, Winter 1996–97, pp. 41–53.

62  'Not So Subtle Reminders of Terrorist Threats to Come', *USA Today*, 4 March 2002, p. 11A; 'Congress Presses Bush on Terror War', *Associated Press Online*, 4 March 2002.

63  Melvin (note 7 above).

64  George W. Bush, 'Presidential Address to the Nation', *Office of the White House Press Secretary*, 7 October 2001; 'Address to a Joint Session of Congress', *Office of the White House Press Secretary*, 20 September 2001.

65  Bill Miler, 'Ridge Close to Unveiling New Warning System', *Washington Post*, 9 March 2002, p. A13.

# [6]

# The Response to Terrorism as a
# Threat to Liberal Democracy[1]

### PETER CHALK
#### *Government, University of Queensland*

When dealing with terrorism as a threat to liberal democracy, it is a common assumption that it is the terrorists — who by definition refuse the rules of the liberal democratic "game" — who pose the greatest threat to the underlying principles and freedoms that are enshrined in this form of political life. However, in instances where the state fails to ensure that its response to terrorism is limited, well-defined and controlled, it is likely that institutionalised counter-terrorist policies will pose an even greater threat to the political and civil traditions that are central to the liberal democratic way of life. This paper demonstrates the potential danger by examining three cases when counter-terrorist policies initiated by (supposedly) liberal democratic entities came dangerously close to transplanting subversive terror from "below" with institutionalised, bureaucratised terror from "above": the "strategy of tension" initiated in Italy between 1969 and 1974; the Spanish "dirty war" against *ETA* between 1983 and 1987; and the abandonment of democratic rule in Peru between 1992 and 1996. The paper concludes that ultimately the effectiveness of the liberal democratic state's response to terrorism depends on its acceptability. It is therefore paramount that any solution which is initiated is made with due regard to the long term impact that it will have on the wider process of liberal democratic life.

Since the late 1960s when terrorism[2] emerged as a significant feature of domestic and international political life, liberal democracies have been struggling with the problem of how to respond in a manner that is consistent with their own norms of legitimacy and acceptability. One of the key foundations of the modern liberal democratic state is the requirement that the government of the day safeguards the

---

[1] It is recognised that to arrive at widely accepted definitions of terrorism and democracy is a contentious and difficult task. It is therefore stressed from the outset that this article proceeds from a Judeao-Christian context and is based on those values and principles which are seen to form the basis of the ethical and legal systems of Western liberal democratic states.

[2] For the purposes of this paper, terrorism is defined as the systematic use of a particular type of illegitimate violence that is employed by sub-state actors as a means of achieving specific political objectives. It is a psychological tactic that seeks to spread fear-inducing effects in a target group wider than the immediate audience through the actual or feared indiscriminate targeting of non-combatant victims. In so doing, it may be regarded as a means of political communication that aims to influence behaviour through the precipitation of a general state of fear and collapse that is exploited to alter political attitudes in such a way that will be beneficial to the group concerned.

security of its citizens by enacting and enforcing laws which are designed to protect their interests. Given the fundamental threat that terrorism poses to any liberal democratic society living under the rule of law, it is generally accepted that such polities must, as a basic principle, respond to acts of terrorism in a firm manner.[3]

Given that the basic task is to defend the community's liberal democratic way of life, however, it is essential that the manner of the state's response to terrorism does not undermine those values and traditions which make such an existence possible in the first place. Indeed, should the government start to use counter-measures of an illegal or unconstitutional manner ("fighting fire with fire"), the state in question runs a very grave risk of undermining its own legitimacy and creating a situation far worse than the one it is attempting to counter.

This paper will examine three specific instances when the state's response to terrorism represented, arguably, a greater danger to the defining principles that underpin liberal democratic forms of government than did the nature of the terrorist threat itself. It will proceed in the following manner. First it briefly examines the central assumptions and principles that underpin liberal democratic systems of criminal law. It then analyses the chief dangers to liberal and democratic principles in state responses to terrorism, illustrating these by reference to three specific case studies: Italy between 1969 and 1974; Spain between 1983 and 1987; and Peru between 1992 and 1996. The paper concludes by developing a model of counter-terrorism that is consistent with liberal democratic norms of social and political legitimacy.

## The Liberal Democratic State and Criminal Law

In essence, the main purpose of criminal law within the modern liberal democratic state is to prevent unconstrained individual behaviour from upsetting the order of society as a whole. Generally speaking, wrongful action can only be made subject to the force of this criminal code in one of two instances: either if it poses an immediate threat to society; or, if left unchecked, it would be likely to cause widespread social harm.[4]

Power conferred to the state in order to curb crime lies at the very heart of the liberal democratic "contractual"[5] conception of political obligation. In return for

---

[3] Paul Wilkinson, "The Role of the Military in Combating Terrorism in a Democratic Society", *Terrorism and Political Violence* 8, 3 (1996), p. 2.

[4] See, for instance, D. Raphael, *Problems of Political Philosophy* (London: Macmillan, 1992), pp. 56-74, 114.

[5] Social contract theories of the state attempt to justify political obligation as an undertaking that is based on an implicit promise to obey the government. State and the citizen, it is argued, have entered into an agreement whereby the government has a duty to provide law and order and a right to expect obedience; and where the citizen has a duty to obey the government and a right to expect its protection. Although there are many problems with such an approach — namely that the theory, in purporting to account for all bonds in society, ignores the psychological fact that the individual is

accepting the security and order that is provided by the state, a citizen bestows upon himself or herself the additional reciprocal obligation both to accept and to obey the legal parameters of that same state.[6]

Although liberal democrats accept the necessity of restricting freedom for the good of society as a whole, they are also adamant that clear limits must be imposed on legal state authority. The absolutist notion of "peace by subjection" that goes back to the omnicompetent philosophy of Thomas Hobbes[7] is firmly rejected in favour of a polity that is characterised by restricted and limited government. It is the essence of liberal democratic thought that checks and balances should form an integral component of the political system in order to constrain the power of the state and prevent abuses of its authority. As Alexis de Tocqueville argued in his commentary on democracy in America:

> In my opinion the main evil present in the democratic institutions of the United States does not arise ... from their weakness but from their overwhelming strength; and I am not so much concerned at the excessive liberty which reigns in that country, as at the very inadequate securities which exist against tyranny. If, on the other hand, a legislative power could be so constituted without necessarily being the slave of its passions; an executive, so as to retain a degree of uncontrolled authority; and a judiciary, so as to remain independent of the other two powers; a government would still be democratic, without incurring any risk of tyrannical abuse.[8]

Legal restraint, justly imposed on the government in the form of constitutional safeguards, thus forms an integral part of any liberal democratic polity. The rights of the accused must be protected; the powers of judicial and police officials must be limited by such imperatives as reasonable suspicion, "minimum force", and due process; and redress must be available for those wrongly accused or imprisoned. It is the existence of such safeguards that legitimise and generate public acceptance of the state's use of coercive violence in the exercise of criminal justice.[9]

---

by nature a social animal with concomitant dispossessions of association towards his/her fellows — it does reveal certain important truths about the reciprocal quality of obligations and responsibilities between government and citizen in democratic states. For further details see Paul Wilkinson, *Terrorism and the Liberal State* (London: Macmillan, 1979), pp. 12-16; and Raphael, *Problems of Political Philosophy*, pp. 182-89.

[6] Peter Chalk, "The Liberal Democratic Response to Terrorism", *Terrorism and Political Violence* 7, 4 (1995), p. 13.

[7] For further details see Thomas Hobbes, "Leviathan", in Jene Porter, ed., *Classics in Political Philosophy* (Ontario: Prentice-Hall Canada, 1989), pp. 261-82; David Apter, *Introduction to Political Analysis* (Cambridge: Winthrop, 1977), pp. 80-83; Wilkinson, *Terrorism and the Liberal State*, pp. 8-10; and Raphael, *Problems of Political Philosophy*, pp. 77-78.

[8] Alexis de Tocqueville, *Democracy in America* (New York: Mentor Books, 1961), pp. 115-16.

[9] Ronald Crelinsten and Iffet Ozkut, "Reconceptualising Security Threats in a Post-Cold War, Integrated Europe: Implications for Counterterrorism and Human Rights". Paper presented at the "European Democracies Against Terrorism: Governmental Policies, Societal Responses and Supranational Cooperation in the Face of an Evolving Challenge", International Workshop, Oñati, Spain, 2-3 May 1996, p. 8.

## Counter-Terrorism in the Liberal Democratic State

Terrorism is a type of behaviour which cannot be tolerated within the legal context of any state. This is especially true of liberal democratic polities. Terrorism, by definition, seeks to disrupt the normal course of social interaction. Its overall aim is not simply to cause immediate destruction but, more intrinsically, gradually to eradicate the solidarity, cooperation and interdependence upon which social cohesion and functioning depend. The hope is that eventually the community will be reduced to pockets of frightened individuals concerned only with their personal safety and thus isolated from their wider social context.[10]

In other words, terrorism seeks to destroy the very structure that enables a liberal and democratic way of life to exist in the first place. By encouraging a general perception that the government is no longer able to fulfill its primary security function, terrorism seeks to undermine the political order which — by freeing each person from the arbitrary will of another — allows individuals to act independently (a right that liberal democrats argue all should enjoy equally). It is therefore vital that in working to counter this threat, liberal democratic governments strive to uphold the legitimacy of their own rule of law. Not do so would be to undermine the very basis that establishes the criminality of terrorism in the first place. As Wardlaw observes:

> To believe that depriving citizens of their individual rights and suspending the democratic process is necessary to maintain 'order' is to put oneself on the same [mistaken] moral plane as the terrorists who believe the 'end justifies the means'.[11]

Characterisations of counter-terrorism typically fall into one of two categories. First there is the criminal justice model. Here terrorism is viewed as a crime with the onus of response placed squarely within the bounds of the state's criminal legal system. Second there is the military model. Here terrorism is viewed as an act of revolutionary warfare with the onus of response placed on the military and entailing the use of retaliatory strikes, campaigns of retribution and troop deployment.[12]

The typical approach adopted by liberal democratic states is to treat terrorism as a crime where punishment takes place within its system of criminal law. In other words, its response conforms to the criminal justice model of counter-terrorism. Most liberal democratic states are reluctant to adopt the war model of counter-terrorism, largely because the powers of the army in a civilian context tend to be ill-defined and could well place soldiers in positions of personal authority which would

---

[10] For further details see Peter Chalk, *West European Terrorism and Counter-Terrorism: The Evolving Dynamic* (London: Macmillan, 1996), chapter 1; and Martha Crenshaw, "The Concept of Revolutionary Terrorism", *Journal of Conflict Resolution* 16, 3 (1972), pp. 383-96.

[11] Grant Wardlaw, *Political Terrorism:. Theory, Tactics and Counter-Measures* (Cambridge: CUP, 1989), p. 69.

[12] Ronald Crelinsten and Alex Schmid, "Western Responses to Terrorism: A Twenty-Five Year Balance Sheet", *Terrorism and Political Violence* 4, 4 (1992), pp. 332-33.

be likely to have serious implications for civil liberties. As a result, military resources are used as a last resort, only to be employed in times of extreme civil unrest or emergency.[13]

The most significant danger that faces the liberal democratic state when it confronts the threat of terrorism as an issue of law is one of over-reaction. Under such circumstances, government officials typically make radical and unjustified departures from conventional judicial and law enforcement procedures, with the state progressively drawn into a parallel grey zone of illegality which mirrors the one in which the terrorist operates.[14] In essence, the criminal justice system is politicised and becomes what Otto Kirchheimer calls an order of "political justice", where the rules and rights enshrined in the principle of due process are either wilfully misinterpreted or completely disregarded.[15]

To guard against such an eventuality, any liberal democratic response must rest on one overriding principle: a commitment to uphold and maintain constitutional systems of legal authority. In instances where the state fails to abide by this fundamental dictum, counter-terrorist responses run the very grave risk of posing even more of a danger to underlying liberal and democratic postulates and freedoms than does extremist political violence itself.

Three examples can be used in support of this basic assertion: Italy between 1969 and 1974; Spain between 1983 and 1987; and Peru between 1992 and 1996. In each instance, the counter-measures initiated by these supposedly liberal democratic parliamentary entities represented a severe departure from accepted constitutional principles of authority and law and order — coming dangerously close to transplanting, as Hacker and Wardlaw put it, insurgent terror from "below" with bureaucratised, institutionalised terror from "above".[16]

## State Responses to Terrorism and the Subversion of Liberal Democracy

*Italy*

The Italian case relates to the initiation of what can best be described as a "strategy of tension" or "counter mobilisation" during the early to mid 1970s. The policy aimed to create and exploit an atmosphere of extreme civil unrest throughout the country in the expectation that this would induce public demand for increased "law

---

[13] Chalk, "The Liberal Response to Terrorism", p. 16.

[14] See Ronald Crelinsten, "Terrorism as Political Communication: The Relationship between the Controller and the Controlled", in Paul Wilkinson and Alasdair Stewart, eds, *Contemporary Research on Terrorism* (Aberdeen: Aberdeen University Press, 1989), p. 9.

[15] See generally Otto Kirchheimer, *Political Justice* (Princeton: Princeton University Press, 1961).

[16] F. Hacker, *Crusaders, Criminals, Crazies: Terror and Terrorism in Our Age* (New York: W. W. Norton and Co., 1976); Wardlaw, *Political Terrorism*, p. 69.

and order" measures against the *Brigata Rossa* (Red Brigades) — an extreme left wing terrorist group that had emerged in 1969.

By the late 1960s, Italy was a country engulfed by extra-parliamentary left wing political activity. Believing that the battle to liberate Italy from fascism had been fought to establish a socialist state, many on the radical left were experiencing an increasing sense of frustration at the paramount rule enjoyed by the moderate conservative Christian Democrats who had dominated a series of coalition governments since 1945. At the same time, there was growing disillusionment among some socialists and communists with the reformist and often pro-Western attitude of the Italian Communist Party to national and international affairs, a stance which effectively excluded the far left from adequate representation in the Italian political system. Together these two factors combined to create a feeling of "betrayed resistance" which, by the mid-to-late 1960s, had crystallised in repeated calls for the mobilisation of extra-parliamentary opposition to achieve fundamental socio-economic change.[17]

Further radicalising the overall political environment in Italy at this time were radical New Left ideologies, which had become entrenched in militant university circles throughout the country. In response to the inherent contradictions and perceived injustices of the post-World War II era, students had begun increasingly to identify with all-embracing anti-Western and anti-NATO ideals. Not only did these dogmas provide a sense of purpose for otherwise bored and undirected intellectuals, they also satisfied an idealism and need for prompt action that was derived from a youthful impatience "with the frustration and confusing complexity of the real world [and] its paucity of hope".[18]

In 1968, this atmosphere of protest and opposition reached critical proportions as hundreds of thousands participated in student-led marches against the Vietnam War, nuclear weapons, neo-colonialism and what was generally seen as an exploitative Western capitalist order. It was against this explosive background that the Red Brigades emerged in 1969 — a militant far left organisation dedicated to the establishment of an armed revolutionary movement of the working classes capable of destroying the Italian capitalist state in favour of a proletarian dictatorship.[19]

---

[17] Alison Jamieson, "The Italian Experience", in H. Tucker, ed., *Combating the Terrorists: Democratic Responses to Political Violence* (New York: Facts on File, 1988), p. 122.

[18] Herbert Kampf, "Appeals of Extremism to Youth", *Terrorism: An International Journal* 4, 1-4 (1980), p. 173. For a detailed account of the factors that contributed to the rise of the New Left throughout Western Europe during the late 1960s see Chalk, *West European Terrorism and Counter-Terrorism*, pp. 31-35; and Benjamin Harrison, "Roots of the Anti-Vietnam War Movement", *Studies in Conflict and Terrorism* 16, 2 (1993), pp. 99-111. Some useful earlier accounts include George Kennan, *Democracy and the Student Left* (London: Hutchinson, 1968); Stephen Spender, *The Year of the Young Rebels* (London: Weidenfeld and Nicolson, 1969); and Alexander Cockburn and Robin Blackburn, eds, *Student Power* (Harmondsworth: Penguin, 1969).

[19] Jamieson, "The Italian Experience", p. 123.

Various Italian government, military and intelligence authorities reacted to these developments by portraying the country as a target of a world-wide Soviet-led offensive, and began to argue for a plan of total defence to meet a combined Red Brigade/communist threat. In particular, considerable discussion was devoted to the idea of recruiting, training and arming "counter-revolutionary" soldiers to fight left wing subversion by all available means.[20] The result was the emergence of a so-called strategy of tension. Carried out under the auspices of the Italian secret service — *Servisio Informazione Democraticia (SID)* — the policy essentially involved "staging" various provocative bombings and other acts of terrorism in the hope that the Italian public would demand more concerted measures against the Red Brigades and other radical Communist groups.[21]

In pursuit of their so-called counter-revolutionary objectives, the *SID* trained, armed and protected various individuals — many of whom were connected with extreme neo-Fascist organisations such as the *Ordine Nuovo*, the *Avanguardia Nazionale* and *Fronte Nazionale*. It was these, *SID*-supported and sheltered, rightist militants who were primarily responsible for the intense wave of terrorism that rocked Italy between 1969 and 1974.[22] Indeed according to one study undertaken by an Italian Member of Parliament, "background" secret service involvement in extreme right wing activities can be traced to some of the worst cases of terrorism ever carried out on the country's soil:

> More or less relevant signs of direct action or involvement by the secret services can be singled out in all the trial records referring especially to the most serious crimes of right wing terrorism, such as the massacre of Piazza Fontana, of Piazza della Loggia, on the train *Italicus*, [and] at the Bologna railway station.[23]

By 1974, concrete evidence had emerged which directly implicated members of the *SID* in the so-called *Rosa dei Venti* organisation. The group had been in the process of organising a nationwide network of armed neo-Fascist groups, the ultimate objective of which was to carry out a fully fledged *coup d'état* and re-establish a Mussolini-style government in a "born again" Salo Republic.[24] Reeling from what was rapidly turning out to be one of the country's worst political crises since the

---

[20] See Franco Ferraresi, "La destra eversiva", in Franco Ferraresi, ed., *La destra radicale* (Milan: Feltrinelli, 1984), pp. 58-59.

[21] Leonard Weinberg, "Italian Neo-Fascist Terrorism: A Comparative Perspective", *Terrorism and Political Violence* 7, 1 (1995), p. 232. See also Jamieson, "The Italian Experience", pp. 118-20.

[22] See, for instance, Donna della Porta, "Institutional Responses to Terrorism: The Italian Case", *Terrorism and Political Violence* 4, 4 (1992), p. 155.

[23] S. Rodata, "La risposta dello stato al terrorismo: gli apparati", in G. Pasquino, ed., *La prova delle armi* (Bologna: Il Mulino, 1984), p. 83. In total, the attacks at Piazza Fontana, Piazza della Loggia, on the train *Italicus* and at the Bologna railway station left 122 people dead with a further 394 injured. See Chalk, *West European Terrorism and Counter-Terrorism*, p. 180.

[24] Weinberg, "Italian Neo-Fascist Terrorism", pp. 233-34. The Salo Republic was a fascist Italian Social state established in the north of Italy under German protection in 1943, with Mussolini as its puppet leader.

war, the Italian Parliament rapidly moved to ban a number of neo-Fascist groups, investigate members of the government and reform the secret services. The *Ordine Nuovo*, the *Avanguardia Nazionale* and *Fronte Nazionale* were all proscribed as "manifestly unconstitutional" entities. The *SID* was also dissolved and replaced with the *Servisio Informazione Sicurezza Democatico*, a new "limited" intelligence organisation which was to be made directly accountable to the democratic authorities.[25]

The Italian case provides a classic example of the dangers inherent in failing to ensure proper democratic control over intelligence agencies employed in the fight against terrorism. In particular, it demonstrates how such entities can be rapidly transformed into "Caliban-type" structures and used to undermine the values, welfare and interests of liberal democracy. As della Porta observes:

> It is usually assumed that a peculiarity of the relations between the democratic state and terrorist organisations is that, because the terrorist organisations, by definition, refuse the rules of the democratic game, the state is — as the main guarantor of these rules — their enemy ... The Italian experience, especially as far as right-wing terrorism is concerned, shows that it is misleading to consider the state as a unitary body fighting against terrorism. Under certain circumstances, parts of the state apparatus may attempt to exploit the presence of terrorism for their own aims.[26]

### Spain

The Spanish case relates to the formation of anti-terrorist death squads by the Socialist Government of Felipe Gonzalez during the 1980s. The groups, known collectively as *Grupos Antiterroristas de Liberación (GAL)*, were utilised as part of Madrid's anti-terrorist campaign against *Euzkadi ta Azkatasuna (ETA)* — a separatist organisation that has been operating in the Basque provinces of Northern Spain since 1968.

The origins of *ETA*'s armed campaign against the Spanish state can be traced back to the brutal suppression of Basque culture and language under General Franco during the 1950s and 1960s. Reacting to what was perceived to be a draconian and wholly illegitimate onslaught against their basic ethnic and linguistic identity, a group of dedicated Basque nationalists announced the beginning of armed insurrection in 1968. Freed from Franco's rigid authoritarian rule by Spain's transition to democracy between 1974 and 1975, *ETA*'s terrorist campaign rapidly developed during the latter half of the 1970s. By the end of the decade, the organisation was routinely targeting government officials, members of the security forces, non-Basque civilians and foreign tourists.[27]

---

[25] *Ibid.*, p. 233.

[26] della Porta, "Institutional Responses to Terrorism: The Italian Case", pp. 167-68.

[27] Chalk, *West European Terrorism and Counter-Terrorism*, p. 55. See also Edward Moxon-Browne, "Terrorism and the Spanish State: The Violent Bid for Basque Autonomy", in Tucker, ed., *Combating the Terrorists*, p. 157; Richard Clutterbuck, *Terrorism, Drugs and Crime in Europe*

Throughout the late 1970s and early 1980s the Spanish Government made a concerted effort to accede to some of the central demands of *ETA*, granting a considerable degree of regional autonomy to the Basque provinces in 1980.[28] These concessions, however, failed to elicit any reduction in Basque-related terrorism, with *ETA* attacks in 1983 double what they had been in 1975.[29] Increasingly frustrated by this lack of progress, and arguing that constitutional safeguards were serving to undermine the effectiveness of the campaign against *ETA*, a number of prominent Spanish politicians and security officials called for the state to abandon legal restraint in its "war" against terrorism.

The decision was taken in 1983, allegedly under the orders of the (then) Interior Minister, José Barrionuevo, and (then) State Security Chief, Rafael Vera, to establish a GAL network within the Spanish police force to launch a "dirty war" against *ETA*. The groups were to be funded by *fondos reservados*, secret resources of the government used for "special purposes", mainly in security matters — and were designed to carry the terrorist war back to *ETA*. Between 1983 and 1987, *GAL* groups carried out numerous bomb attacks, kidnappings and killings in the Basque regions of northern Spain and south-western France, taking responsibility for over two dozen murders during the period. Many of these assaults were perpetrated by Portuguese and French mercenaries who had been directly recruited by undercover Spanish police intelligence agents.[30]

The true extent of the GAL scandal only became apparent in 1996, when two former police officers, José Amedo and Michael Domínquez, confessed to recruiting Portuguese mercenaries to carry out bombings, kidnappings and killings in the Basque provinces of Spain and France. Both Amedo and Domínquez claimed that they were acting on orders from Barrionuevo and Vera and that senior members of the police, military and intelligence services were all involved in the *GAL* scheme. Indeed by 1997, the Bilbao Chief of Police (Miguel Placheulo), the former Chief of the Single Command of the Anti-Terrorist Unit (Francisco Alvarez), the ex-Director of the Security of State (Julian Sancristobal) as well as a number of ex-government ministers, most notably Barrionuevo and Vera, had all been indicted with establishing, leading and coordinating the *GAL* network.[31]

---

*After 1992* (London: Routledge, 1990), pp. 95-99; and Fernando Jiminez, "Spain: The Terrorist Challenge and the Government Response", *Terrorism and Political Violence* 4, 4 (1992), p. 112.

[28] Moxon-Browne, "Terrorism and the Spanish State", pp. 164-65.

[29] Fernando Reinares, "The Political Conditioning of Collective Violence: Democratisation and Insurgent Terrorism in Spain". Paper presented before the "European Democracies Against Terrorism: Government Policies, Societal Responses and Supranational Cooperation in the Face of an Evolving Challenge", International Workshop, Oñati, Spain, 2-3 May 1996, p. 32.

[30] See "Spain: Government Accused of Organising GAL", *Statewatch* 5, 1 (1995); "Spain: The GAL Case", *Statewatch* 5, 4 (1995); "SPAIN: Gal Investigation Goes to Court", *Statewatch* 5, 5 (1995); "SPAIN: The GAL Affair: General Held", *Statewatch* 6, 3 (1996); "Paris Linked to Spanish Hit Squads", *Australian*, 4 October 1995; "Spanish PM Faces Death Squad Probe", *Australian*, 20 October 1995; and "Death Squad Mire Alienates Spanish", *Australian*, 26 January 1996.

[31] "Spain: The GAL Case", *Statewatch* 5, 4 (1995); "Death Squad Mire Alienates Spanish".

The *GAL* affair represented a flagrant violation of the fundamental principle by which police forces operate in the modern liberal democratic state: "minimum force". This essentially requires using the minimum level of force necessary to deter, restrain or contain violence and preserve public order — something that is vital if the state's agents of internal coercion are maintained in a firmly controlled and purely defensive role.[32] By establishing an anti-terrorist "hit squad" within its police structure, the Spanish state severely distorted this basic principle. Indeed, it came dangerously close to institutionalising internal security on the basis of the militaristic (and authoritarian) ideal of maximum force.

While the GAL affair ultimately did not pose as great a threat to liberal democracy as the Italian "strategy of tension", since there was no imminent danger of an intelligence orchestrated *coup d'état*, it nevertheless constituted a major departure from accepted liberal democratic constitutional principles of law and order. Moreover, in many ways its effects have proved to be just as destabilising and counter-productive. Revelations of the dirty war have not only served to "legitimise" *ETA*'s armed struggle in the eyes of many sectors of the Basque population, who accuse the state (quite rightly) of acting in a repressive and dictatorial manner. They were also instrumental in alienating popular support for the Felipe Gonzalez Government and ensuring his political demise in 1996. Sanchez González, Vice-Rector for Research Affairs of the prestigious Universidad Nacional de Educación a Distancia (UNED), is perfectly correct when he argues:

> Of all the possible forms of anti-terrorist struggle [in Spain], the only one that must be rejected from any legal viewpoint is that which uses the same means as the enemy ... Although it may anger some to say so, it is reprehensible, even when it is 'successful,' because it implies an open denial of the Constitutional State and creates a precedent that is a stigma, and which leaves an indelible scar on the democratic political system.[33]

*Peru*

The Peruvian case refers to the enactment of a range of highly repressive anti-terrorism measures by President Alberto Fujimori between 1992 and 1996. Citing what were perceived as fundamental barriers to the resolution of some of the most pressing problems then afflicting the country, Fujimori staged an anti-democratic coup, just twenty months after his election. This self-imposed "autogolpe" was designed, in large part, to eliminate the institutional gridlock and democratic inefficiency that Fujimori felt were constraining the state's ability to act decisively in

---

[32] Chalk, "The Liberal Democratic Response to Terrorism", p. 24. See also Wilkinson, *Terrorism and the Liberal State*, p. 43; Frank Gregory, "Policing the Democratic State. How Much Force?" *Conflict Studies* 194 (1986), p. 1; Wardlaw, *Political Terrorism*, p. 90; and Crelinsten and Schmid, "Western Responses to Terrorism", pp. 334-35.

[33] Santiago González, "Have We Learned from Our Spanish Experience?" Paper presented before the "European Democracies Against Terrorism: Government Policies, Societal Responses and Supranational Cooperation in the Face of An Evolving Challenge", International Workshop, Oñati, Spain, 2-3 May 1996, p. 11.

the face of a growing subversive challenge from the Tupac Amaru Revolutionary Movement (MRTA) and *Sendero Luminiso* (Shining Path).[34]

Terrorism associated with the Maoist-oriented struggles of the MRTA and SL, both of which were essentially aimed at ridding Peru of foreign "imperialist" influences and establishing a revolutionary peasant regime during the 1980s, had consisted primarily of small-scale bombings against the police, banks, state offices, diplomatic premises and political targets. In 1990, however, the two movements, and especially SL, started experimenting with larger, more indiscriminate attacks, carrying out repeated car bombings in wealthy commercial and residential sections of Lima which were specifically designed to inflict mass civilian casualties. By 1992, this increased violence had reached chronic proportions: in the three years since 1990 a total of 1,577 terrorist attacks had been recorded in the country, causing 1,443 injuries and a staggering 3,489 deaths. These instances were so frequent that Peru was designated as the country most severely affected by terrorism, globally, in 1990 and 1991 and the third most affected in 1992.[35]

Arguing that the democratic constraints inherent in the country's system of "partidocracia" were serving to weaken the institutional response to the growing MRTA and *SL* insurgencies, President Fujimori announced the dissolution of Congress on 5 April 1992. Having gained the direct support of the army, he then suspended the Constitution, assumed authoritarian, some would say dictatorial, powers and enacted eleven specific Emergency Anti-Terrorism Decrees. Taken together, these served substantially to enhance the search, arrest and investigative powers of the Peruvian police and security forces while simultaneously allowing for the implementation of a variety of extra-judicial, non-court oriented executive processes.[36]

The anti-terrorism decrees introduced by Fujimori were truly extensive. In specific terms, they sanctioned the following highly repressive measures: A re-definition of terrorism in broad and legally vague terms. A reduction in the age of criminal responsibility for "crimes of terrorism" from 18 to 15. A re-definition of the crime of treason -to include any who "aid and abet crimes of terrorism". A requirement that military tribunals must reach a verdict in terrorist trials within ten days. Provision for the death penalty to be imposed on any person convicted of terrorism. Provision for the police to detain a treason/terrorist suspect indefinitely, without informing anyone except the military justice system. Provision for the police to detain terrorist suspects awaiting trial for up to five years. Provision for teachers

---

[34] Catherine Cozart, "A Persistent but Unconsolidated Democracy: The Case of Peru" [http://www.is.rhodes.edu/modus_vivendi/cozart.html], 1 July 1997, pp. 2-3.

[35] Pinkerton's Risk Assessment Services (hereafter referred to as PRAS), *Annual Risk Assessment, 1990-1992* (Virginia: Pinkerton's, 1991-1993).

[36] Control Risks Group (hereafter referred to as CRG), *Business Security Outlook: The World in 1993* (London: Control Risks Information Services, 1993), p. 102; *Europa Yearbook, Volume II* (London: Europa Publications, 1996), p. 2541; and Cozart, "A Persistent but Unconsolidated Democracy: The Case of Peru", pp. 4-5.

and professors suspected of influencing their pupils by favouring armed opposition groups to be charged with "treason" and tried in military court.[37]

The measures also introduced a strong bias in favour of the prosecution in terrorism cases by forbidding conditional liberty or bail to the accused; preventing lawyers from representing more than one suspect; banning *habeas corpus* petitions on behalf of terrorist suspects; and prohibiting any cross examination by defence lawyers of police and military personnel involved in the detention or questioning of those accused of terrorism. The Emergency Decrees, perhaps most draconian of all, even prevented defendants and their lawyers from challenging, for whatever reason, the impartiality of judges or their decisions.[38]

Although a new Constitution was enacted in 1993, it was not until 1996 that a move was made to relax the above anti-terrorism measures. In 1996, Peru's anti-terrorism laws were modified to permit, inter-alia: Representation by human rights lawyers of multiple defendants charged with terrorism. Cross-examination by defence lawyers of police and security personnel involved in the interrogation of terrorist suspects. The requirement that all those accused of terrorism be brought before a judge or court to determine the lawfulness of their detention (*habeas corpus*). In addition, the age of criminal responsibility for crimes of terrorism was restored to 18 and moves were made to establish an Office of the Public Ombudsman as well as a National Registry of Detainees.[39]

Fujimori justified their retention on the grounds that they had helped to deal a fatal blow to the insurgencies of both SL and MRTA. In purely operational terms, such a claim was valid. By 1996 the structural and logistical support bases of both groups had been effectively destroyed with neither able to pose anything approaching the extent of the threat they had a mere four years previously (the MRTA's siege of the Japanese Embassy in 1996-97 notwithstanding).[40]

At what price, however, had this apparent "success" been achieved? It is now widely accepted by most scholars that the autocratic measures enacted by Fujimori between 1992 and 1996 have, perhaps irrevocably, scarred the democratic process in Peru. Not only did they defy constitutional principles of due process and the rule of law, they also revived the Latin American traditions of personalism, populism and militarism — all obvious impediments to the formation and consolidation of viable parliamentary democratic institutions.[41]

---

[37] Bill Wedemeyer, "Peru's Emergency Decrees of 1992" [http://www.mcs.cornell.edu/~weeds/LawPages/decrees.html], 15 January 1996.

[38] *Ibid.*

[39] For further details see, United Nations Human Rights Committee, "Comments on Peru", [http://www.msc.cornell.edu/~weeds/LawPages/un_hrc_96.html], 1 July 1997.

[40] CRG, *Business Security Outlook 1996* (London: Control Risks Information Services, 1996), p. 115.

[41] Cozart, "A Persistent but Unconsolidated Democracy: The Case of Peru", pp. 1-6.

Certainly the overall legacy of Fujimori's period of authoritarian rule remains controversial. The secret tribunals established to mete out "justice" to terrorists also convicted many innocent persons, often on the flimsiest evidence.[42] The security forces, acting in the absence of any mechanisms of constraint and oversight, exploited their unchecked powers and have since been implicated in countless allegations of serious human rights abuse.[43] By using the armed forces for tasks normally reserved for the police and judiciary, state authority was also heavily militarised and given an overtly offensive character. Finally and perhaps most dangerously, Fujimori's actions have set a bad precedent for future governments and administrations that happen to find themselves, and their political institutions, in similar situations of crisis and difficulty.[44]

It is hardly surprising that these negative effects have significantly undermined popular support for Fujimori, alienating his regime from much of the Peruvian electorate. Indeed, just prior to the successful military assault on the Japanese Embassy in April 1997 (which ended the MRTA hostage crisis that had begun in December 1996), opinion polls had put Fujimori's approval ratings at just thirty-five per cent. This was the lowest figure since the 1992 autogolpe and it came about despite the fact that terrorism within the country had been largely defeated. Such is the reality of attempting to deal with terrorism through an unconstitutional "backdoor". As two Peruvian political commentators cynically observed earlier this year:

> It is important to realise that the [present] storms have not happened because of a mobilised opposition, but the implosion of a regime which has practically monopolised power in this country. Forget about the re-election [of Fujimori]; today it is not even a hope, but simply a tormented dream.[45]

## Philosophical and Strategic Consequences for the Liberal Democratic State

What then are the philosophical and strategic consequences for the liberal democratic state of initiating excessively repressive counter-terrorist measures that fail to abide by accepted constitutional parameters of legal authority?

---

[42] By the end of 1996, a staggering 500,000 people were believed to have been detained by the Peruvian police on suspicion of being involved with the "aims and objectives of terrorism". See "Confident They Had Defeated Guerrillas, Security Forces Let Guard Down", *Vancouver Sun*, 21 December 1996.

[43] For further details see United Nations Human Rights Committee, "Comments on Peru."

[44] Personal correspondence, Mayer Nudell [mnudell@juno.com], Director, Specialized Consulting Services, "Terrorism Reasserts Itself in Peru", 17 March 1997, p. 13; Cozart, "A Persistent but Unconsolidated Democracy: The Case of Peru", p. 6; and Philip Mauceri, "State Reform, Coalitions and the Neoliberal Autogolpe in Peru", *Latin American Research Review* 30, 2 (1995), p. 20.

[45] Quoted in "Fujimori Salvages Flagging Fortunes", *Australian*, 24 April 1997.

Philosophically, it undercuts the essential liberal notion that all human beings have the right to be protected against the arbitrary and coercive actions of institutions which have legal and political power. Ignoring this fundamental dictum brings the liberal democratic polity one step closer to the type of illegitimate and indiscriminate strategies that are characteristically employed by authoritarian states. Systematic fear, aroused by the expectation of institutionalised cruelty, is the very antithesis of the liberal democratic way of life. It is for this reason that liberal democratic political institutions adopt a strong defence of equal rights and their legal protection. If individuals in a civil society do not have the means to assert and protect themselves against official abuse, justice and freedom — those most prized ideals of any liberal democratic polity — are nothing but a forlorn hope.

Strategically, excessive repression runs the very great risk of undermining the perceived legitimacy of the fight against terrorism. This form of political violence thrives on the injustices, both imagined and real, that are inflicted by draconian internal security measures. One of the classic uses of terrorism is the attempt to try and trap authorities into over-reaction by provoking the use of illegal or unconstitutional counter-measures. When authorities do in fact violate accepted constitutional norms they destroy their legitimacy, thus allowing terrorists to set themselves up as the protectors of freedom, while aiding their own cause by drawing popular support from official authorities. Moreover, any victory that is ultimately achieved over the terrorists is likely to be "hollow" as liberal democracy would be perverted into authoritarianism, thus turning it into a regime that threatens the basic civil liberties of all.[46]

## The Liberal Democratic Response to Terrorism

As argued throughout this paper, any liberal democratic response to terrorism has to rest on one overriding maxim: a commitment to uphold and maintain constitutional principles of law and order. Such an undertaking obviously needs to be translated into effective action if it is to secure public support. This is most likely to occur if the initiation of counter-terrorist measures is guided by three over-arching principles of action.

First, the response needs to be limited and well defined. Any counter-terrorist action that is initiated should not go beyond what is demanded by the exigencies of the immediate situation and should only be directed against the terrorists themselves. There should be no question of extending the anti-terrorist campaign to the families or sympathisers of terrorists, a feature characteristic of the counter-insurgency strategies of many dictatorial and authoritarian regimes. A slide into general repression will inevitably serve to alienate the government from the people; encourage moderates to join extremist organisations; and generally give rise to

---

[46] See Chalk, *West European Terrorism and Counter-Terrorism*, p. 162.

suspicions that the state is exploiting the crisis situation for the purpose of enhancing its own political powers.[47]

Second, the response needs to be credible. The general populace has to be convinced that the state's action is necessary and effective in producing results, both with respect to its performance in combating terrorism and protecting civil liberties. If the government is unable to provide justification for implementing and maintaining specialist anti-terrorist measures, it will suffer from a "credibility gap" and will almost certainly fail to gain the level of public support necessary for either their initial creation or continued existence.[48]

Third, the introduction, use and continuance of all counter-terrorist measures, especially those initiated by the intelligence services, need to be made subject to constant parliamentary supervision and judicial oversight. In order to strike a balanced response that does not unduly restrict or abuse individual rights and freedoms, it is absolutely essential that the state be held constitutionally accountable for its actions and that adequate mechanisms exist for the redress of grievance. This is especially important given the covert nature of most anti-terrorism work, an operational reality which obviously leaves little opportunity for public scrutiny.[49]

The best way to achieve legislative and judicial control of anti-terrorism operations is to ensure that they take place within a clear framework of legal controls. In the UK, for instance, an Oversight Committee composed of government ministers, Members of Parliament, senior civil servants and independent members of the judiciary, monitors the activities of the Secret Intelligence Service (SIS), the main body responsible for anti-terrorism in the country. The Committee, which is answerable to Parliament, ensures that the Service operates totally within statute and law, having the power to set up independent tribunals to investigate any aspect of the agency's work that it wishes. This particular form of parliamentary and external scrutiny was enacted in 1993 under the UK Intelligence Services Act to enhance the legislative and judicial provisions of the 1989 Security Service Act.[50] It is similar in

---

[47] Chalk, "The Liberal Democratic Response to Terrorism", p. 36. See also Wilkinson, *Terrorism and the Liberal State*, p. 124.

[48] Chalk, "The Liberal Democratic Response to Terrorism", p. 36.

[49] *Ibid.* See also G. Davidson-Smith, *Combating Terrorism* (London: Routledge, 1990), p. 47; Wardlaw, *Political Terrorism*, p. 70; and Wilkinson, *Terrorism and the Liberal State*, p. 124.

[50] The 1989 Security Service Act was enacted to stem growing public concern over the accountability of the SIS — especially in relation to its activities in Northern Ireland following the "shoot-to-kill" scandal. The 1993 Act aimed to enhance further control over the Service following the 1991 — prompted in part by the release of the Birmingham Six and revelations that the police and intelligence community had deliberately circumvented the rule of law in investigating the bombing of two Birmingham pubs in November 1974. While civil libertarians remain somewhat sceptical of the actual degree of oversight that the 1989 and 1993 acts impose over the SIS, it is generally accepted that the current system of external checks — many of which were initiated by the current head of SIS, Stella Rimmington — has done much to improve the overall legislative and judicial control of the Service. Nevertheless, a number of commentators have argued that there is still need for a more comprehensive system of oversight, particularly in relation to the control of SIS

nature to the oversight function that is undertaken by official "watchdog" committees in other liberal democratic states such as Germany and the Netherlands (which has, in addition, a special Commissioner with the express responsibility of monitoring all the telephone surveillance activities of the Dutch secret services in relation to the tapping of subversives).[51]

Taken together, these three principles of limitation, credibility and accountability will help to ensure that the state's response to terrorism is well defined, controlled and exercised in a manner that is consistent with the imperatives of due process. It is vital that the desire to achieve a "quick fix" to terrorism is not allowed to cloud long term issues and influences — especially if liberal democratic principles of legitimacy are likely to be distorted and abrogated in the process.[52] Only then will anti-terrorist law enforcement action be accepted as a necessary evil that has been forced by the threat of extremist political violence rather than one conveniently excused by it.

---

activities such as the use of paid informants/infiltrated agents, undercover operations, mail opening, communication interceptions and the exercise of "bug and burgle" powers of entry under warrant. Concern has also been expressed over the continuing practice of allowing SIS operatives to testify behind screens in court so as to protect their anonymity. For further details see "Military Intelligence and Northern Ireland", *Statewatch* 2, 5 (1992); "MI5 and Police Carve Out New Roles", *Statewatch* 5, 5 (1995); and "MI5 and Organised Crime", *Statewatch* 6, 1 (1996).

[51] Stella Rimmington, *Security and Democracy — Is There a Conflict?* (London: BBC Education, 1994), pp. 12-13; "Secret Services Unite Against Crime", *Financial Times*, 20 November 1993, and "No Taping of Subversives", *Statewatch* 2, 5 (September-October, 1992).

[52] See, for example, Davidson-Smith, *Combating Terrorism*, p. 231.

# [7]

# TERRORISM AND GOVERNABILITY IN NEW YORK CITY
## Old Problem, New Dilemma

PAUL KANTOR

Fordham University

New York City's experience suggests that the hand of terrorism is profoundly changing urban politics. The events of 9/11 struck a city that was already seriously off balance due to long-building sources of political fragmentation and exclusion that obstruct political leadership, making it difficult to overcome festering social divisions or steer the city in new directions. Despite Mayor Giuliani's image of control during the weeks of emergency, deeply rooted forces conspire against sustained governability. Decaying partisanship, disorganized politics, reliance on exclusionary electoral coalitions, and the proliferation of entrenched special interests powerfully check mayoral leadership and innovative planning for the city as a whole. This is likely to confound the city's recovery and its ability to cope with international terrorism. Since these problems are also found elsewhere, terrorism will pose similar challenges in other cities. Terrorism is combining with an older problem to change urban politics.

**There is little doubt** that the tragedy of 9/11 has thrown New York City off course. The question is how much and in what ways. Despite recent boom years when New York appeared to be rebounding from days of urban crisis, the terrorist act has brought into sharp relief deeply rooted imbalances in the city's governance capacity. This problem assumes greater importance in the wake of the attack and is likely to confound the city's successful recovery. Furthermore, this dilemma will pose dangers elsewhere.

New York City's traditional political strength is its open, competitive, and pluralistic system of governance (Kantor 2002; Sayre and Kaufman 1960). Its traditional weakness is the excessively fragmented character of this political order. All too often, political conflicts are resolved by expanding budgets, launching new programs for special interests, and avoiding necessary fiscal retrenchment at times of declining revenues (Fuchs 1992; Shefter 1985; Siegel 1997). Although political changes during the 1990s helped to check some of these tendencies, they never significantly altered the deeply rooted forces underpinning this system. Consequently, the city is politically unprepared to effectively plan or mobilize support for an effective recovery program.

During the 1970s, the state fiscal monitors that were established to restore the city's credit and contain its appetite for spending more or less displaced elected officeholders from strategic policy making. Their role gradually lifted after New York City reentered the bond market on its own after 1981. What emerged in subsequent years were disturbing signs of increasing fragmentation of decision-making power even as new mayoral electoral coalitions were emerging that seemed to promise greater order. This was due to three countervailing forces: the continued decay of traditional party politics, the flawed character of new mayoral electoral coalitions, and the proliferation of new independent governmental entities.

First, the decline of the Democratic Party as a balance wheel in imposing control over nominations, campaign fund-raising, and elections for local offices has hit an all-time low. Contenders for the major offices increasingly ignore party chieftains in electoral contests that have become increasingly candidate centered. Media campaigns, private fund-raising, and civil service union electioneering have now largely replaced the once-fabled power of the party machines (Savitch and Kantor 2002, chap. 7; Wade 1990). Just how far disorganized politics has come is suggested by the widespread corruption scandal that engulfed Democratic Party bosses and some key mayoral aids during the late 1980s. This led to indictments of many officials, including a member of Congress, and to the suicide of the Queens party boss. Investigations convincingly revealed that the mayor was unconnected to this alternative political system, part of which was being operated from the basement of city hall, but they also showed that greed for personal enrichment alone lay behind most of the kickback schemes (because so little of the take was recycled back into the party machine) (Newfield and Barrett 1988).

The decay of the Democratic Party has enabled recent mayoral contests to become essentially nonpartisan campaigns. On the Democratic side, the mayoral primary has become a catch-as-catch-can match among contenders, some of whom, like Al Sharpton, have had virtually no ties to the Democratic Party yet are able to win large percentages of the primary vote (more than one-third of the vote in Al Sharpton's case). Outside of the Democratic Party, Republican mayoral candidates have been able to mount winning campaigns by assembling their own media-driven electoral machines that owe little to party but much to personal fund-raising. In Giuliani's case, this meant assembling support from big special interest fund-raisers in the uniformed service unions, people who do business with the city, developers, and real estate interests. Michael Bloomberg avoided those financial ties to special interests only by using his vast personal wealth to bankroll his mayoral campaign. In doing so, he conducted the most expensive mayoral campaign in history and gravely weakened or even destroyed New York's model campaign finance system. By spending $75.5 million, mostly his own money, Bloomberg paid the almost unbelievable amount of $100 per vote to win (Cooper 2002).

The decline of party has had the effect of producing new sources of faction and stalemate. As mayoral elections become increasingly nonpartisan and candidate centered, candidates are more dependent on raising their own money to build their own political networks, increasing the role of money and special interests in politics. Simultaneously, however, the decaying Democratic organization has maintained its hold on city council elections and on other political offices at the state and federal levels. The result: growing stalemate between the mayor and city council on many major legislative issues such as budget, education, and finance in a pattern of divided government. This also has produced a lack of unity among officeholders in lobbying for more aid from state and federal sources, undermining the political influence of New York City in intergovernmental politics. The arrival of term limits for members of the city council in 2001 has also helped throw mayoral-council politics out of balance. Last year, 35 incumbents out of the 51 council members were forced to retire and were replaced by new council freshmen. Their ability to work together and pose a counterweight to the mayor remains uncertain.

Second, the Center-Right mayoral coalition that elected three out of the past four mayors is a deeply flawed means of bringing about governability. Since the days of the fiscal crisis, mayors have been unable to build very inclusive electoral coalitions. The city's first African American mayor, David Dinkins, was able to mobilize the poor, minorities, white liberals, and other groups including business in an effort to defuse the racial tensions of the Koch years. Yet his coalition proved unstable, and conflicts over race plagued his administration. After a single term, he lost to Rudolph Giuliani in 1993. In contrast, by winning the support of homeowners, whites, Catholics, and working-class ethnics in the outer boroughs while excluding people of color, white liberals, and the poor, Koch and Giuliani were able to maintain an alliance with leading business interests while containing the demands of service-demanding groups (Green and Wilson 1989; Mollenkopf 1992). This kind of governing coalition is like a keg of gunpowder, however. The longer mayors rely on this electoral strategy, the more they risk bottling up racial resentments and precipitating explosive political confrontations with the very groups whose electoral presence is growing most rapidly (and who already have achieved a majority of the resident, though not the voter, population). During the 1990s, New York became a majority-minority city as white non-Hispanic persons fell from 43.2% in 1990 to 35% in 2000. Due to a large increase in Hispanic births and migration, the number of Latinos surged from 24% to 27% while the African American population dropped slightly to just below one-fourth of the population.

Race relations during the Koch and Giuliani years were almost always poor. Confrontations with Mayor Giuliani were minimized during the later 1990s only by the growth in budget revenues that enabled the mayor to avoid cutting programs and by the rise in private-sector employment opportunities. As time passes and the exclusionary impact of this electoral strategy increases resentment and isolation among marginalized groups, this power base becomes more difficult to sustain. It becomes most unstable at precisely this time, however—after the good economic times are over and the city must pull in its belt. When that happens, mayors who inherit this power structure have two choices. One is to try to maintain this coalition by relying on appeals to white racial and neighborhood resentments, as Mayor Koch did during the fiscal crisis years. The other is to somehow broaden this coalition by uniting groups around issues that have wide appeal.

Mayor Bloomberg has chosen the latter strategy. During the election, Bloomberg won 47% of the Hispanic vote in large part because Democratic candidate Mark Green had been abandoned by minority politicians after a bruising and racially charged campaign. Since 9/11, Bloomberg's challenge has been to broaden his coalition to include Latino and African American voters, but he must do so while contending with a budget gap that approaches $5 billion. Coping with the latter requires across-the-board cuts in virtually all services but especially in the costly social services and in the municipal payroll—areas that are likely to have a disproportionate impact on the very voter groups he needs most to include. Yet those groups feel that their priorities have been postponed long enough after years of exclusionary politics. In effect, Bloomberg's attempt to alter the voter coalition inherited from the past is happening at a time when changes in population and fiscal resources make this most difficult. Mayor Bloomberg has yet to establish a stable political base. The events of 9/11 will make it harder to do so.

The third source of political fragmentation stems from growing reliance on private benefit corporations (PBCs) to buffer the city's economic decision making from mainstream electoral politics. PBCs such as the Port Authority, the Metropolitan Transportation Authority, the Empire State Development Corporation, and others are independent of political and fiscal control of the elected general-purpose government of the city, but they more or less control the city's infrastructure and key economic development projects. They are the city's so-called "money-generating" governments and are highly responsive to bond holders who expect to be paid back from the revenues and user fees that PBC projects are expected to generate from airport fees, rents, transit fares, tolls, and the like (Kantor 1993; 1995, chap. 5).

While reliance on PBCs makes sense for a cash-pressed city at the limits of its borrowing ability, PBCs proliferated dramatically in recent decades, displacing local elected officials from large areas of public policy. In 1960, there were only 6 PBCs in all of New York City, but by the end of the century, there were 36 (Henderson 2001; Walsh 1990). Through them, the city's capability for financing large undertakings has increased, but its ability to govern and remain very accountable to the city electorate has diminished (Savitch and Kantor 2002, chap. 7).

Not surprisingly, the task of rebuilding the World Trade Center site and planning a recovery has been handed over to yet another PBC, the Lower Manhattan Development Corporation (LMDC), a subsidiary of the powerful Empire State Development Corporation. The LMDC has a board that is evenly divided between gubernatorial and mayoral appointees and has access to part of the $20 billion emergency recovery aid promised by federal officials. Studded with blue-ribbon appointees, mostly from the worlds of business and finance, the LMDC rightly sees its role as more than simply cleaning up the trade center site. It has embarked on programs to attract new businesses into Lower Manhattan and assist existing businesses and residents to recover from the losses sustained in the attack. Furthermore, it has organized a number of taskforce committees to consult with interested groups including area businesses, residents of nearby neighborhoods, families of victims, and others in planning a recovery program.

Yet by casting its lot with another independent government corporation that is dedicated to regenerating the downtown business area, state and city officials have bypassed the opportunity to seriously rethink the economic future of the city in a postterrorist world. One effect of 9/11 has been to call into question the competitive advantage of a dense and centralized central business district in which the giant skyscraper is the dominant office site. Several months prior to 9/11, the Group of 35—top leaders from the private and public sector—issued a report on the future of New York City's office sector due to a growing shortage of commercial office space. It predicted that the city would probably need to add 60 million square feet of office space during the next 20 years. Recognizing the limited space for future office construction in Lower Manhattan, the taskforce concluded that priority should be given to dispersing new office construction to other locations in Mid-Town, Queens, Brooklyn, and elsewhere (Group of 35, 2001). The destruction of the World Trade towers has dramatically given impetus to such a plan. In an age of terrorism, global cities like New York, London, and Tokyo provide high-profile "international message" targets for suicide bombers and violent radical groups seeking to dramatize their political demands (Savitch and Kantor 2002, chap. 10). The 9/11 attacks have virtually compelled fundamental reassessment of how far and in what shape the new metropolis will go in the direction of dispersal—not whether the continued building of giant skyscrapers in dense locations will continue to be the norm. Eighteen thousand jobs at stock brokerage firms, banks, and insurance companies have already permanently moved since 9/11, according to a senior economist at the Federal Reserve Bank of New York (*New York Times*, 6 December 2001, A62). The problem, however, is that a nonelected special-purpose government committed to regenerating the old downtown is hardly the kind of planner that is capable of rethinking the future of the city. It stands as yet another instance of planning by special interest and the city's lack of governability.

The events of 9/11 also call into question the adequacy of New York's government for building public confidence in its recovery programs. The death of so many people and the destruction of so much property in a single blow means that decisions over the physical reconstruction of the city cannot be left to only nonelected experts and executives who are used to keeping the public at arm's length in their deliberations. The inevitability of a sustained war on international terrorism requires redesigning cities in ways that can reclaim public confidence in homes, neighborhoods, modes of travel, and places of work. This necessitates greater public participation and oversight in the planning of New York City, not less. Yet the city has already drifted in the latter direction and is not well prepared to cope with the political aftermath of 9/11. Its tradition of fragmenting political power and concentrating management of physical infrastructure in special-purpose authorities is ill-suited to rebuilding public confidence in city building in a postterrorist world.

## URBAN GOVERNANCE IN
## A POSTTERRORISM WORLD

The impact of the terrorist attack and its aftermath goes beyond the immediate damage done to people, business, and security in New York City. The terrible events of September, 2001 struck a city that was already seriously off balance politically. Long-building sources of political fragmentation and exclusion now obstruct the need to assert greater political leadership, overcome festering social divisions, and steer the city in new directions in the wake of 9/11. Although Mayor Giuliani briefly seemed to fulfill this role during the weeks of emergency, the deeply rooted forces of political decay and exclusion conspire against sustained governability. Decaying partisanship, disorganized politics, reliance on exclusionary electoral coalitions, and the proliferation of entrenched special interests powerfully check mayoral leadership and innovative planning for the city as a whole. New York City faces a difficult task of modernizing its political system if it is to successfully cope with twenty-first-century international terrorism.

Since the forms of division and stalemate are not unique to New York City, it is likely that the hand of urban terrorism will pose similar challenges well beyond the borders of the nation's largest city. Urban politics has changed as a result of 9/11. Yet it is because a new dilemma has surfaced in the midst of an older problem.

## REFERENCES

Cooper, M. 2002. Final tally: Bloomberg spent 75.5 million to become mayor. *New York Times*, 30 March, B2.

Fuchs, E. 1992. *Mayors and money.* Chicago: Univ. of Chicago Press.

Green, C., and B. Wilson. 1989. *The struggle for black empowerment in New York City.* New York: Praeger.

Group of 35. 2001. *Preparing for the future: A commercial development strategy for New York* (Final Rep.). New York: Taubman Urban Research Center, New York University.

Henderson, K. M. 2001. Other governments: The public authorities. In *Governing New York State*, edited by Jeffrey M. Stonecash, 187-202. Albany: State Univ. of New York Press.

Kantor, P. 1993. The dual city as political choice. *Journal of Urban Affairs* 15 (3): 231-44.

———. 1995. *The dependent city revisited: The political economy of urban development and social policy.* Boulder, CO: Westview.

———. 2002. The local polity as a pathway for public power: Taming the business tiger during New York City's industrial age. *International Journal of Urban and Regional Research* 26 (1): 80-98.

Mollenkopf, John. 1992. *A phoenix in the ashes: The rise and fall of the Koch coalition in New York City politics.* Princeton, NJ: Princeton Univ. Press.

Newfield, J., and W. Barrett. 1988. *City for sale.* New York: Harper and Row.

Savitch, H. V., and P. Kantor. 2002. *Cities in the international marketplace: The political economy of urban development in North America and Western Europe.* Princeton, NJ: Princeton Univ. Press.

Sayre, W., and H. Kaufman. 1960. *Governing New York City.* New York: W. W. Norton.

Shefter, M. 1985. *Political crisis, fiscal crisis.* New York: Basic Books.

Siegel, F. 1997. *The future once happened here: New York, D.C., L.A., and the fate of America's big cities.* New York: Free Press.

Wade, R. 1990. The withering away of the party system. In *Urban politics, New York style*, edited by D. Netzer and J. Bellush, 271-95. New York: New York Univ. Press.

Walsh, A. H. 1990. Public authorities and the shape of decision making. In *Urban politics, New York style*, edited by D. Netzer and J. Bellush, 188-222. New York: New York Univ. Press.

*Paul Kantor is a professor of political science at Fordham University in New York City. He is a former president of the Urban Politics Section of the American Political Science Association, the author of numerous articles and books including* The Dependent City Revisited *(Westview, 1995), and the coeditor (with Dennis R. Judd) of* The Politics of Urban America *(Longman, 2001). Paul Kantor's most recent work (coauthored with H. V. Savitich) is* Cities in the International Marketplace: The Political Economy of Urban Development in North America and Western Europe *(Princeton Univ. Press, 2002).*

# [8]

# Dying for 'Enduring Freedom': Accepting Responsibility for Civilian Casualties in the War against Terrorism

Nicholas J. Wheeler, *University of Wales, Aberystwyth*

## Abstract

This article examines what moral theories are available to justify the harming of the innocent in war. Focusing on US conduct of the war against the Taliban and al-Qaeda, the article examines how far the US is responsible for the deaths of Afghan civilians. Although US actions have been justified in terms of respect for the Just War principle of non-combatant immunity, the article shows how this principle rested uneasily with alternative moral theories of war that influenced the process of target selection. These are the realist doctrine of necessity in war and Michael Walzer's theories of 'supreme emergency' and 'war is hell'. Just War theory, realism and 'supreme emergency' acknowledge moral responsibility for a state's conduct of war. But the doctrine that 'war is hell' seeks to transfer any responsibility for the cruelty of war to the enemy. The article argues that, whilst the Taliban and al-Qaeda are responsible for exposing Afghan civilians to US attacks, this does not absolve US political and military leaders of responsibility for their conduct of the war.

Keywords: *Just War, moral responsibility, non-combatant immunity, pacifism, realism, supreme emergency*

Perhaps what shocked the world most about the events of September 11 was that the perpetrators of this act deliberately set out to kill innocent civilians. No doubt, it was for this reason (among others) that the US declared 'war' between civilization and the forces of global terror represented by the al-Qaeda network. Less than a month after the attacks on New York and Washington, the Bush administration responded by launching an air and ground war against the Taliban government in Afghanistan. The intervention, primarily justified on grounds of self-defence, had three key objectives: to remove from power the Taliban that had provided a safe haven for Osama bin Laden's terrorist organization; to cripple the capacity of al-Qaeda to strike again; and to send a clear signal to other governments that similar attacks would be visited on them were they to provide a base for global terrorism. President Bush and his senior advisers were in no doubt that they were fighting a just cause, but questions were raised about whether the war was being conducted with just means: put bluntly, why should innocent Afghans die for justice? While the US admitted that civilians were killed as a consequence of its bombing campaign, this was justified on two grounds: the deaths were an unintended consequence of attacks against legitimate targets and the US could not be blamed for these because responsibility rested solely with those who had initiated war on September 11. This has led some commentators to assert a moral equivalence between the killings of September 11 and the deaths of Afghan

206                          INTERNATIONAL RELATIONS 16(2)

civilians: it does not matter to those who were killed whether their deaths were intended or unintended. If the US knows that the means it employs will cause innocent people to die, then is it responsible for these deaths?

The article sets out to investigate this question by considering what moral arguments are available to justify the harming of civilians in war. My starting point is to consider two opposed moral theories of war, namely, pacifism and Just War. The former starts from the premise that it is never permissible to kill anyone in war and that as a consequence war itself is not justifiable. Pacifism is frequently dismissed in discussions of war and intervention. But, against the frequently heard claim that all peaceful means have been exhausted and force is the last resort, it reminds us that we always have moral choices as to whether to fight or resist our enemies non-violently. It is beyond the scope of this article to explore the possibilities of a non-violent strategy in dealing with the threat posed by the Taliban and al-Qaeda. My general contention is that pacifism is too disarming in terms of both preventing states from using force in legitimate self-defence and for purposes of human protection beyond borders. This is the starting point of Just War theory, which is predicated on the view that it is never permissible to deliberately harm the innocent in war. Focusing on Michael Walzer's interpretation of Just War, I examine in relation to 'Operation Enduring Freedom' whether it is possible to reconcile the use of violence with Just War's stipulation that the innocent be protected.

US officials claimed that America's conduct of the war exhibited 'great care' for the lives of Afghans. This judgement is critically assessed in the second part of the article. The norm of non-combatant immunity, which has deep roots in western and non-western traditions of moral thought, and which is enshrined in international humanitarian law, served as a constant legitimating argument for US military strategy. As I show below, there is evidence that this norm constrained targeting policy. On the other hand, it is also the case that the US attacked a range of targets that placed Afghan civilians at great risk. I consider how far US rhetoric of fidelity to the Just War conflicted with its application of alternative moral theories that challenge the idea of restraint in war. The first is the realist doctrine of necessity in war; the other two – 'supreme emergency' and 'war is hell' are taken from Walzer. All these moral conceptions of war justify overthrowing the Just War principle of non-combatant immunity, but only the first two accept responsibility for the deaths of innocents. The latter seeks instead to transfer this solely to the enemy.[1] The article exposes these opposed conceptions of responsibility and considers how far they shaped the conduct of Operation Enduring Freedom.

## Protecting the innocent in war

Since all pacifists establish a very strong moral presumption against killing, it follows that there must be an equally strong presumption against engaging in war itself. Killing is terrible, but critics of pacifism argue that the deontological requirement not to take life has to be set against the moral consequences of refusing to take up arms. The awful dilemma is framed as doing nothing and allowing innocents to die or taking actions that will knowingly kill others in the name of achieving a greater good. The latter is the position adopted by Just War theory. It determines that a war is just if it satisfies the conditions of the *jus ad bellum*: just cause, last resort, right intention, reasonable prospect of success leading to a just peace and right authority. However, states that go to war whether for just or unjust reasons must also meet the requirement of the *jus in bello*. This establishes the absolute and overriding constraint that states are not permitted to deliberately harm the innocent.

How does Just War theory decide who counts as an innocent? The answer rests upon a complex moral distinction that is drawn between combatants and civilians in terms of their capacity to harm others. According to Walzer, those who do not pose a threat to anyone else have a basic and inalienable right to life that should not be violated. Soldiers on the other hand belong to a very different class of persons who have put themselves in a position (he acknowledges that often they may have little choice in this) where they can impose death and destruction on others. Combatants forfeit the right to life once they take up arms and they only regain this right if they lay down their arms and surrender. The problem arises in deciding at what point civilians become so integral to the war-making process that they lose the protection normally granted them. Walzer argues that, 'The relevant distinction is . . . between those who make what soldiers need to fight, and those who make what they need to live, like all the rest of us'.[2] Thus, Bomber Command was permitted to attack German munitions factories during World War II, but it should not have been assigned the mission of area bombing against German cities. Civilians only lose their immunity from direct attack, according to Walzer, whenever they 'are actually engaged in activities threatening and harmful to their enemies'.[3] The problem is that separating out innocent civilians from legitimate combatants is very difficult to sustain when the survival of nations is on the line. In the eyes of political and military leaders, and among wider public opinion in the UK and US, German civilians – whether involved in war-making activities or not – were the enemy.[4]

Despite the bedrock commitment of Just War to protect innocent civilians in war, this protection can never be absolute.[5] Even if states only attack strictly legitimate military targets, it is impossible – even with the most advanced precision weapons – to avoid the unintentional killing of the innocent: there can be no guarantee against human error in programming complex weapon systems; that guidance systems will not malfunction; that targets will prove to have been mistakenly identified; and that the enemy will not place 'human shields' around military installations. Just War accepts that the protection given to civilians cannot be total unless states were to renounce war. However, this position is rejected because it is maintained that those who refuse to fight self-defence or to protect others bear responsibility for the injustice and harm that might have been prevented by using violence. Pacifists mobilize two key responses to this proposition.

208                          INTERNATIONAL RELATIONS 16(2)

The first is to argue that there is a fundamental moral difference between choosing actions that kill civilians in war and refraining from war that has the consequence that others die. Robert L. Holmes writing from a pacifist standpoint asks 'why should I be held accountable if *someone else* kills that same person in circumstances in which I could foresee that by refusing to kill yet another person his death would result?'[6] The second reply to the charge of moral abdication is to challenge the claim 'that the deaths of innocents at the hands of an aggressor are among the consequences of the refusal of [pacifists] *themselves* to kill innocents in the course of responding violently to the aggression'.[7] This reasoning can be applied to the counterfactual case where the US after September 11 had ruled out war on pacifist grounds. The logic of Holmes' position is that it would be wrong to hold the US Government directly accountable for any subsequent deaths of US citizens as a result of terrorist attacks because it refused to kill innocent Afghans in its quest to destroy al-Qaeda. Put differently, would the response of the terrorists in striking the US be a direct consequence of the US decision not to attack Afghanistan?

Yet, if US decision-makers believe that there is a high risk that Osama bin Laden's network will strike again, perhaps with biological, chemical or even nuclear weapons, and there is the prospect of severely reducing this threat by attacking the territory of Afghanistan, could the Bush administration have absolved itself of responsibility for any subsequent deaths of civilians caused by terrorist attacks if it had refused to hit back? On the other hand, given that Just War is premised on protecting the innocent, how can the use of force be justified against al-Qaeda if this places Afghan civilians at risk? The morally uncomfortable answer that Just War provides is to argue that it all comes down to a balancing of evils. Many Just War theorists invoke the doctrine of 'double-effect' that was developed by Catholic theologians in the Middle Ages. It is claimed that it is permitted to perform an act which has both good and evil consequences if the following conditions are satisfied: the evil outcome must not be intended; the adverse effect must not serve as a means to the good achieved; and, crucially, the negative consequence of the act must be outweighed by its good result in preventing further death and suffering.[8] In pressing into service the argument of 'double-effect', Just War comes perilously close to moral incoherence. The principle of non-combatant immunity rests on the proposition that civilians are not engaged in the business of harm. Yet, having done nothing to justify forfeiting their right to life, the theory allows in Theodore J. Koontz's words that '*Non-combatants may be killed but not attacked*'.[9]

The only practical constraint on the doctrine of 'double-effect' is the proportionality rule. It is important to distinguish between the *jus ad bellum* and the *jus in bello* when considering this. According to the former, proportionality relates to whether the use of force produces more good than harm overall; with regard to the latter, it refers to the good of specific military attacks as against the harm imposed by such actions on innocents. The proportionality rule in relation to the *jus in bello* is given its most explicit moral and legal formulation in Additional

Protocol 1 to the 1949 Geneva Conventions (hereafter Protocol 1). Although the US is not a signatory to Protocol 1, the latter is customary international law and hence is binding on all states. This legal instrument enshrines Just War's absolute prohibition against the deliberate killing of civilians. Under Article 52(2), states have a legal obligation to only attack 'objects which by their nature, location, purpose or use make an effective contribution to military action'.[10] And, even if a target is defined as a legitimate military one, Article 51(5)(b) prohibits attacks 'which may be expected to cause incidental loss of civilian life, injury to civilians, damage to civilian objects, or a combination thereof, which would be excessive in relation to the concrete and direct military advantage anticipated'.[11]

The problem is that international humanitarian law (or the laws of war) provides little or no guidance as to what constitutes 'excessive' civilian casualties or 'concrete and directly military advantage' in specific cases. What is clear is that the door is left sufficiently open under Protocol 1 that states can justify the killing of innocent civilians as an unintended consequence of attacks against legitimate military targets. The proportionality rule is the Achilles heel of Just War theory. Walzer's own dissatisfaction with it can be seen in the following passage:

> But we have to worry . . . about all those unintended but foreseeable deaths, for their number can be large, and subject only to the proportionality rule – a weak constraint double effect provides a blanket justification. The principle for that reason invites an angry or a cynical response: what difference does it make whether civilian deaths are a direct or an indirect effect of my actions? It can hardly matter to the dead civilians, and if I know in advance that I am likely to kill so many innocent people and go ahead anyway, how can I be blameless?[12]

He insists that those who take up arms should do more than satisfy themselves that civilian losses are proportionate to the military advantage gained from attacking particular targets. This is a minimal requirement but he argues that political and military authorities incur a positive responsibility to protect those civilians whom their military operations inadvertently threaten. The latter cannot be granted complete protection from the horrors of war, but they have a right that 'due care'[13] is taken with their safety.

A responsibility falls upon military commanders to accept greater risks to their armed forces if this protects civilians who have done nothing to deserve being placed in harm's way. As Walzer puts it, 'if saving civilian lives means risking soldier's lives, the risk must be accepted'.[14] At the same time, he acknowledges that there must be limits to the risks that we can reasonably ask military personnel to run in order to protect the innocent. He suggests that these are 'roughly at that point where any further risk-taking would certainly doom the military venture or make it so costly that it could not be repeated'.[15] Unfortunately, he does not develop his notion of 'due care' beyond the generality that the tolerable level of risk will vary depending upon the target in question, the necessities imposed by the situation and the character of the weapons technology.[16] To try and explore

210                 INTERNATIONAL RELATIONS 16(2)

what is entailed by 'due care' in a practical moral context, the next section examines whether the US bombing campaign against al-Qaeda and the Taliban met this standard of civilian protection in war.

## Operation Enduring Freedom and the requirement of 'due care'

US officials repeatedly emphasized America's caution in avoiding civilian casualties. For example, Department of Defence spokesperson, Victoria Clarke, stated on 23 October 2001 that 'US forces are intentionally striking only military and terrorist targets. We take *great care* in our targeting process to avoid civilian casualties'.[17] According to Under-Secretary of State for Political Affairs, Marc Grossman, 'when the military aspect of the struggle is over, it will be clear that the number of civilian casualties is very, very low'.[18] Secretary of Defence Donald Rumsfeld even went so far as to assert that 'I can't imagine there's been a conflict in history where there has been less collateral damage, less unintended consequences'.[19] He pointed to the recent history of Afghanistan where the struggle for power had been characterized by enormous suffering on the part of the population, considering that the war against the Taliban had replaced 'a repressive government . . . with the fewest civilian casualties of any time in recent decades'.[20] These statements show how the norm of non-combatant immunity has become the legitimating standard against which military operations have to be justified.

Concerns about the public reaction to high levels of collateral damage (the military's euphemism for civilian casualties) can be traced back to the wars in Korea and especially Vietnam. In the case of the latter, President Lyndon Johnson and his advisers exercised very tight control over the selection of strategic targets in North Vietnam. In the eyes of military commanders, this severely handicapped the war effort, but Johnson believed that public opinion at home and abroad would not tolerate high levels of civilian destruction in the North.[21] The development of precision-guided weapons in the last decade has opened up new possibilities for reducing the risks of civilian casualties without sacrificing military effectiveness. The injunction to avoid high levels of civilian casualties was a key feature of the targeting plans developed by Air Force commanders during the 1991 Gulf War. Nevertheless, no matter how tight the controls, there was still a public outcry when the US attacked the Al Firdos bunker killing 200 Iraqi civilians. The target was identified as a command and control centre, but American intelligence was unaware that civilians were also using the facility as a shelter. The presence of civilians in a legitimate military target does not necessarily render such an attack illegal, but, as Ward Thomas points out, it was recognized by senior military commanders that the attack was a public relations disaster. Colin Powell, then Chairman of the Joint Chiefs of Staff, worried that further mistakes of this sort risked losing the moral high ground for the US.[22]

Compared to the deaths of civilians in the Second World War from American and British strategic bombing, the numbers of non-combatants killed in the Gulf War were very low indeed.[23] But, as Thomas argues, what has changed is that the norm of non-combatant immunity has become stronger, raising expectations that war can be fought in a relatively bloodless manner for civilians in the target state.[24] A key consequence of this consensus that unites governments in the developed and developing world (advocates of terrorism remain, of course, outside of this consensus) is that military planners have become increasingly conscious of the requirement that war be fought humanely. The goal of minimizing civilian casualties was an integral part of the operational planning determining target selection in the Kosovo war of 1999. All targets were assessed for their likely collateral damage, and lawyers attached to United States European Command and in alliance capitals scrutinized targets to ensure they were in conformity with international humanitarian law.[25]

President Bush described the limitation of civilian casualties as a key requirement of Operation Enduring Freedom. As in the Gulf War and Kosovo, collateral damage concerns were an integral part of the targeting process. Lawyers in the Pentagon and at the Combined Air Operations Centre at Prince Sultan Air Base in Saudi Arabia scrutinized targets for their legality. Each morning and evening during the operation, General Tommy Franks, Head of US Central Command in Tampa, Florida, and overall commander of the war effort, held a videoconference with Rumsfeld and Chairman of the Joint Chiefs of Staff, General Richard Myers, to discuss the progress and planning of the war. Avoiding civilian casualties was a key factor in these discussions, indicating how the norm of non-combatant immunity had become internalized in the thinking of high-level military leaders.[26] According to one Air Force commander speaking off the record, 'There's been a decision by the people running this war to rely on the advice of lawyers to a greater degree than they have before'.[27] There is evidence that this process went too far for some Air Force commanders who were frustrated that concerns about civilian casualties hampered legitimate military operations. One report cited Air Force officials privately complaining that they were unable to attack 'some of the big boys' because, by the time pilots had gone through the complex approval process, the opportunity was lost.[28] In a normative context where controversial targeting decisions are subject to microscopic scrutiny, one senior officer was reported as saying that concerns about civilian casualties 'become more than considerations. They become the first thing people think about'.[29] As another Air Force official put it, 'When everybody's telling you a civilian structure is nearby . . . there might be refugees in that column . . . we end up not bombing the bad guys'.[30]

The impression that emerges from these insights is of a Pentagon that was exercising 'due care' towards innocent Afghans. The US admitted that civilians had been unintentionally killed during the campaign, but it refused to give any figures claiming that, in the absence of a detailed investigation on the ground, it was impossible to provide reliable figures. This did not deter other commentators.

The most controversial assessment was provided in a highly critical report based on a survey of news reports compiled by Marc W. Herold who claimed that as many as 3000–3600 Afghans had died between 7 October 2001 and 6 February 2002.[31] An alternative study also based on media sources, produced by Carl Conetta of the Project on Defense Alternatives, concluded that 1000–1300 civilians had been killed in the bombing campaign as of January 2002. What is important about Conetta's analysis is that, despite an increased reliance on precision-guided weapons compared to the Kosovo war (60 percent as against 30 percent), he shows that there was a significant increase in the number of civilian casualties compared to NATO's bombing campaign against Yugoslavia. He explains this in terms of the following three factors: first, the switch from laser-guided weapons to the use of smart weapons guided by the Global Positioning System (GPS). These are cheaper than laser-guided weapons, can be used in all weather conditions, but are less accurate.[32] Second, the campaign objectives involved targeting leadership figures hiding in residential areas; third, engaging mobile targets required pilots on occasions to rely on the use of 'dumb bombs' in the absence of laser designation or GPS coordinates.[33]

The above arguments did not figure in Pentagon accounts of civilian casualties. Instead, the US military sought to explain the deaths of innocent Afghans as mistakes in targeting. Fifty percent of the GPS guided Joint Direct Attack Munitions (JDAMs) are expected to land within 32–42 feet of their target. But this does not account for the other 50 percent of the weapons that fall outside this CEP). Several thousand JDAMs were dropped during the campaign, and several of these missed their target and killed civilians. On 12 October, a JDAM missed its designated military target owing to human error and hit a residential area in Afghanistan;[34] 12 days later, a 1000lb bomb dropped by an F-18 airplane missed a vehicle storage depot and hit an old people's home 300 feet away;[35] on 26 October, American planes accidentally destroyed a Red Cross warehouse;[36] and two days later, a further mistake in targeting led to 13 civilians being killed in a neighbourhood in northern Kabul.[37] The fact is that no matter how sophisticated weapons technology becomes, it is impossible to eliminate the risk of machine and human error. One ex-pilot has estimated that 'around five per cent [of these smart weapons] will miss because their guidance systems fail'.[38]

By framing the deaths of innocents as mistakes, the US sought to avoid the deeper moral and legal questions as to whether it was attacking legitimate military targets; whether such actions satisfied the proportionality rule; and whether its air and ground forces were placing themselves at sufficient risk in order to mitigate the horrors of war for innocent Afghans. In reflecting on these questions, it is worth pausing to consider that even a correctly aimed 2,000 lb bomb 'could cause death and casualties for hundreds of yards around the target site'.[39] Thus, even if the vehicle depot attacked on 24 October was a legitimate target, and assuming that it had been successfully hit, would the resulting civilian destruction have been outweighed by the military advantage gained? Balancing these conflicting concerns was the moral and legal challenge faced by American political and military leaders. Subject to the proportionality rule, a grouping of military vehicles is a legitimate target, but what about civilian conveniences that contribute to a state's war making capabilities?

According to Herold, the US 'directly targeted certain civilian facilities deemed hostile to its war success'.[40] This claim directly challenges Rumsfeld's statement on 19 October that the US was 'focused totally on military targets'.[41] To accept the latter statement, it would be necessary to show that the attacks against the main telephone exchange in Kabul; the electrical grid in Kandahar; and the hydroelectric power station adjacent to the Kajaki dam constituted targets that made an 'effective contribution to military action' as defined under Article 52(2) of Protocol 1. The problem is that these facilities are dual-purpose ones that serve the needs of the civilian population but also contribute to the military effort of enemy forces. In the case of the Gulf War, it is estimated that US targeting of Iraq's power-generating facilities resulted in the subsequent deaths of as many as 100,000 Iraqi civilians through the loss of power, water and sewage facilities.[42] The same controversy occurred during the Kosovo campaign. NATO initially refrained from attacking the electrical grid, but, as pressure for a result mounted, it claimed that the military advantage in depriving the Serbian armed forces of electricity justified the resulting disruption to civilian life.[43] The argument that military necessity outweighed concerns about the consequences for civilians clearly persuaded Rumsfeld, Myers and Franks to give the go-ahead for attacks against power-generating stations. Nevertheless, if we apply Walzer's principle that civilians only lose their immunity when they contribute directly to war-making activities, it is hard to justify US attacks against Afghan facilities that directly sustain civilian life.[44] Had US planes not attacked the electrical grid in Afghanistan, the Taliban and al-Qaeda might have proved a more effective fighting force against US and UK forces on the ground. However, if the consequence of reducing the harm imposed on Afghans by not striking the power plants was to increase the exposure of US forces to danger, should military commanders have accepted this in order to protect civilians?

Operation Enduring Freedom raised this question vividly because the Taliban and al-Qaeda forces tried to escape attack by seeking shelter in the homes of civilians, and it was alleged in mosques and hospitals.[45] One of the perverse consequences of the norm against killing non-combatants is that unscrupulous enemies will manipulate for their own ends the reluctance on the part of western states to incur such deaths. Although the US was careful not to attack mosques where it suspected that enemy forces were hiding, it did attack Taliban and al-Qaeda personnel hiding in residential areas. For example, in the first two weeks of November, US planes attacked heavily populated residential areas in Khanabad, one of the last towns still under Taliban control. It is claimed that more than 100 civilians died in these raids. Fleeing refugees said that Taliban fighters were hiding in some of the houses, but others who remained in the town disputed this.[46] In one of the most controversial attacks of the war, dozens of civilians were killed in the village of Qalai Niazi on 29 December. Acting on the basis of intelligence from local allies, US planes attacked with laser-guided bombs six houses where it believed senior Taliban and al-Qaeda leaders were hiding. All of the houses were destroyed, but journalists who arrived on the scene only found evidence of ammunition in three of the destroyed mud-brick houses. The other three on the other side of a ravine about 100 metres away appeared to be civilian dwellings where a feast to end a marriage ceremony had ended only hours earlier. The Pentagon's explanation for the attack was that the target was a legitimate one because it 'housed Taliban and al-Qaeda leadership' who were present in the village at the time of the attack.[47] Local people and village elders denied this, maintaining that rival factions deliberately provided false intelligence to the US in order to bring down air strikes against their enemies. From what reports have emerged so far, it seems that Taliban commanders dumped weapons in the village after fleeing Kabul in mid-November, but had left the village by the time the US attacked in late December.[48] Even if it were accepted that three houses in the village contained Taliban and al-Qaeda forces, would the unintended but foreseeable damage to the houses 100 metres away outweigh any military advantage gained from these attacks? Applying Walzer's standard of 'due care', it should also be asked whether there were other ways of securing the military objective that would have reduced the risks to civilians even if this increased the risk to the US military. Could US ground forces have done more to verify the accuracy of the intelligence acquired from local leaders? The fundamental difficulty confronting the US was distinguishing between members of the Taliban and al-Qaeda and innocent Afghans.[49]

Realism argues that states should override the norm against the killing of civilians if this conflicts with the imperatives of state survival. As Robert Osgood and Robert Tucker put it, 'The appeal to necessity is not incompatible with the acceptance of restraint on state action, so long as these restraints do not jeopardize independence and survival'.[50] This ethic of statecraft accepts moral responsibility for such decisions and acknowledges in David C. Hendrickson's words that breaching the norm of non-combatant immunity should 'not be accepted without the greatest misgivings'.[51] Pentagon spokespersons were careful not to claim that eliminating senior al-Qaeda and Taliban leaders justified jettisoning the principle of civilian immunity in war, but Rumsfeld provided a strong indication that US military strategy was driven by the gravity of the threat facing America after September 11. In response to questions about civilian casualties at a press briefing on 16 October, he denied that the US had any choice in the military strategy it had adopted given the basic requirement to 'defend the United States from the kinds of terrorist attacks which we've experienced'.[52] It is not hard to detect in these words the realist plea of necessity. Is this the answer that the Bush administration would give to those like 14-year-old Jawad who lost his parents, five sisters and a step-brother in one US strike against a Taliban military radar and anti-aircraft batteries? A woman passing by the graves remarked to journalists when asked whether she was a relative, 'That doesn't matter . . . What matters is that they were innocent, and they died'.[53]

An alternative moral argument available to the US to justify overriding the rules of the *jus in bello* is Walzer's idea of 'supreme emergency'. He defines this as 'a threat to human values'[54] that is so horrifying in its nature and so imminent in terms of the danger it poses that any means can be employed to defeat it. The emergency does not only exist for a particular political community as in realism; rather it confronts humanity itself.[55] Walzer cautions that declaring such an emergency does not automatically permit states to override the prohibition against the killing of innocents.[56] If other military strategies are available that stand a good chance of avoiding defeat without breaking the rules of war, then these must be exhausted first.[57] Realism makes no apologies for invoking the doctrine of necessity when the survival of the state is at stake and it offers no feelings of guilt about the actions involved. By contrast, Walzer is emphatic that when leaders override the rule of non-combatant immunity in the name of supreme emergency they are not 'free of guilt [because] were there no guilt involved, the decisions they make would be less agonizing than they are ... A moral theory that made their life easier ... would repress the reality of war'.[58] He gives the example of Nazism as a supreme emergency considering that it posed such a threat to the values of humanity that Britain was right to take the decision in November 1940 to begin bombing German cities.[59] Bomber Command was not capable of precision bombing in 1940–2 and the only effective use of the force was as a weapon of terror against German civilians. Walzer wants us to put ourselves in the shoes of British political leaders who had to weigh up the evil of the 'killing of innocent people' as against 'that immeasurable evil (a Nazi triumph)'.[60] As he points out, no one can know whether, had Britain refrained from using Bomber Command, Nazism would have triumphed. All that can be reasonably asked of political and military leaders is that they carefully consider whether there are alternatives to the use of indiscriminate means that do not increase the likelihood of the threat to humanity represented by the supreme emergency succeeding.

Does the scale of the threat posed by Osama bin Laden's network of global terror – including the risk that the organization might eventually acquire weapons of mass destruction – constitute 'a threat to human values' so radical that it creates a supreme emergency? The justification of US political leaders provides strong support for the proposition that America and the world face an existential threat from the forces of global terrorism. President Bush in his address to Congress on 20 September 2001 made a direct parallel with the threat posed by Nazism:

> Our war on terror begins with al-Qaida but it does not end there. It will not end until every terrorist group of global reach has been found, stopped and defeated ... By sacrificing human life to serve their radical visions ... they follow in the path of Fascism, Nazism and totalitarianism ... We will direct every resource at our command ... to the destruction and the defeat of the global terror network.[61]

A month later, after the war against the Taliban and al-Qaeda in Afghanistan had begun, Vice-President Dick Cheney stated: 'We cannot deal with terror. It will not end in a treaty. There will be no peaceful co-existence, no negotiations, no summit, no joint communiqué with the terrorists. The struggle can only end with their complete and permanent destruction'.[62] Yet this declaration of an apocalyptic threat to civilized values did not lead to the claim that the US was justified in overriding the rules of war. As I discussed earlier, senior Air Force commanders believed that opportunities to destroy Taliban and al-Qaeda leaders were missed because concerns about civilian casualties inhibited prompt and effective action.[63] The argument of these officials was that, whilst a less restrained campaign would lead to higher levels of collateral damage, this would shorten the war and hence save more American and Afghan lives in the long term. This is the type of consequentialist argument that was invoked to justify the dropping of the atomic bomb on Hiroshima and Nagasaki: it saved more lives (American and Japanese) than had the war carried on. Walzer categorically rejects this argument, considering that permission to override the principles of the *jus in bello* only exists in cases of supreme emergency. He writes that 'Deliberately killing civilians in the belief that more civilians will be saved is a fantastic, godlike, frightening and horrendous act'.[64]

The development of precision-guided weapons has ameliorated the awful moral choices that faced American and British decision-makers during World War II. The Bush administration was not required in the 21st century to choose between the deliberate killing of Afghan civilians or risk losing the war against global terrorism. However, what modern technology cannot help the US evade is the balance that it draws between protecting the innocent on the one hand and the destruction of the enemy on the other. If US leaders believed they faced a supreme emergency on the scale of Nazism, then they could have been expected to interpret the proportionality rule in such a way as to define securing their key military objectives as being worth the price in civilian casualties. Having decided that the goal of eliminating al-Qaeda and Taliban forces hiding in civilian areas justified the resulting harm to non-combatants, could these military operations have been carried out differently so as to minimize the risks imposed on civilians?

Given the moral conflict between protecting the lives of NATO aircrews and reducing the risks to Serb civilians that had arisen during the Kosovo conflict,[65] it would not be surprising if this dilemma repeated itself during Operation Enduring Freedom. Herold claims that the US was so obsessed with reducing the risks to its own military personnel that it chose to employ tactics and strategies that maximized the suffering inflicted on innocent Afghans.[66] This critique might have had greater credibility had those Air Force officials who wanted to slacken collateral damage constraints in the belief that this would save the lives of American soldiers won the debate inside the Pentagon. According to Thomas E. Ricks, these officers expressed frustration that 'US Special Forces [were] being forced to go into Afghanistan on the ground to pursue the al-Qaeda terrorist network and Taliban leaders who could have been killed from the air earlier in the campaign'.[67] The difficulty with this assessment is that more extensive use of Special Force operations might have secured US military objectives with less risk of accidentally killing innocent Afghans. It is noteworthy in this respect that in the latter stages of the campaign the US sent in ground forces rather than rely on air strikes in situations where commanders were not confident about the reliability of local intelligence.[68] This suggests that greater use of ground forces in the earlier stages of the campaign might have reduced the numbers who were killed in air raids where the intelligence was wrong or where enemy forces were located in close proximity to civilians. Special Force operations of this kind increased the risk to US ground forces, bringing us back to the hard moral question of how political and military leaders should weigh the lives of their soldiers against those of innocents.

Just War theory is constructed around the moral imperative to protect the innocent. But the reality of war is that the killing (as against the deliberate targeting) of civilians cannot be avoided. Theorists like Walzer try to rescue Just War by attributing a direct responsibility to political and military leaders for the exercise of 'due care'. Without this ascription of responsibility, worries about civilian casualties expressed from the President down during Operation Enduring Freedom would make no sense. Moreover, neither the realist argument of necessity nor the claim of supreme emergency removes responsibility from leaders who decide to sanction actions that break the rules of war. Yet there was an alternative discourse of responsibility at work during Operation Enduring Freedom that can be glimpsed in the occasional public statements of Rumsfeld. In response to questions at a news briefing as to whether the US should have done more to reduce civilian casualties, he retorted: 'We did not start this war. So understand, responsibility for every single casualty in this war, whether they're innocent Afghans or innocent Americans, rests at the feet of the al-Qaeda and the Taliban'.[69] How far this conviction shaped the thinking of senior administration figures is difficult to gauge, but this conception of responsibility represents an even greater challenge to Just War than realism or the theory of supreme emergency.

Walzer named blaming your enemy for the cruelty of war as the 'war is hell' doctrine. He traced the idea to General Sherman's moral justification for the forced evacuation of the population of Atlanta as he razed it to the ground during the Civil War. Sherman claimed to be completely innocent of the harm he and his men had imposed on the citizens of Atlanta, considering that sole responsibility for this rested with those who had started the war, namely, the leaders of the Confederacy. In response to General Hood's plea for restraint on the part of the Unionist forces, Sherman replied: 'War is cruelty and you cannot refine it . . . those who brought war into our country deserve all the curses and maledictions a people can pour out'.[70] The attraction of this conception of war to US decision-makers is that it transfers sole responsibility for any civilian casualties caused by the US bombing campaign to the Taliban and al-Qaeda. An important illustration of the different understandings of responsibility contained in the doctrines of Just War and 'war is hell' can be seen in the response to the Taliban and al-Qaeda using civilians as human shields.

218                          INTERNATIONAL RELATIONS 16(2)

International humanitarian law prohibits belligerents from hiding military forces in civilian areas or seeking sanctuary among the civilian population. But, if such actions take place, combatants are not relieved of their responsibility to honour the principle of civilian immunity. Rather, they still are required to only aim at legitimate military targets and to adhere to the proportionality rule. By contrast, 'war is hell' argues that, if the Taliban choose to put innocent Afghans at risk in this way, then the fault for any deaths of civilians caused by US bombing raids rests with the Taliban alone.[71] Set against this, Just War theory claims that civilians only lose their immunity if they engage in war-making activities that are threatening to the other side. Even if Afghans sympathetic to the Taliban or al-Qaeda voluntarily shelter members of these organizations in their homes, they do not lose their protection as civilians.[72] They can be killed if this is an indirect effect of an attack against a legitimate target, but such strikes would have to satisfy the proportionality rule. It would have to be shown that killing $x$ number of al-Qaeda and Taliban justified the unintended but foreseeable deaths of $y$ number of Afghan civilians. The Pentagon has justified such attacks on the grounds that they were legitimate targets, but it is clear that the definition of legitimacy at work here is wider than Just War. Rumsfeld, Myers and Franks have interpreted what is militarily justified in the context of Bush's declaration that the war against terrorism is a supreme emergency that pits civilization against evil.


## Conclusion

The Bush administration rejected a non-violent response to the events of September 11, believing that the war against terrorism was a just cause that legitimated the use of force. War always involves harming the innocent but does it matter whether civilians are deliberately killed or that they die as the unintended consequence of attacks against legitimate military targets? Just War doctrine would totally reject the equating of terrorist acts like September 11 with the unintended deaths of Afghan civilians in Operation Enduring Freedom. It would claim that these civilian casualties were accidental and did not serve as a means to secure military victory in the war against terrorism. By contrast, the deliberate intention of the terrorists was to kill civilians in their attack on the World Trade Centre: the terrible crime committed on September 11 was a direct means to the ends sought by al-Qaeda. Nevertheless, the moral picture is not as clear-cut as this because the deaths of innocents – however unintended – are always foreseeable in war. The only way to prevent the killing of innocents is to follow pacifism and refuse war itself. Having ruled this position out, Just War seeks to guarantee as high a level of protection as possible by establishing the proportionality rule through the doctrine of 'double-effect'. This has its modern legal expression in Protocol 1.

The problem is that, far from demonstrating the constraint that this imposes on military operations, Operation Enduring Freedom reveals, as did the NATO bombing campaign during the Kosovo conflict, how permissive international humanitarian law can be when it comes to identifying what counts as a legitimate target.[73] Legal advisers have been intimately involved in the process of target selection ensuring that collateral damage concerns were actively considered at all stages of the targeting process. And those Air Force officials who lobbied for the relaxation of targeting restraints were overruled on the grounds that increased numbers of civilian casualties would undermine political support for the war in the international community, especially in the Islamic world. In this respect, the war against the Taliban and al-Qaeda appears to confirm the constraining effect of the norm of non-combatant immunity on US military operations evident in the Gulf War and Kosovo. However, it would be unwise to exaggerate this constraining effect. What is also apparent is that the legal framework in Protocol 1 enabled the US to take on a whole range of targets that look very dubious from the moral standpoint of Just War.

A good illustration is the Pentagon's view that a state's electricity plants constitute a legitimate military target. If one defines the effect on civilians of destroying power plants in indirect terms, then, as Kenneth R. Rizer suggests, 'it might be very difficult to find a concrete and direct military advantage that outweighed the tens of thousands of civilian deaths that might be indirectly caused from loss of electricity'.[74] Given this, it is not surprising that the US Air Force has opted for a definition of civilian harm that only includes the direct injury inflicted by such strikes. This makes it easier to argue that it meets the requirement in Article 51(5)(b) of Protocol 1 that the harm imposed by such strikes is not 'excessive' compared to the direct military advantage of such an attack. Walzer argued that targeting the Iraqi electrical grid during the Gulf War violated the principle of civilian immunity, and would presumably say the same about the attacks on these facilities in Kosovo and Afghanistan. The fact that Protocol 1 does not explicitly prohibit such attacks highlights how involving the lawyers in the process of target selection does not necessarily guarantee greater civilian protection. As Michael Ignatieff puts it, 'moral questions stubbornly resist being reduced to legal ones, and moral exposure is not eliminated when legal exposure is'.[75] Attacks on dual-purpose facilities like electricity plants might be legally justifiable under Protocol 1, but are they defensible in terms of the rules of the *jus in bello*?

The US sought to justify the conduct of the bombing campaign by claiming that the war against terrorism was a supreme emergency. However, given that the attacks against the US on September 11 represented a direct assault on the principle of civilian immunity, the Bush administration could not be seen to be disregarding Just War restraints and retain moral credibility. At the same time, Rumsfeld, Myers and Franks were sufficiently cognizant of the necessity to destroy the Taliban and al-Qaeda that they applied a very permissive interpretation of what counted as a legitimate military target. The problem they faced was balancing the protection of innocent Afghans against the twin moral imperatives of defeating the terrorists and protecting the lives of American soldiers. Until we have more information about the conduct of the operation, judging how well the US reconciled these conflicting moral claims must be a provisional assessment. If the war against terrorism constitutes a supreme emergency on the scale of Nazism, then the decision to attack al-Qaeda personnel hiding in civilian dwellings in the knowledge that innocent civilians would be killed might be justifiable. But can it really be claimed that the threat posed by this network of terror matched the imminence of the Nazi threat to human values in 1940? Moreover, Britain's use of Bomber Command against German cities did not run the risk that it would serve to increase the danger facing Britain from Nazism. However, there are good grounds for worrying that some of those innocent Afghans whose families suffered at the hands of US bombing will seek to extract revenge against the Americans. Put differently, the means employed by the Bush administration to end the threat posed by global terrorism could paradoxically serve to increase the risks facing US citizens.

Having taken the decision to accept whatever level of civilian casualties were necessary to destroy al-Qaeda in Afghanistan, the US was not obviated from meeting Walzer's requirement of 'due care'. It is entirely reasonable that the armed forces should seek to reduce their risks; the problem arises when this has the effect of harming civilians. Is there any evidence that US forces could have done more to protect innocent Afghans even if this meant increasing their exposure to danger? For example, should Special Forces have been tasked with attacking enemy forces in close proximity to civilian areas? Would this have significantly reduced collateral damage as against bombing strikes? Such missions would clearly have been dangerous and it would have to be shown that they did not place US soldiers at undue risk. Moreover, the success of such operations would still have relied on local intelligence, and without reliable information mistakes were inevitable. There is no mathematical formula for quantifying and assessing these risks, and this illustrates how deciding in particular cases what counts as 'due care' will be open to differing interpretations. One way forward is to begin a dialogue between the human rights and military communities on how to balance values of non-combatant immunity and force protection.[76]

In asking whether US military leaders could have done more to protect Afghan civilians, I do not mean to imply that they bear sole responsibility for the deaths of civilians killed during the campaign. They share that responsibility with al-Qaeda and the Taliban because, as Walzer puts it, 'When we judge the unintended killing of civilians, we need to know how those civilians came to be in a battle zone in the first place'.[77] Without the attacks on September 11, there would have been no Operation Enduring Freedom. But what must be rejected is Rumsfeld's assertion that responsibility for the deaths of Afghan civilians rests solely with the terrorists and their supporters. The fact that US planes flew on missions day after day with political and military leaders knowing that civilian deaths were foreseeable means that responsibility for this suffering must also be accepted by US decision-makers. The unintended killing of civilians might be defended on grounds of either Just War, supreme emergency or the realist doctrine of necessity in war. But what is crucial is that none of these justifications seeks to shift sole responsibility for the deaths of innocents to the Taliban and al-Qaeda. The latter are responsible for placing the Afghan people in the hell that is war, but this does not absolve US political and military leaders of their responsibility to protect civilians endangered by the war against terrorism.

## Notes

I wish to thank Alex Bellamy, Mick Cox, Ian Clark, Cori Dauber, Tim Dunne, Toni Erskine, Anne Harris, Andrew Linklater and Colin McInnes for their comments on earlier versions of this article.

1   I owe the idea that responsibility can be viewed as being transferred to the enemy to a conversation with Toni Erskine.
2   Cited in Brian Orend (2000) *Michael Walzer on War and Justice*, p117. Cardiff: University of Wales Press.
3   Michael Walzer (1978) *Just and Unjust Wars*, p146. London: Allen Lane.
4   I wish to thank Colin McInnes for alerting me to this point.
5   Orend, p120 (see note 2).
6   Robert L. Holmes (1989) *On War and Morality*, p202. Princeton, NJ: Princeton University Press.
7   Holmes, p208 (see note 6).
8   A good example of this is Elizabeth Anscombe's classic defence of the killing of the innocent where this is the unintended consequence of one's action. She wrote: 'But if I am answerable for the foreseen consequences of an action or refusal, as much as for the action itself, then these prohibitions [against the killing of the innocent] will break down. If someone innocent will die unless I do a wicked thing, then on this view I am his murderer in refusing: so all that is left to me is to weigh up evils'. Cited in Holmes, p194 (see note 6).
9   Theodore J. Koontz (1997) 'Noncombatant Immunity in Michael Walzer's Just and Unjust Wars', *Ethics and International Affairs*, 11: 59 (original emphasis).
10  Cited in A. Roberts and R. Guelff (2000) *Documents on the Laws of War* (3rd edn), p450. Oxford: Oxford University Press.
11  Cited in Roberts and Guelff, p449 (see note 10)
12  Walzer, p153 (see note 3).
13  This idea of Walzer's is discussed at length in Orend, pp75, 119–20 (see note 2). For Walzer's original discussion of 'due care', see *Just and Unjust Wars*, p156 (see note 3).
14  Walzer, p156 (see note 3).
15  Cited in Orend, pp119–20 (see note 2).
16  Walzer, p156 (see note 3).
17  Quoted in 'Fact Sheet: US Military Efforts to Avoid Civilian Casualties', US Department of State, 25 October 2001 (emphasis added).
18  Under-Secretary of State for Political Affairs Marc Grossman, US Department of State, digital interview with London-based journalists of Arab dailies, 19 October, 2001.
19  Cited in William Arkin (2002) 'Fear of Civilian Deaths may have Undermined Effort', *Los Angeles Times*, 16 January, [http://www.latimes.co], visited on 16 January 2002. This phrase 'collateral damage' has become a euphemism for the death and destruction in civilian areas inadvertently caused by a correctly aimed weapon hitting its intended military target.
20  Secretary of Defence, Rumsfeld, interview with C-Span, [http://www.defenselink.mil/Jan2000], visited on 9 January 2002.
21  Ward Thomas (2001) *The Ethics of Destruction: Norms and Force in International Relations*, pp147–58. Ithaca, NY: Cornell University Press.
22  Thomas, pp87–9 (see note 21).
23  Estimates vary from between 1000 and 15,000, with most commentators agreeing on a figure of 3000. See Thomas, pp158–9 (see note 21).
24  Thomas, p160 (see note 21).

25    Michael Ignatieff (2000) *Virtual War: Kosovo and beyond*, pp197–201. London: Chatto and Windus.

26    Eric Schmitt (2001) 'A Nation Challenged: The Chiefs; Bush's War Troika Seeking Blend of Military and Civilian Decision-making', *New York Times*, 24 October, [http://www.NYTimes.com], visited on 2 November 2001.

27    Esther Schrader (2002) 'War, on Advice of Counsel', *Los Angeles Times*, 15 February, [http://www.latimes.com], visited on 15 February 2002.

28    Thomas E. Ricks (2001) 'Target Approval Delays Cost Air Force Key Hits', *The Washington Post*, 18 November, [http://www.washingtonpost.com], visited on 14 February 2002.

29    William M. Arkin (2002) 'Fear of Civilian Deaths may have Undermined Effort', *Los Angeles Times*, 16 January, [http://www.latimes.co], visited on 15 February 2002.

30    Cited in Arkin (see note 19).

31    Marc Herold (2002) 'Afghan Killing Fields', letter to *The Guardian*, 13 February. Herold published a controversial study of the civilian casualties during the war in early December. See Marc W. Herold (2001) 'A Dossier on Civilian Victims of United States' Aerial Bombing of Afghanistan: A Comprehensive Accounting', 3 December, [http://www.pubpages.unh.edu/~mwherold], visited on 2 January 2002. Other independent commentators have challenged these figures. See Macer Hall and David Wastell, 'Truth and Lies of Taliban's Death Claims', *Electronic Telegraph*, [http://www.portal.telegraph.co.uk], visited on 5 January 2002; Michael Smith, 'Bombing is Successful despite Claims of "Civilian Genocide"', *Electronic Telegraph*, [http://www.portal.telegraph.co.uk], visited on 5 January 2002.

32    Conetta points out that laser-guided bombs achieve a Circular Error Probable (CEP) of 3–8 metres compared to 10–13 metres for GPS guided bombs, and he estimates that this 'equates to being able to put 50 per cent of expended weapons within a 2100 square foot circle *versus* being able to put them in a circle of 3300 feet. Should an intended target sit among a cluster of buildings, the difference between these two circular areas is significant'. Carl Conetta (2002) 'Operation Enduring Freedom: Why a Higher Rate of Civilian Bombing Casualties', Project on Defense Alternatives, Briefing Report No. 11, 24 January, p3, [http://www.comw.org/pda/0201oef.html], visited on 25 January 2002.

33    Conetta, pp3–6 (see note 32).

34    'Satellite-guided Bomb Misses Target, Kills 4 Afghan Civilians', *Space.Com*, [http://www.space.com], visited on 2 January 2002.

35    Rupert Cornwell (2001) 'Pentagon Admits US Jets Bombed Old People's Home in Afghan City', *The Independent*, 24 October, [http://www.independent.co.uk], visited on 4 November 2001; Paul Richter and Peter Pae (2001) 'High-tech US Bombs are Precise but not Perfect', *Los Angeles Times*, 24 October, [http://www.latimes.com], visited on 28 October 2001.

36    Elizabeth Becker and Eric Schmitt (2001) 'US Planes Bomb a Red Cross Site for Second Time', *New York Times*, 27 October, [http://www.NYTimes.com], visited on 4 November 2001; James Palmer (2001) 'Kabul Red Cross is Bombed again by American Jets', *The Independent*, 27 October, [http://www.independent.co.uk], visited on 4 November 2001. A senior military official claimed that the first strike on the Red Cross building was legitimate because 'it is not immediately clear that the warehouse that the ICRC used was not also being used by the Taliban'. Cited in Esther Schrader (2002) 'War, on Advice of Counsel', *Los Angeles Times*, 15 February, [http://www.latimes.com], visited on 15 February 2002.

37    Andrew Buncombe (2001) 'Another 13 Civilians Die in Bungled Bomb Attack', *The Independent*, 29 October, [http://www.independent.co.uk], visited on 1 November 2002.

38    Michael Smith (2001) 'Bombing is Successful Despite Claims of "Civilian Genocide"', *Electronic Telegraph*, 30 October, [http://www.portal.telegraph.co.uk], visited on 15 February 2002.

39    John Nichol (2001) 'The Myth of Precision', *The Guardian*, 29 October, [http://www.guardian.co.uk], visited on 30 October 2001.

40    Herold (2001) 'A Dossier on Civilian Victims of United States' Aerial Bombing of Afghanistan', December, [http://www.pubpages.unh.edu/~mwherold], visited on 2 January 2002.

41    Quoted in 'Fact Sheet, US Military Efforts to Avoid Civilian Casualties', US Department of State, 25 October 2001.

42    The estimate of Iraqi civilians killed by the US strike is cited in Thomas, p166 (see note 21).

43    As NATO spokesperson Jamie Shea put it at a press briefing, 'Command and control or a computer in military hands without electricity simply becomes a mass of metal, wire and plastic'. Quoted in M.R. Gordon (1999) 'NATO Air Attacks on Power Plants pass a Threshold', *New York*

*Times*, 4 May. Also See Ivo H. Daalder and Michael E. O'Hanlon (2000) *Winning Ugly: NATO's War to Save Kosovo*, pp144–5. Washington DC: Brookings Institution.

44    In the case of the Gulf War, Walzer disagreed that the Iraqi power grid constituted a legitimate target, considering that it did not contribute directly to Iraq's war-making activities. See Orend, p117 (see note 2).

45    Martin Bentham (2001) 'Militia Use Civilians as a Shield', *Electronic Telegraph,* 11 November, [http://www.portal.telegraph.co.uk], visited on 13 February 2002; William Branigin (2001) 'Taliban's Human Shields', *The Washington Post*, 24 October, [http://www.washingtonpost], visited on 12 February 2002. Branigin cites one refugee, Mohammed Ali, who claimed, 'the Taliban come at night to the houses of the people and bring their equipment into civilian places'. According to Branigan, Ali said that the Taliban had parked 10 tanks in one mosque.

46    Justin Huggler (2001) 'Legacy of Civilian Casualties in Ruins of Shattered Town', *The Independent*, 27 November, [http://www.independent.co.uk], visited on 15 February 2002.

47    'Terrorists were in Village during Air Attack', *The Washington Post*, [http://www.washington], visited on 16 January 2002.

48    'US Silence and Power of Weaponry Conceal Scale of Civilian Toll', *SMH.com.au*, [http://www.smh.com.au/news/0201/26/world/world3/.html], visited on 25 January 2002.

49    The US had faced exactly this problem in Vietnam: how to identify members of the Vietcong from the civilian population.

50    Robert E. Osgood and Robert W. Tucker (1967) *Force, Order and Justice*, p269. Baltimore, MD: The Johns Hopkins Press.

51    David C. Hendrickson (1997) 'In Defense of Realism', *Ethics and International Affairs* 11: 26.

52    'Rumsfeld Blames Regime for Civilian Deaths', *Guardian Unlimited*, 16 October 2001, [http://www.guardian.co.uk], visited on 3 January 2002.

53    Laura King (2002) 'Review: Afghan Civilian Deaths Lower', *Los Angeles Times*, 11 February, [http://www.latimes..com], visited on 8 March 2002.

54    Walzer, p259 (see note 3).

55    Walzer is frequently interpreted as making a realist argument with his idea of supreme emergency. For example, Michael Smith argues that Walzer 'recognizes the force of the realist argument about necessity because he does intrinsically value the survival of the political community' (Michael Joseph Smith [1997] 'Growing up with Just and Unjust Wars', *Ethics and International Affairs*, 11: 9). However, Walzer's position is more complex than this and his text embodies two distinct understandings of supreme emergency. Walzer can be read as separating out 'a threat to human values' that involves all of us from a specific threat to the survival of a particular political community. He concedes that supreme emergencies can exist for particular states, but does so in a more cautious way than when it comes to describing a threat to the values of humankind that is both close and terrifying. In a telling passage he writes: 'Can a supreme emergency be constituted by a particular threat – by a threat of enslavement or extermination directed against a single nation? Can soldiers and statesmen override the rights of innocent people for the sake of their own political community? I am inclined to answer this question affirmatively, though not without hesitation and worry' (Walzer, p254 [see note 3]). In this passage, Walzer succumbs to a realist ethic of statecraft, but this should be distinguished from his contention that supreme emergency should be defined in terms of a threat to humanity that is so imminent and frightening that the rules of war can be overthrown. In either case, Walzer argues that there is nothing inevitable about such a momentous choice, but considers that few state leaders would be able to resist such a decision (Walzer, p254 [see note 3]). I am grateful to Toni Erskine for suggesting the significance of these two understandings of supreme emergency in Walzer's work.

56    Michael Joseph Smith argues that 'Not only must the proscribed action . . . be the only viable alternative to losing, the action must in some clearly demonstrable way prevent an imminent defeat' (Smith, p10, [see note 55]). Also see Walzer, pp254–55 (see note 3).

57    Walzer is persuaded that Britain had no other realistic military strategy to avoid defeat than area bombing against Germany in 1940. However, Michael Joseph Smith questions this judgement. He writes, 'I wonder whether even in 1940 it [area bombing] was the only way for the British to survive' (Michael Joseph Smith, p10 [see note 55]).

58    Walzer, p326 (see note 3). By arguing that the plea of necessity cannot wipe away the guilt for the evil actions performed in the name of it, Walzer breaks with the consequentialism that underpins

the realist defence of necessity in war. This idea that Walzer's theory of supreme emergency belongs to the tragic is developed by Joseph Boyle (1997) 'Casuistry and the Boundaries of the Moral World', *Ethics and International Affairs* 11: 97.

59  Walzer, pp255–63 (see note 3); Thomas, pp130–6 (see note 21).

60  Walzer, p259 (see note 3).

61  Text of Bush's speech to Congress, *Los Angeles Times*, 20 September 2001, [http://www.latimes.com], visited on 4 November 2002.

62  Cited in Colin Wight, 'Pre-postmodern Terrorism', paper presented at QuinetiQ Workshop, Aberystwyth.

63  Thomas E. Ricks (2001) 'Target Approval Delays Cost Air Force Key Hits', *The Washington Post*, 18 November, [http://www.washingtonpost.com], visited on 14 February 2002. This position echoed Lt Gen. Mike Short's criticism of the air campaign during Operation Allied Force. As commander of the NATO air campaign, Short complained bitterly about the restrictions imposed on his targeting of the Milosevic regime in the early stages of the war. He recognized that his plan risked higher levels of collateral damage, but argued that such a decisive use of force against the 'head of the snake' would have forced the Serbian leader to capitulate much earlier reducing the overall level of suffering (Short's position is cited in A.F. Tully [1999] 'France Faulted for Limiting Targets during Kosovo Conflict', BosNet article, 24 October, [http://www.bosnet.org/archive], visited on 28 June 2001).

64  Walzer, p262 (see note 3).

65  NATO imposed a 15,000 feet limit on air operations to reduce the risks of aircrew being shot down. However, this was criticized on the grounds that it made it difficult to clearly distinguish military from civilian targets, contributing to mistakes like the hitting of the refugee convoy in Kosovo that pilots mistook for armoured vehicles on 14 April 1999. A further illustration of the hard choices that have to be made between the goal of force protection and imposing excessive levels of harm on the civilian population can be seen in the decision to attack Yugoslavia's electrical grid. The US initially used a new specialized CBU-munition that shorts out electrical lines but does not damage the power transmission stations themselves, hence reducing the civilian impact of the strikes. However, as Thomas points out, keeping the power down 'required repeated strikes ... and such a predictable pattern of sorties against fixed targets was seen as posing an increasing threat to the safety of NATO pilots' (Thomas, p166 [see note 21]). On 24 May, the decision was taken to use heavier munitions and knock out the five major power transmission stations creating damage that took weeks to repair. The effect of this strike on the civilian infrastructure was to disrupt electricity and water supplies in many cities, threatening the Serb people with the loss of essential services (Daalder and O'Hanlon, p145, see note 43). For criticisms of this attack as a breach of international humanitarian law, see 'Civilian Deaths in the NATO Air Campaign', Human Rights Watch report, [www.hrw.org/reports/2000], visited on 11 January 2000; Kenneth Roth (2000) letter to *The Guardian*, 1 December.

66  Herold (see note 40).

67  Thomas E. Ricks (2001) 'Target Approval Delays Cost Air Force Key Hits', *The Washington Post*, 18 November, [http://www.washingtonpost.com], visited on 14 February 2002.

68  Employing ground forces to verify intelligence was no guarantee against mistakes. In one incident on 23 January, 16 Afghan fighters who were wrongly identified as members of the Taliban or al-Qaeda were killed. For several weeks, US forces watched the compounds and, according to Rumsfeld, the information was 'persuasive and compelling'. However, it was not sufficiently strong to justify calling in air strikes. Or, perhaps it was believed that the operation could be accomplished at less risk to innocent civilians if it was conducted on the ground rather than from the air. The incident is discussed in Richard T. Cooper (2002) 'Rumsfeld Addresses "Unfortunate" Attack', *Los Angeles Times*, 22 February, [http://www.latimes.com], visited on 8 March 2002; Thom Shanker (2002) 'US Says 16 Killed in Raids Weren't Taliban or Al Qaeda', *The New York Times*, 22 February, [http://www.nytimes.com], visited on 8 March 2002.

69  'Rumsfeld says Taliban to Blame for Casualties', briefing by Donald H. Rumsfeld, US Department of State, 29 October 2001, [http://www.usinfo.state], visited on 3 January 2002.

70  Walzer, p32 (see note 3).

71  This argument is made by Jeffrey Tiel in 'Civilian Casualties as Psychological Warfare', Guest Commentary, October 2001, www.ashbrook.org/tools/printit2.cfm, visited on 13 February 2002.

72  For an excellent discussion of these issues see Koontz, pp65–82 (see note 9).

73   For a discussion of how NATO and its critics interpreted international humanitarian law in the Kosovo conflict see Nicholas J. Wheeler (2003, forthcoming) 'The Kosovo Bombing Campaign: The Limits of Civilian Protection in International Humanitarian Law' in Paul Keal and Christian Reus-Smit (eds) *The Politics of International Law*.

74   Kenneth R. Rizer, 'Bombing Dual-use Targets: Legal, Ethical, and Doctrinal perspectives', [http://www.airpower.maxwell.af.mil/airchronicles/cc/Rizer.html], visited on 15 February 2002.

75   Ignatieff, p199 (see note 25).

76   A welcome development in this respect is the launch of a project by Sarah Sewall, Project Director at the Carr Centre for Human Rights Policy, who plans to investigate the humanitarian implications of military intervention strategies by organizing a series of meetings between human rights groups and the military.

77   Walzer, pp158–9 (see note 3).

# [9]

# Situating the City and September 11th: Military Urban Doctrine, 'Pop-Up' Armies and Spatial Chess

ROBERT WARREN

## Introduction

Critical points in the world's history can be outlined by events related to the capture, control or destruction of urban centers, at least from Troy's fall by deception to the mushroom cloud with the vaporized remains of people and structures rising over Hiroshima (Ashworth, 1991). More recently, urban areas in many nations have experienced decades of formal and guerrilla warfare in varying degrees of intensity. Even so, urban scholars have seldom directed their attention to military-related phenomena. The devastating physical and symbolic effects of the destruction of New York's World Trade Center by suicidal attackers on September 11th 2001, however, has made continued neglect of this topic virtually impossible. Yet focusing only on this event and the ensuing global War on Terrorism, without situating them in a larger context, may exacerbate rather than close the gap in our understanding of military operations in urban space.

Actions and policies pursued in the War on Terrorism have been justified by mantras, propagated by the American government and echoed in the mass media, of 'everything has changed' and the 'world will never be the same'. They also contain subtexts that it will take years to eliminate terrorism and that violations of civil rights and international rules of warfare by the US may be legitimate responses to the unique conditions of fighting terrorists who are organized as networks rather than nations and whose identity cannot always be known.

The destruction of the World Trade Center and its real-time global TV transmission were unquestionably unique and the ensuing War on Terrorism has produced an array of urban-related effects. Cities in Afghanistan were subject to further devastation from unchallenged advanced aerial technology. Municipal governments in the US have assumed unprecedented responsibilities and costs to build capacities for preventing and responding to localized 'terrorist' actions. Residents and visitors in major cities over the world are barred from some spaces and are under intensive state surveillance and control in others. Yet it is misleading to assume that these military and paramilitary operations in urban centers began on September 11th.

Rather than a cause, the 'War on Terrorism' has served as a prism being used to conflate and further legitimize dynamics that already were militarizing urban space. These include the revision of long-standing military doctrine to accept and rationalize multiple missions within urban terrain; turning vast areas of cities into zones of video and electronic surveillance; and the prevention, repression and control of mass citizen political mobilization in cities. These phenomena have expanded and deepened in the aftermath of September 11th. However, the 'War on Terrorism' could be declared at an end tomorrow (its temporal, spatial and behavioral boundaries are subject to continuous and unilateral definition by the US) but these trends would continue.

Situating the 'War on Terrorism' in this broader context offers an opportunity to explore some of the military-related dimensions of cities. Recent changes in military doctrine offer a useful point of departure for framing what can be no more than an incomplete commentary on the increasing state surveillance and control of urban space that may undermine democratic practice rather than end terrorism.

## Military Operations in Urbanized Terrain (MOUT)

Sun Tzu's fourth-century BC warning that warfare in cities should be avoided has remained a basic tenant of military theory to this day. This aversion grows out of the well-documented effects of densely built-up environments: the attacking force's loss of the advantages of numerical and technological superiority; limiting the maneuverability of land and air weapons; the breakdown of communication and command structures in terrain characterized by mazes of unfamiliar streets and buildings that interfere with electronic transmissions; the existence of upper stories, roofs and underground infrastructure that provide the enemy with cover and sniping sites; and the presence of large numbers of noncombatants. These conditions produce high casualty rates, unacceptable or undesirable collateral damage to civilians and structures, negative media coverage and the loss of public political support for such campaigns. Two of the most recent chapters in this 'combat in hell' scenario are the 1993 US incident in Mogadishu and the continuing Russian effort to fully control Grozney (Glenn, 2001).

There has been, however, an evolving and significant revision of military urban doctrine since the end of the Cold War. It is now assumed by the United States and its allies that their military presence in cities, in humanitarian, peacekeeping, policing and homeland security, as well as combat roles, will be unavoidable in the twenty-first century. Probability alone will be a factor given the projected increases in the number and size of urban areas and their importance as control centers. It is expected that urban military action and presence will be required to deal with the aggression of 'rogue' nations, individual and networked acts of terrorism, and civilian riots and disorders. These conclusions generated the need for new military doctrine crafted to overcome the low performance and high costs that have been associated with urbanized terrain in the past (Press, 1999).

The resulting Military Operations in Urbanized Terrain (MOUT) doctrine has been primarily formulated in the US. It was initially based on the assumption that the operations would be located in cities outside dominant industrialized nations. MOUT focuses primarily on combat-related strategies involving asymmetrical encounters in which the inferior forces will seek to gain the advantages of urban terrain as the site of combat and resistance. However, aspects of this doctrine relevant to 'less than war' conditions are of primary interest here: isolating groups and selected city areas; denying adversaries mobility; and utilizing psychological strategies (PSYOP) for dealing with both combatants and noncombatants on site and with political and public opinion at home (Glenn *et al.*, 2001).

## The double switch: targeting first-world urban mass political mobilizations

MOUT doctrine provides a template for describing an increasingly complex and coordinated set of police/military strategies that have been used in the streets of

Barcelona, Brussels, Davos, Genoa, Gothenburg, Los Angeles, New York, Quebec, Washington, DC, and Seattle to respond to large temporary political mobilizations of citizens. The patterns that are emerging in the militarization of urban space can be constructed by reviewing events from Seattle in 1999 to Barcelona in March 2002.

Several tactics are used to deny people engaged in political mobilizations access to specific spaces. One, incubated in Europe to stop the travel of football hooligans, is to prevent the international movement of people who are viewed by authorities as likely to make trouble or engage in violence. However, since it has not been possible to prevent massive mobilizations, creating zones within cities that are off-limits to protesters has been widely used. Mobilization participants are barred by barricade and police or military formations from areas in which the visiting members of privileged organizations (such as the European Union, G8, International Monetary Fund, World Bank or World Economic Forum) will meet, circulate and sleep.

There are official zones allocated to protest activities. These spaces, touted as 'free speech zones', tend to be separated from the meetings that generated the mobilization, not easily accessible to the general public and fenced to make it easier to contain and control dissident groups. Another set of anti-mobilization strategies includes the manipulation of legal rules to enforce a zero tolerance policy, making arrests of leaders, often preemptively, on charges that are usually ultimately dropped, and setting bail high enough to insure they will remain in jail for the duration of the protest.

In city after city, the outcome of increasingly limited legal access to urban space for citizens seeking to exercise political voice has been physical clashes with the police and military. These pitched battles result in injuries to both sides and, at times, the death of demonstrators (Genoa and Gothenburg).

Officials and echoing local media, in almost every case, justify this use of force by adopting a page out of MOUT doctrine's PSYOP tactics. They assert that massive security forces are needed because, no matter how peaceful the intent of most of the thousands of demonstrators, there will be 'anarchists' and others who intend to commit acts of violence against corporate and business properties (Fairness and Accuracy in Reporting, 2002).

The general population in the target city and beyond also may be affected by state actions to limit free spatial mobility. The barricading of streets can deny public access to retail shops and restaurants and produce massive traffic tie-ups in central business districts. Public transportation, especially subway services, to stations in the embargoed zone(s) can be eliminated for the duration of the event. Travel in the airspace above meeting sites can be limited or banned.

## Enter the 'War on Terrorism'

A fully articulated set of responses to political mobilizations reflecting military doctrine was in place when the 'War on Terrorism' was declared. It was normal to close underground, surface and air space to public access in a city to allow non-local privileged organizations to hold meetings for short periods of time without being subject to harassment or even inconvenience from any protesting groups. The same dynamic that privileged one set of actors stigmatized civilian mobilizations as being committed to violence and opposition to the necessary rationalization of the world economy through globalization.

Even so, post-September 11th effects can be noted. Political mobilizations have been further delegitimated. In addition, there has been an expansion of the range of urban phenomena, such as mega-sports and entertainment events, to which military-grade surveillance and control are considered justified and normal. The 2002 professional football Super Bowl in New Orleans, in line with 'War on Terrorism' policies, was declared a National Special Security Event and the Secret Service coordinated local, state and federal security efforts. No amount of control and surveillance was viewed as too much. Eight-foot high fences and concrete barricades were erected all around the sports stadium, direct access to the site by auto was banned, ticket-holders had to arrive hours before the game started to pass through an elaborate search process and air space above the stadium was controlled (Foster, 2002).

Salt Lake City's extensive anti-terrorist arrangements for the 2002 Winter Olympics are expected to be a model for future international mega-events. Well over $300 million in public money was spent on security, and unprecedented coordination among federal, state and local agencies was achieved in planning and carrying out security measures. Extreme constraints were imposed on access to zones within the city and local airspace. Commercial flights were banned at times and private planes could only land in Salt Lake City after first stopping at a regional airport and receiving clearance (Zeigler, 2002). Only weeks later, similar security steps were taken in the world's film capital, Hollywood, for the 2002 motion picture Oscar awards and events. In this case, subway access to the area was shut off and Los Angeles police helicopters patrolled 'potential terrorist hiding places' in adjacent residential areas (Lyman, 2002).

The expansion of events subject to surveillance and control has been accompanied by a well-orchestrated strategy to use the 'War on Terrorism' to justify undermining citizen political mobilizations. Past efforts by state authorities to stigmatize mobilizations as inherently violent and against the public order are now augmented by conflating them with terrorism. The February 2002 World Economic Forum meeting in New York City reflects this phenomenon.

This non-governmental organization of economic luminaries and invited public and private notables has met in Davos, Switzerland, for decades. Its 2001 meeting there was accompanied by a small-scale war between protest groups and security forces. World Economic Forum leaders explained the shift to New York as motivated by a desire to show solidarity with a city that suffered a terrible disaster and to give a boost to its damaged economy.

These were not the only purposes for the move. It offered both a safer venue than Davos and an opportunity to confront and put anti-globalization groups on the defensive. Any violence resulting from protest activities would be splashed over the media as disrespect for the thousands killed in the World Trade Center and as inflicting additional problems on a city that has already suffered enough. In this psychological field, the New York police force, never famous for restraint, made it clear that a zero tolerance policy for any infraction of the law would be used to prevent violence or acts of terrorism. All of these themes were presented and elaborated in the media in the days prior to the World Economic Forum meeting. Tight security was imposed to shield its events and attendees. Areas and streets were closed in the center of Manhattan, creating extensive traffic congestion. No massive mobilization materialized and the media declared the Forum a success on the basis of the ability of the police to shut down demonstrations rather than on anything the meeting accomplished.

## Leaderless networks

The discussion above suggests there is utility in looking at these patterns of militarized responses to civilian mobilizations as multiple networks, ironically without hierarchical leadership, organized in global space but interacting in specific urban sites. One is composed of anti-globalization groups. Its open structure and capacity to organize and act are well known. There is also a network of extra-national hegemonic organizations that direct differing aspects of the globalization project, the World Trade Organization, World Bank, the International Monetary Funds etc. They move among a number of cities to conduct business and create a symbolic presence.

Their actions and policies affect, often negatively, the interests and values of many nations, workers and other groups. Since there is no formal public access to the network's decision-making, citizens, from over the world, periodically assemble where these meetings are held to challenge the policies and legitimacy of entities that are outside of any system of democratic control.

Yet a third network is emerging that is composed of the 'pop-up' armies fielded and paid for by the cities and nations in which the above meetings are held. The initial task of these locally-based security cadres was to protect the visiting agents of globalization. Now, the War on Terrorism has enlarged the array of public events and urban spaces to which they apply MOUT-like surveillance and control. This, in turn, has accelerated the melding of policing with military personnel, tactics and weaponry, and an expansion of mission to be on a continuous alert to stop and respond to terrorists.

These developments have been accompanied by growing national and international linkages among urban law enforcement and military agencies. They include the sharing of experience, data and intelligence, copying of strategies, and cooperation to deny mobility among and within cities to people expected to participate in mass mobilizations or terrorism. Conferences on MOUT doctrine are giving increasing attention to the pacification of civilians and the use of non-lethal crowd control weapons that can 'temporarily' incapacitate large numbers of people (Glenn, 2000). The existing and planned technology for this would not be out of place in science fiction (Lorenz, 1996; Morales, 2001).

## Things to come

This brief discussion, even without touching on the critical phenomenon of actual warfare in cities, indicates the importance of incorporating the militarization of city space and its conflation with the 'War on Terrorism' into urban analysis. Only a few of the many empirical and conceptual matters worthy of exploration are suggested in this commentary.

For example, in spite of the outcome of the World Economic Forum in New York, urban mobilization and militancy have not ended. Massive civilian gatherings have occurred since September 11th in Brussels and Barcelona coincident with European Union summit meetings (BBC1, 2001; Nash, 2002). There is an obvious need to examine and explain this difference in American and European experience. More generally, issues of place, space and democratic practice can be addressed by conceptualizing the three networks noted above as engaged in a multidimensional game of spatial chess. The goal of two of the networks is to exercise hegemonic control of underground, surface and air spaces within cities and movement among cities so that the mobility, presence and actions of agents of globalization are privileged over the mobilization and voice of ensembles of citizens.

The network of hegemonic organizations has exhibited a need to be physically present, temporarily, in urban places. This has produced citizen challenges to their legitimacy by mass mobilizations at the sites of these meetings. The organizations, in turn, attempt to suppress protest with their 'pop-up' armies or seek closed terrestrial places or cyberspaces to conduct business. After its Seattle experience, the World Trade Organization held a subsequent meeting in the Gulf state of Qatar that offered the benefits of a site that was not easily accessible and a government that would provide no welcome to demonstrators from outside the country. The World Bank canceled a mid-2001 meeting in Barcelona and shifted to the internet. Largely closed down on the streets of New York, over 160,000 protesters went online during the World Economic Forum's meeting to carry out a 'virtual' sit-in at the organization's home page (Shachtman, 2002).

In broad terms, then, the efforts of citizen mobilizations to challenge hegemony and infuse democratic practice on a global scale produce extensive military control of space in the cities in which they gather. The extent to which this process, combined with the War on Terrorism and the evolving global network of security forces, will erode democracy through normalizing the closure of urban public spaces and greater state surveillance and control presents an important area for research.

**Robert Warren** (rwarren@udel.edu), School of Urban Affairs and Public Policy, University of Delaware, Newark, DE 19716, USA.

## References

Ashworth, G.J. (1991) *War and the city*. Routledge, London.

BBC1 (2001) *New protests mar EU summit*. 15 December, http://news.bbc.co.uk.hi/english/world/Europe/newsid_1711000/1711350.stm (accessed 16 December 2001).

Fairness and Accuracy in Reporting (2002) *NYC newspapers smear activists ahead of WEF protests*. 28 January, http://www.fair.org/press-releases/pre-wef.html (accessed 30 January 2002).

Foster, M. (2002) Security tighter than ever at super bowl. *Wilmington, DE, News Journal* 29 January, C3.

Glenn, R.W. (ed.) (2000) *The city's many faces*. RAND, Santa Monica, CA.

—— (ed.) (2001) *Capital preservation: preparing for urban operations in the twenty-first century*. RAND, Santa Monica, CA.

——, R. Steeb and J. Matsumura (2001) *Corralling the Trojan horse*. RAND, Santa Monica, CA.

Lorenz, F.M. (1996) Non-lethal force: the slippery slope to war? *Parameters* Autumn, 52–62, http://carlisle-www.mil/usawc/Parameters/96autumn/lorenz.htm (accessed 22 February 2002).

Lyman, R. (2002) Security-prone Oscar ceremony a blight on business. *The New York Times* 23 March, A10.

Morales, F. (2001) Welcome to the free world. *Covert Action* 70 (April–June), 6–13.

Nash, E. (2002) Spain's fighters and warships protect EU summit. *Independent.co.uk* 26 March, http://www.independent.co.uk/story.jsp?story=274171 (accessed 26 March 2002).

Press, D.G. (1999) Urban warfare: options, problems and the future. http://web.mit.edu/ssp/Publications/confseries/urbanwarfare/urbanwarfare.html (accessed 17 May 2001).

Shachtman, N. (2002) Hactivists stage virtual sit-in at WEF web site. *Alternet* 7 February, http://www.alternet.org/print.html?StoryID=12374 (accessed 12 February 2002).

Zeigler, M. (2002) Olympic security sky-high; but some say isolation of Utah, low profile of winter games limit risk. *San Diego Union-Tribune* 6 February, A-1.

# [10]

John Kincaid
*Lafayette College*

Richard L. Cole
*University of Texas at Arlington*

# Issues of Federalism in Response to Terrorism

*The terrorist attacks of September 11, 2001, provoked, among other reactions, considerable commentary about the future of American federalism, particularly predictions of administrative centralization. To assess the potential impact of terrorism on U.S. intergovernmental relations and the ways the federal system should respond, members of the American Political Science Association's Section on Federalism and Intergovernmental Relations were surveyed in late 2001. Generally, these federalism scholars believe the September 11 terrorism will have little effect on intergovernmental relations or on the U.S. Supreme Court's state-friendly jurisprudence, and the surge in public trust and confidence in the federal government will be short-lived. The scholars tend to support a highly federalized response to terrorism, but with intergovernmental cooperation. Partisan differences among the scholars on policy options, however, mirror the party differences in Congress and the resurgence of "politics as usual" less than a year after September 11, 2001.*

The terrorism of September 11 provoked alarm and grief across the United States. The terrorist attacks also seemed to presage major, even fundamental changes in American life and governance. Given the intergovernmental and interjurisdictional responses necessitated by the attacks, it became evident that terrorism is laden with implications for federalism. Newspapers carried headlines such as "States Lack Power to Enforce Airport Guard Rules" (McGraw 2001), "Congress Agrees to U.S. Takeover for Air Security" (Pear 2001), and "Cities and States Say Confusion and Cost Hamper Security Drive" (Belluck and Egan 2001). David Gergen urged "the government" to "launch an urgent and, yes, highly federalized offensive to protect its citizens ..." (2001). Linda Greenhouse, critiquing the U.S. Supreme Court's federalism jurisprudence, declared, "The era of states' rights decisions, a luxury of tranquil times, now seems like a vestige of a bygone era" (2001). The mass media seemed to conclude that terrorism would, and perhaps should, kill federalism.

## Death or Revitalization of Federalism?

Outside the daily newsrooms, many observers felt that (1) the federal system responded remarkably well to the horrific shocks of September 11; (2) the responses of local officials, as well as the civil and heroic behavior of citizens, vindicated the values of local self-government in a federal democracy; and (3) counterterrorism might require more, not less, federalism (Kincaid 2001c; Locke 2001). Jonathan Walters (2001) worried that "there has been far too little talk about preserving the essential roles of local, state, and federal government and getting back to the basics of playing those roles." Donald F. Kettl (2001) concluded that, unlike previous crises such as World War II, which "centralized federalism, this one all but requires ... a new breed of collaborative federalism." The war on terrorism, moreover, is being led by former governors: President George W. Bush of Texas, Homeland Security Director Tom Ridge of Pennsylvania, U.S. Attorney General John Ashcroft of Missouri, and Secretary of Health and Human Services Tommy G. Thompson of Wisconsin. In short, counterterrorism should revitalize federalism.

The White House and Congress responded quickly with aid, especially for New York City, and with promises of more cooperation; yet, regulatory or coercive federalism returned to normalcy rather quickly. Many state and local officials soon complained of a bunker mentality and heavy-

*John Kincaid is the Robert B. and Helen S. Meyner Professor of Government and Public Service and director of the Meyner Center for the Study of State and Local Government at Lafayette College, Easton, PA. He is also the editor of* Publius: The Journal of Federalism. *Email: meynerc@lafayette.edu.*

*Richard L. Cole is the dean of the School of Urban and Public Affairs and acting dean of the College of Liberal Arts and a professor of urban affairs and political science at the University of Texas at Arlington. Email: cole@uta.edu.*

handedness by the Office of Homeland Security, insufficient federal responsiveness to fiscal burdens created by new homeland security needs, and too little information sharing by such agencies as the FBI, the Federal Emergency Management Agency, and the Office of National Preparedness (AP 2001b; Peirce 2001a). A bipartisan group of U.S. senators, with White House sympathy, shocked the states by proposing that Congress decree a 10-day national sales tax holiday beginning the day after Thanksgiving (AP 2001a). In the midst of a recession, and during an era in which states' sales tax bases are eroding, Congress reauthorized the Internet Tax Freedom Act. The *Economist* opined, "Alas, few in Washington seem to care about state finances" (2001). In November 2001, Attorney General Ashcroft sought to nullify Oregon's Death with Dignity law by authorizing the Drug Enforcement Administration to revoke the drug licenses of physicians who assist patient suicides (Eggen and Connolly 2001). These and other federal actions prompted one columnist to resound a familiar critique of the "Republican Revolution" of 1994, the "chief mission" of which "was to disempower the federal government as much as possible and to devolve power to the states." But once they had gained control of Congress, the Republican "devolutionists ... changed their stripes. They now appear to be complete saps for federal power, loving every jot and tittle of regulation and law" (Mathis 2001; Kincaid 2001a; Cole et al. 2001). In short, terrorism seemed to have no impact on Washington-centered federalism. Long-term centralization trends before September 11 proceeded apace after September 11.

What, then, are the implications of terrorism? Is post–September 11 federalism dead, irrelevant, more relevant, or steady on its current course? To gauge possible implications against evolving events, and with the hope of gaining policy insights, this research surveyed members of the American Political Science Association's (APSA) Organized Section on Federalism and Intergovernmental Relations, which includes the nation's leading students of federalism in both political science and public administration.

## Survey Methodology

Because the systemic implications of unprecedented events become most fully evident only over years and decades, it was difficult to formulate questions. Initially, we informally polled members of the editorial advisory board of *Publius: The Journal of Federalism* for ideas. Their responses were helpful. We also monitored news reports and statements by public officials to tap relevant issues. We then formulated a survey focusing on (1) overall and specific implications of the terrorist attacks for federalism and intergovernmental relations; (2) grant-in-aid implications; (3) possible local, state, and federal policy initiatives; (4)

loci of responsibility for various terrorism responses; (5) impact on the U.S. Supreme Court's state-friendly jurisprudence; and (6) changes in public confidence in the federal, state, and local governments. The survey instrument can be obtained from either author of this article.

In November and December 2001, a survey—dispatched and returned by email—was conducted among 295 U.S. members of APSA's Federalism Section for whom usable email addresses were available from APSA's roster of 399 members. Of the 399, 46 were international and were not included in the survey. Twenty-nine members had no listed email address; another 29 surveys were undeliverable. We received 158 usable responses, for a response rate of 53.6 percent, representing 44.8 percent of the 353 U.S. members of the Federalism Section. An examination of the characteristics of nonresponding section members found no systematic response biases. Of the respondents, 81.7 percent were employed by a university or college: 15.4 percent assistant professors, 16.9 percent associate professors, and 46.9 percent professors. Fully 72.9 percent were located in a political science department; 18.6 percent were in a department of public administration. Many of the latter, and some of the former, also belong to the Section on Intergovernmental Administration and Management of the American Society for Public Administration.

Responses were analyzed by gender, region of residence, community size, and political party identification. Other potentially relevant control variables, such as place or sector of employment and departmental affiliation, were not significant. The measure of association reported is the contingency coefficient; the measure of significance is the chi-square test.

## Overall Intergovernmental Implications

APSA's federalism scholars do not believe the terrorist attacks will have a significant impact on U.S. federalism and intergovernmental relations. Two-thirds expect intergovernmental relations to change marginally, while 11.5 percent anticipate little or no change (see table 1). Only 21.7 percent foresee intergovernmental relations changing significantly. Women scholars (34.9 percent) expected, more often than men (17.3 percent), that the attacks will cause significant change. Scholars (31.7 percent) from the country's largest cities (more than one million people) were more likely than those from smaller cities to expect significant change, while scholars from the West (13.6 percent) were far less likely to foresee significant change than were respondents from other regions. Hence, the majority believe the federal system will remain fairly steady on its pre–September 11 course.

Regarding more specific intergovernmental implications, 84.6 percent of the scholars expressed the view that, as a result of September 11, the nation will probably "see more effective cooperation and exchange of information between federal, state, and local officials in the areas of disaster relief and emergency preparedness than otherwise would be the case" (see table 1). Only 10.3 percent said probably not; 5.1 percent were unsure. Similarly (though less proportionately), 73.7 percent anticipated "more effective cooperation and exchange of information between federal, state, and local officials in other policy areas, such as law enforcement and public health than otherwise would be the case."

These questions were asked because problems of intergovernmental coordination became evident during responses to the September 11 attacks. The U.S. General Accounting Office (2001) and national commissions reported poor interagency coordination within the federal government and inadequate and top-down federal/state/local cooperation accompanying the buildup of federal counterterrorism spending and activity after the 1995 bombing of the Alfred P. Murrah Federal Building in Oklahoma City. Many local officials even reported being wary of federal cooperation because they often felt "like canaries in a coal mine. That's because federal plans for domestic terrorism always presumed that the first responders on the scene would be killed or seriously injured," and the types of deaths and injuries they experienced would iden-

tify the presence of particular chemical, biological, radiological, or other weapons (Coburn 1998, 22).

Perhaps the scholars' expectation of greater intergovernmental cooperation in emergency-preparedness and disaster-relief reflects, in part, the imperative for such cooperation if the terrible loss of first-responder lives on September 11, 2001, is to be prevented in the future. Although most scholars also expected increased intergovernmental cooperation in such related fields as law enforcement and public health, fewer expected this outcome, suggesting that enhanced cooperation in the core areas of counterterrorism might not spill over into peripheral policy fields.

At the same time, 62.8 percent of the scholars believed Congress will probably "use this period of national emergency as an opportunity to achieve greater preemption of state regulations and authority in areas like disaster relief, emergency preparedness, and law enforcement" (see table 1). Similarly, though less proportionately, 50.6 percent of the respondents agreed that Congress will seek "greater preemption of state regulations and authority in other areas, such as public health, transportation, and commerce." More than a third (38.6 percent) believed Congress will probably not do so, while 10.8 percent were unsure. These responses are generally consistent with trends of regulatory or coercive federalism since 1968. These trends have

## Table 1 Overall Intergovernmental Implications of September 11, 2001

| Questions | Percent responses | Party ID | Region | Size of community | Gender |
|---|---|---|---|---|---|
| | | | Significant Control Variables [1] | | |
| Will events of September 11, 2001 and their aftermath mark a significant change in U.S. intergovernmental relations? | | | | | |
| A. Yes, significant change | 21.7 | NS | .32** | .28* | .24** |
| B. Yes, marginal change | 66.9 | | | | |
| C. No or very little change | 11.5 | | | | |
| Should the federal government undertake a highly *federalized* effort to protect U.S. citizens from terrorism? | | | | | |
| A. Agree strongly/somewhat | 63.9 | NS | NS | .33* | NS |
| B. Disagree strongly/somewhat | 36.1 | | | | |
| Should the federal government undertake a highly *intergovernmental* effort to protect U.S. citizens? | | | | | |
| A. Agree strongly/somewhat | 85.3 | NS | NS | .35** | .21* |
| B. Disagree strongly/somewhat | 14.7 | | | | |
| Will Congress use this period of national emergency as an opportunity to achieve greater preemption of state regulations in areas such as disaster relief, emergency preparedness, and law enforcement? | | | | | |
| A. Probably yes | 62.8 | NS | NS | NS | NS |
| B. Probably no | 26.3 | | | | |
| C. Not sure | 10.9 | | | | |
| Will we see more effective federal, state, local cooperation in such areas as disaster relief and emergency preparedness? | | | | | |
| A. Probably yes | 84.6 | NS | NS | NS | NS |
| B. Probably no | 10.3 | | | | |
| C. Not sure | 5.1 | | | | |

Note: In all tables, * < .10; ** < .05. The coefficient of association (measuring strength of relationship) shown is the contingency coefficient.

[1] Here and throughout, "Party ID" was coded as Democrat, Republican, or other; "region" was coded as New England or Mid-Atlantic, Midwest, South or Southwest, or West; "size of community" was coded as less than 50,000, 50,000–250,000, 250,000–500,000, 500,000–1,000,000, and over 1,000,000.

included unprecedented levels of federal preemptions of state powers, mandates on state and local governments, crossover conditions of federal aid, and other regulatory measures to ensure state and local compliance with federal policies (Kincaid 1993). Again, most of the scholars see no major change in the federal system's current preemption-prone course, except that terrorism might provide a new rationale for federal preemption.

When asked, however, if the "federal government should undertake a highly federalized offensive to protect U.S. citizens from terrorism," 10.8 percent agreed strongly and 53.1 percent agreed somewhat, echoing David Gergen's advocacy of a highly federalized offensive (see table 1). Yet, when also asked if the "federal government should undertake a highly intergovernmentalized (that is, federal/state/local) offensive to protect U.S. citizens from terrorism," 37.8 percent agreed strongly and 47.5 percent agreed somewhat—an overwhelming majority of 85.3 percent. Only 12.2 percent disagreed somewhat, and 2.5 percent disagreed strongly. Scholars from the largest cities (78.0 percent) were considerably more likely to opt for a highly federalized offensive and less likely (72.5 percent) to support a highly intergovernmentalized approach than were respondents from other localities. A weaker difference appeared along gender lines, with 90.5 percent of women supporting a highly intergovernmentalized offensive compared to 82.7 percent of men.

Although it is clear that some respondents distinguished between federalized and intergovernmentalized offensives, approximately two-thirds of the scholars appear to support a highly federalized, intergovernmental effort to protect citizens against terrorism. These scholars appear to support an effort—led and even dominated by the federal government—that relies necessarily and extensively on intergovernmental cooperation and coordination. All terrorism is local, and local governments primarily, and state governments secondarily, possess the lion's share of first-response responsibility, though rarely the capacity to act alone. These responses may also reflect the fact that, although the federal government's first-response capacity is inherently limited, its pre-attack ability to alert citizens of possible attacks and to prevent terrorism through surveillance, intelligence gathering, domestic apprehension of suspected terrorists, and overseas military action extends far beyond the reach of state and local governments.

A large proportion of the scholars (72.1 percent) agreed that "the federal government should ensure that state Army and Air Guard units are adequately funded and equipped to protect U.S. airspace from terrorist attacks while regular U.S. Armed Forces should concentrate on overseas missions." Only 23.4 percent disagreed somewhat, and 4.5 percent disagreed strongly. The predominant responses are consistent with the historic division of labor between the domestic functions of the National Guard, especially responses to disasters and civil disorders, and the international mission of regular U.S. armed forces. The question was asked, in part, because of longstanding gubernatorial complaints about insufficient federal support for the National Guard, depletions of Guard personnel by federal call-ups, and post–September 11 debates about the costs of increased Air Guard patrols of U.S. airspace.

Similarly, though less proportionately, 58.9 percent of the scholars said that "in terrorist situations such as those occurring on September 11, state Army and Air Guard units should be federalized," compared to 41.2 percent who responded probably or definitely not. Although a majority of the scholars supported federalizing National Guard units in terrorist situations, this option drew less support and more opposition than did federal aid, perhaps because September 11 presented no compelling reasons for federalization, at least on the ground. Governors, however, might be amenable to federalization because it has federal fiscal benefits for the states, especially when units are deployed for long periods. Federalization also might be sensible for massive terrorist events requiring multistate National Guard coordination.

We also asked about the federalization versus privatization of certain public services because of the debate occurring in the fall of 2001 over airport security. In this debate, most congressional Democrats supported federalization; most congressional Republicans and President Bush supported private-sector options. Debate had also emerged in a number of localities and states about the wisdom, in the face of terrorism, of privatizing certain public services such as municipal water systems, mass transit, and security for infrastructure and vulnerable facilities such as nuclear power plants. Concern was expressed, too, about whether privatized services owned by non-U.S. corporations would jeopardize security.

Here, 57.6 percent of the federalism scholars supported "greater *federalization* of some domestic services now performed largely by state and local governments and/or by private enterprise, such as airport security, community health, law enforcement, and public safety." Opposed were 27.8 percent who said "probably no" and 14.6 percent who responded "definitely no." On a counterpart question, only 11.0 percent endorsed increased *privatization* of these kinds of domestic services. Fully 44.8 percent said probably not, and 44.2 percent said definitely not. Hence, a majority of the federalism scholars support federalizing certain domestic functions, while a resounding majority oppose privatization.

Statistically significant partisan differences were found on these questions, even though APSA's Federalism Section is overwhelmingly Democratic (39.2 percent strong Democrats and 24.3 percent leaning Democratic). Fully

76.7 percent of the strongly Democratic scholars supported federalization of the above domestic services, compared to only 11.8 percent of the strong Republicans. A mere 3.4 percent of the strong Democrats supported privatization of such services, compared to 38.9 percent of the strong Republicans. In addition, women (13.9 percent) were more likely than men (2.3 percent) to endorse greater privatization of such domestic services as airport security, community health, law enforcement, and public safety.

In summary, most of the federalism scholars foresee no major changes in the federal system arising from the terrorism experienced so far, though they support a highly federalized—but still intergovernmentalized—response to terrorism, and they generally oppose privatizing most public services relevant to terrorism.

## Grants-in-Aid Implications

Slightly more than half the scholars expected the "events of September 11 and their aftermath will set off a new round of major federal grants-in-aid for state and local governments," though only 5.8 percent said "definitely yes," while 50.3 percent said "probably yes" (see table 2). Another 43.9 percent said probably or definitely not. These split results are consistent with the political and fiscal uncertainties associated with grants-in-aid today.

The need for more federal aid for counterterrorism appears to be undeniable, and additional aid has been approved by Congress and the White House. President Bush's FY 2003 budget requested $38 billion for homeland security, of which 9.2 percent ($3.5 billion) would pass through FEMA primarily to local firefighters, police, and emergency personnel. Other monies, such as $5.9 billion to combat bioterrorism, $722 million to enhance information sharing and technology, and $4.8 billion to fund the Transportation Security Administration, would be spent mostly by federal agencies, but with administrative and communications coordination with state and local governments. The remaining $22.8 billion (60 percent) would be spent almost entirely by federal agencies on federal programs, such as border security and federal-agency security. Thus, the president's budget contemplates limited aid for state and local first-response capacity building compared to other dimensions of homeland security.

Increased direct federal aid to state and local governments for homeland security is also likely to be limited because, while federal aid has increased since 1987, it has shifted decisively from places to persons (Kincaid 1999). In FY 2002, approximately 64 percent of federal aid was dedicated to payments to individuals (for example, welfare and Medicaid). Hence, place-oriented aid, such as highways, education, economic development, and emergency preparedness, has atrophied relative to aid for persons, such

as Medicaid, which alone accounts for more than 40 percent of all aid to states and localities. Because the states receive most of the aid-for-persons grants, local governments—the most crucial for terrorism preparedness—have experienced a precipitous decline in direct federal aid since 1987. The reappearance of federal budget deficits and the squeeze on federal domestic discretionary spending also make major new aid for counterterrorism unlikely, unless a massive terrorist event compels a drastic alteration of federal priorities away from social welfare and tax reductions. Consequently, President Bush's proposed $3.5 billion in homeland security aid would amount to less than 1 percent of all estimated federal aid to state and local governments in FY 2003 (although several billion dollars in terrorism-relevant aid will flow through some other federal programs). In addition, Bush has vowed to balance increased spending on counterterrorism with "slower spending in the rest of government" (quoted in Parks and Dalrymple 2002, 1066). Thus, homeland security aid could reduce other federal aid funding.

If new federal aid flows to states and localities for terrorism-related activities, 51.7 percent of the federalism scholars believe such aid should be delivered through categorical grants, while 48.3 percent believe it should take the form of block grants (see table 2). Although state and local officials usually prefer block grants, and block grants are generally regarded as more devolutionary, it appears that the majority of APSA's federalism scholars are not devolutionists, a finding consistent with the scholars' support for federalization on previous questions. Here, too, there were significant partisan differences. Some 60.0 percent of the Democratic scholars supported categorical grants, compared to 35.5 percent of the Republicans—a difference that parallels party differences in Congress.

The scholars had more disparate views about where grant monies should go. Some 40.7 percent believed that "regardless of type of grant, any increased federal aid for terrorism preparedness" should be allocated "to the states, with each state deciding how to use and allocate the funds among its local governments." Nearly one-third (31.3 percent) said that at least 50 percent of such aid should go to local governments. Ten percent believed that at least 75 percent of such funds should go to local governments, while 18.0 percent said that at least 25 percent of such monies should be awarded to local governments. Thus, a majority of the federalism scholars (59.3 percent) say that some portion of federal grants pertinent to terrorism should bypass state capitals and go directly to local governments. These views are coherent with the scholars' tendency to support categorical grants and a highly federalized, intergovernmental offensive against terrorism. Categorical grants aim to ensure more specific state and local compliance with federal priorities and provide less state and local flexibility than block

| Table 2   Implications for Federal Grants-in-Aid and Other State, Local, and Federal Initiatives | | | | | |
|---|---|---|---|---|---|
| | | | Significant Control Variables | | |
| Questions | Percent responses | Party ID | Region | Size of community | Gender |
| Will events of September 11, 2001 set off a new round of major federal grants-in-aid for state and local governments? | | | | | |
| A. Definitely/probably yes | 56.1 | NS | NS | NS | NS |
| B. Definitely/probably no | 43.9 | | | | |
| Should any new grants be primarily categorical or block grants? | | | | | |
| A. Mostly categorical | 51.7 | .22* | NS | NS | NS |
| B. Mostly block | 48.3 | | | | |
| Should any new grants include in the distribution formula a factor accounting for the likelihood that a state or locality will be the target of attack (such as location of nuclear plants, major dams, and reservoirs, etc.)? | | | | | |
| A. Definitely/probably yes | 82.8 | .34* | NS | .35** | NS |
| B. Definitely/probably no | 17.2 | | | | |
| Should federal, state, and local governments shift resources from the war on drugs to homeland security? | | | | | |
| A. Definitely/probably yes | 63.8 | NS | NS | NS | .23 |
| B. Definitely/probably no | 36.2 | | | | |
| Should each state create a cabinet-level department modeled after the federal Office of Homeland Security? | | | | | |
| A. Yes, definitely | 4.6 | NS | NS | NS | NS |
| B. Yes, probably | 33.1 | | | | |
| C. No | 62.3 | | | | |

grants. Categorical grants also are likely to prevail because (1) they allow members of Congress to target aid to constituents and claim credit for it; (2) there has been a proliferation of suitors for homeland security money; and (3) state and local agencies are repackaging many old aid requests as homeland security necessities.

There was more consensus, though, on one aspect of targeting aid. Fully 82.8 percent of the scholars reported that "it would be appropriate to include in the distribution formula" for such aid "a factor accounting for the likelihood that a state or locality will be the target of attack (such as the Sears Tower in Chicago, location of nuclear plants, major dams and reservoirs, and so forth)." Some 26.5 percent of the respondents said "definitely yes," while 56.3 percent said "probably yes" (see table 2). Again, there was a significant partisan difference, with 87.0 percent of Democrats concurring with this formula, compared to 65.0 percent of Republicans.

Much disagreement was found, however, as to whether "it would be appropriate to include in the distribution formula a factor accounting for the value of each state's or locality's economic base to the national economy." Only 41.5 percent supported an economic-base factor, while 58.5 percent said probably or definitely not. No significant partisan differences appeared, but there was an interesting regional difference. Scholars from the South and Southwest (56.8 percent) and from the West (42.8 percent) endorsed such an economic-base factor more often than did scholars from the presumably more target-rich New England or Mid-Atlantic (31.5 percent) and Midwest (33.3 percent) regions.

In summary, most of the scholars anticipate some increases in federal aid for state and local governments for counterterrorism. By a slight majority, they believe such aid should be categorical, that half or more of the aid should go to local governments, and that grant formulas should include terrorism-vulnerability factors but not necessarily economic-base factors.

## Possible Local, State, and Federal Initiatives

In the wake of the terrorist attacks, the state of New York enacted new antiterrorism laws, and the federal Centers for Disease Control and Prevention proposed a draconian Model State Health Powers Act (Copeland 2001). Fully 89.4 percent of the scholars agreed that other states should "follow New York's lead by enacting new laws to combat terrorism through such means as increased criminal penalties, new means to deny sanctuary and financial support for terrorists, improved surveillance, and enhanced cooperation with other jurisdictions." Some 21.2 percent said "yes, completely," and 68.2 percent said "yes, partially." A lonely 10.6 percent responded "no, not at all." Again, there were significant partisan differences: Republicans were considerably more likely than Democrats to agree that states should follow New York's lead.

Although the federalism scholars support state measures to get tough on terrorists, they are not enthusiastic about states creating "a cabinet-level department modeled after the Office of Homeland Security." Nearly two-thirds regarded this as unnecessary, while 33.1 percent said "yes, probably" and 4.6 percent said "yes, definitely" (see table 2).

A public debate also has developed over whether resources should be shifted away from certain crime-fighting areas, especially the war on drugs, to enhance counterterrorism (AP 2001c; Peirce 2001b). Among the federalism scholars, 63.8 percent generally agreed that federal, state, and local governments should "now shift intelligence and law-enforcement resources from the war on drugs to homeland security" (see table 2). Another 36.2 percent said probably or definitely not. On this question, women (73.1 percent) were more likely to support shifting resources from the war on drugs to homeland security than were men (60.1 percent). There was more division, though, on the proportion of resources to be shifted from the war on drugs. Some 23.0 percent supported a shift of 100 percent–75 percent; 37.0 percent endorsed a shift of 75 percent–50 percent; 30.0 percent supported a shift of 50 percent–25 percent; and 10.0 percent supported a shift of less than 25 percent. Hence, 60.0 percent of the scholars endorsed shifting at least half the drug-war resources to homeland security.

Another debate is whether federal agencies should relinquish certain functions to state and local governments, especially in law enforcement, in order to focus more resources on terrorism. The scholars split almost evenly on whether "Given the allocation of substantial FBI and other federal law-enforcement resources to terrorism, federal law-enforcement agencies should relinquish many domestic law-enforcement tasks now performed by federal agents to state and local law-enforcement officials." A total of 44.8 percent supported such devolution. In contrast, 46.7 percent said "probably not" and 8.6 percent said "definitely not," for a total of 55.3 percent not supporting devolution. As might be expected, Republicans were far more likely than Democrats to support devolution. In reality, it appears the FBI will reduce its street-level crime-fighting significantly, but it will not abandon the streets because state and local officials have urged the FBI to stay engaged against bank robberies, drug trafficking, organized crime, civil rights, corruption, and the like. Although Congress authorized the FBI to hire 966 new agents in FY 2002, partly to maintain street-level activity, Congress also reduced the FBI's drug-fighting budget by 35 percent (Ragavan 2002).

A comparable split occurred in responses to the following statement: "In light of the federal government's need to focus more on terrorism, Congress should halt the federalization of criminal law that is unrelated to terrorism." One-quarter (25.0 percent) said "definitely yes," and 30.3 percent said "probably yes." Hence, a bare majority endorsed such a halt. Meanwhile, 44.7 percent opposed halting the federalization of criminal law unrelated to terror-ism. Not surprisingly, Republicans were much more likely than Democrats to endorse a halt.

This question was asked partly because a massive federalization of traditionally state criminal law has occurred since 1968. There are now more than 3,100 federal criminal offenses and more than 50 offenses subject to capital punishment, including those in the Anti-Terrorism and Effective Death Penalty Act of 1996 and the Defense against Weapons of Mass Destruction Act of 1996. During the 1990s, the Republican Congress and the Clinton White House, along with congressional Democrats, seemed to vie for the electoral rewards of being the toughest on crime. Much of the legislation has been little more than symbolic, though, because of the federal government's limited capacity to combat so many crimes and because of the backlog of criminal cases (such as drug cases) in the federal courts that previously had remained in state courts.

Because of the federal government's focus on terrorism and its limited force of about 75,000 law enforcement personnel (compared to some 748,000 state and local police), questions can be raised about the efficiency and effectiveness of federal homeland security efforts if federal agencies do not share some terrorism-relevant duties with states and localities and relinquish some other law enforcement functions to state and local police. Civil liberties concerns have been raised as well, not only about new statutes such as the USA PATRIOT Act of 2001, but also about expanding federal law enforcement, especially at the expense of local law enforcement (Stuntz 2002). However, the radical grassroots foundation Resist contends that suppressions of civil liberties are quite intergovernmentally cooperative. "Local police departments, often in cooperation with the FBI or other branches of the federal government, are using a heavier hand to deal with organizations wanting to take dissent to the streets" (Boghosian 2002, 1). This "heavier hand," though, is the result of post–September 11 fears, as well as the violence that has occurred in recent years during antiglobalization and anti-abortion protests.

To date, there appears to be no massive centralization of federalism with respect to civil liberties. The persons detained secretly by the federal government have been held on immigration charges, a historic and exclusive federal power. There has been no comparable detainment of U.S. citizens. Many observers have pointed to grave threats to civil liberties embedded in federal antiterrorism statutes enacted since 1995; however, those threats are consistent with the bipartisan federalization of criminal law—another centralizing characteristic of coercive federalism since 1968. Most federal criminal statutes either nationalize punitive state laws or permit more punitive punishment than equivalent state laws. The federal courts, moreover, have been curbing criminal rights for more than two decades. Whether September 11 will accelerate that trend is unknown.

In addition, the kinds of intergovernmentally cooperative assaults on civil liberties reported by Resist may reflect public opinion. Post–September 11 polls have shown that as many as seven in 10 Americans are willing to sacrifice some civil liberties to enhance homeland security. This public sentiment is also reflected in state antiterrorism legislation, which will maintain state footholds in homeland security. At the same time, however, there are no hints from the U.S. Supreme Court that it will overturn the new judicial federalism, whereby some state high courts grant more rights under their state constitutions' declarations of rights than the U.S. Supreme Court grants under the U.S. Bill of Rights. Many state high courts have expanded civil liberties and criminal rights. This area could experience centralization, though. Even if the U.S. Supreme Court sustains the new judicial federalism, federal officials could circumvent and subvert it because they are not controlled by state laws and courts. Thus far, then, civil liberties developments have reflected more continuity than change in American federalism.

In an effort to gauge the extent to which federalism scholars support or oppose federal entry into areas of traditional state and local authority, we asked about the following proposal: "As a result of the September 11 terrorism, Senator Tom Daschle has introduced an amendment to a health and labor appropriations bill that would guarantee collective bargaining rights to firefighters and police officers nationwide." Some 20.7 percent of the scholars agreed strongly, while 32.7 percent agreed somewhat, for a total of 53.4 percent supporting federal imposition of unionization of police and firefighters on all state and local governments. One-quarter (25.3 percent) disagreed somewhat; 21.3 percent disagreed strongly. Again, these results are consistent with the scholars' support for federalization and federal power on most survey items, although there were sharp gender and party differences. Daschle's proposal was endorsed by 72.5 percent of women, compared to 45.8 percent of men. Fully 93.8 percent of the Republicans opposed the proposal, while 68.5 percent of Democrats endorsed it. Recently, many congressional Democrats have proposed to federalize and/or unionize public and private workers deemed relevant to terrorism (for instance, Edward J. Markey's [D-MA] proposal to federalize nuclear-reactor security staff). In contrast, President Bush issued an executive order banning union representation in the offices of U.S. attorneys and four other agencies in the Department of Justice, "out of concern that union contracts could restrict the ability of workers in the Justice Department to protect Americans and national security" (S. Greenhouse 2002).

In summary, majorities of the scholars support state legislation to get tough on terrorists, but they see no need for state cabinet-level offices comparable to the federal Office of Homeland Security. They support a shift of half or more of drug-war resources to counterterrorism, a halt to the federalization of criminal law (though no devolution of federal law enforcement), and federally induced unionization of police and firefighters nationwide.

## Appropriate Loci of Responsibility

The federalism scholars generally favored federal agencies when considering responsibility for such matters as airport security and the appropriate agency to contact when a local hospital concludes that a patient might have a communicable illness possibly caused by a terrorist act.

More than half (59.1 percent) of the scholars reported "that airport security with regard to screening passengers and their baggage should be done by employees" of the federal government. Only 9.7 percent believed that these tasks should be performed by employees of a private company, while 16.9 percent said they should be done by local airport authorities. Another 12.3 percent said they should be performed by the relevant state government, and 1.3 percent said they should be done by the relevant county or municipal government. Democrats (75 percent) were far more likely than Republicans (22 percent) to say that federal employees should administer airport security, while Republicans (39 percent) were much more likely than Democrats (2 percent) to say that employees of private companies should screen passengers and their baggage. In addition, scholars from larger cities more often supported federal responsibility for such airport security; respondents from smaller cities supported private companies more often.

Among those endorsing private companies, 31.8 percent said these companies should be under contract with the federal government; 31.8 percent said they should be under contract with local airport authorities; 27.3 percent said the Federal Aviation Administration; 4.5 percent said state governments; and 4.5 percent picked the airlines.

The scholars also were asked, "If a local hospital concludes that a patient might have anthrax, smallpox, or another illness possibly caused by a yet unknown terrorist act, whom should the hospital call first?" More than half (52.6 percent) said the hospital should first call the federal Centers for Disease Control and Prevention. Only 23.4 percent picked the state health department for the first call; 12.4 percent selected the relevant county health department; and 11.7 percent chose the relevant municipal health department.

Another area that has become a great concern to state legislators since September 11 is the authority to quarantine citizens (and animals) in the event of contagions. Therefore, we asked, "If a municipal or local hospital concludes that a patient might have a contagious illness possibly caused by a yet unknown terrorist act, who should most appropriately be assigned the authority to quarantine the relevant neighborhood or entire municipality, thereby preventing movement into or out of the area?" The scholars' responses were highly disparate, with 22.6 percent choosing the federal Centers for Disease Control and Prevention and 22.6 percent selecting the relevant state health department. Some 19.2 percent selected the governor; 15.8 percent picked the relevant county health department; 8.9 percent chose the relevant municipal health department; 6.8 percent selected the city's mayor or equivalent elected official; 3.4 percent chose the city's manager, if there is one; 0.7 percent said that the president of the United States should make the quarantine decision; and none picked elected county officials.

## Judicial Federalism

A prominent feature of the U.S. Supreme Court since 1990 has been the role of "The Federalism Five"—Chief Justice William H. Rehnquist and Associate Justices Anthony Kennedy, Sandra Day O'Connor, Antonin Scalia, and Clarence Thomas—in forging a new federalism jurisprudence that is highly friendly to the states compared to the eras of Chief Justices Earl Warren (1953–69) and Warren E. Burger (1969–86). This jurisprudence has become controversial, especially for such decisions as *United States v. Morrison* (529 U.S. 598), which struck down the state court civil-remedy provision of the Violence Against Women Act as an overreaching of Congress's commerce power. Indeed, 38 state attorneys general filed *amicus* briefs supporting the act. Consequently, the future composition of the Court was a significant issue underlying the 2000 presidential election (Kincaid 2001b).

Nineteen days after September 11, Linda Greenhouse published an editorial in the *New York Times* (2001) that quoted six "experts" who asserted that terrorism has doomed the Court's federalism jurisprudence. Four of the experts criticized this jurisprudence harshly, with one labeling it "dangerous" in the aftermath of September 11. Another commentator argued that "the Court's near-obsession with the 'dignitary' interests of states and their officials suddenly seems peculiarly misplaced. However much we may revel in quaint notions of federalism during quiet times, in crisis, as history shows, we expect and demand a national, federal response to problems of national scope" (Lazarus 2001). However, no commentator cited a specific state-friendly Court ruling that could conceivably hamper the country's ability to combat terrorism.

Therefore, we asked, "In a number of recent decisions (such as *New York v. U.S.*, 1992; *U.S. v. Lopez*, 1995; and *Alexander v. Sandoval*, 2001), the Supreme Court reached decisions 'friendly' to state governments. If the Court had ruled on these cases and others like them after the terrorist attacks of September 11, do you believe that for most of these, the Court should still rule for the states, as it did earlier, or should the Court now rule for the federal government?" In a marked reversal from their responses to previous questions, 59.2 percent said the Supreme Court should still rule for the states. However, 31.2 percent responded they were "not sure," while only 9.6 percent believed the Court should reverse course and now rule for the federal government. Here also, there were significant party differences. Only 46.9 percent of Democrats believed the Court should still rule for the states, compared to 93.8 percent of Republicans.

When asked if they believed the Supreme Court will discontinue its state-friendly decisions and return to more federal-friendly decisions, however, two-thirds said "probably not." Only 11.5 percent said "probably yes," while another 22.3 percent said they were unsure (see table 3). It did not take long for the respondents' predictions on this point to be proven accurate. In its first important federalism case after the September 2001 attacks, the Supreme Court issued a ruling on May 28, 2002, that significantly expanded the Eleventh Amendment protections granting states immunity from private lawsuits to include protections from actions initiated by private parties brought before agencies of the executive branch (*Federal Maritime Commission v. South Carolina Ports Authority*).

We then asked, "Do you believe that the Supreme Court now should discontinue its state-friendly decisions and return to an era of more federal-friendly decisions?" Here, we did not provide a "not sure" response. As a result, 26.6 percent of the scholars said "definitely not" and 39.6 percent said "probably not." Only 9.7 percent said "definitely yes," and 24.0 percent said "probably yes" (see table 3). Again, party differences were significant. More than half (52.5 percent) of strong Democrats believed the Court should discontinue its state-friendly rulings, compared to 5.6 percent of strong Republicans. Additionally, scholars from New England and the Mid-Atlantic were somewhat more likely than scholars from other regions to say the Court should discontinue its state-friendly rulings.

Considering expectations that Congress would federalize airport security, we asked whether "federal courts will reverse recent decisions stating that federal requirements for airport guards and security training must supersede state requirements, even in those instances where state requirements are more stringent." Only 25.5 percent said "probably yes," while 50.3 percent said "probably no." Another 24.2 percent were not sure. When asked if the federal courts

| Table 3 | Implications for Judicial Federalism and Public Trust and Confidence | | | | | |

| Questions | Percent responses | Significant Control Variables | | | |
|---|---|---|---|---|---|
| | | Party ID | Region | Size of community | Gender |
| *Will* the Supreme Court now discontinue its trend toward state-friendly decisions and return to an era of more federally-friendly decisions? | | | | | |
| A. Probably yes | 11.5 | NS | NS | NS | .30** |
| B. Probably no | 66.2 | | | | |
| C. Not sure | 22.3 | | | | |
| *Should* the Supreme Court now discontinue its state-friendly decisions and return to an era of more federally-friendly decisions? | | | | | |
| A. Definitely/probably yes | 33.7 | .50** | .32* | NS | NS |
| B. Definitely/probably no | 66.2 | | | | |
| Do the high proportions of Americans who say that, following the September 11 attacks, they trust the national government to do "what is right" represent: | | | | | |
| A. Probably a long term shift, lasting for a year or more | 31.8 | NS | NS | NS | NS |
| B. Probably a short term trend, lasting for a year or less | 68.2 | | | | |
| Will the events of September 11 probably: | | | | | |
| A. Cause a decline in the public's trust and confidence in state and local governments? | 4.5 | NS | NS | NS | NS |
| B. Cause an increase in the public's trust and confidence in state and local governments? | 47.1 | | | | |
| C. Have no effect on the public's trust and confidence in state and local governments | 48.4 | | | | |

"should reverse those decisions and give more authority to state governments," 58.6 percent said no, 19.7 percent said yes, and 21.7 percent were not sure.

Thus, a majority of the scholars believe the terrorism of September 11 should not induce the U.S. Supreme Court to reverse its state-friendly jurisprudence. Two-thirds of the scholars believe the Court will not do so anyway. Again, they expect more continuity than disruption in American federalism.

## Public Trust and Confidence in Governments

The post–September 11 surge in public trust and confidence in the federal government "to do what is right" to levels not seen since 1968 (Stille 2001) led us to ask whether the surge will be long or short in duration. More than two-thirds of the scholars said that the surge of confidence will probably be "a short-term trend, lasting for a year or less" (see table 3). Less than a third concluded that it likely will be "long-term, lasting for a year or more." The scholars' views of public opinion are consistent with longstanding findings about the initial "rally around the flag" effects of major wars and crises, effects that usually erode over time (Mueller 1973). Indeed, by May 2002, various polls indicated that public trust and confidence in the federal government and in President Bush had ebbed somewhat. The public, moreover, has long expressed more confidence in the federal government to do what is right in national security and defense than in domestic social policy. Former President George Bush learned this lesson when the after-

glow of the Gulf War was dimmed by the public's domestic economic concerns during the 1992 election.

In light of the post-1970s trend toward greater public confidence in state and local governments relative to the federal government (Cole and Kincaid 2000), we asked about the anticipated impact of the terrorist incidents on trust in states and localities. Here, the scholars offered more closely divided responses. Nearly half said the events of September 11 "will probably have no effect on the public's trust and confidence in state and local governments," while 47.1 percent believed the events "will probably cause an increase in" such trust and confidence. Only 4.4 percent predicted a probable decline in trust and confidence in state and local governments (see table 3). Thus, in the view of most federalism scholars, the post–September 11 surge of confidence in the federal government, which they believe will be short-lived, has not come at the expense of confidence in state and local governments. Perhaps instead, because of the heroic behavior of police officers, firefighters, and other local public servants, as well as the leadership of New York City mayor Rudolph Giuliani, nearly half the respondents believed the terrorist events will probably boost the public's trust and confidence in state and local governments.

## Conclusions

Contrary to the responses of the mass media and many media scholars to the tragic events of September 11, 2001, most members of APSA's Section on Federalism and Intergovernmental Relations do not believe the terrorist attacks will or should significantly alter intergovernmental relations in the United States or reverse the U.S. Supreme Court's state-friendly jurisprudence. For these scholars, terrorism has not killed federalism or rendered it a quaint luxury of quiet times; instead, "continuity in crisis" perhaps best summarizes their overall views.

Generally, the scholars endorse a more federalized than devolutionized approach to counterterrorism, though with substantial intergovernmental cooperation and coordination. At the same time, the disparate responses to many specific policy choices do not offer clear-cut guidance to federal, state, and local policy makers. Perhaps like the real-world situation of the fall of 2001, the scholars were also not sure whom they should call first in the event of a terrorist attack.

This survey also revealed partisan differences on many policy issues. In principle, one would not expect to find many, if any, significant demographic differences among scholars engaged in objective social science. Yet, partisanship was the single most significant variable distinguishing the scholars' responses, especially on policy choices. The scholars' views parallel the real-world political debates and developments that have followed September 11, and they highlight some of the key issues being addressed nationwide by federal, state, and local officials, as well as by citizens and the media.

But the survey results also indicate that the scholars do not share the hysteria that often characterized the media and media-prominent scholars after the terrorist attacks. The results parallel those of most reputable post–September 11 polls, which indicate that the general public, while shocked, angered, and grieved by the terrorism, responded with a "mature and nuanced view" (Langer 2002, 15) of the crisis. The public has not rushed to embrace draconian antiterrorism measures or to demonize the Islamic world and Arabs and Muslims resident in the United States. These poll results are similar to findings during the 2000 presidential election controversy that, despite many media claims of a constitutional crisis, the general public never regarded the controversy as a constitutional crisis. Perhaps a bedrock calmness and stability in public and scholarly opinion in the face of crises accounts for the durability of American federal democracy and its ability to respond rather effectively, to date, to many different kinds of crises.

## Acknowledgments

The authors appreciate the technical assistance of Ms. Patricia Nickel, doctoral student in the School of Urban and Public Affairs, University of Texas at Arlington, in preparation of this article.

## References

Associated Press (AP). 2001a. Senators Call for Sales Tax Holiday to Spur Shopping. *Easton (Pennsylvania) Express-Times*, October 31, A-4.

———. 2001b. Tougher Security Isn't Cheap; States Blowing Their Budgets. *Easton (Pennsylvania) Express-Times*, November 1, A-3.

———. 2001c. War on Terrorism Diverting FBI Staff. *Easton (Pennsylvania) Express-Times*, October 28, A-3.

Belluck, Pam, and Timothy Egan. 2001. Cities and States Say Confusion and Cost Hamper Security Drive. *New York Times*, December 10. Available at *www.nytimes.com*. Accessed December 10, 2001.

Boghosian, Heidi. 2002. The Destruction of Dissent: First Amendment Rights in the Post September 11th Period. *Resist* 11(May): 1–3.

Coburn, Karen Ann. 1998. Rehearsal for Terror. *Governing* 12(February): 22–27.

Cole, Richard L., and John Kincaid. 2000. Public Opinion and American Federalism: Perspectives on Taxes, Spending, and Trust—An ACIR Update. *Publius: The Journal of Federalism* 30(1/2): 189–201.

Cole, Richard L., John Kincaid, Rodney V. Hissong, and Enid Arvidson. 2001. Devolution: Where's the Revolution? *Publius: The Journal of Federalism* 29(4): 99–112.

Copeland, Larry. 2001. CDC Proposes Bioterrorism Laws: States Get Guides to Stop Outbreaks. *USA Today*, November 8, 3A.

*Economist*. 2001. The Economy: A Clash of Wills. October 27, 32.

Eggen, Dan, and Ceci Connolly. 2001. Ashcroft Ruling Blocks Ore. Assisted-Suicide Law. *Washington Post*, November 7, A1, A4.

General Accounting Office (GAO). 2001. *Combating Terrorism: Selected Challenges and Related Recommendations*. Washington, DC: GAO. GAO-01-822.

Gergen, David. 2001. Shoring Up the Home Front. *U.S. News and World Report* 131(October 22): 68.

Greenhouse, Linda. 2001. Will the Court Reassert National Authority? *New York Times*, September 30, 14.

Greenhouse, Steven. 2002. Bush, Citing Security, Bans Some Unions at Justice Dept. *New York Times*, January 16, A15.

Kettl, Donald F. 2001. Devolve and Protect. *Governing* 15(December): 12.

Kincaid, John. 1993. From Cooperation to Coercion in American Federalism: Housing, Fragmentation, and Preemption, 1789–1992. *Journal of Law and Politics* 9(Winter): 333–433.

———. 1999. De Facto Devolution and Urban Defunding: The Priority of Persons over Places. *Journal of Urban Affairs* 21(2): 135–67.

———. 2001a. Devolution in the United States: Rhetoric and Reality. In *The Federal Vision: Legitimacy and Levels of Governance in the United States and the European Union*, edited by Kalypso Nicolaides and Robert Howse, 144–60. Oxford: Oxford University Press.

————. 2001b. The State of U.S. Federalism, 2000–2001: Continuity in Crisis. *Publius: The Journal of Federalism* 31(3): 1–69.

————. 2001c. Terrorism at the W.T.C. New York: Response from a Federal Democracy. *Indian Journal of Federal Studies* 2(2): 166–69.

Langer, Gary. 2002. Touchpoint: Responsible Polling in the Wake of 9/11. *Public Perspective* 13(2): 14–15.

Lazarus, Edward. 2001. Challenges for the Supreme Court in the Wake of Terrorism: Allowing Greater Federal Power, and Minimizing Church/State Ties. Available at *http://writ.news.findlaw.com/lazarus/2001 1002.html*. Accessed October 2, 2002.

Locke, Pamela. 2001. Pentagon Attack Puts Arlington to Test. *PA Times* 24(11): 1–2.

Mathis, Deborah. 2001. Ashcroft Welcomes Punitive Government. *Easton (Pennsylvania) Express-Times*, November 9, A-10.

McGraw, Mike. 2001. States Lack Power to Enforce Airport Guard Rules. *Fort Worth Star Telegram*, November 11, 17A.

Mueller, John E. 1973. *War, Presidents, and Public Opinion.* New York: Wiley.

Parks, Daniel J., and Mary Dalrymple. 2002. New Pot of Federal Dollars Has Admirers from All Over. *CQ Weekly,* April 27, 1066–70.

Pear, Robert. 2001. Congress Agrees to U.S. Takeover for Air Security. *New York Times*, November 16. Available at *www.nytimes.com*. Accessed November 16, 2001.

Peirce, Neal R. 2001a. Mayors Fault Washington on Terrorism Fight. Washington Post Writers Group, October 27. Available at *http://www.postwritersgroup.com/archives/peiro617.htm*. Accessed October 26, 2001.

————. 2001b. To Fight Terrorism: Scuttle the War on Drugs. Washington Post Writers Group, November 4. Available at *http://www.postwritersgroup.com/archives/peiro617.htm*. Accessed November 2, 2001.

Ragavan, Chitra. 2002. Who Ya Gonna Call? *U.S. News and World Report* 132(May 20): 14–16.

Stille, Alexander. 2001. Suddenly, Americans Trust Uncle Sam. *New York Times*, November 3, A10.

Stuntz, William J. 2002. Terrorism, Federalism, and Police Misconduct. *Harvard Journal of Law and Public Policy* 25(Spring): 665–79.

Walters, Jonathan. 2001. Safety Is Still a Local Issue. *Governing* 15(November): 12.

# [11]

# Political geography II: terrorism, modernity, governance and governmentality

## Colin Flint

Department of Geography, Pennsylvania State University, University Park, PA 16802, USA

## I Introduction

The attacks of 11 September 2001 changed many things. Though they will probably change the subject matter of political geography too, most of the reviewed literature in this essay was published either before or too soon after 11 September to provide direct analysis. A series of commentaries in the *Arab World Geographer* provided a forum for initial reflections that offered immediate impressions (Abu-Nimer, 2001; Agnew, 2001a; Flint, 2001a; 2001b; Marston and Rouhani, 2001; McColl, 2001; Nijman, 2001; N. Smith, 2001). In addition, a mixture of historical analysis and policy recommendations has begun to appear (Talbott and Chanda, 2001). However, the most recent scholarship that I was able to review provides the intellectual foundations upon which post-9/11 research will be based. After briefly proposing a geographic research agenda on terrorism, five key themes informed by political geographers are identified; modernity, geopolitics, the state, representation and the public stance of geographers.

## II Terrorism

The academic study of terrorism, like much mainstream social science, has been trapped in a paradigm that equates society with individual states (Taylor, 2000a). Theories of terrorism reviewed by Laqueur (1987: 152–60) all focus upon how changes in particular states may provoke terrorist action against that self-same state apparatus. Not surprisingly, all of these theories are found wanting for one reason or another. In addition, scholars make a consistent contrast between earlier state-based terrorism and the contemporary trans-state, often religiously based, manifestation that is defined as 'senseless' or 'aimless' (Thomson, 2001). One reason for such definitions may be the increasing role of the USA as target, requiring a policy stance denying rationality in case it raises questions of understandable grievances. A theoretical explanation for the confusion lies in the switch from state-centered to global-centered terrorism, a movement of geographic scale that disrupts mainstream state-centric social science.

Geographers are well poised to provide insightful analysis of contemporary terrorism by using three of our comparative disciplinary advantages, the consideration of geohistorical context, geographic scale and territoriality. The attacks of 9/11 provoked surprise and confusion among most US commentators, despite the fact that this was just the latest in a series of terrorist attacks upon US targets, and the alleged perpetrators had made the content of their grievances clear. What is clear is that the attacks were somehow related to America's global role, perceived as brutal unilateral-ism on the one hand, and the export of a lauded way of life that provokes violent jealousy on the other. Both of these perspectives can be understood by noting that American prime modernity, or the most emulated way of life, is exported within the geohistorical context of American hegemony (Taylor, 1999).

Al-Qaeda, the primary focus of policy-makers, is an organization requiring bases in particular localities, preferably (for them) with either state support or ineffective state policing, but with a trans-state range. Furthermore, individuals play a role of debatable importance in maintaining these networks (Lesser, 1999; Sprinzak, 2001). The need for both terrorists and counter-terrorists to operate across a number of geographic scales requires a geographic perspective that understands how scale and conflict are related (Brenner, 2001a; Marston and Smith, 2001). The third theme that is ripe for analysis by geographers is territoriality, especially the spatiality of terrorist networks (Arquilla and Ronfeldt, 1997), the contextual setting of particular nodes in these networks, and how networks interact with the established but dynamic territoriality of nation states (Pillar, 2001).

Geographers have already made significant progress towards establishing knowledge that can be used to investigate contemporary terrorism. The organizing themes of modernity, geopolitics, governance and representation are used to suggest how geographers can make continuing contributions to the understanding of political dynamism during a period of uncertainty and, at the time of writing, increasing geopolitical tensions.

## III   Modernity

One of the questions regarding 9/11 was 'Why now?' This answer is, of course, related to the more basic question of 'Why?' Unpacking the uncritical claims that the terrorists were attacking 'our way of life' is possible through an engagement of modernity from a geohistorical perspective (Taylor, 1999). 'Our way of life' is the expression of the prime modernity of the USA and attempts to globalize its practice (Holloway and Valentine, 2001; Santos, 1999). Yet there is widespread discontentment with the prime modernity expressed by contemporary racist and white separatist groups in the USA (Flint, 2001c), or a feeling of malaise and insecurity that has corrupted our view of children and young adults (Aitken, 2001a; 2001b). The potentials of a changing modernity are manifest in emerging meta-geographies challenging the world political map of nation states (Agnew, 2001b; Taylor, 2000b) maintained by cartographic practices (Shapiro, 1999) and evident in the network of global cities (Taylor *et al.*, 2001). A key catalyst in these geographic changes are the social relations associated with cyberspace, its implications for work practices (Himanen, 2001) and the developing tensions between territorial political entities and virtual ones (Luke, 1999).

The geopolitics of globalization entails the diffusion of particular practices from specific localities across the globe, and place-based and trans-national resistances and acceptances of these practices (Bell and Staeheli, 2001; Santos, 1999). Studies of globalization have concentrated upon economic and political processes, but the religious content of 9/11 and its aftermath requires political geographers to understand the *meaning* attached to these acts. Attention has been focused upon fundamentalist constructions of religious meaning and practice (Armstrong, 2000; Stump, 2000), and the connections between spiritual understandings of conflict and power and the resort to violence (Juergensmeyer, 2001). Though geographers have analysed the role of religion in local politics (Chivallon, 2001; Dunn, 2001; Kong, 2001; Paris and Anderson, 2001; Trigger, 2001) and at the state scale (Secor, 2001), the necessity is to follow the lead provided by Juergensmeyer (2001) and investigate the transnational geopolitics of religion.

A potential pathway has already been set by the suggestion of an International Political Theology (IPT), the 'systematic study of discourses and relations amongst them concerning world affairs that search for – or claim to have found – a response, transcendental or secular, to the human need for meaning' (Kubálková, 2000: 675). IPT recognizes the role of religion in defining multiple modernities that compete with westernization (Eisenstadt, 2000; Thomas, 2000), or the dominance of US prime modernity. This may take the form of inter-civilizational dialogue or geopolitical tensions (Esposito and Voll, 2000; Tibi, 2000) embedded within national identities (Smith, 2000). In general, these reflections on religion and international politics recognize that the search for meaning in modern life (H. Smith, 2001) is a component of contemporary geopolitical tensions, and deserves our immediate attention.


## IV   Geopolitics

Political geographers' engagement with geopolitics is perfectly poised to inform the current developments. The relationship between political geography and geopolitics is now clearly understood (Dodds and Atkinson, 2000; Mamadouh, 1999), and the need and ability to investigate the power relations within geographical visions is axiomatic (Power, 2001; Sidaway, 2001). State conflicts over territory (Chapman, 2000) and resources (O'Lear, 2001) remain, but the geopolitics of contemporary genocide (Wood, 2001) and wars fought through and over access to natural resources (Le Billon, 2001) and technology (Butler, 2001) provide a dynamic and multifaceted view of world conflict.

Retrospectives on geopolitical writings offer an important venue to reflect upon the contribution and future role of geopolitical analysis (Atkinson, 2001; Dalby, 2001; Hepple, 2001; Parker, 2001). Though previous work has made advances in expanding the ontology of geopolitics (with a notable call by Hepple, 2001, not to neglect military

100   Political geography

conflicts), two important debates remain – the epistemology of geopolitics and the uses towards which geopolitical studies should be put. The benefit of the postmodern approach has been the expansion of geopolitical analyses into a multiscalar and multi-process force, but at the expense of creating an approach that accepts and even celebrates the chaotic nature of politics rather than making sense of 'seeming chaos and complexity' (Parker, 2001: 125). This does not demand a singular and hegemonic theoretical template, but does remind us that our role is to offer explanation and under-standing of politics through a geographic perspective, and not merely an observation (lament?) that the world is chaotic. Students, policy-makers, commentators and the public felt bewilderment post-9/11 – what is our role, or even use, if we do not offer competing explanations that provide a way of understanding the chaos? If all we can say is 'You're right, the world is descending into chaos', we have offered no more than the shallowest journalism or even street-corner conversation. Explanation through competing theoretical frameworks adds to the conversation by identifying and evaluating different causes and consequences in what, to an untrained eye, is seemingly unexplainable chaos. This is not to say that we need to be banging the square pegs of actual occurrences into the round holes of theoretical constructs, but that we do need to offer parsimonious theories that help to uncover the multiple roots of all contemporary geopolitical acts.

But who do we tell? Hepple (2001) reminds us of the dilemma of relevance and service to a powerful Prince. Yet the multiplicity of political actors suggests a host of Princes and Princesses. Serving a singular state Prince is a pathway back to intellectual stagnation and imprisonment, but creating knowledge relevant to a host of political actors is a potential spaghetti junction of intersecting theoretical, empirical and applied political knowledges.

## V   The state

Signposts for this approach are replete within political geographies of the state. Brenner's (2001b) engagement of Lefebvre's (2001) writings on the state have made non-French speaking geographers aware of the notion of autogestion – or the political call to democratize the institutions of the state. A parallel contribution is Jones's (2001) use of Storper's (1997) distinction between institutions and organizations, with an emphasis upon considering the perceptions and actions of the personnel of formal state organizations. The spatiality of political strategies to control and alter political and social institutions has also been discussed (Morrison, 2001; Watts, 2001), along with the geographical variation in activism (Fincher and Panelli, 2001) and service provision (Cloke *et al.*, 2001; Peck and Theodore, 2001).

One continuing stream of analysis is the, mainly British, discussions of devolution within the context of the increasing powers of the European Union and the Labour Party's policies of reorganizing government (Raco and Flint, 2001). Attention has been paid to the interaction of geographic scales, their role in both enabling and constraining political actors (Mackinnon and Phelps, 2001a; 2001b), the undemocratic nature of the new institutions (Robinson and Shaw, 2001), and the regional competition over their control (Agnew, 2001c; Biscoe, 2001; Morgan, 2001; Shirlow, 2001). Similar competitions between scales of government are evident in the European Union (Barnett, 2001),

Russia (Mitchnek, 2001) and over the form of the post-apartheid South African state (Ramutsindela, 2001). Attention upon the stresses facing the Australian state concentrates upon the role of public racism and the spatiality of government anti-racism programs (Dunn and McDonald, 2001; Dunn *et al.*, 2001), noting the way that governments can alter the creation of knowledge through the closure of research establishments (Fincher, 2001). The identification of multiple actors in state politics, illustrates that political contests provide opportunities to inform multiple actors.

## VI    Representation

Another stream of analysis is based upon Foucault's concept of governmentality, and its spatiality (Hannah, 2000). Maps (Azaryahu and Golan, 2001; Razin and Hazan, 2001), censuses (Hannah, 2001), housing policies (Dowler, 2001) and racial classification (Winlow, 2001) are all used in projects of governmentality. The representations of subjects, an essential component of governmentality, usually requires a spatializing of an 'other' (Agnew, 2001b; Neumann, 1999), the construction of racialized identities (Gilroy, 2000; Kobayashi and Peake, 2000) or gender identities (Day, 2001), all of which have implications for access to space and territory.

National identity has played a key role in projects of governmentality creating self-defining 'others' (Kearns, 2001) or using symbols to create narratives of in-groups (Crampton, 2001; Webster and Leib, 2001) and bolster the state (Ingram, 2001). The created national group is tied to the state through the legal standing of citizenship, which attempts to include and exclude certain groups to suit governmental projects (Craddock, 2001: Craddock and Dorn, 2001). Alternatively, identities created at the periphery can destabilize nations and states (Howitt, 2001; Paasi, 2001; Painter, 2001) or foster electoral cleavages (Marsh and Warhola, 2001).

It is the future as well as the function of states that has been under investigation (Van Creveld, 1999). The importance of transnational processes and identities (Bebbington and Batterbury, 2001; Rubenstein, 2001) has threatened the power of the state to define the way that we picture political geography (Häkli, 2001). However, Torpey (2000) claims that the state continues to manufacture ways to limit the movement of people, though the global extent of this power of the state is questionable (Herbst, 2000).

Electoral geography is establishing a role in informing how issues of representation are tied to the social construction of space (Flint, 2000; Johnston *et al.*, 2001) over the existing political terrain (Fox and Lemon, 2000). Placing elections in temporal and spatial context (Flint, 2001d), and recognizing that the scale of analysis is an important theoretical (Johnston and Pattie, 2001) and methodological (O'Loughlin, 2001) choice are ways that electoral geographers have used quantitative analysis to illustrate how electoral behavior creates political spaces. Moreover, a focus on the ideology (Morrill, 2001; Secor, 2001) and behavior of parties (Giordano 2001a; 2001b; Shin, 2001), and the role of the geography of electoral systems in the representation of groups and individuals (Forest, 2001), indicates how electoral geographers are analysing the geographies of autogestion (Lefebvre, 2001).

102   Political geography

## VII   Narratives

Claims that the 'world changed' on 11 September 2001 are US-centric. Yet the violence of that day and its aftermath do provide an opportunity for political geographers to enhance their role and leverage within the discipline, in policy-making circles (broadly defined) and in public education. Emphasizing that all politics are 'politics of space' (Purcell, 2001a; 2001b) introduces the multicausality of geopolitical acts, while stressing the particular contribution offered by the discipline of geography (Massey, 2001; Schoenberger, 2001). Of course, the content of political geography is always open to debate (Kirby, 2001; Youngs, 2001). However, this is not a call for a spatial fetishism, and it is essential not to highlight the spatial to the detriment of the 'non-territorial' (Gregson, 2001). What is required are geographies that engage a period of military conflict (Hepple, 2001) without prioritizing the state and including other politics, such as the role of cultural othering (Escobar, 2001) and racialized politics (Kobayashi and Peake, 2000). Geography's global perspective defines a moral responsibility to portray the predicament of peoples often struggling to be heard (Ahmad, 2000; Falah, 2001; Wilson and Bauder, 2001). The time is ripe to illustrate the explanatory power of geography by educating beyond the confines of formal educational and academic arenas to provide a host of real political opportunities and alternatives (Hay, 2001).

## References

**Abu-Nimer, M.** 2001: Another voice against the war. *The Arab World Geographer* 4(2), 89–92.

**Agnew, J.** 2001a: Not the wretched of the Earth: Osama Bin Laden and the 'Clash of Civilizations'. *The Arab World Geographer* 4(2), 85–88.

—— 2001b: *Reinventing geopolitics: geographies of modern statehood. Hettner-Lecture 2000.* Department of Geography, University of Heidelberg.

—— 2001c: How many Europes? The European Union, eastward enlargement and uneven development. *European Journal of Urban and Regional Studies* 8(1), 29–38.

**Ahmad, E.** 2000: *Confronting Empire: interviews with David Barsamian.* Cambridge, MA: South End Press.

**Aitken, S.** 2001a: Schoolyard shootings: racism, sexism, and moral panics over teen violence. *Antipode* 33(4), 593–600.

—— 2001b: Global crises of childhood: rights, justice and the unchildlike child. *Area* 33(2), 119–27.

**Armstrong, K.** 2000: *The battle for God.* New York: Alfred A. Knopf.

**Arquilla, J.** and **Ronfeldt, D.** 1997. *In Athena's camp.* Santa Monica, CA: RAND.

**Atkinson, D.** 2001: Classics in human geography revisited. Commentary 2. *Progress in Human Geography* 25, 425–27.

**Azaryahu, M.** and **Golan, A.** 2001: (Re)naming the landscape: the formation of the Hebrew map of Israel (1949–1960). *Journal of Historical Geography* 27(2), 178–95.

**Barnett, C.** 2001: Culture, policy, and subsidiarity in the European Union: from symbolic identity to the governmentalisation of culture. *Political Geography* 20(4), 405–26.

**Bebbington, A.J.** and **Batterbury, S.P.J.** 2001: Transnational livelihoods and landscapes: political ecologies of globalization. *Ecumene* 8(4), 369–80.

**Bell, J.E.** and **Staeheli, L.A.** 2001: Discourses of diffusion and democratization. *Political Geography* 20(2), 175–95.

**Biscoe, A.** 2001: European integration and the maintenance of regional cultural diversity: symbiosis or symbolism? *Regional Studies* 35(1), 57–64.

**Brenner, N.** 2001a: The limits to scale? Methodological reflections on scalar structuration. *Progress in Human Geography* 25, 591–614.

—— 2001b: State theory in the political conjuncture: Henri Lefebvre's "Comments on a new state form." *Antipode* 33(5), 783–808.

**Butler, D.L.** 2001: Technogeopolitics and the

struggle for control of world air routes, 1910–1928. *Political Geography* 20(5), 635–58.

Chapman, G.P. 2000: *The geopolitics of South Asia: from early empires to India, Pakistan and Bangladesh.* Aldershot: Ashgate.

Chivallon, C. 2001: Religion as space for the expression of Caribbean identity in the United Kingdom. *Environment and Planning D: Society and Space* 19, 461–83.

Cloke, P., Milbourne, P. and Widdowfield, R. 2001: The local spaces of welfare provision: responding to homelessness in rural England. *Political Geography* 20(4), 493–512.

Craddock, S. 2001: Engendered/endangered: women, tuberculosis, and the project of citizenship. *Journal of Historical Geography* 27(3), 338–54.

Craddock, S. and Dorn, M. 2001: Guest editorial. Nationbuilding: gender, race, and medical discourse. *Journal of Historical Geography* 27(3), 313–18.

Crampton, A. 2001: The Voortrekker Monument, the birth of apartheid, and beyond. *Political Geography* 20(2), 221–46.

Dalby, S. 2001: Classics in human geography revisited: commentary 1. *Progress in Human Geography* 25, 423–25.

Day, K. 2001: Constructing masculinity and women's fears in public space in Irvine, California. *Gender, Place and Culture* 8(2), 108–27.

Dodds, K. and Atkinson, D., editors 2000: *Geopolitical traditions: a century of geopolitical thought.* London and New York: Routledge.

Dowler, L. 2001: Preserving the peace and maintaining order: deconstructing the legal landscapes of public housing in West Belfast, Northern Ireland. *Urban Geography* 22(2), 100–105.

Dunn, K.M. 2001: Representation of Islam in the politics of mosque development in Sydney. *Tijdschrift voor Economische en Sociale Geografie* 92(3), 291–308.

Dunn, K.M. and McDonald, A. 2001: The geography of racisms in NSW: a theoretical exploration and some preliminary findings from the mid-1990s. *Australian Geographer* 32(1), 29–44.

Dunn, K., Hanna, B. and Thompson, S. 2001: The local politics of difference: an examination of intercommunal relations policy in Australian local government. *Environment and Planning A* 33, 1577–95.

Eisenstadt, S.N. 2000: The reconstruction of religious arenas in the framework of 'multiple modernities'. *Millennium* 29(3), 591–611.

Escobar, A. 2001: Culture sits in places: reflections on globalism and subaltern strategies of localization. *Political Geography* 20(2), 139–74.

Esposito, J. and Voll, J.O. 2001: Islam and the West: Muslim voices of dialogue. *Millennium* 29(3), 613–39.

Falah, G. 2001: Intifadat al-Aqsa and the bloody road to Palestinian independence. *Political Geography* 20(2), 135–37.

Fincher, R. 2001: Immigration research in the politics of an anxious nation. *Environment and Planning D: Society and Space* 19, 25–42.

Fincher, R. and Panelli, R. 2001: Making space: women's urban and rural activism and the Australian state. *Gender, Place and Culture* 8(2), 129–48.

Flint, C. 2000: Electoral geography and the social construction of space. *Geojournal* 51(4), 145–56.

—— 2001a: Initial thoughts towards political geographies in the wake of 11 September 2001: an introduction. *The Arab World Geographer* 4(2), 77–80.

—— 2001b: Ending in order to begin . . . *The Arab World Geographer* 4(2), 103.

—— 2001c: Right-wing resistance to the process of American hegemony: the changing political geography of nativism in Pennsylvania, 1920–1998. *Political Geography* 20(6), 763–86.

—— 2001d: A TimeSpace for electoral geography: economic restructuring, political agency and the rise of the Nazi party. *Political Geography* 20(3), 301–29.

Forest, B. 2001: Mapping democracy: racial identity and the quandary of political representation. *Annals of the Association of American Geographers* 91, 143–66.

Fox, R. and Lemon, A. 2000: Consolidating South Africa's new democracy: Geographical dimensions of party support in the 1999 election. *Tijdschrift voor Economische en Sociale Geografie* 91(4), 347–60.

Gilroy, P. 2000: *Against race: imagining political culture beyond the color line.* Cambridge, MA: Belknap Press.

Giordano, B. 2001a: 'Institutional thickness', political sub-culture and the resurgence of (the 'new') regionalism in Italy – a case study of the Northern League in the province of Varese. *Transactions of the Institute of British Geographers*

NS 26, 25–41.

—— 2001b: The contrasting geographies of 'Padania': the case of the Lega Nord in Northern Italy. *Area* 33(1), 27–37.

**Gregson, N.** 2001: Missing voices/missing spaces: reflections on a 'new Europe?' *European Journal of Urban and Regional Studies* 8(1), 39–40.

**Häkli, J.** 2001: In the territory of knowledge: state-centred discourses and the construction of society. *Progress in Human Geography* 25, 403–22.

**Hannah, M.G.** 2000: *Governmentality and the mastery of territory in nineteenth-century America.* Cambridge: Cambridge University Press.

—— 2001: Sampling and the politics of representation in US Census 2000. *Environment and Planning D: Society and Space* 19, 515–34.

**Hay, I.** 2001: Editorial: critical geography and activism in higher education. *Journal of Geography in Higher Education* 25(2), 141–146.

**Hepple, L.W.** 2001: Classics in human geography revisited: author's response. *Progress in Human Geography* 25, 428–30.

**Herbst, J.** 2000: *States and power in Africa: comparative lessons in authority and control.* Princeton, NJ: Princeton University Press.

**Himanen, P.** 2001: *The Hacker ethic and the spirit of the information age.* New York: Random House.

**Holloway, S.L.** and **Valentine, G.** 2001: Placing cyberspace: processes of Americanization in British children's use of the internet. *Area* 33(2), 153–60.

**Howitt, R.** 2001: Frontiers, borders, edges: liminal challenges to the hegemony of exclusion. *Australian Geographical Studies* 39(2), 233–45.

**Ingram, A.** 2001: Broadening Russia's borders? The nationalist challenge of the Congress of Russian Communities. *Political Geography* 20(2), 197–219.

**Johnston, R.J.** and **Pattie, C.J.** 2001: 'It's the economy, stupid' – but which economy? Geographical scales, retrospective economic evaluations and voting at the 1997 British General Election. *Regional Studies* 35(4), 309–19.

**Johnston, R.J., Pattie, C.J., Dorling, D.F.L., MacAllister, I., Tunstall, H.** and **Rossiter, D. J.** 2001: Social locations, spatial locations and voting at the 1997 British general election: evaluating the sources of Conservative support. *Political Geography* 20(1), 85–111.

**Jones, R.** 2001: Institutional identities and the shifting scales of state governance in the United Kingdom. *European Urban and Regional Studies* 8(4), 283–96.

**Juergensmeyer, M.** 2001: *Terror in the mind of God: the global rise of religious violence.* Berkeley, CA: University of California Press.

**Kearns, G.** 2001: 'Educate that holy hatred': place, trauma, and identity in the Irish nationalism of John Mitchel. *Political Geography* 20(7), 885–911.

**Kirby, A.** 2001: What in the world? Notes on Peter Taylor's 'Political geography: world-economy, state, and locality'. *Political Geography* 20(6), 727–44.

**Kobayashi, A.** and **Peake, L.** 2000: Racism out of place: thoughts on whiteness and an antiracist geography in the new millennium. *Annals of the Association of American Geographers* 90, 392–403.

**Kong, L.** 2001: Mapping 'new' geographies of religion: politics and poetics in modernity. *Progress in Human Geography* 25, 211–33.

**Kubálková, V.** 2000: Towards an international political theology. *Millennium* 29(3), 675–704.

**Laqueur, W.** 1987: *The age of terrorism.* Boston, Toronto and London: Little, Brown.

**Le Billon, P.** 2001: The political ecology of war: natural resources and armed conflict. *Political Geography* 20(5), 561–84.

**Lefebvre, H.** 2001: Comments on a new state form. *Antipode* 33(5), 769–82.

**Lesser, I.O.** 1999: Countering the new terrorism: implications for strategy. In Lesser, I.O., Hoffman, B., Arquilla, J., Ronfeldt, D. and Zanini, M., editors, *Countering the new terrorism,* Santa Monica, CA: RAND, 85–144.

**Luke, T.W.** 1999: Simulated sovereignty, telematic territoriality: the political economy of cyberspace. In Featherstone, M. and Lash, S., editors, *Spaces of culture: city, nation, world,* London, Thousand Oaks, CA, New Delhi: Sage, 27–48.

**MacKinnon, D.** and **Phelps, N.A.** 2001a: Regional governances and foreign direct investment: the dynamics of institutional changes in Wales and North East England. *Geoforum* 32(2), 255–69.

—— 2001b: Devolution and the territorial politics of foreign direct investment. *Political Geography* 20(3), 353–79.

**Mamadouh, V.** 1999: Reclaiming geopolitics: geographers strike back. *Geopolitics* 4, 118–38.

**Marsh, C.** and **Warhola, J.W.** 2001: Ethnicity, ethnoregionalism, and the political geography of Putin's electoral support. *Post-Soviet Geography and Economics* 42(3), 220–33.

Marston, S. and Rouhani, F. 2001: Teaching and learning the lesson of complexity. *The Arab World Geographer* 4(2), 100–102.

Marston, S.A. and Smith, N. 2001: States, scales and households: limits to scale thinking? A response to Brenner. *Progress in Human Geography* 25, 615–19.

Massey, D. 2001: Geography on the agenda. *Progress in Human Geography* 25, 5–17.

McColl, R.W. 2001: The law of unintended consequences: reflections on some global and national changes following the events of September 11, 2001. *The Arab World Geographer* 4(2), 93–95.

Mitchnek, B. 2001: The regional governance context in Russia: a general framework. *Urban Geography* 22(4), 360–82.

Morgan, K. 2001: The new territorial politics: rivalry and justice in post-devolution Britain. *Regional Studies* 35(4), 343–48.

Morrill, R. 2001: Spaces of the United States election 2000. *Environment and Planning D: Society and Space* 19, 253–57.

Morrison, N. 2001: Introduction: social exclusion and community initiatives. *Geojournal* 51(4), 277–79.

Neumann, I.B. 1999: *Uses of the Other; 'The East' in European identity formation.* Minneapolis, MN: University of Minnesota Press.

Nijman, J. 2001: New York City and the geopolitical transition. *The Arab World Geographer* 4(2), 96–99.

O'Lear, S. 2001: Azerbaijan: territorial issues and internal challenges in mid-2001. *Post-Soviet Geography and Economics* 42(4), 305–12.

O'Loughlin, J. 2001: The regional factor in contemporary Ukranian politics: scale, place, space, or bogus effect. *Post-Soviet Geography and Economics* 42(1), 1–33.

Paasi, A. 2001: Europe as a social process and discourse: consideration of place, boundaries and identity. *European Journal of Urban and Regional Studies* 8(1), 7–28.

Painter, J. 2001: Space, territory and the European Project: reflections on Agnew and Paasi. *European Journal of Urban and Regional Studies* 8(1), 42–43.

Paris, J.W. and Anderson, R.E. 2001: Faith-based queer space in Washington, D.C.: The Metropolitan Community Church – D.C. and Mount Vernon Square. *Gender, Place and Culture* 8(2), 149–68.

Parker, G. 2001: An uneasy relationship: geography and politics at the turn of the Millenium. *Political Geography* 20(1), 120–26.

Peck, J. and Theodore, N. 2001: Exporting workfare/importing welfare-to-work: Exploring the politics of Third Way policy transfer. *Political Geography* 20(4), 427–60.

Pillar, P.R. 2001: *Terrorism and U.S. foreign policy.* Washington, DC: Brookings Institution Press.

Power, M. 2001: Geo-politics and the representation of Portugal's African colonial wars: examining the limits of 'Vietnam syndrome'. *Political Geography* 20(4), 461–91.

Purcell, M. 2001a: Neighborhood activism among homeowners as a politics of space. *Professional Geographer* 53(2), 178–94.

—— Metropolitan political reorganization as a politics of urban growth: the case of San Fernando Valley secession. *Political Geography* 20(5), 613–33.

Raco, M. and Flint, J. 2001: Communities, places and institutional relations: assessing the role of area-based community representation in local governance. *Political Geography* 20(5), 585–612.

Razin, E. and Hazan, A. 2001: Redrawing Israel's local government map: political decisions, court rulings or popular determination. *Political Geography* 20(4), 513–33.

Robinson, F. and Shaw, K. 2001: Governing a region: structures and processes of governance in North East England. *Regional Studies* 35(5), 473–92.

Rubenstein, S. 2001: Colonialism, the Shuar Federation, and the Ecuadorian state. *Environment and Planning D: Society and Space* 19, 263–93.

Ramutsindela, M.F. 2001: Down the post-colonial road: Reconstructing the post-apartheid state in South Africa. *Political Geography* 20(1), 57–84.

Santos, B.d.S. 1999: Toward a multicultural conception of human rights. In Featherstone, M. and Lash, S., editors, *Spaces of culture: city, nation, world*, London, Thousand Oaks, CA, New Delhi: Sage, 214–29.

Schoenberger, E. 2001: Interdisciplinarity and social power. *Progress in Human Geography* 25, 365–82.

Secor, A.J. 2001: Ideologies in crisis: political cleavages and electoral politics in Turkey in the 1990s. *Political Geography* 20(5), 539–60.

Shapiro, M.J. 1999: Triumphalist geographies. In Featherstone, M. and Lash, S., editors, *Spaces of culture: city, nation, world*, London, Thousand Oaks, CA, New Delhi: Sage, 159–74.

Shin, M. 2001: The politicization of place in Italy.

106 Political geography

*Political Geography* 20(3), 331–52.

Shirlow, P. 2001: Devolution in Northern Ireland/Ulster/the North/Six Counties: delete as appropriate. *Regional Studies* 35(8), 743–52.

Sidaway, J.D. 2001: Iraq/Yugoslavia: banal geopolitics. *Antipode* 33(4), 601–609.

Smith, A.D. 2000: The 'sacred' dimension of nationalism. *Millennium* 29(3), 791–814.

Smith, H. 2001: *Why religion matters: the fate of the human spirit.* San Francisco: Harper.

Smith, N. 2001: Ashes and aftermath. *The Arab World Geographer* 4(2), 81–84.

Sprinzak, E. 2001: The lone gunmen. *Foreign Policy* Nov./Dec., 72–73.

Storper, M. 1997: *The regional world: territorial development in a global economy.* New York: Guilford Press.

Stump, R.W. 2000: *Boundaries of faith: geographical perspectives on religious fundamentalism.* Lanham, MD: Rowman and Littlefield.

Talbott, S. and Chanda, N., editors 2001: *The age of terror: America and the world after September 11.* New York: Basic Books.

Taylor, P.J. 1999: *Modernities: a geohistorical interpretation.* Minnesota, MN: University of Minnesota Press.

—— 2000a: Embedded statism and the social sciences 2: geographies (and metageographies) in globalization. *Environment and Planning A* 32, 1105–14.

—— 2000b: Geopolitics, political geography, and social science. In Dodds, K. and Atkinson, D., editors, *Geopolitical traditions: a century of geopolitical thought,* London and New York: Routledge, 375–79.

Taylor, P.J., Hoyler, M., Walker, D.R.F. and Szegner, M.J. 2001: A new mapping of the world for the new millennium. *The Geographical Journal* 167(3), 213–22.

Thomas, S.M. 2000: Taking religious and cultural pluralism seriously: the global resurgence of religion and the transformation of international society. *Millennium* 29(3), 815–41.

Thomson, J.A. 2001: Suddenly, a new NATO agenda. *RAND Review* 25(3), 13.

Tibi, B. 2000: Post-bipolar order in crisis: The challenge of politicized Islam. *Millennium* 29(3), 843–59.

Torpey, J. 2000: *The invention of the passport: surveillance, citizenship and the state.* Cambridge: Cambridge University Press.

Trigger, R. 2001: The geopolitics of the Irish-Catholic parish in nineteenth-century Montreal. *Journal of Historical Geography* 27(4), 553–72.

Van Creveld, M. 1999: *The rise and decline of the state.* Cambridge: Cambridge University Press.

Watts, M. 2001: 1968 and all that . . . *Progress in Human Geography* 25, 157–88.

Webster, G.R. and Leib, J.I. 2001: Whose South is it anyway? Race and the Confederate battle flag in South Carolina. *Political Geography* 20(3), 271–99.

Wilson, D. and Bauder, H. 2001: Discourse and the making of marginalised people: Introduction. *Tijdschrift voor Economische en Sociale Geografie* 92(3), 259–60.

Winlow, H. 2001: Anthropometric cartography: constructing Scottish racial identity in the early twentieth century. *Journal of Historical Geography* 27(4), 507–28.

Wood, W.B. 2001: Geographic aspects of genocide: a comparison of Bosnia and Rwanda. *Transactions of the Institute of British Geographers* NS 26, 57–75.

Youngs, G. 2001: The Taylor guide to globalization: reflections on some of the signposts. *Political Geography* 20(6), 695–707.

# [12]

# "Counterterrorism" and Conventional Military Force: The Relationship Between Political Effect and Utility

CHARLES T. EPPRIGHT

Department of the Navy
Washington, DC, USA

*This paper compares the U.S. national security strategy's vision for counter-terrorism missions to the political realm in which conventional military forces and terrorists operate. Terrorist acts and state responses are analyzed to demonstrate that they have differing political effects, which calls into question the political utility of a conventional military counterterrorist response. Terrorism is placed within context of the present era as, according to Martin van Creveld, evolving historical conditions are wrenching warfare out of the political realm in which Clausewitz's analysis originally posited warfare's extension of political activity based on state power. The article also discusses terrorism's nebulous placement within the levels of war to reveal another aspect of terrorism's different relationship to the political realm. Ultimately, this challenges the U.S. national security strategy's conclusion that conventional military force used in "punitive" or "counterterrorism" operations is an effective political response to terrorism.*

U.S. national security strategy envisions a role for both conventional general-purpose and specialized military response forces for counterterrorism missions, as it comprehends the distinction in the capabilities and approaches that these different military forces can bring to bear within the political arena in which terrorists operate.[1] This dual approach to counterterrorism is based on an understanding of the varied political complexities that contemporary terrorism poses. U.S. strategy envisions both "punitive" and "counterterrorism" missions and recognizes that the international political arena of the United Nations and regional organizations may represent opportunities for political expression against terrorism. Because the violence of terrorism in practice has an immediate impact in the political arena, its effects are more proximate to the political arena than those of the conventional military are. In addition, the political considerations of the "who"

Received 30 June 1996; accepted 10 October 1996.

The opinions expressed in this paper are purely those of its author and do not represent any official position of the United States Department of Defense, its subordinate agencies and commands, or any other United States federal executive branch agency.

Address correspondence to Charles T. Eppright, Department of the Navy, Naval Computer and Telecommunication Station, 901 M St., SE, Building 143–6, Washington, DC 20374.

and "how" of terrorism absolutely determine the nature of the targeted state's response to it. Under these circumstances, it is the degree to which U.S. national security strategy depends on a military response to terrorism that ought to concern us. Recent history and current events reveal how the U.S. national leadership's natural devotion to political matters limits the full extent of the effectiveness of a military response to terrorism. In the final analysis, any military response to terrorism must function in the political environment, in which political utility is the final metric of its effectiveness.

## What Is Terrorism?

Security planners must understand what terrorism is and what ends the terrorist hopes to achieve. Terrorism is best understood as attacks on innocent civilians to produce public fear for its political effect.[2] To accomplish that, terrorists operate secretly and neither abide by the laws of war nor wear uniforms. Terrorists coerce legitimate political systems to change their policies.[3] Terrorists are not guerrillas or irregulars who conduct unconventional warfare against recognized military targets for political purposes; rather, they employ their methods (which are often military in nature) in illegal attacks against primarily civilian targets for political purposes. Therefore terrorists and their methods are an unfamiliar threat for military strategists and planners. The fear that terrorists inspire through their attacks or the threat of attacks to influence the body politic is their principal political weapon, since they seek to force the states they target to modify their policies and actions in order to avoid further attacks.[4]

International terrorism has expanded its threat to Western states and gained in popularity among those inclined to its practice for four principal reasons: Terrorists have achieved political gains; rogue states have actively supported terrorism; the terrorists believe they can spread fear to weaken the resistance of Western citizens and their governments; and the terrorists have noted weak responses at times from the governments they have challenged.[5] It should also be noted that recent terrorist attacks in the Middle East against U.S. and Saudi Arabian targets have begun to reveal an unintended consequence of Western support for the war in Afghanistan against the Soviet Union in the 1980s. The mujahideen in Afghanistan and Islamic fighters from other states who joined them in their struggle against the Soviets and the Soviet-supported regime gained combat experience as well as an impressive amount of sophisticated weaponry with which they have expanded their *jihad* against the West. Recent times have witnessed the advent of new terrorist organizations, about which little is known other than their intended targets, which are Western interests and their coincidental supporters among Arab and Gulf states.[6] The recent attack against U.S. servicemen in Dhahran, Saudi Arabia, reveals this current trend.

But the increased incidences of terrorism in contemporary times do not expose a counterhistorical trend. Rather, the rise of terrorism reveals that states may be less willing to achieve their political goals through *open* warfare, principally because advancements in armaments have made such warfare an unappealing political solution. For states so inclined, however, there is definite appeal in a state-sponsored terrorist program, which enables them, on the political plane, to deny their involvement in such practices. And substate groups are becoming ever more willing to and capable of achieving their goals through war, but likewise not in the formal, Western manner. The nature of warfare in the late twentieth century, as Martin van Creveld presents it, is such that organized formal warfare from states is less likely, since evolving historical conditions in the "new world order" are irretrievably altering the notions that Clausewitz expressed in *On War* (1832) about the state's monopoly on the conduct of organized violence.[7] As distinct from Clausewitz's trinity of the state, the army, and the people, van Creveld notes the "nontrinitarian" nature of terrorism. Terrorists operate in most cases without formal state sanction, without the rational organization for armed forces and the rules for the lawful application of armed force, such as the Geneva Convention, and without anything near the unanimous support of the peoples in whose names they purport to act (van Creveld 59–61).

Although it by no means falls under the strict definition of terrorism, the April 1996 escalation of the fighting between the warlords in Liberia illustrates the changing nature of warfare, showing that an armed rabble can be as effective and destructive as a regular armed force in making war the means to its particular end. Indeed, the guerrilla army of the "wars of national liberation" in the Third World of the 1960s has rapidly given way, after the end of the Cold War, to the armed gang or "criminal enterprise army," by which warmaking has been wrenched out of the "Clausewitzian universe" (van Creveld 33) in which war is an extreme, if not final resort of state-directed and controlled political necessity, and finally made purely an end in and of itself.[8]

Van Creveld's extensive treatise on the mutative nature of war in this era further demonstrates that the distinction between "warfare" and "crime" is beginning to dissolve. News reports about the conflicts around the world demonstrate that "war" is taking on a new meaning in terms of its execution and participants. Theoreticians in the West have labeled this recent phenomenon "low-intensity" conflict, which is conflict lesser in intensity than the type encountered in the clashes of heavily armed conventional military formations, with operations stopping significantly short of the extreme end of the spectrum that represents total state-against-state war.[9] It is in the context of low-intensity conflict that terrorism is effective and may be the preferred mode of operation for some. Substate groups are likely to gravitate toward the practice of terrorism, if they judge doing so to be politically effective.[10] Contemporaneous events provide ample proof of terrorism's ultimate political effectiveness: the Nobel Peace Prize awarded to a (former?) terrorist leader such as Yasser Arafat, and a visit to the White House by Gerry Adams of Sinn Fein, the political front for the Irish Republican Army (IRA).

## Terrorism in Warfare's Mutative Age

The "military technical revolution"—which refers in contemporary defense parlance to the enormous impact that computer and electronic innovations have

wrought on the warfighting environment at the tactical level[11]—though fundamental to the continually modernizing Western-oriented armed forces, could not
be less relevant for substate groups who consider terrorism an option for political
expression. Conventional weapons, the military formations that use them, and the
operational art practiced to employ these will continue to be used by states in
general, and in particular in the Western states, which have developed such evident superiority from these weapons and forces. However, actors in the political
arena that cannot (and need not) compete on the playing field of conventional
forces will of necessity devise asymmetrical responses, which will be as revolutionary in their simplicity as the advancement of the technology so prized by the
West (Cohen 51). In such cases, the dictum that simple is better will hold as an
undeniable truth for those not otherwise restrained by operational reliance on
technological advances.

It is therefore not useful to consider advanced fighting talent at the tactical
level as well as advanced weaponry (both inspired by the operational artistry of
Western forces) important for the practice of terrorism. In terrorism, a blunder at
the tactical level, based on a failure to manage even the simplest type of arma-
ment, can nonetheless carry the same strategic political effect as a tactical success. The February 1996 "accidental" bombing of the London bus by the IRA had
the same effect on the British government as the series of *intentional* Hamas bus
bombings had on the Israeli government in the same time period. That "mistake"
strategically informed the British government that the IRA still has the means to
wage its war of terrorism and at that moment could shatter the peace sustained by
its previous adherence to the truce. Conversely, a tactical mistake by conventional forces means that they did not destroy or neutralize their target. At an
extreme, it may mean that the forces did not survive long enough to engage the
target. In any event, the final political effect of a tactical error in conventional
combat may be negligible and isolated within the larger operational-level context.
But in terrorist practice, a miss is as good as a hit, both tactically and strategically. The political (and strategic) effect of the IRA's mistake is unequivocal:
London has never resembled an armed camp as much as it does now with the
extensive powers granted to its police forces as a result of the public's fear of the
possibility of renewed IRA violence. And Britain will eventually have to consider
other political adjustments at the strategic level to deescalate the violence.

Just as the wider phenomenon of low-intensity conflict illustrates the conduct
of war for its own sake, the reflective nature of terrorism's rejection of the principle of "economy of force" reveals a fundamental distinction between forces that
are embedded in the rules of the Clausewitzian universe from forces that are not.
"Economy of force is the judicious employment and distribution of forces. It is
the measured allocation of combat power."[12] Conventional military practice recognizes this principle of war as fundamental. The recent Israeli incursion into
Lebanon indicates a belief in the possibility of the political defeat of terrorism
through its defeat at the tactical and operational levels. This presumed that the
Israeli economy of force could overwhelm the Hezbollah, whose artillery positions and rocket launchers offered conventional, identifiable targets. But while

the Israeli forces would never hide behind their own people in a cynical manner, the Hezbollah had no compunction about using the Lebanese people in such a way. This terrorist group lured Israel farther into Lebanon with an implicit promise of the trappings of a set-piece battlefield. Yet Hezbollah strategy had no intention of occupying any space in the Clausewitzian universe that would have given Israel an opportunity to defeat the Hezbollah. This illustrates the difficulty in defeating a force that does not recognize the signs of defeat in conventional terms. Because of Israel's incursion, Hezbollah's political stock has risen among the very people whom that group cynically used as shields from Israeli attacks. The only real hope, and a none-too-likely one at that, is that Israel's operational-level success may mitigate Hezbollah's ability to reconstitute itself for effective action at the operational or tactical level, while the Israeli leadership must deal with the unexpected benefit of the increase of Hezbollah's political capital. Unfortunately, for all of the Israeli tactical intensity in Lebanon against the Hezbollah, the Israelis are politically worse off than before this "war."

Likewise, one can only wonder at the tactical intensity that Israel has undoubtedly applied to stop the attacks of the Hamas group within Israel. But Hamas is another terrorist group that refuses to recognize the "economy of force" principle that forces within the Clausewitzian universe cannot avoid. Hamas's cause is apparently borne of such utter desperation that the group has forgone consideration of any other political approach. As long as Hamas can find just one more young man who is willing to strap on explosives and board a bus to kill—and die—for his cause, there may be nothing in the strategic political realm, let alone the operational and tactical levels of war, that can truly stop this. As Hamas and other terrorists conduct it, this may be war for war's sake alone. This is the ultimate form of political self-reflectiveness in which the strategic political cause becomes inextricably aligned with the means of the tactical activity to further it.

My belief is that this marked divergence in the political effect from action at the different levels of war is a distinctive feature of terrorism with which national security planners must contend. Just as tactical "mistakes" are politically effective for terrorists within the larger strategic context, there are few, if any, political constraints that defy the transformation of a terrorist group's desired political approach into tactical action. Similarly, terrorists are not plagued by the political constraints that require states and their conventional armed forces to flow strategic political direction through an operational level of command and control, which then transforms it into the most likely effective tactical action. Terrorist attacks can home in on "centers of gravity" without the degree of agonized planning and estimating in the formative phase of an operational campaign, and without its uncertain post-attack phase, in which conventional military measurements, inadequate as they are, must demonstrate the successful transformation of military action from its initial strategic direction into final political effectiveness.

In its politically unconstrained environment, terrorism's most important metric is the level of coverage and the direction of the commentary from the international media. Since the accelerating boost of this information into the political arena by the media is nearly as immediate in its effect as the terrorists' attack itself, the advent of the information age is the technical revolution that is most relevant for terrorists. This phenomenon reveals the obscurity between terrorism's levels of war as opposed to the conventional military's tactical, operational, and strategic levels. The ability of the terrorist group to transform operational-level planning and estimating into tactical effects is far less constrained by the political awareness of a command and control infrastructure, such as conventional armed forces have, with its absolute need to "integrate strategy, operational design and tactical action . . . [as it considers] the strategic environment during the estimate and planning phase" (JCS Pub 3-0 III-7). Terrorism's actions are so close to the political arena that not a great deal of strategic-to-operational transformation is needed. And with the ubiquitous media presence, there is little need for analysis following terrorist activities to fit the extent of any tactical success into the managed context of an operational-level campaign.

But media attention has a different political effect on a state's use of conventional forces against terrorism. The June 1993 attack on the Iraqi intelligence center carried the appropriate political message from the Clinton administration to Saddam Hussein. However, the media images of the cruise missile parts from the Baghdad hotel lobby allowed some minor technical problems at the tactical level to mitigate the intensity of that political (strategic) message, particularly when the U.S. leadership went into reflexive paroxysms of examination (although not altogether public) over the technical matters related to collateral damage in conventional attacks. In its different political context, one did not hear of and can nonetheless not picture the Provisional IRA command in the same dither about the "accident" on the London bus. Consequently, it must be apparent that the political success of a terrorist attack is immediately evident and effective through reports by the news media. Yet a conventional military attack against terrorists generates its own military operational-level analysis of that attack's effectiveness, which second-guessing at the strategic level about its political utility, brought about in large measure by media imagery, may eventually subsume.

There is some plausibility to the notion that use of the military to send political signals, absent any intent to enable the military to achieve total victory, is a form of limited warfare. And limited warfare cannot work unless it has some significant hope of making an impact on the other side's strategy. A defeat in strategy for terrorists may be the only way to prevail against them.[13] But once again we face a collapsible set of the levels of war with terrorism. It might not be difficult to find terrorism's tactical level, but the obscurity of the operational and strategic levels defies any conclusive distinction, given van Creveld's notion about the nontrinitarian nature of this type of war. Partly because of the collapsible nature of the levels of war as applied to terrorism, and partly because a conventional military response cannot halt media attention to a terrorist attack, there probably is no way to defeat the strategy. The term "CNN factor" is meant to describe the immediate and global nature of news coverage, but it also handily captures the reality of the genie out of the bottle as it concerns the inherent inability of the global village to defeat terrorism's strategy. Censorship is not possible any longer, particularly among the politically capable Western populations against whom terrorist acts are directed. If a state and its people hope to combat terrorism and cannot face the same elements of this "trinity," as so plainly illustrated by Israel's cynical (but practical) attempts to make the Lebanese state (insofar as it is effective) and its people fill in the missing gaps of this "trinity" as the Israeli forces confronted the Hezbollah, the nature of victory in the Clausewitzian universe must therefore remain elusive. The horrible truth is that terrorism may be able to generate political success, but because of its existence outside of the "trinity" in the Clausewitzian universe it may be otherwise immune from suffering political defeat.

## What Is Counterterrorism?

An analysis of the "counterterrorism" and "punitive attack" missions that the *National Security Strategy* suggests as appropriate for "general purpose and specialized units" reveals problems that the United States has experienced with regard to the use of military forces against terrorists and sponsoring states (13). With respect to military action against terrorists, punitive measures can consider the nature of the terrorist act without necessarily duplicating its violence (Gray 22). The *National Security Strategy* proudly points to the June 1993 cruise missile attack on the Iraqi intelligence service's headquarters in retaliation for Iraq's involvement in a failed assassination plot against former President George Bush "in order to send a firm response and deter further threats" (16). The *National Security Strategy* contains some discussion on what media imagery does with respect to public support for military operations, recognizing that "modern media communications confront every American with images that both stir the impulse to intervene and raise the question of an operation's costs and risks" (19). However, one wonders whether the *National Security Strategy* ought to give some consideration to information management after an attack, since a tactically successful conventional attack may slip away on the strategic (political) level by less-than-circumspect information management by the political leadership. In any case, those behind determined causes are undoubtedly aware that the United States, both in image and practice, has never been tremendously effective in deterrence or punishment of terrorism. In the purely political arena, for all of the U.S. interest expressed in the international community's maintenance of a united front against terrorist-sponsoring states, economic sanctions, which are the only usual method acceptable (not to say popular) for broad-based international support, have never had a strong punitive or deterrent effect.[14] Indeed, the final paragraph in the *National Security Strategy*'s discussion on terrorism focuses on the niceties of UN sanctions and international treaties regarding specific sorts of terrorist acts, which ultimately points to the possible political necessity of forgoing a military response (16).

On the purely military front, the United States has never enjoyed anything near the tough reputation on terrorism that Israel has. U.S. practice has been to retaliate only against politically vulnerable state sponsors of terrorism (Gray 23). While Israel has a consistent policy of immediate retaliation, the United States does not have the political focus for concentrated military measures against ter-rorists.[15] Conventional military attacks on state-sponsored terrorist infrastructure have had mixed effects on the states to which they were applied, and typically they have resulted in international outrage and condemnation. Israel's April 1996 Lebanese incursion has had the immediate tactical success of blunting, if not completely stopping, the Hezbollah rocketeers' attacks on northern Israel. But these Israeli operations, aside from some ineffective immediate-term shoring-up of its domestic political position in advance of elections for the Shimon Peres government, were a disaster for Israel on the international political scene as a result of the extensive Lebanese civilian casualties and collateral damage.

Probably for just such a likelihood, the United States has exercised extreme forbearance in pressing for military attacks against suspected terrorist strong-holds, even when military attacks might have had immediately positive effects. The result has been more severe than merely a lost opportunity to silence an immediately apparent terrorist tactical threat. Moreover, on the political front, U.S. leaders' half-hearted approach has at times bolstered the regional standing and political prestige of terrorism's state sponsors. In the early and mid-1980s, the United States conceded some measure of its position in the face of terrorists sponsored by Iran and Syria, and did so at the expense of the firmness of U.S. policy against terrorism (Kupperman and Kamen 85). But we need to be fair to the U.S. leadership in considering the recognized politically "hardened" nature of Syria and Iran at that time in the 1980s (since the U.S. government's interest in retaining any possibility of entente with these states was a factor in that "harden-ing"), which precluded strenuous U.S. counterterrorism measures against them (Martin and Walcott 289). And for all of the continuing U.S. consternation about Syria's sponsorship of terrorism in the Middle East and elsewhere, it was an absolute political necessity to engage Syrian efforts in 1996 to help to secure the truce in Lebanon between Israel and Hezbollah. If the Israeli government at that time had felt as strongly about the Syrian and Iranian genesis of the trouble in Lebanon as does the victor in the Israeli election whose recent book I cite, then the question arises as to why that government did not engage the Syrians in battle. Israel and the U.S. evidently share the understanding that a diplomatic solution through peaceful engagement with Syria is more politically productive than combat. This points out the difficulty in using military forces against a state sponsor of terrorists—not because those forces are inherently ineffective, but simply because the prevalent political climate may negate the ability to use them at all.

Along with the international political image problems, there are international legal problems with a military response to terrorism. The United Kingdom's leaders perceived legal questions about the U.S. response to Libya's People's Bureau terrorist attacks. Those leaders concluded that international law defined the U.S. raid as retaliation rather than as a preemptive response based on Article 51 of the United Nations charter, which defines the inherent right of a state to self-defense (Martin and Walcott 290). A perception based on this legal nuance might be a precondition that could also inhibit future military action against state sponsored or directed terrorism, particularly if the United States depends on international or allied cooperation to conduct such an attack.

Another feature of the ineffectiveness of military forces in fighting terrorism is that military force is difficult to apply precisely for the kind of effects that send the desired political message. Aside from considerations about the use of military forces to send a political message and the tendency this has to reveal a potential motive to conduct limited warfare, there is also the practical hindrance that the collateral death and damage from a conventional attack pose to the focus of such a message. Consequently, there is a definite need to distinguish terrorists from the populations in which they may hide (Farrell "Responding" 52). The 1980 mission to rescue the U.S. embassy hostages in Iran reveals how unproductive a complex military *plan* can be (Martin and Walcott 6–42). Its unfortunate political message to the Iranian ayatollahs was that the United States was still suffering a lack of nerve from the lingering effects of the "Vietnam syndrome." The 1986 U.S. raid on Libya, even with the extensive planning and practice that preceded it, illustrated just how imprecise conventional military *action* is. In that attack the only failure was to execute a level of precision that was tactically impossible but strategically imperative. The attack made a point, but not as fine a point as the U.S. political leadership wanted. It is still difficult to reconcile U.S. efforts to induce an internal revolt against Muammar Qaddafi through the popular Libyan political discontent hoped for as a result of the attack and the belief that his removal from the scene would end Libya's terrorism, with the politically postulated idea in response to media inquiries after the attack that the air raid was not designed to spell his demise. Even if that raid's plans did not include such a feature, the targets chosen in Libya demanded a precision that the air strike simply could not achieve. No matter what the political intent for their use, military forces must nevertheless live within the "fog" and "friction" in the Clausewitzian universe.

In contrast, the military precision of the capture of the perpetrators of the 1985 *Achille Lauro* outrage was unparalleled, although its total effect was disappointing with respect to the vagaries of international politics' foiling the capture of the terrorist mastermind. The eventual international political fallout as a consequence of the very precision of this operation was almost unbearable for the United States and Egypt and absolutely so for the Bettino Craxi government in Italy (Martin and Walcott 256). The lesson is that the tactical transformation of strategic subtlety may still result in activity too blunt for the final political measurement. While in the political arena of the United Nations General Assembly a state may be able to achieve an international understanding of its political subtleties with words in speeches, military forces on operations cannot function with political circumspectness; there will always be political consequences to their use.

Nevertheless, the United States is prepared to use conventional forces to respond to terrorist acts. However, in an explanation that suggests apprehension with the unfamiliar world of counterterrorism, the Department of Defense (DOD) insists that "U.S. agencies involved in combating terrorism follow a principle known as the 'lead agency concept'."[16] Indeed, this oblique maneuvering from final responsibility originates from a broad definition of terrorism that allows agencies to define the limits of their responses.[17] The DOD presumes in defining "counterterrorism" (CT) that those CT forces are specially trained and capable of swift, effective action. Media images from training exercises show elite troops like the Delta Force or the Navy SEALs forming conceptual CT missions with great skill and precision.[18] Indeed, other nations have renowned specialized CT military forces, such as the British Special Air Service or the German Grenzschutzgruppe 9 (Seger 29). The U.S. Special Operations Forces (SOF) have a "counterterrorism mission [that] was mandated by legislation to prevent, deter, and, if necessary, respond to terrorist acts."[19] DOD policy is that such forces are the right answer for specific sorts of terrorist events outside of the United States. For the U.S. SOF, one imagines a mission like the 1976 Israeli rescue at Entebbe. "Punitive" missions against terrorists are likely outside the expertise of these elite troops, given their lethal tactical orientation and the strained U.S. legal niceties concerning pushing CT punitive matters too far.

A military response to terrorism is appropriate if it can be precisely aligned with political goals (Gray 22). The image of the U.S. SOF is not in question as the right precision instrument in a CT mode. What throws doubt into the equation is trying to oppose terrorism by air strikes and naval blockades as "punitive missions," since the international political side effects undermine any chance these have of long-term effectiveness. And yet there is a definite practical political appeal, at least domestically in terms of approval polls, if nothing else, that follows an event like the 1993 cruise missile attack. Likewise, punditry abounded in attempts to find the Israeli incursion into Lebanon in 1996 as principally an attempt to boost the standing of the Peres government prior to elections. As always, conventional military forces can attack "terrorists at their bases abroad or . . . assets valued by Governments that support them" (*National Security Strategy* 15). But to view the deployment of conventional military force against terrorism as something sustainable is not pragmatic in light of the sobering lessons of U.S. involvement in the Middle East in the 1980s, nor from the most recent lessons to be derived from Israel's 1996 incursion into Lebanon.

The final problem with conventional military forces is that they cannot play a CT role within the United States against the nascent domestic terrorism threat. The military could have done nothing to prevent or deter the 1995 Oklahoma City attack. Its perpetrators found a fairly soft target and then acted out their agenda without any concern about military detection or retaliation. In the context of domestic terrorism, conventional military power is therefore completely irrelevant as a deterrent. While the current federal law enforcement system cannot really be effective against domestic terrorism, especially when certain crimes associated with the panoply of terrorist activities may fall under the jurisdiction of several unrelated agencies (Farrell "Organized" 52), the U.S. armed forces have absolute legal prohibitions on their domestic involvement. Certainly while the armed forces could only watch helplessly after the fact, the *National Security Strategy* proudly points out initial legal successes in prosecuting the World Trade

Center bombers (16). Thankfully, we now know that all its perpetrators received stiff punishments. Therefore, the legal apparatus possesses an effect on terrorism that the military never will. Federal legislation under the 1995 and 1996 antiterrorism acts purports to address the military's legal exclusion from action against domestic terrorism, but it remains to be seen whether this will be effective. If the recent Justice Department's pandering to public opinion (exactly whose?) in the now concluded spectacle of its kid-glove treatment of the lunatics in Montana is any indication, one wonders whether our national will not to negotiate with terrorists (considering that the inopportunely named "Freemen" were holding only themselves as hostages) is able to withstand a real test, and whether our law is meaningful. This could lead to a conclusion that law enforcement against domestic terrorism is even less effective in the political sphere than military operations against international terrorism.

Ultimately the United States needs to recognize the political limits of conventional military power as a response mechanism against terrorism. This is a crucial step in determining and executing an effective national strategy. A democracy does not have a choice about whether to counter the terrorist threat (Netanyahu 6). The consequences of failure to do so may be greater than imagined, since a state that does not enact a competent defense is virtually doomed (van Creveld 198). Deciding where the military truly fits best is critical, so that effective, preventive preparations can be made. Effective defensive preparation against terrorism may well prove to be the best kind of prevention that the United States could enact.

## Notes

1. United States, Executive Office of the President, *A National Security Strategy of Engagement and Enlargement,* February 1996, 13. Further parenthetical references in this paper's text provide page sources following an initial citation in documentation endnote format as specified in Joseph Gibaldi, *Modern Language Association Handbook for Writers of Research Papers* (New York: Modern Language Association, 1995), 242–256.

2. Benjamin Netanyahu, *Fighting Terrorism: How Democracies Can Defeat Domestic and International Terrorism* (New York: Farrar, Straus, and Giroux, 1995), 8.

3. Neil C. Livingstone, *The Cult of CounterTerrorism: The "Weird World" of Spooks, CounterTerrorists, Adventurers, and the Not Quite Professionals* (Lexington, MA: Lexington Books, 1990), 24.

4. Robert Kupperman and Jeff Kamen, *Final Warning: Averting Disaster in the New Age of Terrorism* (New York: Doubleday, 1989), 18.

5. Meir Shamgar, "An International Convention Against Terrorism," in *Terrorism: How the West Can Win,* ed. Benjamin Netanyahu (New York: Farrar, Straus, and Giroux, 1986), 158.

6. Mary Anne Weaver, "Blowback," *Atlantic Monthly* 277, May 1996, 26.

7. Martin van Creveld, *The Transformation of War: The Most Radical Reinterpretation of Armed Conflict Since Clausewitz* (New York: Free Press, 1991).

8. Robert D. Kaplan, "The Coming Anarchy," *Atlantic Monthly* 275, February 1994, 72–73.

9. Army/Air Force Center for Low Intensity Conflict, *Joint Low Intensity Conflict Project Final Report,* vol. 1, *Analytical Review of Low Intensity Conflict,* and vol. 2, *Low Intensity Conflict, Issues and Recommendations,* August 1, 1986. Quoted in Michael T. Klare and Peter Kornbluth, "The New Interventionism: Low Intensity Warfare in the 1980s and Beyond," in *Low Intensity Warfare: Counterinsurgency, Proinsurgency, and Antiterrorism in the Eighties,* ed. Michael T. Klare and Peter Kornbluth (New York: Pantheon, 1988), 5.

10. William R. Farrell, Lt. Col. USAF, "Responding to Terrorism," *Naval War College Review,* January/February 1986, 50.

11. Eliot A. Cohen, "A Revolution in Warfare," *Foreign Affairs* 75, March/April 1996, 39.

12. United States, Department of Defense, Joint Chiefs of Staff, *Doctrine for Joint Operations* (Joint Pub 3-0), 9 September 1993, A-2.

13. Colin S. Gray, "Combatting Terrorism," *Parameters,* Autumn 1993, 20.

14. Karl A. Seger, *The Antiterrorism Handbook: A Practical Guide to Counteraction Planning and Operations for Individuals, Businesses, and Government* (Novato, CA: Presidio Press, 1990), 5.

15. David C. Martin and John Walcott, *Best Laid Plans: The Inside Story of America's War Against Terrorism* (New York: Harper Collins, 1988), 312.

16. United States, Departments of the Army and Air Force, *Military Operations in Low Intensity Conflict* (Field Manual 100-20; Air Force Pamphlet 3-20), 5 December 1990, 3–7.

17. William R. Farrell, Lt. Col. USAF, "Organized to Combat Terrorism," in *Fighting Back: Winning the War Against Terrorism,* ed. Neil C. Livingstone and Terrell E. Arnold (Lexington, MA: Lexington Books, 1986), 52.

18. "Nightly News," National Broadcast Corporation, January 30, 1996; featured an extensive report on terrorism and U.S. preparedness activities.

19. United States, Department of Defense, U.S. Special Operations Command, *U.S. Special Operations Forces Posture Statement,* 1994, 20.

# [13]

## The Use of Armed Force Against Terrorism: American Hegemony or Impotence?

Walter Gary Sharp, Sr.*

> Let our actions today send this message loud and clear: There are no expendable American targets; there will be no sanctuary for terrorists; we will defend our people, our interests and our values; we will help people of all faiths in all parts of the world who want to live free of fear and violence; we will persist and we will prevail.
>
> President William J. Clinton[1]

Ironically, while the rest of the world is greatly concerned and annoyed about American military hegemony,[2] some Americans believe U.S. military force is impotent in its fight against international terrorism.[3] It seems as though America's benevolent role as the world's sole superpower should serve as a stabilizing force for international peace and security and a deterrent to terrorists. Instead, its formidable military dominance has antagonized other states and has made America the world's sole super-target of terrorists. In 1997, for example, Americans were the targets of

---

* Principal Information Security Engineer, The MITRE Corporation, McLean, Virginia; Adjunct Professor of Law, Georgetown University Law Center; and Editor-in-Chief, *National Security Law Report*, ABA Standing Committee on Law & National Security. Professor Sharp retired in December 1997 as a U.S. Marine Corps Lieutenant Colonel. His military assignments included service as Deputy Legal Counsel to the Chairman of the Joint Chiefs of Staff, 1994-1997. The opinions and conclusions expressed herein are those of the author and do not necessarily reflect the views of any governmental agency or private enterprise.

1. Concluding remarks of President William J. Clinton, in his Address to the Nation on August 20, 1998 announcing that he had ordered the Armed Forces of the United States to strike at terrorist-related facilities in Afghanistan and Sudan. President's Address to the Nation on Military Action Against Terrorist Sites in Afghanistan and Sudan, 34 Weekly Comp Pres Doc 1643, 1644 (Aug 24, 1998), available online at <http://www.access.gpo.gov/nara> (visited Mar 4, 2000).

2. For a general discussion, see, Evan Thomas and Michael Hirsh, *The Future of Terror*, Newsweek 35 (Jan 10, 2000) ("America entering the 21st century is the strongest, most dominating nation in the world. It is also the biggest and softest target for the dangerous resentments of the left-behind."); David E. Sanger, *America Finds It's Lonely At the Top*, NY Times 1 (July 18, 1999); Samuel P. Huntington, *The Lonely Superpower*, 78 Foreign Aff 35, 42-43 (Mar-Apr 1999) ("[I]n the eyes of many countries [the United States] is becoming the rogue superpower ... [and] the single greatest threat to their societies.").

3. Consider Thomas and Hirsh, *The Future of Terror*, Newsweek at 35 (cited in note 2); Raymond Close, *Hard Target: We Can't Defeat Terrorism With Bombs and Bombast*, Wash Post C1 (Aug 30, 1998); Ralph Peters, *We Don't have the Stomach for This Kind of Fight*, Wash Post C1 (Aug 30, 1998); Gregory Vistica and Evan Thomas, *Hard of Hearing*, Newsweek 78 (Dec 13, 1999) ("Washington has had difficulty finding its most-wanted terrorist, Osama bin Laden, because Islamic extremists use European-made encrypted mobile phones."); Russell Watson and John Barry, *Our Target Was Terror*, Newsweek 24 (Aug 31, 1998).

*Chicago Journal of International Law*

over one-third of all international terrorist attacks.[4]

The United States defines terrorism as "premeditated, politically motivated violence perpetrated against noncombatant targets by sub-national groups or clandestine agents," usually intended to influence an audience, and international terrorism as "terrorism involving citizens or the territory of more than one country."[5] Defined as such, international terrorism is a criminal act committed by non-state actors—and the appropriate response of a victim state to defend against such terrorism is law enforcement. All non-state actors, however, operate within the sovereign territory of at least one state, and when a territorial state is unwilling or unable to cooperate in the suppression of international terrorism, or when it is covertly supporting international terrorism, then the law enforcement option fails. Furthermore, some states openly engage in, or support acts of violence that fall within the U.S. definition of international terrorism,[6] and when a state attacks another state by resorting to or supporting international terrorism, an appropriate response of the victim state may be the use of armed force.

Accordingly, international legal authority for a state to respond to acts of international terrorism is actor-dependent. If it is known that a non-state actor has committed an act of terrorism against the United States, then American law enforcement has the right to apprehend and prosecute the terrorist. However, when the location of a terrorist or a terrorist base camp is known and the territorial state refuses to cooperate with American law enforcement, the law enforcement response is completely ineffective in defending Americans and American interests abroad. In contrast, if it is known that a state actor has committed or supported an act of international terrorism, then American national security organizations have the lead in responding to the use of armed force by another state. Depending upon the severity of the terrorist attack and other circumstances, such a response may range from a diplomatic protest to seeking Security Council condemnation to the use of armed force in self-defense. In practice, however, the identity of the actor and a determination of state-sponsorship can be very difficult to establish. This Article briefly outlines the legal regimes which principally govern U.S. responses to international terrorism when it is established that the terrorist is either a non-state or state actor, and it explores international legal authorities' use of armed force against non-state actors when law enforcement options fail to protect Americans and American interests abroad.

---

4.  See US Department of State, Patterns of Global Terrorism: 1997, Publ No 10535 (Apr 1998), available online at <http://www.state.gov/www/global/terrorism/1997Report> (visited Mar 4, 2000).

5.  22 USC § 2656f(d)(1)-(2) (1994). See also Patterns of Global Terrorism: 1997 (cited in note 4).

6.  For example, in the same year (1984) that Colonel Qadhafi made frequent public statements announcing Libya's right to export terrorism, it was estimated that Libya spent an estimated one hundred million dollars annually operating over a dozen camps where about 1,000 terrorists were trained in guerrilla warfare, explosives, and arms for use in sabotage. See Gregory Francis Intoccia, *American Bombing of Libya: An International Legal Analysis*, 19 Case W Res J Intl L 177, 180-82 (1987).

No state, including the United States, should take a heavy-handed approach toward the use of armed force under any circumstances. All states, however, must be able to exercise their inherent right under international law to defend themselves against all actors—non-state and state alike. Effective deterrence demands that terrorists do not have safe havens and that terrorists must fear that they ultimately will pay a price for their criminal mayhem. This Article does not advocate armed force as an option of first resort; however, when force may be necessary, it details the international legal authority of states to use armed force against states for acts of terrorism and against non-state actors when the more appropriate law enforcement option is ineffective against terrorist threats to the national security of our great Nation.

## I. THE LAW ENFORCEMENT RESPONSE TO NON-STATE-SPONSORED TERRORISM

Non-state-sponsored terrorism[7] committed against the citizens, property, or territory of a state is rarely a criminal violation of international law per se, but it is usually a violation of the domestic criminal law of the victim state or of the state where the act of terrorism occurs. States must therefore rely upon one another to effectively combat international terrorism. Although the international community began a concerted effort to control international terrorism in the late 1920s, it has never been able to agree on a definition of international terrorism.[8] Consequently, the international community has taken a piecemeal approach and addressed the problem of international terrorism by identifying particular criminal acts inherently terrorist in nature to be prevented and punished by domestic law.[9] The result has been the adoption of a number of global treaties, regional conventions, and bilateral agreements which are relevant to the suppression of international terrorism, and corresponding domestic laws which implement those arrangements.[10]

The basic function of all of these arrangements is to establish a framework for international cooperation among states to prevent and suppress international terrorism by requiring state parties to cooperate in the prevention and investigation of terrorist acts, to criminalize terrorist acts, to assist other states in the prosecution of terrorists, and to either prosecute or extradite terrorists found in their territory.[11] The

---

7. The US Secretary of State has designated 30 groups as foreign terrorist organizations. See Patterns of Global Terrorism: 1997 (cited in note 4). This report provides a complete listing and detailed description of each of these terrorist organizations.

8. See John Norton Moore, et al, eds, *National Security Law Documents* 446-47 (Carolina Academic 1990).

9. Id at 447, 455.

10. Id at 455. At pages 455-62, this text provides a detailed discussion of these global, regional, and bilateral arrangements as well as proposed conventions. For a collection of documents relevant to the suppression of international terrorism, see John Norton Moore, et al, eds, *National Security Law Documents* 293-322 (cited in note 8).

11. See Moore, *National Security Law* at 456-59 (cited in note 8).

*Chicago Journal of International Law*

goal is to ensure that the accused terrorist is apprehended and prosecuted, but even when all states cooperate in good faith, it is very difficult to obtain the necessary evidence to convict an international terrorist, and the effectiveness of these arrangements as deterrents is questionable.[12]

The U.S. Congress has taken an increasingly active role in criminalizing international terrorism[13] based upon four internationally recognized principles of extraterritorial jurisdiction.[14] Indeed, the jurisdiction that the United States claims over international terrorism is the most far-reaching of any of its extraterritorial statutes.[15] Regardless of where the act occurs, for example, terrorists who kidnap, assault, or murder an American citizen are subject to U.S. criminal prosecution.[16] Similarly, terrorists who assist in the making of any biological agent, toxin, or delivery system for such agents or toxins anywhere in the world are subject to U.S. criminal prosecution if the intended victim is an American citizen.[17] The United States also criminalizes terrorist acts that damage aircraft or injure airline passengers of any nationality, regardless of where the incident occurs.[18]

Nevertheless, despite the practical difficulties of multi-jurisdictional efforts to investigate, identify, capture, and prosecute international terrorists,[19] when states cooperate in good faith the only appropriate and legal response to non-state-sponsored international terrorism is domestic law enforcement. Such a law enforcement response permits a state to rely upon its military or intelligence capabilities to discharge its law enforcement responsibilities, but it must do so consistent with the international law obligations that define the character of a law enforcement response.

## II. THE USE OF ARMED FORCE AGAINST STATE-SPONSORED TERRORISM

State-sponsored terrorism[20] committed against the citizens, property, or territory of another state is a violation of the international law of conflict management which invokes the victim state's inherent right of self-defense. This international law of conflict management is codified in Articles 2(4), 39, and 51 of the Charter of the United Nations ("Charter"), which governs the use of force between states.[21] Article 2(4) of the Charter prohibits the threat or use of force by any state against the

---

12. Id at 456-57.
13. See Howard M. Shapiro, *Terrorism in a Democratic Society*, 1 J Natl Sec L 95, 96 (1997).
14. See James S. Reynolds, *Expansion of Territorial Jurisdiction: A Response to the Rise in Terrorism*, 1 J Natl Sec L 105, 106 (1997).
15. Id at 107.
16. See Shapiro, 1 J Natl Sec L at 96 (cited in note 13).
17. Id at 97.
18. Id at 96.
19. Reynolds, 1 J Natl Security L at 108 (cited in note 14).
20. The US Secretary of State has designated seven countries as state sponsors of terrorism: Cuba, Iran, Iraq, Libya, North Korea, Sudan, and Syria. Patterns of Global Terrorism: 1997 (cited in note 4).
21. See Bruno Simma, ed, *The Charter of the United Nations: A Commentary* 111 (Oxford 1994).

territorial integrity or political independence of another state, except as authorized by the U.N. Security Council ("Security Council") under its Article 39 authority or in self-defense as authorized by international law and recognized by Article 51 of the Charter.[22] A state can sponsor an act of terrorism by directing the action of its regular armed forces, armed bands, irregulars, mercenaries, or private groups.[23]

No international convention interprets or defines the thresholds of Articles 2(4), 39, and 51. Thus, a heuristic analysis of interdependent, subjective, and politically volatile interpretations of state practice is required to determine what acts of state-sponsored terrorism constitute an unlawful use of force under international law or what acts of state-sponsored terrorism invoke a state's right of self-defense.[24] Inherently, this analysis usually results in conclusions of law that fail to maintain any international consensus or provide any concrete precedent. For example, in response to the murder of seven Americans in two Libyan-sponsored bombings in Rome and Vienna in December of 1985 and the terrorist bombing of a West German discotheque in April of 1986, the United States justified the lawfulness of its April 1986 air strikes against terrorist training camps and military targets in Libya as an exercise of its right of self-defense as recognized by Article 51 of the Charter.[25] The air strikes were widely denounced, however, by the international community primarily

---

22. These articles must be read together to determine the scope and content of the Charter's prohibition on the use of force, the responsibility of the Security Council to enforce this prohibition, and the right of all states to use force in self-defense. Articles 2(4), 39, and 51 provide:

    *Article 2*

    The Organization and its Members, in pursuit of the Purposes stated in Article 1, shall act in accordance with the following Principles: . . . .

    (4) All Members shall refrain in their international relations from the threat or use of force against the territorial integrity or political independence of any state, or in any other manner inconsistent with the Purposes of the United Nations. . . . .

    *Article 39*

    The Security Council shall determine the existence of any threat to the peace, breach of the peace, or act of aggression and shall make recommendations, or decide what measures shall be taken in accordance with Articles 41 and 42, to maintain or restore international peace and security. . . . .

    *Article 51*

    Nothing in the present Charter shall impair the inherent right of individual or collective self-defense if an armed attack occurs against a Member of the United Nations, until the Security Council has taken the measures necessary to maintain international peace and security. Measures taken by Members in the exercise of this right of self-defense shall be immediately reported to the Security Council and shall not in any way affect the authority and responsibility of the Security Council under the present Charter to take at any time such action as it deems necessary in order to maintain or restore international peace and security.

    UN Charter Arts 2(4), 39, 51.

23. Simma, *The Charter of the United Nations* at 674 (cited in note 21).

24. For a general discussion, see Walter Gary Sharp, Sr, *CyberSpace and the Use of Force* (Aegis Research 1999) (This text provides a detailed heuristic analysis of how the international law of conflict management is defined by state practice.).

25. See Intoccia, 19 Case W Res J Intl L at 179, 182-85, 191-92, 200-13 (cited in note 6).

*Chicago Journal of International Law*

because of the concern that it would perpetuate the cycle of violence.[26] A Security Council resolution condemning the U.S. action was vetoed by Great Britain, France, and the United States, but the U.N. General Assembly adopted a resolution condemning the air strikes by a vote of 79 to 28, with 33 abstentions.[27]

In addition to relying upon their inherent right of self-defense, states may seek Security Council authority to use armed force to combat international terrorism. Every act of international terrorism proscribed by Article 2(4) is, per se, a threat to international peace and security within the meaning of Article 39.[28] Accordingly, the Security Council has the coercive authority to authorize states to impose coercive sanctions or to use armed force in response to any act of terrorism that violates Article 2(4).[29] Most importantly, the authority of the Security Council to use force extends beyond violations of Article 2(4). Indeed, the Article 39 threshold extends considerably below the Article 2(4) threshold,[30] giving the Security Council the power to authorize states to use armed force under circumstances where states do not independently have the right to use armed force in self-defense. For example, threats to international peace and security within the meaning of Article 39 even include the failure of a state to surrender terrorists in accordance with an order of the Security Council.[31]

Regardless of which international legal authority a state relies upon to use armed force to defend itself against terrorism, customary international law requires that all uses of force be necessary for either individual or collective self-defense and proportional, and it prohibits the use of force for retaliatory or punitive actions.[32] For example, the requirement of necessity for a state to use armed force in self-defense could clearly be met when a pattern of state-sponsored terrorism is established.[33] In contrast, if a single act of state-sponsored terrorism occurs, and it is evident from the circumstances that it is indeed an isolated act, then the principle of necessity would not justify the use of force in the absence of a continuing threat.[34] For example, in justifying the lawfulness of its April 1986 air strikes against military targets in Libya as an exercise of its right of self-defense, the United States emphasized Libya's policy on exporting terrorism and "compelling evidence of Libyan involvement in other planned attacks."[35]

---

26. Id at 186-89.
27. Id at 189.
28. See Simma, *The Charter of the United Nations* at 119 (cited in note 21).
29. Decisions taken by the Security Council under Article 39 are binding on all Member States. Id at 407-18; see also UN Charter Art 25.
30. Simma, *The Charter of the United Nations* at 119 (cited in note 21).
31. Id at 113, 611-12.
32. See John Norton Moore, *Crisis in the Gulf: Enforcing the Rule of Law* 156-157 (Oceana 1992); Simma, *The Charter of the United Nations* at 677 (cited in note 21).
33. See Intoccia, 19 Case W Res J L at 200-12 (cited in note 6).
34. See id at 200-12.
35. Id at 191.

Similarly, international law requires that a state's use of force be proportional in intensity and magnitude to what is reasonably necessary to promptly secure the permissible objectives of self-defense.[36] The principle of proportionality does not unreasonably limit the use of force that can be used between combatants. Nor does it limit the use of force to destroy a military objective to the strength or firepower of that objective. Proportionality is a limitation on the use of force against a military objective only to the extent that such a use of force may cause unnecessary collateral destruction of civilian property or unnecessary human suffering of civilians.[37] The principle of proportionality is a balancing of the need to attack a military objective with the collateral damage and human suffering that will be caused to civilian property and civilians by the attack.[38] Proportionality categorically imposes *no* limitations on the use of force between combatants in the absence of any potential effect on civilians or civilian property.[39]

States have a number of response options when they are the victim of a terrorist attack by another state. Victim states may publicly denounce the terrorist act; sever diplomatic relations with the terrorist state and expel its diplomats; terminate trade or impose economic sanctions; or, seek civil redress in the International Court of Justice. They may also seek the public denouncement by the United Nations or other regional organizations; request the Security Council to impose mandatory sanctions on the terrorist state; or, request the Security Council to authorize the use of force against the terrorist state. However, even without Security Council authority, a state which has been the victim of a state-sponsored terrorist attack has the inherent right under international law to use necessary and proportional armed force to defend itself.

---

36. See Moore, *Crisis in the Gulf* at 158 (cited in note 32).

37. While civilian property and civilians may not be the *object* of an attack as such, states may use force against civilian property and ·activities that support or sustain an enemy state's war-fighting capability during armed conflict. States may use force during armed conflict, for example, against economic targets such as enemy lines of communication, rail yards, bridges, rolling stock, barges, industrial installations producing war-fighting products, and power generation plants. See US Dept of the Navy, NWP 1-14M, The Commander's Handbook on the Law of Naval Operations paras 8.1.1–8.1.2 (1995) (hereinafter Commander's Handbook). In today's modern society, much of a state's civilian infrastructure is used for military purposes, and is thus subject to lawful attack during armed. See US Department of Defense, Conduct of the Persian Gulf War: Final Report to Congress Pursuant to Title V of the Persian Gulf Conflict Supplemental Authorization and Personnel Benefits Act of 1991, Pub L No 102-25, Appendix O at 613 (Apr 1992) (hereinafter Conduct of the Persian Gulf War: Final Report).

38. It is not unlawful to cause *incidental* injury to civilians, or collateral damage to civilian property, during an attack on a legitimate military objective. The balancing of proportionality does require, however, that such incidental injury or collateral damage not be excessive in light of the advantage anticipated by the attack. See Commander's Handbook para 8.1.2.1 (cited in note 37).

39. Indeed, one of the four strategic concepts of the national military strategy of the United States is to use decisive force to overwhelm an adversary. See Chairman of the Joint Chiefs of Staff, National Military Strategy of the United States of America 3 (1997). Even more notably, in December 1990, U.S. Secretary of Defense Dick Cheney threatened Saddam Hussein that the U.S. response to an Iraqi use of weapons of mass destruction would be "absolutely overwhelming and ... devastating." Conduct of the Persian Gulf War: Final Report, Appendix Q at 641 (cited in note 37).

*Chicago Journal of International Law*

## III. THE USE OF MILITARY FORCE AGAINST NON-STATE ACTORS—DEFINING STATE-SPONSORSHIP

While the international legal regime requires a law enforcement response toward non-state actors, it operates under the core precondition that states will act in good faith and will not covertly sponsor or harbor non-state actors who engage in international terrorism. When a state fails to act in good faith and cooperate with a state that has been the victim of international terrorism, the issue arises as to when its lack of cooperation constitutes state sponsorship. On one extreme, it is clear that a state has sponsored an act of terrorism if it is established that it explicitly ordered the commission of the terrorist act.[40] At the other extreme, the inability of a state that attempted in good faith to locate a terrorist in its territory does not constitute state-sponsorship. In between these two extremes, when states refuse to cooperate in good faith and law enforcement fails, the simple and powerful guidepost is that a state never loses its inherent right to use necessary and proportional armed force in self-defense.[41] For example, state sponsorship could be established if a state aids and abets by encouraging, inducing, inciting, or soliciting a terrorist act against another state; assists in the planning or otherwise facilitates the commission of a terrorist act; or, knowingly receives, harbors, or assists in the escape of a non-state terrorist.

The most recent and perhaps the most instructive precedent that demonstrates how a state's refusal or unwillingness to cooperate in good faith may constitute sponsorship of a terrorist act is Afghanistan and Sudan's failure to cease their cooperation with the known terrorist Osama Bin Laden. On August 7, 1998, twin truck bombs struck the U.S. Embassies in Kenya and Tanzania, killing more than 200 people, including twelve Americans.[42] President Clinton announced that the United States had "convincing information" that Osama Bin Laden was behind the embassy bombings and "compelling evidence" that Bin Laden was planning further attacks on Americans.[43] Bin Laden has been linked to a number of other major international terrorists incidents such the 1995 and 1996 bombings of U.S. military facilities in Saudi Arabia and plots to kill Egyptian President Hosni Mubarak and Pope John Paul II.[44] He also supplied troops to fight U.S. forces in 1993 in Somalia,[45] and had publicly threatened to strike more American targets.[46]

Investigations, bolstered by the confessions of defectors from Bin Laden's terrorist network, determined that he had an extensive terrorist training complex in Afghanistan and ties to a pharmaceutical plant in Sudan determined to produce

---

40. See Simma, *The Charter of the United Nations* at 674 (cited in note 21).
41. See Sharp, *Cyberspace and the Use of Force* at 48 (cited in note 24).
42. Vernon Loeb, *U.S. Wasn't Sure Plant Had Nerve Gas Role*, Wash Post A1 (Aug 21, 1999).
43. Watson and Barry, *Our Target was Terror*, Newsweek at 24 (cited in note 3).
44. See Sam Skolnik, *The Law Behind the Bombs: Experts Debate Legality of U.S. Airstrikes Against Terrorists*, Legal Times 8-9 (Aug 24, 1998).
45. See Watson and Barry, *Our Target was Terror*, Newsweek at 24 (cited in note 3).
46. See Skolnik, *The Law Behind the Bombs*, Legal Times at 8 (cited in note 44).

precursors for nerve agents.[47] Soil samples established the presence at this Sudanese plant of a synthetic chemical that has no use except in making nerve gas.[48] "Highly reliable evidence" also established that Bin Laden poured millions of dollars into Sudan and had reached an agreement with the Sudanese government enabling him to produce chemical weapons in Sudan with government assistance.[49] The United States made repeated efforts to convince the Sudanese government and the Taliban regime of Afghanistan to cease their cooperation with Bin Laden.[50] Afghanistan insisted that Bin Laden had clean hands and that he had no terrorist training camps in Afghanistan.[51] It also stated it could never hand Bin Laden over to the United States.[52] Similarly, Sudan denied any connection with Bin Laden and insisted the pharmaceutical plant produced medicines.[53] In response to the unwillingness of Afghanistan and Sudan to cooperate, President Clinton ordered cruise missile attacks on August 20, 1998 against the training facilities in Afghanistan and the pharmaceutical plant in Sudan.[54] The U.S. Federal Bureau of Investigation has put Bin Laden on its Ten Most Wanted list, and the U.S. Department of State has offered a $five million reward for information leading to his capture.[55] Bin Laden and eight other co-defendants have been indicted by the United States for plotting the bombings of the U.S. Embassies in Kenya and Tanzania.[56] These eight codefendants are in custody in New York and London awaiting trial by the United States.[57] Bin Laden, however, still resides in Afghanistan "as a guest of the fundamentalist Taliban militia."[58]

The United States justified the lawfulness of its August 1998 missile strikes in Afghanistan and Sudan as an exercise of its inherent right of self-defense in response to an attack and a continuing threat of attack.[59] It had been established that Bin Laden was responsible for the attacks on two of its embassies and the murder of 12 Americans, and he publicly threatened future attacks against Americans. Despite the evidence and the urging of the United States, Afghanistan provided Bin Laden a safe haven, and Sudan refused to terminate its support of Bin Laden.

When a state, such as Afghanistan or Sudan, supports terrorism or interferes

---

47.  See Watson and Barry, *Our Target was Terror*, Newsweek (cited in note 3).
48.  See Loeb, *U.S. Wasn't Sure*, Wash Post at A1 (cited in note 42).
49.  See id at A2.
50.  See Frederic L. Kirgis, *Cruise Missile Strikes in Afghanistan and Sudan*, Am Socy Intl L Flash Insight (Aug 1998), available online at <http://www.asil.org/insight.htm> (visited Mar 4, 2000).
51.  See Watson and Barry, *Our Target was Terror*, Newsweek (cited in note 3).
52.  See id at 26.
53.  See id.
54.  See id.
55.  Barbara Slavin, *U.S. Must Deal with a New Facet of Terrorism*, USA Today 7A (Aug 4, 1999).
56.  Bill Nichols, *U.S. Builds Bombing Case as Bin Laden Still at Large*, USA Today 7A (Aug 4, 1999).
57.  Id.
58.  See Daniel Klaidman and Evan Thomas, *Americans on Alert*, Newsweek 10 (Jan 1, 2000).
59.  See Skolnik, *The Law Behind the Bombs*, Legal Times at 9 (cited in note 44).

with the ability of the United States to defend itself through law enforcement channels, then the United States has the right under international law to defend itself with the use of armed force. The Security Council could have authorized coercive measures to include the use of armed force against the terrorist infrastructures of Bin Laden in response to his terrorist acts because they constitute threats to international peace and security.[60] It was very unlikely, however, that the Security Council would have authorized armed force to root out Bin Laden or have taken any other effective action to prevent him from engaging in future terrorist acts.[61] Accordingly, the United States had to rely upon its inherent right of self-defense. The U.S. attack on Bin Laden's terrorist infrastructure within Afghanistan and Sudan was a necessary and proportional exercise of its inherent right of self-defense.

## IV. CONCLUSION

Even horrific acts of international terrorism committed by non-state actors remain a law enforcement issue. Despite what their destructive effects may be, acts of international terrorism committed by non-state actors do not constitute a use of force within the meaning of the law of conflict management. Similarly, the ineffectiveness and practical difficulties of law enforcement arrangements among cooperative states to address the problem of international terrorism do not change a crime to a use of force or the basic nature of the legal issues. In the absence of any state sponsorship of terrorist or criminal activities, a use of force by a state against those non-state actors in the sovereign territory of another state without that state's consent may very likely be an unlawful use of force against that territorial state.

The U.S. bombing of Libya in April 1986 was a stern warning to states who openly sponsor terrorism that they could not attack Americans and American interests abroad with impunity. Accordingly, the issue of state and non-state sponsorship has become very factually complicated by a number of circumstances such as the activities of state-owned commercial enterprises and surrogate actors, as well as the anonymity afforded by clandestine operations and technology. Determining when state-owned commercial enterprises, for example, are acting as commercial enterprises or at the direction of a state is a determination surrounding facts, such as who controls the enterprise, who directed the activity, and the nature of the activity. It is not an issue of law.

Consequently, the legal analysis remains rather straightforward. From a legal

---

60. See Daniel Pickard, *When Does Crime Become a Threat to International Peace and Security?*, 12 Fla J Intl L 1, 14-19 (1998).

61. See Michael J. Glennon, *The New Interventionism: The Search for a Just International Law*, Foreign Aff 2-3 (May-Jun 1999) ("When American embassies were bombed in Kenya and Tanzania last August, world attention focused entirely on the propriety of American air strikes against perpetrators allegedly ensconced in Afghanistan and Sudan; the idea that the United Nations might actually do something to combat such bombings was never even raised, so conditioned had observers become to expect it to do nothing.").

perspective, *all* acts of international terrorism are either non-state sponsored and thus a crime addressed by national and peacetime treaty law, or are state sponsored and thus a use of force governed by the law of conflict management. The complete refusal or unwillingness of a state, for example, to cooperate in the suppression or prevention of an acknowledged non-state-sponsored terrorist activity that originates in its sovereign territory constitutes state-sponsorship of a use of force ipso facto—thereby invoking the law of conflict management which authorizes a use of necessary and proportional force in self-defense against such a state or the non-state actors in that state. A state either cooperates and is a part of the solution to control non-state-sponsored terrorism, or it becomes a part of the problem and a sponsor of terrorism by aiding and abetting or offering a safe harbor.

International law requires that states first consider law enforcement, diplomacy, and other peaceful mechanisms to control international terrorism and resolve threats to international peace and security, but international law does not require timidity in the face of senseless murder and slaughter by non-state actors or states. The United States is far from being impotent in its fight against terrorism—and it must continue to prevent and deter terrorism sponsored by non-state actors and states with the use of necessary and proportional armed force when states fail to cooperate and cause the law enforcement option to fail to protect Americans and American interests abroad.

# [14]

# Pragmatic Counter-terrorism

Jonathan Stevenson

By their sheer scale, the 11 September attacks drew a bright line between the 'new terrorism' practised by al-Qaeda and the 'old terrorism' exemplified by groups like the Palestine Liberation Organisation (PLO), the Provisional Irish Republican Army (IRA), *Euskadi ta Askatasuna* (ETA) and the Liberation Tigers of Tamil Eelam.[1] The distinction itself, however, is nothing new. Since Osama bin Laden surfaced in the 1990s, terrorism experts have noted that his apocalyptic vision of the United States and its allies internationally debilitated by radical Islam is not amenable to political negotiation. Bin Laden does not make demands as such, and only elliptically claims credit for acts of terror, often long after the fact. What drives him to kill is essentially religious hatred. Older groups like the PLO or the IRA are generally constrained by nationalist or irredentist goals – a Palestinian state, a united Ireland – that are negotiable. They present their demands clearly, and generally take direct responsibility for their acts in order to make it clear to their adversaries that the bloodletting will stop when those demands are met. What motivates their violence is the desire to obtain a particular political result. Old terrorists are looking to bargain; new terrorists want only to express their wrath and cripple their enemy.[2]

Before 11 September, the policy implication of this dichotomy could be summarised like this: whereas political approaches to representatives of 'old' terrorist groups could sometimes help tame them, only hard counter-terrorist measures such as law-enforcement and intelligence cooperation could contain the threat of new terrorism. The formula was only selectively applied. But within ten days of the attacks on the World Trade Center and the Pentagon, in his inspiring speech to Congress, President George W. Bush proclaimed: 'our war on terror begins with al-Qaeda, but it does not end there. It will not end until every terrorist group of global reach has been found, stopped and defeated'.[3] An understandable reaction to the worst single terrorist attack in history, his pronouncement galvanised a grieving and traumatised American public. Despite the sweeping cast of the 'Bush doctrine', however, the qualification 'with global reach' gave him the leeway to circumscribe the operative definition of terrorism, and on 25 September Secretary of Defense Donald Rumsfeld confirmed that the elimination of all species of terrorism would be 'setting a threshold that is too high'.[4] Never–theless, many 'old' terrorist groups could be construed as having

**Jonathan Stevenson** is the editor of *Strategic Survey* and a Research Fellow at the IISS.

'global reach'. For instance, the IRA has links with ETA and now apparently with the Revolutionary Armed Forces of Colombia (FARC).

Post-11 September, then, is a terrorist just a terrorist, or a state sponsor just a state sponsor? Plenty of people living in Belfast and London might be viscerally inclined to place Gerry Adams – president of Sinn Fein, the IRA's political arm – and the IRA in the same category as bin Laden and al-Qaeda. Practical considerations militate against any policy that does so. The counter-terrorism effort against al-Qaeda alone will require diverse and sustained military, law-enforcement and intelligence resources that will stretch the capacities of the United States and its allies.[5] On account of shifts in public opinion and new diplomatic imperatives occasioned by the 11 September attacks, the US and its allies enjoy greater leverage over some terrorist groups, and less over others. Further, the diplomatic exigencies of building and maintaining the international coalition required to disable al-Qaeda will, paradoxically, require the United States to court nations like Pakistan and Syria, which have supported terrorism. The upshot is that different policies will fit different terrorist groups and sponsors.

## Terrorism's heightened profile

During the 1990s, old-style terrorist groups atrophied due to the withdrawal of the Cold War's ideological impetus, were compromised when the uncovered records of complicit communist regimes exposed their operations, or were tamed in peace processes. Al-Qaeda was perceived in most European capitals (though not in Washington) as a remote and sporadic threat. The 11 September attacks vaulted terrorism back to international centre stage. Its re-ascendance has had two cross-cutting effects.

On the one hand, it has re-awakened dormant or demoralised terrorist groups and potential recruits to the considerable power of showcasing grievances by lethally attacking unsuspecting civilian targets. Bin Laden himself, of course, is not primarily motivated by grievances pressed by other terrorists or terrorist sponsors. For example, the escalation of the Israeli–Palestinian conflict would seem a natural source of his inspiration, yet the 11 September operation was apparently planned, and other al-Qaeda operations committed, during hopeful phases of the Oslo process.[6] Nevertheless, in videotapes released shortly after the United States and the United Kingdom began their assault against Afghanistan on 7 October, he and his lieutenants cited the Israeli–Palestinian conflict and US enforcement of sanctions and the no-fly zones against Iraq as reasons for the attacks, and threw in implicit Western backing for Hindus against Muslims in Kashmir for good measure. Presumably the idea was to rally popular Islamic support, incite more localised Arab terrorist operations and weaken the US coalition with moderate Muslim states. To an extent, the gambit worked. Popular protest increased throughout the Islamic world, notably in Pakistan, the Palestinian territories and Indonesia.[7]

On the other hand, 11 September also has shown most of the world – non-Muslims and Muslims alike – the cruelty and danger that terrorists pose and mobilised wider public opinion against terrorism of all kinds. Americans, who have been suggestible about whom they deem 'terrorists' as opposed to 'freedom fighters', are now prepared to support substantial curtailments of civil liberties to decrease their vulnerability. Irish-Americans – traditionally a major source of financial, political and occasionally operational support for anti-British groups in Northern Ireland – are abandoning their wink-and-nod tolerance of the IRA and the dissident Real IRA.[8] Even sympathetic US politicians called on the IRA to disarm, and thus break the impasse in the Northern Irish peace process.[9] In the United Kingdom, an October 2001 Gallup poll indicated that 80% of British residents consider the IRA and bin Laden common enemies, and two-thirds believe the early release of IRA prisoners to seal the Good Friday Agreement, which was signed in April 1998 and has not been fully implemented due to the IRA's refusal to disarm, was a mistake.[10] The IRA's disarmament gesture on 23 October, which prompted unionists to return to devolved government and thereby rejuvenated the peace process, should be read in significant part as the IRA's response to political pressure intensified by 11 September.

While this groundswell of disgust for all forms of terrorism is salutary, its significance is tempered by the fact that the small minority of radical Muslims attracted to al-Qaeda and its ideas still potentially number in the millions. Further, the hallmark of terrorists is that they need only a relatively small core of support for sustenance, and may care little about broader public opinion. Indeed, in most cases, if terrorists enjoyed anything approaching a majority or plurality following, they would have no political need for terrorism. Thus, their very unpopularity can fuel their resolve.

## The possibility of terrorist cross-fertilisation

Al-Qaeda is far more dangerous to the United States in particular, and strategic stability in general, than is the IRA, ETA or even Hamas. Yet it would be a grave mistake to assume that they and al-Qaeda are completely different animals. While these other groups have purposefully been more constrained than al-Qaeda in their violence, and their intent is to persuade their targets rather than to destroy them, the two classes of terrorist do share a methodology: to cow public support for legitimate government objectives by instilling fear in the civilian population. The epochal events of 11 September may have hardened the distinctions between new and old terrorist groups. Left unimpeded, however, new terrorists and old terrorists could cross-fertilise.

Al-Qaeda's aims diverge thoroughly and qualitatively from the IRA's and those of most other 'old' terrorist groups. They would not make a ready fit. At the same time, if most terrorists remain fanatically dedicated, they will also forge highly pragmatic and flexible alliances to attain the results they seek. That a politically frustrated ETA, say, would accept attenuated al-Qaeda assistance – for example, weapons, training or financial assistance rather than actual oversight – should not be ruled out. In this vein, it is sobering to recall the IRA's long and intimate relationship with Libya and Colonel Muammar Gaddafi, which began in 1973. In 1986–87, after the US bombed targets in Libya in retaliation for a Libyan-sponsored terrorist attack killing

*38* **Jonathan Stevenson**

American soldiers at a nightclub in Germany, the IRA eagerly accepted large arms shipments from Libya that now constitute the bulk of the IRA's 100-tonne arsenal. There were also reports that IRA men were being trained in Libya.[11] Tripoli was then a major sponsor of anti-American transnational terrorism, and later engineered the mass slaughter of Americans and others on Pan Am Flight 103 in December 1988.[12] And some groups like Hamas, while geographically confined in their concerns and responsive to political movement, are more natural al-Qaeda partners.[13]

From al-Qaeda's perspective, existing secure alliances with groups such as Egyptian Islamic Jihad and alumni of Algeria's Armed Islamic Group suggest that the need for new non-Muslim partners is not acute. Nevertheless, backing outfits as divergent as Hamas and the IRA could be attractive as a means of diverting resources from the heightened international law-enforcement and intelligence effort to thwart al-Qaeda, as well as to help with the work of disrupting and economically impairing Western societies. Alternatively, with a mass-casualty keynote now emphatically struck and al-Qaeda's operations compromised by the heightened counter-terrorist campaign, al-Qaeda could choose to bide its time until the next major attack with a protracted low-technology terrorist campaign on American soil. This would serve to distract law-enforcement efforts from planned mass-casualty attacks that serve bin Laden's eschatological vision and to corrode US public support for those efforts.[14] For these respective purposes, groups like Hamas, the IRA, ETA and the Tamil Tigers would make excellent accessories or tutors, and there are quite plausible circumstances in which some of them could be inclined to contract out.[15]

## Applying distinctions

Americans have sometimes accused Europeans of being 'soft on terrorism'. After 11 September, it became clear that this accusation was true with respect to 'new' terrorism. There are some understandable reasons. European countries have faced mainly ethno-nationalist and left-wing terrorism over the past 30 years. Thus, countries such as the United Kingdom and Spain have had to concentrate anti-terrorist efforts on the more traditional type of terrorist threat, and over the past decade, Europe has perceived the threat from al-Qaeda and related groups as modest, in contrast to the US assessment.[16] As a result, al-Qaeda appears to have found European countries more useful as recruitment and planning points than as direct targets. Existing statutory and operational counter-terrorism resources set up to deal with old terrorist threats do give European governments a head start on helping to establish an international coalition against terrorism and a transnational law-enforcement and intelligence network to contend with al-Qaeda. And more effective transnational law-enforcement and intelligence in response to the 11 September attacks will diminish the operational capabilities of all terrorist groups.[17] To liberate those resources for primary application to al-Qaeda, however, political engagement remains a useful tool of counter-terrorism for controlling the old-style groups. Governments ought to stay politically engaged with groups that are capable of being tamed.

Contrary to some of the soaring post-traumatic rhetoric, then, 11 September has in fact increased the need to segregate groups that respond to political suasion from those that do not. It will be far easier for, say, Britain – which, along with Germany, seems to be a key locale for bin Laden's recruiting and planning – to focus its attention on al-Qaeda if the IRA is neutralised by way of a political process. Yet because diplomatic resources are also limited, it is not enough to distinguish terrorist groups merely in terms of old and new, political or expressive, apocalyptic or constrained. Old terrorist groups must be further differentiated according to their willingness – as a function of negotiation prospects, financial backing and diplomatic support – to participate in serious political dialogue. Those that are willing will be less likely to impede the global effort against international terrorism (whether by diverting resources through ongoing terrorist operations or establishing some form of synergy with al-Qaeda), provided interested outside powers exploit or create opportunities to bring them to the negotiating table.[18]

A number of questions bear on the likelihood of a terrorist group's linking-up with al-Qaeda. First, are the group's grievances related to Islam? Second, is the prospect of a political solution to its grievances remote? Third, are the group's political stakes high – in other words, is it angling for something as basic and radical as a change in sovereignty or independence, and is there a prevailing sense that time for achieving success is running out and a resulting attitude of desperation? Fourth, are its indigenous sources of political, financial or other support scarce? Fifth, are the group's external sources of support scarce? Sixth, does the old terrorist group operate in a country or region in which an active al-Qaeda presence has been uncovered? Affirmative answers would indicate a degree of susceptibility on the part of a given terrorist group to al-Qaeda influence and co-optation.

Abu Sayyaf, in the Philippines, would qualify on most of the criteria, and in fact substantial links between the group and al-Qaeda have been established.[19] The radical Muslim makeup of Islamic Jihad, its military weakness against a US-backed Israel and its political marginalisation within the Palestinian territories may make it ripe for al-Qaeda assistance. Hamas, in contrast, has considerable political support among Palestinians and from outside sponsors, and appears to be more responsive to political developments than the other Palestinian groups, though it does share some ideological roots with al-Qaeda.[20] Hizbullah is supported by Iran, which is hostile to bin Laden, and by Syria, and has recently enjoyed considerable success as a legitimate political party in Lebanon. Hizbullah therefore might not be apt to tilt al-Qaeda's way.[21] Given the fierce mutual hostility between Hindus and Muslims, the Tamil Tigers are broadly unsusceptible to al-Qaeda influence.[22] Chechen rebels are Muslim and have established al-Qaeda links, but many Chechens are uncomfortable with the Islamic law that the rebels have imposed. In the hope that this discomfort could spell political flexibility, the Russian government opened negotiations without preconditions in November 2001.[23]

Among European terrorist groups, ETA might be moderately susceptible. Although it has nothing to do with Islam, ETA has dismal political prospects and an increasingly desperate tone, its indigenous and external sources of support have been squeezed, and at least one al-Qaeda cell is known to have operated in Spain. Conversely, the National Liberation Army (NLA) in Macedonia, while predominantly Muslim in composition, does not have a fundamentalist bent, has relatively good political prospects, has partially disarmed and enjoys strong outside support from diaspora in Europe and the United States. But since the fall of Milosevic, it has become less likely that the Kosovo Liberation Army (KLA), which has close ties to the NLA, would attain its goal of independence in the near term. There is also evidence of al-Qaeda's interest in the Balkans as a lucrative drug-trafficking route, fertile ground for spreading the puritanical Wahhabi brand of Islam that bin Laden practises, and a target of opportunity on account of deployed American forces. The KLA therefore merits close attention.[24] The IRA constitutes only a low-level threat. The eleventh of September has diminished support among Irish diaspora in the United States, and three Libyans and one Algerian suspected of having ties to al-Qaeda were arrested (but soon released) in Dublin in October. But the chances that the Good Friday Agreement will survive tilts towards the extremes of both pro-British unionism and pro-Irish nationalism have improved since the IRA rendered unusable weapons stored in one or two dumps in October 2001. The group has a large existing arsenal and proven means of generating funds within Ireland.[25]

Burgeoning world opinion against terrorism since 11 September has rendered more credible threats by governments to old terrorist groups that further terrorist activity will only guarantee their political failure. Consequently, these governments, on balance, enjoy greater political leverage over old terrorist groups. Peace processes and other, less intensive political instruments, such as the State Department's list of foreign terrorist organisations, are appropriate vehicles for applying this leverage.[26] Prior to the 11 September attacks, US diplomatic support appeared important to the IRA's political strategy for extracting concessions from unionists and the British government, but also seemed to embolden the IRA to commit or threaten violence when politics moved too slowly to suit it. In attacking Canary Wharf in 1996, the IRA arguably bombed its way back to the conference table. America's new hypersensitivity to terrorism means that the IRA cannot expect to receive any appreciable support from the United States if it uses terrorism or threats of violence to advance its political agenda. Indeed, it is conceivable that had the Provisional IRA continued to refuse to disarm, the State Department might have restored the group to its official list of terrorist organisations, triggering the application of statutes authorising financial controls and deportation. Recognition of these realities – and their confirmation to Sinn Fein officials by the Bush administration – is probably what moved the IRA to make its recent disarmament gesture.[27]

Broader intolerance of terrorism may also work in favour of the Aznar government's firm stance against ETA, renewed efforts by the Sri Lankan government to bring the Tamil Tigers to the negotiating table and American pressure on the Palestinian Authority to assert control over Hamas, Islamic Jihad and the PFLP to facilitate a new peace process.

## Coalition considerations

Targeting state sponsors of terrorism, as opposed to the terrorist groups themselves, poses a different set of policy challenges. The military campaign to end state support for al-Qaeda began in October 2001 against the Taliban – the fundamentalist Muslim group that controlled most of Afghanistan, harboured bin Laden and other al-Qaeda commanders, and permitted al-Qaeda training camps to operate in Afghanistan. In prosecuting the wider 'war' on terrorism, Deputy Secretary of Defense Paul Wolfowitz has suggested that the United States should hit Iraq as well as Afghanistan. Columnist Charles Krauthammer has an even more ambitious agenda:

> After Afghanistan, we turn to Damascus. What then? Stage three is Iraq and Iran
> ... All we do know is that history, cunning and cruel, will demand that if this
> president wants victory in the war he has declared, he will have to achieve it on
> the very spot where his own father, 10 years ago, let victory slip away.'[28]

Yet there are countervailing diplomatic imperatives for waging a campaign against a global terrorist network that claims to draw legitimacy from religious principles. Chief among them is the need to rally Muslim government leaders against al-Qaeda terrorists. Most American officials – some of them considered 'unilateralist' – recognised on 11 September that accomplishing this calls for an international coalition that would not be feasible were the United States to extend its military effort to Iraq and other state sponsors of terrorism, at least not in the absence of incontrovertible evidence of their complicity in the 11 September attacks or in the spread of anthrax. By mid-November, expectations of a lengthy follow-on engagement in Afghanistan strengthened the case for holding off on Iraq.

In their own calculations, Muslim states derive moral weight against the United States by virtue of not only US action against Iraq but also ongoing Israeli aggression in the Palestinian territories. Diplomatic and moral pressure – for example, President Bush's statement on 20 September that the nations of the world must take a decisive stand on terrorism, 'either you are with us or you are with the terrorists' – is insufficient for winning such states as coalition partners. Rhetorical condemnation of the 11 September attacks and operational neutrality would be enough to indemnify most countries against US economic or diplomatic retaliation. After registering their obligatory disgust with the World Trade Center and Pentagon strikes, Kuwait has not been penalised for its subsequent reticence, nor Saudi Arabia for its refusal to allow the United States to sortie from bases there into Afghanistan. So Washington has found it necessary to extend affirmative rewards to fence-sitting Muslim countries in exchange for their active participation in the US-led global campaign.

So far, the most prominent such 'deal with the devil' has been Washington's enlistment of Pakistan into the coalition, despite the conclusion of a congressionally commissioned study in June 2000 that it was 'not cooperating fully on counter-terrorism'.[29] Pakistan was the only official state sponsor of the Taliban until it backed away after 11 September. Pakistan also backs Islamic terrorist groups in Kashmir, where one such outfit, the Pakistan-

42 **Jonathan Stevenson**

based Jaish-e-Muhammed group, killed 38 people with a car-bomb attack on the state legislative assembly building in Srinagar on 1 October.[30] The United States had to form a partnership with Islamabad in order to establish the operational requirements for moving militarily against Afghanistan and the political conditions for developing a regionally acceptable replacement for the Taliban. The principal carrot dangled in front of Islamabad was the lifting of American bilateral sanctions imposed on Pakistan after its nuclear test in May 1998. Sanctions were lifted on 23 September, after Pakistan disowned the Taliban and in plain anticipation of Pakistan's logistical and political cooperation.

In addition to coalition partners required for military operations, other partners will be needed to improve transnational intelligence and law-enforcement and to facilitate diplomacy. The United States has also stepped out of character with respect to Iran, Syria, Libya and Sudan – perennial entries on the State Department's list of state sponsors of terrorism. Iran's Shi'ite Muslims have a history of enmity with Wahhabi Sunnis like bin Laden and Deobandi Sunnis that make up the Taliban, and Iran shares a 900-km (560-mile) border with Afghanistan. Thus, Washington has informally sought Iran's intelligence cooperation and accelerated its review of the 'dual containment' policy, even though Iran is believed to have been involved in the 1996 bombing of the Khobar Towers in which 19 American airmen were killed.[31] The United States abstained from blocking Syria's membership on the United Nations Security Council in the hope of winning similar cooperation from Damascus, and acquiesced in the UN's lifting of sanctions against Sudan to show its appreciation for Sudan's arrest and expulsion of terrorist suspects. Syria and Iran both support Hizbullah and Hamas, Sudan has backed anti-American Islamic groups (including al-Qaeda), and Libya, while showing signs of relenting over the past several years, has a long history of sponsoring anti-American and anti-British terrorism. But by late October, the CIA's 'secret' delegation to Damascus and cautious overtures to Sudan and Libya were showing signs of bearing fruit in terms of intelligence cooperation.[32]

Such compromises may hardly reflect an 'ethical foreign policy'. Yet even if such a thing were possible this wouldn't be the time for it.[33] The threat of terrorism that al-Qaeda poses to the United States and its allies is an existential one that calls for short-term self-defence and a long-term policy of containment. While this should not politically skew alliances and special relationships to the extent that the Cold War did, the degree to which another country is willing to help prosecute the war on terrorism will be the most important single determinant of US relations with that country. Conversely, to ensure that its counter-terrorism coalition is inclusive enough to stave off something approaching a 'clash of civilisations', Washington will have to tolerate – for a time, anyway – some state conduct that may be adverse to subordinate US interests. Some friends in the battle against terrorism, for instance, may hinder the war on drugs (Tajikistan) and the campaign against human-rights abuses (Uzbekistan).[34]

Nevertheless, if the United States and its allies provide too many sweeteners for cooperation, they could risk losing a principled grip on regional diplomacy that may need to be tightened once the current security crisis has receded. The question remains how many concessions constitute too many. Unfortunately, the cost-benefit ratio may be possible to know only in hindsight. For example, given Iran's religious differences with bin Laden's Wahhabism and its geopolitical difficulties with the Taliban, it may have been gratuitous for the Justice and State Departments to ask a federal judge to dismiss a civil suit brought against Iran by the 52 Americans held hostage for 444 days beginning in 1979. Washington may also have gilded the lily in declining to freeze the assets of Iran-supported Hizbullah and Hamas.

On the other hand, absent these moves, the United States might have been unable to secure a pledge from Tehran to rescue any American soldiers in distress in Iranian territory.[35] Such reassurances could be useful in maintaining domestic public support for ground operations against the Taliban and other terrorist collaborators. Further, turning a temporary blind eye to a certain level of support for terrorist groups – particularly Islamic ones – with circumscribed regional grievances may make them less rather than more susceptible to the depredations of al-Qaeda. And should Iraq turn out to be complicit in the 11 September atrocities or other attacks, the US would likely feel compelled to respond with major leadership strikes on Baghdad at some stage. In the absence of substantial inducements to Arab states, it is extremely unlikely that Washington could carry out such strikes and still maintain a broad counter-terrorism front that included even a delicate sufficiency of Muslim countries.

Distasteful compromises are far from irreversible. Tools such as US State Department official lists of terrorist organisations and terrorist sponsors, the sanctions that these lists activate, and political conditionality on economic aid can be re-imposed as well as de-activated. The state-sponsor listing system could also be revamped to reflect differing degrees of support for terrorism or non-cooperation in counter-terrorism, which would afford Washington greater precision in punishing undesirable state conduct and rewarding state reform.[36] The events of 11 September argue for foreign policies that employ positive incentives selectively and conditionally, and subject to credible penalties, with respect to terrorist sponsors. More broadly, certain forms of more open-ended, or 'unconditional', engagement may prove useful with respect to authoritarian regimes (particularly 'friendly tyrants' like the governments of Egypt and Saudi Arabia) that require political reform if they are to become stable coalition partners or allies and less fertile recruiting grounds for terrorists.[37]

## Coalition-building and peace processes

Warmer relations generated by *ex ante* American confidence-building – the euphemistic term for placating dubious actors – could pay important diplomatic and operational dividends. In addition to Pakistan's political and operational cooperation in *Operation Enduring Freedom*, examples might include enlisting Iran's cooperation as part of a contact group overseeing Afghanistan's political transition, or securing intelligence-sharing from Syria. Some blowback is inevitable. Improving US relations with state sponsors of terrorism could

44 **Jonathan Stevenson**

mean both reduced support for their terrorist clients and the hardening of their adversaries' positions. In turn, the terrorist groups could look increasingly to al-Qaeda for backing as prospects for political progress dwindled. For instance, courting Syria and Iran could both make Hamas anxious about its outside backing and drive Israel further from the negotiating table. In other cases, the geopolitical repercussions could be substantial. The American tilt towards Pakistan could not only make India less inclined to negotiate on Kashmir with Pakistan, but also impel New Delhi to seek alternatives to a strategic alignment with the United States.[38]

To minimise the perverse effects of coalition diplomacy, the United States will need to offset its tolerance for the dubious behaviour of expedient partners (like Iran and Pakistan) with intense engagement of ambivalent allies (like Israel and India). This task will involve pushing such reluctant parties hard for establishing or energising peace negotiations to resolve terrorist conflicts and making the case that entering into them is in that party's interest. Heavy diplomatic maintenance will be required. For example, convincing New Delhi that re-engagement with Islamabad on Kashmir makes sense for India in the post-11 September context would entail sustained dialogue and perhaps some material inducements to reassure Indians that US diplomacy on the subcontinent will remain balanced, then a resolute peace initiative on Kashmir.[39] Where the United States is diplomatically hindered – as it is *vis-à-vis* a number of Arab states due to its support for Israel and its hostile relationship to Iraq – Washington could also profitably enlist the aid of coalition partners in advancing diplomatic objectives to counter-terrorist effect.[40]

The eleventh of September revealed the apocalyptic intent, global scope, organisational sophistication and operational capabilities that make al-Qaeda an unprecedented terrorist threat, and necessitated an equally unprecedented global counter-terrorism agenda. Given the direness of al-Qaeda's threat, the United States and its allies must nurture finite counter-terrorist resources frugally. Constructive but cautious engagement with lesser evils – be they terrorist groups or their suspected state sponsors – is a price worth paying for the capacity to confront the greater evil without quarter.

## Notes

1 The 11 September attacks have intensified the ongoing debate on what constitutes 'terrorism'. A serviceable definition is 'the use of violence, often against people not directly involved in a conflict, by groups operating clandestinely, which generally claim to have high political or religious purposes, and believe that creating a climate of terror will assist attainment of their objectives'. IISS, 'Defining Terrorism', *Strategic Comments*, vol. 7, issue 9, November 2001. While reasonable minds may differ on particular applications, there is a substantial consensus that *method* (as opposed to, say, historical background, goals or context) is the most important criterion. If, in undertaking a given operation for a political purpose, an armed group specifically intends to place civilian non-combatants in harm's way, it's safe to say that the group is committing a terrorist act. See Timothy Garton Ash, 'Is There a Good Terrorist?', *New York Review of Books*, 29 November 2001.

2 See especially Steven Simon and Daniel Benjamin, 'America and the New Terrorism', *Survival*, vol. 42, no. 1, Spring 2000, pp. 59–75. Certain chronologically old terrorist groups resemble al-Qaeda in the limited sense that they appear to lack political goals that are subject to negotiation. The one that comes immediately to mind is the left-wing Revolutionary Group 17 November, which seeks a Greek polity that is free of American and European involvement and willing to confront Turkey – hardly a negotiable outcome. See Jonathan Stevenson, 'Terrorism: New Meets Old', *Survival*, vol. 43, no. 2, Summer 2001, pp. 153-59 (review essay). In contrast to ethno-nationalist groups like the PLO and the IRA, the Italian and German left-wing terrorist groups prominent

in the Seventies and Eighties, now largely rolled up, also lacked a coherent political agenda. See Bruce Hoffman, *Inside Terrorism* (New York: Columbia University Press, 1998), pp. 172–76.

3 'President Bush's Address on Terrorism Before a Joint Meeting of Congress', *New York Times*, 21 September 2001, p. A4.

4 See Neil King Jr. and Jim VandeHei, 'Allies Hope Antiterror Effort Won't Ignore Local Fights', *Wall Street Journal*, 26 September 2001, p. A10.

5 On the severe resource constraints facing US domestic law-enforcement alone, see Kevin Sack, 'Focus on Terror Creates Burden for Police', *New York Times*, October 28, 2001, p. A1; Joby Warrick et al., 'FBI Agents Ill-Equipped to Predict Terror Acts', *Washington Post*, 24 September 2001, p. A1.

6 See Daniel Benjamin and Steven Simon, 'Myths of American Misdeeds', *Financial Times*, 2 October 2001, p. 14.

7 See 'The Propaganda Front', *Jerusalem Post*, 10 October 2001, p. 8.

8 See, e.g., 'Made in Manhattan', *Economist*, 20 October 2001, p. 34.

9 See, for example, Toby Harnden, 'Adams in Danger of Losing US Allies', *Daily Telegraph*, 28 September 2001, p. 12. For a forthright challenge to Boston Irish to wake up to the IRA's reprehensible *modus operandi*, see Joan Vennochi, 'Time to Question the IRA's Tactics', *Boston Globe*, 11 October 2001, p. A15.

10 See, e.g., Anthony King, 'Treat the IRA Like bin Laden', *Daily Telegraph*, 4 October 2001, p. 1.

11 E.g., W.D. Flackes and Sydney Elliott, *Northern Ireland: A Political Directory, 1968–1993* (Belfast, Northern Ireland: Blackstaff Press, 1994), p. 210.

12 Admittedly, the IRA would be reluctant to alienate Irish-American supporters (who have been

### 46 Jonathan Stevenson

profoundly affected by the horrific losses suffered by New York's heavily Irish-American fire and police contingents) by embracing al-Qaeda's aid, just as it balked at accepting Soviet support during the Cold War. Both the IRA and ETA publicly sought to distance themselves from al-Qaeda after 11 September. See, e.g., Oliver Wright, 'IRA and ETA Condemn US Attacks', *The Times*, 1 October 2001, p. 14.

[13] Similarly, the networked character of al-Qaeda has drawn in insurgencies not normally considered terrorist groups and states not ordinarily regarded as terrorist sponsors. For example, Sierra Leone's Revolutionary United Front, with help from Liberia and possibly Senegal, appears to be engaged in illicit diamond transactions with al-Qaeda. Clearly such groups and states now merit greater scrutiny as possible al-Qaeda partners. See Douglas Farah, 'Al Qaeda Cash Tied to Diamond Trade', *Washington Post*, 2 November 2001, p. A1.

[14] The transmission of anthrax bacteria through the US mail that began in September 2001 demonstrates how substantially the public's fear of frequent small-scale terrorist operations can disrupt daily life.

[15] The breadth of the network of terrorist training camps that developed in flourished in the 1990s gives some indication of the general potential of groups with widely differing causes and areas of primary activity to establish operational bonds. See Thomas Hunter, 'Bomb School', *Jane's Intelligence Review*, March 1997, p. 134.

[16] See Bruce Hoffman, 'Is Europe Soft on Terrorism?', *Foreign Policy*, no. 115, Summer 1999, pp. 62–76. Among European countries, Greece has been singularly uncooperative with the United States on counter-terrorism.

On the Greek public's apparent sympathy with al-Qaeda post-11 September, see Taras Michas, 'Is Greece a Western Nation?', *Wall Street Journal Europe*, 23 October 2001, p. 8.

[17] By the same token, since more effective law enforcement in Europe will make European countries less suitable for recruitment and planning, they could become more attractive direct al-Qaeda targets.

[18] Impasses even in relatively successful peace processes can still produce backsliding. For example, the August 2001 arrests of three Provisional IRA men in Colombia for assisting the FARC suggest that at least some IRA members have lost faith in the peace process and are inclined to re-insert themselves into an international terrorist family, which they did to a degree during the Cold War.

[19] See, e.g., Victorino Matus, 'Al Qaeda's Filipino Branch Office', *Weekly Standard*, 26 November 2001.

[20] See generally Khaled Hroub, *Hamas: Political Thought and Practice* (Washington DC: Institute for Palestine Studies, 2000), pp. 145–208.

[21] Syria explicitly and Iran implicitly discouraged Hizbullah from undertaking operations against Israel after 11 September, but subsequent hard-line statements from Iran's religious leadership have given Hizbullah a pretext for providing Palestinian groups with military advice and financial, arms and logistical support. No significant links between Hizbullah and al-Qaeda have emerged. See Daniel Sobelman, 'Hizbullah Lends its Services to the Palestinian Intifada', *Jane's Intelligence Review*, November 2001, pp. 12–14.

[22] Nevertheless, the fact that the Tamil Tigers have contemplated airborne suicide attacks and to have purchased light aircraft and explosives to further that objective, and staged a suicide attack on a government-chartered oil

tanker reminiscent of the al-Qaeda-engineered attack on the *USS Cole* in Yemen in October 2000, suggests that another probative criterion could be terrorist methodology. See Rohan Gunaratna, 'Terror from the Sky', *Jane's Intelligence Review*, October 2001, p. 8.

23  Daniel Williams, 'Russia Opens Face-to-Face Negotiations with Chechnya', *Washington Post*, 19 November 2001, p. A18.

24  See Marcia Christoff Kurop, 'Al Qaeda's Balkan Links', *Wall Street Journal Europe*, 1 November 2001, p. 8.

25  While the IRA's move jump-started a nearly dead peace process, it neither guaranteed political stability to Northern Ireland nor foreclosed the possibility of future IRA terrorism. Unionists expect the first gesture to be merely the beginning of a process of disarmament, while the IRA almost certainly regards it as something that will not be repeated until Ireland is virtually united or the British army is withdrawn wholesale from Northern Ireland. Unionists retain the power to withdraw from the executive and collapse the devolved assembly, and may do so when further decommissioning of weapons is not forthcoming. Conversely, the IRA has not forsworn the use of violence in the future, and terrorism presumably remains its fallback position should non-violent politics prove inadequate for its purposes. Finally, the IRA's disarmament gesture, token though it was, symbolised surrender to many hard-line Irish republicans and is likely to produce some defections from the Provisional IRA to the Real IRA, which opposes the peace process, if political crisis (over decommissioning or policing) again threatens the devolved government. But Sinn Fein and the Provisional IRA's ambitious all-Ireland political agenda has blunted Real IRA

accusations that the republican movement is merely settling for a partitionist solution, and the statesmanlike character of the decommissioning gesture has elevated the political stature of Irish republicanism. Thus, the Real IRA's incentive to heighten terrorist activity is now relatively low. On balance, then, the late October developments in the Northern Ireland peace process were highly positive from the standpoint of nurturing resources for the global counter-terrorism campaign.

26  See especially Paul R. Pillar, *Terrorism and U.S. Foreign Policy* (Washington DC: Brookings Institution Press, 2001), pp. 140–56. See also Jonathan Stevenson, 'Northern Ireland: Treating Terrorists as Statesmen', *Foreign Policy*, no. 105, Winter 1996–97, pp. 125–40.

27  See, e.g., Toby Harnden, "IRA Acted After Bush Warning on Terrorism," *Daily Telegraph*, October 25, 2001, p. 9.

28  Charles Krauthammer, 'The War: A Roadmap', *Washington Post*, 28 September 2001, p. A39.

29  See U.S. Department of State, Daily Press Briefing, 5 June 2000, www.state.gov/www/global/terrorism/000605_reeker_terrorism.html

30  See Jim Hoagland, 'An Ally's Terrorism', *Washington Post*, 3 October 2001, p. A31. The need to gain Russia's acceptance of American deployments in Central Asia to defeat the Taliban also required the US to mute criticism of Moscow's use of force against Chechen rebels, which has been widely criticised as excessive.

31  Alan Sipress and Steven Mufson, 'U.S. Explores Recruiting Iran into New Coalition', *Washington Post*, 25 September 2001, p. A1.

32  James Risen and Tim Weiner, 'C.I.A. Is Said to Have Sought Help from Damascus', *New York Times*, October 30, 2001, p. A3.

[33] On the unsustainability of an ethical foreign policy, see Robin Harris, 'Blair's "Ethical" Policy', *The National Interest*, no. 63, Spring 2001, pp. 25–36.

[34] See Alan Cullison and James M. Dorsey, 'Washington Faces Dilemma in Central Asia Heroin Trade', *Wall Street Journal Europe*, 3 October 2001, p. 3; C.J. Chivers, 'Alliance With U.S. Spotlights Uzbek Rights Abuses' *New York Times*, October 30, 2001, p. A1.

[35] See Elaine Sciolino and Neil A. Lewis, 'Iran Dances a "Ballet" with U.S.', *New York Times*, 15 October 2001, p. B1.

[36] See Pillar, *Terrorism and U.S. Foreign Policy*, pp. 178–86. The flexible use of the State Department list could be particularly useful in curbing counter-productive official conduct or policies in countries that are putative allies, such as Greece.

[37] Richard Haass and Meghan O'Sullivan distinguish 'unconditional' from 'conditional' engagement strategies, noting that the former do not require reciprocity while the latter broadly do require it and are therefore more contractual in nature. But they emphasise that conditional engagement need not be a slavishly tit-for-tat affair, and use the term to signify 'strategies of reciprocity with focused, policy objectives in mind'. Thus, they cite the Agreed Framework reached with North Korea in 1994 – a comprehensive arrangement whereby North Korea is to end its nuclear weapons programme in exchange for economic rewards – as a good example of conditional engagement. Richard N. Haass and Meghan L. O'Sullivan, 'Introduction', in Haass and O'Sullivan (eds.), *Honey and Vinegar: Incentives, Sanctions and Foreign Policy* (Washington DC: Brookings Institution Press, 2000), pp. 4–5. On applying the conditional engagement approach to Pakistan in particular, see Gerald F. Seib, 'Pakistan, America and the Meaning of Friendship', *Wall Street Journal*, October 31, 2001, p. A26.

[38] See IISS, 'India and the War on Terrorism', *Strategic Comments*, vol. 7, issue 9, November 2001.

[39] The case to be made is that New Delhi's re-engagement with Islamabad on Kashmir, with the US acting as mediator, would lower immediate tensions near the Line of Control, open up the possibility of a sustainable settlement and provide President Musharraf with political cover needed to mollify conservative Islamic elements in Pakistan opposed to Pakistan's cooperation in the counter-terrorist effort. Such a move would help manage a radical Islamic threat that is inimical to India, potentially erode a rich recruiting ground for al-Qaeda and make a valuable diplomatic contribution to the counter-terrorism campaign. The difficulties inherent in post-11 September US diplomacy on the subcontinent were illustrated by Secretary of State Powell's visit to India in October 2001. See Jesse Pesta, 'Powell Offers Words of Reassurance to New Delhi', *Wall Street Journal*, 18 October 2001, p. 1; Patrick E. Tyler and Celia W. Dugger, 'Powell's Message: America's Courting of Pakistan Will Not Come at India's Expense', *New York Times*, 18 October 2001, p. B3.

[40] For an example of how concerted European Union involvement in the Middle East could eventually be constructive in reining in Hizbullah, see Steven N. Simon and Jonathan Stevenson, 'Declawing the "Party of God"', *World Policy Journal*, vol. XVIII, no. 2, Summer 2001, pp. 31–42.

# [15]

# American Grand Strategy in the Age of Terror

## G. John Ikenberry

The surprise attacks on the World Trade Center and the Pentagon have been called this generation's Pearl Harbor, exposing America's vulnerabilities to the outside world and triggering a fundamental reorientation of foreign policy. President George W. Bush's speech to Congress on 20 September has likewise been seen by some as the most important statement of American grand strategy since President Harry Truman's Greece and Turkey speech of 12 March 1947, when the United States declared its determination to fight communism world-wide. Indeed, to some, 11 September marks the end of the post-Cold War era. The 1990s was a decade of peace and prosperity during which the 'new economy', budget surpluses and momentary geopolitical stability bred a sort of naïve liberal optimism about the future. But in reality, according to this view, these years were merely an historical interlude between eras of struggle. After a decade of drift, the United States has finally rediscovered its grand strategic purpose.[1]

This evocative image of historical transition in American foreign policy and world order is misleading. The events of 11 September and the Bush administration's declaration of war on terrorism will have an enduring impact on world politics, but primarily in reinforcing the existing Western-centred international order and providing new sinews of cohesion among the great powers, including Russia and China. The most profound diplomatic achievement of the 1990s was the preservation of relatively stable and cooperative relations among the major states. Cold War bipolarity turned into American unipolarity without great geopolitical upheaval. The Bush administration's coalition strategy of fighting terrorism relies on and – if Washington plays its cards well – promises to strengthen this structure of cooperative relations. Europe, Japan and the United States form the core of this order. If Russia becomes more tightly connected to the West, there will be a 'critical mass' among the great powers committed to international order organised around alliance partnership and cooperative security. If China follows its strategic interests that favour continued integration into the

**G. John Ikenberry** is Peter F. Krogh Professor of Geopolitics and Global Justice at Georgetown University. He is the author, most recently, of *After Victory: Institutions, Strategic Restraint and the Rebuilding of Order after Major Wars* (Princeton, NJ: Princeton University Press, 2001).

international system, and the United States remains committed to an inclusive global strategy of anti-terrorism, it is possible that engagement and accommodation – rather than balance of power and security rivalry – will continue to define great-power relations well into the future.

The most immediate consequence of the recent terrorist events could be within the Bush administration itself, pushing it back toward a more centrist foreign policy. Divergent philosophies of international order and American leadership coexist uneasily within the administration. A pragmatic orientation – that stresses alliances, multilateral cooperation and a commitment to building order around practical and mutually beneficial rules and institutions – competes with a more unilateral orientation that stresses military preponderance, selective engagement and national autonomy. In its first six months in office, the Bush administration signalled a move towards a more hard-line unilateralist position. It rejected a series of international treaties and agreements, championed missile defence and stated its desire to abrogate the ABM Treaty. However, the administration's new ambition to lead a global coalition against terrorism makes unilateralism untenable. Much as leadership of the free-world coalition during the Cold War forced the United States reluctantly to make policy compromises and commitments, so too will its leadership of an anti-terrorist coalition.

The rise of a unipolar American order after the Cold War has not triggered a global backlash, but it has unsettled relationships world-wide. Europeans worry about the steadiness of American leadership. Other governments and peoples resent the extent and intrusiveness of American power, markets and culture. Some intellectuals in the West even suggest that an arrogant America brought the terrorism of 11 September on itself.[2] Aside from diffuse resentments, the practical reality for many states is that they need the United States more than it needs them – or so it would seem. In the early months of the Bush administration, the political consequences of a unipolar superpower seemed all too obvious. It could walk away from treaties and agreements with other countries – on global warming, arms control, trade, business regulation and so forth – and suffer fewer consequences than its partners. But to conduct a campaign against terrorism successfully, the United States now needs the rest of the world. This is a potential boon to cooperation across the board.

The core of today's international order – what might be called the 'American system' – is built on two grand bargains that the United States made with other countries around the world. One is a 'realist' bargain that grew out of the Cold War. The United States provides its European and Asian partners with security protection and access to American markets, technology and supplies within an open world economy. In return, these countries agree to be stable partners who provide diplomatic, economic and logistical support for the United States as it leads the wider American-centred post-war order. The other is a 'liberal' bargain that addresses the uncertainties of American power. Asian and European states agree to accept American leadership and operate within an agreed-upon political-economic system. In return, the United States opens itself up and binds itself to its partners, in effect, building an institutionalised coalition of partners and reinforces the stability of these long-term relations by making itself more 'user friendly' – that is, by playing by the rules and creating ongoing political processes with these other states that facilitate consultation and joint decision-making. The United States makes its power safe for the world and in return the world agrees to live within the American system. These bargains date from the 1940s but continue to undergird the post-Cold War order.

To pursue a global campaign against terrorism successfully, Washington will need to renew these two critical bargains. How Washington fights the war on terrorism matters. Cooperative strategies that reinforce norms of international conduct do constrain the ways in which the US uses military force, but they also legitimate that use of force and make other states more willing to join the coalition. If the United States acts with an eye on the logic and historic bargains of the existing international order, the terrible events of 11 September will provide an opportunity to strengthen the pillars of democratic community and great-power peace.

## Post-Cold War Orders – Real and Imagined

Many observers expected that the end of the Cold War would usher in dramatic and destabilising shifts in world politics. But despite the collapse of the Soviet Union – and despite great swings in the international distribution of power – the United States and its partners navigated their way into a new era while maintaining stable and cooperative relations. Indeed, the most important characteristic of the current international order is the remarkable absence of serious strategic rivalry and competitive balancing among the great powers. At the core of this order are the major industrial democracies of Europe, North America and East Asia – a community of states with stable governments, liberal societies and advanced market economies, linked by security alliances, economic interdependence and a variety of multilateral governance institutions.[3] The United States – whose military, technological and economic superiority increased during the 1990s – sits at the order's epicentre.

Stable peace among the great powers was not a widely anticipated outcome. One group of 'realist' analysts forecast the return of great-power rivalry.[4] Without the cohesion provided by a common external threat, the argument went, the major powers would revert to competitive strategies driven by the underlying structure of anarchy. In this view, Germany and Japan would rearm and loosen their subordinate security ties to the United States, NATO and the US–Japan alliance would unravel, and a competitive multipolar scramble for power would emerge. The post-Cold War world would look more like the late-nineteenth-century system of shifting alliances and great power conflict. Security cooperation and the willingness of European and Asian partners to operate within an American-centred global order were considered artefacts of the Cold War.

Another scenario of breakdown in the American security system has focused on shifting geopolitical ambitions in Europe and the United States. The United States may be 'indispensable' to the stable operation of global order, but American voters are not really aware of this or much impressed by

22 **G. John Ikenberry**

its imperatives. Charles Kupchan argues that a shrinking American willing–
ness to be the global protector of last resort will be the primary engine of a
change to that order.[5] Today's hegemonic order will crack from a growing
mismatch between domestic support and external commitments.

> The foundation is shaky because America has a dwindling interest in paying the
> construction and upkeep ... Rather than pursue a hollow hegemony that misleads and
> creates unmet expectations, it is better for the United States to give advance notice
> that its days as a guarantor of last resort may be numbered.[6]

The big oak tree of American hegemony has grown steadily over the decades.
Others still want it and benefit from it and the fact of its existence makes
alternative ordering systems less viable – but it still depends on a subterranean
water supply – United States public support – that could be drying up. The rise
of a united Europe that seeks an independent security role and its own
leadership presence around the world adds to the coming conflict.

A second group of analysts has focused on shifts in the economic structure
of the existing order. This group anticipated that the world would return to
the problems of the 1930s: open multilateralism would give way to rival geoeconomic regions. Europe and East Asia would each pull away from the
United States and pursue their own visions of regional economic order.
Markets would become more political, trade conflict would rise and the three
major regions would compete for supremacy.[7] The severity of these regional
clashes would be intensified – in the view of some – because of deep
differences in the character of each region's capitalism. Continental Europe,
Anglo-America and East Asia each has its own values and institutions that
gives each a distinctive approach to state and market. Chalmers Johnson, for
example, has argued that with the end of artificial Cold War constraints,
Japan will eventually reassert its economic independence from the United
States, triggering greater conflict across the Pacific.[8]

The themes of both these post-Cold War visions are fragmentation and
conflict. The 'problems of anarchy' will reassert themselves: economic closure,
hyper-nationalism, arms races and regional competition and strategic rivalry.

Yet these grim predictions have not come to pass. Despite losing the
Soviet Union as a common threat, Japan and the United States during the
1990s reaffirmed their alliance partnerships, contained political conflict,
expanded trade and investment across the Atlantic and Pacific, and avoided
a return to balance-of-power politics. Germany and other European states are
reducing their defence expenditures rather than increasing their independent
military capacity. Japan is rethinking its defence posture in Asia but not
questioning its fundamental alliance link with the United States. Russia and
China remain outside the core community of industrial democracies, but
even as they voice opposition to America's hegemonic global presence they
are also seeking greater integration into the Western-oriented world system.
This stable peace among the great powers is noted by Robert Jervis:

> Although the causes can be debated, the fact is striking: we are experiencing the
> longest period of peace among the great powers in history ... This is a breathtaking

change in world politics, which previously consisted of the state of war among the great powers.[9]

Part of this stability was achieved in the decades after the Second World War, a response to Cold War bipolarity and nuclear weapons. But since the end of superpower struggle, it is clear that this stable order among the great powers is rooted in the more general relationship between the United States and the outside world.

## Political Foundations of the American System

Forecasts of post-Cold War breakdown and disarray missed an important fact: in the shadow of the Cold War, a distinctive and durable political order was being assembled among the major industrial countries. This order might be called the American system – evoking the multifaceted character of this American-centred order organised around layers of security alliances, open markets, multilateral institutions and forums for consultation and governance. It is an order built on common interests and values and anchored in capitalism and democracy. But it is also an engineered political order built on American power, institutional relationships and political bargains.

The American system is a product of two post-war order-building exercises. One – commonly seen as the defining feature of the era – was containment. Truman, Dean Acheson, George Kennan and other American foreign-policy makers were responding to the spectre of Soviet power, organising a global anti-communist alliance and fashioning an American grand strategy. America's strategy was to 'prevent the Soviet Union from using the power and position it won ... to reshape the postwar international order'.[10] This is the grand strategy, and international order based on it, that was swept away in 1991.

But there was another order created after the Second World War. American officials worked with Britain and other countries to build new relationships among the Western industrial democracies. The political order among these countries, aimed at solving the problems of the 1930s, was articulated in such statements as the Atlantic Charter of 1941, the Bretton Woods agreements of 1944 and the Marshall Plan speech in 1947. Unlike containment, there was not a singular statement of strategy and purpose. It was a collection of ideas about open markets, social stability, political integration, international institutional cooperation and collective security. Even the Atlantic Pact of 1949 was as much aimed at reconstruction and integrating Europe and binding the democratic world together as it was an alliance created to balance Soviet power.[11]

The American system is based on a vision of open economic relations, intergovernmental cooperation and liberal democratic society. But the most consequential aspect of the order is its security structure. Although the United States remained deeply ambivalent about extending security guarantees or forward-deploying troops in Europe and Asia, it ultimately bound itself to the other advanced democracies through alliance partnerships.[12] This strategy of security binding has provided a structure of commitments, restraints and mechanisms of reassurance.

24 **G. John Ikenberry**

The American-centred alliances have always been doing more 'work' than is usually appreciated.[13] The traditional understanding of alliances is that they are created to balance against external power and threats. But America's post-war alliances with Europe and Japan were created to achieve a lot more. Stabilising and managing relations between alliance partners was as much a function of these alliances as countering hostile states. This was true even during the Cold War, but it is even more fundamentally the case today. The alliances serve to bind Japan, the United States and Western Europe together and thereby reduce conflict and the potential for strategic rivalry between these traditional great powers. The alliances help these states establish credible commitment to a cooperative structure of relations and provide institutional mechanisms that allow each state to gain access to the policy making processes in the others. Moreover, by binding Germany to Western Europe and Japan to the United States, the alliances helps prevent security dilemmas and strategic rivalry that might otherwise break out in Europe and East Asia.[14] The alliances allow the United States to both project power around the world and to limit and channel how that power is exercised. These functions of the alliances fit together, constituting a long-term institutional bargain between the United States and its European and Asian partners.

The durability of the American system rests on preponderant American power and a distinctive form of open and institutionalised hegemony. American power has been essential to the building and maintenance of the existing order. After the Second World War, the United States commanded about 50% of the world's wealth. While the other major powers were destroyed or diminished by war, the United States economy reached new levels of growth and technological advancement. Again today, the United States has only about 4% of the world's population but produces approximately 27% of global output. Its nearest rivals – China and Japan – produce about half this amount with four times the population between them.[15] As in the 1940s, America's military and technological supremacy is unchallenged and unprecedented.[16]

One explanation for the durability of the American system involves an appeal to a version of the 'democratic peace' thesis: that open democratic polities are less able or willing to use power in an arbitrary and indiscriminate manner against other democracies.[17] The calculations of smaller and weaker states as they confront a democratic hegemon are thereby altered. Fundamentally, power asymmetries are less threatening or destabilising when they exist between democracies. This might be so for several reasons. Open polities make the exercise of power more visible and easy to anticipate. Accountable governments make the exercise of power more predictable and institutionalised. Democracies are more externally accessible than non-democracies. Leaders who rise through the ranks within democratic countries are more inclined to participate in 'gave and take' with other democratic leaders than their counterparts in autocratic and authoritarian states. Processes of interaction between democracies make the crude and manipulative exercise of power less likely or consequential. Institutions and norms of consultation and reciprocal influence are manifest in relations across the democratic world. These facets of democracy are stressed by John Gaddis:

> Negotiation, compromise, and consensus-building came naturally to statesmen steeped in the uses of such practices at home: in this sense, the American political tradition served the country better than its realist critics – Kennan among them – believed it did'.[18]

This system of alliances and multilateral institutions are the core of today's world order. American power both undergirds this system and is transformed by it. By enmeshing itself in a post-war web of alliances and multilateral commitments, the United States is able to project its influence outward and create a relatively secure environment in which to pursue its interests. But that order also shapes and restrains American power and makes the United States a more genial partner for other states. Likewise, the array of institutions and cooperative security ties that link Europe, the United States, Japan and the rest of the democratic community create a complex and stable order that by sheer size overwhelms any alternative. Russia, China, or any other combination of states or movements are too small to mount a fundamental challenge to the American system. This order provides the ready foundation for a concerted campaign against terrorism.

## America's Competing Grand Strategies
The Bush administration has still not completely come to terms with – or accepted the logic of – the American system. The events of 11 September expose the deep divides within the Bush administration over the exercise of American power and visions of international order. Two distinct strategies are competing for primacy. One is the liberal multilateralism that generally characterised the approach of the previous Bush and Clinton administrations as well as American policy towards the West during the post-Second World War era . This is the strategy that gave rise to and reinforces the American system. But some Bush administration officials embrace a more unilateral – even imperial – grand strategy, based on a starkly realist vision of American interests and global power realities. In this view, American preponderance allows it selectively to engage Europe and Asia, dominating world politics with military forces that are both unchallenged and less bound to United Nations or alliance controls. Cooperative security, arms control and multilateral cooperation play a reduced role in this global strategy. But the events of 11 September have rendered this strategy deeply problematic. The logic of the Bush administration's war on terrorism – with its emphasis on leading an international coalition of states – necessarily reorients the administration's foreign policy in ways that will push it back in the direction of post-war liberal multilateralism.

Grand strategies are really bundles of security, economic and political strategies based on assumptions about how best to advance national security and build international order. Administrations inevitably pursue a mix of

26 **G. John Ikenberry**

policies and strategies.[19] In general, however, the strategy of liberal multilateralism has been the dominant strand of American policy in the decade after the Cold War, with the elder Bush and Clinton administrations drawing on ideas and commitments from the post- Second World War era that gave shape to the American system. This liberal grand strategy is based on the view that American security and national interests can be best advanced by promoting international order organized around democracy, open markets, multilateral institutions, and binding security ties.

James Baker, Secretary of State in the previous Bush administration, captured aspects of this strategy in his reflections on American policy in the immediate aftermath of the Cold War, likening the first Bush administration's thinking to American strategy after 1945.

> Men like Truman and Acheson were above all, though we sometimes forget, institution builders. They created NATO and the other security organizations that eventually won the Cold War. They fostered the economic institutions ... that brought unparalleled prosperity ... At a time of similar opportunity and risk, I believed we should take a leaf from their book.[20]

This strategy was reflected in the first Bush administration's support for the North American Free Trade Area (NAFTA), Asia-Pacific Economic Cooperation (APEC), the World Trade Organisation (WTO) and its initial steps to expand NATO's association with countries in the former Soviet Union. The Clinton administration pursued an even more ambitious and explicitly articulated version of liberal multilateralism under various rubrics such as 'enlargement' and 'engagement'.[21]

The new Bush administration speaks with a more mixed voice on grand strategy.[22] To be sure, it has reaffirmed basic aspects of the multilateral economic and security order and America's leadership position within it. It has moved forward aggressively with freer trade and investment in the Western hemisphere and called for a new round of global multilateral trade negotiations. But lurking in some quarters of the government is a deep scepticism about operating within a rule-based international order and a preference for unilateralism and selective engagement. 'It is not isolationist but unilateralist, unashamed of using military power', one journalist notes.[23] It is a unilateral grand strategy that resists involvements in regional and multilateral entanglements that are deemed marginal to America's own security needs. It envisions American power acting in the world but not being entangled by it.

The most visible sign of this tendency was the dramatic sequence of Bush administration rejections of pending international agreements, including the Kyoto Protocol, the International Criminal Court, the Biological Weapons Convention and UN action on the trade in small arms and light weapons. In pushing national missile defence, the administration has also signalled its willingness to withdraw from the 1972 Anti-Ballistic Missile Treaty, which many regard as the cornerstone of modern arms-control agreements. There is room for serious debate about the merits of various aspects of these agreements. But together the chorus of rejections underscore the misgivings the Bush administration has about multilateral and rule-based cooperation in general.[24]

The current administration is also retooling defence strategy in a way that will inevitably loosen alliance partnerships. The high-tech revolution in military capabilities will increasingly allow the United States to project force from the United States rather than from platforms in Europe, Asia and the Middle East. These include more long-distance bombers, precision missiles and space-based weapons. Missile defence – depending on which options are pursued – can also loosen alliance ties by making the United States more secure without a forward-based presence. Missile defence has been defended by some as a technology that will strengthen America's defence commitment to its European and Asian allies. If the United States feels secure from counter-attack from North Korea, they say, it is more likely to come to the defence of Japan and Korea. But in the longer term, a comprehensive national missile defence capacity will have the opposite effect: with its own homeland protected, American political leaders will be less certain why the United States needs to be spending money protecting people in faraway places.

The vision that lies behind this grand strategy and military posture is deeply rooted in old ideas about the country's place in the world – ideas that over the last 50 years have been pushed to the sidelines.[25] It is a vision of a country that is big enough, powerful enough and remote enough to go it alone, free from the dangerous and corrupting conflicts festering in all the other regions of the world. It is a vision that is deeply suspicious of international rules and institutions. 'It is the difference between those who would rely on lawyers to defend America and those who rely on engineers and scientists', observed Newt Gingrich, in explaining why his 'Contract with America' included a commitment to national missile defence.[26] The dream that propels many missile-defence proponents is not a limited missile shield that might stop an errant missile launched by a rogue state, but a national shield that will abolish the post-war system of nuclear deterrence – based as it is on the ugly logic of mutual assured destruction.

The tension between the liberal multilateral and unilateral grand strategies has been heightened in the aftermath of 11 September, but it has also been altered by these events. Richard Perle, the Bush administration's head of the Defence Policy Board at the Pentagon, suggested that there were real limits on a coalition-based approach to fighting terrorism: 'It's wonderful to have the support of our friends and allies, but our foremost consideration has to be to protect this country and not take a vote among others as to how we should do it.' When Perle's remark was brought to the attention of Secretary of State Colin Powell, he responded:

> I have not scheduled a vote for any members of this coalition to participate in …
> But the President has made it very clear that the kinds of things that will probably
> be most successful in the campaign against terrorism are intelligence-sharing,
> controlling people going across borders, financial transactions and how to get at
> their financial systems. You can't do this, America alone. You need coalitions.[27]

*28* **G. John Ikenberry**

This embrace of multilateralism does not mean that the United States submits itself fully to a rule-based order on an equilateral basis. In the American system, the United States accepts restraints on its power, but this is not the same as the absolute and across-the-board acceptance of formally binding rules. The restraint is manifest in more subtle ways that entail conducting foreign policy in a way that is sensitive to norms and processes of multilateral cooperation. Some administration officials – embracing unilateralist ideas – have bridled at the constraints that an alliance and coalition-based approach implies, particularly the limitations that it imposes on the countries and targets that the United States can go after. But the logic of the situation has strengthened the hand of those seeking to pursue American interests through multilateral and alliance-based tools.

It is unclear whether the Bush administration's discovery of the virtues of a multilateral coalition in fighting terrorism will spill over to its grand strategy. But there will be pressures and incentives for it to move back to a more general multilateral orientation. At least, it will be difficult for the US to ask for new forms of cooperation – intelligence, logistical support, political solidarity – from other states and resist their strongly-held views on missile defence, global warming and other major issues. American unilateralism – exhibited in the first six months of the Bush term – was built on ideology and a practical reality. The ideology was a unilateral or imperial grand strategy embraced by a vocal and articulate group of officials. The practical reality was that the United States could in fact say no to agreements and not pay a huge price. Today, that ideology has not disappeared but it is less credible. The new practical reality is that the United States does want something from its partners, so it will need to give things in return.

To fight terrorism on a global scale, the Bush administration will need to rediscover the two bargains that the United States has made with the world. The realist bargain exchanges America's security support and access to markets and technology for the diplomatic and logistical support needed by the United States to pursue its geopolitical objectives. To fight terrorism effectively, the United States needs partners: the military and logistical support of allies, intelligence sharing and the practical cooperation of front-line states. The transnational character of modern terrorism makes a national strategy impotent. Fighting terrorism entails tracing bank accounts, sharing criminal information and other basic tasks of transnational law enforcement. As Fareed Zakaria has indicated, 'the crucial dimensions of the struggle are covert operations, intelligence gathering and police work. All of this requires the active cooperation of many other governments. US Marines cannot go into Hamburg and arrest suspects. We cannot shut down banks in the United Arab Emirates. We cannot get intelligence from Russia except if the Russians share it with us'.[28] The simple logic of problem-solving moves the United States into the realm of multilateral, rule-based foreign policy. Aerial bombing may root out terrorists and destroy their camps, but the long-term demands of a campaign against terrorism is to work within and strengthen rules, laws and institutions.

The liberal bargain also needs to be renewed. The United States obtains the cooperation of other states by offering to restrain and commit itself in return. To the surprise of many observers, the Bush administration did not rush the use of force after 11 September, but waited while Secretary of State Powell built an informal coalition of support and defined the war aims in sufficiently precise and limited terms to keep other states on board. While reserving the right to act unilaterally, the United States signalled patience and restraint. There are practical incentives for the United States to do so. If the world perceives the war on terrorism to be between an arrogant and narrowly self-interested America and an aggrieved Islamic people, the war will be difficult to win. A war between the civilised, democratic world and murderous outlaws, on the other hand, can be won. Coalitions do not just aggregate power, they also legitimate it, particularly when they are organised around shared principles and values.

## The Future of Great Power Cooperation

'One knows where a war begins but one never knows where it ends' – so remarked a diplomat looking back on the bloodiest war in history, the collapse of European empires and the chaotic spectacle of Versailles, all of which seemed to follow from a single shot fired in Sarajevo in 1914. States rarely finish wars for the same reasons they start them. To build support for the waging of war, leaders need to define the struggle in terms that will make the sacrifice worthwhile. Leaders tend to promise that if their countrymen are willing to bear the burdens of war, a better world awaits on the other side. In the Atlantic Charter of 1941, Churchill and Roosevelt articulated ideas for war-weary Britain and war-wary America of a prosperous and stable peace built on a united community of nations. If history is a guide, the American-led war on terrorism will lead Western leaders to cast their actions in terms of broad principles and values which will in turn influence the response to future conflicts.

The war on terrorism is different from the great wars of the past and likening it to the Cold War obscures as much as it reveals. In one sense, today's terrorism is more disturbing than the violence of past wars. If it is rooted in a clash between Western modernity and failed and threatened Islamic fundamentalism, the war will not end soon.[29] Wars between states are easier to understand, and if it is territory that is in dispute, they are easier to settle. In another sense, the struggle today is not a war at all, but is more like fighting organised crime. The solution is not deploying troops but traditional law enforcement. If this is true, the impact of this war will be primarily within societies, reshaping the balance between civil liberties and the reach of the state. Governments will have greater incentives to coordinate their domestic security and law-enforcement operations. They will also need to tackle the problems of failed states that harbour terrorists, promoting responsible regimes and the rule of law. This is an important agenda, but it does not evoke the memory of 1815, 1919 or 1945.

Nevertheless, the aftermath of 11 September will have important impacts beyond the immediate struggle with terrorism – impacts within the Western democratic world and between that world and the outside powers. The Bush

*30* **G. John Ikenberry**

administration's response to the attacks is illuminating the logic of the American order. In seeking partners in its struggle, the United States is rediscovering that the strategic partnerships it has built over the decades still exist and are useful. After NATO voted its support of the American campaign, Secretary of State Powell remarked that 50 years of steady investment in the alliance had paid off.[30] When the United States ties itself to a wider grouping of states it is more effective, but this requires some compromise of national autonomy. The US must both restrain and commit its power. The logic of this grand strategy is captured by Robert Jervis:

> Binding itself to act multilaterally by forgoing the capability to use large-scale force on its own would then provide a safeguard against the excessive use of American power. This might benefit all concerned: the United States would not be able to act on its own worst impulses; others would share the costs of interventions and would also be less fearful of the United States and so, perhaps, more prone to cooperate with it.[31]

The struggle between unilateral and multilateral grand strategies today is a debate over the costs and benefits of binding American power to wider alliance and global groupings. The United States may give up some discretion but gains partners. The coalition-based struggle against terrorism is providing an object lesson in how best to strike the balance.

The American system is encouraging this collaborative approach to terrorism. European and other world leaders trooped into Washington in the weeks following the 11 September attacks. Each offered its support but also weighed in on how best to wage the coming campaign. The actions of Prime Minister Tony Blair exemplify this strategy of engaging America. The British leader has tied himself to the American anti-terrorist plan but in doing so, he has made it a Anglo-American – and even alliance-based – campaign. By binding itself to the superpower, Britain gains a stake in the struggle but also a voice in the policy. America's allies are surely hoping that the administration's new-found embrace of multilateralism is not a single-issue affair. At least for now, post-11 September allied diplomacy shows the dynamic character of the American system: the United States has ready friends and America's allies have ready access to American decision-making. Allied interactions tend to moderate policy, soften the sharp edges of allied disagreements, and move the countries toward a more concerted strategy.

The American campaign against terrorism is also changing the wider terms of great power cooperation. Russian President Vladimir Putin is the best example of a leader seeking to exploit this new opportunity to bargain. By throwing his support to the American cause, he is opening the way for support and accommodation by the United States on a range of issues crucial to the Russian agenda: economic aid, Chechnya, NATO expansion and missile defence. Prior to 11 September, the United States had been seeking to recast its strategic relationship with Russia. While the Bush strategy has been to offer that strategic relationship in exchange for accommodation on missile defence, the ultimate result might be some more expansive form of cooperative security between Russia and the West. Indeed, Russian cooperation on terrorism may in the long run strengthen the argument that Russia should be brought fully into the Western security framework, including perhaps NATO membership.[32] China is more quiet but it too may find ways to exchange its support of the American anti-terrorist campaign for a stable policy of engagement by the United States. This was the first call to arms by an American president where the enemy was not another great power, or a totalitarian ideology linked to a great power. This new transnational threat offers incentives to deepen strategic cooperation among all the great powers.

All this could go sour. The United States could decide that its desire to oppose terrorist regimes such as Iraq was more important than maintaining the coalition. In this case it might use force in a way that split the allies into fragmented groups each seeking a separate settlement. The United States could also return to its unilateral ways on other issues, allowing the deep disagreements and latent antagonisms between America and Europe – currently not visible because of the temporary united front against terrorism – to break out into the open. The deals that the United States and its allies make with repressive regimes in the Middle East and South Asia could also come back to haunt the Western democracies by undercutting the credibility of the West's commitment to democracy and human rights and creating locales for breeding the next generation of terrorists.

Yet overall, the events of 11 September do not seem to signal the unravelling of the old international order. The Bush administration is launching its war on terrorism from a foundation of stable and cooperative relations built over many decades. It may well be that historians remember the global response to 11 September more than those dramatic events themselves. Certainly the terrorist events present the United States, Europe and other states with an opportunity to renew and expand the political bargains on which the current international order rests.

32 **G. John Ikenberry**

## Acknowledgements

The author wishes to thank Joe Barnes and Victor Cha for comments on an earlier draft of this paper.

## Notes

1  See Steven Mufson, 'Foreign Policy's 'Pivotal Moment', *The Washington Post*, 27 September 2001; Joel Garreau, 'Hinges of Opportunity', *The Washington Post*, 14 October 2001.

2  See for example, Steven Erlanger, 'In Europe, Some Say the Attacks Stemmed from American Failings', *The New York Times*, 22 September 2001; and Elaine Sciolino, 'Who Hates the US? Who Loves It?', *The New York Times*, 23 September 2001. For imperial views of American power, see Chalmers Johnson, *Blowback: The Costs and Consequences of American Empire* (New York: Henry Holt and Co., 2000); and Michael Hardt and Antonio Negri, *Empire* (Cambridge, MA: Harvard University Press, 2000).

3  For descriptions of this democratic core, see Daniel Deudney and G. John Ikenberry, 'The Nature and Sources of Liberal International Order', *Review of International Studies*, Vol. 25 (Spring 1999); Bruce Cumings, 'Trilateralism and the New World Order', *World Policy Journal*, Vol. 8, No. 3 (Spring 1991), pp. 195–222; James M. Goldgeier and Michael MacFaul, 'A Tale of Two Worlds: Core and Periphery in the Post-Cold War Era', *International Organization*, Vol. 46 (Spring 1992), pp. 467–91; and Richard L. Kugler, 'Controlling Chaos: New Axial Strategic Principles', in Kugler and Ellen L. Frost (eds), *The Global Century: Globalization and National Security* (Washington, D.C.: National Defence University Press, 2000), Vol. 1, pp. 75–107.

4  See Kenneth Waltz, 'The Emerging Structure of International Politics', *International Security*, Vol. 18, No. 2 (Fall 1993); Waltz, 'Structural Realism after the Cold War', *International Security*, Vol. 25, No. 1 (Summer 2000); John J. Mearsheimer, 'Back to the Future: Instability of Europe after the Cold War', *International Security*, Vol. 15 (Summer 1990), pp. 5–57; Mearsheimer, 'Why We Will Soon Miss the Cold War', *The Atlantic*, 266 (August 1990), pp. 35–50; Christopher Layne, 'The Unipolar Illusion: Why New Great Powers Will Arise', *International Security*, Vol. 17, No. 4 (Spring 1993), pp. 5–51; and Christopher Layne, 'What's Built Up Must Come Down', *The Washington Post*, 14 November 1999. For a new statement of this view, see John J. Mearsheimer, *The Tragedy of Great Power Politics* (New York: W.W. Norton, 2001).

5  Charles A. Kupchan, 'After Pax Americana: Benign Power, Regional Integration, and the Sources of Stable Multipolarity', *International Security*, Vol. 23, No. 3 (Fall 1998), pp. 40–79.

6  See Charles Kupchan, 'Fractured US Resolve', *The Washington Post*, Outlook Section, 13 June 1999, B1, B4.

7  For one version of coming regional economic conflict, see Lester Thurow, *Head to Head: The Coming Economic Battle among Japan, Europe, and America* (New York: William Morrow and Company, 1992).

8  Chalmers Johnson, 'History Restarted: Japanese-American Relations at the End of the Century,' in Johnson, *Japan: Who Governs? The Rise of the Developmental State* (New York: Norton, 1995).

9  Robert Jervis, 'America and the Twentieth Century: Continuity and Change,' in Michael J. Hogan (ed.), *The Ambiguous Legacy: US Foreign Relations in the 'American Century'* (New York: Cambridge University Press, 1999), p. 100.

10  John Lewis Gaddis, *Strategies of Containment: A Critical Appraisal of*

*Postwar American National Security Policy* (New York: Oxford University Press, 1982), p. 4.

[11] See Mary N. Hampton, 'NATO at the Creation: US Foreign Policy, West Germany, and the Wilsonian Impulse', *Security Studies*, Vol. 4 No. 3 (Spring 1995), pp. 610–56; and Hampton, *The Wilsonian Impulse: US Foreign Policy, the Alliance, and German Unification* (Westport, Conn.: Praeger, 1996).

[12] On the complex, ambivalent, and evolving American thinking on its post-war security commitment to Europe, see Marc Trachtenberg, *A Constructed Peace: The Making of the European Settlement, 1945–1963* (Princeton: Princeton University Press, 1999); and Melvin Leffler, *A Preponderance of Power: National Security, The Truman Administration, and the Cold War* (Stanford: Stanford University Press, 1992).

[13] This argument is developed in G. John Ikenberry, *After Victory: Institutions, Strategic Restraint, and the Rebuilding of Order after Major War* (Princeton: Princeton University Press, 2001).

[14] For discussion of security dilemmas, see John Herz, 'Idealist Internationalism and the Security Dilemma', *World Politics*, vol. 2 (1949/50); and Robert Jervis, 'Cooperation under the Security Dilemma', *World Politics*, vol. 30 (1978), pp. 167–214.

[15] World Bank figures cited in Gerard Baker, 'Liberty's Triumph,' *The Financial Times*, 23 December 1999.

[16] On global power disparities and America's preeminent position, see William Wohlforth, 'The Stability of a Unipolar World', *International Security*, Vol. 24, No. 1 (Summer 1999), pp. 5–41.

[17] See Bruce Russett and John O'Neal, *Triangulating Peace: Democracy, Interdependence, and International Organizations* (New York: Norton, 2001).

[18] John Lewis Gaddis, *We Now Know: Rethinking Cold War History* (New York: Oxford University Press, 1997), p. 50.

[19] A large and growing literature has emerged on American grand strategy. For surveys, see Barry R. Posen and Andrew L. Ross, 'Competing Visions for US Grand Strategy', *International Security*, Vol. 21, No. 3 (Winter 1996–97); and G. John Ikenberry (ed.), *American Unipolarity and the Future of the Balance of Power* (Ithaca: Cornell University Press, forthcoming).

[20] James A. Baker, *The Politics of Diplomacy: Revolution, War and Peace 1989–92* (New York: G.P. Putnam's Sons, 1995), pp. 605–6.

[21] See White House, *A National Security Strategy of Engagement and Enlargement* (Washington, DC: White House, July 1994).

[22] The US State Department's Director of Policy Planning, Richard Haass, has coined the term 'à la carte' multilateralism to describe the administration's approach, but important differences in thinking exist across the administration. See Thom Shanker, 'White House Says the US is Not a Loner, Just Choosy', *The New York Times*, 31 July 2001.

[23] Stephen Fidler, 'Between Two Camps', *Financial Times*, 14 February 2001.

[24] See Gerard Baker, 'Bush Heralds Era of US Self-Interest', *International Herald Tribune*, 24 April 2001.

[25] See Thomas E. Ricks, 'US Urged to Embrace an 'Imperial' Role', *International Herald Tribune*, 22 August 2001.

[26] Stephen Fidler, 'Conservatives Determined to Carry Torch for US Missile Defence', *Financial Times*, 11 July 2001.

[27] Secretary of State Powell, National Public Radio Interview, 27 October 2001.

[28] Fareed Zakaria, 'Back to the Real World', *The Washington Post*, 2 October 2001.

[29] See Martin Wolf, 'The Economic

34  **G. John Ikenberry**

Failure of Islam', *Financial Times*,
26 September 2001.

30  Secretary Colin Powell, public
statement, 10 October 2001.

31  Robert Jervis, 'International Primacy:
Is the Game worth the Candle?',
*International Security*, Vol. 17 (1993),
p. 66.

32  See Quentin Peel, 'Washington's
Balancing Act', *Financial Times*,
1 October 2001; and Timothy Garton
Ash, 'A New War Reshapes Old
Alliances', *The New York Times*,
12 October 2001.

# [16]

# Democratic Regimes, Internal Security Policy and the Threat of Terrorism

FERNANDO REINARES[1]

*Politics and Sociology, Universidad Nacional de Educación a Distancia, Madrid*

Since terrorism poses a serious threat to the processes of liberal democracy governments should act decisively to curb terrorist groups. This article examines the range of political, judicial and enforcement measures available, assesses the problems associated with them and the conditions for their success. Political measures include reforms in response to popular unrest, negotiations with terrorist groups and amnesties to encourage an end to violence. Since terrorists seek to influence domestic and international public opinion, the authorities need to counter that propaganda and in particular to explain and justify the political, judicial and enforcement measures they adopt. Governments have to choose between treating terrorism like other forms of criminal behaviour or setting up special courts and passing emergency legislation, with the attendant dangers to civil liberties. Enforcement of anti-terrorist measures has quite often been inept. Coordination is required to prevent police anti-terrorist units and other security agencies from engaging in institutional rivalry. But if these agencies are efficient in their intelligence gathering, and politically supervised to ensure that they act within the law, they can be decisive in the reduction of terrorism, as in Western Europe at the end of the 1970s.

Although relatively limited in scope when compared with other manifestations of collective violence, terrorism can nonetheless exert a significant impact on the fundamental political processes which characterise democratic forms of government. Indeed, the avowed aim of small-scale, clandestine organisations that engage in terrorist practices is precisely to alter the structure and distribution of power. When terrorism becomes a systematic, long-term activity, the individual's entitlement of public liberties may be curtailed, the human rights of citizens are recurrently violated, institutions may be disrupted in their functioning, elected representatives prevented from carrying out their duties and civil society otherwise diverted from the course along which it had been developing. Taken in combination with other factors that seriously disrupt the existing political arrangements, terrorism represents a threat not only to the stability of democratic regimes — especially those in the process of consolidation — but also to the structural underpinnings of the state. It follows, therefore that any legitimately constituted government should take

---

[1] This paper has been translated from Spanish by Robert Latona.

immediate steps to deal with an emerging terrorist threat to a tolerant political order and to the state's monopoly on the use of physical coercion. Special efforts are required to ensure that terrorist groups do not persist beyond their initial emergence, an eventuality always possible and extremely difficult to anticipate.

The emergence and consolidation of these types of armed groups is often preceded by progressively radicalised stages of collective mobilisation. In theory, by exercising a minimum of prudence, it would seem feasible for authorities to monitor a potential terrorist threat while it is in the process of formation and take measures to bring it under control. In actual fact, however, it usually proves quite difficult for democratic governments to anticipate the course of events, and often they have no choice but to take reactive measures after the groups have made their invariably violent and attention-grabbing public debut.[2] The secrecy, small size and unpredictability which have characterised terrorist activities in industrialised societies from the 1960s onwards poses serious dilemmas for authorities given their responsibility for devising consistent, long-range policies aimed at neutralising the phenomenon. Cross-currents of public opinion, legal guarantees enjoyed by the citizens, and the interplay of articulated interests present in the internal security field, are critical factors in the formulation and implementation of anti-terrorist policies. In the case of democratic regimes, as they exist in industrialised societies, such state responses have included a certain number of essentially political measures, along with others of a judicial or law-enforcement character, many of which have been applied in a framework of active cross-border cooperation.[3] In light of the foregoing discussion, we may consider: Of what exactly do these measures consist? What type of problem underlies each of them? and What criteria should be used in evaluating their effectiveness?

## Reforms to Address Discontent and Negotiations

It falls within the mandate of democratic governments to devise and implement measures of political expediency in order to regulate and to resolve peacefully social conflicts that have reached violent extremes. A timely and proper response to more or less generalised situations of popular discontent or unrest may be enough to satisfy demands expressed in this fashion. It might possibly, for instance, strengthen

---

[2]  Regarding this point, see Fernando Reinares, "Estado, democracia liberal y terrorismo político", *Revista del Centro de Estudios Constitucionales* 16 (1993), pp. 113-32. Likewise, Ehud Sprinzak, "The Process of Delegitimization: Towards a Linkage Theory of Political Terrorism", in Clark McCauley, ed., *Terrorism Research and Public Policy* (London: Frank Cass, 1991), pp. 50-68.

[3]  Ronald D. Crelinsten and Alex P. Schmid have detailed a scheme for classifying models of anti-terrorist policy adopted by democratic governments in "Western Responses to Terrorism: A Twenty-five Year Balance Sheet", in Alex P. Schmid and Ronald D. Crelinsten, eds, *Western Responses to Terrorism* (London: Frank Cass, 1993), pp. 307-40. See also Fernando Reinares, "Fundamentos para una política gubernamental antiterrorista en el contexto de regímes democráticos", *Sistema. Revista de Ciencias Sociales*, 132, 3 (1996), pp. 111-28.

the hand of more moderate groups sharing the same ideological space as the terrorists. It may even allow them to acquire some additional degree of influence over events. In such fashion, the instigators of violence are deprived of the leverage they would otherwise derive from the prevailing climate of dissatisfaction. Experience, however, shows that all this implies no guarantee that as a direct result of such measures, terrorist groups will simply wither away. To a certain extent, this is because the effectiveness of the measures tends to vary as a function of the time it takes to implement them. Another factor is the degree of resource mobilisation which the terrorist group has achieved in the meantime.

Chances for the reformist approach appear best whenever the group has failed to muster any significant degree of support from the society in which it is embedded. In these instances, there are better grounds for supposing that by diligently addressing underlying grievances and rectifying where necessary, the appeal of the violent option can be substantially reduced. At the very least, it makes the instigators of that violence more vulnerable to coercive and conciliatory measures by the state. Such was the case of a handful of tiny, far-left terrorist cells active in the United States around the early 1970s. In that instance, young radicalised intellectuals whose ideological agenda might have impelled them to choose the violent option, instead took the personal and political decision to work within the framework of reforms undertaken by state and federal governments in response to public protests.[4] Something similar occurred towards the middle of the same decade where young militants, acting in the name of the ethnic Moluccan community settled in the Netherlands, carried out a limited number of terrorist activities. Fortunately, these incidents were resolved with a limited use of state force. Without having to give into any of their major demands, the government came through with a series of programmes to upgrade living conditions for immigrants from this former Indonesian colony and to integrate them into the larger fabric of Dutch society.[5]

When a terrorist organisation has solidly anchored itself in the society whose grievances it claims to set right, and obtained the tolerance, overt support or protective collusion of a substantial segment of the population, it is far less probable the group will wither away simply because reforms have been made, no matter how extensive they may be. In this respect, we may cite the case of the Provisional Irish Republican Army (PIRA), which emerged in Ulster during the latter part of the 1960s, building on the long-established foundations of anti-British insurgency. Just as the PIRA was emerging, many movements which sought to defend the civil rights of the province's catholic minority were being severely repressed by a semi-

---

[4]   Jeffrey I. Ross and Ted R. Gurr, "Why Terrorism Subsides. A Comparative Study of Canada and the United States", *Comparative Politics* 21 (1989), pp. 405-26; Richard E. Rubenstein, *Alchemists of Revolution: Terrorism in the Modern World* (New York: Basic Books, 1987), pp. 83-85.

[5]   Valentine Herman and Rob van der Laan Bouma, "Nationalists Without a Nation: South Moluccan Terrorism in the Netherlands", in Juliet Lodge, ed., *Terrorism: A Challenge to the State* (New York: St Martin's Press, 1981), pp. 119-45.

autonomous local government, which turned out to be rather less than a model of democracy. Yet, despite the fact that Catholics have now received many guarantees that their civil rights will be respected, violence continues in Northern Ireland. This is because for essentially unrelated reasons, relatively significant though undoubtedly minoritarian segments of society have acquiesced in the PIRA's persistence.[6] The experience of Spain during its transition to democracy offers another case in point. The Basque country was granted an historically unprecedented degree of self-rule under a power-sharing arrangement which was endorsed in a 1979 referendum by the vast majority of its inhabitants. This spurred the majority (the so-called "political-military") sector of the terrorist organisation known as *Euskadi ta Askatasuna* (*ETA*, Basque Homeland and Liberty), to lay down its arms. But the so-called "military" faction of ETA, the remnant of a terrorist group that emerged during the latter part of the Franco dictatorship, is doggedly carrying on the armed struggle, thanks to a continuing, though declining, degree of residual support among the Basque population.[7]

Political reforms may appear less successful than they really are if judged solely on their effectiveness as an element of anti-terrorism policy. That is because except at relatively early stages in a terrorist group's evolution, self-perpetuation tends to prevail over all other aims. This is a truism that holds for almost all types of political organisations, but specially so in the case of clandestine ones whose leaders as often as not stake their own personal authority on maintaining the group's operational viability.[8] But it is equally true that, by and large, as time passes, militants in small, hermetic groups dedicated to conspiracy and violence become increasingly impervious to political argument and respond more to the logic of internal solidarity. It is for this reason that terrorist organisations so often outlast the circumstances invoked to justify their violence, though such persistence may carry a price in the form of recurrent internal conflicts. Persist they do, however, despite having failed to accomplish their original objectives and deliberately ignoring

---

[6]  Martha Crenshaw, "The Persistence of IRA Terrorism", in Yonah Alexander and Alan O'Day, eds, *Terrorism in Ireland* (London: Croom Helm, 1984); Robert W. White, "From Peaceful Protest to Guerrilla War: Micromobilization of the Provisional Irish Republican Army", *American Journal of Sociology* 94 (1989), pp. 1277-302; John Darby, "Northern Ireland: The Persistence and Limitations of Violence", in Joseph V. Montville, ed., *Conflict and Peacemaking in Multiethnic Societies* (Lexington, Mass.: Lexington Books, 1991).

[7]  Fernando Reinares, "Nationalism and Violence in Basque Politics", *Conflict* 8, 2-3 (1988), pp. 141-55, and "Democratización y terrorismo en el caso español", in José F. Tezanos, Ramón Cotarelo and Andrés de Blas, eds, *La transción democrática española* (Madrid: Sistema, 1989), pp. 611-44; also, "The Political Conditioning of Collective Violence: Regime Change and Insurgent Terrorism in Spain", *Research on Democracy and Society* 3 (1996), pp. 297-326. See, as well, Fraciso J. Llera, "Violencia y opinión pública en el País Vasco, 1978-1992", *Revista Internacional de Sociología* 3 (1992), pp. 83-111.

[8]  James Q. Wilson, *Political Organizations* (New York: Basic Books, 1973), pp. 30-55. Martha Crenshaw, "An Organizational Approach to the Analysis of Political Terrorism", *Orbis* 29 (1985), pp. 465-89.

changes in the social, political and cultural circumstances once invoked as a justification for their stance. Terrorism thus becomes the end rather than the means, and the imperatives of self-survival impel its leaders to branch out into predatory sidelines such as blackmail and extortion that, rather than seeking to influence the conduct of public affairs, fall more properly within the sphere of organised crime.

The foregoing analysis may give some idea of the obstacles inherent in any attempt to negotiate directly with terrorists in a bid to arrive at political arrangements and impose them on the remainder of the people affected by the conflict. Another point to bear in mind when the state devises and implements its response to violence is that by no means all of the terrorists' aims and ambitions are necessarily explicit. Those demands which they do articulate often appear either far too vague or far too extreme, emotionally charged enough to serve as the raw material for slogans, but not as a basis for serious transactions. Indeed it sometimes happens that if any of their demands should be satisfied, the terrorists perceive it not as a victory won but as a threat to their own continuity and survival. We notice a tendency periodically to redefine their aims, dismiss out of hand as unreal or inadequate efforts to satisfy the original demands, and inflate their exigencies until they become, for all intents and purposes, too big for the bargaining table.[9]

Any attempt by the representatives of a democratic regime to negotiate with the leaders of a terrorist group may give rise to a number of unforeseen and undesirable consequences. First of all, should the government publicly acknowledge its willingness to discuss issues of substance with a group of armed insurgents, it will almost certainly be perceived as a sign of weakness by the group's hard-liners. At the same time, other extra-parliamentary organisations with a political agenda to pursue may be emboldened by the terrorists' success and decide to proceed with more overtly aggressive acts, while those already committed to violence remain hardened in their conviction. On the other hand, it may happen that the terrorists make the overtures, fully aware they have very little to lose in the event the talks should fail. It is not uncommon for them to call a temporary cease-fire as a "good will gesture", although the objective of such a move is probably quite otherwise. Here we may cite the short-lived truce announced by *ETA* in June 1996. It was designed and timed to serve as a pretext for seizing the political initiative and fracturing the consensus reached by the Basque nationalist and non-nationalist parties opposed to violence, a factor that had clearly diminished the terrorists' ability to mobilise support.[10] Similarly, during the eighteen-month long cease-fire which it ostensibly observed to create a propitious climate for all-party Northern Ireland peace talks, the Provisional Irish Republican Army used the interval from

---

[9] Crenshaw, *ibid.*, p. 474. Nathan Leites, "Understanding the Next Act", *Terrorism: An International Journal* 3 (1979), pp. 1-46.

[10] See the information published in El País for 1 April 1997. This report reproduces *ETA*'s leadership considerations, as they appeared in *Zutabe*, the internal bulletin of the terrorist group.

September 1994 to February 1996 to reorganise its people and stockpile more arms and explosives.

Second, any type of parley invariably suggests that the terrorist group has been implicitly recognised by the government as a valid negotiating partner. This discredits those who opted to make use of constitutionally acceptable means in pursuing a political agenda. It likewise undermines the legality and legitimacy to which a democracy lays claim. Negotiating under such conditions shatters the ground rules under which democracy exercises its authority and gives rise to disquiet among its constituent institutions. Such a course amounts to nothing less than putting the rule of law on hold, with all the unforeseeable consequences this entails. Nevertheless, margin enough exists to allow for preliminary contacts to be held under certain circumstances for the purpose of sounding out the clandestine leadership with a view to determining whether they might be responsive to government initiatives directly affecting themselves and their underlings. In fact it was just such an initiative at the beginning of the 1980s that led to the self-dissolution of the "political-military" wing of *ETA* and the gradual reintegration into society of most of its militants and collaborators, nearly three hundred people, none of whom are known to have subsequently taken part in terrorist activities. Much more recently, a similar approach led to the break-up of the *Fronte di Liberazione Naziunale di a Corsica (FLNC)* in January 1997. In this case, it would appear the French authorities were not adverse to offering monetary inducements to encourage leaders of this significant part of the Corsican separatist movement to lay down their arms.

Finally, there are those exceedingly difficult instances in which, having once entered into some kind of talks, the terrorist group creates an on-the-ground advantage that gives them the upper hand. This could coerce the government into a situation where it has little or no choice but to go along with this group's demands. There have been many episodes highlighting the fact that democratic governments encounter grave difficulties in making the right decision in a moment of crisis, such as when terrorists resort to kidnapping or hostage-taking, actions that inevitably put the onus on the state if lives are lost. Under such circumstances, a government is sometimes obliged to take actions not always as clear-cut as the attitudes they express in words. Put bluntly, democratic governments sometimes have no choice, for humanitarian reasons, but to give in to terrorist blackmail.[11] However, the sight of a freely-elected government capitulating to a minority that represents only itself carries too high a political price tag and sets a precedent for more of the same. Over the middle and long-term, this will only serve to put more victims within reach of the terrorists' violence.

---

[11] Paul Wilkinson examines in detail this and other related problems concerning anti-terrorist policy in the eighteenth chapter of his *Terrorism and the Liberal State* (London: Macmillan, 1986).

*Fernando Reinares* *357*

## Anti-Terrorism and Communicative Action

A modern democracy is entitled to uphold and defend the legitimising basis that sustains its authority, as long as it maintains the utmost respect for the principles and procedures proper to a form of government based on tolerance and respect for human rights. To do otherwise is tantamount to undermining society's support for the system and playing into the hands of extremists such as terrorists. It therefore follows that the institutional response should also place a high priority on communication in order to counteract terrorist propaganda that the enemy state is incapable of fulfilling one of its primary functions, that of generating a reasonable degree of security for its citizens.[12] More to the point: the authorities who draw up security policy should bear in mind the implicit messages being communicated when terrorism, by small clandestine groups, becomes a sustained activity. In industrially-developed societies, these messages are interpreted in different ways by different segments of society both inside and outside the country.

By focusing on the terrorists' external audience, especially in like-minded democracies, it should be possible to expunge the self-justifying propaganda which terrorists put out, and at the same time deprive them of some of their active or passive international support. As for the internal audience, it is essential to develop effective, informative policies and educational mechanisms as an adjunct to the anti-terrorist struggle. These should explain the need for measures which the government is obliged to take and clarify the extent to which the populace's own lives will be affected as a result. At the same time, they should drive home the difference between democratic values and the despotic attitudes of clandestine terrorist groups, and muster support for the rule of law. In this manner, it should be possible to mitigate the tendency of public opinion to demand immediate, extreme and ultimately counter-productive steps following attacks that provoke a greater than usual degree of outrage and fear.[13]

Security authorities have no doubt that the coverage the terrorist groups receive from the mass media impacts significantly on their efforts. They should therefore seek to orient it in the right direction. Censorship, however, tends to be self-defeating as well as unjustified, especially for democratic governments. That is one conclusion to be drawn from the experience of the British authorities who banned the direct broadcast or quotation of remarks by terrorists or their sympathisers in October 1988. This ban was soon extended to restrict media access to individuals at home or abroad who were likely to express criticisms of the government's Northern Ireland policy. It would therefore seem more productive to stimulate informal bridge-

---

[12] The reader may consult, about this issue, Joanne Wright's study *Terrorist Propaganda: The Red Army Faction and the Provisional IRA, 1968-1986* (Basingstoke and London: Macmillan, 1991).

[13] Concerning the influence of the mass media, especially television, on crisis situations provoked by terrorist groups, see Ronald D. Crelinsten, "The Impact of Television on Terrorism and Crisis Situations: Implications for Public Policy", *Journal of Contingencies and Crisis Management* 2 (1994), pp. 61-72.

building efforts between government and the news media, while respecting the freedom which journalists require, as well as the right of the citizenry to be informed about the events that affect them. This implies that journalists should voluntarily accept certain restrictions on the dissemination of information which might serve the terrorist group's aims, such as the details of police operations still in progress. These restrictions should go hand-in-hand with the watchdog function that should be exercised by the press and its duty to guard against power excesses.[14]

## Undermining Cohesion of Terrorist Groups

More positive than misdirected attempts at negotiated solutions with the terrorists, and no less relevant to the goal than communicative institutional actions, are endeavours by the government to influence the internal cohesion of terrorist organisations. Such a strategy is based on a working hypothesis: an ambivalence exists within terrorist groups that can be exploited and used to exhaust their potential for recruiting new members.[15] Taking political initiatives which sought to persuade individual militants to renounce their links to the terrorist organisation, for example, was an approach that worked extremely well for Italian authorities.[16] Correct timing, however, is of critical importance to this approach. The militant has to be "caught" just at the moment when he has begun to question his commitment or when the government is disposed formally to consider amnesties, pardons or reduced sentences to those who make a clean break. Sometimes the sole condition is that the individual explicitly renounce violence as a means of obtaining goals. Since the early 1980s, this has been the bottom-line policy of Spanish authorities. Although measures of this nature have proved their effectiveness in helping democratic governments to mitigate or neutralise long-standing terrorist activity, a number of potential drawbacks must be acknowledged. For instance, the defection or renunciation of violent methods by some members of the group may lead those who remain to escalate their violence as a show of defiance and resolve. This is what happened in Corsica in the early 1980s after France decided to grant an autonomy statute for the island and declared a blanket amnesty to jailed members of the *FLNC*.[17] On another level, when the reinsertion offer is open-ended and prolonged, it may become a factor that brings down the individual's perceived cost of joining the

---

[14] Some interesting considerations regarding how democratic governments have dealt with the mass media within the context of a comprehensive anti-terrorist policy can be found in Jennifer J. Hocking, "Governments' Perspectives", in David L. Paletz and Alex P. Schmid, eds, *Terrorism and the Media* (Newbury Park and London: Sage, 1992), pp. 86-104.

[15] Christopher Hewitt, *The Effectiveness of Anti-terrorist Policies* (New York: University Press of America, 1984).

[16] In this regard, see Franco Ferracuti, "Ideology and Repentance: Terrorism in Italy", in Walter Reich, ed., *Origins of Terrorism: Psychologies, Ideologies, Theologies, States of Mind* (Cambridge: Cambridge University Press, 1990), pp. 59-64.

[17] Michel Wieviorka, *Sociétés et terrorisme* (Paris: Fayard, 1988), p. 45.

terrorist organisation rather than enhancing the inducements to defy its iron-clad discipline.

In 1989, Spanish authorities had considerable initial success in disrupting the terrorist organisation's internal cohesion by both offering generous terms to allow *ETA* militants to re-enter society, and dispersing inmates to penitentiaries scattered throughout Spain. In this way, they succeeded in creating fissures and fractures in the iron discipline maintained by *ETA* over militants serving long prison sentences. Prospects for the survival of terrorist groups depend greatly on maintaining the internal cohesion and unconditional submission of jailed members; these members constitute the main asset for marshalling support and sympathy from the society whose destiny they claim the right to determine. This is not so much a matter of exploiting a political consensus as a pre-existing network of friendship and family structures which is uncommonly cohesive with an intense sense of collective identity. Therefore, when the authorities arrange for the dispersal of terrorist prisoners as part of a concerted anti-terrorist policy, the reaction by the group's leadership tends to be extreme. Their usual tactic is to start out by accusing the government of depriving the prisoners of their basic human right to have regular access to family members by jailing them far from their former places of residence. If this agitation should not produce the desired result, the leaders order their jailed members to stage hunger strikes or employ other coercive measures. Finally, they strike back by attacking prison administrators, guards and employees. That is exactly what happened in Spain after such a policy was applied to members of *ETA* and the October 1st Anti-fascist Group (GRAPO). The frenzy of these groups' reaction gives some idea of the degree to which these measures subverted the internal discipline of the two organisations. It is nonetheless true, that the degree of success achieved in such instances is extremely contingent on external factors, and needs to be modified as circumstances require. Social reinsertion measures such as these are much less effective when the jailed militants are convinced — either rightly or wrongly — that all they have to do is sit back and wait for political negotiations in which a generous amnesty is bound to be one of the issues.

Despite all these inherent difficulties, there can be little doubt that this type of political move, especially when complemented by other judicial and law-enforcement measures, has played a fundamental part in Spain and Italy in sending long-established and particularly virulent forms of terrorism into an irreversible decline. In Spain, however, the continuity and effectiveness of reinsertion measures designed to strike at terrorist group cohesion has, to some degree, been compromised by two factors. First, there is the fact that the moral legitimacy of such moves has been called into question by those who speak on behalf of the terrorists' victims. In Spain, these people have organised themselves into an influential lobby, which the government has been unable to ignore. The second factor is that the country's political parties are in less than complete agreement over the expediency of the reinsertion policy. This has served to reduce its overall effectiveness.

None of the measures to which the government has recourse will prove entirely effective unless working alliances and bargains are struck among those parties whose differences are of less consequence than their overriding loyalty to the democratic system. Then and only then will they have achieved the kind of consensus that is a prerequisite for all initiatives undertaken at the institutional level. Logically, this consensus is difficult to achieve as long as there are important sectors that either implicitly or explicitly have reservations or doubts as to the legitimacy of the democratic system, or maintain an ambivalent stance towards terrorist violence. Here we might take note of the ambiguity maintained by the Italian Communist Party during the 1970s regarding the wave of far-left terror. Turning once again to Spain, ambivalence could also describe the attitude towards *ETA* manifested over the past two decades by certain influential sectors within the Basque Nationalist Party. The same construct would doubtless hold true in other European countries where right-wing parties that have enjoyed a not insignificant degree of support at the polls might take an equivocal attitude to terrorist violence of the type perpetrated nowadays by neo-Nazi groups.

**The State, Law and Terrorism**

In formulating a response to the terrorist challenge, advanced democracies have at their disposal a certain number of interrelated dissuasive or coercive measures assigned to and administered by different judicial or law-enforcement institutions. Each of these categories of measures is supported by an entirely different set of criteria. Moreover, responsibility for putting them into practice is commonly assigned to different government agencies and organisms. For both these reasons, anti-terrorist policies are frequently affected by structural tensions that can cause the pendulum to swing between the twin poles of over-zealous excess and lack of resolve.[18] The latter extreme may arise from perspectives that reduce terrorism to an ordinary type of criminal behaviour, denying its political content and disdaining anything other than standard legal procedures to deal with it. At the other extreme, there is a tendency that pushes for the excessive use of force to address the problem. No matter how small the group that provokes such a response, no measure is ever deemed too disproportionate or heavy-handed, according to such a perspective. The inevitable outcome is the constant impulse to over-react and exceed democratic limits for the sake of obtaining results.[19]

---

[18] Didier Bigo and Daniel Hermant, "La relation terroriste", *Etudes Polémologigues* 30 (1984), pp. 44-63, and *Etudes Polémologigues* 31 (1984), pp. 75-100. See also, Peter Chalk, "The Liberal Democratic Response to Terrorism", *Terrorism and Political Violence* 7 (1995), pp. 10-44, in particular pp. 17-19.

[19] Ronald D. Crelinsten, "Terrorism, Counterterrorism and Democracy: The Assessment of National Security Threats", *Terrorism and Political Violence* 1 (1989), pp. 242-69.

One relatively common characteristic of anti-terrorist policies implemented by democratic governments over the past quarter-century is the establishing of separate courts to try terrorist crimes. Though controversial, these special tribunals have been able, where established, to deliver verdicts more independent and less inhibited by the threat of reprisal than ordinary courts. Witness and jury intimidation, opening the way for perverse acquittals were precisely what led the British Government to create the Diplock Courts in 1973. These are overseen by a single judge who hears cases relating to crimes likely to have been carried out by terrorist groups.[20] In February 1977, Spain's *Audiencia Nacional* held its first sessions in Madrid. At present it shares with the *Juzgados Centrales de Instrucción* exclusive competence for preparing and trying cases involving terrorist activities carried out anywhere on Spanish territory by individuals who are members of armed organisations or otherwise acting in collusion with them. Though controversial at the time of its creation, this tribunal set an important precedent in helping to remove jurisdiction over terrorist crimes from the military courts, barely two years after Franco's death, at a time when the transition to democracy was by no means complete or even on a solid footing.[21] Other countries have opted for more intermediate solutions. In 1986, France set up a Paris-based special bench for terrorist crimes that specifically excludes acts of violence carried out in exclusively regional or local jurisdictions. By contrast, Germany appears only partially convinced of the advisability of special courts. The Italian judiciary is an example of a court system that has proved itself perfectly capable of dealing with terrorism without recourse to special tribunals, even when terrorist activity was at its height. Terrorist crimes continue to be tried by the Corti de Assise, ordinary tribunals assigned routine jurisdiction over a given district.

Anti-terrorist legislation in general has often been undermined by improvisation, heterogeneous policy directives, relative technical imprecision, and its transitory nature. Many jurists see such legalism as a violation of the fundamental principles of law, since it allows a certain type of crime to be dealt with in a fashion markedly different from other forms of delinquent behaviour.[22] These same critics also consider the punitive aspects of such legislation a perversion of the fundamental postulates of the classical liberal model. This is because they allow political considerations to prevail over exclusively juridical ones in singling out types of

---

[20] On the peculiarities of the Diplock Courts, see Antonio Vercher, *Antiterrorismo en el Ulster y en el País Vasco. Legislación y medidas* (Barcelona: Promociones y Publicaciones Universitarias, 1991), chapter five.

[21] Esteban Mestre, *Delincuencia terrorista y Audiencia Nacional* (Madrid: Ministerio de Justicia, 1987), p. 93.

[22] In this respect, see Luigi Ferrajoli, "Emergenza penale e crisi della giurisdizione", *Dei delitti e delle pene* 2 (1984), pp. 271-92; Diego López Garrido, *Terrorismo, política y derecho. La legislación antiterrorista en España, Reino Unido, República Federal de Alemania, Italia y Francia* (Madrid: Alianza, 1987); José A. Martín Pallín, "Terrorismo y represión penal", *Claves de Razón Práctica* 23 (1992), pp. 26-34.

illegal conduct for special treatment. In answer to these criticisms, it may be countered that systematic violence carried out by armed clandestine organisations in developed industrial societies does indeed constitute an exceptional case that demands rather exceptional remedies. Not only can terrorism disrupt the balance of power and cause mass panic among the populace, it also interferes with the individual and collective dynamics which ensure the normal functioning of democracy. Legitimately established governments are under the obligation to defend the authority of the state and protect their citizens. On that basis, it follows that some kind of emergency legislation may be the only effective method of defending or even reestablishing the constitutional order damaged by a campaign of sustained terrorist violence.[23] Maintaining or restoring internal legal stability is an essential political task and may require modifications to the preordained judicial system to carry it out. These changes might well include, for example, restricting the rights of certain individuals under a given set of circumstances as long as basic democratic principles and procedures are observed. In periods of political instability provoked by terrorism, it is more imperative to defend democracy, its constituent structures and institutions, than to maintain as inviolate specific statutes and edicts that may well have been formulated before such a threat was in evidence.

From a critical perspective, this latter aspect is the one which is most often stressed. In all the anti-terrorist legislation which has been adopted by Western democracies during the past few decades, a certain number of constitutional guarantees have inevitably been restricted. These include the maximum length that a suspect can be held in preventative detention without right of *habeas corpus*; guarantees against unreasonable search and seizure of private property; the inviolability of private communications; and even freedom of speech. It is understood that when these guarantees are damaged, it is in the course of investigating what are commonly considered terrorist and terrorist-related crimes. Even when these suspensions are accompanied by formal guarantees subordinating them to control by the judiciary or the legislature, one still hears arguments that these will have only a limited effectiveness, while containing considerable potential for abuse. This may indeed be the case when judges adopt a passive attitude or if these legal provisions are implemented at a time when the law-enforcement agencies prove incapable of obeying the letter of the law they are sworn to uphold. Certainly problems are likely to occur when police agents have been influenced by notions of public order that do not mesh all that well with the moral imperatives underlying a system based on political tolerance. Emergency laws which notably restrict civil rights may lead, and in fact on more than one occasion have led, the police to over-react, and to stage mass round-ups of suspects. In the majority of cases those arrested were neither themselves terrorists, nor had anything to do with terrorism.

---

[23] On this argument, with particular reference to the British and German cases, see John E. Finn, *Constitutions in Crisis: Political Violence and the Rule of Law* (New York and Oxford: Oxford University Press, 1991).

One of the legal measures most likely to give rise to civil rights abuses by the state security apparatus is that of allowing suspects to be held without charge and without access to legal counsel for prolonged periods.[24] Regardless of whether this type of policy is tolerated for long or short periods of time, it is indeed one of the most widespread measures adopted by democratic governments as a means of reinforcing their anti-terrorist policies. It has given rise to cases such as the death of an *ETA* militant in February 1981 as a result of the mistreatment he received during the nine days he was held in isolation at police headquarters in Madrid. The legislation in force at the time allowed for ten days of arrest under the supervision of a judge, but obviously the judicial authority either could not, or chose not, to exercise this responsibly. It is disconcerting to see how the vast majority of those detained in the mass round-ups authorised by any of several special measures passed in Northern Ireland were subsequently set free with no charges filed against them.[25] This tends to suggest that special detention powers given to British law-enforcement agencies were, in large measure, either being misdirected or else used for purposes entirely different from those intended by their framers.

One of the most controversial moves taken by the British authorities, as part of anti-terrorist policy in Northern Ireland, has been the "supergrass" system. Under this strategy, suspects were offered inducements to inform against their comrades after criminal proceedings had been brought against them. In exchange for testimony, the informer had charges reduced or dropped. From 1983 to 1986, a good many of the sentences handed down by Northern Ireland tribunals were supported by testimony of the supergrasses. It appears that initially the information thus obtained may have been useful for generating intelligence and disrupting the terrorist organisations. Increasingly, however, it fell into disuse, not only on account of its limited effectiveness in bringing in guilty verdicts, but also because it had scarcely any effect on reducing the level of violence. On the contrary, it had a profoundly negative influence on the intensification of the Ulster conflict. Another factor contributing to its decline was the Anglo-Irish accord signed in November 1985. This protocol focused on a package of measures which sought to reconcile the communities involved in the Northern Ireland conflict by establishing guarantees

---

[24] In this respect, see the work of Stanley Cohen and Daphan Golan, *The Interrogation of Palestinians During the Intifada: Ill-treatment, Moderate Physical Pressure or Torture* (Jerusalem: The Israeli Information Centre for Human Rights in the Occupied Territories, 1995). Israel is the only democratic country which allows presumed terrorists to be subjected to physical pressure to obtain information. The authorities justify such techniques by pointing to the unusual degree of violence they face. Nevertheless, these practices are condemned by the international treaty making torture illegal that took effect in 1987.

[25] According to data published by the British Home Office, between 1974 and 1990, more than 7,000 were detained under the Prevention of Terrorism Act in relation to the conflict in Northern Ireland. Eighty-six per cent of these were set free, and only three per cent were accused of crimes covered by this Act. The rest received exclusion orders or were charged with other offences. See *Statewatch* 1, 2 (1991), pp. 10-11.

with respect to public-safety measures and the administration of justice.[26] In light of this far-reaching political development, it was inevitable that the scant reliability and inherent precariousness of informers would be questioned. Such a situation is conducive to serious judicial errors, deterioration in the public image of the state institutions, and possibly a crisis in the state's legitimacy which terrorists may seek to turn to their advantage.

Britain's criminal justice system has been strongly criticised since the end of the 1980s, as a series of unjustified verdicts came to light that had been handed down during the 1970s, many of them in relation to crimes carried out by the IRA on British soil. Some, such as the cases of the Guildford Four, the Seven Maguires and the Birmingham Six, acquired a great deal of notoriety. Those convicted spent large periods behind bars for crimes which they never committed, only being freed after other tribunals set aside the verdicts under which they had unjustly been condemned. The miscarriages of justice revealed a series of machinations carried out by police officers investigating the crimes, ranging from concealing evidence to falsifying testimony and obtaining confessions by the use of intimidation and trickery. The judges' bias in favour of the law-enforcement establishment, and an intense campaign of orchestrated hostility by the popular press, further contributed to the false verdicts.[27] These mistakes were only retroactively rectified (at an extremely late date) thanks to the determination of the suspects' friends and family members, a part of the liberal press, Anglican clergymen, and the efforts of a few eminent jurists and politicians with national clout.

It is true that democratic institutions may unwittingly magnify the political and social repercussions of terrorism when they are over-zealous in their legal response. The problem that needs to be addressed, then, is how to respect legal constitutional guarantees in force, without allowing them to stand in the way of meeting the citizen's rightful demands for justice — particularly those who are the victims of violent crime.[28] There can be no question that in formulating and implementing internal security policies, democratic governments need to adopt legal measures that are flexible enough to allow them to establish sanctions that are proportionate to the seriousness of the offence in question. It is essential that judicial organisms are agile and competent enough to oversee and direct law-enforcement activities and support them within the valid legal framework. There are also ample ethical as well as

---

[26] David Bonner, "Combating Terrorism: Supergrass Trials in Northern Ireland", *Modern Law Review* 51 (1988), pp. 23-53; Steven Greer, *Supergrasses: A Study in Anti-terrorist Law Enforcement in Northern Ireland* (Oxford: Clarendon Press, 1995); Anthony Jennings, ed., *Justice Under Fire: The Abuses of Civil Liberties in Northern Ireland* (London: Pluto Press, 1990).

[27] Steven Greer, "Miscarriages of Justice in the United Kingdom: A Very British Affair?", in Dario Melossi, ed., *Social Control, Political Power and the Penal Question: For a Sociology of Criminal Law and Punishment* (Oñati: International Institute for Sociology of Law, 1995).

[28] See José R. Recalde, "Problemas de legitimidad: provocación terrorista y respuesta del Estado", in Fernando Reinares, ed., *State and Societal Reactions to Terrorism* (Oñati: International Institute for the Sociology of Law, 1997).

purely practical considerations, however, (and there is no reason why either one of these criteria need be applied at the expense of the other) for arguing that all "dubious" elements should be excluded from the juridical facet of the anti-terrorist struggle. It is too easy for these to get out of hand and in the end they may prove counter-productive. This is especially likely to occur when they are carried out by state security apparatus' that are inadequate for the task at hand. In such instances, the tendency is to stretch the rules to abusive lengths and even far beyond the limits established by law.[29] These measures are thus difficult to administer impartially and in many cases it would not be going too far to assert that they represent a greater threat to democracy than the terrorism they are supposed to combat.[30] Such dubious provisions should be excluded out of hand, despite the objections of those who argue that the bending of the rule of law ought to be accepted as the lesser of two evils and one that is essential to contain and defeat terrorism. There is no doubt that sustained terrorism affects society's willingness to accept restrictions on its liberties for the sake of the personal safety of its members and the survival of the political system.[31] But this does certainly not thereby free the state from all restraint on legal action.

## Security Agencies and Terrorism

It is perfectly natural and reasonable that democracies should use the legal forms of violence which they monopolise and administer to combat illegal violence. Unlike dictatorships, or regimes which are more representative but operating within highly fragmented societies, however, consolidated democracies have rarely had occasion to call on the armed forces in order to face the terrorist challenge. Military force usually only entered the equation where the terrorist threat emerged suddenly and the other state security agencies were caught off guard unprepared to deal with acute crisis situations, such as a mass hostage-taking or hijacking. Even this limited degree of intervention has tended to recede as regular police forces have acquired the skills and experience required to deal with this type of incident. International cooperation between parallel state agencies has helped speed the process along. As an example, the first anti-terrorist elite squads in the Netherlands, the *Landelijke*

---

[29] As an illustration, between 1980 and 1983 the anti-terrorist legislation then effective in Spain was applied to 443 common criminals in Madrid alone. On the factors that made these and other abuses possible during the period from the crisis of Francoism to the consolidation of democracy, see Oscar Jaime-Jiménez, "Legislación antiterrorista y agencias estatales de seguridad: un análisis preliminar de la experiencia española, 1960-1996", *Revista de Derecho Penal Criminology* 6 (1996), pp. 569-97.

[30] On these matters, see Andrew Mack, "The Utility of Terrorism", *Australian and New Zealand Journal of Criminology* 14 (1981), pp. 197-224; Antonio Vercher, *Terrorism in Europe: An International Comparative Legal Analysis* (Oxford: Clarendon Press, 1992).

[31] Irving L. Horowitz, "The Routinization of Terrorism and its Unanticipated Consequences", in Martha Crenshaw, ed., *Terrorism, Legitimacy and Power: The Consequences of Political Violence* (Middletown, Conneticut: Wesleyan University Press, 1983), pp. 38-51.

*Bilstandsteam Terreurbestrijiding*, benefited from the training and expertise of the West German Federal Police, who at that time — the early 1970s — were far more experienced in this area.[32]

Throughout the 1980s and 1990s, army troops have sometimes played a secondary role in certain anti-terrorist missions, being temporarily deployed to control international borders (this has occurred in Spain) or guarding embassies when the police have had their resources strained to the utmost by extended mobilisation. This is what happened in France during the wave of terror attacks blamed on Algerian Islamic militants that swept the country between July and October 1995. But other than these specific circumstances it is generally accepted that involving the armed forces in the anti-terrorist struggle amounts to a dangerous over-reaction, at least as far as democratic countries are concerned. This is because such a response proceeds from the fallacious assumption that terrorism is a type of warfare, and therefore it is a task properly within the competence of the armed forces. This ignores the fact that terrorism is practiced by small groups that do not recognise any international convention regulating battlefield behaviour, nor are their members subject to military discipline.

However, to return to situations where the anti-terrorist effort is entrusted to existing law-enforcement agencies. The first consideration here is that special pains must be taken to coordinate their efforts if, as happens in Europe and North America, more than a single police-type organisation is involved in anti-terrorist activities. Apart from competition at the institutional level, personal rivalries are often brought to bear on the outcome, since the dangers and the sacrifices inherent in this special type of law enforcement work are often seen as a short-cut to promotion. Comparing experiences in various European countries shows a roughly similar approach to easing inter-agency tensions. Most commonly a system of checks and balances has been established.[33] The effectiveness of such an approach, however, is conditioned by external factors such as changes of government. Politicians' predilection for one of the security agencies at the expense of another may also be a factor. Generally, a centralised command centre has been used to coordinate the activities of anti-terrorist agencies.

Given the clandestine and unpredictable nature of terrorism, however, all these resources may not be effective unless they are accompanied by mechanisms for detecting and preventing future threats.[34] Reliable intelligence is an essential tool. Experience shows that, as long as the other components function as they should, success in the state's counter-terrorism campaign is directly proportional to the

---

[32] Herman and van der Laan Bouma, "Nationalists Without a Nation", p. 139.

[33] An excellent approach to this question can be found in Natalie Cettina, *Les enjeux organisationnels, de la lutte contre le terrorisme* (Paris: Université Panthéon-Assas, 1994).

[34] As noted by, among others, Irving L. Horowitz, "Political Terrorism and State Power", *Journal of Political and Military Sociology* 1, 1 (1973), p. 149.

emphasis placed on the gathering and analysing of reliable information.[35] On the contrary, when intelligence is insufficient or inadequate, the terrorist group may sense the window of opportunity they are being offered and will not hesitate to exploit this advantage by escalating its campaign of insurgent violence. In 1976, for reasons that have never been sufficiently clarified, the Italian Government decided to dismantle the special anti-terrorist units it had created only a few years earlier and ordered a far-reaching reorganisation of its secret services. Terrorist attacks, which until then had been diminishing in frequency, immediately began to pick up and did not ease again until the early 1980s. Not coincidentally, by that time, revamped intelligence services put under greater supervisory control of the legislative and executive branches, had begun to produce results.[36]

The upsurge in violence registered during Spain's transition to democracy, especially during the 1978-80 period, was to some extent a consequence of the transfers of command, personnel shuffles, and organisational restructuring involved in the orderly and peaceful change-over from an authoritarian to a democratic regime.[37] This, in parallel with other developments on the domestic and international scene, provided the terrorists with a window of opportunity to escalate their activities. Besides being hamstrung by inadequate mandates, it was clear that a number of senior officers in the security apparatus were by no means reconciled to a process of democratisation, the outcome of which was uncertain at the time. In a similar fashion, some analysts have linked the upsurge in both domestic and foreign terrorism in the United States from the early 1990s onwards to the problems that have assailed that country's intelligence services.[38] These agencies were hampered not only by a surge of negative public opinion produced by their controversial involvement in events that received a great deal of unfavourable media coverage, but they were also left with an organisational structure and operational mechanism that, with the end of the Cold War, had suddenly become obsolete, not to mention inadequate for dealing with the tactics of contemporary terrorist groups.

It is true that the functions which secret intelligence services may be required to perform to combat terrorism may well raise more than a few problems *vis-à-vis* the basic freedoms and civil rights of a democratic society. The experiences of various

---

[35] Edwy Plenel, "Police et terrorisme", *Esprit* 11 (1986), pp. 7-20; Bruce Hoffman and Jennifer Morrison-Taw, *A Strategic Framework for Countering Terrorism and Insurgency* (Santa Monica, California: The RAND Corporation, 1992); Chalk, "The Liberal Democratic Response to Terrorism", pp. 27-31.

[36] Leonard Weinberg and William L. Eubank, *The Rise and Fall of Italian Terrorism* (Boulder, Colorado: Westview Press, 1987), pp. 125-26.

[37] Reinares, "Democratización y terrorismo en el caso español, pp. 611-44.

[38] Joseph L. Albini, Roy E. Rogers and Julie Anderson, "The Sicilian Mafia, the Russian Mafia, the Evolution of Espionage Networks and the Crisis of International Terrorism and Global Organized Crime: An Application of Albini's Patron-client Model". Paper presented at the Workshop on Global Organized Crime and International Security, International Institute for the Sociology of Law, Oñati, 3-6 June 1997.

European and North American countries, however, show that these agencies can, in fact, carry out their activities within the legal and constitutional framework, providing that the executive and legislative branches exercise strict oversight.[39] Apart from non-classified data and the fruits of high technology surveillance, the type of intelligence most likely to be of use to the anti-terrorist struggle is often that which is furnished by informers and by agents infiltrated into the terrorists' own ranks. Both of these sources come with a set of inherent difficulties. Wittingly or not, informers may provide misleading information or become *agents provocateurs*, where the "moles" may find themselves forced to participate directly in criminal activities in order to "worm" their way deeper into the organisation.[40] Both types of operation run grave personal risks for the agents involved. One thinks of the informer within the French terrorist group *Action Directe* who was murdered in 1982 when its leaders discovered he had been supplying information to the *Reseignements generaux*, the state security agency.

Yet the fact remains that reliable intelligence can be a key element in the government's efforts to suppress terrorist violence. It is essential, however, that citizens only circumstantially involved, or not involved at all in the anti-terrorist campaign should not suffer harm as a result. An excessively repressive and indiscriminate response that fails to distinguish between the terrorists themselves and the society in which they operate only serves to alienate significant sectors of that society, turning them against the government. This, in turn, creates problems regarding the government's institutional legitimacy that may contribute to the terrorist group's mobilisation capability. Without first-rate intelligence, the security services will not be able to make the necessary distinctions between terrorists and innocent civilians. Instead they may tend to fall back on heavy-handed procedures such as suppressing the right to *habeas corpus* for extended periods or denying suspects legal counsel. Such measures are more than likely to be counter-productive, stirring up support for the insurgents, at least in social segments already emotionally or ideologically in sympathy with them. One need only look at the end results of the British crackdowns in Northern Ireland or Israeli mass detentions in the Occupied West Bank to confirm the truth of this observation. In the end, excesses and abuses

---

[39] On this problem, see John B. Wolf, "Controlling Political Terrorism in a Free Society", *Orbis* XIX, 4 (1976), pp. 1289-308; H. A. Cooper, "Terrorism and the Intelligence Function", in Marius H. Livingston, Lee B. Kress and Marie G. Waneck, eds, *International Terrorism in the Contemporary World* (Westport, Connecticut and London: Greenwood Press, 1978), pp. 287-96; K. G. Robertson, "Intelligence, Terrorism, and Civil Liberties", in Paul Wilkinson and Alasdair M. Stewart, eds, *Contemporary Research on Terrorism* (Aberdeen: Aberdeen University Press, 1987), pp. 549-69; Peter Gill, *Policing Politics: Security Intelligence and the Liberal Democratic State* (London: Frank Cass, 1994); Laurence Lustgarten and Ian Leigh, *In From the Cold: National Security and Parliamentary Democracy* (Oxford: Clarendon Press, 1994).

[40] On the problems raised by the use of informants and concealed agents, see Steven Greer, "Towards a Sociological Model of the Police Informant", *British Journal of Sociology* 46, 3 (1995), pp. 509-27; Cyrille J. Fijnaut and Gary T. Marx, eds, *Undercover Police Surveillance in Comparative Perspective* (La Haya: Kluwer Law International, 1995).

simply give rise to more insecurity, more public order problems and more polarisation in the society. This is not only a negation of the principles of democratic government that they are supposed to defend; it also makes it that much easier for the terrorists to gain public support.

It often turns out that security force structures which act haphazardly or bend or break the laws they are supposed to uphold are actually not particularly well qualified for the task they have been given. One recurrent problem is the inability (largely due to poor intelligence) to identify accurately those who are really responsible and to bring them before the courts with the evidence required to secure a conviction. In such situations, pressures from above and below — politicians and public opinion demanding tangible results at all costs — may lead security forces to contemplate mass arrests and other unwise moves. A good example of this was the British response to an upsurge in PIRA terrorism in 1971.[41] Mass detentions carried out by the army, characterised by the round-up of young males in neighbourhoods where republican sympathies were running strongest, were complemented by special interrogation techniques that had been developed in Britain's former colonies. Keeping suspects hooded, subjecting them to loud noises, depriving them of sleep and proper food, and forcing them to stand against the wall for extended periods of time were the usual practice. It was only after five years had gone by, when these techniques had been shown to be not only futile but also counter-productive, that they were formally banned in the wake of protests over the mental and physical degradation which they entailed.

An inept response to the terrorist threat can equally be related to a lack of adequate control by the executive branch over the activities of its security agencies. Cases of abuse reported from Spain's Basque provinces, especially during the crucial years of the democratic transition, appear to fall within this category. These were mostly attributed to agents and officials who had been trained and steeled in a system that was authoritarian and quasi-military in its approach to the maintenance of law and order.[42] A further problem is likely to occur when, either through inhibition or manipulation, the security agencies augment the impact of terrorist crimes on public opinion for their own private interest. Such cases serve to show how misleading it can be to evaluate the state's response to terrorism as if it originated from a single source.[43] For example, after the heads of Italy's secret services were sacked following the kidnap and murder of the Italian President Aldo

---

[41] Peter Taylor, *Beating the Terrorists? Interrogation in Omagh, Gough and Castlereagh* (Harmondsworth: Penguin Books, 1980), p. 19. On the maintenance of the public order in a society so divided and affected by terrorism as Northern Ireland, see Adrian Guelke, "Policing in Northern Ireland", in Brigid Hadfield, ed., *Northern Ireland: Politics and the Constitution* (Buckingham: Open University Press, 1992), pp. 94-109

[42] See Manuel Ballbé, *Orden público y militarismo en la España constitucional (1812-1983)* (Madrid: Alianza, 1985), chapter 12.

[43] As Donatella della Porta has observed, when analysing the Italian case, in his "Institutional Responses to Terrorism: The Italian Case", *Terrorism and Political Violence* 4 (1992), p. 167.

Moro by the Red Brigades, it emerged that they had all been members of a Masonic lodge implicated in a campaign to destabilise and eventually force the collapse of the democratic government. The same lodge was also implicated in neo-fascist terrorist acts of which some resulted in major massacres.[44] When terrorism of the far right could no longer exploit privileged relations with the Italian secret service, it went into decline and all but disappeared.[45]

On other occasions we can observe how the illicit use of public resources is meant to enhance and complement existing legal measures through methods that can scarcely be distinguished from those employed by the terrorists themselves. Some police officers or individuals holding political office may consider these to be extremely effective in the short term, despite their obvious illegality. In point of fact, not only are these morally reprehensible but also exceedingly counter-productive in that they tend to feed the social unrest from which the terrorists draw their ideological sustenance. This is what occurred in Spain when members of the state security forces secretly set up illegal anti-terrorist groups, known as Anti-Terrorist Liberation Groups (GAL), with the passive acquiescence, if not the active complicity, of some high ranking politicians. The anti-terrorist consensus among Spain's political parties took a long time to recover from the consequences of this illegal violence, practiced around the mid-1980s. The credibility of the state security apparatus suffered great damage while at the same time providing *ETA* with new pretexts for justifying its own terrorism just when support for the organisation had sunk to an all-time low. Spain is, of course, far from the only country in which those who enforce the law are less successful in obeying its strictures. Elsewhere officials have either violated the law themselves or stood by and let others do so with impunity. In that regard, it has been shown that loyalist Protestant paramilitary groups operating in Ulster have clearly benefited over a considerable period of time from the deliberate passivity and documented cases of collusion on the part of the British security services.[46]

## Conclusion

The above considerations make it clear that the ineffectiveness or incompetence of state law-enforcement agencies have been a key factor in determining why terrorism

---

[44] See especially, Weinberg and Eubank, *Rise and Fall of Italian Terrorism*, pp. 119-33. See also, Stefano Rodotá, "La risposta dello stato al terrorisms: gli apparati", in Gianfranco Pasquino, ed., *La prova delle armi* (Bolonia: Il Mulino, 1984), pp. 77-91; Luciana Stortoni, La repressione del terrorisms in Italia: l'intervento delle Forze dell'ordine fino all'inizio degli anni ottanta, unpublished doctoral thesis, European University Institute, 1992.

[45] As Rosario Minna has corroborated in "Il terrorisms di destra", in Donatella della Porta, ed., *Terrorismi in Italia* (Bolonia: Il Mulino, 1984), especially pp. 59-61.

[46] See Steve Bruce, *The Red Hand: Protestant Paramilitaries in Northern Ireland* (Oxford: Oxford University Press, 1992), especially chapter 8. See also the information published in *Statewatch* 3, 4 (1993), pp. 12-13.

should have taken root in certain democracies rather than in others. If, on the contrary, the state takes pains that its security apparatus should respond in a limited, well defined and credible fashion to the challenge while scrupulously respecting the legal framework, its response could become a serious obstacle for a terrorist group in its efforts to consolidate or perpetuate itself.[47] It even becomes possible to imagine the terrorist group's definitive dismemberment or its eventual collapse. For instance, there seems little doubt that the decline of terrorism in Western Europe dating from the end of the 1970s onward coincided to a great extent with the development and implementation of sophisticated and comprehensive internal security mechanisms that, applied in conjunction with other measures of a political or juridical nature, have managed to narrow substantially the favourable opportunity structure available to these types of armed clandestine organisations.

Recent variations of the terrorist phenomenon, such as those that derive their inspiration from racist and xenophobic ideologies, have begun to taken centre stage. These are in part a side-effect of the imbalances produced as advanced industrialised societies are acquiring a multi-cultural dimension and in part the result of national governments becoming involved in conflicts beyond their borders. The changing nature of terrorism amounts to a new and important test for the conjunction of measures that typically characterise the state response to terrorism in the context of a democratic regime. The response has to adapt as the nature of the criminal activity changes. To be sure, however, the real validity of the law enforcement and other measures eventually adopted against terrorism tends to be objectively limited as a result of the increasing transnational character of that phenomenon. This necessarily makes effective cooperation on the international level of the greatest importance.

---

[47] John B. Wolf, *Fear Of Fear: A Survey of Terrorist Operations and Controls in Open Societies* (New York and London: Plenum Press, 1981); Wilkinson, *Terrorism and the Liberal State*, especially chapter 8; Chalk, "The Liberal Democratic Response to Terrorism".

# [17]

# The Discourse and Practice of Counter-Terrorism in Liberal Democracies

RONALD D. CRELINSTEN

*Criminology, University of Ottawa*

This article examines the post-Cold War tendency to broaden the counter-terrorism mandate to include other phenomena such as organised crime, drug-trafficking and illegal immigration. This redefinition has important implications for democracy, both at the level of discourse and at the level of practice. At the level of discourse, the plasticity of the word "terrorism" and its application to a wide variety of phenomena is a form of claims making activity by a variety of agencies fighting for budgetary allocations in an era of cost-cutting and deficit reduction. At the level of practice, the counter-terrorism mandate is being expanded to include the range of phenomena covered in the widening discourse and this, in turn, has led to a blurring of boundaries between internal and external security, police and military models of control, and public and private sectors. All this has an impact on the openness of government, the accountability of agencies of social control, the adherence to the rule of law in the fight against terrorism and related phenomena, and the possibility of informed consent by a public made fearful by the claims-making discourse as it is disseminated through the mass media.

With the end of the Cold War and the disintegration of the Soviet Union, the bipolar lenses with which many viewed the world of political violence and terrorism are gone. As a result, the definitional and typological complexities that were so cavalierly papered over during the 1970s and 1980s have begun to resurface in the discourse of those concerned with counter-terrorism. Phenomena such as drug trafficking, organised crime and illegal immigration are being included along with the more traditional objects of concern for those responsible for dealing with terrorism. In addition, new kinds of threats have been formulated, ranging from infectious diseases[1] to information warfare.[2] The recognition of new/old threats has,

---

[1] See, for example, Andrew T. Price-Smith, "Infectious Disease and State Failure: Developing a New Security Paradigm". Paper prepared for the annual meeting of the International Studies Association, Toronto, 18-22 March 1997.

[2] See, for example, Matthew G. Devost, National Security in the Information Age. MA thesis in Political Science, The University of Vermont, May, 1995. For an electronic version, see <http://www.terrorism.com/documents/devostthesis.html>. See also Matthew G. Devost, Brian K. Houghton and Neal Allen Pollard, "Information Terrorism: Political Violence in the Information Age", *Terrorism and Political Violence* 9, 1 (1997), pp. 72-83.

in turn, been translated into a broader operational mandate for agencies responsible for counter-terrorism and the blurring of mandates between different control agencies that previously were quite distinct, such as customs agencies, border control, security intelligence, defence and policing. This tendency to place disparate phenomena into the same security basket has also been reflected in recent analyses of terrorism. For example, Richard Clutterbuck[3] lumps drug trafficking, international crime, ethnic cleansing, religious fanaticism, rural guerrilla and urban terrorism all together as legitimate concerns for counter-terrorism policymaking in the post-Cold War world.

In this article, I will examine the implications of these changes, both at the level of discourse and at the level of practice, for the development of counter-terrorism policy within liberal democracies. For the purposes of this analyis, I shall consider liberal democracies to be characterised by the following principles: the rule of law; openness and accountability of government; and the maintenance of a bond of trust and confidence between citizen and government that results from an electorate that is informed about public affairs. While these are all ideals that fall short in practice in most, if not all, liberal democracies, they are the central principles which distinguish such regimes from authoritarian or totalitarian ones. Inherent in these principles are many of the human rights that have been entrenched in a number of international conventions since the Second World War, most notably the Universal Declaration of Human Rights and the International Covenant on Civil and Political Rights. These rights include, among others, freedom of opinion and expression, freedom of thought, conscience and religion, freedom of assembly and association, equality before the law, the right to privacy and the right to take part in the government of the country and in the conduct of public affairs.

In the sections which follow, I shall first examine in greater detail the relationship between terrorism and criminal phenomena such as drug trafficking and organised crime, with a view to understanding why they might lend themselves to a common approach by police and security agencies. Next, I shall discuss how the assimilation of criminal phenomena into the counter-terrorism mandate might affect the two most common models of counter-terrorism: the criminal justice model and the war model. I shall also look at the related phenomenon of the increasing involvement of the military in internal security and the resultant conceptual blurring of internal and external security that stems from this. Next, I shall examine the relationship between what Jean-Paul Brodeur[4] has called "high policing", or political policing, and "low policing", or the policing of ordinary crime. This will involve a discussion of the recent trend towards increased cooperation between security agencies and police agencies and its implications for the rule of law, openness of government and public accountability. Then, I shall look at the wider issue of the relationship between

---

[3] Richard Clutterbuck, *Terrorism in an Unstable World* (London: Routledge, 1994).

[4] Jean-Paul Brodeur, "High Policing and Low Policing: Remarks about the Policing of Political Activities", *Social Problems* 30 (1983), pp. 507-20.

social action and political action and the distinction that has been made between societal security and national security.[5] Are all threats to social order necessarily threats to the state? At what point can we say that organised crime or drug trafficking or illegal immigration, for that matter, threaten national security, as opposed to the social order (or societal security)? If social or criminal phenomena are depicted as national security threats by those in authority, what impact does this have on public opinion and public attitudes about social activism or crime?

Finally, I shall examine how these definitional and operational changes impact on the different elements of democratic acceptability identified above: the rule of law; openness of government; public accountability; and public trust and confidence in government. These features of a democratic society, in turn, highlight other issues, such as the protection of minority rights in a society where majority rules; the concept of "loyal opposition" whereby dissent is valued as long as it follows certain rules; the role of the media in promulgating moral panics and creating public fear and loathing of outsiders; and the polarisation of freedom and security, rights and duties, privacy and surveillance in a society increasingly concerned about security.

**Placing Terrorism in Context**

Definitional ambiguity is an inherent feature of national security threat assessment since, at the operational level, terrorism merges with other phenomena, such as crime, subversion, advocacy, protest and dissent. To illustrate this, Figure 1 places terrorism along a continuum of phenomena that includes social, political, coercive/violent and military forms of control and deviance.[6] The upper part of the figure refers to state agents and agencies, i.e. governments or the "controllers". The lower part refers to citizens and groups operating outside government, i.e. opposition groups or the "controlled".[7]

Figure 1 identifies four domains that typify the ways in which controllers and controlled interact: the social, the political, the penal and the military. Within these domains lie the institutions of social control that regulate daily life. Yet as David Garland[8] points out, social institutions are porous in that they are "only partly self-contained":

---

[5]  See Didier Bigo, "Security(s): Internal and External, the möbius ribbon". Paper presented at the International Studies Association annual meeting, Toronto, 18-22 March 1997, especially pp. 13-15.

[6]  For earlier versions of this model, see Ronald D. Crelinsten, "Terrorism, Counter-Terrorism and Democracy: The Assessment of National Security Threats", *Terrorism and Political Violence* 1, 2 (1989), pp. 242-69; "Terrorism as Political Communication: The Relationship Between the Controller and the Controlled", in P. Wilkinson and A. M. Stewart, eds, *Contemporary Research on Terrorism* (Aberdeen: University of Aberdeen Press, 1987), pp. 3-23.

[7]  Crelinsten, "Terrorism as Political Communication".

[8]  David Garland, *Punishment and Modern Society: A Study in Social Theory* (Oxford: Clarendon Press, 1990), p. 283.

They open up on to other worlds and connect into a social network which extends well beyond their particular domain. Each institution occupies a particular place in the wider social field and routinely relates to its social environment, affecting and being affected by the social forces which surround it. Institutions link up with other institutions and with the world outside.

|  |  |  |  |  |  |  |
|---|---|---|---|---|---|---|
|  |  |  |  |  |  | $C_1$ ↓ |
|  |  |  | $B_1$ ↓ |  | State Terrorism "from above" |  |
|  | $A_1$ ↓ |  | Security Intel. |  |  |  |
|  | Politics |  |  | Criminal |  |  |
| Social Control | ←→ | Government | ←→ | Justice | ←→ | Internal War |
| Deviance | ←→ | Dissent | ←→ | Crime | ←→ | Revolution |
|  | Protest ↑ |  | Subversion ↑ |  | Insurgent Terrorism "from below" ↑ |  |
|  | $A_2$ |  | $B_2$ |  | $C_2$ |  |

**Figure 1.** Placing terrorism in context: insurgent terrorism falls within Zone $C_2$ that separates the violent fringe of political protest, for which the control model is usually a criminal justice one, and fullblown revolution, for which the control model is usually a military one. State terrorism falls within a reciprocal zone, ($C_1$), that separates a judicial model of control which respects due process and a military model that follows the rules of war. Human rights abuses are greatest in this middle zone, though they can occur within both the criminal justice and war models of control.

Similarly, in Figure 1, we see how the range of institutions of social control — from the most coercive ones of the military and the criminal justice system, through the police and the security intelligence agencies, to the political institutions of government and the social institutions of the media, work, school, church and home — all operate and cooperate within a wider environment. The grey zones at A, B, and C attempt to map out some of the ways in which different institutions at each point along the spectrum link up and, at times, supplant, distort, mirror or otherwise influence one another.

Unfortunately, a linear model cannot capture the full complexity of these interactions. This is because institutions more widely separated from one another — at different zones — also mutually influence each other, shaping and being shaped by those social forces that surround them. Nevertheless, it is this inherent porousness of social institutions and the particular domains that they represent which is the primary focus of my analysis. Much of the impetus of democratic life is directed at the maintenance of clear demarcation zones between different policy domains and the institutions of social control that characterise them — despite their inherent interrelatedness. As such, any explicit attempts by agents of specific institutions to facilitate the blurring of operational mandates or policy domains are by their very nature potentially anti-democratic. In similar fashion, any deliberate attempt to blur spheres of protest or dissident activity by those at the bottom of the figure can also pose a threat to the democratic principles at issue here, if only because they can serve to justify a reciprocal blurring in the realm of control.

Terrorism is one part of this complex spectrum of interaction between controller and controlled, lying in the grey zone between the penal and military domains (zone C). In Figure 1, I take a *behavioural* approach to defining terrorism, as a form of coercive, violent communication, rather than a motive-based or perpetrator-based approach. It then becomes clear that terrorism can occur in the context of criminal activity, as much as within a political or a war context. It can also be committed by state agents as much as by insurgents or political criminals. In fact, the use of torture has often been justified as a necessary weapon against insurgents and terrorists and has played a central part in regimes of terror that have evolved from counter-terrorism or counter-insurgency campaigns.[9]

Using this behavioural approach, terrorism can be defined as the combined use and threat of violence, planned in secret and usually executed without warning, that is directed against one set of targets (the direct victims) in order to coerce compliance or to compel allegiance from a second set of targets (targets of demands) and to intimidate or to impress a wider audience (target of terror or target of attention). The act of victimising captures the attention of particular audiences and allows the terrorist to communicate more specific messages tailored to each one. The message need not be articulated in words; it can be symbolic (conveyed by the target selected, for example) or simply shocking (conveyed by the indiscriminate nature of the attack). This is classic propaganda of the deed.

With such a definition, one can easily argue that organised crime syndicates and drug cartels use terrorism in the pursuit of goals that are primarily aimed at ensuring a propitious environment for their criminal activities. Corruption rather than subversion is their goal and they more often than not would actually prefer the government to survive and prosper, as long as they can continue their activities unimpeded. Even before the post-Cold War focus on such activities, earlier terrorism scholars have recognised the existence of criminal terrorism as a distinct phenomenon.[10] Criminal terrorism, however, received scant attention during the Cold War compared with political terrorism, particularly its ideological and nationalist variants. Now, as the definitional lens broadens to include organised

---

9 See Ronald D. Crelinsten and Alex P. Schmid, eds, *The Politics of Pain: Torturers and Their Masters* (Boulder, CO: Westview Press, 1995) for an examination of the use of torture.

10 See, for example, Frederick Hacker, *Crusaders, Criminals, Crazies* (New York: W. W. Norton, 1976). See also the typology on the front cover of Alex Schmid's texts on terrorism, e.g. Alex P. Schmid and Albert J. Jongman, *Political Terrorism: A New Guide to Actors, Authors, Concepts, Data Bases, Theories and Literature* (New Brunswick: Transaction Books, 1988).

crime and drug trafficking, it is important to ask whether they are really relevant to a counter-terrorism mandate.

## Common Features of These and Other Seemingly Unrelated Phenomena

Terrorism clearly involves the commission of criminal acts such as bombing, kidnapping, murder and extortion. Acts of terrorism can also be part of the arsenal used by organised crime organisations and drug cartels. In cases where criminal organisations use violence *instrumentally*, for communicative purposes such as coercion, intimidation or extortion, rather than for purely vindictive, revengeful or retributive purposes, such action would be consistent with the behavioural definition of terrorism presented above. However, much of the instrumental violence used by organised crime syndicates or drug cartels does not differentiate between the direct victims and the targets of demands or the targets of attention. In protection rackets, for example, the direct victim of threats and violence is also the one who must accede to demands for money. On the other hand, when the Italian Mafia assassinated judges investigating their activities, this was a message to others not to get involved in the investigation. As such, these murders would conform to the above definition.

Ethnic cleansing, too, is usually planned in secret and inflicted on its victims without warning, though usually in a war context. To the extent that such activity communicates a message of terror to others sharing the same ethnic origin, one can even argue that it fits the definition of terrorism provided above. It is arguable, however, whether mass murder and genocide are strictly terrorism, since the main goal is elimination of a people, not the communication of messages of intimidation, terror or specific demands. Peter Merkl[11] refers to the Serb policies of ethnic cleansing as "a combination of direct genocide and expulsion by terror", thereby distinguishing between these two quite different goals.

As for terrorism itself, the involvement of terrorist groups and sympathisers in the drug trade and other forms of criminal activity has contributed to the widening of the counter-terrorism mandate to include purely criminal phenomena. Many terrorist groups do engage in criminal activity such as bank robberies, credit fraud forgery or drug trafficking in order to raise funds for their cause. Some groups involved in insurgent campaigns in their home states extort funds from fellow nationals who have fled the homeland and sought refugee status in the West. For example, in April 1996, Swiss police arrested fifteen members of the Liberation Tigers of Tamil Eelam who are conducting a guerrilla campaign against the Sri Lankan Government.

---

[11] Peter H. Merkl, "Radical Right Parties in Europe and Anti-Foreigner Violence: A Comparative Essay", *Terrorism and Political Violence* 7 (1995), p. 100.

They were charged with causing physical injury, intimidation and extortion directed against Tamil refugees in Switzerland.[12]

While the term "narcoterrorism" probably goes too far in its implication that a new form of terrorism has emerged,[13] as long as terrorist groups do profit from the drug trade and other phenomena such as money laundering and arms smuggling, security agencies will have an interest in tracking the movement of such goods and the people who engage in their distribution. In this sense, it is simply a logical step to increase police and security cooperation in areas where the methods of investigation are similar.

One aspect of the above definition of terrorism that all these phenomena share, whether political or criminal or a mixture of both, is the element of secrecy. From an operational perspective, this is the most important. All such groups involve organisational structures that are clandestine. Membership often requires oaths of secrecy or the commission of criminal acts by new recruits to ensure fidelity to the organisation's norms and values rather than "mainstream" ones and to render exit from the group more difficult. Because of these characteristics, such phenomena are resistant to traditional methods of policing and usually require more intrusive techniques such as electronic surveillance and mail-opening which, by their very nature, infringe on the personal liberties of those under surveillance. Such intrusive techniques are admissible within the rule of law, but there are strict legal procedures that must be followed before they are allowed, usually involving the obtaining of judicial warrants.

Because members of clandestine organisations do not usually divulge information about what they are up to, control agencies have to rely on providing incentives to informers to break their oaths of secrecy and to betray the trust of their colleagues. The use of informers, however, is fraught with difficulties and dangers,[14] some of which have direct bearing on the protection of individual rights. Informers sometimes provide false or misleading information that incriminates innocent people. In other cases, informers become *agents provocateurs*, encouraging or convincing those in the groups they inform upon to engage in activities they might otherwise not have considered. Beyond the use of informers, there is the ultimate weapon whereby control agencies use their own agents to penetrate secret organisations in order to collect information "from the inside". This often leads to the same ethical dilemmas alluded to above, whereby the agent must commit criminal acts, sometimes even murder, to gain entry into the organisation.

---

[12] Victor Biro, *Weekly Terrorism Profile* (*WTP*), 22 April 1996.

[13] In similar fashion, the term "computerror" or "computer terrorism" has sprung up in the wake of highly publicised incidents whereby individuals have managed to break into computer data banks. Such activities, including the use of computer viruses, are more a kind of sabotage rather than a new form of terrorism. The use of a term such as "computerror" only introduces more definitional confusion into an already confused area.

[14] See Gary T. Marx, *Undercover: Police Surveillance in America* (Berkeley: University of California Press, 1988).

One reason for including certain kinds of criminal activity in a counter-terrorism mandate might therefore relate to these shared characteristics. Especially from an operational point of view, this makes a lot of sense since expertise gained in the fight against organised crime can be applied to the fight against terrorism and vice versa. As an example, Richard Ericson and Kevin Haggerty describe how

> records on organized criminals inevitably tie in with records on political criminals and terrorists. Much of the activity scrutinized by police intelligence units is explicitly political, racist meetings being one example. Many organized criminals are treated as potential terrorists. Of course, separate records are kept on suspected terrorists, the data files being similar to those for organized crime figures.[15]

Here we see how, from a strictly operational point of view, such as record-keeping, organised crime, political crime and terrorism are all treated in a similar fashion. Furthermore, those suspected of one are automatically suspected of the other.

The question remains, however, why all of a sudden counter-terrorism discourse is focused so much on criminal phenomena. This brings us back to the end of the Cold War.

**Finding a New Enemy**

During the Cold War, the world of terrorism and political violence was viewed through the bipolar East vs West lens. Definitional and typological complexities were papered over by Cold Warriors intent on forcing all conflicts onto a Procrustean bed of a Soviet-sponsored, international terror network intent on destabilising and subverting the West. This resulted in several distinct trends in the terrorism literature, particularly during the 1970s and early 1980s: a tendency to focus exclusively on international and transnational terrorism and to ignore domestic terrorism or to cast it in a transnational light;[16] a tendency to ignore right-wing terrorism and to focus exclusively on left-wing terrorism;[17] a tendency to focus primarily on insurgent terrorism and to ignore state terrorism, particularly of the

---

[15] Richard V. Ericson and Kevin D. Haggerty, *Policing the Risk Society* (Toronto: University of Toronto Press, 1997), p. 246.

[16] This often involved stripping national conflicts of their social, political and cultural contexts so as to characterise more easily the conflict as the result of Soviet influence. This may be why the state terrorism of the Shah of Iran was tolerated (and, it may be argued, facilitated, through technology transfer and police training) — until the Khomeini Revolution put an end to it (and replaced it with another form). For an excellent analysis of both regimes of terror, see Darius Rejali, *Torture and Modernity: Self, Society, and State in Modern Iran* (Boulder, CO: Westview Press, 1994).

[17] This was facilitated by the first trend, since many left-wing terrorist groups either cooperated internationally/transnationally or else used an internationalist rhetoric, claiming common goals with comrades and brethren throughout the world in their common fight against Western (US) imperialism and colonialism.

variety used by Western[18] and especially US-sponsored "authoritarian" regimes; and a wilful blindness to any evidence of a US-backed terror network intent on destabilising and subverting the Eastern bloc. Much of the terrorist literature took on a Manichean flavour with titles such as "How the West Can Win". The enemy was clear and academic analysis often tended to cast itself in a cheering mode for increasingly militaristic policy solutions to the terrorist problem.[19] With the end of the Cold War, the old enemy was gone, the war was won. When the bipolar lenses were removed, the world looked quite different. Domestic conflicts were more easily seen in their social, political and cultural contexts; right-wing terrorism became more apparent; state terrorism was more easily seen to cross ideological divides and to have its own set of unique variables; and the idea of terror networks sponsored by superpowers was more easily seen to be a simplifying myth that conveniently obscured the complexity of the terrorism phenomenon.[20] The problem was that the world suddenly became more complicated. As a result, the enemy became more diffuse.

The creation of an external enemy is one of the most important elements in motivating soldiers to fight and in galvanising societies to support a war effort. This is as true for counter-terrorism and criminal justice as it is for warfare — conventional or unconventional. At the definitional level of analysis, much of the impetus for broadening the scope of counter-terrorism discourse to include phenomena such as organised crime and drug trafficking is the need to create a new enemy to replace that of the Cold War. Many Western security intelligence agencies are even promoting the importance of economic espionage as a new and rising threat to national security. According to Lustgarten and Leigh,[21] this new focus on economic interests represents a dangerous broadening of the meaning of national security. By focusing on criminal syndicates and international drug traffickers intent on destabilising the Western social and economic system, we return once again to

---

[18] For a comparison of American and Soviet views on terrorism at the end of the 1980s, see Brian Jenkins, "Setting the Scene", in J. Marks and I. Beliaev, eds, *Common Ground on Terrorism: Soviet-American Cooperation Against the Politics of Terror* (New York: W. W. Norton, 1991), pp. 30-49. While the United States focused on international terrorism, primarily because United States nationals were prime targets, the Soviet Union focused mainly on the danger of domestic terrorism. Now, we find that terrorism at home has become a prime focus of the Americans in the wake of the New York World Trade Center bombing and especially the Oklahoma City bombing, while the Soviet fears have been justified by the Chechen use of terrorism in their ongoing rebellion.

[19] For more on the militarisation of counter-terrorism in the late 1980s, see Ronald D. Crelinsten and Alex P. Schmid, "Western Responses to Terrorism: A Twenty-Five Year Balance Sheet", in A. P. Schmid and R. D. Crelinsten, eds, *Western Responses to Terrorism* (London: Frank Cass, 1993), pp. 307-40, especially pp. 315-22.

[20] For a more recent attempt to transcend some of these Cold War-inspired distortions and to view terrorism in its historical, social, political and economic context, see Martha Crenshaw, ed., *Terrorism in Context* (Philadelphia: University of Pennsylvania Press, 1995).

[21] Laurence Lustgarten and Ian Leigh, *In From the Cold: National Security and Parliamentary Democracy* (Oxford: Clarendon Press, 1994), pp. 27-30.

many of the features of the old simplifying myth: one, that our domestic and international problems can be blamed on a state-sponsored, international terror network of evil outsiders who are difficult to track and to capture, and two, that the only way they can be countered is through international cooperation and the relaxing of the rule of law to allow our police and security intelligence agencies to do their job. Herein lies one of the dangers that such thinking poses for democratic society. By promulgating the notion of an increased level of threat, a new kind of danger, agencies of social control engage in claims-making activity. They claim that they need new powers, new jurisdictions, new networks of cooperation, new power sharing arrangements, all because of the transnational nature of the threat. Suddenly, experts claim that the level of lethality has increased,[22] although their statistics are not convincing due to the fact that high casualties have occurred before. One expert who, in the 1970s, coined the phrase "terrorism as a new mode of warfare", was still using the word "new" in an address to a conference in 1997. Clearly, the newness of the threat is in large part a semantic construction designed to justify increased funding and expanded powers at the operational level.

During the Cold War, *internal* threats were never taken as seriously as external ones, even to the point of excluding domestic incidents from incident chronologies and data bases. This promoted a kind of blindness to domestic terrorism (and its causes/solutions) that was typical of the Cold War period. When serious domestic terrorism does break out, it can then easily be seen as a symptom of an external threat, much as the Oklahoma bombing was first attributed to Muslim extremists rather than "home-grown" militia men. What was fundamentally troubling to most Americans when they first learned who the prime suspects actually were was that the alleged perpetrators of the Oklahoma bombing were "clean-cut", white, all-American boys. It is always easier to vilify someone when he or she is perceived to be inherently alien. Some of the recent domestic cases in the United States highlight this variable as well. For example, it was striking to see how the authorities dealt with the Montana Freemen standoff in March-April 1996 and to contrast their approach with their treatment of the Waco standoff three years earlier. In Waco, a negotiations approach which tried to bridge the gap between David Koresh's clearly "deviant" world view and that of the negotiators was ultimately swept aside by an assault approach. This was justified primarily by a supposedly growing threat to the children (threat amplification), but was also clearly fuelled by a view of Koresh as "alien" and therefore unredeemable.[23] In Montana, despite a similarly fundamental schism between the world views of the Freemen and the authorities, a negotiations strategy prevailed and the incident was resolved peacefully after a considerable

---

[22] See, for example, Bruce Hoffman, "The Confluence of International and Domestic Trends in Terrorism", *Terrorism and Political Violence* 9, 2 (1997), pp. 2-3.

[23] For an excellent analysis of the Waco incident, see Michael Barkun, "Millenarian Groups and Law Enforcement Agencies: The Lessons of Waco". *Terrorism and Political Violence* 6, 1 (1994), pp. 75-95.

period of time. One element that may have been decisive was that, among the local inhabitants, there appeared to be an underlying assumption that the Freemen were basically good people, not unlike everyone else.

In the section which follows, I shall look more closely at the relationship between crime and terrorism by examining the two principal control models that have been used to counter terrorism.

## Two Models of Counter-Terrorism

Figure 2 illustrates the relationship between a criminal justice and a war model of counter-terrorism. In a criminal justice model, the rule of law is paramount, while in a war model, it is the rules of war that prevail. In the criminal justice model, it is the police who exercise the state's monopoly on the use of violence. The rules of engagement, so to speak, involve the use of *minimal* force, which requires an exercise of judgement on the part of the officer(s) involved. Military rules of engagement, on the other hand, require the *maximal* use of force, designed to overpower the enemy.

It has primarily been via deformations of the criminal justice model that liberal democracies have moved away from the rule of law and democratic acceptability.[24] Special courts have been used in France and Spain. Special procedures have been adopted, such as internment without trial in Northern Ireland. Limiting the rights of the defence, such as in Germany, or allowing certain witnesses to testify on videotape, thereby making it impossible for the defence to cross-examine, have undermined the traditional prerogatives of due process.

Excessive use of force has been the primary problem within the war model of counter-terrorism, particularly in the case of political killings whereby a suspect is shot rather than arrested, as in cases of alleged shoot-to-kill policies. This often arises when elite commandos, who may be either police personnel with special training or military personnel, are used to capture suspected terrorists. It is clear that the rule of law is breached in such incidents, but it is not always clear whether such breaches are an unintended consequence of using personnel accustomed to employing "maximal force" or the result of an explicit policy.

If one looks at the bottom of Figure 2, it is clear that criminal phenomena do merge with political ones. As a result, those agencies whose mandate it is to counter them can have a vested interest in sharing information, intelligence and operational techniques. While jurisdictional conflicts and turf battles have traditionally impeded such cooperation, the new discourse that conflates a variety of disparate threats into one composite framework has created a new incentive for cooperation. This, in turn, has led to a blurring of mandates. Two complementary trends can be identified: the

---

[24] See Crelinsten and Schmid, "Western Responses to Terrorism", pp. 333-34 , note 20.

militarisation of the police mandate and the "policification"[25] of the military mandate.

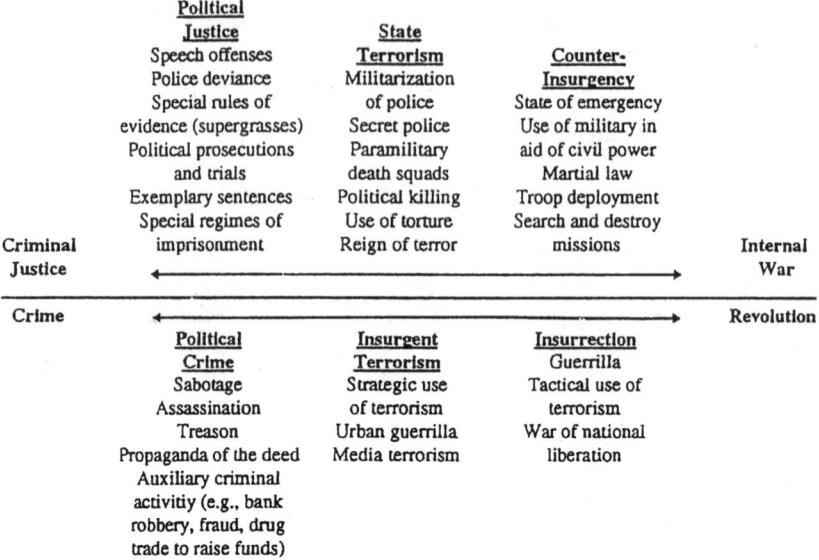

**Figure 2.** The zone that separates the more individual acts of political violence that are traditionally treated as crimes and those forms of political violence that, because of the involvement of larger numbers of people and weaponry, are treated more as war. While auxiliary criminal activity is placed on the more purely criminal side of the diagram, it is true that terrorist groups and guerrilla and national liberation groups do sometimes engage in more purely criminal activities, such as drug trafficking, money laundering and the kinds of protection rackets or criminal enforcement more typical of organised crime. The same can also be said for some paramilitary forces and death squads, as well as some police forces and military units.

## A Blurring of Security Mandates

Martin Woolacott has recently argued that "crime is beginning to be dealt with as if it were an insurgency, a thesis that is supported by moves in a number of countries

---

[25] Bigo, "Security(s)", p. 12, note 5, coins the term "policiarisation" to refer to the tendency for the military to use proactive policing techniques in dealing with external trouble spots such as Bosnia. Here, I am using an Anglicised version of his term to refer to the increasing involvement of the military in matters that would normally be dealt with by the police. Another possible term would be "civilianisation", which emphasises the use of the military in peacetime.

to bring their espionage services into the crime fight".[26] This shift from a more law-based model of crime control to a counterinsurgency model in the fight against *ordinary* crime parallels a similar shift that occurred in counter-terrorism, especially during the 1980s, from a criminal justice model to a war model.[27] The assimilation of criminal phenomena into the counter-terrorism mandate has the potential to reinforce a counterinsurgency approach to anti-terrorism by importing this militarisation of crime control along with the definitional shift. The "war on crime" takes on a whole new dimension when police, military and other control agencies begin to cooperate more closely and the predominant model of control is a counterinsurgency one. Terms such as "information warfare", "cyberwar" "cyberterrorism", "narcoterrorism", the "war on drugs" all blur together previously distinct mandates, casting them in the same insidious, transnational, ruthless and unpredictable mould.

Didier Bigo argues convincingly that there has been an "interpenetration of internal and external security"[28] such that internal security has taken on an increasingly military flavour, while external security has begun to resemble proactive policing, such as in the area of peacekeeping.[29] He argues that this interpenetration reflects "an attempt at insecuritisation of daily life by security professionals in order to increase a sense of societal insecurity and thereby justify increased intervention of policing in a wide variety of areas.[30] At the level of practice, because of the increasing militarisation of crime control and counter-terrorism models, the end result is what Bigo calls "a militarisation of the societal", whereby the same coercive solutions are proposed for any number of social problems.

A central element of a war or counterinsurgency model of counter-terrorism is the importance of intelligence about the enemy. We have seen how identification of a new post-Cold War enemy has led to a proliferation and intermingling of a variety of threats. Another aspect of this and one that has important implications for human rights, is a tendency to focus more and more on "outsiders" as the enemy to be tracked and controlled — whether they be immigrants, refugees and asylum-seekers[31] or inner-city dwellers and the underclass of industrial society. Didier Bigo

---

[26] Martin Woolacott, "The Long Army of the Law", *Globe and Mail* (Toronto), 27 January 1996, p. D4. Reprinted from the *Guardian* (date unknown).

[27] For more on this latter shift, see Crelinsten and Schmid, "Western Responses to Terrorism", pp. 315-22.

[28] Bigo, "Security(s)", p. 12.

[29] *Ibid.*, p. 11.

[30] *Ibid.*, p. 12.

[31] See Ronald D. Crelinsten and Iffet Özkut, "Counterterrorism Policy in Fortress Europe: Implications for Human Rights", in Fernando Reinares, ed., *European Democracies Facing Terrorism: Government Policies and Supranational Cooperation* (Dartmouth/Oñati Series in Law and Society, forthcoming).

refers to this as "a lowering of the level of acceptability of the other".[32] The implications of this will be explored in greater depth later.

## Two Kinds of Policing: Proactive and Reactive

When we turn to the question of policing per se, two models of policing can be identified. While I have mentioned proactive policing already, the more traditional is actually reactive policing. This involves the arrest of someone suspected of having committed an act proscribed in criminal law. It is reactive because control agents only respond once a criminal act is committed and then reported to them. The ensuing police investigation focuses on gathering evidence that can be used in a court of law and this process of data collection is regulated by due process. In proactive policing, the gathering of information is not directed at building a criminal case against a person accused of committing a crime. It is directed at determining whether individuals targeted by the investigation are planning to commit a crime. So *reactive* policing is related to crime *solving*, while *proactive* policing is related to crime *detection*. Elsewhere, I have described how proactive policing resembles security intelligence, particularly in terms of the investigative techniques used.[33] Figure 3 illustrates this similarity between proactive policing and security intelligence in greater detail. In both cases, the kinds of concerns related to the determination of the guilt or innocence of a suspect, subsumed under the notion of the rule of law, are less important than the gathering of information per se.

In proactive policing (as well as in security intelligence), information is not gathered for evidentiary purposes but for intelligence purposes. The ultimate goal is not necessarily criminal prosecution (though it can be), rather it is to learn more about what the targets are up to. This relates directly to what was said before about clandestine organisations. Intrusive techniques of surveillance are often the only way to gather any kind of information about such groups and their activities. The result is that when enough evidence to support a criminal prosecution is gathered, it is not a foregone conclusion that an arrest will be made. In many cases, potential suspects are allowed to bargain away arrest and criminal charges for continued cooperation as informers. Sometimes, particularly in the area of security intelligence, individuals are even protected from prosecution for ordinary crimes (including violent ones), that are unrelated to the sphere of activity for which they are providing intelligence. As such, the imperatives of information gathering often conflict with the imperatives of criminal investigation and due process. The most common example of this is the dropping of criminal charges rather than revealing sources during a trial. The necessity to allow the defence the right to cross-examine witnesses clashes here with the needs of protecting intelligence sources. The dropping of charges undermines the

---

[32] Bigo, "Security(s)", p. 12.

[33] See Crelinsten, "Terrorism, Counter-Terrorism and Democracy" , pp. 254-55, note 7.

chances of a successful prosecution while allowing intelligence-gathering to continue. The alternative would be to have a successful prosecution but to lose the opportunity of gathering any more intelligence.

| **Proactive Policing** | **Security Intelligence** | **Reactive Policing** | |
|---|---|---|---|
| Surveillance | Surveillance | Arrest | |
| Target hardening | Countersubversion | Searches and | |
| Criminal intelligence | Infiltration | seizures | |
| Intrusive technique | Covert | Riot and crowd | |
| Use of informers | facilitation | control | |
| Entrapment | "Gray policing" | | **Criminal** |
| Political policing | | | **Justice** |

Government ⟷

Dissent ⟷ Crime

| **Legal Dissent** | **Illegal Dissent** | **Violent Dissent** |
|---|---|---|
| Opposition parties | Disturbing the Peace | Violent strikes and demonstrations |
| Extra-parliamentary opposition (labour, intellectuals, media, etc.) | Disorderly conduct Illegal assembly Nonviolent, mass radical protest | Vandalism Property damage Intimidation |
| Radical politics | Civil disobedience | Riots |
| Interest groups and lobbyists | General Strikes Violent rhetoric Sedition, conspiracy and subversion | Resisting arrest Assault |

**Figure 3.** The zone separating political forms of dissent from criminal ones and the corresponding models of social control. The close similarity between proactive policing and security intelligence highlights the similarity between investigating covert, clandestine activities of a subversive nature and those of a purely criminal nature, such as drugs traffic or organised crime. Legal forms of dissent are often targets of security intelligence or political policing because they are viewed as potential threats to national security or fronts for covert activity. Furthermore, many forms of dissent which are criminalised are not inherently violent, but are treated as crime so as to frustrate their further development.

Of course, some defendants and their lawyers try and take advantage of this dilemma by demanding secret information from the prosecution, hoping that they will decide to drop charges rather than reveal the information. Lustgarten and Leigh[34] call this practice "greymail" (a lighter shade of blackmail). In the area of counter-terrorism, this inherent conflict between prosecution goals and intelligence goals has led to compromises that tend to undermine strict adherence to the rule of law, such as the videotaping of intelligence sources' testimony; this protects the identity of the source but also deprives the defence of the opportunity for cross-

---

[34] See Lustgarten and Leigh, *In From the Cold*, chapter 11, note 22, for a more detailed discussion of the kinds of techniques used in prosecutions and trials to balance the rights of the defence with the needs of national security.

examination. The end result has been a trend to circumvent the controls built into the criminal justice system by the classical (deterrent) approach to punishment and an increasing reliance on certain kinds of expertise that are tailored to the identification of dangerous "enemies".[35] In the worst cases, those identified as extremely dangerous have been killed rather than brought to trial.

Van Outrive[36] has also pointed to what he calls "grey policing", whereby more and more police functions, particularly in the areas of guarding (such as at soccer games), surveillance and investigation, are being privatised. The result has been an increased ambiguity between private and public policing and a resulting lack of accountability. A "Dirty Harry mentality" in which efficiency supplants legality, partly because the profit motive prevails in the private sector, has led to abuses of power. The distinction between public and private becomes even greyer in cases of "sunlighting" (as opposed to "moonlighting"), whereby public police do private work during working hours. There is also the phenomenon of the "blue drain", whereby police leave the public sector to join the private sector. The situation is further aggravated when what should be *collaboration* between public and private becomes, in essence, a domination by the private sector. This typically occurs when the latter gains access to information held by the former in return for favours granted in the past. Corruption resulting from conflict of interest between the public and private sectors as well as the primacy of professional secrets shared by a common subculture only serve to increase the possibility that the rights of those who are the object of such policing will be compromised. One area where this is particularly evident is that of policing immigrants and ethnic minorities.

## Police Violence Against Foreigners: The Problem of Selective Targeting

When police and military, public sector and private sector, internal and external security agencies increasingly view their mandates as overlapping and interpenetrating, the concepts of security and its converse, insecurity, tend to take on new and increasingly diffuse meanings. This is quite clear in the area of targeting, where the post-Cold War redefinition of security threats has led to a widening of the counter-terrorism mandate to include illegal immigration as a potential source of terrorism. This has resulted in a pernicious kind of selective targeting of foreigners or outsiders (which in most cases means immigrants, refugees and asylum-seekers). This selective targeting of an easily identifiable class of people — the "enemy" — by police and security agents has in turn led to abuse.

This is well exemplified by a 1995 Amnesty International report on the Federal Republic of Germany which states that from January 1992 to March 1995, it

---

[35] For more on this trend, see Crelinsten and Özkut, "Counterterrorism Policy in Fortress Europe", note 33.

[36] Lode Van Outrive, La police grise (The Grey Police). Lecture presented to the Department of Criminology, University of Ottawa, Ottawa, Canada, 21 March 1996.

"received over 70 reports of separate incidents in which it was alleged that German police officers had used excessive or unwarranted force in restraining or arresting people, or had deliberately subjected detainees in their custody to cruel, inhuman or degrading treatment or punishment".[37] While most of the cases occurred during arrest, some occurred while the detained person was being taken to the police station, with others occurring in the station itself. In the vast majority of cases reported, "the victims ... [were] foreign nationals, including asylum-seekers and refugees, or members of ethnic minorities". Amnesty International concluded that, in these cases at least, the ill-treatment in question may have been racially motivated. As for the likelihood of any kind of official investigation or redress for abused victims, the same Amnesty International report cites figures from a German newspaper[38] that suggest a lack of accountability: "Out of 646 complaints of police ill-treatment made in Berlin in 1992, 572 had been rejected by the middle of the following year. In nineteen cases officers were charged and tried. All were acquitted." Similar findings were reported with respect to Switzerland, France and Italy.

In many of the individual cases reported by Amnesty International, arrests appear to have occurred when police asked a foreigner or a person from a visible minority for his or her identity papers and then used force to arrest them when the individual questioned why they were being singled out. Similarly, in cases where a person has been arrested on suspicion of having committed a particular offence, they are often beaten or ill-treated during the arrest process or on the way to the police station. Many are abused during the period of detention (usually within twenty-four hours) before they are brought before a judge or other judicial authority. Typically, if they state that they intend to lodge a formal complaint, they are either beaten even more or they are charged with resisting arrest or assaulting/insulting an officer (see also Figure 3, bottom right). Many of these cases occur during police searches for drugs or on suspicion that an individual is smuggling drugs. Here we see how the assimilation of drug-trafficking into a counter-terrorism mandate can lead to abuse of individual rights.

Stanley Cohen and Daphan Golan[39] list a set of legal conditions under which gross human rights violations are likely to occur once an individual is arrested or detained. The first of these is " a long period in incommunicado detention, particularly without access to a lawyer". In the area of counter-terrorism, Crelinsten and Schmid[40] point out this is the most common "special power" to be adopted by liberal democracies in their fight

---

[37] Amnesty International, *Federal Republic of Germany: Failed by the System: Police Ill-Treatment of Foreigners* (London: Amnesty International, International Secretariat, 1995), AI Index: EUR 23/06/95.

[38] *Der Tagesspiel*, 21 July 1994.

[39] Stanley Cohen and Daphan Golan, *The Interrogation of Palestinians During the Intifada: Ill-treatment, "Moderate Physical Pressure" or Torture?* (Jerusalem: B'TSELEM — The Israeli Information Center for Human Rights in the Occupied Territories, 1991), p. 110.

[40] Crelinsten and Schmid, "Western Responses to Terrorism", p. 334, note 20.

against persistent or serious terrorism. Clearly, the assimilation of drug trafficking and organised crime into the counter-terrorism mandate can only increase the probability of such prolongations occurring under declared "states of emergency" (see Figure 2, top right). Couple this with the assimilation of illegal immigration into the security mandate, and the possibility of selective targeting of foreigners (or those who appear to be foreign) increases dramatically. Clearly, policing that relies on the identification of "dangerous classes" is very likely to impinge on the rights of large numbers of people, many of whom are completely innocent.

The rise in police violence against foreigners or European citizens of foreign origin has coincided with a more generalised rise in politically opportunistic racism and anti-foreigner violence within Europe.[41] Peter Merkl[42] raises the important point that many of those who attack foreigners also attack homosexuals, the homeless, the handicapped and a variety of random victims who may be perceived as foreigners, but who are not. This highlights the fact that "foreigner" can often be a mere label, socially constructed by the media, politicians or others as a vehicle for promoting hatred, scapegoating or intimidation. As Merkl points out: "'Foreigners' are created by a deliberate process of exclusion and labelling".[43]

It is troubling enough to see how right-wing political parties can fan the flames of hatred and prejudice in this way, often trying to recruit skinheads, hooligans and similar perpetrators of anti-foreigner violence — usually *after* they commit the violence.[44] But when the police show similar signs of hatred or stand by and tolerate racist attacks by others, the problem is far worse. The social construction of dangerous categories is the stuff of moral panics, media-driven and fuelled by official sources— usually the police or politicians — who construct images of crime waves, epidemics, invasions or mass threats to collective security. This is a complex process and one that is difficult to map precisely. Something akin to this seems to have occurred, however, within Europe during the 1990s and the object of the moral panic is refugees, immigrants and asylum-seekers.[45] The role of the media in this process is crucial in that it serves as the crucible within which public images and discourse are forged, shaped and channelled into particular themes and agendas. This leads to our final consideration: the relationship between social action and political action.

---

[41] See Tore Bjørgo, ed., *Terror from the Extreme Right*, special issue of *Terrorism and Political Violence* 7, 1 (1995) for a collection of articles dealing with the rise in right-wing violence in Europe and beyond.

[42] Merkl, "Radical Right Parties in Europe", pp. 104-05, note 12.

[43] *Ibid.*, p. 99.

[44] *Ibid.*, p. 113.

[45] See also Crelinsten and Özkut, "Counterterrorism Policy in Fortress Europe", note 33; Peter Chalk, "EU Counter-Terrorism, the Maastricht Third Pillar and Liberal Democratic Acceptability", *Terrorism and Political Violence* 6, 2 (1994), pp. 103-45.

## Two Kinds of Security: National Security and Societal Security

The above discussion of police violence against foreigners and its link with racism and xenophobia in the wider society highlights the fact that selective targeting of visible minorities in the name of national security or counter-terrorism can have serious consequences for individual liberties. What is more, the *leitmotif* that runs through the examples given is the labelling of certain social classes or groups as potential security threats. But what security? Is the security of the state in question or is it more a kind of societal security that is linked to some kind of cohesive identity, such as ethnic, religious or cultural? Figure 4 illustrates the relationships between purely social phenomena of control and deviance and those of a more explicitly political nature. It is precisely in this grey area separating the social and the political that the distinction between national and societal security[46] takes on significance. It is here, for example, that many of the issues surrounding immigrants, refugees and asylum-seekers can impact on security threat analysis. Immigrants, migrant workers, refugees and asylum-seekers do frequently import their conflicts — along with their customs and values — into the countries where they seek asylum, residence or work. The communities in which they live and work can therefore constitute a pool of sympathisers, supporters or active members for groups who promote or use violence against the states from which they came. Fund-raising for such groups can easily be disguised as fund-raising for cultural or social events. It can also involve the use of extortion and intimidation, as mentioned previously.

Figure 4 makes it clear that any kind of deviant group or community can become the target of security intelligence if they are deemed to be the source of potential security threats. This includes not only immigrant and refugee communities, but also different ethnic communities, gay and lesbian communities, religious and cultural minorities, or deviant subcultures such as punks, skinheads, or rockers. They can all become targets of security intelligence, both as a perceived source of potential security threats and as a pool of informers or recruits. They can also become targets of proactive policing of drug trafficking and other forms of clandestine criminal activity. Clearly, as these forms of policing tend to merge into a broadened mandate, the opportunities for this type of targeting can only increase. Such deviant groups, subcultures or communities can also become flashpoints for campaigns of harassment and violence by hate groups or racist political movements.

---

[46] See Bigo, "Security(s)", pp. 13-18.

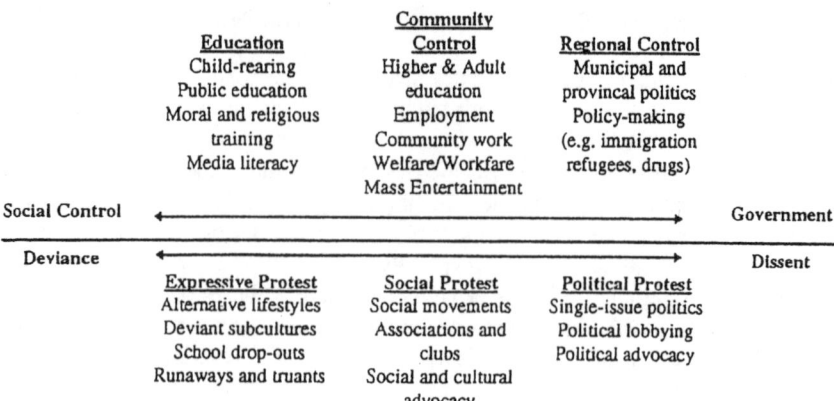

**Figure 4.** The zone that separates the purely social, individualised forms of deviance and protest from the more strictly political, more organised forms. The corresponding forms of social control range from the traditional ones of family, school and church for the more individual, expressive forms of protest and rebellion, through the socialising influences of job, profession, community life and the mass media, to the more strictly political ones of municipal, provincial and state policy. It is in this zone that many immigration and refugee issues arise.

The role of the media is important here too, as such campaigns can sometimes be exacerbated, even triggered, by moral panics generated by sensationalistic reporting.[47] If the media reproduce official discourse that conflates terrorism with drug trafficking and organised crime, then the public is more likely to support the kind of blurred operational mandates described above and to turn a blind eye to the excesses or abuses that may derive from them. By promoting public fear and loathing of dangerous outsiders, the media can shape public attitudes both about the controller — the government agencies that deal with security threats — and the controlled — the targets of control by those agencies. What Figure 4 makes clear is that while the social is intimately related to the political, the exact nature of this link is not always obvious, not only to the security analyst, but also to the politicians and the public at large. It is one thing to recognise an operational relationship between social movements and terrorist groups. It is an entirely different thing to treat what are inherently social problems as if they are criminal problems or to use police and security agencies to monitor and track selected classes of citizens because they may be a source of trouble.

As the boundary between external security and internal security begins to blur, so too does the notion of national security begin to fuse with that of societal security, where society itself rather than the state, per se, is perceived to be threatened. Instead of the classic external enemy or subversive agent acting within society to overthrow the state, one finds an internal enemy — elements within society — who threatens the identity, and by inference, the cohesion of that society. Didier Bigo

---

[47] Mediatised attacks by France and Germany on Dutch drug policy as promoting drug-trafficking within Europe could be included here.

found that for security professionals in post Cold-War Europe the distinction between national or state security and societal security simply does not exist:

> the actors pass permanently from one kind of threat to another, fusing the two objects of reference into one ... To their minds, of course terrorism is an attack on societal identity with its logic of hate, but it also indirectly attacks sovereignty by challenging the security pact. The same applies to the fight against drugs which not only attacks the youth of a country, but may also be the result of new strategies to weaken the country's defence potential. Immigration is perceived as a potential attack on identity if the integration processes are insufficient, but it is also seen by some as the strategy of certain Southern countries seeking to set up a kind of Fifth Column.[48]

Figure 4 captures this grey zone between the social and the political, between the perceived threat to society and identity and that directed against sovereignty and the state. Bigo makes it clear that it is not just at the level of discourse that this blurring occurs, but at the level of practice. This is why I have emphasised the intimate relationship between definitional or conceptual issues, operational issues, and what is actually happening in the real world. The abstract, intellectual problems interface with the concrete, practical problems in the area of policy. Figure 4 highlights the fact that there are many other forms of social control that are involved in the wider context within which counter-terrorist policies operate. In the post-Cold War era, these different forms of control and the institutions within which they are exercised are increasingly interacting and interdependent.

## Conclusion: Implications for Liberal Democracy

Returning to Figure 1, there are three grey zones (A, B and C) in which traditional models of control tend to blur into one another, raising important questions about the rule of law, accountability, openness and public trust and confidence in government. Each zone highlights a different set of sometimes overlapping issues.

### Zone A (Figure 4)

Figure 4 depicts the grey zone between the strictly social and the explicitly political, highlighting the difficulty of clearly demarcating society from polity, deviance from dissent, private from public, and societal security from national or state security. For example, is a social movement or a cultural association a legitimate organisation involved in social or cultural activity or is it a front for illegitimate, subversive or organised criminal activity? In a surveillance society that values security over privacy, many troubling questions arise concerning individual rights and freedoms and how they balance with the duties and responsibilities of a public citizen. Prevention is particularly problematic, especially when selective targeting of particular segments of society deemed to be potential security threats — however

---

[48] Bigo, "Security(s)", p. 18.

defined — can infringe on individual rights and create social divisions that can, in turn, constitute security threats themselves. The role of the media is crucial here in that an informed public can also be a misinformed or a "disinformed"[49] one. If security professionals or other official voices characterise security threats in particular ways, and the media reproduce and amplify this discourse, the result can be the creation of moral panics.

The dangers for democracy in this zone are as follows: undermining public trust in government by misinforming the public about the nature of security threats or by deliberate disinformation campaigns; promoting public anger and outrage at scapegoat targets, thereby creating social divisions; creating public fear and moral panics as a means of garnering consent for certain control programmes; undermining minority rights; creating a surveillance society that by its very nature infringes on freedom of expression, assembly and movement; and finally, criminalising certain kinds of dissent and protest activity that in a less security-conscious society would be considered tolerable and could be controlled by less coercive means.

*Zone B (Figure 3)*

Figure 3 distinguishes between proactive or political policing and reactive policing and highlights the similarity between the former and security intelligence. The rise of a counterinsurgency model of counter-terrorism leads to a blurring of police and military functions. As the police become more militarised and the military assume more policing functions (policification or civilianisation of the military), the problems that proactive policing poses for due process and the rule of law can only be exacerbated. This is particularly true in the case of the military, where traditional judicial control is lacking. These problems include: lack of adequate judicial control of surveillance techniques; the need for secrecy undermining openness and accountability; the problem of selective targeting (see also Zone A); the use of informers and covert facilitation; and impunity for law-breaking (crime management rather than crime control). As for reactive policing, problems include: determining reasonable grounds for arrest; discrimination, racism, and anti-immigrant/foreigner violence; and selective enforcement based on the identification of dangerous classes of people.

The dangers for democracy in this zone are: a lack of openness and accountability that are a direct result of the nature of political policing and security intelligence; infringement of individual rights and freedoms by discrimination due to selective targeting and the identification of dangerous classes; a widening of the net of surveillance to include legitimate organisations or "secondary targets", i.e., those who communicate with individuals and groups already targeted; law-breaking or crime creation through covert facilitation or infiltration, resulting in the undermining of public trust and confidence; and the inherent conflict between security intelligence

---

[49] As in "disinformation".

and criminal prosecution which again undermines public trust and confidence, but this time because of ineffectiveness.

Some of these dangers have been addressed in liberal democracies by the creation of oversight committees and the requirement of judicial warrants for intrusive techniques of surveillance. Another principle that tries to alleviate some of the inevitable problems surrounding security intelligence is that agencies must use the least intrusive techniques that are still effective, resorting to more intrusive ones only when the lesser ones are ineffective. In essence, a delicate balance exists between two opposing concerns. On one hand, a fear of false negatives (failure to detect a security threat) leads to widening the surveillance net as much as possible, thereby running the risk of infringing upon civil liberties of those targeted and, ultimately, facilitating the commission of human rights violations by control agents. On the other hand, a fear of false positives (targeting innocent individuals, organisations or communities) leads to the imposition of judicial restrictions upon intelligence gathering and the creation of oversight committees, thereby running the risk of attenuating the effectiveness of intelligence gathering operations. Clearly, both fears can be socially constructed by organisations with a stake in the outcome. This is why the media can play such an important role in tipping the balance one way or the other.[50]

### Zone C (Figure 2)

Figure 2 highlights the difference between the criminal justice model and the war model of counter-terrorism. With the merging of police and military mandates in the post-Cold War era, we see the blurring of internal and external security that parallels the blurring of societal and national security discussed in Zone A. While the military act more as peacekeepers or peacemakers, they sometimes commit gross human rights violations in the process, such as the case of Canadian peacekeepers in Somalia who tortured and killed a Somali teenager.[51] Similarly, as special police units are called on to fight terrorism, police begin to move away from the doctrine of minimal force and adopt special weapons and tactics that mirror the military doctrine of maximal force. In doing so, they take on the aura of hit squads that follow shoot-to-kill policies, rather than police officers intent on apprehending a suspect for criminal prosecution.

---

[50] In Zone A (Figure 4), top left, media literacy is identified as an important element of education. If members of the public were more aware of how the media can distort political discourse, they might be more immune to these media effects. See Ronald D. Crelinsten, "The Impact of Television on Terrorism and Crisis Situations: Implications for Public Policy", *Journal of Contingencies and Crisis Management* 2, 2 (1994), pp. 61-72.

[51] For a detailed study of this case, see Donna Winslow, *The Canadian Airborne Regiment in Somalia: A Socio-cultural Inquiry. A Study Prepared for the Commission of Inquiry into the Deployment of Canadian Forces to Somalia* (Ottawa: Minister of Public Works and Government Services, Canada, 1997).

As criminal phenomena such as organised crime and drug trafficking are incorporated into the counter-terrorism mandate, the question arises as to when such phenomena become a threat to national security. It can be argued that illegal organisations that are able to corrupt a government to look the other way have come to the point of constituting a parallel power that undermines the legitimacy of the government, thereby constituting a national security threat. The question remains, however, as Lustgarten and Leigh suggest,[52] whether this broadening of the concept of national security constitutes a dangerous distortion or a realistic assessment of a changing threat.

The dangers to democracy in this zone include: sidestepping the rule of law in the name of security (the primacy of security over freedom, and effectiveness over democratic acceptability); the commission of gross human rights violations such as torture or extrajudicial killings (the primacy of necessity over proportionality); the emergence of a cult of clandestinity (primacy of government secrecy and cover-ups over openness and disclosure); and a lack of accountability (primacy of authority over legitimacy — we know what's best; just trust us).

In sum, then, the rule of law is threatened by the complementary trends of militarisation of the police and civilianisation of the military and the fusing of police and military mandates, as well as the need to use intrusive techniques for investigating clandestine organisations. Openness and accountability are threatened, in turn, by the need for secrecy in intelligence operations and the bureaucratic imperatives of multiple and interlocking institutions of control. Finally, the maintenance of public trust and confidence in government, achieved primarily by the fostering and nurturing of an informed public, is undermined by the trend towards a surveillance society that selectively targets certain groups deemed to be outsiders, thereby creating social divisions, moral panics and emotional swells of fear and loathing that hinder information flow and hamper public education. This trend is often fuelled by sensational media coverage of doomsday predictions and dire warnings from security professionals and politicians whose discourse is designed to garner public support for their control efforts.[53]

In such an environment, the concept of the loyal opposition becomes an oxymoron as all opposition is deemed to be a security threat. The notion of representative democracy gives way to majority rule as individual conscience and minority opinion are swept aside by a tidal wave of consensus that democratic principles and the rule of law are impediments to the effective control of a terrible threat. It is here that the level of discourse and practice merge and what is said becomes what is done. When

---

[52] Lustgarten and Leigh, *In From the Cold*, pp. 27-30.

[53] At a recent seminar on the future of terrorism, sponsored by the US Department of State, one of the participants suggested that the entire US population be vaccinated against anthrax, since he was convinced that an anthrax attack was inevitable given the ease with which terrorists could acquire and deliver the deadly bacterium. Happily, no one else found the suggestion had any merit, but one can imagine the panic if some major media outlet published an interview with this "security expert" and framed it as a prediction with high credibility.

consensus is achieved by playing on the fears and suspicions of ill-informed people, then the concept of democracy loses its meaning and freedom is reduced to a mere word.

# [18]

## SPECTRES OF 'TERRORISM'

*Saree Makdisi*
University of Chicago

'A spectre', we might say – at once borrowing from and modifying the opening lines of a seemingly forgotten nineteenth-century pamphlet – 'A spectre is haunting the world: the spectre of terrorism. All the Powers of the world have entered into a holy alliance to exorcize this spectre.'[1]

In today's global war, however, the concept of 'terrorism' has acquired a new function, a new meaning, and an altogether different kind of existence than those that applied to it in other times and places. 'Terrorism' is a term that was once used – and sometimes it still is – as a label to identify the actions of a specific enemy or group of enemies. The US State Department,

for example, maintains a list of America's current enemies, who are, by definition, guilty of engaging in or supporting 'terrorism'. That countries are placed on the list not necessarily according to their actual behaviour but rather according to the degree of their cooperation with US foreign policy suggests that here the term 'terrorism' lacks substance, let alone that quality known as meaning. It is merely one among many phrases coined by US policymakers and disseminated by the media; phrases such as 'Weapons of Mass Destruction', 'Middle East Peace Process', 'Moderate Arab States'. Such phrases are meaningless in that they have no meaning other than those supplied by the US government and the various policy 'experts' (who decides, for example, what counts as a 'Weapon of Mass Destruction', and, more importantly, *whose* weapons of

1 Earlier versions of this essay were presented as lectures at Oxford University in November 2001 and the American University of Beirut in January 2002.

mass destruction count as 'Weapons of Mass Destruction'?).

However, the use of 'terrorism' to label an enemy can go beyond mere rhetorical expediency to transform an enemy into an existential Other. This use of the term derives from an older colonial and radical understanding of sovereignty and identity. The best example of it is Israel's use of the term 'terrorism' as a blanket description for the Palestinians. Here the label is not restricted to specific acts of violence but functions instead as an ontological category. Since the primary target of the current Israeli assault on the Palestinians is the Palestinian people's will to resist the Israeli occupation – as manifested in any trace of a Palestinian collective existence on terms not dictated by Israel – it is only by identifying all Palestinians, and their collective being, with 'terrorism' that Israel could describe its repression of the *intifada* as an attack on 'terrorism' as such. For it is only in ontological and existential terms that one could possibly imagine the near total obliteration of the Jenin refugee camp in April 2002, for example, as a blow against 'terrorism' in the way that Israelis so fervently use that phrase; it is only in such terms that one could understand the mass destruction of people's homes, the murder of hundreds of unarmed men, women and children, the new displacement of already displaced refugees, the endless curfews, the mass detentions of men and boys, the prohibition of ambulances, the prevention of rescue operations, and the pathological uprooting of the traces of collective existence, as components of a 'war on terrorism'. In keeping with Israeli policies going back to Oslo and long before, the aim of the current Israeli assault on 'terrorism' is to disperse the Palestinians into dozens of territorially discontinuous cantons and hence to extirpate their collective political being – if

not their actual physical existence – once and for all.

But in America's recent declarations, and in much of the talk surrounding the recent (and still ongoing) war in Afghanistan and across the globe, 'terrorism' has been used in a calculatedly undefined and indefinite, rather than specific, way. It names not a specific external enemy, a specific Other, but a general and omnipresent threat, of which Ussama bin Laden happened to serve as a kind of focal point for a certain time, a role that will now probably be played by the proliferating agents of what the US has recently identified in official terms as the axis of Evil. Indeed, perhaps not surprisingly, such is America's influence that not one of the recent United Nations resolutions, proclamations, and conventions on 'terrorism' offers a proper and usable definition of the term. Since the passage of UN Security Council 1373 shortly after the September 11 attacks, for example, those states all over the world that did not rush to sign have been prodded, cajoled, and coerced into signing these conventions, not one of which defines its object. Such a situation would be somewhat reminiscent of those puritanical sexual laws in several American states that prohibit 'moral turpitude' and 'crimes against nature' except that at least in those cases everyone knows what the referent for those laws is, and its not being named only adds to the equally puritanical thrill of convicting people of it. Whereas, in the case of 'terrorism', the fact that no one knows what it is has everything to do with the fact that all are being asked to exorcise it, on pain of being 'ended', to use the memorable term of Paul Wolfowitz, US Deputy Secretary of Defense.[2]

For the very fact that the US is working so hard to make all other states sign what might look like a totally meaningless set of

SPECTRES OF TERRORISM
Saree Makdisi

conventions indicates precisely their meaning, and the new meaning of 'terrorism' itself. Terrorism today, in the global American usage, no longer refers merely descriptively to a label for specific acts of violence as such, nor does it name and stigmatize a specific external enemy or even a group of such enemies. For it turns out that the purpose of all those otherwise meaningless UN conventions on terrorism is to name a spectre, a ghost, and in so doing to call into being the exorcist or rather the league of exorcists appropriate to it. Terrorism has now assumed not merely a descriptive or a discursive, but really a properly *spectral* existence. For if it exists everywhere, it has to be hunted down everywhere, and hence its existence offers not merely the ideological justification but rather the politico-juridical foundation for a universal campaign of investigation, interrogation, confiscation, detention, surveillance, torture, and punishment, on, for the first time, a genuinely global scale, and at that a scale that allows for no exceptions, no neutralities. It is in this sense that such a ghostly and spectral terrorism may be seen as one of the founding conditions for a properly global network of power meant to counter it, not only wherever it *does* manifest itself, but wherever it *might* manifest itself, which could, of course, be anywhere.

To elaborate this admittedly somewhat abstract claim, it is worth considering the status of 'terrorism' in the current war, of which the American bombardment of

Afghanistan is supposed to mark only the first stage. This is, as various politicians have told us, not a war in the conventional sense, but a war unlike any we have ever seen. Not only will it last for years to come, they say – for our lifetimes, according to some European politicians – but it will have no climactic outcomes, it will take place on and off the record, visibly and invisibly, and its objectives will continually be renewed as the fight shifts between political, economic, and military modes as circumstances require, engaging targets both latent and manifest, all over the world. Taken at face value, in other words, the newly declared war against terrorism really is nothing less than the proposal for a new system of governance and control whose declared enemies are indefinite and spectral. It offers, to be more specific, a potentially permanent and global system of governance that – precisely like the spectre that it promises to eliminate – recognizes no outsides, no externalities, and no neutralities: 'you're either with us or you're against us', as President Bush famously said. This permanent and global war against terrorism, then, is not a war against an ontologically constituted Other – like the Israeli war against the Palestinians – but rather a war against a thoroughly internalized threat, a spectral presence immanent in and indeed potentially constitutive of a newly founded global order. With this, we have in a sense returned full circle to the original meaning of the word 'terrorism', which was coined in the 1790s to refer to a *system of government* and was only relatively recently appropriated by governments to describe their own enemies.

That this war is being waged against a spectral foe does not mean, of course, that real and actual people will not be targeted and killed. But perhaps we can think of such casualties as what US policy-makers call

---

2 Wolfowitz says that 'it's not just simply a matter of capturing people and holding them accountable, but removing the sanctuaries, removing the support systems, ending states who sponsor terrorism. And that's why it has to be a broad and sustained campaign. It's not going to stop if a few criminals are taken care of' (Paul Wolfowitz, US Department of Defense News Briefing, 13 September 2001: http://www.defenselink.mil/news/Sep2001/t09132001_t0913dsd.html).

'collateral damage' in a war against an indefinite and all-pervasive enemy. Here we should bear in mind, for example, everything that has happened over the past months – not only the repeated strikes at civilian targets in towns and cities across Afghanistan on a scale that we would probably not have known about had it not been for the coverage provided by Al-Jazeera (at least until its Kabul offices were bombed by the US Air Force, settling the controversy over its coverage once and for all), but also the wholesale slaughter of Taliban soldiers. For, other than the hundreds, and possibly thousands, of civilians killed by American bombers, by some counts up to 10,000 Taliban troops may have been killed as well, the vast majority of whom, we can be sure, had barely even heard of New York or Washington, much less had any complicity in the murderous events of September 11. In addition to this, we have to count the repeated massacres of prisoners, including what I think is the unprecedented use of air power in the mass execution, at Qalat-i-Janghi, of prisoners-of-war many of whom still had their hands tied behind their backs; but then, as US Secretary of Defense Donald Rumsfeld explicitly stated, the US had no intention of taking prisoners in this war, and sought instead to prevent what Rumsfeld prosaically called 'bad folks' from perpetuating their terrorist menace.[3]

All this extraordinary bloodletting happened in the name of the great ghost hunt for Ussama bin Laden.

3 See Rumsfeld's comments at Pentagon press briefings on 19 November and 11 December 2001, available at http://www.defenselink.mil. For more on the massacre at Qalat-i-Janghi, see Françoise Chipaux, 'Qala-e-Janghi: questions sur un carnage', in *Le Monde*, 1 December 2001. For more on the civilian death toll from the American bombing, see, among others, *Irish Times*, 10 January 2002, *The Times*, 2 January 2002, *Sydney Morning Herald*, 12 January 2002, and *Chicago Tribune*, 28 December 2001.

Bin Laden could well have been the mastermind behind the terrible September 11 attacks, which are fully appropriate to his violent Manichean worldview. But, if he is guilty of a criminal act, no matter how appalling, he should have been prosecuted and tried as a criminal. There are mechanisms, however inadequate, available to prosecute criminals at an international level, though it should be remembered that the US itself has systematically opposed such mechanisms (as, for example, an international court for war crimes), just as it has rejected out of hand previous rulings of the World Court of Justice in the Hague (as, for example, in the case of the US mining of Nicaragua's harbours in the 1980s). However, the fact that the Taliban's repeated offers – both long before and during the recent crisis – to turn bin Laden over for trial in a neutral country, in return for some modicum of evidence as to his guilt in the long list of crimes of which he has been accused, were rejected out of hand by the US suggests that, in fact, his guilt or innocence with regard to those attacks is really quite besides the point.

Several commentators and analysts have pointed out that, if the US is successful in eliminating the Taliban and replacing it with a more pliable government sympathetic to American interests – as it has now done with the new Afghan regime, several members of which may be US citizens and the interim president a former consultant for the US oil company Unocal, which had negotiated rights for the construction of an oil and gas pipeline through Afghanistan – the US would be able to extend its geopolitical domination from the Persian Gulf right into the very heart of Central Asia, and hence to park its army at the back doors of China, Russia, India, and Iran all at once.[4] In 1998, Richard Cheney, then the CEO of Halliburton, a major oil

SPECTRES OF TERRORISM

services company, but now of course the Vice President of the United States, pointed out that 'the Caspian may be the first world class oil province to open since the North Sea', a fact which presented exciting new possibilities for US foreign policy, since 'the United States wants to see more diversity in the sources of the world's oil supply and encourage opportunities for U.S. commercial interests'. It is 'in our strategic and economic interest to encourage the opening up of new areas of supply,' Cheney added, since 'this can create a more balanced and less vulnerable world market'.[5] Indeed, if it were to achieve dominance over Afghanistan and Pakistan, the US would also find itself in control of the most likely route for pipelines carrying Central Asia's vast and as yet relatively untapped oil and gas reserves – supposedly second only to the entire supply of the Middle East and larger than those of either Alaska or the North Sea.[6]

To conclude, however, that the hunt for bin Laden was just an excuse, an argument made in bad faith, in order to justify the destruction of the Taliban, the conquest of Afghanistan, and the subsequent American geopolitical and geoeconomic domination of Central Asia, would be to miss the point entirely. As I have already suggested, the war against terrorism must not be understood as hypocrisy or cover up: it is the name given to what is being offered as a system of global governance. We are not only being asked to believe that everything that has happened in Afghanistan had to do with the war against terrorism, and

hence the hunt for bin Laden, we should believe it, because it is true: true in the sense that the 'war against terrorism' is the real and actual – not merely the ideological and rhetorical – foundation for what is happening today. What is being hunted down in Afghanistan, of course, is not only the real Ussama bin Laden – whose actual existence, as much as his guilt or innocence in the events of September 11, is quite besides the point – but the *spectral* Ussama bin Laden, whose ghastly image had been banned from television screens in Europe and America lest, we were told, he send secret messages to his fanatical followers with a wink of the eye, a twist of the hand, or a pull of the beard. What happened, or what happens, to the real Ussama bin Laden is in this sense almost entirely irrelevant: he might run away, he might be killed, he might be captured. Bin Laden's organization, such as it is, is merely part of the residue of a large network of similar organizations which US policymakers were happy to encourage, finance, and take advantage of when their energies were directed against America's enemies. Until the US changes its approach to – or its desire for – regional dominance, as well as its unqualified support for Israeli militarianism, there will continue to be people and groups who will vomit forth more violence in response to the belligerency of the US and its allies; but such violence should not be allowed to overshadow all the Arab and Muslim attempts to refuse America's aggressive ambitions in ways that engage with all those – including all those Americans – who are also struggling for a fairer and more equitable and non-violent world order, one more closely approximating America's own democratic ideals.[7] What we are seeing now is violence contending with and producing more violence.

4 For more on the Unocal connection to the present Afghan government, see *Le Monde*, 6 December 2001, on http:www.lemonde.fr/article/0,5987
5 See Richard Cheney, 'Geopolitical overview', on the U.S.-Azerbaijan Chamber of Commerce website (http://www.usacc.org/azerbaijan/intro-geopolitical.htm#geopo14).
6 See, for example, Cohen (1997). Also see Rashid (2001: esp. pp. 143–82).

7 See Makdisi (2002).

In the meantime the global project to exorcise the spectre of terrorism will carry on – and not only in Afghanistan, for terrorism is being exorcised from televisions and newspapers, schools and universities, parliaments and congresses, airport immigration queues and courts of justice around the world. 'Terrorism', it turns out, not only poses a threat from within (rather than from without) the world system, but, just as the threat that it poses can take any number of forms, the 'insides' that it can inhabit include not only countries and territories, but also computer networks, financial systems, discursive formations, texts, and even our very intellectual and emotional centres of being. 'Terrorism' henceforth includes not only acts of violence and murder, but also acts of speech, of writing, of thought, even of emotion. The war against it will therefore involve not only smart bombs and fuel-air explosives (or 'daisy cutters'), and not only judicial detention and torture, but also intellectual warfare, and, potentially, forms of censorship so severe that one will not even recognize them any longer because one will reside within them, one will inhabit them.

I am thinking here, for example, of the extraordinary self-censorship that has been imposed on American civil society in the wake of the September attacks, not at the behest of a fascist dictatorship, but voluntarily in the name of the war against terrorism, and in the name of the need to purge the nation and civil society itself of any possible taint of terrorist sympathy. The full spectrum of America's civil institutions is now part of the war effort against terrorism. At universities across the US, faculty members and even students who have questioned American foreign policy are being publicly reprimanded and threatened with various sanctions. Moreover, with the full cooperation of universities across the country – unprecedented in any previous

crisis, including the second Gulf War – the grades, records, transcripts, and movements of foreign students are being carefully monitored by law enforcement and intelligence groups. With only a little pressure from Condoleeza Rice and others in the Bush administration, the American media establishment, while complaining bitterly about al-Jazeera's supposedly biased coverage, has in the meantime openly aligned itself with the US government's war aims and methods (hence the repeated editorials in *The Washington Post* and *The New York Times* supporting the war and calling for the continuation and even the extension of the bombing campaign when questions started being asked about the terrible civilian death toll resulting from attacks that could only have been indiscriminate or incompetent, attacks burning Red Cross food warehouses, destroying UN de-mining offices, entombing whole families – mothers, fathers, babies, and all – in the rubble of their mud-brick village houses). 'Civilian casualties are historically, by definition, a part of war, really' one well-known American journalist has pointed out; and therefore, 'they're not really news' (Hume 2001).

Nor, clearly, is the arrest in the United States of over 1,100 people – of whom perhaps nine or ten are directly suspected of, and only one so far actually charged with, complicity in the September 11 attacks – a newsworthy event, since what little coverage it has received has had more to do with the lopsided debate over the relaxation of laws against torture than with the fact that these people have been held for months without being charged, in solitary confinement, and without access to either lawyers or family members. Meanwhile, a further 5,000 people, singled out solely on the basis of gender, age, and national origin, are slowly being interrogated by American law enforcement agencies, even though none of

SPECTRES OF TERRORISM
Saree Makdisi

them is suspected of having broken the law (and the US government and media have already made it clear that, although Arabs are the prime suspects for now, in future the dragnet will be extended to other Asians as well as Africans). In addition to the newly passed anti-terrorism laws, which provide draconian new powers to a military and political surveillance system now freed from judicial oversight, and besides the newly created Office of Homeland Security which will coordinate the war on terrorism with the FBI, the CIA, and military intelligence agencies, President Bush has been granted extraordinary war powers for what we must remember is still an undeclared, indeterminate, and open-ended war. He has, for example, authorized the creation of military tribunals, which will be empowered to dispose of – that is, to arraign, detain, imprison, and execute – those accused of terrorist crimes without any of the usual judicial procedures, requirements for evidence, or public access to the proceedings. The historian Arthur Schlesinger once called Nixon's the Imperial Presidency, but, whereas the powers that Nixon wielded were often illegal, underhanded, and unofficial, the extraordinary powers that Bush will leave for future US presidents are now fully authorized.

The fact that the new military tribunals are supposed to operate not only within the US but outside it as well might serve to confirm the suspicion that a key component of the global war against terrorism represents the extension of US sovereignty, directly or indirectly, over the rest of the world, and hence a new kind of American imperialism, as suggested, for example, by America's abduction of the prisoners of war from Afghanistan and their transportation to Guantanamo Bay, where the US claims the unilateral right to judge their fate (in flagrant violation of the provisions for prisoners-of-war stipulated by the Fourth Geneva Convention, whose applicability the US, again unilaterally, claims the right to decide for itself). Certainly it often seems as though the US finally has its chance to put into place its plans for the rest of the world, beginning with the Middle East and Central Asia, and then moving on to other regions.

Here, however, particularly insofar as a potential American imperialist plan overlaps with Israel's own vision of the Middle East – and indeed, with more or less explicit US support, the Israelis have rhetorically insinuated their spring 2002 assault on the Palestinians into the larger 'war on terrorism', although, as I have suggested, it invokes a very different concept of 'terrorism' – a number of problems present themselves, of which it is worth taking note. First, one would have thought that the main lesson to be learned from the recent history of the Middle East is that one-sided visions cannot be imposed, or at least not for very long, and not without running into potentially disabling popular resistance. Despite all the violence at its disposal, for example, Israel has yet to succeed in imposing its will on the Palestinians, just as it failed to do on the Lebanese, even after decades of merciless occupation. After all, one lesson from the Israeli occupation of Lebanon, and indeed from the current *intifada*, is that the most hopeless looking odds in the world will not necessarily break a people's will to resist and that even the most lopsided violence fails at least as often as it succeeds. It is too early, of course, to see what the result will be of the current American attempt to impose its will on Afghanistan and Central Asia more generally, but the Afghans are not noted for their deference to foreign powers.

The second problem facing the US will to dominate the world brings us back to the question of the 'war against terrorism' itself, which, I have suggested, may be thought of as the name of a proposed new global system of governance. As it is presently being proposed, however, such a global system of governance includes many non-American parties, and it would not necessarily be compatible with a resurgent American imperialism, and may well be at odds with it. Even if we were to imagine that the US could somehow hijack the 'war on terrorism' for its own purposes (which is not out of the question), or indeed even if we imagine that the 'war on terrorism' is nothing more than an extension of US domestic and foreign policy under a different name (which is also possible), a further and much more significant problem is that this is *not* the only system of governance that seeks to extend its sovereignty over the world. The worldwide debate over the World Trade Organization (which completed its most recent ministerial meeting in Qatar as the war on Afghanistan got under way) may have been pushed out of the headlines, but the WTO's project, and that of a fully globalized capitalist economy, of which the WTO is only one agent among many others, is far from complete – just as the resistance it faces is far from vanquished, and has in fact been gathering strength ever since the virtual uprising in Seattle two years ago, resistance which manifested itself with renewed intensity in recent gatherings in Washington, Quebec City, Prague, and Genoa.

Indeed, globalization as an economic, social, and cultural process and globalization as a political and military process are not to be confused with each other. Certainly, there have been many times in the history of capitalism and of imperialism in which political, cultural, and economic forms of domination have worked together with extraordinary efficiency until they run into crisis. But there have also been times when military and political forms of domination have come into contradiction –

and even into conflict – with economic and cultural forms of domination and exploitation (the British empire provides us with a good example in the period from 1790 to 1815 or so). Today, it seems to me, we are witnessing the beginning of a new crisis in world governance. However coordinated they may have been since the end of the Cold War, the political-military process of globalization and the economic-cultural process of globalization seem now to have separated, and to be developing in different, contradictory, and possibly antagonistic ways.

*Empire*, the new book by Antonio Negri and Michael Hardt (2001), provides us with one of the most provocative, brilliant and sweeping analyses of the process of globalization to emerge in recent years. I want now briefly to paraphrase and reconstruct their argument, and I will do so not necessarily because I agree with it in all respects but rather because it provides us with an excellent way to articulate sympathetically an alternative point of view. Hardt and Negri argue that we should distinguish a properly postmodern form of sovereignty, into which we have now entered – and to which they give the name Empire – from the modern forms of sovereignty appropriate to, and indeed constitutive of, the imperialist politics of an earlier era. In those modern forms of sovereignty, modernity itself was articulated through the struggle between a colonial European Self and its non-European Others, a struggle whose dynamics were given their most cogent formulation in the work of Frantz Fanon. As Fanon points out in that famous passage in *The Wretched of the Earth*, the colonial world is a world cut in two, a world articulated by a series of binary divisions given their clearest expression in the dividing line articulating the site of the colonial encounter. Today the best surviving example of the violent encounter between

SPECTRES OF TERRORISM
Saree Makdisi

colonizer and colonized is to be found all along the borders of Palestine and Israel, which is why, as I remarked earlier, the Israeli use of the discourse of 'terrorism' expresses a modern mode of sovereignty, and defines this conflict as a struggle between Self and Other – and which is also why the Israeli war against the Palestinians is so often articulated in terms of an existential antagonism.

According to Hardt and Negri, such a racist and imperialist dynamic must be regarded as truly the exception rather than the rule in the contemporary world order. For they base their argument for a genuinely postcolonial and post-imperialist Empire on what they regard as the new postmodern form of sovereignty proposed by Empire itself, which we can see most clearly perhaps in what they say is the anti-foundationalist and anti-essentialist discourse par excellence, namely, that of the free market. Of course, as Marx noted long ago, capitalism has always tried to overcome boundaries, divisions and limitations to the sphere of its rule. In this sense, Hardt and Negri argue, the realization of the world market can be taken to constitute the point of arrival of a tendency much older than itself, for 'in its ideal form there is no outside to the world market: the entire globe is its domain' (2001: 190). Whereas modernity constructed places that were necessarily engaged in and founded on a dialectical play with their others, their outsides, the space of what Hardt and Negri call imperial sovereignty is smooth – smooth not in the sense that all struggles and crises have been resolved, but precisely in the sense that the many crises and conflicts constitutive of modernity have now given way to an ever-present sense of omni-crisis enveloping the entire world.

One of the key features of the argument proposed in *Empire*, however, is that this smooth space must not merely be understood in economic and financial terms, but also in political,

military, and indeed juridical terms as well. Empire is therefore not simply the latest stage or the perfection of the older imperialist projects but rather an entirely new phenomenon, marked by the emergence of a single power that overdetermines all other forms of power (especially the power of the various nation states, imperialist and otherwise), and that structures them all in a unitary way (Hardt and Negri 2001: 9). Here Hardt and Negri are very careful to distinguish what they see as the new role played by the US in the politico-juridical order of Empire. Having abandoned its earlier properly imperialist project as a result of the defeat inflicted on it by the people of Vietnam, the US, they say, now serves not in its own national interest as such, that is, not to project its own national sovereignty in an older sense, but rather as the ultimate guarantor of global peace, as the policeman of Empire.

Hence the significance of the second Gulf War of 1990–1, whose importance, Hardt and Negri argue, 'derives from the fact that it presented the United States as the only power able to manage international justice, *not as a function of its own national motives but in the name of global right*. Certainly,' they concede, 'many powers have falsely claimed to act in the universal interest before, but this new role of the United States is different. Perhaps it is more accurate to say that this claim to universality is false, but it is false in a new way. The U.S. world police acts not in imperialist interest but in imperial interest' (2001: 180). It is in this move that we start to run into possible problems with the analysis provided by Hardt and Negri, especially but not only in view of the immediately contemporary crisis. There are, in particular, two key potential difficulties that we now need to address.

First of all, although the discourse of globalization seems to have become all-

pervasive, there are some problems with thinking of the free market's gradual infiltration of
virtually the entire planet in the smooth and
seamless terms apparently provided by Hardt
and Negri. We must remember here, however,
that they are not saying that conflict and contradiction have disappeared from a smooth
world system now supposedly open to all
flows (such a view is, rather, appropriate to the
fantasy of the free market itself) but rather
that conflict and contradiction – and their hallmark, crisis – have been absorbed into the
structure of the world system and are now
omnipresent, and take place everywhere,
rather than marking the outer limits of sovereignty. Many other recent accounts of the
global economy and of the phenomenon of
globalization, however, have stressed the persistence of large and dramatic striations and
discontinuities in the global system, many of
which suggest the endurance of a distinction
between a smooth economy of world trade
and its exteriors, zones not yet incorporated
into it and hence not subject to its form of
sovereignty.

Saskia Sassen, Manuel Castells, and others
point out that, despite the tendency towards
the formation of a fully globalized space of
flows, the world economy has been developing
in a deeply and ever more asymmetrical way.[8]
Indeed, Paul Hirst and Grahame Thompson,
among many others, have argued compellingly
that the discourse of globalization itself is a
myth (2000: 68–75). World trade, they point
out, is overwhelmingly concentrated in the
OECD region comprising the US, Western
Europe and Japan, which, together with a few
other key nodes in the world economy,
account for less than 16 per cent of the world's
population but over 80 per cent of world trade

– 80 per cent of which in turn is managed by
500 giant companies. The G7 countries
account for 91 per cent of the world's high-
tech manufacturing capacity, as well as 80 per
cent of the world's computing power.[9] There
are also clearly growing asymmetries between
informational and affective labour, on the one
hand, and older or cruder forms of manufacturing, on the other, the kind of lopsided-
ness which produces, for example, the curious
statistic that Michael Jordan makes more
money from his Nike ad campaign in the US
than all the tens of thousands of Nike's southeast Asian workers earn in a year of their
pitiful wages. Partly as a result of all these
asymmetries, the absolute contradiction
between ever more concentrated wealth and
economic power, on the one hand, and ever
greater impoverishment, on the other, can be
recognized as a key feature of the world today,
when the richest 20 per cent of the world's
population receives 90 per cent of the world's
income, and the ratio of rich to poor has gone
from 1 to 30 in 1960 to 1 to 74 in 1997.[10]
What remains unclear as yet is whether we
should think of this as a kind of contradiction
taking place *within* the world system, or rather
*between* that world system and its others,
those vast swathes of humanity excluded from
the prosperity enjoyed by only a tiny minority
of the earth's population.

Addressing this point, Robert Keohane has
recently argued for what he refers to as a 'partially Hobbesian' world, in which a smooth
'inside' space of peace, prosperity, and justice
– not unlike the space of Empire discussed by
Hardt and Negri – is contrasted with a turbulent and chaotic world beyond its boundaries
(2000: 109–23). But there are severe problems
with Keohane's Hobbesian argument, at a

8 See Sassen (1998: esp. 195–218) and Castells (2000: 259–73).

9 See Castells (2000: 265). Also see Miyoshi (1998: 249).
10 See Ellwood (2001: 101).

SPECTRES OF TERRORISM
Saree Makdisi

philosophical as well as a political and historical, level. For Keohane, clearly, the turbulent space of nature is assumed to be not only exterior to, but also in a sense *prior* to, the smooth civilized space of commercial prosperity. Yet it is not at all evident that the contrast between an inside of a prosperous and interconnected global space of flows and a chaotic world where life remains nasty, brutish and short is a contrast between a sovereign system and an external space of nature representing its prior condition. Hardt and Negri argue that what looks like the space of nature is, like all nature in the postmodern world, the product of sovereignty, internal to it rather than marking its natural Other, its outside. Perhaps, then, all these contradictions, disarticulations and asymmetries should be thought of as interior to and even constitutive of the sense of omnipresent crisis in Empire itself.

The belief in a smooth process of globalization faces another potential critique from what has been identified as the Realist school in international relations, according to which the process of globalization must be understood precisely in terms of what Hardt and Negri argue are the older forms of sovereignty pertaining to modern nation-states. As long ago as 1948, George Kennan, whom many regard as the father of all Realists, pointed out that 'we [that is, the US] have about 50 percent of the world's wealth, but only 6.3 percent of its population. In this situation,' Kennan continues, 'we [must] devise a pattern of relationship[s] which will permit us to maintain this position of disparity without positive detriment to our national security.'[11] From such a standpoint, any talk of globalization eroding the power and the sovereignty of the powerful (as opposed to the weak) states is misguided.

11 George Kennan, quoted in Miyoshi (1998: 251).

As against Ulrich Beck's contention that 'a globally disorganized capitalism is continually spreading out', for example, that is, the argument that 'there is no hegemonic power and no international regime, either economic or political', so that globalization has come to mean a 'world society without a world state and without world government' (2000: 99–103), the enormous political and economic power still available to many states, above all the US, is evidence that the world is not as lacking in governance as it might seem.

Hardt's and Negri's account of the world system differs from that of globalists like Beck in that they argue that there is a mode of sovereignty, and hence a political and juridical system, appropriate to the fully globalized world market. But they differ from the Realist argument insofar as they seek to argue that any possible tendencies towards an older and properly imperialist projection of state power – and especially American imperialist power – have been overdetermined by America's new role as a global police force.

This, of course, brings us back to the war against the spectre of terrorism. Especially in view of the latest sets of American actions, and the attempt to project geopolitical power in the oldest possible imperialist sense (and, at that, in the central Asian playground of what Kipling called the 'Great Game' of the older imperialist struggles), it seems as though the US is using the current war to establish not only a new global system of governance, but one in which it will reign supreme. Such a move would, of course, fly in the face of what Hardt and Negri argue will be the post-imperialist role of the US in the new world order of Empire. But, although this looks like the ultimate validation and confirmation of the Realist argument that the world economic system is neither as chaotic nor as free as it might seem, such an argument, it seems to me, also misses the point.

Certainly, the US as the dominant political and military presence in the world may do whatever it can to impose its will on the WTO or to refuse unilaterally to sign conventions like Kyoto or treaties on disarmament and non-proliferation, not to mention refusing the jurisdiction of genuinely international legal bodies. But, although there are times and places when it can translate political and military power into economic clout, the nature of America's power is in some ways actually becoming increasingly fragmented – not in its effects, necessarily, nor in the way it is deployed, but rather in the purposes and the functions it serves. We can well regard the US project to exert geopolitical dominance in the Persian Gulf or Central Asia as an exercise in imperialist power of the old school. On the other hand, it is not clear that the US will benefit as a nation-state in the old school sense appropriate to that older mode of (imperialist) sovereignty. After all, the old imperialisms were also national projects, and served to benefit the national population at home, in however uneven a fashion, and at whatever the cost, so that an empire's growing power eventually (and with whatever kinds of lag) translated into growing prosperity at home, and vice versa.

But the time of America's extraordinary rise to unparalleled global dominance – particularly the period from 1990 to the present – has coincided with a remarkable *deterioration* in America as a national project, with the result that, even though their country dominates the planet in a political and military sense, the majority of the American people are working harder than ever before, in jobs that are more transitory and less secure than ever before, with less health insurance coverage than ever before, and hence living in greater fear than

ever before – fear, in fact, has become the great driving principle of contemporary American culture, society, and politics. All around them, in the meantime, they have been watching their national social infrastructure (including health care, public health, transportation, and education) slowly deteriorating, while the gap between rich and poor has grown wider than ever before, mirroring, in fact, the growing gap between rich and poor on a global scale.

While, for example, median family incomes in the US grew by around 100 per cent across the board in the period from 1947 to 1979, in the period from 1979 to 1998, median family incomes stagnated for the bottom 60 per cent of families – though they grew by 64 per cent for the top 5 per cent of families.[12] Around a quarter of all American workers – and a third of all women workers – earned poverty-level wages in 1999.[13] At 21 per cent, in fact, the US has more of its population living in poverty than any other Western country – double the poverty rate of Europe; moreover, according to a 1999 OECD report, the US population has the lowest escape rate from poverty of any industrialized nation, which shows that the story of upward social mobility offered in the American dream is little more than a myth.[14] These and other factors have led to a situation in which the share of wealth owned by the top 1 per cent of the US population has grown to almost 40 per cent, up from 34 per cent in 1983, which is more than the share of wealth owned by the bottom 95 per cent of the population, the growth of whose share remained flat over the same period.[15] Even conservative

12 See Economic Policy Institute, *The State of Working America, 1998–99*, based on US Census Bureau data.
13 See Economic Policy Institute, *The State of Working America, 2000–1*.
14 UNICEF data; also see Howard Oxley, Thai-Thanh Dang, and Pablo Antolin's OECD paper (Paris: OECD, 1999).
15 See Collins et al. (1999), based on Federal Reserve data.

SPECTRES OF TERRORISM
Saree Makdisi

and business-oriented magazines like *Forbes* and *Fortune* and *Businessweek* are starting to voice concern at the dramatic gap in wealth and incomes in the US, pointing out, for example, that, whereas the average CEO made twenty times what the average worker made in 1965, by 1997 the ratio had gone to 115 times: the average production worker's pay in 1998 was just under $23,000; the average CEO pay was close to $11 million.[16] 'Since 1975, practically all the gains in household income have gone to the top 20 percent of households,' the CIA notes in its 2001 *World Factbook*; 'long term problems include inadequate investment in economic infrastructure, rapidly rising medical costs of an ageing population, sizeable trade deficits, and stagnation of family income for the lower income groups.'[17]

Thus, although the US is in absolute terms the greatest superpower the world has ever known, it is one that, unlike previous great powers, is growing both stronger and weaker at the same time, which is a highly unusual development – and a development, at that, which reminds us that the US itself, superpower though it may be, is not immune to the dramatic and often deleterious changes imposed by global economic transformations *across* as well as *within* national boundaries. Indeed, we can read these developments, I think, as the telltale signs of the contradiction between a political process of globalization, on the one hand – a process now given renewed strength in the global war on terrorism, a war that recognizes no outsides and that has witnessed and will witness the deployment of power across the world – and, on the other hand, an economic and cultural process of

globalization that also seeks to override borders and rewrite international regulations, but ultimately for an altogether different set of objectives, in which concepts such as geopolitical dominance and military strategy – and even national interest, in the traditional sense of that term – may have little or no role to play, and in which a nation's economy and social fabric, even those of America itself, may be eaten away from within even as it is projecting its baleful political and military power without.

The long assault, led by the advocates of free-market liberalism and privatization all through the 1990s on the institutions of the American state, is showing the toll they have taken on America as a collective national project through the attempts not only to dismantle the welfare state but to privatize virtually all the functions of the state – education, health care, insurance, social security, even prisons – with the solitary exception of military planning and national defence, to which ever greater sums of money have been dedicated; even counting the huge increase in defence spending over the years (including the Star Wars programme), public investment as a share of GDP has fallen by over a third since the early 1980s, and is projected to fall by another third or more by 2007.[18] One result of all this is the contradiction we have already noted, namely, that America's increasing capacity to project its enormous military and political power over the world has coincided with an ever-increasing sense of crisis and insecurity at home, and at times even a sense of imminent social collapse, of which the riots, school shootings, mass suicides and other episodes of random and otherwise inexplicable violence are sometimes taken to be the harbingers.

16 See *The New York Times*, 9 April 1998.
17 See 2001 CIA *World Factbook* (http://www.cia.gov/cia/publications/factbook).

18 See Baker (1998).

Perhaps, then, we are witnessing in the ongoing war against the spectre of terrorism an attempt by the US to impose its will on the world, to redefine, seize control of, and determine the apparatuses of global governance, and hence to impose the war on terrorism precisely as a new mode of global governance, as I have been arguing all along. Such an attempt to reassert political imperatives over economic ones would certainly explain the recent calls by the US government for citizens to express their patriotism and their rejection of the spectre of terrorism by spending their money rather than holding back for fear of a recession which would then be a self-fulfilling prophecy. In this way even shopping has been drafted to the cause of national defence against terrorism, and consumption recoded as a patriotic duty. Here we are witnessing the reassertion of the political over and against an economic order that seems increasingly out of control, and now more than ever, and in spite of the enormous power being brought to bear on the world, the war against the spectre of terrorism starts to look like a desperate effort to project American political and military power on to a world in which such power – for all its devastating potency in human and material terms – may no longer offer effective control.

What this bundle of contradictions leaves us with is the possibility that such projects of domination may start to run into and unravel each other, even as they have also to contend with a determined opposition whose equally global presence is only just beginning to be felt. Here I am certainly not referring to the likes of Ussama bin Laden, but rather to all those movements, in America, in Europe, and across the world, to unify the planet in the name of cooperation rather than competition,

solidarity rather than antagonism, and hope rather than the gloom of world orders that recognize no limits to their own acquisitive power and dreams of domination.

## References

Baker, Dean (1998) *The Public Investment Deficit*, Economic Policy Institute.
Beck, Ulrich (2000) 'What is globalization?', in David Held and Anthony McGrew (eds) *The Global Transformations Reader*, Cambridge: Polity.
Castells, Manuel (2000) 'The global economy', in David Held and Anthony McGrew (eds) *The Global Transformations Reader*, Cambridge: Polity.
Cohen, Ariel (1997) 'U. S. policy in the Caucasus and Central Asia: building a new "silk road" to economic prosperity', *Heritage Foundation Backgrounder* 1132, 24 July (http://www.heritage.org/library/categories/forpol/bg1132.html).
Collins, Chuck, Leondar-Wright, Betsy and Sklar, Holly (1999) *Shifting Fortunes: The Perils of The Growing American Wealth Gap*, Boston, MA.
Ellwood, Wayne (2001) *The No-Nonsense Guide to Globalization*, London: Verso.
Hardt, Michael and Negri, Antonio (2001) *Empire*, Cambridge, MA: Harvard University Press.
Hirst, Paul and Thompson, Grahame (2000) 'Globalization – a necessary myth?', in David Held and Anthony McGrew (eds) *The Global Transformations Reader*, Cambridge: Polity.
Hume, Brit (2001) 'Special Report with Brit Hume', Fox News Channel, 5 November.
Keohane, Robert (2000) 'Sovereignty in international society', in David Held and Anthony McGrew (eds) *The Global Transformations Reader*, Cambridge: Polity.
Makdisi, Ussama (2002) ' "Anti-Americanism" in the Arab world: an interpretation of a brief history', *Journal of American History* summer.
Miyoshi, Masao (1998) ' "Globalization," culture, and the university', in Fredric Jameson and Masao Miyoshi (eds) *The Cultures of Globalization*, Durham, NC: Duke University Press.
Rashid, Ahmed (2001) *Taliban: The Story of the Afghan Warlords*, London: Pan.
Sassen, Saskia (1998) *Globalization and its Discontents*, New York: New Press, esp. pp. 195–218.

# [19]

William L. Waugh, Jr.
*Georgia State University*
Richard T. Sylves
*University of Delaware*

# Organizing the War on Terrorism

*The network of public agencies, private firms, nonprofit organizations, ad hoc groups, and individual volunteers that deals with natural and technological hazards and disasters did a remarkable job of responding to and helping us recover from the September 11th attacks. That national emergency management network, along with the national security and law enforcement networks, provides a foundation for our war on terrorism, helps us mitigate the hazard of terrorism, and improves our preparedness for future violence. However, coordinating the efforts of the networks will be a real challenge for the director of homeland security and his or her state and local counterparts. Coordination will necessitate using legal authority to assure compliance, economic and other incentives to encourage compliance, formal partnerships to encourage collaboration, informal understandings to encourage cooperation, and personal encouragement to influence appropriate action. A top-down, command-and-control approach to the war on terrorism, such as the proposed Department of Homeland Security is intended to provide, may be counterproductive.*

The United States is now at war with terrorists and terrorism. It is, therefore, vital to inquire about whether the war effort is organized in a manner that will prove effective, and whether post–September 11 national investments in programs to reduce the hazard of terrorism are changing national, state, and local policy priorities for the better. Is the war organized to assure that we are prepared for the next attacks? Will the tidal wave of new federal laws and the mammoth increase in terrorism budget authority help federal, state, and local authorities address the threat of terrorism? Will the new emphasis on counterterrorism complement or undercut state and local governments' capacities to manage the many common hazards that are more likely to befall them?

The federal government is investing tens of billions of dollars in developing antiterrorism capabilities, based on the presumed potential for catastrophic terrorism rather than on measured risk. The identification of cities needing counterterrorism training, for example, was based on population and not on their likelihood of becoming terrorist targets. Indeed, notwithstanding the events of September 11, the concern about nuclear, biological, and chemical terrorism has largely shaped the war effort. Such agents, including plutonium and other radioactive materials, were left in the rubble of the Soviet war machine and have been sold,

lost, and temporarily misplaced. Nuclear, biological, and chemical agents also have been created by so-called "rogue states" and by independent terrorist organizations. Although delivery systems may still pose problems, terrorists do have the wherewithal to obtain such weapons and to carry out mass casualty attacks. Perhaps more important, some terrorist organizations have demonstrated their willingness to kill hundreds—if not thousands—of people in order to achieve their political goals.

We used to think, because many experts had surmised, that political terrorists "want a lot of people watching and not a lot of people dead." The attacks by Islamic fundamentalists on the World Trade Center in 1993, the Aum Shinryko sarin gas release in the Tokyo subway system in

*William L. Waugh, Jr., teaches public administration in the Andrew Young School of Policy Studies at Georgia State University. His research focuses on the design of disaster policies and hazard-reduction programs and on the coordination of multiorganizational and intergovernmental operations. His publications include Living with Hazards, Dealing with Disasters (2000), Terrorism and Emergency Management (1990), and International Terrorism (1982). Email: padwlw@langate.gsu.edu.*

*Richard T. Sylves teaches environmental, energy, and disaster policy and public budgeting in the Department of Political Science and International Relations at the University of Delaware. His recent research has focused on the politics and economics of presidential disaster declarations. He has authored and coauthored many publications, including two books, Disaster Management in the U.S. and Canada (1996) and Cities and Disaster (1990). Email: sylves@udel.edu.*

1995, the attack perpetrated by Timothy McVeigh and Terry Nichols against the Alfred P. Murrah Federal Building in Oklahoma City in 1995, and the multiple attacks on the World Trade Center, the Pentagon, and the passengers of Flight 93 on September 11, 2001, manifestly demonstrate the willingness of terrorists to kill large numbers of people. The FBI and other agencies warned of possible incidents, and President Clinton signed Presidential Decision Directive 39 (PDD 39) in June 1995, which took on the threat of nuclear, biological, chemical, and radiological (that is, weapons of mass destruction) terrorism. In 1996, Congress passed and President Clinton signed the Nunn-Lugar-Domenici or Defense against Weapons of Mass Destruction Act, which further defined agency responsibilities and provided initial funding for the implementation of the national program to meet the threat of terrorism. Presidential Decision Directives 62 and 63 followed in 1998 to provide mechanisms for dealing with the threat of terrorism to America's critical infrastructure. Following the September 11 attacks, President Bush created the Office of Homeland Security and the Homeland Security Council by executive order, and a plethora of programs have been created to protect airports, seaports, public buildings, and other potential terrorist targets and to engage the American public in the war. Immigration policies are being reexamined as well. Political and administrative mechanisms to deal with the threat of terrorism are being designed, implemented, and refined.

In essence, the "war on terrorism" creates a new set of organizational structures to address the threat of nuclear, biological, chemical, and radiological terrorism. The FBI houses the interagency program and coordinates its operations. The Department of Defense has a key role because of its expertise with nuclear, biological, and chemical warfare and with external threats, and the Department of Health and Human Services has a key role because of its expertise in dealing with public health hazards. The Federal Emergency Management Agency (FEMA) also has a key role in coordinating federal efforts and supporting state and local efforts. Washington basically directs the program such that federal agencies assume the lead in helping state and local governments improve their ability to respond to terrorist incidents involving weapons of mass destruction.

There has been some disagreement about the progress of the war. Some have opposed federal efforts because they discount the need to spend billions of dollars on programs to deal with the threat of weapons of mass destruction or because they do not trust the Defense Department and federal law enforcement agencies. Because of September 11, some of this opposition has waned, but there is an increasing challenge to any new security measures that might infringe on civil liberties and affect political and administrative prerogatives. Clearly, the September

11 event may mean for quite some time that any bill with the word "terrorism" in the title is assured congressional support. However, the design and implementation of the counterterrorism program, even before September 11, has been controversial.

For example, prior to September 11, the General Accounting Office reported some problems in priority setting and in how the Defense Department and other federal agencies were dealing with state and local agencies. Spending priorities sparked debate. Initially, there were concerns that the "Defense of the Homeland" was not integrated into the national emergency management system. The program was accused of dedicating too many resources to the threat of weapons of mass destruction and too little to the conventional weapons threat. Fertilizer bombs and other homemade devices are well within the capabilities of most domestic and international terrorists, while nuclear, biological, and chemical weapons are not; automatic rifles, plastic explosives, and other military weapons are readily available on the commercial and black markets. In short, while weapons of mass destruction may pose the greatest threat, less sophisticated attacks are more probable (see, for example, Smithson and Levy 2000).

Only days after the September attack, many were asking whether federal interagency competition and conflicts, combined with differences in organizational cultures and missions, would confound the homeland security initiative. The threat of terrorism elicits a military crisis-management response in terms of the potential scale and nature of attack. However, the American political system requires a law enforcement approach to domestic threats (unless the scale is so large that government function and national survival are threatened). September 11 has muddled this considerably. The military presence at airport security checkpoints is only one of the changes that has occurred. The U.S. mail is irradiated to counter anthrax contamination, and almost every facet of daily American life has been affected by the threat of terrorism. Americans do not know whether the next terror attack against the nation will transpire thousands of miles away from the homeland or simply down the block. Perhaps the most important lesson from the World Trade Center and Pentagon attacks is that terrorism cannot be prevented entirely. Some acts can be thwarted and some effects can be lessened, but there are too many potential targets to protect, and our open society affords opportunity for enemies to attack.

Fortunately, a national emergency management system has been in place to deal with catastrophic disasters of natural and unnatural origin for quite some time. When incidents at the state or local level exceed the capabilities of first responders, additional resources are brought to bear from adjacent jurisdictions and from the federal government. Emergency managers are well practiced in coordinating their work in multijurisdictional and multiorganizational operations. There are lessons to be learned from that system, and first among them is that emergency management is a bottom-up process. Capacity building has to begin at the level of the first responders who will be responsible for dealing with crises and their consequences until support arrives. The second lesson is in how multiorganizational, multisector, and intergovernmental operations are coordinated.

The increased professionalization of state and local emergency managers has encouraged movement away from the command-and-control approach that was common two or three decades ago, when civil defense against nuclear attack was the paramount concern. Coordination, rather than command and control, has become the more common approach (Waugh 1993, 1994, 2001a). Indeed, it is a concern of emergency management professionals that the response to September 11 will bring back that earlier era rather than produce a more consensually based and elegantly interlaced emergency management system—one that does not superimpose overbearing command systems riddled with secrecy requirements that complicate the collaboration and public involvement essential to dealing with hazards and disasters.

Will a post–September 11 emergency management system break down the networks of public, nonprofit, and private disaster organizations, or will it empower state and local governments and their partners to contribute to the counterterrorism effort in a reasonable way? If the war on terrorism inadvertently undercuts or distorts an emergency system designed to deal with so-called routine disasters, it may well weaken current capabilities to manage conventional hazards *and* the hazard posed by terrorism. FEMA's Office of National Preparedness may assure that the threat of natural and technological hazards is not forgotten in the rush to prepare for terrorist-sponsored catastrophes, but it is also important that the war on terrorism be understood in the context of all of the other major hazards that face America.

## The War on Terrorism

In large measure, current U.S. counterterrorism policy is a direct reaction to the events of September 11. The war on terrorism was announced, and the U.S. government responded with air strikes against al-Qaeda and Taliban bases in Afghanistan and police raids on suspected terrorist cells in Europe and elsewhere. In essence, national policy became a multilevel operation to kill or apprehend those associated with Osama bin Laden and his organization. Historically, this has been the pattern of U.S. policy making. Crisis—whether precipitated by national security threat

or natural disaster—gives the impetus for policy makers to act, and they, as a rule, define the policy problem narrowly. In the parlance of the military, policy makers always prepare to fight the last war. In this case, they are responding to the kind of terrorism experienced on September 11 without necessarily addressing the broader threat posed by terrorist violence. To be sure, we have had recent acts of domestic terrorism, evidently including the anthrax attacks, and there are other terrorist organizations operating in the world that pose threats to U.S. citizens at home and abroad. Not all terrorist groups have the same objectives, modus operandi, or capabilities, as al-Qaeda, and, if our programs are to address future threats, they should be focused broadly enough to accommodate at least the most serious known threats.

The question, then, is how to organize the war on terrorism to best meet the range of threats posed to the United States and its citizens by terrorists. In the March/April 2002 issue of *Public Administration Review*, Charles Wise examines the organizational issues surrounding the Office of Homeland Security and suggests the homeland security program might best be structured in a less hierarchical manner than many believe. At present, the coordinator of homeland security has little real authority over the myriad of departments, agencies, and offices that are involved in dealing with the terrorist threat. Governor Ridge has to rely on the cooperation and resources of others in order to design, implement, and maintain a coherent set of programs. Wise concludes that a network approach will be more appropriate and likely more effective.

Network management is an emerging art in public administration and is particularly appropriate—if not absolutely necessary—when officials lack the direct authority to pursue policy goals. The sheer number of actors involved makes coordination a serious problem, particularly when many view the task as a peripheral mission. Coordinating agencies might use direct authority when it is available, direct influence (such as financial incentives) when circumstances permit, indirect influence (such as technical assistance) when feasible, and less formal support (such as expressions of personal support) when more formal and substantive support is not appropriate. Goals are pursued through some combination of regulatory relationships, contractual relationships, formal and informal partnerships, and personal relationships (see, Waugh 2002). As Wise points out, direct command-and-control approaches may even be counterproductive (142). Control encourages resentment and resistance, while collaboration encourages commitment and cooperation.

So, again, how should the war on terrorism be organized? The discussion to follow will describe the current national emergency management system and how it deals with hazards such as terrorism, the new counterterrorism structures that are part of the "Defense of the Homeland" programs, and the poor fit between the new structures and the national emergency management system. It will conclude with an examination of the policy implications of the current war on terrorism.

## Crisis Management before September 11

When three airliners struck the World Trade Center towers and the Pentagon on September 11 and a fourth crashed in Pennsylvania, the national emergency management system was activated. While military aircraft were positioned to protect New York City and the national capital from aerial attack, and security forces were positioned to protect the nation from land and sea attack, thousands of first responders were mobilized to deal with the immediate crisis and the consequences of the attacks. Tens of thousands of additional emergency responders followed to provide support for the rescue and recovery efforts. The emergency response included the agencies identified in the National Response Plan as having lead and supporting responsibilities, including the American Red Cross. It also included state and local government agencies, nongovernmental organizations, ad hoc groups that emerged to provide assistance and tens of thousands of unaffiliated volunteers who wished to assist. Medical volunteers and search and rescue teams came from all over the United States and even from outside. In most respects, the response was similar to what might be expected following a major natural disaster, such as an earthquake, although the scale and nature of the World Trade Center disaster likely increased the attraction of outside groups. The point is simply that a national emergency management system was already in existence and offered remarkable capacity to respond to the events on September 11. The system was able to deal with a terrorist disaster.

### The National Emergency Management System

The national emergency management system has expanded and evolved over the past two decades. Throughout American history, when disasters have occurred, communities have relied on nongovernmental organizations, private firms, individual volunteers, and the ad hoc groups that emerge in response to need, as well as their public safety agencies. The disaster network is loosely structured, organizationally diverse, motivated by a broad range of interests, and, in part, ad hoc. It is also flexible and very capable. Most communities still rely on the American Red Cross, the Salvation Army, and a few other general-purpose relief agencies to take care of the victims of smaller disasters and to assist public agencies during larger disasters. In other words, FEMA and its state and local counterparts are only the tip of the proverbial iceberg.

The network is extensive. There are thousands of organizations, large and small, in the United States that are engaged in disaster-related activities. Nonprofit voluntary organizations range from large environmental groups to small faith-based groups. Some have highly specialized skills, such as search and rescue, amateur radio communications, and emergency feeding or shelter, and others are much broader in scope. The American Red Cross has a national network of offices, intensive training programs for volunteers, and capabilities to respond to many kinds of disaster. Smaller organizations may operate out of the basements of churches, synagogues, or mosques, or even out of members' garages, but they often provide critical services. Coordination and cooperation among nonprofit, voluntary groups has been increasing at the national and state levels. The National Volunteer Organizations in Action in Disaster was formed to provide a vehicle to coordinate the planning of disaster responses and to minimize duplications of effort. State volunteer organizations fulfill similar regional and local roles. Members range from the American Red Cross and the Salvation Army to smaller organizations such as the Mennonite Disaster Services, the Phoenix Society for Burn Victims, Volunteers in Technical Assistance, and the Second Harvest National Network of Food Banks. State and local emergency management agencies are relying more on such groups to provide essential services that are unavailable through government offices.

Professional organizations are also involved. Some of the more prominent organizations are the National Emergency Management Association (representing state emergency management agencies and managers), the International Association of Emergency Managers (representing local emergency managers), the American Planning Association, the American Psychological Association's Disaster Response Network, the American Public Works Association's Council on Emergency Management, and the American Society for Public Administration's Section on Emergency and Crisis Management. The network also includes organizations representing engineers, architects, airline pilots, floodplain managers, funeral home directors, dam safety officials, local government officials, insurance companies, fire chiefs and firefighters, risk managers, and other professions with disaster skills and concerns. Many of these groups assisted in the World Trade Center and Pentagon response and recovery operation. Private-sector organizations provide a variety of services ranging from technical assistance to debris management, and associations from particular industries—for instance, the Chemical Manufacturers Association—provide resources. The threat of terrorism to business is being addressed through the training programs of the American Society for Industrial Security, for example.

Ad hoc or "emergent" groups of volunteers also form in the aftermath of disaster, as they did following the September 11 attacks. Some groups can be highly organized, and others may be amorphous groupings of volunteers. Such groups and individual volunteers can provide needed manpower for disaster operations if they are integrated into the existing emergency management system, but they may interfere with operations if they are not organized and used effectively. Coordinating the activities of volunteer and other nonprofit groups, for-profit organizations and individuals, and government agencies is a complex and difficult task. Emergency managers have to anticipate the emergence of such groups and individuals and find ways to utilize the financial, administrative, and political resources they bring to hazard reduction and disaster management. It is a complex network with fragmented authority. Formal partnership arrangements, memoranda of understanding, contractual relationships, personal connections, and informal agreements to cooperate and share resources hold the network together. While some agencies use command-and-control mechanisms (such as the incident command system) in their own operations, most are loosely structured, consensually oriented, and dependent on trust and commitment from professional and volunteer staff to maintain organizational purpose.

## The Counterterrorism System

U.S. policy on terrorism has evolved over the past half-century. President Nixon and Secretary of State Henry Kissinger formally enunciated a "no negotiation, no compromise" policy in the early 1970s following an international terrorist incident in which two American diplomats were killed. The policy was also applied to domestic terrorist incidents. Nonetheless, there have been incidents in which negotiations were held and terrorist demands were met in order to secure the release of hostages (see Waugh 1982, 1990). In response to increased international terrorism, President Reagan signed National Security Directive 207 in 1986, assigning responsibility for coordinating the U.S. response to international terrorist incidents to an Interagency Working Group under the auspices of the National Security Council. The State Department was the designated lead agency for terrorist incidents outside the United States, and the FBI was the designated lead agency for incidents within the United States.

In June 1995, President Clinton signed Presidential Decision Directive (PDD) 39, reaffirming U.S. policy on terrorism and spelling out the strategy to "reduce vulnerabilities and prevent and deter terrorists acts before they occur; respond to terrorist acts that do occur, including managing crises and apprehending and punishing terrorist perpetrators; and manage the consequences of terrorist attacks" (GAO 1997, 2). The directive reaffirmed the lead responsibilities for the Department of State and the FBI for crisis management and assigned lead responsibility for domestic consequence management to FEMA.

As the lead agency for domestic terrorist incidents, the FBI can call upon virtually any federal agency that has needed expertise. The Bureau may also request the activation of a Domestic Emergency Support Team with representatives from agencies that can provide specialized expertise (GAO 1997, 43). Partial Domestic Emergency Support Teams have been deployed for major events, including the 1996 Olympics and the 1997 presidential inauguration, to involve agencies with expertise that might be needed in the event of a terrorist incident (GAO 1997, 45). The Department of Defense can provide assistance through a variety of facilities and units, including the Chemical, Biological Defense Command, the U.S. Army Explosive Ordnance Disposal group, the Defense Technical Response Group, and the U.S. Army Technical Escort Unit (GAO 1997, 45). The Defense Department also provides Civil Support Teams to support state and local first responders early in a crisis. Ten regional teams were created initially, each with 22 full-time National Guard personnel, to identify biological and chemical agents and to assess situations so that additional resources can be brought in. More teams have been added, and there is increasing pressure to expand the number even more—eventually, perhaps, to permit each state to create its own team. The Environmental Protection Agency has response teams and research laboratories to deal with chemical and radiological incidents, and the Department of Energy can use its radiological monitoring and response units (GAO 1997, 61). The Department of Energy also can activate a nuclear incident team, if needed.

If an incident exceeds FBI capabilities, the attorney general and the secretary of defense may agree that an exception to the Posse Comitatus Act is necessary and ask the president to sign an executive order and issue an emergency proclamation for the use of the military to enforce civilian law. Draft documents are held for the president's signature, should action be required on very short notice (GAO 1997, 47). The counterterrorism effort is largely top-down, with the lead agencies deciding what resources are needed and who should participate.

By contrast, dealing with the consequences of terrorist attacks more closely resembles the response to natural and technological disasters. FEMA coordinates the consequence management operation following the Federal Response Plan and its Terrorism Annex or, if it is a radiological incident, the Federal Radiological Emergency Response Plan. The Department of Health and Human Services can activate Disaster Medical Assistance Teams to provide emergency medical care. In cooperation with FEMA, the Departments of Defense, Veterans Administration, and

Health and Human Services can activate the National Disaster Medical System to locate hospital beds for victims and Disaster Mortuary Teams to assist in processing deceased victims. The Defense Department's medical facilities and research institutes also may be called upon. The Health and Human Services Department's National Pharmaceutical Stockpile program provides necessary pharmaceutical supplies to local, state, and federal authorities in the event of a disaster, including incidents involving nuclear, biological, or chemical contamination.

Other federal agencies are tasked under the Federal Response Plan to provide emergency medical care, temporary shelter, search and rescue, and measures to restore critical lifelines, as well as providing traditional disaster assistance (for example, public assistance, small business loans, and individual assistance) to the victims. It is important to note that, as in other kinds of disasters, the federal government is not the lead government in managing the consequences of terrorist incidents. State and local governments have primary responsibility for disaster response and recovery from domestic terrorist incidents, and host nations have those responsibilities following international terrorist incidents. When the resources of state and local governments are overwhelmed, the governor can request assistance from the federal government. The Robert T. Stafford Disaster Relief and Emergency Assistance Act permits the president to issue a presidential disaster declaration or designate an incident as a "major emergency." The declaration or designation permits FEMA and other federal agencies to provide a range of disaster assistance to individuals, businesses, communities, and governments. Following the September 11 attacks, presidential disaster declarations were issued for affected counties in New York, New Jersey, Connecticut, Virginia, and Maryland, and for the District of Columbia.

To some extent, PDD-39 does recognize that crisis management and consequence management functions may be carried out at the same time. An Interagency Consequence Management Group is included in the Joint Operations Center to advise officials. The differentiation between crisis management and consequence management is an important one for a variety of reasons, not least of which is that it suggests a two-phase process. The comprehensive emergency management model currently used in dealing with natural and technological disasters was originally conceptualized as having four phases: mitigation (hazard reduction), preparedness, response, and recovery. Increasingly, however, it is recognized that the four functions are not separate or sequential. Mitigation should begin before there are consequences, so that officials can minimize loss of life and reduce property loss and, thereby, speed recovery. In the "Homeland Security" program, there is some consideration of consequences, but until the FBI

decides the "crisis" is under control, consequence management may be a low priority. Fortunately, the creation of FEMA's National Preparedness Office seems to reflect an understanding of the need for mitigation before terrorist incidences.

Congressional "Homeland Security" (or Domestic Preparedness) priorities were spelled out in the 1996 Nunn-Lugar-Domenici or Defense Against Weapons of Mass Destruction Act (an amendment to the National Defense Authorization Act for FY97, P.L. 104-201). Under the act, "weapons of mass destruction" are defined in Section 1403 as "any weapon or device that is intended, or has the capability, to cause death or serious bodily injury to a significant number of people through the release, dissemination, or impact of (1) toxic or poisonous chemicals or their precursors; (2) a disease organism; or (3) radiation or radioactivity." The act specifically cites the potential transfer of devices, materials, and information on nuclear, biological, and chemical weapons from the former Soviet states to terrorist organizations and hostile nations.

The act requires the secretary of defense to implement a program to train and provide technical assistance to local, state, and federal civilian personnel so they can respond to emergencies involving the use or threatened use of such an attack (see Section 1411a). The assistance to federal, state, and local agencies includes training to use equipment for the detection of chemical and biological agents or nuclear material; protecting emergency responders and the public; decontamination; establishing a "hot line" for information dissemination; using the National Guard and Reserves; and loaning equipment (Section 1412e).

The secretary of defense was designated the responsible official for implementing the program until October 1, 1998, when President Clinton assigned responsibility to the attorney general and a new FBI-led interagency office was created for the National Domestic Preparedness program. The act reaffirmed the legal restrictions on the use of military personnel and units in civilian law enforcement (that is, the Posse Comitatus Act) and the acceptability of using military personnel for the "immediate protection of human life" when law enforcement officials are unable to do so (Section 1416d). The act goes on to mandate that the president assist in building the capacities of federal, state, and local agencies to deal with the use or threatened use of "weapons of mass destruction," and it provides additional funding to support efforts to interdict, control, and coordinate policies and measures designed to stop the proliferation of such weapons, as well as to support the cooperative threat-reduction program with the former Soviet states. It was unclear that funding would be more than one year, and the limited definition of weapons of mass destruction defined spending priorities.

The Department of Defense was also tasked with training local first responders to deal with terrorist incidents involving weapons of mass destruction. The Chemical Defense Training Facility at Fort McClellan, Alabama, was designated as the site for training, and training sessions began in October 1995. The Domestic Preparedness Program began in FY 1997, with the goal of training police, fire, and emergency medical services personnel in 120 designated U.S. cities by 2001. Under the program, each city received $300,000 in equipment from the Defense Department. FEMA also began providing grants to states for terrorism-preparedness activities, including consequence management planning, exercising, and training, and to state fire-training centers for first-responder terrorism training courses (NDPO 1999a, 2). The Department of Health and Human Services, through the Public Health Service, began setting up Metropolitan Medical Response Systems and providing equipment and pharmaceuticals (NDPO 1999b, 3–5).

On May 22, 1998, President Clinton signed PDD-62, establishing the Office of the National Coordinator for Security, Infrastructure Protection, and Counterterrorism to oversee counterterrorism, infrastructure protection, consequence management, and preparedness programs. The national coordinator works within the National Security Council, reports to the president through the assistant to the president for national security affairs, and makes recommendations on budgets and policies regarding terrorism (White House 1998a). On the same day, President Clinton also signed PDD-63 on protecting America's critical infrastructures to address the vulnerability of the nation's information system infrastructure. The National Infrastructure Protection Center was created by the FBI to deal with attacks, with a national coordinator to oversee efforts to reduce vulnerabilities (White House 1998b).

More than 40 federal departments and other agencies were involved in combating terrorism prior to September 2001, and the number has increased since. Now there is a homeland security chief, Governor Tom Ridge, and a Homeland Security Council with a rapidly expanding staff. There is also a Transportation Security Administration in the Department of Transportation to oversee efforts to protect the nation's transportation systems. The Defense Department has created a Northern Command to oversee military efforts to defend the nation and to coordinate those efforts with other agencies. FEMA has been given an enhanced role in the homeland security program as officials have come to appreciate the magnitude of the effort and the need to coordinate with state and local agencies. FEMA has developed a strong information technology system to support disaster operations (Lisagor 2002), and its new Office of National Preparedness will have a lead role in preparing first responders to deal with terrorism, coordi-

nating federal programs, and supporting the development of the Citizen Corps (U.S. House 2002).

## How Should We Organize the War on Terrorism?

Prior to September 2001, the General Accounting Office had identified a number of serious problems with the "Defense of the Homeland" programs, including the lack of a common definition of terrorism among the lead agencies (GAO 1997, 16); the selection of cities for first-responder training without appropriate attention to the existing emergency management networks that would be involved in any major incident (GAO 1998, 2); confusion about the "loan" of equipment by the Defense Department (even though the department considers the loans to be permanent) (GAO 1998, 2); and the lack of a systematic assessment of the risk of attack by terrorists using biological or chemical weapons and the vulnerability of potential targets (GAO 1999). Problems in the relationships among the Defense Department and other agencies and the complexity of the weapons of mass destruction program were also noted (GAO 1998, 2–3). The TOPOFF ("top official") exercise in 2000 revealed many of the same coordination problems. Turf battles, communication problems, and differences in how the threat was defined raised serious questions about the nation's capability to respond to catastrophic terrorist incidents. Another TOPOFF exercise is planned.

The 120 cities designated for first-responder training were selected based on population (all over 144,000 based on the 1995 census estimate) and represented 22 percent of the U.S. population, 38 states and Washington, D.C., and one-quarter of the cities in California and Texas. No threat or vulnerability analyses were conducted to choose the cities. In fact, the General Accounting Office concluded that training in fewer cities and including the local emergency management networks responsible for dealing with disasters would speed the process and be more effective (GAO 1998, 6–8). Some of the problems identified by the General Accounting Office have already been addressed, such as the need to broaden the training to include metropolitan response networks. However, threat assessments are still needed. Using worst-case scenarios to set training priorities and allocate funding is not good policy.

PDD-39 and the Nunn-Lugar-Domenici Act of 1996, as well as PDD-62 and 63, created a national-security-focused counterterrorism structure that was, in effect, layered over the national emergency management system, with little attempt to integrate the two. For minor incidents of terrorism, the system will likely work as intended. For major incidents of terrorism involving mass casualties and/or large areas of contamination or destruction (whether caused by the use of nuclear, biological, or chemical weapons or the use of more conventional weapons), the system will be much less effective than it might be. As Charles Wise suggests, coordinating such diverse elements will require considerable political and administrative skill. The principal reasons for concern are the shifting of decision-making responsibilities from agencies with strong working relationships with their state and local counterparts to agencies (such as the Defense Department and, perhaps to a lesser extent, the Department of Justice) that do not have strong records of cooperation with state and local government agencies, nongovernmental organizations, private firms, volunteers, and victims. The focus on crisis management will not encourage attention to preparedness and mitigation measures and, even with a consequence management team participating in the response, to recovery needs. If a catastrophic terrorist event occurs, consequence management may well be the immediate priority, with law enforcement concerns being secondary.

Homeland security suffers from the variety of perspectives on terrorism that its constituent agencies bring to the table. The focus on weapons of mass destruction is problematic because the definition permits the inclusion of agents that pose threats to only a very small number of people. Poison-dipped bullets and small quantities of biological agents with little or no potential for wide dispersal have been termed weapons of mass destruction, for example. Radiological material might conceivably contaminate large numbers of people if dispersed widely, such as in a "dirty bomb" incident, or concentrated in large-enough quantities in a heavily populated area, but the imprecise definition deems virtually all radiological material as weapons of mass destruction. After the Oklahoma City bombing, explosive devices were added to the list, although analysts all too frequently revert to the old nuclear, biological, and chemical definition. While the terminology, in and of itself, may facilitate legal action, it also may lessen the likelihood that such threats will be taken seriously by responders and potential victims.

The focus on weapons of mass destruction is also distracting state and local emergency management agencies from their responsibility to address more common hazards. Terrorism is a serious hazard that should be addressed, but emergency managers in California have to concentrate their efforts on the earthquakes that are certain to occur, emergency managers in Florida have to concentrate on the next Force 5 hurricane, and emergency managers in Texas, Pennsylvania, and elsewhere have to concentrate on their next floods, tornadoes, and other hazards. To justify the attention that homeland security requires, state and local emergency managers need to build capacities to deal with the more common and certain hazards and to expand their networks and resource bases. They need to integrate essential emergency response elements into their networks and pro-

vide mechanisms to facilitate a collaborative effort. The definition of "consequence" is vague and certainly makes it unclear whether such efforts should include the kinds of hazard management activities that would be used in dealing with natural and technological hazards. Homeland security needs to be based on a broad perspective on the phenomena of terrorism and integrate a broad range of mitigation and preparedness programs into the antiterrorism effort.

There is a decided tendency to define the terrorist threat in law enforcement and military terms only. That is the nature of war, perhaps. However, if we are dealing with a hazard that will remain with us well after the al-Qaeda network and its sponsors are subdued, we should be prepared for whatever form the next round of violence takes. History has, in fact, demonstrated that terrorism is relatively common, and there is no reason to think it will disappear. Therefore, we should be prepared to manage the hazard in the long term (Waugh 2001a). The war effort should include law enforcement and military options to prevent acts of terrorism against the United States and its citizens, and against others in the world, but it should also include those actions that may facilitate security. For example, the principles of Crime Prevention through Environmental Design can be used to reduce the threat to public buildings by controlling access and facilitating security. We can be protected from terrorists, disgruntled employees, abusive spouses, and other criminals at the same time (Waugh 2001b).

Lastly, any weapon that can cause mass casualties or large-scale economic or social loss is a weapon of mass destruction. A computer virus that shuts down critical services can be a weapon of mass destruction. A ship aimed at port facilities or dams can be a weapon of mass destruction. The World Trade Center disaster involved airplane crashes, high-rise fires, and structural collapses. In many respects, the disaster response was similar to what has occurred during major earthquakes. The threat of chemical weapons has often been described as similar to a hazardous materials accident, and in many respects that is probably true. The difference, however, is in the number of potential casualties. The threat of bioterrorism is usually defined in terms similar to a major pandemic, such as the Spanish flu outbreak of 1918; again, in many respects, the analogy may be well chosen. We have capabilities to respond to hazardous materials spills and even pandemics.

The real issue may be the scale of the disaster. A serious chemical attack could cause mass casualties and require a much larger response than fire departments and hazmat specialists generally understand. In short, the attack and its consequences may be much more than a large hazmat incident. Trying to extrapolate from our familiar disasters to far larger catastrophes may be a serious problem. Focusing on large events such as the World Trade Center tower collapses, which required resources far beyond those of New York City, from federal and state assets to small community groups and unaffiliated volunteers, may be the key. A national system to deal with the threat of terrorism should include those who are responsible for the less obvious mitigation, preparedness, response, and recovery efforts. Many lessons can be drawn from our experience with natural and technological hazards, if we are willing to broaden our view of the terrorism hazard (Sylves 2002).

The proposed Department of Homeland Security is intended to assure coordination of the counterterrorism effort. However, the new bureaucracy is already excluding those without security clearances in hand and legally defined roles in homeland security. Law enforcement and national security agencies are not noted for their openness to public participation, their willingness and abilities to work with communities and to integrate volunteers into operations, and their sensitivity to the plights of victims. Notwithstanding the call for a Citizen's Corps of volunteers, there has been little indication that the homeland security apparatus knows how to integrate civilians into its operations. Whether the department will be open to those with expertise and resources when a catastrophic disaster occurs, be it terrorist-spawned or a natural disaster, is also a serious question. Many of the organizations that assisted in the September 11th rescue and recovery operation are already out of the loop. Whether the commitment to disaster mitigation, preventing or reducing the effects of disaster, will continue is also a serious question. Efforts to encourage communities to become more disaster resistant and resilient have been based upon formal and informal partnerships. The imposition of federal or state authority would be fatal to many of those relationships. Lastly, the American public has come to expect a great deal of transparency and sensitivity when dealing with FEMA and other disaster agencies. However the war on terrorism is organized, will it be open, building upon decades of investment in community capacity-building, or will it be yet another classical closed bureaucracy, preparing to respond for rather than with communities?

# References

General Accounting Office (GAO). 1997. *Combating Terrorism: Federal Agencies' Efforts to Implement National Policy and Strategy.* Washington, DC: Government Printing Office. GAO, GAO/NSAID-97-254.

———. 1998. *Combating Terrorism: Opportunities to Improve Domestic Preparedness Program Focus and Efficiency.* Washington, DC: Government Printing Office. GAO, GAO/NSIAD-99-3.

———. 1999. *Combating Terrorism: Observations on Biological Terrorism and Public Health Initiatives.* Washington, DC: Government Printing Office. GAO/T-NSIAD-99-112.

Lee, Deborah. 1998. Integration of Reserve Components Responds to New Threat. *Defense Viewpoint* 13(29). Available at *http://www.defenselink.mil/speeches/1998/s19980s07-Lee.html.* Accessed June 14, 2002.

Lisagor, Megan. 2002. Reinventing FEMA. *Federal Computer Week,* March 25. Available at *http://www.fcw.com.* Accessed June 14, 2002.

National Domestic Preparedness Office (NDPO). 1999a. FEMA Terrorism-Related Grants. *The Beacon,* January 22, 2. Available at *http://www.ndpo.gov/beacon/1999/jan99.pdf.* Accessed June 14, 2002.

———. 1999b. Department of Health and Human Services Role at the NDPO. *The Beacon,* June 15, 1–5. Available at *http://www.ndpo.gov/beacon/1999/jun99.pdf.* Accessed June 14, 2002.

Smithson, Amy, and Leslie-Anne Levy. 2000. *Ataxia: The Chemical and Biological Terrorism Threat and the U.S. Response.* Report no. 35. Washington, DC: Henry L. Stimson Center.

Sylves, Richard T. 2002. Comments on "Countering Terrorism: Lessons Learned from Natural and Technological Disasters." National Academy of Sciences Natural Disasters Roundtable, February 28–March 1.

U.S. Congress. 1996. Defense Against Weapons of Mass Destruction Act of 1996. *National Defense Authorization Act for Fiscal Year 1997, Conference Report,* 104th Cong., 2d Sess., July 30, 303–21.

U.S. House Committee on Transportation and Infrastructure. 2002. New Office Will Better Coordinate Domestic Terrorism Response, According to Government Officials. Press Release, April 11.

Waugh, William L., Jr. 1982. *International Terrorism: How Nations Respond to Terrorists.* Salisbury, NC: Documentary Publications.

———. 1990. *Terrorism and Emergency Management.* New York: Marcel Dekker.

———. 1993. Co-ordination or Control: Organizational Design and the Emergency Management Function. *International Journal of Disaster Prevention and Management* 2(2): 17–31.

———. 1994. Regionalizing Emergency Management: Counties as State and Local Government. *Public Administration Review* 54(3): 253–58.

———. 2001a. Managing Terrorism as an Environmental Hazard. In *Handbook of Crisis and Emergency Management,* edited by Ali Farazmand, 659–76. New York: Marcel Dekker.

———. 2001b. *Terrorism and Emergency Management.* Emmitsburg, MD: FEMA, Emergency Management Institute. Available at *http://training.fema.gov/emiweb/edu/Terrorism.zip.* Accessed June 14, 2002.

———. 2002. *Leveraging Networks to Meet National Goals: FEMA and the Safe Construction Networks.* Washington, DC: PricewaterhouseCoopers Endowment for the Business of Government.

White House, Office of the Press Secretary. 1998a. *Fact Sheet: Combating Terrorism: Presidential Decision Directive 62,* May 22. Available at *http://www.fas.org/irp/offdocs/pdd/index.html.* Accessed June 14, 2002.

———. 1998b. *Fact Sheet: Protecting America's Critical Infrastructures: Presidential Decision Directive 63,* May 22. Available at *http://www.fas.org/irp/offdocs/pdd/index.html.* Accessed June 14, 2002.

———. 1998c. *White Paper: The Clinton Administration's Policy on Critical Infrastructure Protection: Presidential Decision Directive 63,* May 22. Available at *http://www.fas.org/irp/offdocs/pdd/index.html.* Accessed June 14, 2002.

Wise, Charles R. 2002. Organizing for Homeland Security. *Public Administration Review* 62(2): 131–44.

# [20]

M. Shamsul Haque
*National University of Singapore*

# Government Responses to Terrorism: Critical Views of Their Impacts on People and Public Administration

*Following the tragic, massive terrorist attacks on the United States in September 2001, many antiterrorist laws, policies, and institutions have emerged to wage war on terrorism. These antiterrorist initiatives have major consequences for individuals, societies, and nations all over the world. Although controversies have proliferated with regard to the implications of counterterrorism for people's basic rights, the debate remains fragmented and often unfocused. This article examines the critical impact of new antiterrorist initiatives on the fundamental rights and responsibilities of citizens and others, with special reference to public administration.*

Citizenship has been a central concern in both practical and academic public administration in most constitutionally democratic societies, emphasizing people's rights and responsibilities in relation to the state and to society in general. It is argued that citizenship represents the fundamental basis of constitutional democracy in terms of the reciprocal relationships between the state and people; thus, it provides the framework within which public administration functions as one of the basic domains of the state (Oliver and Heater 1994). During recent decades, in response to remarkable sociohistorical events—especially various movements and demands for civil liberties, economic opportunities (including union rights), gender equality, and ethnic representation—the nature of these relationships has undergone considerable change, especially in terms of expanding people's rights and entitlements, in almost all societies. In this regard, T.H. Marshall (1950) explains how the scope of citizenship began to expand to incorporate civil rights, political rights, and social rights. In line with this overall progress in the configuration of citizenship, the public service in most countries expanded to implement diverse policies and programs—ranging from basic needs and services to equal employment opportunity and affirmative action—to serve the public with fairness, equality, responsiveness, and accountability.

Recently, however, concerns have grown about newly emerging challenges to the principles of citizenship that are posed by market-driven reforms in governance, the re-definition of citizens as utilitarian customers, and the replacement of collective public interest by individual choice (Eriksen and Weigard 1999; Denhardt and Denhardt 2000). While concerns about the diminishing value of citizenship in public management were already on the rise, the September 11 terrorist attacks on the United States have raised new questions about public governance and the democratic principles of citizenship. While policy makers attempt to justify antiterrorist laws and institutions in the name of internal and external security, critics argue that such measures may pose a considerable challenge to various domains of people's rights, especially privacy, freedom of expression, political dissent, racial equality, and social entitlement (Dempsey 2001–02). According to the United Nations High Commission for Human Rights, new antiterrorist provisions may undermine basic human rights (Robinson 2002). In short, the growing debate questions the trade-offs between liberty and security in the aftermath of September 11 (Dempsey 2001–02).

Public administration is greatly affected by the September 11 event, especially in terms of articulating and implementing varied legal provisions, strategies, and programs

*M. Shamsul Haque is an associate professor in the Department of Political Science at the National University of Singapore. His most recent articles on governance and public administration have appeared in Public Administration Review, International Review of Administrative Sciences, International Journal of Public Administration, International Journal of Politics and Ethics, and other refereed journals. He is currently studying public governance in Asia. Email: polhaque@nus.edu.sg.*

adopted in many countries in response to terrorism. However, the event is too recent to expect much substantive literature. One major edited volume published immediately after the event is *Governance and Public Security* (Roberts 2002). Although this volume includes several articles that are useful in terms of their analysis of the potential administrative repercussions of September 11, it hardly deals with greater concerns such as the change in the nature of relationships between people and administration that is caused by new antiterrorist measures. A short commentary published in *Administration and Society* by Zahid Shariff (2002) includes hardly anything substantive in this regard except the author's prediction that September 11 might have strengthened the credibility of public administration professionals because of a renewed recognition of their role in serving people, which had been tarnished by bureaucrat bashing during the past few decades. In its March/April 2002 issue, *Public Administration Review* published a special report titled "Organizing for Homeland Security" (Wise 2002), which examines major approaches to organizational management in coordinating and managing public institutions involved in antiterrorist policies and programs. A broader analysis can be found in an earlier article titled "Fanatical Terrorism versus Disciplines of Constitutional Democracy" (Newland 2001), which also appeared in *Public Administration Review* (November/December 2001).

Some controversies have also emerged with regard to the favorable and adverse effects of September 11 on public administration as both a practical and an academic field. Few scholars emphasize that responses to terrorism have positive implications for the field or for the restoration and expansion of public trust in the credibility and necessity of public agencies and employees (Gordon 2002; Boaz 2001). Critics point out the failure of agencies and officials (especially those related to international and external security) to anticipate and prevent such a terrorist attack (Boaz 2001). These scattered arguments hardly explain how state–citizen relations have been affected by the new antiterrorist measures. In any case, these are examples of how some piecemeal studies are gradually emerging in relation to the impact of September 11 on public administration.

Needed are in-depth, comprehensive studies to examine the implications of the war on terrorism for various dimensions of public administration, including patterns of its relationships with people in different circumstances. However, an objective assessment of the impact of new antiterrorist measures is difficult because some have been presented emotionally by their proponents and opponents, making it difficult to gather impartial information, interpretations, and viewpoints. In fact, it is a common challenge in public administration to go beyond what L.E. Lynn (2001) calls "stylized facts, stories, conjectures, and ideo-

logical glosses" and to "ascertain whatever lessons and meanings might lie beneath." This article attempts to present a balanced assessment of the impact of antiterrorist measures on public administration, especially on its role to protect people's rights and to facilitate their performance of responsibilities. Because the existing views largely offer a favorable explanation of the war on terrorism, this study focuses more on the other perspectives, analyzing some of the adverse effects of antiterrorist laws, executive orders, and other measures on the principles of people's fundamental responsibilities and rights in relation to the theory and practice of public administration. In this attempt, the next section of this article briefly describes the background of the war on terrorism and the antiterrorist measures adopted after September 11.

## The Current War on Terrorism: Initiatives, Measures, and Significance

The terrorist attacks on September 11 were an unprecedented event that intensified antiterrorist initiatives and policies, mobilized world opinion, ushered in a newly formed worldwide coalition, and globalized the discourse on terrorism. However, terrorism is not a new phenomenon—terrorist incidents and antiterrorist measures have been present for decades. For instance, between 1981 and 2000, the total number of terrorist attacks globally was 9,179 (an average of 459 attacks a year), with the highest number (630 attacks a year) in the mid-1980s (Center for Data Analysis 2001). Regionally, during 1995–2000, the average number of terrorist attacks per year was 122 in Latin America, 101 in Western Europe, about 45 in Asia, and only 15 in North America (ibid.).

A series of international antiterrorist conventions emerged prior to September 11, including the Convention for the Suppression of Unlawful Acts against the Safety of Aircraft in 1971, the Convention against the Taking of Hostages in 1979, the Convention for the Suppression of Terrorist Bombings in 1997, and the Convention for the Suppression of Financing Terrorism in 1999 (CEC 2001). At the national level, terrorism was a major American concern for over two decades, leading to various government initiatives reflected in documents such as *Managing Terrorist Incidents* (1982), *National Program for Combating Terrorism* (1986), *U.S. Policy on Counterterrorism* (1995), and *Terrorism, the Future, and U.S. Foreign Policy* (2001) (Richelson and Evans 2001).

Despite the existence of such a long list of antiterrorist conventions and legal provisions, the colossal terrorist attacks on September 11 could not be predicted or prevented. On that day, through the global media, the whole world observed the horrifying actions that destroyed New York's World Trade Center, damaged the Pentagon building, and caused the deaths of thousands of people. Subsequently, the episode unfolded with its worldwide condemnation by political leaders and policy makers, the announcement of a "war on terrorism" by President Bush, the formation of an antiterrorist coalition among various nations, a global search for the terrorists responsible for the attack, massive military operations in Afghanistan to eliminate the al-Qaeda terrorist networks led by Osama bin Laden, and the adoption of multifaceted legal provisions against terrorists and their sympathizers worldwide (Gordon 2002).

In the history of terrorism, the September 11 attack was the most significant event because it altered the structures of interstate relations, transformed perceptions of security, redefined the identities of friends and enemies in world politics, restructured the criteria of state–citizen–resident relations, and reprioritized the mission of public governance. At the international level, the United Nations passed Security Council Resolution 1373 (September 28, 2001) immediately, calling on all states to prevent and suppress the financing of all terrorist acts, criminalize the provision or collection of funds for terrorists, freeze funds and assets of individuals involved in terrorism, and so on (UNSC 2001). This resolution also requires all states to exchange information regarding terrorist networks, false travel documents, traffic in sensitive materials, and communications technologies used by terrorist groups.

In the United States, the national government has adopted a series of antiterrorism measures since September 11, including the Financial Anti-Terrorism Act, Airport Security Federalization Act, Bioterrorism Response Act, Preparedness against Domestic Terrorism Act, Aviation Security Enhancement Act, Airline Security Act, Bioterrorism Preparedness Act, and United States Security Act. One of the most important legal provisions is the so-called USA PATRIOT (Uniting and Strengthening America by Providing Appropriate Tools Required to Intercept and Obstruct Terrorism) Act, signed by the president on October 26, 2001. As the next section will explicate, this act enhances the government's authority and capacity to redefine terrorism, conduct surveillance, gather intelligence, determine crimes and penalties, detain immigrants for lengthy periods, and verify financial transactions and accounts (Chang 2001; White House 2002a). Another significant antiterrorist measure adopted in the United States after September 11 was the creation of the Office of Homeland Security, which aims to "develop and coordinate the implementation of a comprehensive national strategy to secure the United States from terrorist threats or attacks" (Wermuth 2002, 31). Other related organizations and initiatives have also emerged, including the Anti-Terrorism Task Forces, Customs Trade Partnership Against Terrorism, Citizen Corps, and so on (White House 2002a).

Other Western countries also have strengthened and expanded antiterrorist laws since September 11. For example, the European Commission adopted the Framework Decision on Combating Terrorism (2001), which prescribes the definition of terrorism, extent of penalties and sanctions, extradition procedures, and means of exchanging information to be followed by the member states of the European Union (CEC 2001). After September 11, Canada introduced the Anti-Terrorism Act (2001), which prescribes measures to define and designate terrorist groups and activities, prosecute and punish terrorists, facilitate the use of electronic surveillance, and allow the arrest and detention of suspected terrorists (Canada, Department of Justice 2001). Likewise, the British government adopted the Anti-Terrorism, Crime and Security Act (2001). In Australia, the government has introduced various amendments in its antiterrorist laws, including the *Security Legislation Amendment (Terrorism) Act (2002) and Border Security Legislation Amendment Act (2002)* (CEC 2001). Similar amendments in antiterrorist laws have been pursued in France to expand the powers of police to conduct investigation, monitoring, and surveillance.

In the case of developing countries, the United Nations's Security Council Resolution 1373, adopted after September 11, requires these nations to comply with its provisions and strategies to eradicate terrorist groups and networks, refrain from any form of support to such groups and networks, and share and exchange information in this regard (UNSC 2001). Some developing countries have also adopted their own antiterrorist measures. In particular, following the September 11 event, India introduced the Prevention of Terrorism Ordinance (2001), which broadens the definition of terrorism and empowers law enforcement agencies to investigate and punish terrorist activities. The Indonesian government is also pushing for a controversial antiterrorism bill that would provide expansive power to its security forces to manage radical religious groups (Asmarani 2002). The Malaysian government has promised to cooperate with the United States in information sharing, military operations, intelligence, and law enforcement. In terms of global support to the American antiterrorist campaign, 23 countries have agreed to host U.S. forces to conduct military operations, 89 countries have granted overflight authority, 76 countries have approved landing rights, and 142 have issued orders to freeze the assets of suspected terrorist organizations (White House 2002b).

This brief description above of new antiterrorist laws, institutions, policies, and strategies shows how September 11 has fundamentally changed national and international priorities and concerns, perceptions of internal and external security, roles of the state and bureaucracy, and the nature of relationships between the state and society.

In America, the broad scope of these antiterrorist measures has serious implications for how the nation-state relates to the international community, makes public policy, allocates federal budgets, prioritizes expenditures, delivers services, relates to its own citizens and other residents, and defines human rights and responsibilities. In other words, the antiterrorist measures not only have affected foreign policy and internal policy priorities, they have also affected the basic principles of people's constitutional rights as the essence of democratic governance. While it is too early to assess the effectiveness of these legal provisions to combat terrorism, critics are concerned that such measures may have consequences for people's rights and entitlements in each country. The next section examines how these measures are affecting the basic tenets of people's constitutional protections, with special reference to public administration.

## New Measures of War on Terrorism: Impact on People's Rights and Public Administration

The impact of antiterrorist measures on the rights and responsibilities of citizens, other residents, and visitors are crucial concerns in a constitutionally democratic nation-state. In Western democracies, these fundamentals include civil rights (freedom from state intervention in the private sphere), political rights (effective political participation, expression, and influence), and social rights (access to basic goods and services through reallocation by the state) (Eriksen and Weigard 1999; Oliver and Heater 1994). In the United States, through various constitutional amendments and laws, an expanded definition of civil rights has emerged that encompasses freedom of speech and assembly, the right to vote, and the right to equality in public places irrespective of race, religion, gender, age, and national origin. This broad scope of civil rights covers political rights as well as social rights. The evolution and expansion of these basic rights took many decades and involved popular struggles and movements.

In other nations, such rights have often changed depending on major historical events affecting the nature of state formation, mode of governance, and structure of state–citizen relations. The terrorist attack on September 11 is undoubtedly such a historical event that has an impact on relationships between the state, its citizens, and other people. This section of the article examines how the antiterrorist measures adopted in response to September 11 have affected the mode of civil, political, and social rights and responsibilities of citizens and other residents. It is followed by an analysis of how these changes may affect public administration.

## Critical Impacts on People's Rights and Responsibilities

First, with regard to people's *civil rights*—especially the right to privacy and other freedoms from state interference—it is observed that the antiterrorism legislation adopted after September 11, especially the USA PATRIOT Act (2001), has significant consequences. That act grants unprecedented powers to the executive branch to conduct surveillance, including gathering sensitive personal records, tracking email and internet usage, monitoring financial transactions, practicing sneak-and-peek searches, and using roving wiretaps (Chang 2001). Under Section 213 of the act, the sneak-and-peek searches of physical property can be conducted as normal criminal investigations without prior knowledge of the property owner (Levy 2001). Similarly, under Section 215, sensitive personal records can be obtained by certifying their relevance to the investigation of international terrorism. The scope of such investigation may cover American citizens and permanent residents, and provisions can apply to nonterrorist activities such as drug cases, tax fraud, and other federal crimes (Dempsey 2001–02).

Similarly, in Europe, the European Union's justice and home affairs ministers decided in a meeting on September 20, 2001, to combat terrorism by assigning new surveillance powers to law enforcement agencies, especially by retaining data from emails, phone calls, faxes, and internet usage (Statewatch 2001). In particular, the British government now requires all telecommunications providers to retain such data for 12 months. This is basically an initiative to put various modes of electronic communications under close surveillance or scrutiny by the government. The French National Assembly has also approved antiterrorism provisions that allow more intensive investigation and monitoring of private communications. In the developing world, the Prevention of Terrorism Ordinance (2001) in India has expanded the power of the police to detain people without trial and to search premises and intercept vehicles without warrant.

The adoption of a national ID card system has been discussed in the United States to enhance airport security, which could involve various biometric surveillance mechanisms such as digital fingerprinting, voice-authentication techniques, handprint scans, computer registries, software data collection, and electronic retinal scans (Thierer 2001). Although some experts consider such expanded surveillance power to be essential to counterterrorism, others think that it violates people's privacy and fails to provide for governmental accountability (Cave and Mieszkowski 2001). In Britain, the home secretary recently reinforced the possibility of introducing such ID cards, which is opposed by human rights advocates on the grounds that such a provision would compromise people's civil liberties (Johnston and Jones 2002). In response to measures of intercepting communications and gathering information adopted after September 11, 2001, strong opposition has emerged from various privacy and civil liberties organizations, including those in Austria, Britain, Denmark, Germany, and the Netherlands, which have urged the European Council to maintain people's freedoms, privacy, and civil liberties (Evers 2001).

Second, in terms of people's *political rights*, critics argue that recent antiterrorist provisions represent a threat to any form of political protest, movement, and activism. For example, according to Levy (2001), although the USA PATRIOT Act has not replaced the principle of separation of powers in America, it has adversely affected the protection of due process under the Fifth Amendment and the safeguards against "unreasonable searches and seizures" guaranteed by the Fourth Amendment. Similarly, Chang (2001) is concerned that Section 802 of the act compromises political freedoms (especially freedom of speech and political association) because of its broad definition of domestic terrorism, which may cover political dissent, civil disobedience, and environmental activism and allow investigation and surveillance of such political activities and groups. To be more balanced, one needs to examine situations in other countries.

In Australia, under the Security Legislation Amendment (Terrorism) Act, the government can detain and question people for two days without legal representation. In Britain, although the government takes pride in the Anti-Terrorism, Crime and Security Act adopted after September 11, the critics are concerned that, under this law, people can be jailed if the home secretary suspects them of having terrorist connections, and one may consider political protesters or demonstrators to be terrorists (Nag 2001). Similarly, it is argued that under the new European Commission's Framework Decision on Combating Terrorism (2001), the definition of terrorism—that is, any act of altering the political, economic, or social structure and causing unlawful damages to state facilities—may cover various forms of political dissent and protests (such as anti-war or animal rights protests), thus undermining democratic freedoms (CEC 2001).

In the developing world, according to critics, some states have used the events of September 11 as a pretext to justify internal political repression in the name of controlling terrorism. For example, the proposed antiterrorist bill in Indonesia is criticized on the ground that it may undermine human rights and can be used by the elites to purge opposition voices (Asmarani 2002). In India, there are serious reservations that its Prevention of Terrorism Ordinance may criminalize legitimate political protests of vulnerable social groups, serve the ruling party against the press and political opponents, and weaken the protection of civil liberties and human rights (POTO 2001). According to Klingner (2001), current antiterrorism efforts in many developing countries are likely to adversely affect people's participation in democratic governance and their peaceful resistance against varied forms of injustice.

In addition, it is observed that, in the process of building an antiterrorist coalition after September 11, the United States has extended military or financial assistance to some countries, including Pakistan, India, the Philippines, and Uzbekistan, which allegedly practice political repression, ethnic inequality, and/or caste discrimination (HRW 2002). Specifically, there are restrictions on political parties under the military rule in Pakistan, continued caste discrimination in India, abuses of military and police powers in the Philippines, and a repressive political system in Uzbekistan (ibid.). Although organizations such as Human Rights Watch may not always succeed in objective reporting, such political conditions in these countries are widely known facts, and, prior to September 11, some of them were criticized for human rights violations by the American government itself.

Third, in relation to political rights, *minority rights* are also affected in different countries in the context of the war on terrorism. In the United States, for instance, the terrorist attacks on September 11 and the images and expressions that followed, influenced some Americans to become intolerant and aggressive toward Muslim Americans, Arab Americans, Sikh Americans, and South Asian Americans (U.S. Department of Justice 2002). These minority groups experienced some violent assaults, physical attacks, death threats, and vandalism (HRW 2002). Although the government has undertaken certain joint interdepartmental initiatives to combat such discrimination based on ethnicity, religion, and national origin (U.S. Department of Justice 2002), the rise of such racial assaults may represent a new challenge to minority rights in America. Cave and Mieszkowski (2001) argue that these discriminatory attitudes toward minorities may not be isolated from the racial and religious profiling publicized in the global media and implicated in certain antiterrorism initiatives.

With regard to immigrants, according to Chang (2001), the USA PATRIOT Act tends to deprive some of due process and First Amendment rights by expanding categories of immigrants that are subject to removal on terrorism grounds and by increasing the attorney general's authority to detain immigrants suspected of terrorist activities. In Russia, although the government's human rights abuses in Chechnya were condemned by most Western countries before September 11, after the event, these countries began to downplay them because of alleged Chechnyan links with terrorist networks (HRW 2002). Similarly, in China, the government now tries to defend its crackdown on the ethnic separatist movement of the Muslim population in the Xinjiang Uighur Autonomous Region by portraying them as terrorists (Amnesty International 2002, 5). Similar tendencies to deny minority rights in the name of antiterrorism may be found in India under the newly introduced Prevention of Terrorism Ordinance. These are only a few of many critical observations of how current antiterrorism campaigns may be affecting minority rights in various countries and how some governments may use them to deny such rights.

Finally, with regard to people's *social rights,* the war on terrorism may have certain indirect impacts on people's entitlement to basic services as a result of the restructuring of budgets in favor of defense and law enforcement at the expense of social programs. In terms of defense spending, compared to 2001, the proposed defense budgets for 2003 represent increases of $4 billion in Russia, $2.5 billion in China, $8.5 billion in Saudi Arabia, and so on (CDI 2002). However, it is the United States where the defense budget is the world's largest and has expanded the most. According to the U.S. Department of State (2002a), in the proposed federal budget for 2003, the defense budget is about $379 billion, which amounts to a 14 percent increase in defense spending over 2002, and it represents the largest increase in 21 years. Other gainers in the proposed budget are the Federal Aviation Administration, Coast Guard, Customs Service, Justice Department, and Federal Emergency Management Agency, which are mostly related to safety and law and order (U.S. Department of State 2002b). In addition, in this budget, the requested allocation was $37.7 billion for homeland security (increased from $19.5 billion in 2002), $11 billion for border security, $2.3 billion for the inspection of customs services, and $6 billion for protection against bioterrorism (Bush 2002).

Although it is too early to conclude whether such increases in government spending on major sectors and organizations related to external and internal security may affect spending on social programs in America, the fact remains that, in the proposed 2003 budget, the government outlines significant cuts in highway programs, federal payments to hospitals, and job training programs (U.S. Department of State 2002b). In this regard, Twight (2002) emphasizes that, under the war on terrorism, the federal government has adopted a series of new law and order programs that might adversely affect the funds available for social programs. However, this problem is likely to be more serious in low-income countries such as India and Pakistan, where any increases in the use of resources for military, security, and law and order are likely to diminish the availability of such resources for services like education, health, housing, and other basic needs.

## Impact of Terrorism Responses on Public Administration

It is clear from this discussion that under the war on terrorism, the antiterrorist laws, institutions, and budgets have expanded in an unprecedented manner. Although these measures have been presented as necessary to combat terrorism, they have serious implications for people's basic rights, including their rights to individual privacy, to free press and speech, to political participation and association, to equal representation, and to basic goods and services. The erosion of these basic rights implies a form of citizenship that Hadenius (2001) calls "weak citizenship." This section of the article explores how nations' responses to terrorism have affected civism and public administration. It must be noted here that, in line with the impact on macro-level democratic rights discussed previously, the impact in public administration may be on micro-level administrative provisions and processes such as accountability, participation, trust, attitude, and so on.

*Constitutional Claims to Public Accountability.* In the field of public administration, one major manifestation of popular sovereignty in constitutional governance is political and administrative accountability, realized through legal and political means (including the legislative and judicial processes), administrative means, and informal devices such as the media. Since September 11, critics charge that the adoption of antiterrorist provisions in the United States has seriously affected this authority of people to enforce public accountability, especially because of the rise of executive power challenging the powers of other branches of the national government.

According to Chang (2001), the far-reaching USA PATRIOT Act was introduced and adopted without sufficient public hearings, debate, and committee reporting, although the act has serious outcomes in terms of expanding the powers of the executive and insulating the exercise of such powers from effective judicial and legislative oversight. Critics say that it represents a challenge to the capacity of the legislative and judicial branches to counterbalance the executive power and hold it accountable to the public. In the aftermath of September 11, similar trends of expanding executive power in relation to other branches of the government can be observed in countries such as Australia and Britain, which also have adopted varied antiterrorist measures. Once again, the point is that such an increase in executive power poses a challenge to public accountability.

*Public Participation versus Bureaucratic Power.* The realization of people's political rights, which basically implies their empowerment, is often enhanced through their participation in public policies and decisions. Nigro and Richardson (1990) observe that the issue of legitimacy often depends on how public officials promote broadly based public participation. Today, the opportunity for such participation and access may be challenged by the aforementioned antiterrorist laws and institutions, which stress bureaucratic secrecy rather than transparency. In the current antiterrorism context, in fact, state agencies, especially those related to law enforcement, have more access to sensitive information about people, while people's access to information regarding these agencies has become limited. In this atmosphere, overwhelmed by concerns for security, surveillance, investigation, suspicion, and distrust, it is unrealistic to expect greater public participation in public administration.

Public participation may also be affected because, since September 2001, power relations between people and the bureaucrats enforcing law and order have changed. Although one may not agree with critical views that some governments have used the event of September 11 as a pretext to expand national police powers (Levy 2001), the fact remains that, under the USA PATRIOT Act (2001), the power of law and order bureaucracy has increased considerably. As discussed earlier, while the authority of law enforcement agencies has expanded to conduct surveillance and investigation, the scope of people's rights to privacy has weakened correspondingly. For Gormley (2002, 5), although people are being encouraged to participate in administration to fight terrorism by informing law enforcement agencies of suspicious activities, the situation may become complicated "where citizens report on fellow citizens." Although the traditional mode of public participation based on volunteer services still continues, the atmosphere of information gathering through expanded surveillance and monitoring may create doubts or distrust in this participatory process.

*Popular Confidence in Public Service.* An important dimension of public administration is the level of public trust in civil and military services. During recent decades, although one of the main objectives of market-led reforms under initiatives such as reinventing government and "reengineering bureaucracy" was to restore public confidence in governance, the outcomes have not been that remarkable. In the United States, between 1987 and 1992, the number of people with a fair degree of confidence in the federal government declined 26 percent, and in state-level governments that number declined 22 percent (Thompson 1993, 11–14). Similar declines in public trust occurred in Canada, Britain, and Norway (Haque 2001). However, some observers believe that, in the context of the war on terrorism, a growing sense of patriotism and increasing trust in public agencies has occurred. For instance, the percentage of people reporting they "always" trust the government increased from 18 percent in 1994 to 51 percent in 2001 after September 11 (Moynihan and

Roberts 2002, 133). Following the event, a growing sense in the United States and some other countries appears to be that the role of government is seen, once again, as a solution rather than a problem (Hamilton 2001).

However, according to critics, this increased confidence in government is not clear because, after all, the September 11 attacks represented "a massive failure of the government" to anticipate or prevent them (Boaz 2001). After the event, it is being realized that serious deficiencies are present in various public agencies related to intelligence, law enforcement, immigration and border control, and emergency situations (Moynihan and Roberts 2002). In this regard, Carter finds the recent approaches to antiterrorism adopted by the U.S. federal administration (including those after September 2001) inadequate, and he concludes that certain fundamental weaknesses are present in dealing with terrorism (Carter 2001–02, 9–12). In any case, in an atmosphere of severe external threats, most people tend to rally behind the government, but the long-term sustainability of this public support is uncertain. The terrorist attacks of September 11 represent one such episode, which was so horrifying, disastrous, and emotional that only the government could address it and take the necessary national and international measures to limit future threats. An opinion poll conducted by ABC News after September 11 shows that, although 68 percent of respondents expressed trust in government to handle national security and terrorism, only 38 percent showed such trust in the government handling of issues such as health care, economy, social security, and education (Palmer and Samples 2002, 12). In other words, the war on terrorism has not necessarily improved people's overall trust in government.

*Global Orientation of Public Service.* According to Mameli (2002), after September 2001, the parochial, inward-looking view of public service has proven inadequate, and there is a need for exposing the profession to the global atmosphere to deal with transnational issues such as the environment, health, and terrorism. In the United States, although some public administrators have embraced cross-cultural collaboration through international bodies and professional associations, gaps remain in understanding the views of American counterparts in other countries (Mameli 2002). A similar point is emphasized by Gordon (2002), who thinks that the terrorist attacks on September 11, which led to worldwide cooperation among heads of state and public officials, provided an impetus for pursuing national policy agendas based on cross-national collaboration, especially for preventing and addressing such attacks in the future.

Beyond a doubt, the September 2001 assault has brought together varieties of political leaders, policy makers, and public administrators to take preventive and remedial measures against terrorism. But as far as the public service is concerned, one needs to think carefully to strike a balance between the need for reorienting public employees to the global atmosphere and cross-national linkages on the one hand, and the importance of their responsiveness and accountability to domestic public interests and demands on the other. It certainly has become essential for public employees to think globally in this relatively borderless world, where many countries are simultaneously affected by common international issues ranging from environmental catastrophes to terrorist attacks.

*Civism and Administrative Theory.* Beyond the practical concerns of public administration reviewed here, how does the war on terrorism affect the citizenship principle in academic public administration, especially with regard to administrative theory building? First, as in other fields and disciplines of study, in public administration, practical realities and experiences interact with academic concepts and theory building. Developments since September 2001 in the domains of practical citizen–administration relations—including the aforementioned constraints to accountability, participation, and entitlement—now affect academic discourse. Public administration scholars may encounter pressure or influence to reorient public administration to global responses to terrorism.

Second, in line with the above emphasis on the need for a global orientation of the public service to face events such as September 11, recognition is growing that such a global perspective needs to be incorporated into academic articulation of administrative theories and concepts. In this regard, Mameli (2002) suggests that public administration scholars should understand and utilize international relations theories and perspectives. It is pointed out that such an approach, combining public administration and international relations, would better explain rapidly changing global events such as international terrorism. However, it may be necessary to go beyond the mechanical integration of public administration as a field focusing on domestic policy issues and international relations as a field dominated by statecentric foreign relations. To meet today's needs, it may not be necessary to "reinvent the wheel." The heritage of comparative public administration that was strong in the 1950s through the 1970s persists, and it can be revived more vigorously. In the past, comparative public administration made considerable progress in training public managers in cross-national administrative systems, generating literature in comparative administration and constructing useful analytical frameworks. This valuable tradition can be utilized to perform much-needed cross-national comparative studies.

Third, evidence is that, since September 2001, the notion of public governance has changed in terms of a more active and expansive public sector, greater popular acceptance of the public service, more positive images of public

agencies, and stronger public trust in American government (Moynihan and Roberts 2002, 132). One must be cautious in drawing such conclusions because, as explained earlier, increased public acceptance or trust may not encompass the whole of public administration, and it may be a transitional phenomenon. After all, it was not that long ago that public service was blamed nearly worldwide for its alleged inefficiency, indifference, rigidity, and elitism, and it was considered inferior to the business sector. Although such allegations were hardly credible, one should not be too excited about the new surge or revival of active public governance, because, as discussed in this article, overwhelming concerns for security under changed modes of governance could weaken practices of popular participation in governance based on basic democratic rights and responsibilities.

Finally, thinking is emerging that the current shift toward a greater role and positive image of public administration may promise a new paradigm—evident in the growing appreciation and conviction of public servants, diminishing belief in private-sector superiority, and enhanced coordination and cooperation among public agencies (Gormley 2002, 2–5). In addition, the market-led paradigm of New Public Management, also known as the reinvention paradigm, is now in doubt (Moynihan and Roberts 2002). However, in the end, it is concluded that emergence of a changed and enduring post–September 11 paradigm is not yet certain, and the validity and credibility of such a new paradigm may lie, ironically, in more costly terrorist attacks to prove its worth (Gormley 2002; Moynihan and Roberts 2002).

Even if such a changed paradigm of public administration emerges, according to Gormley (2002, 7–8), it may not be compatible with varied forms of postbureaucratic accountability and with the notions of decentralization and service orientation. What warrants major attention is the principle of popular sovereignty and limited government in forming a reliable paradigm of "public" administration under constitutional democracy. This is critical because major foundations in the field have always been associated with citizenship-related issues of civic duty and public service, including principles of responsiveness, accountability, fairness, participation, representation, human dignity, and justice. These basic tenets of constitutional government service, which have come under scrutiny since September 2001, must remain central to sustain a practical paradigm of public administration.

## Conclusions

First, because contemporary challenges to citizenship principles in politics and administration are related to the war on terrorism, it is essential to understand the causes and remedies of terrorism itself. Existing antiterrorist strategies in the United States are largely based on the assumption that superior American values such as freedom, openness, and affluence make it vulnerable to terrorism; that there are clashes between civilizations and their cultures, between good and evil, which lead to terrorism; and that such terrorism can be eradicated mainly by force and military means (Bush 2002; Eland 1998). But there are alternative views that terrorism often thrives in countries where people are oppressed and impoverished (Hamilton 2001, 14; Newland 2001, 648). In addition, based on a study of all major terrorist attacks on the United States between 1915 and 1998, Eland (1998, 21) concludes that such actions were mostly the result of American military involvement and intervention in other countries, and that the frequency of such attacks could be substantively reduced by lowering its military profile overseas. According to Ford (2001), one major factor leading to terrorism is the anti-American hatred in many Arab and Muslim countries, which is caused by people's perceptions that American foreign policies and military strategies are often responsible for adverse human conditions in these countries, especially the suffering of the Palestinians under Israeli policies. The point here is that alternative perceptions of the causes of terrorism warrant serious consideration, because the causes and motivations behind terrorism must be addressed to combat it effectively. As Carter (2001–02, 7) emphasizes in references to September 11, 2001, "the motivations and root causes of catastrophic terrorism—inscrutable as they may now seem—must eventually yield at least part of careful study."

Second, visible strategies against terrorism are predominantly based on military force, including preemptive strikes, commando actions, rescue operations, special reaction forces, and so on (UNODCCP 2001). There are also international conventions, laws of nation-states, rules of engagement, surveillance and investigation, intelligence gathering, police cooperation, strict law enforcement, suspension of civil rights, and so on. Although these strategies and tactics may be essential, they should be complemented by nonconfrontational options such as understanding the political and socioeconomic grievances of terrorist groups, reducing poverty and unemployment in countries prone to terrorist activities, creating international pressures on repressive regimes to practice constitutional democracy and respect human rights, reducing self-serving foreign interventions, addressing the paradox of localization and globalization, and adopting public awareness programs regarding the costs and dangers of terrorism (Newland 2001; UNODCCP 2001). This multidimensional approach to control terrorism is necessary because past experiences show that primary reliance on force is not often effective.

Third, in the case of the terrorist attacks of September 11, the event was so immense and tragic that the adoption of extreme antiterrorist laws and initiatives (discussed earlier) was to be expected. However, in adopting such provisions, it is necessary to have a strict and clear definition of terrorism; in many instances, the definitions are so vague and broad that they may lead to the criminalization of peaceful movements and unreasonable restrictions on basic human rights (Amnesty International 2002, 6). While terrorism usually means "any act of violence or threat" with the motive of terrorizing people to harm them or impair their freedom, security, property, and honor, activities such as legitimate political protests and liberation movements should not be considered terrorist acts (OIC 1999). In short, careful interpretation is necessary to ensure that innocent people are not being harassed and that their basic civil and political rights are not compromised. In other words, a balance must be reached between people's need for security against terrorism and their constitutional rights and responsibilities.

Finally, people's rights and involvement in overall governance, including participation in transparent public administration, should not be sacrificed under any threats, including terrorist attacks. Although debate continues about security versus liberty in the aftermath of September 11, these should not be seen as a zero-sum equation: The absence of liberties often becomes the breeding ground for terrorism, and the expansion of people's basic rights may be conducive rather than constraining to the eventual defeat of terrorism (Hamilton 2001). In fact, in public administration, concerns have grown in recent years regarding how to recognize the public interest, reinforce people's empowerment, strengthen democratic citizenship, and ensure public accountability, in order to create a "new public service" (Denhardt and Denhardt 2000, 553–56). Given new challenges to these fundamental values posed by security measures under the war on terrorism, today it is even more essential for public administration scholars to safeguard the spirit of constitutional democracy, including respect for people's rights and responsibilities.

# References

Amnesty International. 2002. *Rights at Risk: Amnesty International's Concerns Regarding Security Legislation and Law Enforcement Measures*. London: Amnesty International.

Asmarani, Devi. 2002. Muslims Oppose Jakarta Anti-Terror Bill. *Straits Times* (Singapore), May 11.

Boaz, David. 2001. Turning to Government. *Cato Daily Commentary*, November 2. Available at *http://www.cato.org/current/terrorism/political.html*. Accessed April 3, 2002.

Bush, George W. 2002. *Securing the Homeland, Strengthening the Nation*. Washington, DC: White House. Available at *http://www.whitehouse.gov/homeland/homeland_security_book.html*. Accessed May 31, 2002.

Canada, Department of Justice. 2001. Government of Canada Introduces "Anti-Terrorism Act." Ottawa: Department of Justice. October 15. Available at *http://canada.justice.gc.ca/en/news/nr/2001/doc_27785.html*. Accessed May 31, 2002.

Carter, Ashton B. 2001–02. The Architecture of Government in the Face of Terrorism. *International Security* 26(3): 5–23.

Cave, Damien, and Katharine Mieszkowski. 2001. The End of Liberty. *Salon.com*, September 22. Available at *http://www.salon.com/tech/feature/2001/09/22/end_of_liberty/index.html*. Accessed May 31, 2002.

Center for Defense Information (CDI). 2002. *World Military Expenditures*. Washington DC: Center for Defense Information. Available at *http://www.cdi.org/issues/wme/*. Accessed May 20, 2002.

Commission of the European Communities (CEC). 2001. *Council Framework Decision on Combating Terrorism*. September 19. Available at *http://www.statewatch.org/news/2001/sep/terrorism.pdf*. Accessed May 31, 2002.

Center for Data Analysis. 2001. *Facts and Figures about Terrorism*. Washington, DC: Center for Data Analysis, Heritage Foundation. Available at *http://www.heritage.org/shorts/20010914terror.htm*. Accessed May 31, 2002.

Chang, Nancy. 2001. *The USA PATRIOT Act: What's So Patriotic about Trampling on the Bill of Rights?* New York: Center for Constitutional Rights.

Dempsey, James X. 2001–02. Civil Liberties in a Time of Crisis. *Journal of the National Council of Jewish Women*, Winter 2001/2002. Available at *http://www.ncjw.org/news/winter2002/dempsey.htm*. Accessed April 3, 2002.

Denhardt, Robert, and Janet V. Denhardt. 2000. The New Public Service: Serving Rather than Steering. *Public Administration Review* 60(6): 549–59.

Eland, Ivan. 1998. *Does U.S. Intervention Overseas Breed Terrorism? The Historical Record*. Foreign Policy Briefing, no. 50. Washington, DC: Cato Institute.

Eriksen, Erik Oddvar, and Jarle Weigard. 1999. *The End of Citizenship? New Roles Challenging the Political Order*. Working paper, no.99/26. Oslo, Norway: ARENA. Available at *http://www.arena.uio.no/publications/wp99_26.htm*. Accessed May 31, 2002.

Evers, Joris. 2001. Euro Civil Liberty Campaigners Urge Restraint. *IDG News Service*, Amsterdam Bureau, September 21. Available at *http://www.idg.net/ic_697701_1794_9-10000.html*. Accessed May 31, 2002.

Ford, Peter. 2001. Why Do They Hate Us? *Christian Science Monitor*, September 27, 1.

Gordon, Paula D. 2002. International Relations and National Agendas After September 11, 2001. *PA Times* 25(2): 6.

Gormley, William T. 2002. Reflections on Terrorism and Public Management. In *Governance and Public Security*, edited by Alasdair Roberts, 1–16. New York: Campbell Public Affairs Institute, Maxwell School, Syracuse University.

Hadenius, Axel. 2001. *Institutions and Democratic Citizenship*. Oxford: Oxford University Press.

Hamilton, Mary R. 2001. Government Matters More than Ever. Paper presented at the First International Congress of Political Science and Public Administration, November 28, Universidad Autonoma del Estado de Hidalgo, Mexico.

Haque, M. Shamsul. 2001. The Diminishing Publicness of Public Service under the Current Mode of Governance. *Public Administration Review* 61(1): 65–82.

Human Rights Watch (HRW). 2002. *World Report 2002: Events of 2001*. New York: Human Rights Watch.

Johnston, Philip, and George Jones. 2002. Blunkett Plans ID Card. *Daily Telegraph*, February 6, 1.

Klingner, Donald. 2001. International Relations in the Aftermath of Terror. *PA Times* 24(10): 7–8.

Levy, Robert A. 2001. The USA PATRIOT Act: We Deserve Better. *Cato Daily Commentary*, November 27. Available at *http://www.cato.org/current/terrorism/justice4terrorists.html*. Accessed April 3, 2002.

Lynn, L.E. 2001. Globalization and Administrative Reform: What is Happening in Theory? *Public Management Review* 3(2): 191–208.

Mameli, Peter A. 2002. American Public Administration in a Globalizing World. *PA Times* 25(2): 3.

Marshall, T.H. 1950. *Citizenship and Social Class, and Other Essays*. Cambridge, UK: Cambridge University Press.

Moynihan, Donald P., and Alasdair Roberts. 2002. Public Service Reform and the New Security Agenda. In *Governance and Public Security*, edited by Alasdair Roberts, 128–46. New York: Campbell Public Affairs Institute, Maxwell School, Syracuse University.

Nag, D. 2001. Arrest without Any Reason under Blair's Regime. *People's Democracy* (India), 25(49): 12.

Newland, Chester A. 2001. Fanatical Terrorism versus Disciplines of Constitutional Democracy. *Public Administration Review* 61(6): 643–50.

Nigro, Lloyd G., and William D. Richardson. 1990. Between Citizen and Administrator: Administrative Ethics and *PAR*. *Public Administration Review* 50(6): 623–35.

Oliver, Dawn, and Derek Heater. 1994. *The Foundations of Citizenship*. New York: Harvester Wheatsheaf.

Organization of the Islamic Conference (OIC). 1999. Convention on the Organization of the Islamic Conference on Combating International Terrorism. Geneva, Switzerland: OIC. Available at *http://www.oic-un.org/26icfm/c.html*. Accessed April 4, 2002.

Palmer, Tom G., and John Samples. 2002. Limited Government After 9-11. *Cato Policy Report* 14(2): 1–14.

POTO. 2001. Amnesty Urges India Not to Adopt Controversial Law. *Dawn* (Pakistan), December 1.

Richelson, Jeffrey, and Michael L. Evans, eds. 2001. *Volume 1: Terrorism and U.S. Policy*. National Security Archive Electronic Briefing Book, no. 55, September 21. Available at *http://www.gwu.edu/~nsarchiv/NSAEBB/NSAEBB55/index1.html*. Accessed March 31, 2002.

Roberts, Alasdair, ed. 2002. *Governance and Public Security*. New York: Campbell Public Affairs Institute, Maxwell School, Syracuse University.

Robinson, Mary. 2002. Introductory Statement, United Nations High Commissioner for Human Rights. March 20. Available at *http://www.statewatch.org/news/2002/mar/12unhchr.htm*. Accessed May 31, 2002.

Shariff, Zahid. 2002. Reflections on Public Administration in a Time of Crisis. *Administration and Society* 34(1): 4–7.

Statewatch. 2001. EU: Data Protection or Data Retention in the EU? London: Statewatch. Available at *http://www.statewatch.org/news/2001/sep/01data.htm*. Accessed May 31, 2002.

Thierer, Adam. 2001. National ID Cards: New Technologies, Same Bad Idea. *Techknowledge*, no. 21, September 28. Available at *http://www.cato.org/tech/tk/010928-tk.html*. Accessed April 3, 2002.

Thompson, Frank J. 1993. Critical Challenges to State and Local Public Service. In *Revitalizing State and Local Public Service*, edited by Frank J. Thompson, 1–40. San Francisco, CA: Jossey-Bass.

Twight, Charlotte. 2002. It's Not Just about Terrorists. *Cato Daily Commentary*, March 8. Available at *http://www.cato.org/current/civil-liberties/index.html*. Accessed April 3, 2002.

United Nations Office of Drug Control and Crime Prevention (UNODCCP). 2001. *A Classification of Counter-Terrorism Measures*. Vienna, Austria: UNODCCP. Available at *http://www.undcp.org/terrorism_measures.html*. Accessed May 31, 2002.

United Nations Security Council (UNSC). 2001. *Security Council Resolution 1373 (2001)*. Adopted by the Security Council at its 4385th meeting on September 28. Available at *http://www.un.org/Docs/sc/committees/1373/*. Accessed April 4, 2002.

U.S. Department of Justice. 2002. Joint Statement against Employment Discrimination in the Aftermath of the September 11 Terrorist Attacks. Washington, DC: U.S. Department of Justice. Available at *http://www.usdoj.gov/crt/legalinfo/jointstatement.htm*. Accessed May 31, 2002.

U.S. Department of State. 2002a. Bush Sends $379,300 Million Defense Budget Request to Congress. February 4. Available at *http://usinfo.state.gov/topical/pol/terror/02020402.htm*. Accessed May 19, 2002.

———. 2002b. *Fact Sheet on Fiscal 2003 Budget Proposals*. February 4. Available at *http://usinfo.state.gov/topical/pol/terror/02020414.htm*. Accessed May 19, 2002.

Wermuth, Michael A. 2002. Mission Impossible? The White House Office of Homeland Security. In *Governance and Public Security*, edited by Alasdair Roberts, 29–36. New York: Campbell Public Affairs Institute, Maxwell School, Syracuse University.

White House. 2002a. Strengthening Homeland Security Since 9/11. Available at *http://www.whitehouse.gov/homeland/six_month_update.html*. Accessed May 31, 2002.

———. 2002b. Campaign Against Terrorism: A Coalition Update. March 11. Available at *http://www.whitehouse.gov/march11/coalition/*. Accessed May 31, 2002.

Wise, Charles R. 2002. Organizing for Homeland Security. *Public Administration Review* 62(2): 31–44.

# [21]

# Perspectives on privacy and terrorism: all is not lost—yet

## Robert Gellman*

*Privacy and Information Policy Consultant, 419 Fifth Street SE, Washington, DC 20003, USA*

**Abstract**

Antiterrorism legislation passed at the end of 2001—the U.S.A. Patriot Act—has serious implications for privacy. Many of the law's provisions expand the government's existing ability to intercept wire, oral, and electronic communications relating to terrorism and other crimes, to share criminal investigative information, and to conduct electronic surveillance. While the changes are controversial, and some are of questionable constitutionality, the surveillance provisions of the new law mostly make changes in degree and not kind. Other aspects of privacy and privacy law remained unchanged. Laws affecting how the private sector gathers, stores, and uses personal information for private purposes were not modified. After passage of the antiterrorism law, other legislation expanded privacy protections in other areas. Further events and legislation will affect privacy rights and interests, and some protections may be eroded while others are improved. © 2002 Elsevier Science Inc. All rights reserved.

## 1. Introduction

Too often, casual observers treat privacy as a singular trait. We either have privacy or we do not. Personal information is either within the control of the data subject or privacy does not exist. One of the most famous recent quotes about privacy is from Scott McNealy, the president of Sun Microsystems. In 1999, McNealy said: "You have zero privacy. Get over it."[1]

Analyzing privacy is considerably more complex than examining a light switch to see if it is on or off. McNealy's observation about privacy is clearly wrong. In 1999, we had the same basic constitutional protections for privacy that we had in previous years. Supreme Court decisions may have added a bit here and subtracted some there, but the core of constitutional privacy interests found in the Bill of Rights remains.[2] Looking beyond

---

* Corresponding author.

256                    *R. Gellman / Government Information Quarterly 19 (2002) 255–264*

constitutional rights, many other privacy protections remain. Bathroom doors still have locks, and confidential communications with physicians have the same privilege as before.[3] Privacy rights have actually increased in recent years with the passage of new federal laws[4] such as the Children's Online Privacy Protection Act[5] and the financial privacy provisions of the Financial Services Management Act, popularly known as the Gramm-Leach-Bliley Act.[6] Without question, other developments have been less favorable to privacy.

One of those less favorable developments is a major piece of antiterrorism legislation—the U.S.A. Patriot Act—passed during the first session of the 107th Congress in December 2001.[7] In this essay, I propose to take a casual look at some of the privacy implications of that legislation for the purpose of offering alternate ways of cutting up the privacy pie. No point-by-point review of the antiterrorism law will be provided. What follows is a broad evaluation of the law's consequences for privacy that will leave out many of the details and will allow considerable room for other points of view. The goal here is to consider perspectives on privacy that go beyond the *zero privacy* approach.

## 2. What is privacy anyway?

Privacy is a difficult term to define, mostly because it represents a context-specific value and not a fixed concept. Privacy interests recognized in the U.S. Constitution include such diverse matters as freedom of religion, freedom of speech, freedom from unreasonable government searches and surveillance, the right against self-incrimination, and the right of association. Privacy rights and interests with respect to nongovernmental activities, while not constitutionally based, are even more diverse. The earlier point about bathroom door locks is not silly. It reflects one aspect of privacy. The ability to review a credit record protects a privacy interest. Many also believe that telemarketing telephone calls during dinner or even basic junk mail is an invasion of privacy. A list of privacy rights and interests could continue for pages. For most people, the personal details of their lives can be found scattered in the files of dozens or perhaps even hundreds of record keepers, and a privacy interest can be connected to nearly all of those files. The list of privacy rights would be considerably shorter, but the privacy list would have considerable substance nevertheless.

Like other complex value-laden objectives, such as justice, security, and ethics, the level and quality of privacy change over time. We continue to have a core of significant privacy protections even though those protections may increase or decrease in response to public opinions, current events, legislation, judicial decisions, new technologies, and other factors. Privacy will not and cannot disappear entirely as a concern for individuals or as a public policy issue. Antiterrorism legislation diminished some privacy protections, but many privacy laws and principles remain unchanged.

In 1976, the Supreme Court offered a summary of its own decisions affecting privacy in a way that offers a constitutionally-based perspective. In *Whalen v. Roe,* the Court found that there are two categories of privacy interests. One is the interest in independence in making certain kinds of important decisions (e.g., matters relating to marriage, procreation, contraception, family relationships, child rearing, and education), and the other is the individual

R. Gellman / Government Information Quarterly 19 (2002) 255–264 257

interest in avoiding disclosure of personal matters.[8] Privacy can be categorized in other ways, but the Supreme Court's analysis is useful.

The first of the Supreme Court's categories, relating to individual autonomy, seems wholly unaffected by the events of September 11 and their aftermath. The right of individuals to make fundamental decisions about their personal lives is the same as it was.

The second category is sometimes referred to as information privacy or data protection.[9] This is the aspect of privacy that may be most threatened by responses to terrorism. However, before we can assess the effect of terrorism on information privacy, we still need to know the elements of information privacy. In most places around the world, the substance of information privacy law and policy can be described using the principles of fair information practices (FIPs).

A federal advisory committee at the Department of Health, Education, and Welfare first proposed a FIPs code in a 1973 report.[10] The work of the committee had a great impact worldwide,[11] and, by 1980, FIPs had become the core of nearly all international privacy policy documents. A 1980 restatement of FIPs by the Organization for Economic Cooperation and Development[12] (OECD) is now generally recognized as a prime statement of FIPs.[13]

We can use the eight principles of FIPs to begin to break down the concept of information privacy into digestible parts. The OECD FIPs principles are: (1) collection limitation; (2) data quality; (3) purpose specification; (4) use limitation; (5) security safeguards; (6) openness; (7) individual participation (access and correction); and (8) accountability. Much more can be said about these principles than can fit in the available space. However, even a cursory review of the FIPs checklist shows that many core principles of privacy are not affected at all or in any major way by the antiterrorism measures enacted by Congress. Thus, personal records that are more secure have some better privacy protections even if the records can be used in antiterrorism investigations. Regardless of specific authorized uses, privacy protections remain when record keepers are held accountable for complying with privacy rules, if other use limitations remain in force, or if record keeping practices must be disclosed publicly.

The Privacy Act of 1974, a law that principally applies to personal information maintained by federal agencies, was the first statute anywhere in the world to implement FIPs.[14] The same committee that developed the idea of FIPs recommended passage of the act, and Congress followed the committee's recommendations closely. Most other privacy (or data protection) laws around the world today are implementations of FIPs.

What did the antiterrorism legislation do to the Privacy Act and to FIPs? Nothing. The act and the principles on which it was based were unchanged. Well before September 11, information privacy laws everywhere around the world already included significant exemptions for law enforcement and national security activities.[15] The Privacy Act has always applied to the Central Intelligence Agency (CIA), to the Federal Bureau of Investigation (FBI), and to every other federal agency. At the same time, the Privacy Act has always allowed personal records of the CIA[16] and of law enforcement agencies[17] to be exempted from some of its requirements. The exemptions are broad, but they are not complete. No personal records covered by the Privacy Act are completely exempt from the act's basic requirements concerning openness, purpose specification, use limitation, security safeguards, and data quality. Nothing in the antiterrorism legislation changed the way that the Privacy Act applies to intelligence and law enforcement agencies.[18] The Privacy Act's implementation of FIPs for federal agencies was unchanged, including the scope of the act, its protections, and its exemptions.

## 3. Privacy and Government

Many of the antiterrorism law's provisions with privacy implications increased the surveillance powers of government.[19] Legislation authorizing and regulating government surveillance activities for criminal law enforcement and national security matters can be found in several previous statutes, including the Foreign Intelligence Surveillance Act of 1978,[20] the Electronic Communications Privacy Act,[21] and the Omnibus Crime Control and Safe Streets Act.[22] Allowing reasonable government surveillance under defined conditions balances the public interest in fighting crime and protecting national security against privacy in a traditional manner. At higher levels of abstraction, balancing is often noncontroversial. No one asserts that privacy is an interest that outweighs other societal values and objectives. The controversies arise over the details of the balancing.

The antiterrorism law enhances the government's ability to intercept wire, oral, and electronic communications relating to terrorism and other crimes, to share criminal investigative information, to conduct electronic surveillance, and for other purposes. These changes were among the most hotly contested and most controversial parts of the law, and the constitutionality of some of the provisions has been called into question.[23] For the most part, however, the surveillance provisions of the new law only make changes in degree and not kind.

Most of the changes relating to surveillance found in Title II of the legislation were accomplished by revisions to existing statutes and not through the enactment of new sections of law. The distinction between a cut-and-paste amendment of an existing section of law and the enactment of a new section of law is not always a reliable indicator of the significance or scope of the change. In this instance, however, it shows that existing laws already granted surveillance powers to federal agencies, and that the new law expanded those powers by changing procedures and burdens of proof. Without question, the changes represent a significant loss for some aspects of privacy protection, but the changes were relatively narrow when measured broadly against privacy rights and interests.[24] The antiterrorism law enhanced government surveillance powers, but limitations, controls, and procedures continue to exist. Government surveillance is not unlimited or unrestricted. The privacy barriers were moved, perhaps too far, but they were not eliminated.

Another set of statutory changes affected privacy matters that relate to financial institutions. The antiterrorism law changes rules governing maintenance, disclosure, and sharing of information about international money laundering and the financing of terrorism.[25] The law also requires financial institutions to meet minimum standards to verify the identity of customers opening accounts.[26] Other provisions encourage financial institutions to report suspicious activities.[27] The law also makes credit reporting available for counterterrorism purposes.[28]

*R. Gellman / Government Information Quarterly 19 (2002) 255–264* 259

The provisions of the antiterrorism law affecting financial institutions are much more extensive that can be discussed here. Here, too, many of the new requirements are extensions of existing rules, laws, or practices. Antimoney laundering provisions have been in place for years. The new law enhances them. Many banks already undertake investigations of new customers,[29] and the law's new requirements may not greatly change existing practices. The Fair Credit Reporting Act already allows for the disclosure of credit reports to the FBI for counterintelligence purposes.[30] The expansion of the law to cover disclosures for counterterrorism investigations is not significantly different.

In general, the antiterrorism law will directly affect the way that personal information is collected, maintained, and disclosed by banks, and the effects on privacy will be viewed by most as negative. The growing interrelationship between private sector record keepers and the government is clearly troubling from a privacy perspective, and further developments that enhance the flow of personal data from the private sector to the government will be even more unwelcome to privacy advocates. However, the antiterrorism law did not modify the financial privacy provisions of the Gramm-Leach-Bliley Act or change the principal consumer protections in the Fair Credit Reporting Act. One conclusion is that the antiterrorism law eroded some privacy protections, but other protections remain unaffected.

Not everything in the antiterrorism law can be casually swept into the *incremental change* category. One provision of the antiterrorism law changes the rules for use of statistical records by the National Center for Educational Statistics (NCES).[31] This relatively obscure provision may be one of the most radical antiprivacy parts of the entire law.

NCES is one of a number of existing statistical agencies operating under laws making the information that they collect unavailable for all administrative uses. The Census Bureau is perhaps the best known example of a statistical agency whose records cannot be disclosed for administrative uses.[32] The antiterrorism law makes NCES records available for the investigation and prosecution of terrorism. A court order is required, but the court is obliged to issue the order if the government certifies that there are specific and articulable facts giving reason to believe that the information is relevant to an terrorism investigation or prosecution.[33] The standard is much weaker than probable cause or reasonable cause.

The NCES amendment is a significant change because it allows a new use for an entire category of hitherto protected statistical records. The justification for strict privacy laws for statistical and research records is the recognition that guaranteeing protection of the records from administrative or law enforcement uses is essential to the ability to collect the records from voluntary providers.[34] By requiring that NCES records be available for law enforcement purposes, the antiterrorism law, for the first time, takes a class of statutorily protected statistical records and turns them into administrative records available for law enforcement purposes. All NCES records collected in the past under a statutory guarantee of confidentiality may now be used in a way that is directly inconsistent with the terms of collection and the assurances provided to data providers and data subjects. A particularly unfortunate aspect of the change in status for NCES records is that NCES management reportedly instigated the amendment.

Congressional willingness to allow statistical records collected under strict confidentiality rules to be used in other ways is a major blow to the privacy of all statistical records. It establishes a precedent that could be used to change the protections for records of other

260                        *R. Gellman / Government Information Quarterly 19 (2002) 255–264*

statistical agencies. The change to the NCES law represent a major breach of a long-standing statutory privacy protection. The amendment may also undermine the availability of data for educational research and the mission of NCES.

## 4. Privacy and the private sector

For all of the negative consequences for privacy wrought by the antiterrorism legislation—and it is worth repeating, again, that, although many of the changes were incremental, the consequences are still significant—it is important to take note of what was not changed. Most existing information privacy laws were not changed at all by the antiterrorism legislation,[35] although several were amended to enhance government access for terrorism investigations.[36] However, laws affecting how the private sector gathers, stores, and uses personal information for private purposes were not changed. Basic policies of fair information practices reflected (albeit inconsistently) in existing privacy laws remain unchanged by the antiterrorism law. The balance between privacy and law enforcement that was always a part of public policy was adjusted to reflect new concerns. However, the framework in which that balancing has traditionally been conducted was largely untouched.

Events of September 11 changed public views in many ways. The passage of the legislation strongly suggests that the public is more willing to accept diminished privacy protections to permit government surveillance in terrorism investigations and prosecutions. How public attitudes will adjust over time is uncertain. Public opinion polls indicate that the public was much more willing to support adoption of a national identification card shortly after the terrorist attack, but public support began to wane as time passed.[37]

No matter how recent events may have modified public views about some privacy issues, it seems likely that some types of privacy concerns are likely to remain unaffected. People still expect that bathroom doors will have locks, that medical records will receive confidential treatment, and that their tax returns will not be freely shared throughout government. Public concerns about private sector collection, use, and disclosure of personal information have probably not changed either. There is no reason to believe that people are any more willing than they were before September 11 to share personal information with companies over the Internet, to disclose Social Security numbers, or to receive telemarketing calls during dinner. Strong evidence of continuing public concern about privacy can be found in legislation passed several months after the passage of the antiterrorism law.

The No Child Left Behind Act of 2001 is a major education law passed after September 11, 2001, that includes new privacy protections for the collection of marketing information through schools.[38] The law requires local educational agencies to adopt and notify parents about privacy policies for surveys that collect some personal information from students and for activities involving the collection, disclosure, or use of personal information collected from students for marketing purposes.[39] Parents also have the right to review marketing collection instruments in advance and to refuse to allow their children to participate in marketing surveys.

The passage of this law indicates that privacy has not disappeared from the congressional agenda. Indeed, the school privacy provisions were passed in the face of strong opposition

R. Gellman / Government Information Quarterly 19 (2002) 255–264 261

from marketers and school boards. The opposition was able to weaken the privacy provisions, but it was not strong enough to remove them entirely. Privacy continues to be seen by Congress as a value of importance to the public. Even the antiterrorism law itself includes some provisions designed to make sure that privacy interests are reflected in rulemaking and data sharing activities.[40]

## 5. Conclusion

Perhaps the most insidious aspect of any legislation that reduces privacy protections is that it moves the privacy baseline.[41] The *incremental change* analysis presented here should not be too reassuring even if it were an entirely fair characterization of the antiterrorism law. A series of incremental changes can, and will, completely erode a statutory protection enacted in good faith. The privacy provisions of the tax code[42] and the limited protections in the Right to Financial Privacy Act of 1978[43] have both been substantially undermined by a torrent of incremental amendments over the years. However, incremental change can work in both directions. The privacy protections of the Driver's Privacy Protection Act were enhanced through later amendments.[44]

It is safe to predict that future events and legislation will affect privacy rights and interests. Some privacy rights and interests are likely to be diminished, and serious losses in privacy protection are possible. Improvements are also a possibility. It is not unusual to find public policy moving in different and, sometimes, contradictory directions at the same time. In considering the effects of any of these possible changes, it is useful to break down the analysis into smaller components. By using the elements of privacy (e.g., fair information practices), the domains of privacy (individual autonomy and information privacy), and the types of record keepers (public sector and private sector), the consequences of change can be more clearly evaluated, and the result will be a better understanding of what has been gained or lost.

## Notes

1. Quoted in James Freeman, "You Have Zero Privacy . . . Get Over It," *U.S.A. Today,* Aug. 9, 1999, ⟨http://www.usatoday.com/news/comment/columnists/freeman/ncjf30.htm⟩.
2. See, e.g., the famous statement of Associate Justice William O. Douglas from a 1965 decision of the Supreme Court: "The foregoing cases suggest that specific guarantees in the Bill of Rights have penumbras, formed by emanations from those guarantees that help give them life and substance . . . . Various guarantees create zones of privacy. The right of association contained in the penumbra of the First Amendment is one, as we have seen. The Third Amendment in its prohibition against the quartering of soldiers 'in any house' in time of peace without the consent of the owner is another facet of that privacy. The Fourth Amendment explicitly affirms the 'right of the people to be secure in their persons, houses, papers, and effects, against unreasonable searches and seizures.' The Fifth Amendment in its Self-Incrimination

Clause enables the citizen to create a zone of privacy which government may not force him to surrender to his detriment. The Ninth Amendment provides: 'The enumeration in the Constitution, of certain rights, shall not be construed to deny or disparage others retained by the people.' " *Griswold v. Connecticut,* 381 U.S. 479, 484 (1965) (citation omitted).

3. The value of the privilege has been questioned, but it continues to exist much the same as it has in the past. See, for example, Robert Gellman, "Prescribing Privacy: The Uncertain Role of the Physician in the Protection of Patient Privacy," *North Carolina Law Review,* 62 (January 1984): 255.

4. The value of the legislation is a matter of considerable controversy, but there can be no question that some improvements in privacy protections were achieved.

5. 15 U.S.C. 6501 et seq.

6. 5 U.S.C. 6801 et seq.

7. Uniting and Strengthening America by Providing Appropriate Tools Required to Intercept and Obstruct Terrorism (U.S.A. PATRIOT ACT) Act of 2001, P.L. 107–056, 115 Stat. 272. http://frwebgate.access.gpo.gov/cgi-bin/getdoc.cgi?dbname=107_cong_public_laws&docid=f:publ056.107.

8. 429 U.S. 589, 599–600 (1976).

9. *Data protection* is a term widely used in Europe and around the world to refer to information privacy. The word *privacy* does not exist in every language.

10. Secretary's Advisory Committee on Automated Personal Data Systems, *Records, Computers, and the Rights of Citizens* (Washington: Department of Health, Education & Welfare, 1973), at http://aspe.os.dhhs.gov/datacncl/1973privacy/tocprefacemembers.htm.

11. David Flaherty, *Protecting Privacy in Surveillance Societies* (Chapel Hill, NC: University of North Carolina, 1989, p. 310.

12. Organization for Economic Cooperation and Development, *Council Recommendations Concerning Guidelines Governing the Protection of Privacy and Transborder Flows of Personal Data,* 20 I.L.M. 422 (1981), O.E.C.D. Doc. C (80) 58 (Final) (Oct. 1, 1980), at http://www.oecd.org//dsti/sti/it/secur/prod/PRIV-EN.HTM.

13. Colin J. Bennett, *Regulating Privacy: Data Protection and Public Policy in Europe and the United States* (Ithaca, NY: Cornell University Press, 1992), pp. 130139.

14. 5 U.S.C. 552a.

15. For example, the European Union's core data protection rules also allow national government to provide for some exemptions for national security, defense, public security, and law enforcement matters. *Directive on the Protection of Individuals With Regard to the Processing of Personal Data and on the Free Movement of Such Data,* Council Directive 95/46/EC, 1995 O.J. (L 281) 31, Article 13 ⟨http://europa.eu.int/comm/internal_market/en/dataprot/law/index.htm⟩.

16. 5 U.S.C. 552a(j)(1).

17. Id. at 552a(j)(2).

18. Indeed, a provision in section 310 of the antiterrorism law regarding the Financial Crimes Enforcement Network expressly provided that rules on information use and disclosure must comply with the Privacy Act of 1974.

19. U.S.A. Patriot Act at Title II (Enhanced Surveillance Procedures).
20. 50 U.S.C. 1801 et seq.
21. See 18 U.S.C. chapter 119.
22. See 18 U.S.C. chapters 119 and 121.
23. See, for example, American Civil Liberties Union, *U.S.A. Patriot Act Boosts Government Powers While Cutting Back on Traditional Checks and Balances* (New York, NY: November 2001) ⟨http://www.aclu.org/congress/L110101a.html⟩.
24. The long-term effects of some of the act's provisions may not be clear before the end of 2005. A number of amendments relating to government surveillance expire at that time and will disappear if not renewed by a subsequent statute. U.S.A. Patriot Act at section 224.
25. U.S.A. Patriot Act at Title III (International Money Laundering Abatement and Financial Anti-Terrorism Act of 2001).
26. Id. at section 326.
27. Id. at section 351.
28. Id. at section 626.
29. See, for example, Paul Beckett, "Banks Are Using a National Database to Blacklist Customers For Slip-Ups," *Wall Street Journal,* Aug. 1, 2000: A1 (Eastern edition).
30. 15 U.S.C. 1681u.
31. 20 U.S.C. 9007.
32. 13 U.S.C. 9.
33. U.S.A. Patriot Act at section 508 (amending 20 U.S.C. 9007).
34. See, for example, U. S. Privacy Protection Study Commission, *Protecting Privacy in an Information Society* (Washington: GPO, 1977) at chapter 15.
35. These privacy laws were not changed by the antiterrorism law: Privacy Act of 1974, 5 U.S.C. 552a; Video Privacy Protection Act, 18 U.S.C. 2710; Driver's Privacy Protection Act, 18 U.S.C. 2721 et seq.; Telecommunications Act, 47 U.S.C. 222; Children's Online Privacy Protection Act, 15 U.S.C. 6501 et seq.; Gramm-Leach-Bliley, 15 U.S.C. 6801 et seq.; Health Insurance Portability and Accountability Act, 42 U.S.C. 1320 days-2 note; 45 CFR Parts 160 & 164.
36. The Fair Credit Reporting Act was changed slightly as described above and in some other minor ways. The Right to Financial Privacy Act, 12 U.S.C. 3414, was also modified slightly. See U.S.A. Patriot Act at section 505. The Family Educational Rights and Privacy Act, 20 U.S.C. 1232g, was modified to allow disclosure of school records for terrorism investigations pursuant to court order. See U.S.A. Patriot Act at section 507. The Cable Communications Policy Act, 47 U.S.C. 551, was amended to permit limited disclosure of subscriber records to government entities. Even here, the law prohibited disclosure of records revealing cable subscriber selection of video programming from a cable operator. See U.S.A. Patriot Act at section 211. Of course, the surveillance amendments in the antiterrorism law significantly amended the Electronic Communications Privacy Act, which prescribes the rules for government access to electronic communications. See U.S.A. Patriot Act at Title II passim.
37. Donna Leinwand, "National ID in Development," *U.S.A. Today,* Jan. 22, 2002, http://www.usatoday.com/life/cyber/tech/2002/01/22/id-cards.htm.

38. P.L. 107–110, January 8, 2002.

39. Section 1061 of the act amending 20 U.S.C. 1232h.

40. See U.S.A. Patriot Act at section 403 (amending 8 U.S.C. 1105(d)(2) to require that sharing of National Crime Information Center information will "ensure the security, confidentiality, and destruction of such information" and will protect privacy rights).

41. Professor Paul Schwartz makes a similar point about technology, arguing that ever-increasing technological capabilities can erode expectations of privacy because the technology is often in place, accepted, and profitable before anyone can argue that it is unreasonable. Paul Schwartz, "Privacy and Participation: Personal Information and Public Sector Regulation in the United States," *Iowa Law Review,* 80 (March 1995): 553, 573.

42. 26 U.S.C. 6103.

43. 12 U.S.C. 3401 et seq.

44. 18 U.S.C. 2721 et seq.

# [22]

# The Coming War on Terrorism*

LAWRENCE FREEDMAN

AT the start of June 2002 President George W. Bush described for the graduates of the US Military Academy, West Point, how they would have to fight the developing war on terror. They would confront an enemy that, unlike those of the past, lacked 'great armies and great industrial capabilities'. Not pausing to query whether this might undermine the rationale for the great army of the United States, he continued:

The gravest danger to freedom lies at the perilous crossroads of radicalism and technology. When the spread of chemical and biological and nuclear weapons, along with ballistic missile technology—when that occurs, even weak states and small groups could attain a catastrophic power to strike great nations. Our enemies have declared this very intention, and have been caught seeking these terrible weapons. They want the capability to blackmail us, or to harm us, or to harm our friends—and we will oppose them with all our power.

Such enemies could be beyond deterrence or containment, the mainstay doctrines of the Cold War, because they have no 'nation or citizens to defend'. Then, indicating perhaps that nations might be involved, Bush complained that this threat could not be mitigated by putting 'faith in the word of tyrants, who solemnly sign non-proliferation treaties, and then systemically break them'. His conclusion: waiting was dangerous. 'We must take the battle to the enemy, disrupt his plans, and confront the worst threats before they emerge. In the world we have entered, the only path to safety is the path of action. And this nation will act.' The enemy, however would be difficult to find—'hidden in caves and growing in laboratories'. There were terror cells in sixty countries. Every instrument of power, including diplomacy, would be needed to deal with it. Nonetheless, the US military must therefore be 'ready to strike at a moment's notice in any dark corner of the world'.[1]

So, almost nine months after the most audacious and costly terrorist attack ever, which had led to the President first declaring his war on terror, and after what he considered to be a successful first stage of that war in Afghanistan, he set out the core themes for the war's future development. The most important feature of this speech as far as commentators were concerned was its pre-emptive quality, the readiness to go out and deal with enemies before they could do damage. This fitted in with the expectation, created by the State of the Union speech the previous January, that the United States was gearing up

---

* An early version of this chapter was delivered as the Ramsay Murray Lecture, Selwyn College, Cambridge, on 26 April 2001.

THE COMING WAR ON TERRORISM

for an attack against Iraq, as a key member of the 'axis of evil', a drive stalled for the moment precisely because this was an enemy with a 'great army', or at least one large enough to cause the United States serious difficulty when defending its homeland.[2]

Another theme, which fitted in with a raft of alarming warnings from senior administration officials, was that the attacks on 11 September could well be repeated. Director of Homeland Security Tom Ridge observed that this was a matter of when and not if. Defense Secretary Donald Rumsfeld asserted that 'inevitably' terrorists would acquire and use chemical, biological or nuclear weapons. The timing of these warnings in late May 2002 could be seen as a response to revelations about the poor work of intelligence agencies, which had had evidence of the preparations being made by the suicidal hijackers but had failed to 'join the dots'. While ensuring that next time there could be no accusations of complacency, the imprecise and all-encompassing nature of these warnings meant that they were useless in terms of defensive planning.[3] It should be noted that it was not only in the United States that the assumption of 'when but not if' was made. Europeans assumed that their major cities and nationals abroad were as likely to be targeted as those of the United States.

The conclusion that in critical respects the United States could not yet concentrate solely on the offensive but was still on the defensive was confirmed by the major reorganisation of government proposed to improve the flow of critical intelligence and bring together a number of agencies under a new Office of Homeland Security. The other clear message was that the greatest danger lay in terrorists getting access to weapons of mass destruction. Yet the attacks of 11 September, as Bush himself had observed, had been mounted by a few dozen men, acting on behalf of a movement rather than a state, with low technology and at minimal cost. Al-Qaeda could claim some involvement in practically all conflicts, large and small, in which there was an Islamic element, which is why this war had such a wide geographical spread. Their tactics in all these conflicts derived from those long used in guerrilla warfare and its more terroristic variants. Nor was there real novelty in organising a number of simultaneous attacks and persuading the most accomplished militants to base their plans on suicide. All this came together to produce attacks that commanded attention because of their location and scale. There was evidence of an interest in chemical or biological weapons, and a reasonable assumption that if these weapons were acquired they would be used, but there was no reason to suppose that this was a high-probability threat. Even when a scare was raised over a suspected plot to explode a radiation bomb, something which had clearly interested al-Qaeda from 1993,[4] reports suggested that this was at an elementary stage and that, even if some device were constructed, the effects would be modest, becoming severe only if panic ensued. The management of the anthrax attacks that followed 11 September, probably from an indigenous US source, indicates that when anxiety levels have been raised it can become even more difficult for

LAWRENCE FREEDMAN

governments to manage effectively the communication of risk. The responses to the spate of warnings in May and June 2002 suggested that if, once anxiety levels have been raised, little happens, then the credibility of warnings declines.

Although Iraq may have tested a radiological device at some time, reportedly with poor results, like the other states which constituted the 'axis of evil' it had not, as far as could be ascertained, played any direct role in the 11 September attacks. Yet Iraq, undoubtedly guilty of developing the most noxious technologies, seemed to have become the target for the coming stage of the war on terror. This could be justified only on a pre-emptive basis: not because the 'perilous crossroads of radicalism and techno-logy' had been reached, but because we dare not let it be reached. Al-Qaeda's diffuse, non-state radicalism and Iraq's state-generated technology were on separate paths. They did not have to meet for either to cause trouble, but it was their potential combination that was deemed to be most frightening.

The two were not natural allies, despite their shared loathing of the United States and Israel, with the secular/religious divide of considerable import-ance. Iraq, as a country, could expect to enjoy international rehabilitation once Saddam Hussein was no longer in power. Al-Qaeda has no *raison d'être* other than denying unbelievers and apostates any influence in the affairs of the Islamic world and working towards the creation of a series of mighty theocratic states. Since the fall of the Taleban in Afghanistan, the only regime Osama bin Laden considered truly Islamic, it is bound to follow a subversive, radical route to power, as part of a network of like-minded but more nationally based groups. In this it is not unlike the leftist groups of the 1970s, which were also sustained through a loose, ideologically based and at times truly global network.

It would, therefore, have been possible to specify the enemy in terms of its ideology and objectives. Instead the enemy was defined in terms of terrorism rather than just one group of terrorists. If that is the case, then it is the tactic rather than the objective that is most at fault, and the purpose of the current war would be to establish a new anti-terrorist norm in international politics. Though terrorism covers a wide range of activities adopted by many diverse actors, on this view all these activities would be judged illegitimate and deserving of special attention by an international anti-terrorist coalition. We can note, for example, that of the 346 international terrorist attacks in 2001 (other than those of 11 September) as counted by the US State Department, 178 were bombings against a multinational oil pipeline in Colombia— constituting 51 per cent of the year's total number of attacks.[5] Once it becomes necessary to distinguish between forms of terror, on the grounds that some acts are more iniquitous than others, by what criteria should they be evaluated? This chapter attempts to establish a framework for thinking about the future of the war on terror.

## Humanitarian intervention

Prior to 11 September 2001, it seemed to be the case that whereas the security problems of the past could be blamed on strong states which wished to get stronger through conquest and hegemony, the sources of most contemporary problems were weak states, unable to manage their own affairs and thus descending into the old apocalyptic scourges of persecution, war, famine and disease. Even famine and disease, on close inspection, often turned out to be the result of 'political' as much as 'natural' disasters. To mitigate the effects of these disasters and to eliminate their causes would require a considerable effort. It meant acting to stop large-scale abuses of human or minority rights by repressive states, calm civil wars or other forms of intercommunal violence, and help reconstruct shattered societies.

This could be presented as a matter of obligation as well as interest. If these situations are left to fester and intensify, the scourges not only rebuke the international conscience but also spread and begin to impinge directly on our own societies. The instability they generate is rarely localised or readily contained, with refugees, drugs, small arms, every imaginable form of criminal activity and also terrorism soon flowing to the rest of the world. This developing agenda posed a direct challenge to the traditional assumptions of international affairs, and in particular the privileged position of the state. The doctrine of non-interference in internal affairs was undermined by the evident problems many new states had in managing their internal affairs and the steady elevation of minority and human rights above state rights.

At the same time, the strong incentives to deal with these political disasters have always been balanced by the high costs and military risks of intervention, and the lack of means of addressing their root causes, short of taking over these weak states in a quasi-imperial role. The multiplication of cases meant that there was little to be done but to pick and choose about where and how to intervene, and a certain amount of effort has gone into setting tests for where available resources might best be applied. Prime Minister Tony Blair notably set out in Chicago in 1999, at the height of the war in Kosovo, five tests, relating to confidence in the analysis, exhaustion of diplomatic efforts, availability of military options, a readiness for the long haul and some connection with national interests.[6]

By and large, the leading European countries had the will to intervene in these conflicts, but only limited means with which to do so. The Americans were far better endowed with means, but lacked the will. Even before the second Bush presidency, the ascendant view in the United States was that only the most extreme cases should be addressed, and then with great caution.[7] Western countries could do little to solve such deep-seated social cleavages and economic mismanagement, and to the extent that they tried they probably made things worse. The fear was of a succession of 'quagmires', so that even before entrance into distant quarrels was contemplated, an 'exit strategy' had to be designed. The American preference, in line with

LAWRENCE FREEDMAN

the classical realist preoccupation with power balances, and reinforced by the sensitivity of its role as the lone superpower, was to focus foreign policy on the challenges to Western hegemony that might be posed by strong states. This meant not just rising great powers, such as China (very much the preoccupation of the first months of the Bush term), but those that were acquiring an artificial strength, notably by acquiring weapons of mass destruction. In the first months of the Bush administration these were already identified as the rogue states of Iraq, Iran and North Korea.

## Is this a war?

Both sides to this debate viewed the attacks of 11 September as confirming the validity of their approaches. Liberal internationalists could claim that the limits of classical realism had been brutally demonstrated. Out of Afghanistan, one of the most miserable, factionalised and conflict-prone of third world countries, serially abused by neighbours and outsiders alike, came a precision attack directed against the greatest symbols of American economic and military power, the World Trade Center and the Pentagon. To deal with this challenge the United States had to become a player in Afghan politics, exactly the sort of place the Pentagon planners expected to be able to disregard. Lesson one: great powers ignored the poor and the wretched at their peril. No country can be dismissed as irrelevant to security. Indeed, the more forbidding and the more chaotic the society, the more (it seemed) it is able to provide safe havens for terrorists as well as criminals. Lesson two: it is vital to work closely with other states—in this case, those that shared borders with Afghanistan or appeared also to have been infected by al-Qaeda or could offer specialist intelligence or military resources in support.

Yet could liberal internationalism reassert itself on the basis of a 'war on terrorism'? The very language focused on the role of force and violence in political affairs. War is the ultimate realist experience. It sharpens divisions and ensures that multilateralism is at best only partial, in the form of an alliance. Beyond the alliance is the enemy. The purpose of war is to eliminate the enemy, or at least to render it incapable of exercising its malign influence. The possibility of attempting to accommodate its political agenda so that it no longer needs to be deemed hostile has been precluded. Such accommodation can easily be represented as 'appeasement', thereby encouraging rather than buying off threatening behaviour. Other significant or potentially significant actors may be reluctant to accept a role as allies; but once war has been declared, neutrality invites charges of appeasement and consorting with the enemy. At war, the United States expects its allies to be 'with us or against us' but nowhere in between.[8]

Because of the implications of such thinking, some have queried whether it is useful to think of the current conflict as a war at all. A number of arguments have been made here. First, redefining obnoxious criminal acts as warlike dignifies them and gives the perpetrators an unnecessarily heroic status.

Second, instead of objectives being framed in terms of law enforcement and the successful prosecution of the perpetrators, they are framed in terms of military victory.[9] Third, in a war the gloves are off and governments can do things that they cannot do when problems are described in more civilian terms, for example in finding ways to bypass the civil rights of anyone, including foreign nationals, suspected of being implicated in terrorism. This leads in exactly the opposite direction to a judicial approach. Fourth and finally, power within government shifts to the military and the Pentagon civilians, leading to a harsh foreign policy with scant scope for diplomatic initiatives, let alone attention to the conditions which breed terrorism.

There is something to all these arguments; but, after an attack on such a scale, mounted by a political entity based in a distant country, war was not a matter of choice but a strategic imperative. It was Osama bin Laden who had declared war, some years earlier; he had just not been taken seriously until he reached new levels of terrorist achievement. When the United States suffered a surprise attack, with severe casualties, there was no holding back. This was more than just a large crime or an affront to common decency. The US government could also point to the limits of an alternative approach. It had dealt with the 1993 attack on the World Trade Center through the courts, but this successful prosecution had palpably failed to stop a second attack. In 2001 it was hard to take seriously calls for hard evidence before any action was taken when the whole operation stank of al-Qaeda, or to begin to imagine how a broad-based militant movement, with many activist cells dispersed around the globe, could be put in the dock. In the event an attempt was made, although without great conviction, to ask the Taleban regime in Afghanistan to hand over the prime suspect. This was rebuffed in a disingenuous manner. In practice the Taleban and al-Qaeda had fused over the previous few years. It was impossible to deal with the terrorists without first overthrowing the regime.

By invoking Article 5 of the Atlantic Charter—that an attack on one should be considered an attack on all—the established allies of the United States signalled their understanding of this position. There was a general wish to show solidarity with the United States, and certainly a sense that at least it was prudent to do so. 'We are all Americans,' declared *Le Monde*, in a famous and unlikely headline of 12 September. Many governments were all too aware of how they might become victims of similar attacks, possibly also from al-Qaeda. Yet through these declarations of sympathy and sorrow for the Americans, made by many people of many countries, often despite themselves, there ran an undercurrent that the United States must not jeopardise this solidarity by moving too quickly or ruthlessly—'lashing out' was the phrase used. While the Americans did not rush to action, the declaration of war sent a signal that there was no intention of playing the victim.

A more substantial criticism was that it was a mistake to declare war on a tactic.[10] There is a tendency to declare war on problems, as a means of focusing attention and mobilising resources—hence the war on drugs, or

Lawrence Freedman

cancer, or poverty. The war on terrorism was never quite understood in those terms, because the prominence of intelligent opponents capable of fighting back provides an essential feature of any war. Nor is it unusual for wars conducted against specific political entities to be assigned much wider and grander objectives—encouraging the hope that victory will ensure that some basic values will have been upheld. Positively, wars are fought for democracy, liberation, civilisation (at one point a contender in this case), and negatively they are fought against aggression, colonialism and now terrorism.

## Defining terror

If declaring a war against terrorism is comparable to, say, a war against aggression, then that might mean not so much constant conflict as that a marker is in place. When the norm is violated, as was the norm of aggression when Iraq invaded Kuwait in August 1990, then there would be an expectation of collective action. We shall return to this issue of establishing an anti-terrorist norm later, but for the moment we can note one important difference. Cases of pure aggression, when one state invades another, are extremely rare, and becoming more rare. Terrorism, on the other hand, in some shape or form, is ubiquitous, because it can refer to small acts of violence as well as the catastrophic sort. It is one thing to fight al-Qaeda as a particularly noxious form of terrorism. It is another then to feel obliged to take on all forms of terrorism, especially given the notorious problem of deciding what is to be included in this category.

The question of how to define terrorism has become familiar to the point of tedium. The term is both descriptive and pejorative, hence the regular observation about how terrorists from one perspective are freedom fighters from another. Because 'terrorist' is such a natural insult it is used extremely loosely, covering all types of violent activity, or even just potentially violent activity. Its use is certainly not confined to groups who mainly target civilians. Those who concentrate on members of the security services or known agents of the state are regularly denounced for their terrorism. Even groups who have adopted unambiguously terrorist strategies can barely resist resorting to the abusive use themselves, as when governments are castigated as terrorists for repressive measures or for refusing to bow to secessionist movements or for not redressing economic or political inequities.

Nor is terrorism confined to those with overtly political agendas. It can be applied by those who expect their actions to be eloquent in themselves, without any accompanying manifesto or demands. Their motives may not be straightforward but rather intensely personal, perhaps reflecting a desire for vengeance on a cruel world, the peculiar attractions of a clandestine life, social alienation, the fantasies of millennial movements or the machinations of organised crime. Methods suitable for sniping at soldiers and bombing government buildings can serve racketeers (as impoverished 'freedom fighters' have often discovered).

A final problem is that much terrorist activity is barely terrifying while most regular combat is. Some individuals or groups may aspire to cause panic and chaos but they simply fail to generate enough notice or interest. To the extent that the IRA campaign in mainland Britain succeeded, it was because they attacked economic targets. Obviously they were responsible for much loss of life, and risked much more, so this should not be played down; yet for most of us living through this campaign it became another hazard of modern life, along with strikes on the railways, extremes of weather and flu epidemics, with its own familiar routines of alerts and evacuations. It was known that the IRA, and on occasion other groups, would mount 'spectaculars', but these events were so unexpected and infrequent that there were few adjustments to normal life that could be made to accommodate them, other than to tolerate the inconveniences of bag searches at department stores and intrusive airport security.

When terrorism is used effectively as a strategy it serves as a coercive means of obtaining political effects by using threats of violence against civil society. It is only when occasional outrages turn into sustained campaigns, and a recognisable pattern of activity emerges, that the effects on public life become palpable. This is evident in Israel as unnecessary trips to city centres are avoided, tourism drops off, uniformed men with guns suddenly appear at street corners and, on occasion, political initiatives are set in motion in order to isolate the terrorists or take the edge off their hostility. So, for the coercion to work, an irresistible and ruthless reputation must be generated. Occasional outrages do not have the same political effects. Without a substantial measure of support in the community on whose behalf it is perpetrated, a campaign may well succumb to improved security and weariness. Even then, the track record of terrorist methods serving the ambitious political goals with which they are usually associated is poor.

So while it may be the case that terrorism is a strategy adopted by the desperate and the marginalised to fight against the strong, it is not necessarily a good strategy. Alternatives are to appease, persuade, appeal to a better nature, embarrass or frustrate, as well as cause havoc and economic dislocation through non-violent action. A sophisticated strategy, especially in these days of complex interdependence and instant communications, will be as mindful of the effects of measures and countermeasures on the governments of allies and spectators, and the mood within international organisations, as of those on the notional 'enemy'.

What does this mean for attempts to develop criteria to indicate when a particular group should become a target of the 'war on terrorism'? President Bush initially attempted to focus on 'international' terrorism, or 'terrorism with a global reach', and this has the advantage of addressing those groups that wish to use terrorism to internationalise otherwise localised conflicts by taking advantage of modern forms of transportation and communication. Yet Bush had to walk back from the implication that terrorism mattered only when the United States was vulnerable. In addition, it was apparent that not

LAWRENCE FREEDMAN

all of those associated with al-Qaeda were interested in mounting attacks on the other side of the world; many, on the contrary, were content to engage in geographically restricted campaigns. This has led the Americans to be drawn into quite specific campaigns in the Yemen, Philippines and Georgia.

If one objective of the current campaign is to establish a new norm of international politics, to the effect that terrorist methods are illegitimate in all circumstances, then almost any cause might be invalidated by their adoption. If this is the way we want to move, then some way has to be found of limiting the concept and the imperatives for action. This is to some extent what has been going on with the attempt to create a norm of humanitarian intervention during the 1990s. Indeed, there are important links between the acts which prompt humanitarian intervention and those that prompt a war on terrorism. In both cases the victims are most likely to be defenceless civilians. The moral objection lies in the use of violent means against non-combatants for political objectives. In both cases taking action will probably mean ignoring inhibitions against interfering in the internal affairs of other states.

In another sense, however, there is an important difference. Vicious domestic persecution or ethnic cleansing are weapons used by the strong against the weak, so that the weak can find redress only if those who are attacking them are in turn attacked by even stronger powers, which is why this becomes a test for a contemporary form of internationalism. Victim status is becoming a prized commodity in international politics, because it is a means by which a group with no capacity of its own can acquire powerful external allies.

Terrorism, by contrast, is a weapon habitually used by the weak against the strong. It is a form of response that does not rely on taking on the enemy at its strongest point but instead looks for vulnerabilities in its social structure. So, while the victims of ethnic cleansing and other human rights abuses have by definition already been marginalised, the victims of terrorism are more likely to be found in the cities of the strong. This is why it is more likely to prompt a response by the strong, and why a war to ease humanitarian distress may well be against an established regime yet a war against terrorism may well be in its support.

I observed earlier that tests have had to be developed as to when humanitarian intervention is warranted, and they might also serve as a starting point for consideration of how to take forward a war on terrorism. I am suggesting that there is a shared norm that organised violence should not be used against civilians. There is much to be said for seeking to establish such a general norm, given that over the past century we moved from a situation where 90 per cent of the casualties of war were combatants to one where 90 per cent are civilians. It is also the case that the trend in Western military thinking is to emphasise capabilities to deal with enemy armed forces, and to stress the importance of restraint in situations where innocent civilians may get harmed. Leaving aside the fact that the strong would always prefer to confine conflict to open battle between regular forces, there are still

THE COMING WAR ON TERRORISM

difficulties in upholding this approach, even allowing for the greater precision of modern military technology. The distinction between hurting civilians by aiming for them and hurting them through aiming for something else, and then missing, which invariably happens in air campaigns, is not always appreciated, and there are also many dual-purpose targets, connected with energy supplies and communications, that can cause harm to the civilian and military sectors at the same time. In addition, terrorists hide within civil society as well as targeting it, and invite attacks upon civilians so as to radicalise the victims. So further tests are still needed. What might these be? Some guidance might be found by following Blair's Chicago criteria for humanitarian intervention.

On this basis, the first test suggests that if battle is to be joined against a particular group then there must be confidence that the violence it employs is truly illegitimate, so that we have not simply been beguiled by an authoritarian regime that is rhetorically accomplished. Will a cry of terrorism be used as a cry of communism was in the past by inadequate and repressive governments to suppress any inconvenient dissent? Second, we will want to know if opportunities for political dialogue have been rejected. If the cause is serious enough, and has a head of steam behind it, then at the very least alternative and credible means of political resolution must be explored. Third, are there useful forms of forceful action available that will not simply make things worse, by generating more recruits for the terrorists and gaining them political sympathy?

Fourth, there will also be a need to hang in for the long term, if for no other reason than that terrorism, by its nature, rarely succumbs to a decisive battle. These are not battles fought between organised armies whose troops are sufficiently disciplined that they can be ordered to surrender or sufficiently unmotivated that they may simply skulk home after a defeat. Terrorist campaigns tend to depend on small numbers of highly motivated people operating in cells. Demotivation takes time as cells are captured or killed. The campaign is most likely to end by petering out. Thus the IRA has agreed to a ceasefire and political negotiations, and is now putting arms beyond use, but some of its members still do not want a ceasefire. Only over time can they be neutralised. Arguably, this is what has happened in Afghanistan. American, British and other Western troops have been engaged in large-scale sweeps along the border with Pakistan to finish off al-Qaeda, but they have found little. On the other hand, remaining al-Qaeda and Taleban activists have not deemed it prudent to attempt any serious actions of their own.

With regard to humanitarian intervention Blair's final test, that of relevance to national interests, was to some extent always easy to pass because in another part of his speech he had argued how national and international interests could coincide. More realistically, the test remains significant because the campaigns of terror that bother us most are apt to be those that are directed against our own societies, or those of our closest allies and

LAWRENCE FREEDMAN

partners, or those that threaten to upset a country which is important to us in economic, security or resource terms.

When we apply these tests we soon find that the easiest cases are those in which violence is used against the stable liberal democracies of the West, which contain ample non-violent mechanisms through which to promote causes and redress grievances. Not only does the violence lack legitimacy, but it is also likely to be manageable without calling upon the assistance of an international coalition, except in such areas as intelligence, extradition and frustrating fundraising (where the assistance has not always been forth-coming). By and large this is how the 'red' activists of the 1970s and 1980s, or the more durable IRA and ETA, were handled. These groups were never able wholly to destabilise the political and social structures they were attacking, even though they could on occasion inflict some harsh blows.

The hardest cases are those in which activities that might be warranted by resistance to oppression or self-defence have become so unacceptable that they move beyond justification. It is therefore not surprising to find that contemporary conflicts can involve a sort of competitive victimology, whereby the strong claim to be victims of terrorism, while the weak claim to be victims of inhuman persecution. Thus in early 1998 the United States was prepared to describe the Kosovo Liberation Army as terroristic,[11] yet not much more than a year later it was in effect in alliance with them as it responded with the rest of NATO to the disproportionate campaign waged against the Kosovan people by Serbia in the name of rooting out the KLA terrorists. In the two most testing international issues of the first half of 2002, the issue of whether the resort to terror deprives a cause of its legitimacy has been central. Israelis point to a society traumatised by suicide bombings, while the Palestinians point to the daily humiliations and harsh measures taken by the Israelis in the West Bank, territory that they are not supposed to occupy. Indians point to outrages perpetrated by Islamic militants, including an attack on their parliament, while Pakistanis point to the rigidity of the Indian hold on the disputed Kashmir.

The similarities do not stop there, and indicate the wider difficulties of the war on terrorism. Certainly the ascendance of the anti-terrorist norm has helped the Israelis and Indians gain sympathy from the United States, and to a lesser extent from its allies. Yet the extent to which the leaders of the Palestinians and Pakistanis, Yasser Arafat and General Musharraf respect-ively, could be held responsible for all acts of militancy became itself a matter of dispute. These leaders had to balance the risks to their regimes from hard-liners if they appeared to sell out a sacred cause with the risks of losing vital international support if they failed to crack down on terrorists. Even then, for the United States a tough stance against the Palestinians undermined the wider Middle Eastern backing required if the influence of extremists was to be weakened and Iraq challenged, while in the first stage of the war on terror Musharraf had played a central role by disassociating Pakistan from the Taleban in Afghanistan and allowing the United States to use his country's facilities. In his West Point speech Bush spoke of the importance of moral purpose. 'There can be no neutrality', he insisted, 'between justice and cruelty, between the innocent and the guilty. We are in a conflict between good and evil, and America will call evil by its name.' Yet conflicts involve power as well as morality, and so while Bush's assertion that 'targeting innocent civilians for murder is always and everywhere wrong' stresses the normative element, the power element still requires compromises and occasional concessions to regimes whose own moral record is, to say the least, imperfect.

## The war on terrorism: past and future

While it is useful, then, to have some tests because they might at some point be needed to distinguish deserving from not so deserving cases, it is important not to lose sight of the wider political context in which they will have to be applied. Terrorism is a tactic that often comes naturally to radical political movements. It is most likely to be defeated when these movements have run their course and begun to fade away through constant rebuffs and frustration. It is arguable that on this basis two past wars on terrorism have already been largely won since the phenomenon reasserted itself as a direct threat to Western societies (rather than their colonial administrations) in the late 1960s.

At that time the ideological shift to the left in the youth movements of the West, prompted largely by the war in Vietnam, combined with a new assertiveness by a variety of deprived racial and other minority groups. The theorists of the anti-globalisation movement, in many ways the ideological inheritors of the anti-capitalist left, do not argue in favour of a violent insurrection, and to the extent that these movements have become associated with violence it is because of the rioting that, until 11 September, appeared to be the natural accompaniment to any international summit.

A more difficult question concerns secular Arab terrorism, linked to the Palestinian cause. Following the 1967 war and the Israeli occupation of the West Bank, the Palestine Liberation Organisation was unable to mount much of a guerrilla campaign. Twenty years passed before the first *intifada*, and that was largely a spontaneous uprising rather than an organised campaign. Nor were neighbouring states anxious to allow the PLO to use their territory as a base for mounting operations against the Israelis, as they were the ones that suffered retaliation. After almost unseating King Hussein in Jordan in 1970, before he got the upper hand, the PLO moved into Lebanon, where it proceeded to unsettle the country's delicate political balance, an event from which Lebanon has yet to recover fully. Even before then, Palestinian groups and their supporters had attempted to attack Israelis wherever they could be found, a campaign of which the Munich Olympic Games massacre of 1972 was the most conspicuous example. As Israeli security was generally tight, internationalising the conflict generally meant hijacking aircraft and making a

51

LAWRENCE FREEDMAN

nuisance. The result was generally to leave the PLO outlawed and discredited.

Israel's offensive into Lebanon in 1982, leading to the massacres and the Sabra and Chatila refugee camps, and the radicalisation of the country, raised the temperature further, with suicide bombers much in evidence, directed against the US presence in Beirut. In addition, the old radicals, Syria and Libya, still toyed with terrorism, partly as revenge for real and imagined slights against themselves as much as the Palestinians. In June 1985 flight TWA 847, carrying 153 passengers and crew, largely American, was seized by two Hizbollah extremists taking off from Athens en route to Rome. After a tortuous journey, during which some hostages were released and one was murdered, the aircraft ended up in Beirut. The hostages were removed into the city and then bargaining began, effectively for prisoners held by Israel who were at any rate due for release. Interviews were regularly given to the media.

It was at this point that the United States almost declared war on terrorism. Caspar Weinberger, then the US Secretary of Defense, remarked that 'it is a war and it is the beginning of a war.' When the crisis was effectively resolved, President Reagan made a nationwide broadcast, demonstrating to would-be hijackers the influence this tactic could bring. This was followed by the seizure of the US cruise ship *Achille Lauro*, and the killing of an invalid American. When the hijackers managed to get a deal to fly to Egypt, the Americans intercepted the aircraft and forced it to land in Italy, much to the dismay of the Italian government. Reagan went on TV with a message to terrorists: 'You can run but you can't hide.'[12] Sounds familiar?

By now the United States was focused on Libya as the most voluble pro-terrorist state. Secretary of State George Shultz said: 'My opinion is that we need to raise the cost to those who perpetrate terrorist acts . . . so they will have to think more carefully about it.' After an attack on a Berlin nightclub that left a US soldier dead, the United States bombed Tripoli. This move was immensely popular and judged a success, in that little was heard from Colonel Qadhafi for some time thereafter; but it was also followed by the bringing down of a transatlantic flight, Pan Am 103, over the Scottish town of Lockerbie in 1988, killing 259 passengers and 11 local people, as well as by arms shipments to the IRA. Even so, the diplomatic isolation of Libya as Britain and the United States demonstrated its complicity in Lockerbie led to Qadhafi working hard to demonstrate that his regime had changed its ways. Whatever Israel may have thought, even Arafat managed to present himself as a suitable interlocutor in the Middle East peace process by demonstrating that the PLO had put terrorism behind it. Moreover, in relation to its past lists of state sponsors of terrorism, by early 2002 the United States was prepared to acknowledge that, in addition to Libya, Sudan also understood the need to get out of the terrorism business. Syria was deemed to be making some limited moves in the right direction, and in fact has been reported to have made some significant contributions to the US intelligence effort;

nevertheless, as with Iran, the problem was not so much a readiness to support international terrorism as support for radical groups apt to attack Israel, such as Hizbollah and Hamas. So, while Israeli society has been under a sustained terrorist bombardment, neither the PLO nor secular radical Arab states now see terrorism as a sensible way of internationalising the conflict. This is more likely to be achieved by drawing attention to the illegitimacy of Israel's position in the West Bank and Gaza, leaving the question for Palestinian strategists as to whether this is put at risk by the ferocity of the suicide bomber campaign against Israeli civilians. Saddam Hussein is, of course, another product of 1960s secular Arab radicalism, and he tries to use the Palestinian campaign to boost his standing (including by giving subventions to the families of suicide bombers); yet he got into conflict with the West only because of some old-fashioned aggression against another Arab state, Kuwait, and thereafter the issue became the survival of the regime and the elimination of its capacity to inflict mass destruction rather than any ideological argument.

The current campaign concerns a different ideological tradition, originating in but not confined to the Middle East. It is further confused by representing one strand of Islamic militancy, distinct, for example, from the Iranian version which first made an international impact and got into arguments with the United States in the late 1970s. This strand was, if anything, in a form of alliance with the United States during the 1980s during the campaign to undermine the Russian position in Afghanistan. The fight against the Soviets was the training ground for committed young Arabs, such as Osama bin Laden, and the source of their Islamic zealotry. Its political importance initially seemed to rest more in the challenge posed to regimes in Muslim countries that were deemed to be failing in their promotion of Islamic law. It was certainly anti-Israel but elsewhere, for example in the Balkans, if anything it was again working with the United States to back the Muslim cause. Its anti-American character derived first from abhorrence of the way of life the United States represented and more particularly from objections to the strong American presence in Saudi Arabia, seen as a desecration of Islam's holiest places, after the Iraqi invasion of Kuwait. Its future depends on a series of ideological and political battles being fought within Muslim countries, as well as the evolution of the conflicts that animate it—in Central Asia as well as the Middle East.

In its war against the United States, this strand of Islamic militancy may not see many options other than terrorism. Since the end of the Cold War the United States has been confident of defeating all-comers in regular war, and now looks forward to spending as much as the rest of the world combined on its armed forces. Other than Saddam Hussein, who in 1991 allowed himself to be misled about the quality and combat proficiency of American forces, opponents have generally preferred to avoid open battle with the United States. Instead they have adopted guerrilla tactics. The objective in all cases has been to persuade the United States to take itself out of a particular fight,

LAWRENCE FREEDMAN

and this has generally been successful. This was the purpose of communist tactics in Vietnam. The same tactics can also be said to have worked in Beirut in October 1983, when a suicide bomber drove a truck into the US marine barracks, and then a decade later in Somalia when US Rangers were caught and eighteen were killed. In both cases these incidents were followed by US withdrawal.

What conclusions might be drawn from this? The United States has demonstrated in the past that when it comes to wars of choice it is vulnerable to guerrilla tactics, elements of which may be characterised as terrorism. These have the effect of making casualties suffered disproportionate to the stakes involved. The mistake made by al-Qaeda, therefore, was to go for a spectacular attack that turned a war of choice into a war of necessity, so that instead of being encouraged to leave the Middle East and Central Asia, as would have been hoped, the United States became drawn into those regions more deeply than before. This was the opposite of what had been intended.

This leaves open the question, which clearly perturbs the Bush administration, as to whether 11 September has set new standards for terrorists, obliging all those who follow to raise their game, which means looking at chemical, biological and radiological weapons. This is the spectre of the combination of radicalism with technology, as described by President Bush, with which this chapter opened. While it is the case that the Bush administration had Saddam Hussein in its sights before 11 September, the attacks led to the case that the logical next step in any escalation would be the ultimate in superterrorism, and Iraq was the most likely source of the wherewithal for such an attack. It is simply too dangerous, runs the argument, to wait until that happens; the self-defence has to be anticipatory. Dealing with this risk is also conceptually undemanding, even if militarily possibly extremely demanding. The demands of regime change in Iraq are substantial, but in its military aspects at least this is a problem of a type that the United States understands. While the solution may be expensive and complex, and risk great loss of life, taking on Iraqi armed forces will involve operations the US knows how to conduct and with which, unlike guerrilla warfare, it is comfortable.

There is, however, another possibility, and that is that the lesson to be learned from the fate of al-Qaeda is not to raise the level of violence excessively high, so as to create a retaliatory imperative for the victims, but to keep it focused and carefully targeted, for example on American (and other Western) personnel and assets in places where they might be convinced that they are not at all welcome and would rather not stick around. Although this has yet to happen, a similar conclusion might be drawn by Palestinian militants (and should have been drawn from the Lebanon) that it is sustained guerrilla operations against exposed positions, rather than city-centre spectaculars, that eat away at public resolve to sustain these positions.

This is not to deny that these groups would be delighted to acquire weapons of mass effect, or that the retributive urges could overcome strategic sophistication when contemplating their use, or that there are other grounds for fearing the success of Iraqi effort to acquire such weapons. Rather, it is to warn that that the war on terrorism may well continue to take the United States into the sort of operation it dislikes, without an enemy in the field to be annihilated or obliged to surrender, into remote and inhospitable areas where struggles for local political power provide radical groups with the opportunity to define their identifies and refine their tactics. This brings us back to the parallels between the debate on humanitarian intervention as it developed during the 1990s, and that currently raised by the war on terrorism, including the attempt, in the midst of such chaos and political upheaval, to divert violence away from civilians. I have pointed to the differences, in the sense that one is about protecting the weak from the strong while the other, potentially, involves protecting the strong from the weak. In both cases we keep on being drawn back into the complex affairs of unstable regions and mismanaged states, where are to be found deep social and political cleavages and enduring conflicts that demand intensive diplomatic attention. In the end the central issue remains the same: whether to get involved in difficult and demanding parts of the world, accepting the drain on our resources, our energy and our political skills, on the firm understanding that if we do not these are not only places where people get viciously angry with each other but also provide havens and inspiration for those who are angry with us.

## Notes

1 Remarks by the President at the 2002 Graduation Exercise of the United States Military Academy, West Point, New York, 1 June 2002, at http://usinfo.state.gov/topical/pol/terror/02060201.htm.

2 President Bush's State of the Union Address, 29 January 2002, at http://usinfo.state.gov/topical/pol/terror/02012914.htm. On the difficulties faced by US military planners, see William Arkin, 'US Military; Planning an Iraqi War but Not an Outcome', *Los Angeles Times*, 5 May 2002.

3 Ivo Daalder and Michael O'Hanlon, 'Let's Cool Those Terrorism Alerts', *Newsday*, 23 March 2002.

4 A. Oppenheimer, 'Weapons of Mass Destruction: Radiological Devices', *Jane's Terrorism and Security Monitor*, May 2002. This notes that as early as 1993 bin Laden operatives tried and failed to buy enriched uranium, and in recent times appear to have been sold some useless material in the belief that it was weapons-grade.

5 The number was down from 2,000 when 426 had been counted. US State Department, Counterterrorism Office, *Patterns of Global Terrorism 2001*, May 2002, at http://www.state.gov/s/ct/rls/pgtrpt/2001.

6 *The Doctrine of International Community*, 22 April 1999, at http://www.number-10/public/info/index.html.

7 See e.g. the pre-election article by Bush's National Security Advisor, Condoleeza Rice, 'Promoting the National Interest', *Foreign Affairs*, vol. 79, no. 1, Jan.–Feb. 2000.

8 Address by the President to a Joint Session of Congress and the American People, 20 Sept. 2001: 'Every nation, in every region, now has a decision to make. Either

Lawrence Freedman

you are with us, or you are with the terrorists': http://usinfo.state.gov/topical/pol/terror/01092051.htm.
9 Michael Howard, 'What's in a Name? How to Fight Terrorism', *Foreign Affairs*, vol. 81, Jan.–Feb. 2002.
10 I took this line in Lawrence Freedman, 'The Third World War?', *Survival*, vol. 43, no. 4, Winter 2001.
11 Richard Caplan, 'International Diplomacy and the Crisis in Kosovo', *International Affairs*, vol. 74, no. 4, Oct. 1998, pp. 753–4.
12 Jeffrey D. Simon, *The Terrorist Trap*, Bloomington, Indiana University Press, 2001.

# [23]

# Finance Warfare as a Response to International Terrorism

MARTIN S. NAVIAS

FINANCE warfare emerged as a major instrument of anti-terrorist strategic operations almost immediately following the 11 September attacks in the United States. It drew upon legislative, regulatory and policing instruments already in place, though these had long been geared primarily to financial battles little connected with terrorist funding. The refinement and development of this stratagem as a means of combating international terror, its implementation and global integration, involve and continue to demand enormous efforts by political, financial and policing authorities.

To be sure, attacks upon an enemy's economic infrastructure and assets have always been elements of grand strategy. Economic targeting is a form of indirect approach whose object is to undermine the opposition's capacity for conducting operations by assaulting one of the key pillars of fighting power and political will. Finance warfare as it has emerged in the context of counterterrorist operations after 11 September is a form of economic warfare whose context is the global financial markets and whose aim is to constrain the enemy's capability both to generate funds and to shift monies across borders for the purposes of supporting and sustaining international operations. The institutions mobilised in this counterterrorist campaign are those very organisations that facilitate and underpin the global markets themselves. The legislative and regulatory means are the means deployed to counter non-political criminal money-laundering activities. Thus finance warfare has achieved a new salience since 11 September, but its strategic pedigree and the tools of its implementation are to be traced back prior to that infamous date.

The early financial emphasis of the broader counterterrorist campaign derived from the fact that the money trail leading from the hijackers not only helped establish their political origins but also served to expose all too clearly the vulnerabilities of the international banking system to terrorist fund generation, money laundering and general financial logistics. The 11 September atrocities were revealed to have been made possible by a sophisticated financial operation, one that relied at least partially on correspondent banking and alternative remittance systems, backed up by a diffuse network of legal and illicit associations consisting of an amalgam of private organisations, corporate shell companies and charitable bodies straddling the globe. The central hub of this network was located in the loose banking arrangements in a number of developing states in North Africa and the Gulf but extended to financial networks situated in Europe and North America.

MARTIN S. NAVIAS

The interconnectedness of the laxer, less regulated banking and finance frameworks in the developing world with the more orderly complexes in Europe and North America confirmed that internationally the financial system was vulnerable to penetration by terrorist organisations intent upon supporting worldwide operations, including operations in areas where financial controls were thought rigorous.

This chapter reviews a number of the main international, regional and national efforts undertaken both before and since 11 September to constrain terrorist exploitation of the international financial system and to assess continuities and discontinuities in method. In terms of regional and domestic approaches to the problem it will focus on various steps taken in Europe and in the United Kingdom in particular, but will show the linkages to developments in the United States. It will analyse some of the essential legislative and regulatory measures which have been adopted since the terrorist attacks and place them in the context of anti-money-laundering efforts before 11 September. In so doing it will outline the main parameters of operations but also seek to address the question of how measures which have until recently been geared in the main to constraining financial practices in the context of non-political criminal activities have been amended to meet the demands of what amounts to a politically and ideologically driven financing process.

## The immediate response: declaring financial war and freezing assets

Prior to the first ordnance being dropped on enemy positions in Afghanistan and well before substantial ground forces were deployed in theatre, financial war was publicly declared by the United States and its allies on international terrorism. The declaratory opening of a financial front against terrorists and their supporters, the explicit characterisation of financial methods as relevant techniques of combat and the drafting into the battle of international financial institutions can be traced to President Bush's executive order on terrorist financing, issued on 24 September, less than two weeks after the attacks on New York and Washington. 'Because of the pervasiveness and expansiveness of the financial foundation of foreign terrorists,' Bush argued, 'financial sanctions may be appropriate for those foreign persons that support or otherwise associate with these foreign terrorists.' The need existed, said the President, 'for further consultation and cooperation with, and sharing of information by United States and foreign financial institutions as an additional tool to enable the United States to combat the financing of terrorism.'[1]

This focus on financial countermeasures certainly served the expedient purpose of demonstrating resolve and commitment to a public expectant of imminent action at a time when military plans were still incubating. It was uncontroversial, as its core argument that finance underpinned terrorist operations and therefore needed to be constrained was well understood. In

© The Political Quarterly Publishing Co. Ltd. 2002

## FINANCE WARFARE AND INTERNATIONAL TERRORISM

terms of implementation the policy carried little attendant physical risk or danger, and in the short term at least involved the agreement and assistance of only the more amenable of like-thinking allies. Visible victories and apparent progress could be declared with rapidity.

From the start of the counterterrorist financing operations it was evident that while the focus was on al-Qaeda, the net was cast much wider and sought to capture not only operations supporting al-Qaeda but those of a broad range of Islamic and non-Islamic groups. Terrorist organisations were thus quickly identified and their bank accounts blocked. On 17 September the FBI provided a list of terrorist suspects to various banking supervisory agencies, while all banks operating in the United States were requested to report immediately on any transactions with the specified individuals. On 24 September the US government publicly identified twenty-seven such individuals and institutions, closing their bank accounts and freezing their assets. This was followed shortly thereafter by EU measures which sought to freeze funds held by a similar number of organisations and individuals believed to support terrorist financing activities and aimed at also ensuring that these funds could not readily be shifted around the EU banking system for purposes of evading the freeze. Various alternative remittance systems and charitable organisations believed to have links with terrorist organisations were shut. By 8 January 2002 the United States had frozen more than $33 million in assets belonging to more than 150 individuals and organisations, while a similar amount was frozen by European and other countries.

The US authorities had in fact been interested in identifying and freezing bin Laden's assets since the East Africa embassy bombings in 1998, but lack of political will and sense of urgency meant no steps had ever been taken towards this end. The freezing of terrorist funds after 11 September thus certainly represented an upgrading of financial efforts aimed at terrorist organisations, but it was short-term financial firefighting and was recognised as such. While the measures demonstrated national and international resolve and also cut off funds to terrorists, the amounts involved were relatively tiny, and the effects on terrorist financing capabilities—given their recognised sophistication and complexity as well as their extensive scope—could not be expected to be anything but negligible. What was needed was a more sustained and globally coordinated campaign that addressed systemic vulnerabilities in the international financial system and specifically targeted the generation and accumulation of funding by terrorist organisations, as well as their ability to launder funds and otherwise transfer monies across borders.

At an extraordinary summit in Brussels in October 2001, heads of the EU reached agreement on fast-track measures against terrorist funding. Specifically, the council of finance ministers emphasised the need 'to take the necessary measures to combat any form of financing for terrorist activities'. European countries were called upon not only to implement a framework decision on freezing terrorist assets but also to adopt a new and improved anti-money-laundering directive and to support global initiatives in this

Martin S. Navias

regard by signing and ratifying a UN convention on suppressing terrorist financing. In addition, the joint statement indicated that measures would be taken against states identified as having lax controls in relation to their financial systems such that those systems could be readily exploited by terrorist organisations. Concomitantly, EU justice and home affairs authorities agreed to cooperate better in the area of intelligence information exchange as to the sources of terrorist funding and to ensure that the banking system was not used for the transfer of terrorist funds. The European Central Bank made similar declaratory pronouncements. The intent was there to improve coordination and to begin upgrading regulatory controls at a variety of levels, as well as to start closing off regulatory loopholes that could be exploited for purposes of terrorist financing logistics.

## Systemic vulnerabilities exposed

Both immediate and medium-term financial responses to the 11 September attacks were conditioned by a recognition of the vulnerabilities in the financial system that made terrorist financing and ultimately terrorist operations possible. The focus on reining in correspondent banking relationships, shutting down alternative remittance systems and paying more attention to fundraising and disbursing organisations of a charitable or other legal nature came from a belated recognition that steps would need to be taken against such systems as they provided access to the North American and west European banking environment. As noted by US Senator Carl Levin in evidence before the Senate Committee on Banking, Housing and Urban Affairs on 26 September 2001, 'The evidence is clear that terrorist organisations are using our own financial institutions against us, and we need to understand our vulnerabilities and take new measures to protect ourselves from similar abuses down the road.'[2] The vulnerabilities were many, but three stood out: the problems posed by correspondent banking systems; challenges related to alternative remittance systems; and the use of legal entities for fundraising and disbursement purposes.

Correspondent banking systems clearly highlighted the vulnerability of Western national banking to external penetration. Correspondent banking involves the provision by one bank of financial services to another bank so as to move funds across borders or carry out a variety of other financial transactions. If, for example, a bank in Saudi Arabia had a client who wanted sterling in the United Kingdom, the Saudi bank would employ a bank in London with which it had a correspondent relationship to make sterling available in the United Kingdom. Undoubtedly, such relationships facilitate and ease movement of capital, but they clearly have their costs. A major weakness of the system was that at least prior to 11 September banks may not have always carried out proper due diligence procedure in respect of the correspondent bank with which they had a relationship, even if such a bank was located in a jurisdiction with known lax regulatory controls. By

FINANCE WARFARE AND INTERNATIONAL TERRORISM

'nesting' in a bank with a correspondent banking relationship in a targeted country, a terrorist can access the banking system of that country, a strategy that was facilitated by not only poor but in many cases effectively non-existent investigatory procedures exercised by banks over their correspondent relationships.

If such controls were less effective than expected or required in the formal banking sector, the whole purpose of the informal sector was to avoid them. The term 'alternative remittance systems' refers to the non-bank financial institutions that transfer funds for entities or individuals mainly through their own network. This is an essentially paperless system involving unregistered lenders in at least two countries prepared to move money across borders. As there are no official bank records or statements, there is no proper trail to the source of the funds. Groups such as terrorist organisations intent upon distancing themselves from their money and keeping the finance out of the formal regulated sector found such systems extremely useful. Jeffrey Robinson, for example, has shown how the *hawala* network operating between London and the Punjab and Kashmir has served not only to channel finance in relation to drug trafficking, but also to support Sikh and Kashmiri secessionists.[3]

It should be emphasised that not only was all this well known by Western banking and regulatory authorities prior to 11 September, but it was also well known before 11 September that al-Qaeda engaged in correspondent banking activity and alternative remittance systems as means of transferring funds across borders in order to support terrorist operations. Indeed, by the late 1990s it was common knowledge that bin Laden's main area of technical specialisation was his experience of money transfer techniques in support of terrorist attacks, techniques which had been honed during his involvement in the war against the Russians in Afghanistan and conflicts in East Africa and the Balkans, as well as in relation to the financing of numerous other cross-border terrorist strikes.[4]

The importance of correspondent banking to the al-Qaeda network can be seen by examining the case of the al Shamal Islamic Bank in Khartoum. The bank was capitalised by bin Laden himself in the early 1990s when he provided an estimated $50 million to secure a major shareholding in the new institution. Foreign currency accounts were set up at al Shamal for a number of companies belonging to bin Laden, including the al Hijra Construction and Development Co. Ltd, which was involved in major construction work in Sudan, and a company called Wadi al Aqiq, which served as a holding company for various legitimate businesses including furniture, bakery and cattle breeding. These accounts appear to have been constantly replenished from sources in the Gulf. Then, by relying on al Shamal's correspondent banking relationships with a variety of reputable institutions with global reach—including in the United States, Citibank, American Express and Arab American Bank (since acquired by the National Bank of Egypt); in Africa, Standard Bank of South Africa; in Europe,

MARTIN S. NAVIAS

KommerzBank in Germany and Crédit Lyonnais in Switzerland; in the Middle East, Saudi Holland in Jiddah (in which ABN Amro had a 40 per cent stake); and in Asia, ING Bank in Indonesia—all of which had their own various correspondent banking relationships, al-Qaeda was able to move money rapidly and relatively unimpeded around the world.[5]

Alternative remittance systems were also important to al-Qaeda's ability to move funds. In relation to a *hawala* known as al Tarqua, a US government source stated that 'we believe that al-Qaeda has been skimming off that [*hawala*] network.' Al-Qaeda was thought to have actually established the network and funded it, as well as getting a percentage of every transaction that it made. Here the *hawala* served the dual purpose of moving finances as well as generating funds.

Finally, and very significantly, bin Laden set up another separate financial system for fund generation and transference, grounded in legal and quasi-legal charitable organisations, businesses and educational foundations. These organisations were originally based upon the al-Qaeda Foundation, a charity established by bin Laden in the 1980s whose purpose was to steer funds to Islamic fighters in Afghanistan and Pakistan. As Bodansky has noted, 'this quasi legal system also quickly evolved into a multitude of seemingly unrelated charities and multilayered organizations that interacted and moved people and funds back and forth as security authorities in the West struggled to untangle the web.' As will be described in greater detail below, a key factor in relation to this system was that it circumvented most banking and anti-money-laundering regulatory controls as they existed during the 1990s.

That a general knowledge of systemic vulnerabilities and an appreciation of the efforts international terrorist organisations were making to exploit these vulnerabilities did not result in successful actions specifically to identify terrorist financing operations and shut them down is partially to be explained by lack of political will at the national level, coupled with bureaucratic inertia when it came to implementing regulatory reforms and the fact that existing anti-money-laundering systems were not particularly appropriate to the particularities of the terrorist financing phenomenon.

## The anti-money-laundering roots of the finance war against global terrorism

The roots of the finance war against global terrorism are to be found not in specific anti-terrorist financing measures but in the anti-money-laundering initiatives adopted globally, regionally and nationally during the 1990s. Prior to 11 September, anti-money-laundering procedures were certainly receiving increasing attention from the then G7 countries, though the motivation was not primarily counterterrorism. More significant in making the coordination of anti-money-laundering efforts a major policy objective were the declining

### FINANCE WARFARE AND INTERNATIONAL TERRORISM

revenues arising from taxation and increasing recognition of the massive amount of funds being laundered from the proceeds of criminal drug dealing. It was recognised that the opportunities for criminals to hide the illegal origins of their funds were being radically enhanced by the rapid and apparently inexorable move towards integration of international banking and capital markets. According to the IMF these circumstances were resulting in between $600 billion and $1.5 trillion of funds (equal to 2–5 per cent of global GDP) being laundered each year.

Money laundering is defined as the process by which the proceeds of crime are converted into assets that appear to have legitimate origins so that they can be retained permanently or recycled to fund further crimes. Technically, money laundering involves three distinct stages. First, there is placement— the process whereby unlawful proceeds are inserted into legitimate financial institutions, whether by means of wire transfers, actual deposits or a variety of other means; second, there is layering—the process whereby the launderer begins the intricate task of separating the proceeds of the criminal activity from their origin by means of layers of complex and sophisticated financial transactions; and third, there is integration, the process whereby the launderer employs transactions which appear legitimate to disguise the illicit proceeds. It is by way of a combination of these processes that the monetary proceeds derived from illicit activities are transformed into funds with an apparently legal source. An element of criminality is thus central to this definition of money laundering, and therefore, not surprisingly, anti-money-laundering initiatives in both their regulatory and bureaucratic expressions were from the start grounded in efforts to contain non-political criminal activity.

The institutional centrepiece of the bureaucratic mechanism driving international efforts to tackle money laundering is the Financial Action Task Force on Money Laundering (FATF), an independent international organisation set up in 1989 by the G7 countries with its secretariat in the OECD. It has twenty-nine member states plus the European Commission and the Gulf Cooperation Council, representing all the main financial centres in North America, Europe, Asia and the Middle East, who band together for the purposes of investigating means to combat money laundering in all its forms. FATF coordinates global anti-money-laundering activities by working together with a variety of regional and international organisations. At the same time FATF helped to set up and coordinates anti-money-laundering actions with a number of regional anti-money-laundering bodies located in the Caribbean, central and eastern Europe, Asia and the Pacific, southern and eastern Africa, and South America. Initially, efforts focused on criminal activity such as organised crime gangs and drug cartels and little attention was paid to the specifics of terrorist financing, though the general prescriptions obviously had an impact.

In 1990 FATF published the so-called Forty Recommendations (later amended in 1996) for all states and territories to adopt; these are now

MARTIN S. NAVIAS

regarded as constituting the appropriate international standard for anti-money-laundering behaviour. They include requirements for states to criminalise money-laundering activities, to adopt customer identification and record-keeping practices, and to commit themselves to cooperating with other states and international organisations in anti-money-laundering activities. FATF members are committed to the implementation of these recommendations, and adherence is monitored by way of a combination of self-assessment and mutual evaluation, focusing on the implementation of the key legal, financial and international cooperation measures as expressed in the twenty-eight recommendations that require specific action by member states.

The nature of the problem was identified in the 2001 FATF annual review, which stated that 'the limited statistics available suggest that money laundering is actively investigated and prosecuted in a limited number of countries, but elsewhere, the offence is not frequently prosecuted.' In addition to this general implementation problem, which impacts on anti-money-laundering activities including efforts against terrorist financing, the particular point was noted that while the recommendations were properly implemented in relation to banks, they were not always applied in relation to non-bank institutions such as money remittance companies. This latter weakness appears to have been readily exploited by terrorists.

A major task of FATF which, while originally not directly responding to the terrorist financing challenge, undoubtedly has had implications for anti-terrorist-financing measures is the FATF identification of what are known as non-compliant countries and territories (NCCT). These NCCTs are jurisdictions which do not cooperate in combating money laundering, and FATF members are obliged to take financial countermeasures against them. FATF currently blacklists as NCCTs nineteen jurisdictions (including Russia, Egypt, Ukraine, Nigeria, Guatemala, the Philippines, Dominica, Indonesia, Hungary and Lebanon). In order to be removed from the blacklist the NCCT must be able to demonstrate that it has undertaken specific actions in financial supervision, criminal law, customer identification, suspicious transaction reporting requirements and international cooperation. Not surprisingly, the NCCT focus has sometimes strained relationships between FATF and regional organisations, thus demonstrating the political/ideological element that complicates proper implementation of FATF anti-money-laundering prescriptions—something that is particularly acute in relation to political terrorist as opposed to non-political criminal organisations.

For FATF recommendations to have bite, implementation and enforcement must be effected at the national level. Two jurisdictions which have above average FATF records are the United States and the United Kingdom. In both the focus has until recently been on criminal rather than terrorist activities.

The United States undoubtedly possesses the most complex and diverse anti-money-laundering system in the world.[6] As noted in a FATF report, there exist in the United States 'a large number of law enforcement and regulatory

### FINANCE WARFARE AND INTERNATIONAL TERRORISM

agencies, [a] huge number of financial institutions, [and] a diversity of federal and state laws'. The anti-criminal focus of this system is certainly evident, but not surprising since about 60–80 per cent of federal money-laundering cases in the United States involve narcotics proceeds—though significant proceeds are also generated by offences connected with organised, white-collar crime and foreign crimes. Prior to 11 September, efforts to enhance the system included measures such as a new and improved 'suspicious activity' reporting system, modifications to the currency transaction reporting system, new funds transfer record-keeping rules, and efforts to encourage improved cooperation between government and industry and between states: measures which, it can be argued, improved the United States' capability to deter, detect and punish terrorist money-laundering activities. Where, however, the United States approach remained weak—due to, *inter alia*, the pressures of both banks and civil liberties groups—was in the area of client and beneficial ownership identification, a lacuna that terrorist groups could exploit. It was also recognised that effective anti-money-laundering measures needed to be extended to non-bank financial institutions which, as noted above, were of the kind exploited by terrorist organisations.

To point out all this is not to argue that the US authorities did not recognise that terrorist groups laundered money. Indeed, in the Terrorism Prevention Act of 1996 the list of money-laundering predicate offences was extended to cover terrorism as well. To make such an extension is, however, not the same as adopting specifically sensitive counterterrorist financing measures. Consequently one government analyst writing in May 2001 described money laundering as being defined 'Legally . . . as any attempt to engage in a monetary transaction that involves criminally derived property. To convict, prosecutors must show that the defendant engaged in financial transactions . . . that involved funds from a "specified unlawful activity".'[7] This, as will be argued below, was not necessarily appropriate to the problem posed by terrorist financing.

While not as complex as that of the United States, the anti-money-laundering systems of the Europeans and the United Kingdom in particular reflected similar values and priorities. Specifically, British efforts aimed at countering terrorist financing also had their foundations in anti-money-laundering legislation primarily dedicated to constraining the activities of criminal organisations such as drug cartels (legislation, for example, such as the Drug Trafficking Act 1994, which makes it an offence to conceal or transfer the proceeds of drug trafficking) rather than global terrorist networks. Indeed, prior to the Proceeds of Crime Bill (see below) becoming law, the centrepiece of UK primary legislation dealing with money laundering has for some time been the Criminal Justice Act 1988 as amended by the Criminal Justice Act 1993. In respect of money laundering the legislation focused on the handling of the proceeds of crime and creates offences relating thereto. The core offences were those in relation to the knowing acquisition of proceeds of criminal conduct, abetting arrangements facilitating the retention of proceeds

MARTIN S. NAVIAS

of criminal conduct, failure to disclose the provision of financial assistance for criminal conduct and the tipping off of money launderers of any investigation into their activities. The nuts and bolts of constraining money laundering in the United Kingdom are centred on the Money Laundering Regulations 1993, issued pursuant to the 1993 Criminal Justice Act, and in continued implementation into English law of the 1st EU Directive on Money Laundering. These regulations apply to institutions such as banks and building societies carrying on relevant financial business and require the institutions to deter money launderers from using the financial system and catch those that do. The three main methods employed are: (1) the 'know your customer' requirement, which demands that the financial institution be able to identify positively the original source of funding that is entering their business; (2) the identification and reporting of transactions that appear to the financial institution to be suspicious; and (3) the need for the financial institution to consider the requirements of subsequent money-laundering investigations by ensuring the creation of an audit trail. Failure to comply with these requirements is a criminal offence.

There is no doubt that these methods and rules, while not originating in an anti-terrorist framework, provided an appropriate base for dealing specifically with terrorist money laundering. In theory they should have helped identify terrorist funding and made its prosecution easier, though it should be noted—certainly on the basis of experience with the al-Qaeda network—that of all the organisations employing money-laundering techniques, terrorist organisations are probably the most trained and adept at disguising their own origins as well as those of their funds.

Unfortunately, even in relation to their traditional objectives the impact of anti-money-laundering initiatives has been questionable. Studies have shown that outside the United States very little wealth has been interdicted and permanently put beyond the reach of criminals. For example, it has been noted by one UK legal academic that only a third of cases where there has been a conviction on indictment for a crime that involves a profit motive result in a confiscation order. Furthermore, the amount confiscated is usually extremely small. In cases not involving drugs it has been estimated that the sums taken out of criminal circulation are less than 0.0001 per cent of the amounts that theoretically are subject to the law.[8] While this in itself does not indicate that the actual impact on the targeted organisation is negligible, it must raise questions as to the usefulness of the method itself—especially if it is to be used against terrorist organisations whose objectives are not ultimately financial gain and who are presumably less sensitive to financial setbacks.

Part of the problem can no doubt be traced to laxities and inefficiencies in implementation of existing legislation due to complexity, confusion or tardiness rather than to any conceptual failure inherent in the legislation itself. However, at the same time, while the smuggling of illicit narcotics and the laundering of the extensive profits that result from that lucrative trade are international crimes par excellence, they differ in their functioning from practices of global terrorism in that the genesis, motivations and objectives of the former are at root neither political or ideological in character but rather mercantile. For terrorists, on the other hand, the pecuniary consequences of their actions are secondary, while the methods by which they raise and distribute finance sometimes differ from those of criminal organisations.

## The terrorist financing typology

The question then arises as to whether relevant statute, regulation and bureaucratic structure primarily geared to constraining financial practices in the context of non-political criminality are those best suited and most responsive to the demands of what amounts to a politically driven finance process which is both broader and independent of money laundering as presently construed. An analysis of the financial underpinning of the 11 September attacks demonstrated that the financial war against terrorist financing was at least partially being hampered by the inappropriateness of the tools at hand. For money laundering as a concept does not encapsulate the problems posed to the integrity of the international financial system by terrorists, while extant anti-money-laundering measures could not cope with their operational strategies.

There is little dispute that major terrorist operations involve a significant financial element. Terrorist organisations are of course known to tap into illegal sources of funding such as drug trafficking, extortion, kidnapping, robbery, fraud, gambling and smuggling of contraband goods. The Peruvian Shining Path has long funded its activities with sales of cocaine, and other groups such as the Revolutionary Armed Forces of Colombia, the National Liberation Army and United Self Defense Forces of Colombia have engaged in similar activities. The advantages of drug trading were not unknown to al-Qaeda. In this, terrorist funding practices are indistinguishable from those of various large-scale non-political criminal organisations. In theory, then, there should be little difficulty in expanding the scope of domestic and international anti-money-laundering measures and other relevant legislation to cover the funding and laundering activities of terrorist networks. Indeed, there is an argument that there exists a critical nexus between terrorism and organised crime, and that many of the skills and equipment needed to combat the financing of organised crime are applicable in combating the financing of international terrorism; all that is required is improved coordination and implementation.

While such a nexus does of course exist—methods of generating and transferring funds may in some circumstances be similar—and enhanced coordination between agencies and governments and improved implementation will lead to better results, the fact remains that there are significant differences between terrorist groups and criminal organisations engaged in money laundering. One key factor here is the important role played by

MARTIN S. NAVIAS

'legitimate sources' of financing within the broader funding operations of terrorist organisations. This analysis, if it is correct, or indeed even partially correct, immediately calls into question the relevance of anti-money-laundering legislation as a tool for combating terrorist financing as such legislation is essentially based on the assumption that the funds in question are illicit. Thus, for example, where sources of funding are legal there may be few if any indicators that would identify any individual financial transaction, or even a series of such transactions, as being linked to terrorist operations.

Three sources of funding do appear unique to terrorist organisations and serve to complicate the picture severely from a control point of view in that they do not in themselves constitute criminal activity in a domestic context.

First, there is the issue of state financial sponsorship of the terrorist organisation. There are a number of examples of nation-states in the developing world providing support and succour to terrorist organisations for political and/or military reasons. Indeed, each year the US State Department provides Congress with a list of these countries and there may well be others. This support is given in the form not only of training and logistics but also of finance—and not only in supplying funds but also in providing financial services and integrating state and terrorist financial services (for example, in the cases of al-Qaeda and the government of Sudan and the former Taleban government of Afghanistan) or using state financial services to cloak those of the terrorist organisation. Obviously, such action breaks no domestic law, and by providing the full range of complex and integrated state-controlled financial services to support the terrorist organisation large sums of money may readily be integrated on behalf of the terrorist organisation into the international financial system, whether the origin of that funding be the state itself or some other legal or illicit source. The use of state apparatus both to provide and to launder money poses serious challenges to efforts aimed at constraining such financing, both in terms of foreign policy considerations and in terms of actual control mechanisms.

Second, as noted above in relation to al-Qaeda, terrorist organisations can rely on donations and contributions from supporters as a means of funding activities. Because of their political and military objectives, terrorist groups are able to attract funds from supporters—some central, some peripheral—of the organisation. This is unlike criminal organisations, which where they seek to acquire such funds need to do so by coercive techniques such as protection rackets which are themselves illegal (though this is not to argue that coercion of some kind is not present when terrorists generate funds, for example by so-called 'revolutionary taxes'). Significantly, such funds may be generated in terrorist host states or in states that are the target of the terrorist group's activities or are at least hostile to them. In this latter situation, the resort to funding is often abetted by the terrorist organisation's strategy of disguising (from the authorities and in some cases even from the contributors) the true object of the finance. This is done by differentiating between political and

### Finance Warfare and International Terrorism

military arms of the organisation, the political wing often having a legal basis, or by creating charitable or educational foundations which appear as the object of the contribution (this often being at least partially the case) and which also act as a means of siphoning the funds to the true object, the terrorist organisation itself. By adopting such techniques terrorist groups seek to minimise the suspicion and intervention of the local authorities, escape asset-freezing measures, take advantage of various tax concessions and also establish a means useful in any later money-laundering process. In addition, and importantly, as noted above in relation to al-Qaeda, the establishment of charitable and educational organisations serves the additional purpose of enhancing local support for the terrorist group by actually providing services of the kind to which it is ostensibly directed. Anti-money-laundering techniques have not always been entirely relevant to such strategies, being as they are directed at activities more ostensibly and unqualifiedly criminal. The legal funding approach is beyond the radar screen of much of the anti-money-laundering legislation in place before 11 September.

Third, terrorist organisations may engage in legitimate business activities for purposes of raising and distributing funds. While other criminal organisations may of course seek to move from illegitimate activities into legitimate business activities for both financial and security reasons, it is sometimes the case with terrorist organisations that the businesses themselves may be legitimate from the start and that only the purposes to which the funds generated are ultimately put are illegal. The obvious example here is the al-Qaeda network, whose source of funding was originally based not upon the proceeds of crime but upon a legitimate bin Laden family inheritance (estimated at anywhere between $50 million and $300 million) and legitimate construction, engineering and other corporate concerns. Again, traditional criminal and anti-money-laundering approaches have not been best suited to dealing with such kinds of activities as their focus is elsewhere.

The problem lies not only in the different sources of terrorist funding but in the purposes to which the funding is put and the manner in which it is done. The funding needed to finance even a large-scale terrorist operation may be small and the associated transactions supporting such operations may not be complex. Much of the funding received by the 11 September hijackers was carried out in transactions valued at under $10,000. Some terrorists were ostensibly students who, it appeared, were receiving money to support their studies. The transactions would not be either quantitatively or by category of the type requiring, without other indicators, additional scrutiny by those financial institutions involved in the transaction. Indeed, it should be noted that a US bank filed reports to the relevant authorities on transactions undertaken by the leader of the 11 September hijackers, Mohammed Atta, but these reports did not lead to an investigation.

As argued above, it would be wrong to state that the international community was unaware of the particular need to combat this specific typology of financing. The UN definitely played a role in this area throughout

MARTIN S. NAVIAS

the latter half of the 1990s. The Declaration on the Occasion of the Fiftieth Anniversary of the United Nations contained in General Assembly Resolution 50/6 of 24 October 1995 referred to the problem; General Assembly Resolution 49/60 of 9 December 1994 and its annex on the Declaration on Measures to Eliminate International Terrorism included a general condemnation of terrorist activities and called for a review of international legal measures to combat its outbreak. It provided the framework for approaching terrorist financing issues. Most significantly, General Assembly Resolution 51/210 of 17 December 1996 recognised the specific nature of terrorist financing itself when in paragraph 3 it called upon states to take appropriate domestic legislative measures to prevent the financing of terrorism, not only where it was linked to drug dealing, arms trafficking and other criminal methods, but also where the financing was associated with ostensibly legal and non-criminal institutions of a charitable, cultural or social nature. General Assembly resolutions were additionally backed up by those of the Security Council. UN Security Council Resolution 1373 (2001) called for member states to freeze or block terrorist funds or assets.

This UN focus was given primary expression in 1999 in the International Convention for the Suppression of the Financing of Terrorism.[9] The convention aimed less at defining the specific typology of terrorist financing than at enhancing cooperation between states in adopting effective measures specifically in relation to terrorist financing and its suppression through the prosecution and punishment of its perpetrators. It called upon state parties to adopt domestic measures for the purposes of identifying, detecting, freezing or seizing funds used for committing the (defined) terrorist offences; and also to ensure that financial institutions within their territories 'utilise the most efficient measures' for the identification of their customers and to 'pay special attention to unusual or suspicious transactions'. It further required state parties to establish regulations prohibiting the opening of accounts for unidentified holders or beneficiaries, and to rely upon verification procedures in relation to clients and legal entities. 'Unusual large transactions and unusual patterns of transactions, which have no apparent economic or obviously lawful purpose', were to be reported to the relevant authorities, while financial institutions were to maintain for at least five years all relevant records of their transactions. Significantly, there was also a demand that there be licensing of all money-transmission agencies.

In 2001, prior to the September attacks, and for the first time, FATF too started to take an interest in terrorist financing. It began to investigate the terrorist financing typology and how specifically terrorist groups moved or concealed their funds. One of the main objects of the investigation was to determine whether the reliance by terrorists on legal sources of funding impacted on countries' ability to employ existing anti-money-laundering measures to target terrorist-related money laundering. The conclusions of these discussions revealed a definite lack of consensus. Material discussed by the experts appeared to indicate that there were more similarities than

FINANCE WARFARE AND INTERNATIONAL TERRORISM

differences in the sources of funding for both types of groups. The report noted that 'there is little difference in the sources used for both terrorist and organised crime groups.'[10] Of the ten identified sources of funding of terrorist organisations, six (drug trafficking, extortion and kidnapping, robbery, fraud, gambling, and smuggling and trafficking in counterfeit goods) were identical to those funding criminal organisations. Four, however, were unique: direct sponsorship by states, contributions and donations, sale of publications and funds derived from legitimate activities. The 2001 report further argued that there was a decline in state sponsorship of terrorism (though no evidence was made public of this assertion) and that in fact 'terrorist groups have increasingly resorted to criminal activity to raise the funds needed to support their activities.' Less controversially, the report argued that there were similarities in money-laundering methods between terrorists and criminal groups.

Some FATF experts argued that what terrorists were in fact doing did not actually constitute money laundering per se as the source of funding was not criminal. Following therefrom it was reported that 'There [was] no agreement on whether anti-money-laundering laws could (or should) play a direct role in the fight against terrorism' as '[s]ome countries, for example, are not able to use anti-money-laundering legislation for tracking or restraining suspected terrorist money if the source of the funds was a voluntary contribution and not a criminal act.'[11] In addition, there was a recognition by FATF of the political problem of definitions as to what constituted a terrorist.

In the final analysis there appeared significant differences of opinion among experts as to how to categorise and deal with the problem of terrorist financing. The details of the discussions were not made public, but there was no disguising the fact that consensus was lacking. Thus it was reported that 'Certain of the FATF experts were of the opinion that terrorist related money laundering is a distinct sub-category of money laundering. Others held the opposite view and believed that terrorism can be adequately targeted under existing laws.' As we shall see, this latter approach was to change dramatically following the events of 11 September.

Of course, it was one thing passing UN resolutions and FATF proposals which recognised the particular nature of terrorist financing and called attention to its particular attributes. It was another to put these, with all their imperfections, into action both domestically and internationally. The events of 11 September were to focus attention on the terrorist typology in a dramatic fashion and to act as a powerful spur to the implementation of ideas that were already being considered.

## Enhancing global cooperation

The need to focus specifically on terrorist financing as a specific typology and to develop particular countermeasures to deal with the terrorist financing threat was given obvious urgency by the events of 11 September. Previous

MARTIN S. NAVIAS

debates as to whether existing laws were adequate for the purpose of dealing with terrorist financing or whether in fact such measures should be used at all to combat terrorist financing were rapidly resolved. Problems of definition relating to who or what constituted a terrorist group were in many cases pushed aside—at least temporarily and perhaps superficially—as the United States forced through its own definitions of terrorist organisations. Both the EU and the G8 finance ministers recommended that the lead in the global campaign against terrorist financing be taken once more by FATF and within the context of international effort already taken to combat money laundering.

At an extraordinary plenary on the financing of terrorism held in Washington on 29 and 30 October 2001, FATF delegates demonstrated their intention to use existing anti-money-laundering initiatives as a basis for tackling terrorist financing while at the same time implicitly recognising the inadequacy of the measures for dealing with the specific problem. It was now unequivocally stated that 'FATF [has] expanded its mission beyond money laundering. It will now focus its energy and expertise on the world-wide effort to specifically combat terrorist financing.' An additional 'Eight Special Recommendations' setting new international standards to combat terrorist financing were adopted by FATF and were to be appended to the existing Forty Recommendations. These new recommendations not only committed FATF members to be more expeditious in terms of adopting and enforcing new legislation and enhancing cooperation with other states, but broadened the scope of the regulatory ambit by specifically targeting terrorist financing in terms of funds generation and transfer. At their core was a recognition that terrorists may rely upon legal sources of funding but at the same time utilise financial networks in similar ways to other criminal groups. Specifically, FATF members are now called upon to ratify and implement the 1999 UN International Convention for the Suppression of the Financing of Terrorism, as well as relevant UN Security Council Resolutions; initiate domestic legislation to criminalise terrorist financing, with such offences to be designated predicate offences for money laundering; freeze and confiscate terrorist assets and the assets of their supporters; require financial institutions within their jurisdictions to report suspicious transactions linked to terrorism; commit themselves to engage in cooperation with other countries' law enforcement agencies and financial regulators in terrorist financing investigations; apply anti-money-laundering controls to alternative remittance systems; improve customer identification data transmitted by wire transfers; and take measures to ensure that organisations, especially non-profit bodies, are not abused by terrorist groups.

In November 2001 FATF typology experts meeting in New Zealand sought to provide to financial institutions a means 'to detect transactions potentially related to terrorists and terrorist groups, as well as the persons and entities that support them'. It was intended that the outcome of their discussions would inform the ongoing review of the Forty Recommendations. The substance of their view prior to 11 September was not, however, changed.

## Finance Warfare and International Terrorism

The experts continued to reaffirm the view that state sponsorship of terrorism was declining, but without publicly providing evidence for that assertion. Personal wealth was recognised as a source of terrorist financing, but no example other than that of bin Laden was publicly provided. The role of legitimate sources of finance was emphasised, though it was noted that this varied according to the terrorist group and whether the source of funds was in the same geographical location as the terrorist acts. The list of potential legal sources of funding of terrorist groups was expanded and included collection of membership dues and/or subscriptions, sales of publications, speaking tours, cultural and social events, door-to-door solicitation within the community, appeals to wealthy members of the community and donations based upon a portion of personal earnings. According to one expert present, the most effective means of raising funds in his jurisdiction was through community solicitation and fundraising. Examples of legitimate businesses supporting terrorists included publishing, food production, construction and computers. Also reaffirmed was the view that terrorist groups use the same laundering methods as criminal organisations. More specifically, terrorists were relying on cash smuggling, purchases of various types of monetary instruments, structured deposits to or withdrawals from bank accounts, use of debit and credit cards, wire transfers and reliance on *hawala* systems. It was recognised that the identification of terrorists by means of suspicious transactions would be very difficult and that financial institutions would need to be provided with 'other intelligence' as well in order for them to make identifications.

These and other steps taken by FATF received widespread international support. In Europe the need to counter terrorist finance began permeating a wide range of economic discussions. Thus, for example, a commitment was made by the European council of finance ministers (ECOFIN) to reach political agreement on a new proposed market abuse directive 'paying particular attention to the financing of terrorism when it examines the proposed directive'. According to internal market commissioner Bolkestein, this approach 'would be a significant step towards reinforcing safeguards against market abuse, including by terrorists'. A new EU money laundering directive is also construed as having a counter-terrorist-financing objective as it expands the range of predicate offences and seeks to impose additional requirements on professionals working outside the financial services sectors (such as auditors, lawyers and estate agents) whose financing services may be used by terrorists. These professionals will now need to comply with requirements relating to client identification, the keeping of relevant records and the reporting to the relevant authorities of suspicious transactions. This has been made necessary by the fact that as banks have become more stringent in relation to anti-money-laundering controls, money launderers have turned to less regulated sections of the financial services industry such as professionals. Again according to Bolkestein, 'The new directive will be a crucially important measure in the fight against the financing of terrorism and

MARTIN S. NAVIAS

organised crime. [It] will set an international benchmark for the fight against money laundering.'

Certainly, since 11 September urgency has been given to EU efforts in relation to constraining terrorist financing. This can also be seen in ongoing steps, *inter alia*, to extend Europol's mandate to include all types of money laundering, irrespective of the predicate offence underlying the laundering activity; to improve cooperation between national financial intelligence services; and to develop a protocol to the EU Mutual Legal Assistance Convention which would among other matters deal with the vexed issue of banking secrecy and money-laundering reporting. The EU, however, cannot itself monitor compliance with anti-terrorist money-laundering efforts, which has to be carried out at the national level.

## Upgrading domestic regulation

The UN and FATF recommendations set the tone and direction for national efforts aimed at reducing the vulnerability of domestic financial systems to terrorist manipulation. Anti-money-laundering legislation was supplemented and buttressed by steps taken specifically to deal with terrorist financing.

In the United States the USA Patriot Act, signed into law by President Bush on 26 October, sought to abet existing US anti-money-laundering measures by targeting terrorist financing in particular. Various other pieces of legislation are currently being reviewed by the House of Representatives and the Senate in support of this objective. The general thrust of the US approach involves allowing for the tracking of information in relation to accounts of foreign persons if there are suspicions that such persons are involved in terrorist financing. Long-arm jurisdiction is established over foreign money launderers. There is also a greater focus on correspondent bank accounts, with requirements for far more enhanced due diligence by domestic US banks when opening correspondent accounts for offshore entities, especially banks situated in jurisdictions where it is known there are in place weak anti-money-laundering controls. This has been complemented by efforts on the part of customs to target *halawas* and by the US Treasury better to track and monitor international terrorist financing. FATF recommendations therefore play a central role in helping US financial institutions prevent, detect and report instances of terrorist and other money laundering.

In the United Kingdom, there already existed prior to 11 September a stream of legislation that focused directly on terrorist groups but which for many years was aimed primarily though not exclusively at Irish terrorism. The key legislation was for some time the Prevention of Terrorism (Temporary Provisions) Act 1989 (as amended by the Criminal Justice Act 1993). This was replaced by the Terrorism Act 2000 which has been used *inter alia* to implement the UN International Convention for the Suppression of the Financing of Terrorism and which was in turn amended by the Anti-Terrorism, Crime and Security Act 2001. This latter new Act includes

### FINANCE WARFARE AND INTERNATIONAL TERRORISM

measures to give police powers to freeze funds under investigation, monitor accounts and seize assets. It also incorporated some of the provisions in the Proceeds of Crime Bill, including the negligence test.

The Proceeds of Crime Bill, which at the time of writing is in legislative passage, is arguably even more significant from the perspective of the finance war against international terrorism. The bill does not amend the 1993 Money Laundering Regulations but consolidates provisions in the Drug Trafficking Act and the Criminal Justice Act. Legislation as currently drafted applies only to laundering the proceeds of serious crime, but this is to be widened to include any criminal conduct. One of the bill's most important contributions, however, is its emphasis on suspicious transaction reporting requirements and its attempt to increase the importance and seriousness accorded to such requirements in financial institutions. It does this by the establishment of a negligence test in relation to failing to report cases where a person has 'reasonable grounds for knowing or suspecting that another person is engaged in money laundering'. An individual who fails to report such suspicions (in the context of reasonable grounds showing that he or she *should* have known that a money-laundering offence was being committed) to a money-laundering reporting officer who would then pass the information on to the National Criminal Intelligence Service (NCIS) could be subject to the imposition of a five-year custodial sentence—a severe sanction indeed. It is irrelevant that the person who should have reported the activity did not actually know that money laundering was taking place. It is, of course, hoped that the authorities will be able to absorb and process increased numbers of suspicious transaction reports, which can now be expected to rise substantially as financial institutions submit defensively.

New legislation has also been complemented by the introduction of new regulatory structures, though again plans for this were already in place prior to 11 September. Certainly for some time efforts were being undertaken in the United Kingdom to modernise the regulatory framework and to include within the new and strengthened regulator's objectives the goal of reducing financial crime. The new regulatory activities of the Financial Services Authority (FSA) are set out in the Financial Services and Markets Act 2000, which came into force on 1 December 2001. In line with the regulatory objective of reducing financial crime, a specific focus on money laundering was also introduced, the significance of which was reinforced by the terrorist attacks. Under section 146 of the Financial Services and Markets Act 2000 the FSA was given the responsibility to make relevant rules for the purposes of the prevention and detection of money laundering. It was also tasked with monitoring compliance by banks and other authorised financial institutions with respect to money-laundering matters. Specifically, financial crime is defined in the new Act to include fraud and dishonesty, misconduct and misuse of information relating to a financial market, and handling of the proceeds of crime. Failure to comply with these rules is a regulatory offence and the FSA can impose fines, withdraw authorisation or publicly censure the

Martin S. Navias

relevant party. At the same time the 1993 Money Laundering Regulations remain in force and the FSA now has the authority to prosecute for breaches of these regulations. The FSA is certainly cognisant of the particular problems posed by terrorist financing; indeed, 'within the FSA the term "money laundering" is now short-hand for money laundering and terrorist finance.'

Bureaucratic and specifically intelligence capabilities are being enhanced in terms of both funding and interdepartmental coordination. In October 2001 it was announced that the NCIS would focus increasingly on the specific issue of terrorist financing. Furthermore, a new 'multi-agency terrorist finance unit' would be set up within the NCIS. This financial intelligence unit would be backed by 'additional special branch investigative resources' and would employ academic, financial and commercial expertise to review various relevant banking regulatory matters. In February it was announced that the Treasury is to chair a money-laundering advisory committee to oversee the UK's anti-laundering strategy. New anti-terrorist financing legislation and regulation are to be given teeth.

## Conclusion

Despite all these massive national and international efforts, there continue to be reports that terrorist fund generation capabilities remain in place. Thus, for example, there are indications that numbers of *halawas* are still able to function outside national control, while accounts and funds in various jurisdictions, although identified, remain active. Nor is there as yet any suggestion that national intelligence authorities have a full grasp of either the scale or the scope of terrorist financing networks and practices.

The response to the terrorist attacks on the United States involved the creation not only of international military and political coalitions but of a global financial coalition as well. It was recognised from the start that the goal of constraining terrorist fund generation and distribution demanded a level of international cooperation far greater than that required even at the military and diplomatic levels, where disparities in military and political power allowed Washington a more generous freedom of action. National unilateralism in such a finance war, even by the strongest economic power, could never be effective in the context of interconnected global capital markets that increasingly bypass national boundaries and limit the interventionist efforts of local authorities.

Tensions as a result of unilateralism exist but have never had the significance they attained in the military and political spheres. Conversely, the requirement for effective global cooperation has made counterterrorist finance warfare just as strong as its weakest national links. Technical problems stem from the inability of many states actually to identify, control and enforce measures against terrorist financing in their less regulated financial systems, though these difficulties are in many (though not all) cases being addressed with US and European assistance. The conceptual problems are

76

## FINANCE WARFARE AND INTERNATIONAL TERRORISM

obviously more serious and are linked to the definitional issues that inevitably arise whenever there are attempts to identify and categorise what constitutes terrorism. Without agreement as to such definitions effective cooperation at the financial level spheres is difficult, as it becomes subject to other, more powerful, political and ideological considerations.

Disputes between the US and various Middle Eastern and Islamic countries are unsurprisingly the most public of these definitional debates. For example, there are arguments in relation to the desirability of shutting off Hizbollah funds, especially in the Lebanese banking system, while Saudi Arabia has been criticised for not acting vigorously in relation to certain accounts and funds identified by the Americans.

Even where there may not be great differences in definitions, resentments have arisen over Washington's attempt to set the pace in the finance war. Thus, strains have emerged between the United States and a number of European allies, including Germany and France, over what Washington regards as tardiness when it comes to closing down accounts and constraining funds flow. While some of these latter difficulties are a result of differing legal and bureaucratic practices rather than conceptual variations, they nevertheless still hinder effective counterterrorist operations by creating loopholes through which terrorist finances may pass.

Even more fundamentally, the general principles of counterterrorist campaigning which are embodied in the various FATF recommendations and UN resolutions and conventions are not all uncontroversial, either as principles or as effective counterterrorist tools. This can be seen in the attitude of many international financial institutions, the structural linchpins of the global markets and the frontline soldiers of the anti-terrorist finance campaign, which have found themselves mobilised in a war for which they are both practically and conceptually unprepared. This is not to say that the financial services industry objects to the anti-terrorist focus of the political authorities. On the contrary, the industry recognises the dangers that terrorist financing poses to the integrity of the global banking system and financial markets. However, there is scepticism in relation to the potential effectiveness of some of the new measures and the practicalities of implementation. There is concern as to the costs, in terms of both money and efficiencies, that the anti-terrorist financing measures entail. Thus the practicalities of significant reporting requirements in relation to suspicious transactions (especially where there is an objective test for such reporting), issues of customer identification (which touch upon highly sensitive client confidentiality) and fears as to loss of competitiveness (to less regulated jurisdictions) make this a difficult period for these organisations.

Ideologically, the counterargument in its most general construction, at both the political and the institutional financial level, is that market abuse and organised crime will never be totally removed from the global markets and the extent of regulation required to serve such a goal actually undermines the functioning of those very markets that the regulation seeks to protect. The

Martin S. Navias

essence of this type of perspective is that regulatory measures must not be allowed to impede the movement of legitimate capital. If they do, the costs to the global political economy will be enormous and the terrorists, as a result, would succeed in their aim of subverting the international financial system.

Finance warfare remains a critical component of the global struggle against international terror, as the logistical infrastructure of international terrorist organisations must be destroyed if ultimately their operational capabilities are to be degraded. While to date many successes have been claimed in the counterterrorist finance campaign, these in reality represent small battles in what promises to be a long-drawn-out and complicated war where success cannot in any way be guaranteed. The ongoing finance war against non-political money laundering is not a source of optimism in this regard, but in the war against terrorism the stakes are arguably far larger and therefore the war must continue to be prosecuted with vigour. Technical, bureaucratic, political, conceptual and coordinational obstacles will nevertheless need to be overcome before terrorist financing capabilities can be seriously eroded.

## Notes

1 For use of war terminology to describe the financial battle, see also statements by Jimmy Gurule, Treasury Under Secretary for Enforcement. According to Mr Gurule, 'The Treasury Department is now waging a multi-lateral battle to break the financial backbone of terrorist groups and their financiers . . . [it] is playing a key role in this new and unconventional war with respect to dismantling the maze of money that makes these atrocious acts possible.' The establishment by the Treasury of the Foreign Terrorist Asset Tracking Center was described as 'a new proactive, preventative strategy for waging financial war': 'Treasury's Gurule on Strategy to Fight Money Laundering', in *US Department of State: International Information Programs*, 22 Oct. 2001.
2 'Sen. Levin Testifies on Money Laundering and Terrorism', *US Department of State: International Information Programs*, 26 Sept. 2001.
3 Jeffrey Robinson, *The Laundrymen*, New York, Pocket Books, 1998, p. 18.
4 For a survey of these issues see Yossef Bodansky, *Bin Laden: The Man Who Declared War on America*, California, Prima, 2001.
5 Anita Ranasastry, 'Follow the Money and Follow it Fast', *Findlaw's*, 15 Oct. 2001; John Willis, 'Trail of Terrorist Dollars that Spans the World', *Financial Times*, 29 Nov. 2001.
6 For a description see Paul Bauer, 'Understanding the Wash Cycle', in *Economic Perspectives: The Fight Against Money Laundering*, vol. 6, Washington DC, US Department of State, May 2001. The main legislative pieces of US anti-money-laundering legislation prior to 11 September include the 1970 Banking Secrecy Act, the 1984 Racketeer Influenced and Corrupt Organisations Act, the 1986 Money Laundering Act, the 1988 Anti-Drug Abuse Act, the 1992 Annunzio–Wylie Anti-money-laundering Act, the 1994 Money Laundering Suppression Act, the 1996 Health Insurance Portability and Accountability Act, and the 2000 Civil Asset Forfeiture Reform Act. Also, the National Money Laundering Strategy for 2001 was mandated by the Money Laundering and Financial Crimes Act of 1998.

## FINANCE WARFARE AND INTERNATIONAL TERRORISM

7 Bauer, 'Understanding the Wash Cycle'.
8 Editorial comment by Professor B. Ryder in *Money Laundering Monitor*, no. 25, Oct. 2001.
9 International Convention for the Suppression of the Financing of Terrorism, United Nations General Assembly Resolution 54/109 of 9 Dec. 1999.
10 *FATF-XII Report on Money Laundering Typologies (2000–2001)*, p. 19.
11 Financial Action Task Force on Money Laundering, *Annual Report 2000–2001*, 22 June 2001, p. 16.

# [24]

# HOW USEFUL IS THE ECONOMIC MODEL OF CRIME IN ASSISTING THE WAR AGAINST TERRORISM?

## Dorothy Manning

This article considers whether the economic model of crime can be applied to terrorist activity. It concludes that the model does explain both secular and religiously motivated terrorism: policy-makers wishing to reduce terrorist activity should aim at devising policies which increase costs and/or decrease benefits to change terrorist incentives. The 'war' should continue as long as the probable costs to society incurred by terrorist activity are greater than the costs of abatement.

## Introduction

Following the horrific events of 11 September and the subsequent ongoing 'war on terrorism' pursued by the West, the world has become very aware of the modern-day problem posed by terrorism. But how great is the threat of terrorism? Is the problem more acute in 2002 than in previous years? What can and should be done to alleviate the threat? Has the Western world overreacted? Terrorism, because of its very nature of 'creating terror,' is charged with negative connotations so is often treated emotively rather than in objective terms. Whilst addressing the above questions this article will focus on how valid the economic model of crime is in explaining terrorist activity and consider if it can aid policy-making institutions formulating policies to counter terrorist activities.

## What is the economic model of crime?

Any economic model deliberately simplifies and generalises in order to gain a better understanding of the real world. Every model is based on a set of assumptions and, if the model is meaningful, it will generate predictions to which behaviour conforms more often than it does not. The economic model of crime is no exception to this. This model, originally developed by Becker,[1] is based on a set of assumptions, the main one being that criminals

are rational actors who will only engage in crime if it is beneficial for them to do so. Criminals weigh up their expected private costs and benefits of participating in illegal and legal activities and when the expected net benefit of illegal activity is greater than that from legal activity they will choose the criminal option. The decision to participate in crime is then a calculated decision by a rational individual. The criminal is not, therefore, a hapless victim of socio-economic circumstances driven into a life of crime, totally beyond his own control absolved of all responsibility for his actions. He is not pre-programmed by his physiological makeup, being born 'bad' with genes which dictate a life of crime; nor is he suffering from any psychological illness ('mad'). The criminal deliberately chooses to pursue the criminal route as it maximises his own self-interest. This view of an individual's behaviour is common to all individuals, so is indifferent to a person's wealth, education, religion, culture and society. According to the model we are all potential criminals; the people who become criminals do so not because their basic motivation differs from those of others but because their costs and benefits differ.

The economic model of crime is a predictive model of criminal behaviour. The fundamental hypothesis in the economic approach to crime is that offenders will alter their behaviour in response to a change in incentives. According to the deterrence hypothesis, an increase in costs and a decrease in benefits will lower the willingness of a person to

348                                    *War on Terrorism*

22    HOW USEFUL IS THE ECONOMIC MODEL OF CRIME IN ASSISTING THE WAR AGAINST TERRORISM?

engage in criminal activity. As costs include the chance of being caught and punished the model asserts crime rates will respond in a predicted manner to changes in the probability of apprehension, conviction and severity of punishment, thus giving clear guidance for criminal justice policies.

Does the economic model of crime explain terrorist activities? If it does, then it will be of use to governments and other institutions formulating counter-terrorist policies. Empirical studies show the model best explains property crimes; that is, those with a money motive. Terrorism, as it is an illegal activity, is a crime but it is not motivated by personal monetary gain. Does this invalidate the model in explaining terrorist behaviour? Theoretically the model does not require that pecuniary motives are the only, or even dominant, motive in the decision to participate in crime.[2] Pecuniary and non-pecuniary factors are included in the definitions of costs and benefits. Does it matter that decisions made by terrorists involve the death of innocents? The economic approach does not distinguish between major decisions involving life and death and minor decisions such as choosing a brand of coffee, or between these decisions involving strong or weak emotions.[3] So there is no need to discard the model on these counts.

All models are sensitive to assumptions, and changing any of the assumptions will generate different results. The cornerstone of the economic model of crime is that the criminal is rational and self-interested, aiming to maximise his own personal welfare and is the best judge of what this constitutes. Is the terrorist a rational person? Is terrorist activity rational? If the answer is no, does it then render the model invalid for explaining terrorism? In order to assess this, the characteristics, structure and objectives of terrorists and their organisations need to be considered.

## Is the individual terrorist a rational being?

What makes a person become a terrorist? Why do some people become terrorists whilst others with the same religion or beliefs do not? There are tens of thousands of terrorists in the world coming from all walks of life – from the poor slums in Egypt to the fabulously wealthy from Saudi Arabia. So they are not all hapless victims of socio-economic circumstances.

Are they all psychologically disturbed or genetically disposed to terrorise? The literature abounds with studies that conclude terrorists are not suffering from psychological abnormalities. Long[4] states terrorists do not share a personality type. No work has revealed a particular psychological type or uniform terrorist mind-set. Similarly, Sarraj,[5] after examining many people identified as potential suicide bombers, found no psychological problems among them. Merari's[6] research found the only common characteristics of suicide terrorists were that they were young and unmarried. They had no common socio-economic background, coming from a cross-section of society. None of the terrorists in his study were found to be suffering from psychological abnormalities. Horgan[7] too claims there are no personality traits that will allow you to predict that one person or another is more likely to become a terrorist. It is likely that the terrorist groups do not actually want psychopaths or mentally unstable members in their group as this poses far too great a risk to security and operations.

Most terrorists join an organisation while young and are predominantly male. Why do they join an organisation and take risks when they personally do not gain benefit by achieving their objective? O'Brien[8] states the sentimentalist thinks of the terrorist as driven to violent acts as a result of being a victim of oppression or to ratify a grievance. But the pursuit of a cause is not the sole motive for becoming a terrorist. There are other more immediate rewards. Many terrorists come from poor backgrounds where unemployment is high and prospects are few. Terrorism offers them the opportunity for gratification of a grievance and also, from the moment they become terrorists, it offers them access to significant amounts of power, prestige and wealth. It is, therefore, more realistic to see the terrorist as bettering himself. O'Brien[9] writes:

> 'For an unemployed young man . . . the most promising channel of upward social mobility is . . . the national terrorist organisation . . . In this situation the terrorist option is a rational one . . . you don't have to be a nut, a dupe or an idealist.'

Hence when terrorism receives a glare of publicity it improves recruitment because it enhances the prestige and glamour of terrorism. According to Johnson[10] the media glorify terrorism and have elevated Osama bin Laden into an 'invincible sort of person.' And with more than half the population in the Middle East below the age of 20 years there is no shortage of potential recruits. The model would seem appropriate here as the opportunity costs of legitimate employment are lower for unemployed, poorly educated, young people.

On the other hand, some terrorists are extremely wealthy and/or well educated and, while they may seek other non-pecuniary rewards such as personal glorification, they primarily seek gratification of hatred or pursuit of a quest. This hatred/grievance may or may not be rational. A terrorist's beliefs and way of thinking may be based on false information, flawed assumptions and/or irrational inferences but this does not invalidate him making rational decisions based on irrational beliefs. The trend now is a rise in the Islamic fundamentalist religious groups with a vehement hatred of the US; whether or not this hatred is justified is irrelevant to the workings of the economic model of crime.[11]

## Are suicide bombers rational?

Although incidents of suicide terrorism have occurred for hundreds of years, the present era of suicide bombings began in the early 1980s most notably with those in Beirut in 1983 when hundreds of servicemen were killed. There have been many other incidents since then. The trend is on the increase but they still remain only the minority of acts. Most terrorist acts are not suicide missions. Most terrorists are willing to risk their life by taking part in terrorist acts but most want to get out alive. What about the minority of individuals willing to take their own life in pursuance of their cause? Is readiness to take your own life in an act of terrorism the behaviour of a rational individual or irrational fanatic?

Harrison[12] has addressed this question and concludes that suicide terrorists are rational and self-interested. His explanation is that it is human nature to adopt an identity and some people will go to great lengths to defend it, some even being willing to die rather than relinquish it. Sprinzak[13] too believes suicide terrorists are rational individuals. He states people who would never consider killing themselves for the more normal reasons for taking your own life, 'opt for suicide terrorism as a result of cold reasoning.'

The terrorist does not see deliberately killing himself as an act of suicide but rather as an act of self-sacrifice; martyrdom for a cause he or she vehemently

believes is right and just. He or she may actually despise people who take their own life for other reasons and see them as weak, pathetic individuals. The religiously motivated suicide terrorists see their life on earth as only a small part of their entire existence – their life after death being more important. Islamic fundamentalist terrorists' interpretation of Islamic religion is such that they see being a suicide terrorist as an opportunity to secure for themselves a place in Paradise. By perpetrating an act against the enemy entailing sacrificing their own life they will reap their rewards in heaven, while on earth, after their death, they will be revered as heroes bringing honour and glory on themselves and their family.[14] This is why it is essential for Islamic religious terrorists to receive the sanction of the religious clerics before going on a suicide mission.

It may be argued that once in the terrorist organisation individuals are deliberately indoctrinated and brainwashed, manipulated by leaders, so they can no longer be thought of as rational decision-makers. However, suicide terrorists are always volunteers. They are never coerced into it. There is far too much planning at stake for the leaders to risk using people against their will. Suicide bombers have usually trained with the intention of sacrificing their life for a long time before they actually do so. Merari[15] maintained that no organisation could create a person's basic readiness to die. The task of recruiters is not to produce but rather to identify and reinforce a person's predisposition to suicide. During the 1990s Merari changed this view and now believes that suicide terrorists have been deliberately indoctrinated by the terrorist organisation.

So is becoming a terrorist rational or irrational behaviour? Many experts argue that terrorists are not crazy but are rational people pursuing goals. 'They are rational, they are not insane . . . they have goals and they are moving towards those goals,' writes Pearlstein.[16] Sprinzak[17] states, 'The perception that terrorists are undeterrable fanatics . . . belies the reality that they are cold rational killers who employ violence to achieve specific political objectives.' And what about the reformed ex-terrorists who have relinquished terrorist tactics and are now integrated back into society? Are these people, some of whom are now well-known politicians, deemed to be irrational beings?

It is often argued that suicide terrorists are irrational fanatics but there are other acts of suicide

350                                      *War on Terrorism*

24      HOW USEFUL IS THE ECONOMIC MODEL OF CRIME IN ASSISTING THE WAR AGAINST TERRORISM?

and these perpetrators are not condemned outright as irrational. As Harrison[18] points out, in other cases of suicide perpetrators are often seen as heroic or tragic, not 'mad' or 'bad.' The *kamikaze* pilot laying down his life is a hero in his country; a person dying rather than bringing shame on his family is tragic. So there is no reason to assume a suicide bomber is not rational. However, even if they are irrational, a few participants whose behaviour does not comply with the assumptions of the model does not invalidate the model. A model is a generalisation only. The theory allows for irrational behaviour but argues that groups of individuals behave as if they are rational. The economic approach does not contend that all individuals are rational; rather, economic man is an average in which extremes of behaviour are evened out.[19]

## Is terrorist activity rational?

When is terrorist activity resorted to rather than using legal methods? When it is cheaper, more effective and quicker than political ways. When, because of asymmetric military strengths, one party stands no chance of winning an outright war. Terrorists will utilise every possible method that will further their cause. Given they possess relatively few resources compared to governments terrorism is the easiest and most effective form of insurgency. Is it ever justified? Are any terrorists really honourable freedom fighters? This is another story and not relevant to the application of the economic model of crime in explaining terrorist behaviour.

Terrorist groups differ in their structure and characteristics but mainly they are well organised and members well disciplined. They operate in cells with terrorists having information on a need-to-know basis for security reasons. There can be thousands of terrorists operating in many cells, all pursuing the same mission. Members of an organisation receive training so they become skilled in terrorist activity (although there is an increase in the use of amateurs now). In larger organisations, the financial side is well organised with personnel dedicated to raising, managing, investing and distributing funds via front companies.

Acts themselves are well thought out and meticulously planned and are usually part of an overall strategy to achieve some desired end result. The growing trend in using suicide terrorism is because this is a very effective and cost-efficient weapon of terrorism.[20] It has an immense impact on spreading terror because it is seen as so hard to defend against and is usually successful. It can be used to inflict mass casualties and extensive damage and it can also be used for precise targeting. The Tamil Tigers killed two heads of state in the early 1990s this way.

Terrorist organisations do not keep repeating the same behaviour. They are evolving organisations as they consciously learn, develop, adapt and react to improve effectiveness. They research and develop better tactics and more effective weapons to keep ahead of the authorities. Bombs are now smaller, more lethal, easier to detonate and harder to detect. Small, inconspicuous bodysuits have been designed for suicide bombers. They learn from mistakes and change their behaviour accordingly. Transcripts of terrorist trials are meticulously combed through for information on how authorities operate and why a terrorist was caught. They learned this way that fingerprints can be taken from inside refrigerators and underneath toilet seats.[21] The most famous lesson learned is possibly the Stockholm Syndrome when terrorists learned not to talk to hostages and to change guards frequently to prevent personal relationships being established. New information is recorded in training manuals and communicated between groups.

Although the economic model of crime can account for spontaneous crime to some extent it most certainly accounts for premeditated crimes better. Terrorist activity indisputably comes under the category of premeditated crime as sometimes years of training, planning and preparation take place before the execution of an act. The definition of terrorism used by the US Department of State is 'premeditated, politically motivated violence.'[22] Merari[23] compares different forms of insurgency and determines that terrorism is not spontaneous but a strategy of protracted struggle over the long term. Grenshaw[24] describes terrorism as 'systematic, deliberate and sustained over time; it is not spontaneous . . . engaging in terrorism usually requires a sustained commitment.' Using terrorism itself is a rational decision given the difference in resource endowment between the terrorists and the authorities. Using terrorist methods puts those few resources into good effect, targeting a few yet impacting on many.

Is it rational to engage in an activity where the chance of success is very remote? A group aiming to overthrow a government or change a political/economic system cannot realistically expect to win. Or can they? Osama bin Laden has often stated that one of his goals is to destroy the US. This is not unobtainable in his view. He believes he is carrying out the will of God and with God on his side he will succeed. According to Johnson,[25] bin Laden sees US society as evil, a hollow shell that, if hit in the right spot, will collapse. Bin Laden himself has often stated that the USSR was defeated in the war in Afghanistan and that victory can be repeated: 'I am confident that Muslims will be able to end the legend of the so-called superpower that is America.'[26] The majority of terrorists have additional reasons for their behaviour so their reward is not reliant on the achievement of their long-term objective.

The economic model of crime does not require decision-makers to be aware of consciously calculating the costs and benefits of their actions, only that their behaviour can be explained as if they do.[27] Terrorist activity, by both secular and religious terrorists, does seem to comply with the requirements of the model.

### Can terrorism be deterred?

The economic model of crime predicts changing terrorist incentives by increasing the costs and lowering the benefits of terrorism will deter activity, thus giving a clear goal for counter-terrorist policies. The benefits to terrorist organisations are achievement of end goals and any interim goals such as withdrawal of the military from an area, receipt of ransom money, release of prisoners, etc. To the individual terrorist it is the glamour, prestige and access to wealth being a terrorist brings. To the suicide bomber it is eternal life in Paradise. Any policies to lower these should reduce terrorist activity.

In accordance with the deterrence hypothesis increasing the probability of apprehension and conviction and the severity of punishment raises costs. The US government aimed to do this by showing terrorists they would be caught and brought to justice no matter how long it took. It took over ten years to bring the terrorists accused of the Pan Am 103 bombing to court. The more a terrorist is convinced that there is a high probability of response and it will be of great severity, the greater the deterrence effect.

Weinberger[28] claims that the weak response of the US government in the past has encouraged more attacks.

Even suicide bombers can be deterred this way. Harrison[29] points out the desire of terrorists to sacrifice their life would fall if religious clerics could be persuaded not to sanction suicide attacks as the benefits of eternal life would become more uncertain. Sprinzak[30] believes terrorist organisations can be deterred from using suicide acts. He sees these organisations as rational, calculating decision-making units. If you make the costs to them of using suicide terrorism as a weapon so great by sanctions and military reprisals this will serve as a deterrent.

The most active groups at present are the religiously motivated groups and it is not easy to manipulate their costs and benefits sufficiently to change incentives. Their benefits, being spiritual and eternal, are very high. A traditional method of lowering benefits such as a policy of non-negotiation and not complying with terrorists' demands is ineffective with these groups, as they do not try to negotiate demands. It is also hard to put pressure on these terrorists by raising their costs as the conventional tools used by the authorities are less effective. Sanctions have limited impact as these groups have access to private wealth and income from drugs trafficking so are less dependent on state sponsors. Covert intelligence operations are more difficult to operate as it is virtually impossible to infiltrate their groups. Key targets can be hardened and additional security measures put in place but as their objective is causing maximum lethality and destruction they are more indiscriminate about targets and so have a much wider scope for attack. Even military reprisals are made difficult as the terrorists are not often visible and located in an area that can be attacked as their networks are spread out in small cells around the world.

### How many resources should be allocated to combating terrorism?

There is a risk of overreacting to terrorism due to overestimating the extent of the threat it poses. Economic theory can demonstrate how many resources to devote to countering terrorist activity and how these resources should be allocated to each policy choice. The stated objective of the Bush administration is to put an end to all terrorist networks. President George W. Bush, in his now

352                           *War on Terrorism*

26      HOW USEFUL IS THE ECONOMIC MODEL OF CRIME IN ASSISTING THE WAR AGAINST TERRORISM?

famous speech on 21 September to Congress, announced,

> 'We will direct every resource at our command, every means of diplomacy, every tool of intelligence, every instrument of law enforcement, every financial influence and every necessary weapon of war – to disruption and defeat of the global terrorist network.'

Is this a reasonable response or an over-reaction to albeit the worst terrorist attack in history? Should the aim be to extirpate terrorism? There are other demands on government resources, other risks to citizens, and resources are limited. How many resources should be devoted to combating terrorism?

Economic theory states that terrorism should only be abated as long as the marginal social benefits of abating the terrorist activity are greater than the marginal social costs of abatement. That is, if it is going to cost more to stop a terrorist act than the value of the damage done to society by the act taking place, then allow the terrorist act to go unabated. This concept of an optimal level of terrorism can cause outrage from non-economists, appalled at the thought of permitting some criminal activity to occur. But some criminal acts confer only low costs to society. This concept applies to all areas of policy. Only a certain level of pollution should be abated. Why go to the expense of fitting anti-pollution equipment if the damage done by pollution is less than the cost of the abatement? So too terrorism should only be abated to the point where marginal social cost of abatement equals marginal social benefits.

So how great is the threat of terrorism? Terrorism endangers human life and property but does not pose a significant threat to democracy, Christianity or the state. Until recently the actual damage caused by terrorism was relatively small, with the majority of acts being domestic incidents killing and injuring a small number of people. However, now with the increase in activity by religiously motivated groups with different motives and characteristics, the actual and potential costs have increased.[31] Figure 1 shows the upward trend in deaths and injuries as a result of international terrorist attacks. The new terrorists engage in spectacular acts, often occurring in swarms, intent on causing greater lethality and destruction. The events on 11 September are a prime example.

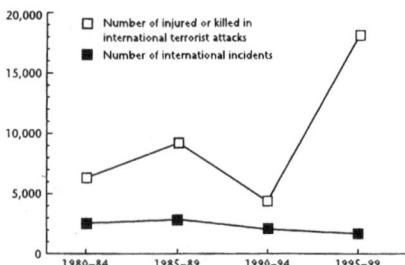

**Figure 1:** Terrorism becoming more dangerous
Source: *Countering the Changing Threat of International Terrorism,* Report of the National Commission on Terrorism.

What about the future potential costs of terrorist activity? To date, the bomb has been the most favoured weapon of the terrorist.[32] Terrorists will continue using conventional weapons but many experts warn there is a real danger that weapons of mass destruction (WMD) will be used in the near future. Most terrorist groups have so far vied away from WMD, not only because of the logistical difficulty in acquiring, transporting and distributing them but also because the old-style terrorists are concerned about the backlash of public opinion.[33]

The signs are that the willingness amongst terrorist groups to use WMD has increased and their access to them is easier than ever. The new religious terrorist groups now have a new type of motive. They see themselves as operating in a 'war paradigm' with a goal to kill as many of the enemy and to wreak as much havoc and destruction as possible. They are unconcerned with public reaction. And they justify it to themselves as carrying out the will of God so any crime is acceptable in their mind-sets. Osama bin Laden has made it clear in his numerous declarations that he considers it is his religious duty to seek to acquire WMD and if he manages to acquire them then it is God's will that he has done so and God means him to use them against his enemies. It is the holy duty of all Muslims to use 'any means available to kill all Americans.'[34]

At the present time it is relatively easy to acquire WMD. The dissolution of the old Soviet bloc and the ending of the Cold War means there are stockpiles of chemical, biological and nuclear materials in the ex-Soviet Union, ineffectively accounted for and poorly guarded. Unemployed scientists previously employed

**iea** ECONOMIC AFFAIRS SEPTEMBER 2002          27

on WMD R&D programmes were known to be looking for jobs in the global labour market, both legal and illegal. The spread of the global information economy and IT developments means that information on methods to produce WMD is available on the Internet.[35]

Terrorists may launch a nuclear attack in the future but a more realistic threat in this arena is that they will use a 'dirty bomb,'[36] which would be much simpler to produce and deploy, and the results would be devastating. It is rumoured that the bombs used in the first attack on the World Trade Centre in 1993 contained sodium cyanide.[37] The use of chemical or biological weapons seems a likely option. Smallpox, anthrax, plague and mustard gas, for example, are quite easily manufactured and require only fairly unsophisticated equipment to do so. Another alternative that could cause immense damage to Western economies is cyber-terrorism. Laqueur[38] sees this as a credible threat and questions why terrorists would use violent acts if they can produce chaos by 'electronic switching,' stating,

'If the new terrorism directs its energies toward information warfare, its destructive power will be exponentially greater than any it wielded in the past – greater even than it would be with biological and chemical weapons.'

## Is there a real danger of terrorists resorting to using WMD?

The US treats it as a real threat and sees itself as the prime target for an attack using WMD. It has established units/instigated training to deal with attacks by WMD on civilians. The US offers assistance to Russia to ensure all nuclear materials are accounted for or disposed of properly. Merari[39] seems to suggest that they will be used if given the opportunity, as

'Al Qaeda has made the jump to mass casualty terrorism and the only factors constraining their actions in terms of the scale of casualties they seek to create are practical and technical, not political and moral.'

Hoffman[40] states that the different objectives, values, justifications and mind-set of the new type of terrorists suggest they will be more likely than their secular counterparts to use WMD. Terrorists used to want more people watching than dead; now it is the other way. Alibek[41] too believes 'there is no doubt that

we will see future uses of biological weapons by terrorist groups, as there have been several attempts already.' Laqueur[42] predicts it will be the unsuccessful groups that turn to WMD in despair.

In contrast, however, Sprinzak[43] sees it as an over-rated threat stating, 'Whereas the threat of WMD terrorism is little more than overheated rhetoric, suicide bombing remains a devastating form of terrorism.' Johnson[44] warns the threat of terrorism is 'over-heated' and blames media coverage for distorting the problem. He argues it is only Osama bin Laden and Al-Qaeda specifically targeting and killing Americans and they are not able to commit acts with greater frequency than once a year. And Al-Qaeda is not a particularly sophisticated organisation as 'footsteps the size of elephants' were left after 11 September.

So the growth in religiously motivated terrorism with the objective of causing greater lethality and destruction indicates future costs could be very much higher which suggests the optimal level of abatement has increased.

## Summary and conclusion

This article asks if terrorism, being an illegal activity, can be encompassed by the economic model of crime and concludes it can. It is whether or not it explains the new religious terrorism that is contentious. This article suggests there is a body of evidence that demonstrates the model's main assumption of rationality is met at both the individual and organisational level of both secular and religious terrorist groups. Having established that the model is valid in explaining terrorist behaviour, it then aids the authorities by giving a clear signal that the level of terrorist activity can be manipulated by changing costs and benefits. Faced with higher costs and/or lower benefits, terrorists, as rational, calculating decision-makers, will be deterred and choose to participate in a lower level of terrorist activity.

It is difficult to find evidence to support or refute the deterrence hypothesis as applied to terrorism as you cannot measure how many acts have been deterred. Even if evidence showed counter-terrorist policies have not been a deterrent it does not necessarily invalidate the model. It could be that costs have not been raised and benefits lowered sufficiently to alter behaviour.

In determining how many resources should be devoted to deterring terrorism the optimal level of abatement the government should aim at is where marginal social costs of terrorism equals the marginal social cost of abatement. With the growth in religious terrorism operating in a war paradigm and intent on destruction of their enemies the possibility of terrorists using WMD in the future is now much higher than before. And if even one act is not deterred it would have catastrophic consequences. It seems the 'war on terrorism' is justified from an economic perspective at the present time, as the potential costs to society if the most dangerous groups are not deterred are enormous. The costs incurred by the secular terrorists will probably remain relatively small so it may be inefficient to abate all terrorism. Any abatement of terrorist activity should only occur if the cost of doing so is less than the costs the act would confer on society.

1.  G. S. Becker (1968) 'Crime and Punishment: An Economic Approach,' *Journal of Political Economy*, 76, 2, 169–217.
2.  I. Ehrlich (1984) 'The Economic Approach to Crime – A Preliminary Assessment,' in A. I. Ogus and C. J. Veljanovski (eds.) *Readings in the Economics of Law and Regulation*, Oxford: Oxford University Press.
3.  G. S. Becker (1984) 'The Economic Approach to Human Behaviour,' in Ogus and Veljanovski (eds.) op. cit.
4.  In 'The Psychology of Terrorism Understanding Evil,' University of Wisconsin, posted 20 September 2001 (http://whyfiles.org/140terror-psych).
5.  E. Sarraj, cited in 'Inside the Minds of Suicide Bombers' (www.npr.org).
6.  A. Merari, cited in 'Inside the Minds of Suicide Bombers' (www.npr.org).
7.  In 'Serving a New Audience Understanding Evil,' University of Wisconsin (2001) (http://whyfiles.org/140terror-psych).
8.  C. C. O'Brien (1986) 'Thinking About Terrorism,' *The Atlantic Monthly*, June.
9.  Ibid.
10. Frontline: Hunting bin Laden. Interviews: Larry C. Johnson (http://www.pbs.org/wgbh/pages/frontline).
11. See, for example, the article by B. Lewis (1990) 'The Roots of Muslim Rage,' *The Atlantic Monthly*, September. For a different viewpoint see William Blum (2002) *The Rogue State*, London: Zed Books.
12. M. Harrison (2001) 'The Economic Logic of Suicide Terrorism,' University of Warwick (Draft).
13. E. Sprinzak (2000) 'Rational Fanatics,' *Foreign Policy*, September/October.
14. Families may also receive a financial reward.
15. A. Merari, cited in 'Fletcher Hosts Israeli Suicide Terrorism Expert,' by A. Moghdan (http://fletcherledger.com/

archive); and also 'Who is the Suicide Terrorist?' by R. Litwak (http://wwwics.si.edu). Also E. Sprinzak, op. cit.
16. In 'The Psychology of Terrorism Understanding Evil,' op. cit.
17. Sprinzak, op. cit.
18. Harrison, op. cit.
19. C. J. Veljanovski (1984) 'The New Law-and-Economics: A Research Review,' in Ogus and Veljanovski (eds.) op. cit.
20. Although some terrorist groups never use suicide acts and others use them only on an ad hoc basis, there are some groups such as the Tamil Tigers that have permanent suicide squads.
21. B. Hoffman (2001) 'Combating Terrorism: In Search of a National Strategy,' *Rand Testimony Series CT-175*.
22. *Patterns of Global Terrorism 2000*, released April 2001.
23. A. Merari, 'Terrorism as a Strategy of Insurgency.'
24. M. Grenshaw (ed.) 'Terrorism in Context' (http://www.psupress.org/books).
25. Frontline: Hunting bin Laden, op. cit.
26. Ibid.
27. Becker (1984) op. cit.
28. Interview with C. Weinberger in Frontline: Target America: 'Lessons Learned in the 1980s' (http://www.pbs.org/wgbh/pages/frontline).
29. Harrison, op. cit.
30. Sprinzak, op. cit.
31. For databases see *Patterns of Global Terrorism*, The Rand–St. Andrews Chronology of International Terrorism, DCI Counterterrorist Centre.
32. According to the Political Terrorism Database, 46% of total terrorist attacks between 1968 and 1993 were bombings.
33. So far the main incidents using WMD seem to be the attempts by the Japanese religious sect Aum Shinrikyo, who made several unsuccessful attempts to spread botulism, anthrax and sarin gas and who eventually succeeded in dispersing sarin gas in the Tokyo underground in 1995 killing several people and injuring thousands. The most famous will probably be the anthrax postal attacks in the US after 11 September.
34. Frontline: Hunting bin Laden, op. cit.
35. For example, information on the production of sarin gas is available on the Internet.
36. A 'dirty bomb' being a conventional explosive containing low-grade fissionable material.
37. S. H. Leader, 'The Rise of Terrorism' (www.securitymanagement.com).
38. W. Laqueur (1996) 'Postmodern Terrorism: New Rules for an Old Game,' *Foreign Affairs*, 75, 5.
39. In R. Litwak, 'Who is the Suicidal Terrorist?' summary of presentation by A. Merari (http://wwics.si.edu/NEWS).
40. B. Hoffman, 'Old Madness, New Methods' (www.rand.org).
41. K. Alibek (1998) 'Terrorist and Intelligence Operations: Potential Impact on the US Economy' (http://www.house.gov).
42. Laqueur, op. cit.
43. Sprinzak, op. cit.
44. Frontline: Hunting bin Laden, op. cit.

**Dorothy Manning** is Senior Lecturer in Economics at the University of Northumbria, UK.

# [25]

# THE THERAPEUTIC POTENTIAL OF NARRATIVE THERAPY IN CONFLICT TRANSFORMATION

CATHIE J. WITTY, Ph.D.

*Recent acts of terrorism and violence on U.S. soil have left citizens, politicians, and professionals asking similar questions. Why did this happen to us? What can we do to keep this from happening again? This article provides one answer to those questions by calling for greater involvement of systemic therapists in violence prevention of and intervention at home and abroad. Therapists have unique skills that are desperately needed in the prevention of and recovery from violence, war, and terror. Therapists can heal, teach people how to hear and transform, and listen. Conflict resolution theory, steeped in realism, modernism, and a structural perspective of change, dominates conflict analysis abroad even though it has been largely ineffective. Structural changes in government do not address the fear, anger, and destruction of human relationships generated by war and terror. The transformation of the root causes of war, violence, and hatred lies in integrating the analytical and transformational perspectives of conflict resolution and systemic therapy, particularly the narrative deconstruction of hate, with existing structural problem-solving models.*

As we enter the 21st century, the field of conflict resolution has accumulated more than 50 years of community conflict resolution and postwar peace-building experience. Lessons have been learned on the domestic front in schools and communities saturated by violence, racism, and intolerance, as well as in protracted conflict in communities worldwide. Nationally, after September 11, we have begun to understand what many indigenous global communities have known for years: There are no impenetrable social or technological boundaries against violence and hatred. Locally, conflict resolution practitioners wonder why conflict resolution skills and cross-cultural education have not been enough. Internationally, peacemakers struggle to create peace dialogues and changes to reform governments. The question is the same: How do we transform rage and heal people's recovery from terror and violence? Family therapists, from their

Address correspondence to Cathie Witty, Ph.D., Associate Professor, Nova Southeastern University, 3301 College Avenue, Fort Lauderdale, FL 33314.

agencies and private practices, speak to these issues in their local communities, but they seem unengaged in the opportunities to apply systemic thinking, therapy, and intervention to issues of postwar conflict, trauma recovery, and family and community reconstruction.

As a veteran conflict resolution specialist with a degree in family therapy, I recognize the powerful transformative qualities of both fields. From a theoretical and clinical perspective, integration of these two fields holds incredible promise for an effective solution to the ongoing struggle to understand and eliminate protracted, repetitive cycles of violence. We desperately need the systemic, second-order change that collaboration of our two fields and other relevant disciplines can provide at this critical junction in human history. Such collaboration would reflect the awareness of groups like the World Health Organization that effective responses to war and trauma need to be multilevel and multimodal. Bringing systemic knowledge and techniques to the transformation of human relationships is one practical way to build foundations for sustainable futures. We have structural strategies in place and continue to improve them, but diplomats and relief planners resist dealing with human pain and suffering. As therapists, we can help diplomats, humanitarian relief workers, policy planners, peacemakers, and international donors such as the United Nations and the European Union understand the critical necessity of hearing and responding to the needs of traumatized survivors. Healing is the critical element missing from current peace-building efforts, because the transformation of human relationships is the social foundation for sustainable peace.

## CONFLICT ANALYSIS AND COMMUNITY BUILDING

In conflict resolution and international relations, there is substantial work being done in America and abroad in crisis intervention, restorative justice, conflict transformation, and peace building. These are the interdisciplinary frontiers, which blend conflict resolution, international relations, reconciliation, social justice, and healing. The international community is rebuilding homes, infrastructures, social institutions, and economic structures, but it makes little financial or moral commitment to rebuilding relationships within communities (Galtung, 1996).

Sustainable peace and conflict transformation, both here and abroad, require interdisciplinary efforts. No one field has the answers to such complex issues, which operate throughout the larger systems at multiple levels. Sustainable peace requires that people change their minds in meaningful ways so that they can act as catalysts and challenge existing cultures of corruption, violence, and hatred. Systemic family therapy and the transformational perspective within conflict resolution (Bush & Folger, 1994), both of which focus on helping people modify their views of their beliefs and relationships, are ideally suited to this task. Domestic forms of trauma and violence, as well as international rage from theological fascists and intolerant state governments, will continue unabated until we acknowledge the essential need to heal relationships between people so they can change their own futures. There is urgency in this call for collaboration because there is clear evidence that trauma and violence, unhealed, will escalate exponentially into successive generations (Bower. 1996; Perry, 1996; van der Kolk, 1989; Volkan, 1997).

Much of the systemic family therapy being done today has not yet lifted its vision to the landscape of meaning and action on the international horizon; clinical practice is largely confined to the private clinical practice; work with individuals and families in medical, community, university, and specialized clinics (substance abuse, HIV); and work with children in schools, residential care facilities, foster care, jail, and other programs for "at risk" youth. While a focus on larger social systems, client-centered perspectives, and second-order change characterizes family therapy and systemic interventions in general, much of our work remains focused on domestic U.S. issues at the family and, occasionally, at the community level. This is important work, but it is not enough.

Currently, psychiatrists and psychologists who generally do not bring systemic approaches to postwar recovery dominate the field of trauma intervention and treatment. Second-order change (Watzlawick, Weakland & Fisch, 1978), the healing of trauma at family levels, and the restorying of family and community relationships ultimately hold the key to resolving violent community conflict (Freeman & Combs, 1996; Mercham, 2000; Volkan, 1988). Without healing, the need for revenge festers just under the surface, fueled by people's pain (Maynard, 1997; Smyth, 2001). Systemic therapeutic approaches, particularly the narrative conversation, are the cornerstone of relationship-focused techniques that help people change from those who *react* to each other to those who can *relate to* one another. We need to think outside the box and, as therapists, outside our country as well.

## TRAUMA AND VIOLENCE: THE SYSTEMIC CONNECTION

In thinking about the implications of ignoring the pain of traumatized war survivors, consider this brief list of the long-term effects of trauma left unwitnessed and unhealed:

- aggression toward self and others
- inability to modulate impulses
- problems with social attachment and attention
- dissociation and numbing
- heightened, increased defensive fear responses
- loss of trust, hope and sense of agency

- loss of meaningful attachments, loss of identity
- lack of participation in preparing for the future. (modified from van der Kolk, 1996a, p. 184)

The strength of systemic therapy is its ability to focus on the whole person, work within local cultural and meaning systems, and create space in which families can reevaluate their relationships with themselves and external social systems. Conflict resolution practice does not effectively see the pain of the whole person, does not link people to larger systems, and underestimates the significant role that survivors must play in redefining the sustainable transformation of their communities. People suffering from "irrational" trauma-based behaviors are excluded from public peace dialogues. However, if the wounded, numb, repressed, and enraged are not included in community reconstruction, the inevitable outcome is more violence, hate, and revenge. To include them requires building healing into the reconstruction of violence communities everywhere.

## SYSTEMIC SOLUTIONS

The narrative deconstruction of traumatic events, intense pain, loss, and bereavement can be integrated into current clinical practices and local efforts to rebuild communities if we have the will to do so. But first, therapist, diplomats, and peacemakers have to understand why it is essential. There are three reasons why narrative transformational conversations, as I am reframing narrative therapy for this context, are critical to sustainable peace:

1. They are a family-centered, systemic approach that accommodates family-focused, high-context social systems; they are equally application to clinical practice in this country because families and communities also experience the group trauma and mourning (Oklahoma City, World Trade Center, postal anthrax).

2. Therapeutic healing from trauma and reconciliation of war related experiences must precede community peace building. Current programs do not develop the trust sufficient to transform violent ethnic groups into enduring, peaceful civil communities. Without healing, we are building fragile new social systems on the tenuous emotional pillars of fear, rage, intolerance, and hate.

3. Narrative conversations can model transformational processes that families can continue well into the future, as well as prepare families for transition into community-based peace-building discussions, dialogues, and development projects currently practiced by humanitarian agencies.

Narrative therapy skills can be integrated into existing local practices such as EMDR, body-focused, psychomotor therapy, and cognitive-behavioral models, and create an expanding, sustainable therapeutic process in local communities.

The Balkan Trauma Recovery Project and the Integrated Rehabilitation Model used at the Coalition for Work with Psychotrauma and Peace in Vukovar, Croatia (Witty & Tauber, 2002) and the Centre for Ubuntu in South Africa (Kayser, 2000) are excellent examples of integrated, multimodal programs that work. Narrative approaches complement current psychological protocols that help clients achieve safety, develop coping skills, control impulses, develop trust, explore attempted solutions, relieve anxiety, and alter self-image and identity; they should not threaten current practitioners. But systemic interventions are relatively noninvasive ways to help families and larger groups of people develop a belief that there "is" a future for them. The conjoint creation of new futures within a family or other close-knit group is cumulative and contagious. The ripple effect can be powerful and sustaining.

Conflict resolution and family therapy practitioners must not abandon trauma and crisis intervention to individually focused, medication-driven diagnosis and medically defined models. After years of critical debate, EMDR has struggled to gain acceptance from the psychiatric and psychological establishment; it has done so because it has proven effective in working individually with abuse, war, and torture survivors (Silver & Rogers, 2002); this technique was developed by Shapiro at MRI in Palo Alto, California, as a trauma intervention technique integrated within the context of family therapy (Shapiro, 2001; Shapiro & Ramsey, 1997). This example serves to remind us that systemic therapies belong in the conflict, trauma, abuse, rape, torture, crisis, and violence prevention and intervention fields.

## TRANSFORMATION OF INDIVIDUALS, FAMILIES, AND COMMUNITIES

Some domestic organizations have reached their own independent conclusions that healing people is more effective than giving up on them or building more prisons. The State of Ohio, for example, has recently applied for a grant to offer trauma assessment and defusion in every elementary school in the state. They realized, through teaching conflict resolution skills in the schools, that these skills alone are inadequate to prevent and heal violence in human relationships. The grant recognizes that schools must reach out and treat the underlying, short- and long-term effects of trauma on children (and their parents), because without such healing, students never develop the cognitive skills necessary for social and emotional learning.

In prolonged, or even single-trauma events, there are good reasons that people may develop impulse-driven, aggressive self-defense responses. Initially, it saves their lives. However, people suffering from the effects of prolonged trauma cannot immediately connect with work projects, peace dialogues, or problem-solving activities. They often cannot even connect with themselves.

This is the pivotal nexus: relationships. Our mistaken focus on changing govern-mental and legislative structures while failing to heal relationships is painfully reflected in the global array of protracted conflicts, which continually erupt in violence and defy resolution. *The fundamental strength of systemic therapy is that it focuses on relationships* as the client and the therapeutic focus. Collabora-tive solutions are based on the "client's expertise on themselves and the thera-pist's expertise on a process"(Anderson, 1996, p. 96) which allows local com-munities and families to heal themselves through indigenous conversations that transform relationships rather than dialogues that solve problems. Problem solv-ing outside of relationships will not last if people have not changed their percep-tions of the old political order, the impact of their unique war or violent experi-ences, the causes of prior violence and aggression, and their new roles in a different future. All such first-order change is doomed to failure in the long run. People must be given space and the opportunity to develop resources to resist the dominant discourse and culture of violence that permeate their communities. They can do this by transforming their relationships with others and the dis-course of intolerance and hate, and by creating new self-identities that challenge dominant definitions of "the enemy."

Problem solving in conflict resolution practice makes the fundamental error of "separating the person from the problem." Not only are issues of hate and violence imbedded in community relationships, but the problem solving exercise also lulls us into a false sense of security and allows us to assume that once the problems are resolved, things will move naturally toward a better future; but they cannot, because fundamental values and beliefs that contradict peaceful solutions have not been changed. Conflict resolution practice has much to learn from the process of externalizing.

## NARRATIVE TRANSFORMATIONAL CONVERSATION

Language and conversation are the core concepts in the narrative definition and approach to conflict. We create conflict and violence with language, and we can transform them the same way (Freeman & Combs, 1996). For the conflict reso-lution specialist, narrative therapy has two major contributions to bring to the field. First, transformational change, or change that brings about a shift in peo-ple's perception of their relationships with one another, involves a change in language before change in behavior and perception. People need a safe place to explore, ask questions that are not asked in "normal" discourse, and speak the as yet unspoken. Problems are not obstacles to be overcome; they must be em-braced, explored, and deconstructed to create the opportunity for change. Prob-lems cannot be solved, but must be "dissolved" in the transformation of people's view of themselves in relation to the problems. How were these problems cre-ated, how did I accept the argument that strangers are always suspect, and, most importantly, are those beliefs working for me today? If not, what do I need to change? Change is created through shifts in the use of language; people can, in transformational conversations, reshape their present violence-, terror-, and war-saturated stories into more meaningful and action-based stories that heal and empower. In changing their stories, they also change themselves. This is the epistemological basis of narrative therapy (Anderson, 1997; Epston, 1993).

Second, the narrative conversation is always an externalizing conversation. This is not the same as "separating the person from the problem," which implies that the problem exists outside the person and his or her relationships. Narrative externalizes the problem but works with the family system to understand the dynamics of how the identified "problem" is stabilized, strengthened, or challenged by the social relationships of the group. Systemic therapy knows that you can externalize the problem by speaking of it as "outside" the person, but you cannot separate the problem from the person's meaning or relationship systems.

## OPENING TRANSFORMATIONAL DIALOGUE

Systemic therapists must empower themselves to open transformational dialogues. Opening conversations about peace, tolerance, and violence in our own communities is a good first step. Education and dialogues about different religious and ethnic experiences is also a good place to start as well; larger discussions of international relations and misconceptions can follow. This work can flow from current work in schools, churches, clinics, and jails into the communities. Listen to the anger and pain; show communities that they must really hear the pain of the other before it will diminish. In developing group conversations, our systemic focus on relationships is essential and connective because it is a central, positive value among many Americans and peaceful peoples worldwide. We must not only remain open to transformational dialogues in the privacy of the therapeutic relationship, but we must also take such conversations and externalized focus on "sparkling moments" of change out into the broader community.

## SYSTEMIC FAMILY-BASED PEACE BUILDING

Operating in postconflict communities where trauma reactions are endemic and widespread and trust is incredibly low, the narrative approach to transformational conversations can begin with individuals or families. Many successful programs (Agger, 1995; Salem, 2000; Wessells, 1998) begin with children; as parents support their children's healing, they enter into and encourage an expanded dialogue. How this is organized and named is a function of local com-

munity decision making. Agger (1995) held conversations in quilting groups
because that was where women gathered to talk and process community life. As
we do at home, let local values and people guide your work; families need to
feel safe to become active partners in their own recovery.

Although the narrative therapeutic concept is Western (Australia), systemic
therapists understand that the facilitator does not operate from the position of
outside expert and does not rely on preconceived knowledge; he or she learns
to create a process in which the distinctive, unique experience of the people
involved in the conversation redefines and changes the problem. Rather than
listening and learning to communicate across two different systems of meaning,
as conflict resolution tends to do, narrative has the transformational aim of
working within the other's ordinary indigenous language to produce change
from the inside out. It is a conjoint process, but driven by local knowledge,
perceptions, and concepts (Freeman & Combs, 1996; Lederach, 1995, 1997;
White & Epston, 1990). The conflict parties are the "experts" and the solutions
lie in their narratives, myths, cultural metaphors, values, and beliefs. Although
the facilitator brings skill to guiding the conversation and asking the right kinds
of questions, her or his knowledge, experience, and values are no more valid or
true than the other parties'.

This is the final strength of the systemic family therapy perspective, because
narrative or any other form of intervention can be more effective and sustainable
in local cultural contexts if extended to family groups. This process can be
taught to local community members and healing professionals and expand sustainable therapeutic conversational skills. Families and local practitioners can
sustain the practice well into the future.


## THE LANDSCAPE OF THE FUTURE

Healing and recovery from trauma is a process that takes patience, an understanding of culture and larger social systems, and an ability to see relationships
as the key element in sustainable peace. It involves giving people the space and
time to see themselves, their culture, and their past from new perspectives in
order to envision the possibility of a new future. This is systemic theory and
practice in action and at its best. Its absence remains a critical weakness of
modern, linear, structural thinking in conflict resolution theory and practice.
Peace-building efforts desperately need the perspectives and the skills of narrative transformational conversations.

The following are some practical strategies for implementing proposed
changes; I offer them for dialogue and discussion:

- Develop local community-based conflict assessment tools focused on the
  resilience, stress, and reactivity of the local population. Systemic family

therapists working with local nongovernmental organizations would be ideal in this role; from the conflict resolution point of view, this type of local community assessment and prevention mirrors the current international focus on conflict prevention.

- Incorporate nonpathologizing, family-based trauma intervention activities into recovery and reconstruction plans. These can begin before international and national diplomacy efforts have concluded (if safety warrants) and before community reconstruction begins. Narrative family conversations would prepare families for and facilitate transition to subsequent peace-building conversations at the community level.
- Train conflict specialists and peacekeeping forces in group-based community trauma assessment.
- Train systemic therapists in conflict transformation, peace building, the goals of social reconstruction, and trauma intervention skills.
- Develop cultural assessment tools that incorporate local knowledge such as storytelling, myth, proverbs, and cultural beliefs and values to assist in developing family-based transformation strategies that are culturally viable to increase local participation in community programs. Local people must develop these tools.

None of these suggestions precludes providing individual attention for people at risk for self-harm or violence. The local, indigenous nature of the necessary healing cannot be overemphasized. Conflict resolution theory acknowledges this, but it practices a more culture- and gender-bound, first-order process of making "them" more like "us." Transformation must come from within, assisted by training of local practitioners and working to integrate local processes into well-meaning international relief efforts.

*Here is where foreign practitioners have an important role*: training local practitioners and running interference between local communities and international reconstruction efforts that believe conflict can be solved by building different kinds of social institutions based solely on replicating Western models of civil society. If you leave the culture of violence unchallenged in people's belief systems and in the community, and also fail to heal the survivors, changes to the larger system will be meaningless.

## CONCLUSIONS AND BEGINNINGS

Many of the questions raised here are raised every day in American homes, in our clinical practices, in Rwanda and Kosovo. How can we stop the violence? What can we do about *them*? Those angry violent teens, adults, those neighbors down the street, those terrorists? Our efforts to transform violence, change ourselves at home, and engage in relief activities abroad are in part stymied by our own ambivalence about facing the problem. It is not just about them; it is about all of us.

None of us is so far removed from the problems facing refugees in Bosnia, Kosovo, Rwanda, and now Afghanistan; people are abused, traumatized, subjected to violence and oppression, and die in American cities and communities every day. This perceived difference is just a matter of degree, and ethnic or racial identity; as Americans, we tend to see the conditions of the "other" from a position of privilege and power. Deconstruct this perception. We have learned not to see the violence, oppression, and ethnic cleansing in the world; it is too painful and we turn back to our comfortable lives. One hopes that this perception changed on September 11, 2001. The problems of displaced persons, refugees, civilian casualities of war, domestic and family violence, victims of rape and torture, traumatized children, the terrorized, and the victims everywhere are our problem. We cannot escape from them; they are us.

Individuals and families hold the key to a sustainable peace, particularly the children, if they are not already lost to us. This is the rightful domain of family therapy and any other philosophy that believes that people create change, not social systems. It is people who envision peace and make it happen by building communities and struggling for better lives for themselves and their children. The social structures and institutions we create are a reflection of the care and attention we give to children, in particular, and families in general. In the final analysis, they will be the reflection of how much, or how little, we care about ourselves and the rest of humanity.

## REFERENCES

Agger, I. (with Vuk, S., & Mimica, J.). (1995). *Under war conditions: What defines a psycho-social project? In theory and practice of psycho-social projects under war conditions in Bosnia-Herzegovina and Croatia* European Community Humanitarian Office (ECHO), Geneva: European Community Task Force, Psycho-Social Unit (ECTF).

Anderson, H. (1996). *Collaboration in therapy: Combining the client's expertise on themselves and the therapist's expertise on a process.* In T. Keller & N. Greve, (Eds.), *Social psychiatry and system thinking: Cooperation in psychiatry.* Bonn: Psychiatric Verlag.

Anderson, H. (1997). *Conversation, language, and possibilities: A postmodern approach to therapy.* New York: Basic Books.

Bower, B. (1996). Trauma syndrome traverses generations. *Science News, 149*(20), 310–318.

Bush, R. B. & Folger, J. (1994). *The promise of mediation: Responding to conflict through empowerment and recognition.* San Francisco, CA: Jossey-Bass.

Epston, D. (1993). Internalizing discourses versus externalizing discourses. In S. Gilligan & R. Price (Eds.), *Therapeutic conversations* (pp. 161–177). New York: Norton.

Freeman, J. & Combs, G. (1996). *Narrative therapy. The social construction of preferred realities.* New York: Norton.

Galtung, J. (1996). *After violence: 3R, reconstruction, reconciliation, resolution. Coping with visible and invisible effects of war and violence.* www.transcend.org

Kayser, U. (2000). *What do we tell our children? The work of the Centre for Ubuntu in Cape Town.* Centre for the Study of Violence and Reconciliation. *www.csvr.org.za/papers*

Lederach, J. P. (1995). *Preparing for peace. Conflict transformation across cultures.* Syracuse: Syracuse University Press.

Lederach, J. P. (1997). *Building peace: Sustainable reconciliation in divided societies.* Washington, DC: United States Institute of Peace Press.

Maynard, K. (1997). *Rebuilding community: Psychological healing, reintegration, and reconciliation at the grassroots level.* In K. Kumar (Ed.), *Rebuilding war-torn societies: Critical areas for international assistance* (pp. 227–238). Boulder, CO: Lynne Rienner.

Merscham, C. (2000). Restorying trauma with narrative therapy: Using the phantom family. *Family Journal 8*(3), 282–287.

Perry, B. (1996) Incubated in terror: Neurodevelopmental factors in the 'cycle of violence.' In J. D. Osofsky (Ed.), *Children, youth, and violence: Searching for solutions.* New York: Guilford Press.

Salem, R. (2000). *Witness to genocide, the children of Rwanda: Drawings by child survivors of the Rwanda genocide of 1994.* New York: Friendship Press.

Shapiro, F. (2001). *Eye Movement Desensitization and Reprocessing: Basic principles, protocols, and procedures.* New York: Guilford Press.

Shapiro, F. & Silk-Forest, M. (1997). *EMDR: The breakthrough therapy for overcoming anxiety, stress, and trauma.* New York: Basic Books.

Silver, S., & Rogers, S. (2002). *Light in the heart of darkness: EMDR and the treatment of war and terrorism survivors.* New York: Norton.

Smyth, M. (2001). Putting the past in its place: Issues of victimhood and reconciliation in Northern Ireland's peace process. In M. Biggar, (Ed.), *Burying the past. Making peace and doing justice after civil conflict* (pp. 107–130). Washington, DC: Georgetown University Press.

van der Kolk, B. (1989). The compulsion to repeat the trauma: Re-enactment, revictimization, and masochism. *Psychiatric Clinics of North America, 12*(2), 389–411.

van der Kolk, B. (1996). The complexity of adaptation to trauma. Self-regulation, stimulus discrimination, and characterological development. In B. A. van der Kolk, A. C. McFarlane, & L. Weisaeth (Eds.), *Traumatic stress: The effects of overwhelming experience on mind, body and society.* New York: Guilford Press.

van der Kolk, B. (1996b.). The body keeps the score. Approaches to the psychobiology of posttraumatic stress disorder. In B. A. van der Kolk, A. C. McFarlane, & L. Weisaeth (Eds.), *Traumatic stress: The effects of overwhelming experience on mind, body and society.* New York: Guilford Press.

Volkan, V. (1988). *The need to have enemies and allies: From clinical practice to international relationships.* Northvale, NJ: Aronson.

Volkan, V. (1997). *Bloodlines: From ethnic pride to ethnic terrorism.* New York: Farrar, Straus and Giroux.

Watzlawick, P., Weakland, J., & Fisch, R. (1974). *Change.* New York: Norton.

Wessells, Michael G. (1998). Humanitarian intervention, psychosocial assistance, and peacekeeping. In H. J. Langholtz (Ed.), *The psychology of peacekeeping.* New York: Praeger.

White, M. (1991). Deconstruction and therapy. *Dulwich Centre Newsletter, 3,* 211–240.

White, M., & Epston, D. (1990). *Narrative means to therapeutic ends.* New York: Norton.

Witty, C. J. & Tauber, C. D. (2002). Psycho-trauma and non-violent conflict resolution: ECPCR5. *Conflict Resolution Notes, 19*(3), 32–34.

# [26]

# The Architecture of Government in the Face of Terrorism

*Ashton B. Carter*

On September 11, 2001, the post–Cold War security bubble finally burst. In the preceding ten years, the United States and its major allies failed to identify and invest in the prevention of "A-list" security problems that could affect their way of life, position in the world, and very survival. Instead they behaved as if gulled into a belief that the key security problems of the post–Cold War era were ethnic and other internal conflicts in Bosnia, Somalia, Rwanda, Haiti, East Timor, and Kosovo. Peacekeeping and peacemaking in these places, although engaging important humanitarian concerns, never addressed the vital security interests of the United States, and none of these conflicts could begin to threaten its survival. As if to confirm this point, the official military strategy of the United States during the last decade centered not on peacekeeping but on the challenge of fighting two Desert Storm reruns, one in Korea and one in the Persian Gulf, at the same time. The two-major-theater-war doctrine at least had the virtue of addressing threats to vital U.S. allies and interests. But as the decade wore on, it was increasingly apparent that although important interests were at stake in both major theaters, in neither was U.S. survival in question. The A-list seemed empty, so policy and strategy focused on B- and C-level problems instead.[1]

A-list threats, such as the threat posed by the Soviet Union for the preceding half-century—were indeed absent, but only if threat is understood as the imminent possibility of attack defined in traditional military terms. If taken instead to denote looming problems that could develop into Cold War–scale dangers, the A-list contained at least four major underattended items in the

*Ashton B. Carter is Professor of Science and International Affairs at Harvard University's John F. Kennedy School of Government and Co-director of the Preventive Defense Project, a research collaboration of the John F. Kennedy School of Government and Stanford University.*

The author is grateful for the support of the Carnegie Corporation of New York, the John D. and Catherine T. MacArthur Foundation, the Packard Foundation, the Simons Foundation, and the Herbert S. Winokur, Jr., Fund for support of this work. The author has benefited from discussions with William J. Perry, John P. White, and Herbert S. Winokur, Jr., and from the editorial and research assistance of Gretchen M. Bartlett in the preparation of this article.

1. This argument and the corresponding A-, B-, and C-lists are derived from Ashton B. Carter and William J. Perry, *Preventive Defense: A New Security Strategy for America* (Washington, D.C.: Brookings, 1999).

*International Security 26:3* | 6

1990s: (1) the collapse of Moscow's power, (2) the growth of Beijing's military and economic might, (3) proliferation of weapons of mass destruction, and (4) the prospect of catastrophic terrorism. Upon taking office, George W. Bush and his administration claimed to be formulating their strategy around the first two of these items, in a self-proclaimed return to big power realism. But in the wake of the World Trade Center and Pentagon attacks of September 11, the Bush administration is instead finding its agenda dominated by catastrophic terrorism, for which it appears no more or less prepared than its predecessor Bush, Sr., and Clinton administrations.

The challenge of catastrophic terrorism is destined to be a centerpiece of the field of international security studies, and thus of the readers and writers of the pages of this journal, for the foreseeable future. Today the focus is a particular nest of Islamic extremists operating freely from the lawless failed state of Afghanistan. But the last time that a building in the United States was destroyed in a terrorist attack, the Alfred P. Murrah Federal Building in Oklahoma City in April 1995, the perpetrator was homegrown, an embittered American nihilist operating in the vast anonymity of modern society. One month earlier, an obscure cult in Japan put sarin nerve gas in a Tokyo subway and attempted an airborne anthrax release. Indeed the varieties of extremism that can spawn catastrophic terrorism seem limitless, and they have not been studied as thoroughly by social scientists as have the dynamics of great power rivalry. What is clear is that war-scale destructive power is becoming increasingly available as technology advances. The same advances heighten the complexity and interconnectedness of civilization, making society more vulnerable at the same time it delivers to small groups destructive powers that were formerly the monopoly of states. Thus if security is understood to be the avoidance and control of mass threat, catastrophic terrorism must occupy a central place in security studies, a status that "ordinary" non-mass terrorism never achieved.[2]

---

2. Studies dealing with catastrophic terrorism include: Richard A. Falkenrath, Robert D. Newman, and Bradley A. Thayer, *America's Achilles' Heel: Nuclear, Biological, and Chemical Terrorism and Covert Attack* (Cambridge, Mass.: MIT Press, 1998); "A False Alarm (This Time): Preventive Defense against Catastrophic Terrorism," in Carter and Perry, *Preventive Defense*, pp. 143–174; Ashton B. Carter, John M. Deutch, and Philip D. Zelikow, "Catastrophic Terrorism: Tackling the New Danger," *Foreign Affairs*, Vol. 77, No. 6 (November/December 1998), pp. 80–94; Robert T. Marsh, John R. Powers, Merritt E. Adams, Richard P. Case, Mary J. Culnan, Peter H. Daly, John C. Davis, Thomas J. Falvey, Brenton C. Green, William J. Harris, David A. Jones, William B. Joyce, David V. Keyes, Stevan D. Mitchell, Joseph J. Moorcones, Irwin M. Pikus, William Paul Rodgers, Jr., Susan V. Simens, Frederick M. Struble, and Nancy J. Wong, *Critical Foundations: Protecting America's Infrastructures: The Report of the President's Commission on Critical Infrastructure Protection* (Washington, D.C., October 1997); The Gilmore Commission, James S. Gilmore III, James Clapper, Jr., L. Paul Bremer, Raymond Downey, George Foresman, William Garrison, Ellen M. Gordon, James Greenleaf, William Jenaway, William Dallas Jones, Paul M. Maniscalco, Ronald S. Neubauer, Kathleen

*The Architecture of Government* | 7

The resulting agenda of analysis and policy development is wide. First, the motivations and root causes of catastrophic terrorism—inscrutable as they may now seem—must eventually yield at least in part to careful study.[3] Second, the potential of catastrophic terrorism to transform traditional international relations should also be studied and its policy consequences propounded, as the great powers—the United States, Europe, Japan, Russia, and China—set aside some of the lesser issues that divide them and acknowledge a great common interest in protecting their homelands.[4] This article concerns a third dimension of policy: the need to reengineer the architecture of governance—security institutions and their modes of operation—when war-scale damage results from terrorism.[5]

## The Governance Issue

Post–Cold War complacency was only one reason that the United States found itself so surprised by, and so unprepared for, the onset of catastrophic terrorism and the mission of homeland security. A deeper reason is that the security institutions of the U.S. federal government are particularly ill-suited to deliver

O'Brien, M. Patricia Quinlisk, Patrick Ralston, William Reno, Kenneth Shine, and Ellen Embrey, *First Annual Report to the President and the Congress of the Advisory Panel to Assess Domestic Response Capabilities to Terrorism Involving Weapons of Mass Destruction I: Assessing the Threat* (Washington, D.C., December 15, 1999), http://www.rand.org/nsrd/terrpanel/terror.pdf; The Gilmore Commission, James S. Gilmore III, James Clapper, Jr., L. Paul Bremer, Raymond Downey, Richard A. Falkenrath, George Foresman, William Garrison, Ellen M. Gordon, James Greenleaf, William Jenaway, William Dallas Jones, Paul M. Maniscalco, John O. Marsh, Jr., Kathleen O'Brien, M. Patricia Quinlisk, Patrick Ralston, William Reno, Joseph Samuels, Jr., Kenneth Shine, Hubert Williams, and Ellen Embrey, *Second Annual Report to the President and the Congress of the Advisory Panel to Assess Domestic Response Capabilities to Terrorism Involving Weapons of Mass Destruction II: Toward a National Security for Combating Terrorism* (Washington, D.C., December 15, 2000), http://www.rand.org/nsrd/terrpanel/terror2.pdf; and The National Commission on Terrorism, Ambassador L. Paul Bremer III, Maurice Sonnenberg, Richard K. Betts, Wayne A. Downing, Jane Harman, Fred C. Iklé, Juliette N. Kayyem, John F. Lewis, Jr., Gardner Peckham, and R. James Woolsey, *Countering the Changing Threat of International Terrorism*, report of the National Commission on Terrorism (Washington, D.C., June 5, 2000), http://www.fas.org/irp/threat/commission.html.
3. Jessica Stern, *The Ultimate Terrorists* (Cambridge, Mass.: Harvard University Press, 1999); and Philip B. Heymann, *Terrorism and America: A Commonsense Strategy for a Democratic Society* (Cambridge, Mass.: MIT Press, 1998).
4. See Stephen M. Walt, "Beyond bin Laden: Reshaping U.S Foreign Policy," in this issue.
5. Ashton B. Carter and William J. Perry with David Aidekman, "Countering Asymmetric Threats," in Carter and John P. White, eds., *Keeping the Edge: Managing Defense for the Future* (Cambridge, Mass.: MIT Press, 2001), pp. 119–126; and The Hart-Rudman Commission, Gary Hart, Warren B. Rudman, Anne Armstrong, Norman R. Augustine, John Dany, John R. Galvin, Leslie H. Gelb, Newt Gingrich, Lee H. Hamilton, Lionel H. Olmer, Donald B. Rice, James Schlesinger, Harry D. Train, and Andrew Young, *Road Map for National Security: Imperative for Change: The Phase III Report of the U.S. Commission on National Security/21st Century* (Washington, D.C., February 15, 2001).

homeland security. Greater awareness of the threat since September 11 alone will not rectify this problem. There is a fundamental managerial inadequacy, as basic as that of a corporation with no line manager to oversee the making of its leading product.

Pundits have been debating whether the campaign to prevent catastrophic terrorism is a "war" or not. If one sets aside semantics and asks the practical managerial question, Can U.S. preparations for war be easily adapted to preparation for catastrophic terrorism? the answer is no. Preparations for war in the military, diplomatic, and intelligence senses are the province of institutions—the Departments of Defense and State, and the intelligence community—whose focus and missions have been "over there" in the fields of Flanders, the beaches of Normandy, the jungles of Vietnam, and the desert of Kuwait. Their opponents have been foreign governments, and even against them they have not been asked to defend the U.S. homeland in recent history except through the abstraction of nuclear deterrence.

If catastrophic terrorism cannot really be treated as a war, then perhaps it should be conceived as a crime. But the U.S. law enforcement paradigm is also ill-suited to deal with catastrophic terrorism. This paradigm centers on the post facto attribution of crimes to their perpetrators and to prosecution under the law. So deeply entrenched is this model that four weeks after the September 11 attacks, the attorney general had to prod the Federal Bureau of Investigation publicly to shift its efforts from "solving the case" to preventing another disaster.[6] Additionally, if the focus of the war model is foreign perpetrators, the focus of the law enforcement model is the American citizen. Neither model encompasses the transnational drifter that is characteristic of the al-Qaeda operative.

Early in the Bush administration, the new director of the Federal Emergency Management Agency (FEMA) asserted that catastrophic terrorism was not a war or a crime, but a disaster, and thus the province of his agency, even obtaining a presidential directive to that effect.[7] In so doing, he reversed the previous FEMA management, which regarded catastrophic terrorism as a new mission with no funding and thus to be avoided. But even armed with a presidential directive, FEMA seemed unable to convince anyone that acts of God and acts of terror were similar enough that a managerial solution was to be found in combining them.

---

6. Philip Shenon and David Johnston, "F.B.I. Shifts Focus to Try to Avert Any More Attacks," *New York Times*, October 9, 2001.
7. Vernon Loeb, "Cheney to Lead Anti-Terrorism Plan Team: New FEMA Office Will Coordinate Response Efforts of More Than 40 Agencies, Officials Say," *Washington Post*, May 9, 2001, p. A29.

*The Architecture of Government* | 9

Thus the federal government lacked a managerial category for catastrophic terrorism, which is neither war, crime, nor disaster, as conventionally understood. Preparations for mass terrorism therefore proceeded haltingly in the 1990s. Some progress was made when preparedness was tied to specific events, such as the 1996 Atlanta Olympics.[8] But elsewhere the preparations were more the result of the efforts of a few well-placed individuals—in the Departments of Defense, Justice, and Health and Human Services—who had become concerned about the problem, than of any overall managerial scheme. As the decade wore on, money did begin to flow to such programs as training state and local governments in weapons of mass destruction.[9] But these efforts were largely the result of congressional initiative and inevitably reflected constituent interests. They did not lead to the development of a program to build a national capability for combating catastrophic terrorism.

Outside the federal bureaucracy, even less was done. State and local governments, key to both prevention and response to this new threat, generally lacked the resources and specialized knowledge to combat catastrophic terrorism. The role of the private sector—for example, in protecting critical infrastructures such as communications and power networks from disruption or in funding protection through insurance—remained undefined.

Before September 11, 2001, therefore, the U.S. government did not have a managerial approach (i.e., a framework for bringing responsibility, accountability, and resources together in sharp focus) to deliver a key public good—security in the homeland against catastrophic terrorism. This managerial deficiency was not unique to catastrophic terrorism. The post–Cold War world spawned a host of novel security missions for government: peacekeeping and post-peacekeeping civil reconstruction, counterproliferation, threat reduction, information warfare, and conflict prevention (or "preventive defense"). Although it is widely agreed that the United States needs to be able to accomplish these missions (even if debate continues over exactly when and where it should perform them), no fundamental changes have been made in the security architecture to create better institutions and capabilities for them.

---

8. Kennedy School of Government case authored by John Buntin, Parts A–C: "Security Preparations for the 1996 Centennial Olympic Games (Part A)," Case No. C16-00-1582.0; "Security Preparations for the 1996 Centennial Olympic Games: Seeking a Structural Fix (Part B)," Case No. C-16-00-1589.0; and "Security Preparations for the 1996 Centennial Olympic Games: The Games Begin (Part C)," Case No. C16-00-1590.0.
9. Defense against Weapons of Mass Destruction Act 1996 (Nunn-Lugar-Domenici), Public Law 104-201 (H.R. 3230), September 23, 1996, National Defense Authorization Act for Fiscal Year 1997, 104th Cong., 2d sess., http://www.fas.org/spp/starwars/congress/1996/pl104-201-xiv.htm.

*International Security 26:3* | 10

Indeed, at least on paper the federal structure has changed little since the first burst of innovation in the aftermath of World War II and the onset of the Cold War. No comparable burst occurred in the 1990s. It is as though corporate America was managing the modern economy with the structures of the Ford Motor Company, the Bell System, and United Fruit. Company managements spend a great deal of thought and energy on organizing their functions to align executive authority with key products. The federal government disperses executive authority so thoroughly that few individuals believe they are accountable for any of the government's key security outputs. People rise to the top of the Washington heap because of their policy expertise, not their managerial expertise. Those senior executives who are managerially inclined find their tenures so short and precarious that there seems to be little reward in making changes in "the system" that will make it possible for their successor's successor to be more effective.[10]

Above all, the federal government in the past few decades has eschewed creating new institutions for new missions such as preparedness for catastrophic terrorism. The political climate in the United States has been hostile to "big government," and existing cabinet departments staunchly defend their heritages and authorities, many of which are enshrined in two hundred years of statute. The sense of departmental entrenchment is mirrored on Capitol Hill, where separate authorization and oversight committees protect each "stovepipe"—national security, law enforcement, disaster relief, public health, and so on—as jealously as the executive agencies themselves.

It is not surprising, therefore, that the specter of catastrophic terrorism occasions deep reflections on the nature and structure of governance in the United States. What needs to be done next cannot be understood without reference to these problems, and to past attempts to overcome them.

## Four Failed Approaches

In broad outline, four approaches to managing the mission of homeland security have been proposed: the command and control approach of the Clinton administration, the lead agency approach, the establishment of a Department of Homeland Security, and the appointment of a White House coordinator or "czar." To date, the Bush administration appears to be focusing on the last, which like the other three has inherent deficiencies.

---

10. Ashton B. Carter, "Keeping the Edge: Managing Defense for the Future," in Carter and White, *Keeping the Edge*, pp. 1–26.

*The Architecture of Government* | 11

The Clinton administration defined its approach in command and control terms: Which federal agency should be in charge of dealing with catastrophic terrorism? Initially, the administration determined that the Department of Justice would "have the lead" in domestic terrorist incidents, while the Department of State would do so in incidents abroad. This approach both reinforced the false distinction between domestic and foreign terrorism and focused on acts in progress rather than on advance detection, prevention, and protection. Later, the Clinton administration promulgated two presidential directives, PDD-62 and PDD-63, which further apportioned the matter of "who's in charge" among the existing agencies according to their traditional functions.[11] Thus, for example, PDD-63 assigned protection of the financial system to the Treasury Department. The fact that this department had no funds, no technology, and little authority to regulate in the field of cybersecurity did not deter the authors of PDD-63. In fact, by focusing on the question of who is in charge, the command and control approach presumed that the government possessed the capabilities to combat catastrophic terrorism; all that was required was to marshal them effectively under a clear command system. The result was the creation of a host of unfunded mandates, responsibilities assigned with no plan for providing the means to fulfill them. The administration made no provision to build new capability, which was—and remains—the crux of the matter.

A second approach considered was to designate a single lead agency as having the homeland defense mission. In this approach, the proposed lead was usually the Department of Defense. DoD was presumed to have already much relevant technology, an ample budget, and a reputation for carrying out its mission more effectively than most other government agencies.[12] But this approach failed because too much of the relevant capability—for example, for surveillance of potential terrorists on U.S. territory—fell beyond DoD's traditional purview. The Pentagon shared the disinclination to arrogate such sweeping new authorities to itself and proclaimed itself willing to take a strong, but follower, role if another agency would lead the effort.

---

11. Address by President Bill Clinton at the U.S. Naval Academy, May 22, 1998; White House fact sheet, Combating Terrorism, PDD/NSC-62, Protection against Unconventional Threats to the Homeland and Americans Overseas, May 22, 1998, http://www.fas.org/irp/offdocs/pdd-62.htm; and White House fact sheet, PDD/NSC-63, Critical Infrastructure Protection, May 22, 1998, http://www.fas.org/irp/offdocs/pdd/pdd-63.htm.
12. See Joseph S. Nye, Jr., Philip D. Zelikow, and David S. King, eds., *Why People Don't Trust Government* (Cambridge, Mass.: Harvard University Press, 1996), p. 9 and references therein.

*International Security 26:3* | 12

A third approach called for the creation of a Department of Homeland Security.[13] This approach sought to escape the problem of interagency coordination by concentrating the catastrophic terrorism mission in a single agency. It recognized that none of the existing cabinet departments was a natural lead agency, and that their ingrained cultures would not easily incline them to adopt the new mission. The fallacy in this approach is that interagency coordination could be thus avoided. Suppose, for example, that the Department of Homeland Security sought to develop a more rapid means of determining whether someone was exposed to anthrax. It would soon discover that this effort was redundant with DoD's efforts to develop the same detector technology for battlefield exposure in accordance with its traditional mission. The problem of interagency coordination would not have been eliminated, but only complicated by the introduction of a new agency. Aggregating functions such as customs, immigration, border patrol, and coast guard into a new agency might be efficient, but it can hardly be said that such an entity should have the lead in homeland defense, or that its creation eliminates the inherently interagency nature of catastrophic terrorism.

A fourth approach to organizing the federal government for catastrophic terrorism is to appoint a White House coordinator or "czar." President Bush named Pennsylvania Governor Tom Ridge to such a post within a month of September 11. This approach is the least problematic, because it recognizes that the essence of the solution is the coordination of a wide range of government functions behind a new priority mission. White House czars, however, have usually been ineffective. With no resources or agencies of their own, they are easily reduced to cajoling cabinet departments into doing what the czar prescribes. The czar's instructions inevitably compete with other needs and tasks of the department, and the final outcome of the competition is determined by the cabinet secretary (invoking legal authorities, usually of long standing) and the relevant committees of Congress, not the czar. After the czar is thus overridden a few times, lower-level bureaucrats conclude that the czar's directives can be ignored. As the Washington saying about czars goes, "The barons ignore them, and eventually the peasants kill them."

## The Crux of the Managerial Challenge

A solution to the managerial challenge of catastrophic terrorism should have two features that the approaches outlined above lack. First, it should acknowl-

---

13. Hart-Rudman Commission, *Road Map for National Security*.

*The Architecture of Government* | 13

edge the inherent and ineluctable interagency nature of the problem and abandon any idea of creating a single lead agency.[14] Second, the approach should begin the long process of providing the United States with a stock of essential capabilities—tactics, technology, and institutions—that the federal departments, state and local governments, and private sector currently lack. Interagency coordination implies a White House focus. But this focus should not be a "czar" who tries to assume or direct the daily functions of all the agencies involved but an "architect" who designs the capabilities that these agencies need to address the problem. This approach gives the architect budgetary authority (the key to his influence) and applies that influence where it is needed most: to creating needed capabilities rather than stirring up empty command and control disputes over who is in charge of capabilities that are woefully inadequate or do not exist at all. In short, the important function of the White House architect is *program* coordination, not policy coordination or command and control. The program in question is a multiyear, multiagency effort to develop tactics, technology, and where required new institutions for the ongoing struggle against catastrophic terrorism.

Perhaps the most apt analogy for the job required of the White House is provided not by any war that the United States has fought, but rather by the Cold War. In 1949 Josef Stalin's Soviet Union exploded an atomic bomb over the steppes of Kazakhstan. Although no U.S. citizens died in that distant blast, Americans were suddenly gripped by the prospect of warlike damage being visited upon their homeland by a shadowy enemy with global tentacles. George Kennan warned of a long twilight struggle that would test U.S. patience and resolve. The nation mobilized over time a response that was multifaceted, multiagency, and inventive. Nuclear bombers, missiles, and submarines were built for deterrence and retaliation. Spy satellites were launched for warning. Air defenses were deployed around the nation's periphery, and missile defenses were attempted, to raise the price of attack. Civil defense programs sought to minimize casualties if the worst happened. Special relocation sites and procedures were instituted to ensure continuity of constitutional government if Washington was destroyed. NATO and other alliances were formed to get more friends on the U.S. side, and the Marshall Plan sought to ensure that economic desperation did not become an ally of Stalin. U.S. lead-

---

14. This does not rule out the possibility of creating an agency that combines the functions of such border-related agencies as the Coast Guard, Border Patrol, Immigration and Naturalization Service, and Customs. Accomplishing this bureaucratic feat, however useful, would require the full-time attention of a senior manager with presidential and congressional support. If Governor Ridge were to assume this task, he would have no time for anything else.

*International Security 26:3* | 14

ers further recognized that this new reality was so dangerous that they needed a capacity to analyze, reflect, and learn, not merely react. They founded such think tanks as the RAND Corporation to devise innovative methods for coping with the era's new danger. In time, ideas such as the theory of deterrence and the theory of arms control were elaborated that were not obvious in 1949 but that helped navigate the world through fifty years of Cold War. With difficulty and many mistakes, the nation also learned to deal with fear of a threat at home without hunting "reds" in the State Department and Hollywood. The Cold War effort was massive, extended throughout most of the federal government, and was coordinated by the White House.

Designing a similar long-range program to counter catastrophic terrorism is the task of the Bush White House in the aftermath of September 11, 2001. The National Security Council (NSC) cannot do the job for two reasons. First, it does not normally convene the full range of departments, especially Justice and Health and Human Services, required for this effort. The NSC has largely focused on foreign problems. More fundamental, since Dwight Eisenhower's day the NSC has slowly lost the capacity for program coordination and become a policy coordination body only.[15] That is, it brings the national security agencies together to decide upon a common policy but does not oversee or influence their internal capabilities or budgets. Indeed the NSC's staff is renowned for its diplomatic and policy expertise, but few have experience managing programs or agencies.

President Bush was therefore correct not to give the homeland security job to the NSC, but instead to found the Office of Homeland Security with a broader membership, chaired by Governor Ridge. It is up to Governor Ridge to avoid the fate of White House czars who try to "run things" from the White House. Instead of taking a command and control approach, Ridge should adopt the architect's programmatic approach, designing a multiyear, multiagency plan that will materially increase the capabilities of the existing departments and agencies so that they can play their part in the campaign against catastrophic terrorism. Such an approach would have the additional salutary effect of overriding the tendency, prevalent as the fiscal year 2002 budget was finalized in the aftermath of September 11, for individual agencies and their oversight committees to craft their own response to the counterterror challenge. In many cases, these responses amounted to little more than long-standing budgetary requests to

---

15. John Deutch, Arnold Kanter, and Brent Scowcroft with Chris Hornbarger, "Strengthening the National Security Interagency Process," in Carter and White, *Keeping the Edge*, pp. 265–284.

*The Architecture of Government* | 15

which the label "counterterrorism" was conveniently applied. Elsewhere, multiple agencies vied to make redundant subscale investments where a single large investment by only one of them is needed.

The homeland security program might be organized functionally according to a time line extending from before a hypothetical incident of catastrophic terrorism to its aftermath. In the first phase, the United States needs better capabilities for *detection* of catastrophic terrorism. This involves surveillance of persons and motives—a delicate matter—but also surveillance of potential means of destruction such as crop dusters, germ cultures, and pilot instruction. Surveillance of means raises far fewer civil liberties issues than does surveillance of persons, and it might be much more effective. A group that evades surveillance becomes subject to *prevention* by efforts to keep destructive means out of their hands. The Nunn-Lugar program to safeguard Russian nuclear weapons and fissile materials is an example of a prevention program. The next stage is *protection*, making borders, buildings, airplanes, and critical infrastructures more difficult to breach, disrupt, or destroy through technical design and procedures. Protection might also mean making people more resilient to disease through vaccination and other public health measures. *Interdiction* or "crisis management" seeks to disrupt and destroy potential perpetrators of catastrophic terrorism and their base of support before they can mount an attack, as in the current campaign in Afghanistan. *Containment* or "consequence management" means limiting the level of damage and the number of casualties by organizing emergency response, public health measures, and restoration of critical functions in the aftermath of a terrorist attack. *Attribution* refers to the capability to find the perpetrators of an act (e.g., by typing an anthrax culture or performing radiochemical analysis of nuclear bomb debris) and choosing retaliation, prosecution, or other response. Finally, as with the RAND Corporation in the Cold War, the nation will need a capacity for *analysis and invention*: studying terrorist tactics and devising countermeasures, understanding motivations and modes of deterrence, drawing lessons from past attacks, creating new technologies, and developing a systematic plan.

Schematically, the result of such an effort by the Office of Homeland Security would resemble a simple matrix, in which functions are arrayed in columns and the agencies involved in carrying them out in rows (see Figure 1). In each box would appear the agency's responsibility, if any, for possessing capability in that function, with a plan to develop that capability over a period of years. The president would approve such a matrix for each fiscal year extending five years into the future, and would send it to the Congress with his annual bud-

Figure 1. Dimensions of a Homeland Security Program: The Architect's Program Plan.

| | Detection | Prevention | Protection | Interdiction | Containment | Attribution | Analysis and Invention |
|---|---|---|---|---|---|---|---|
| Justice/FBI | | | | | | | |
| Defense | | | | | | | |
| Intelligence | | | | | | | |
| Health and Human Services | | | | | | | |
| Border (Coast Guard, Border Patrol, Customs, Immigration, etc.) | | | | | | | |
| FEMA | | | | | | | |
| Other (Energy, Transportation, Agriculture, State, etc.) | | | | | | | |
| New Federal Agencies or Nonprofit Institutions | | | | | | | |
| State and Local Government (supported by federal grants) | | | | | | | |
| Private Sector (via regulation, subsidy, and indemnification) | | | | | | | |

get submission. Although Congress would of course have the last word on the budget, experience shows that it makes only marginal adjustments where there is a strong and clear presidential program on a subject of great national importance.

## Key Ingredients of the Homeland Security Program

The homeland security program will have many key components. Below are a few illustrative examples.

### RED TEAM, BLUE TEAM

Most Americans were probably not shocked to learn on September 12 that the U.S. government did not have advance information about the dozen or so individuals residing in the country who plotted and took part in the airline suicide attacks of September 11. They probably were deeply disturbed to learn, however, that the government was as heedless of the tactic used as it was of the perpetrators. The airline security system inspected for guns and bombs, not knives; aircrews were trained to deal with hijackers who sought hostages or conveyance to Cuba, not kamikaze attack. In retrospect, a huge gap existed in the U.S. air safety system. Terrorists detected it before the security system did—and exploited it.

To avoid tactical surprise of this kind, the homeland security effort needs to adopt a standard mechanism of military organizations: competing red and blue teams. The red team tries to devise attack tactics, and the blue team tries to design countermeasures. When the United States developed the first stealth aircraft, for example, the air force created a red team to try to detect and shoot them down. When the red team identified a weakness in the stealth design, the blue team was charged to fix it, systematically balancing risk of detection against the cost and inconvenience of countermeasures.

A comparable red/blue team mechanism should be the central feature of the program for homeland security. To work, the mechanism must be systematic and institutionalized, not ad hoc. It must be independent of the interests— airlines, for example—that stand to be inconvenienced by its findings. It must have the money to conduct experiments, tests, and inspections, not just paper studies. It must be knowledgeable about the technologies of terrorism and protection. Above all, it must be inventive. These criteria all argue for a new institutional founding outside of, but close to, government. Models include the National Academies of Sciences, the RAND Corporation, the Mitre and

Mitretek Systems Corporations, the Institute for Defense Analyses, and other nonprofit research organizations established during the Cold War.

SCIENCE AND TECHNOLOGY

American society has many weaknesses in the battle against catastrophic terrorism. It is large and open. Its infrastructures are complex and interconnected. It values free movement, free speech, and privacy. Its commanding international position is a lightning rod for many international grievances. The United States must therefore draw on its key strengths in ensuring homeland security, among which inventiveness, deriving from its huge science and technology base, is probably most important. The U.S. military has long sought to use superior technology to offset opponents' favorable geography, superior numbers, and willingness to suffer casualties.[16] The homeland security effort requires a program of contract research and technology development that should be conducted outside of government, in universities and private companies. The contracting methods should permit small and entrepreneurial commercial companies that are the drivers of new technology, and not just large government contractors, to participate in the effort. Biotechnology companies, which unlike the aerospace and information technology industries have never had strong ties to national security, should be induced to participate.[17] Finally, "centers of excellence" in counterterrorism should be established. These centers should set out to develop the same depth of expertise represented by the Los Alamos, Livermore, and Sandia National Laboratories in the field of nuclear weapons design during the Cold War.

TRANSNATIONAL INTELLIGENCE

A number of studies have called attention to the problem of combining information derived from foreign intelligence collection with information derived from domestic law enforcement.[18] The rules governing collection in the two categories differ for the important reason that U.S. persons enjoy protections from surveillance that do not apply to the overseas activities of the intelligence community. There is no reason, however, why information of both types col-

---

16. William J. Perry, "Desert Storm and Deterrence," *Foreign Affairs*, Vol. 70, No 4. (Fall 1991), pp. 64–82; and Ashton B. Carter with Marcel Lettre and Shane Smith, "Keeping the Technological Edge," in Carter and White, *Keeping the Edge*, pp. 129–163.
17. Joshua Lederberg, ed., *Biological Weapons: Limiting the Threat* (Cambridge, Mass.: MIT Press, 1999), chap. 1.
18. Gilmore Commission, *First and Second Annual Reports to the President and the Congress*; Carter, Deutch, and Zelikow, "Catastrophic Terrorism"; Hart-Rudman Commission, *Road Map for National Security*; and Heymann, *Terrorism and America*.

The Architecture of Government | 19

lected by the U.S. government in accordance with the respective rules for each cannot be combined and correlated. The barriers to doing so are largely bureaucratic. These barriers need to be surmounted in an era when individuals move easily across borders, and when groups fomenting terrorism are likely to be transnational in their membership.[19]

INTELLIGENCE OF MEANS

Surveillance of the *means* that terrorists employ is potentially more important than surveillance of *persons*, and raises far fewer civil liberties issues. Placing all Middle Eastern male noncitizens resident in the United States under surveillance, for example, is both objectionable and impractical. But inquiring after all those persons, of whatever nationality, who take flying lessons but are not interested in learning to take off or land, who rent crop dusters, or who seek information on the antibiotic resistance of anthrax strains or the layout of a nuclear power plant is feasible and might be extremely useful.

Likewise, it is undesirable to restrict access by citizens to the Capitol building and congressional office buildings, but there is no fundamental technical barrier to seeding these buildings with sensors that would promptly, and with a low rate of false alarms, detect the presence of anthrax on surfaces and in ventilation systems. Nuclear weapons are much harder to detect, but the streets in the vicinity of the White House could be laced with sensitive detectors that would stand a good chance of finding a nuclear weapon or radiological weapon. Although these detectors would individually have a high rate of false alarms, when networked so that their outputs are correlated in space and time, they could comprise an effective warning system. Such a system is preferable to registering truck drivers or other methods of surveilling persons in the White House vicinity.

CONTROL OF WEAPONS AND MATERIALS

Ten years into the Nunn-Lugar program to safeguard nuclear, chemical, and biological weapons and materials in the former Soviet Union, a job remains to be completed.[20] In addition to continuing to support and greatly expand this

---

19. A specific proposal for combining CIA and FBI intelligence on transnational terrorism is contained in "A False Alarm (This Time)," pp. 143–174; and Carter, Deutch, and Zelikow, "Catastrophic Terrorism."

20. See Matthew Bunn, *The Next Wave: Urgently Needed New Steps to Control Warheads and Fissile Material* (Washington, D.C., and Cambridge, Mass.: Carnegie Endowment for International Peace and Harvard Project on Managing the Atom, April 2000); and Howard Baker and Lloyd Cutler, cochairs, *A Report Card on the Department of Energy's Nonproliferation Programs with Russia* (Washington, D.C.: U.S. Department of Energy, Secretary of Energy Advisory Board, January 10, 2001).

*International Security 26:3* | 20

program, the effort must be extended to Pakistan, where an arsenal of substantial size might fall prey to growing extremism.

THE COSTS OF PROTECTION

Protective measures for homeland security cover a wide spectrum of possibilities: vaccines, air defenses around the White House and nuclear power plants, electronic firewalls around information networks, to name just a few examples. The investments required could be enormous. Who will pay? Private investment could be mandated by regulation. Government could bear or subsidize the costs. Or apportionment of risk and blame could be left to the insurance marketplace and tort courtrooms. The answer will vary from case to case, but the federal government needs to devise a strategy. Crafting the right regulation and legislation, as well as putting the right subsidies in the federal budget, will be a key responsibility of the homeland security architect.

NATIONAL INFORMATION ASSURANCE INSTITUTE

A major ingredient of the protection effort must be safeguarding the information infrastructure that resides overwhelmingly in private hands. Developing protective tools and techniques, sharing information on threats between government and private network operators, and establishing the proper balance between regulation and government spending to strengthen networks will require a public-private partnership. These objectives could be accomplished through a nonprofit institution dedicated to this purpose and funded jointly by government and participating private network operators. Several such institutions have already been proposed.[21]

INTERDICTION

Soon after September 11, President Bush enunciated a principle of U.S. policy against catastrophic terrorism that, if pursued to its logical conclusion, would establish interdiction as an ongoing effort rather than an episodic response to actual attacks. In his first major public pronouncement following the September attacks, the president said, "Either you are with us, or you are with the terrorists."[22] This would seem to imply the need for a continuing program to preempt attack from groups that profess an intention to carry out mass terror-

---

21. "A False Alarm (This Time)," pp. 164–165.
22. President George W. Bush, Address to a Joint Session of Congress and the American People, U.S. Capitol, September 20, 2001.

*The Architecture of Government* | 21

ism and to apply pressure, including attack, against those who actively support or harbor them. Taken literally, such a program of interdiction would have profound consequences for U.S. foreign policy, for alliances such as NATO, and for international organizations such as the United Nations.

PUBLIC HEALTH SURVEILLANCE AND RESPONSE

Containment of the damage from an incident of mass terrorism requires that the public health and agricultural systems establish capabilities that go well beyond their accustomed mission of protecting against naturally occurring dangers. The powers of the public health authorities to mandate disease surveillance and impose such remedies as quarantine are broad, a holdover from the nineteenth century. These authorities need to be updated to encompass man-made pandemics. The private health care system overall, which under the doctrine of managed care is designed to have the least possible excess capacity during normal times, will need to provide such surge capability as extra hospital beds and stockpiled medications carefully chosen and sized for possible bioterrorism.

STATE AND LOCAL FIRST RESPONSE

The Nunn-Lugar-Domenici legislation, passed in 1996, began providing state and local first responders with the equipment and training needed to enhance their vital role in consequence management.[23] Defining the ongoing federal role in supporting state and local government is a major task of the counterterrorism program.

FORENSICS FOR ATTRIBUTION

Ever since the U.S. Air Force sampled the first residue from the Soviet Union's nuclear weapons testing in the 1950s and deduced their detailed design, radiochemical analysis of bomb materials and debris has developed into a sophisticated science. A corresponding effort to type bioterror agents and their chemical preparations is required to attribute attacks to their perpetrators. At this time the FBI, DoD, and the Centers for Disease Control and Prevention all have forensic programs, but none is adequate for counterterror purposes. The

---

23. Falkenrath, Newman, and Thayer, *America's Achilles' Heel*; and Richard A. Falkenrath, "The Problems of Preparedness: Challenges Facing the U.S. Domestic Preparedness Program," BCSIA Discussion Paper 2000-28, ESDP Discussion Paper 2000-05 (Cambridge, Mass.: Belfer Center for Science and International Affairs and Executive Session on Domestic Preparedness, John F. Kennedy School of Government, Harvard University, December 2000).

counterterror program architect will need to decide which of these programs will be funded to provide the greatly expanded capability the nation needs.

MOBILIZATION AND SUNSET

Until the mid-twentieth century, successful prosecution of war depended on the ability to mobilize nations and armies. A similar concept is useful in the war on terrorism. In the face of reasonably credible and specific information about actual or imminent mass terrorism, extraordinary measures might be advisable that are undesirable when there are no such warnings. In an emergency, the government will assume special authorities, restrict movement and other freedoms, and impose economic disruptions as the nation hunkers down. It is important to the quality of civil society in the long run that this mobilized state be clearly distinguished in statute and procedures from "normal" times when catastrophic terrorism is an ever-present, but not specifically anticipated, contingency. Experience in the United Kingdom during its century-long struggle against Irish terrorism suggests that even in liberal democracies, powers granted to the government in the name of imminent terrorism are seldom rescinded when the threat recedes.[24] It is therefore important to write into any statute or regulation conferring extraordinary powers on the government a sunset clause describing the time and method of demobilization, placing the burden for extending the mobilization squarely on the government's ability to produce credible and specific information of imminent threat.

## Conclusion

Merely coordinating the existing capabilities of the United States to counter catastrophic terrorism is not adequate to protect the nation or the international order from this major new challenge, because the existing capabilities fall far short of what is needed. Nor is it practical to imagine having someone in the federal government who is truly in charge of a mission that inherently cuts across all agencies of the federal government, state and local government, and the private sector. What is required instead is a multiyear, multiagency program of invention and investment devised in the White House, embedded in the president's budget submissions and defended by him to Congress, and

---

24. Laura K. Donohue, "Civil Liberties, Terrorism, and Liberal Democracy: Lessons from the United Kingdom," BCSIA Discussion Paper 2000-05, ESDP Discussion Paper 2000-01 (Cambridge, Mass.: Belfer Center for Science and International Affairs and Executive Session on Domestic Preparedness, John F. Kennedy School of Government, Harvard University, August 2000).

*The Architecture of Government* | 23

supported by appropriate law and regulation. This program should cover all phases in the war against catastrophic terrorism—detection, prevention, protection, interdiction, containment, attribution, and analysis and invention. If President Bush's director of homeland security assumes the role of architect of such an effort, he will provide future presidents with the tools they will need to cope with this enduring problem.

# 27

# Military Deterrence of International Terrorism: An Evaluation of Operation El Dorado Canyon

HENRY W. PRUNCKUN, JR.

Slezak Associates
Wayville, South Australia

PHILIP B. MOHR

University of South Australia
School of Psychology
Adelaide, South Australia

*This study addresses the question of whether Operation El Dorado Canyon, the April 1986 U.S. air raid on Libya, influenced the pattern of international terrorism in the period that followed. Specifically, the study documents the frequency and severity of acts of international terrorism over a forty-one-month period centered on the date of the raid. Findings indicate that the level of activity of Libyan-associated terrorist groups and, after a brief up-surge, the frequency of attacks against U.S. targets both declined after the raid. Whereas the number of acts of international terrorism worldwide was similar for the periods before and after the operation, the postraid period was characterized by a shift from acts of medium and high severity to acts of low severity in violence. Although findings are inconclusive, they are consistent with the view that the raid had a generalized deterrent effect on international terrorism for the period examined.*

International terrorism is a phenomenon that governments around the world have come to fear.[1] The problem of how to deal with the threat of terrorism has been grappled with by political leaders of virtually every democratic nation.[2] For example, since the Second World War there have been hundreds of terrorist groups operating worldwide, each pursuing its own political agenda.[3] Likewise, the cases involving terrorism are seemingly endless.[4] There have been aircraft hijackings, hostage takings, embassy and department store bombings, and the assassination of political leaders and diplomats.

Combating this continuing stream of terrorist events has proved a trouble-some political issue for democratic governments, especially when trying to protect their citizens and property overseas.[5] Governments can usually enact leg-islation to guard against terrorism at home[6] and develop their domestic law

Received 15 July 1996; accepted 10 October 1996.
Address correspondence to Henry W. Prunckun, Jr., Slezak Associates, 57 Daven-port Terrace, Wayville, South Australia 5034. E-mail: slezak@dove.net.au

enforcement agencies to detect and deter potential local events.[7] Governments can also exercise a large measure of control when resolving events such as hostage situations that have already unfolded domestically.[8] However, when faced with an event overseas, far from their geographic sovereignty, governments are especially vulnerable, and terrorists know this.[9]

### State-Sponsored Terrorism

The potential of terrorist groups to inflict damage against a state is increased by the support—active or passive—given to such groups by other states. State-sponsored terrorism, the most extreme manifestation of such support, has been described in the context of international relations as low-intensity conflict—a form of warfare that does not draw national armies into confrontation on the battlefield.

> It is a category of conflict that has become ever more prominent in an era of weapons of mass destruction, in which the penalties of escalated hostilities loom prohibitively. Low-intensity conflict permits avoidance of those penalties. And state-sponsored terrorism recommends itself especially as a means of waging clandestine, undeclared war.[10]

The use of terrorists as agents of their foreign diplomacy entails few risks, and it is an association that the employing state can easily deny in public.

Although the existence of individual cases of state-sponsored terrorism may be difficult to establish,[11] it is apparent that some states, Libya notably among them, have regarded terrorism as one means of conducting foreign relations.[12] According to Brian L. Davis,[13] Libya, under Muammar Qaddafi, established a large network of training camps which at times gave support to specific attacks. Davis reported that during the 1980s Libya trained as many as seven to eight thousand terrorists and guerrillas per year, spent approximately US$100 million on arms and financial disbursements to Palestinian terrorists, shared intelligence with terrorist groups, provided transport aboard Libyan airliners, supplied false passports, and safe-housed terrorists operating in Europe. In the middle and late 1980s Libya's financial support to terrorists reportedly surpassed that of all other terrorist-supporting countries with the exception of Iran.[14]

Whereas state sponsorship adds to the potential extent of terrorist activities, it may also, paradoxically, increase the options available to the states against which terrorism is directed. Over the years, the policies adopted by target states for dealing with international terrorism have been predominantly based on a law enforcement model.[15] As was the case for insurgent movements of the 1950s and 1960s, terrorism has been found to be difficult to counter using traditional law enforcement methods.[16] However, the knowledge or belief that terrorism is, directly or indirectly, the hostile act of another state provides the target state with a visible putative foe and creates the circumstances for the exercise of diplomatic or military responses. Those responses include, at the diplomatic level, the imposition of military, economic, or political sanctions, and at the military level, retaliation with the aim of deterring future terrorist attacks.

## Operation El Dorado Canyon, 1986

The issue of state-sponsored terrorism was prominent in the antagonistic relations that existed between the United States and Libya in the mid-1980s and that culminated in the bombing by the U.S. military of the Libyan capital, Tripoli, on 14 April 1986. In the sequence of events leading up to the bombing, the United States had accused Libya of having been involved, through the provision of bases and training, in the simultaneous terrorist attacks on Rome and Vienna airports on 27 December 1985.[17] Relations between the two nations worsened to the point of a limited naval engagement on 24 and 25 March 1986 in the Gulf of Sidra, where the U.S. Sixth Fleet exercised in defiance of a Libyan-imposed "Line of Death" exclusion zone. On 2 April 1986 a bomb exploded in the passenger cabin of a TWA jet flying over Greece; four Americans were killed.[18] Then on 4 April 1986, at the La Belle Discotheque in West Berlin, a powerful bomb exploded, killing three people, including two American servicemen, and wounding 261 others, including 79 Americans. On 7 April 1986 the U.S. ambassador to West Germany, Richard Burt, announced that the United States had evidence that Libya was involved in the incident.[19]

On April 14 the United States, having announced its intention to raise the costs of terrorism, launched an attack on Libyan targets in what President Ronald Reagan would later say was in retaliation for the direct Libyan role in the West German nightclub bombing.[20] In all, 100 U.S. aircraft took part in the operation, code-named El Dorado Canyon. Of this number, thirteen Air Force F-111 tactical strike bombers based in England and twelve carrier-based Navy A-6 Intruder attack aircraft simultaneously bombed five specific ground targets in and around the cities of Tripoli and Benghazi and struck at numerous surface-to-air missile sites dotted across northern Libya.[21] According to Davis,[22] the raid was intended to be punishing, with high-visibility target damage, and to demonstrate to present and future enemies that the United States did not need to have an aircraft carrier nearby for them to fear retaliation.

## The Principle of Deterrence

The raid attracted the interest of political and military analysts as an application of the military doctrine of deterrence to the problem of international terrorism.[23] Deterrence theory is used in international foreign relations to contain the aggressive behavior of an opponent state through the threat of retaliation[24] and generally has two applications. The first is where one state keeps another state from acting in an unacceptable way by having a position of strength; the second is where a state threatens its opponent with dire consequences if it does not comply with certain demands or does not stop doing particular deeds.[25] The Libyan raid appears to fit the second application of the theory.

"Deterrence or dissuasion is intended to affect calculations—to convince the terrorists that the costs of striking or committing acts of terrorism are exceeding their benefits."[26] Such intent is evident in the Reagan administration's counter-terrorist policy of February 1986, which threatened the supporters of terrorist acts aimed at Americans and U.S. property abroad with direct retaliation if culpability could be established. The policy addressed what it termed "the growing threat of terrorism"[27] and cited recent threats by Qaddafi against the United States to underscore what it saw as a worsening climate. The range of responses the president was prepared to take when managing terrorist incidents, the task force report stated, included preemption (i.e., preventive measures), delaying tactics, the use of third-party arrangements, negotiating, and finally, counterattacking.[28] With regard to the counterattack option, the report said, "A successful deterrent strategy may require judicious employment of military force to resolve an incident."[29]

Deterrence theory rests on three premises.[30] The premise of *unacceptable damage* requires that a state must be able to deliver great harm upon its opponent in order for the opponent to be deterred. The second premise is that the threat has to be *perceived* by an opponent. Thirdly, the threat must be *credible* to succeed. Credibility, in turn, comprises two elements: that the country making the threat is *capable* of delivering the "dire consequences" and that it has the *will* to do so. This may require a demonstration.

Until the attack on Libya, the theory of deterrence had been applied almost exclusively[31] to military matters.[32] The U.S. administration stated that the raid against Libya would become a warning, signaling to other nations that sponsored international terrorism that they could now expect to receive the same punishment for their involvement, punishment that had previously been reserved for the terrorists themselves. States sponsoring or aiding terrorism, the Reagan administration warned, would hereafter find it counterproductive to their interests to be involved.[33]

## Evaluation of the Effects of Operation El Dorado Canyon

Views of the likely success of this strategy were highly varied. France expressed the fear that the U.S. military strike would lead to an escalation of violence; indeed, both France and Spain had refused a request by the Americans to allow the F-111s to fly over their countries en route to Libya.[34] In many circles the reaction was openly hostile and critical,[35] the raid described as a frustrated move by the United States to deal with the terrorist problem,[36] and the claimed justification for it rejected.[37] Political commentators disagreed on whether the operation would have any effect on the level of terrorist activity and, if so, what the direction of that effect would be.[38] There was also a fear that other terrorist groups, not associated with Libyan terrorism, would take the opportunity to contribute to a new wave of violence that would spiral out of control. A short time after the Libyan raid, Jeffery A. McCredie stated, "Despite the short-term gains of such an act, the long-term gain appears not to be deterrence, but further instigation."[39] Later assessments were more favorable.[40]

In 1988 the United States published its own positive assessment of the effectiveness of what it called its antiterrorist policy.[41] Without referring directly to the Libyan operation, the report claimed a 25 percent reduction in the number of anti-U.S. terrorist attacks from 1986 to 1987. Similar reductions in international terrorism after 1986 were claimed for Western Europe and Latin America. Although these data appear to support the view that Operation El Dorado Canyon had not given rise to a sustained increase in the amount of terrorist activity, they contain too little information to permit an assessment of the effectiveness of the operation in its own right. For this purpose, the figures have two main limitations.

Firstly, because the analysis is conducted in terms of calendar years, it uses a benchmark period (1986) that is itself, for the most part, postraid. Consequently, if Operation El Dorado Canyon did, as some commentators believed, give rise to an increase in the number of terrorist attacks, any reduction noted for 1987 may merely have reflected a reversion to preraid levels. Secondly, a report of counts of terrorist acts is only meaningful when supplemented by information about the nature of the acts. It is conceivable, for example, that a reduction in the numbers of acts might be accompanied by a shift to more violent acts, or vice versa. In either case, the *amount* of terrorist activity might ill represent the *level* of terrorist activity.

The purpose of the present study is to attempt a more detailed evaluation of the effects of Operation El Dorado Canyon on international terrorism. As an isolated, prominent act linked to a single point in time, the raid was felt to lend itself to a comparison, within an interrupted time-series framework,[42] of the frequencies and nature of terrorist events that preceded and followed it. Specifically, the study seeks to identify changes, pre- and postraid, in the frequencies of terrorist events associated with Libyan-sponsored anti-American groups and, overall, in the frequencies of terrorist attacks directed against Americans and U.S. property abroad. In addition, the study addresses the possibility that the raid was associated with a change in the pattern of terrorist activity worldwide, as indicated by both frequencies and level of severity of acts of terrorism.

## Method

### Data Collection

The first phase of the study consisted of the documentation of all acts by terrorists that threatened or caused harm to people or property in the time preceding and following Operation El Dorado Canyon. Data were collected for a forty-one-month period, that is, twenty and a half months before and twenty and a half months after the 14 April 1986 air raid. This period was dictated in part by the availability, at the time the study was carried out, of data to the end of 1987. In addition, it was considered a good compromise between sufficient observation points to reveal any seasonal trends and proximity to the event in question.

The main source of the data was a chronology compiled by Edward F. Mickolus,

Todd Sandler, and Jean M. Murdock.[43] This chronology was assembled from material from the Associated Press, United Press International, Reuters tickers, the *Washington Post*, the *New York Times*, the *Foreign Broadcast Information Service Daily Reports*, as well as the American Broadcasting Company's, National Broadcasting Company's, and the Columbia Broadcasting Company's evening news services. Mickolus et al. also utilized chronologies supplied to them by the U.S. Nuclear Regulatory Commission, the U.S. Federal Bureau of Investigation, and what the authors described as several "foreign embassies."[44]

We supplemented these data with James P. Wotton's[45] chronology of terrorist events involving Americans and U.S. property abroad. At the time his chronology was published, Wotton was a researcher with the Foreign Affairs and National Defense Division, Congressional Research Service, U.S. Library of Congress. In his introduction, Wotton stated that the chronology was compiled as background information "for Congress as it considered a wide range of legislation designed to combat terrorism."[46]

### Severity Classifications

The second phase of the study was the classification of terrorist incidents according to level of severity. The data consisted of the rating, by independent judges, of the perceived severity of violence of the twenty-three most common terrorist tactics (e.g., assassinations, bombings, hostage-taking, etc.) cited in Mickolus et al.[47] The ratings were provided by eighteen adult judges (seven women and eleven men), drawn from various professional and nonprofessional backgrounds, and ranging in age from twenty-two to forty-eight years.

The respondents rated each terrorist tactic on a ten-point scale for its perceived severity as an act of violence. The mean ratings for each act were then converted to standard scores, on the basis of which the acts were trichotomized into classifications of high, medium, or low severity, corresponding to locations in the upper, middle, or lower thirds of the distribution, respectively. This division resulted in ten high severity tactics ($z > .43$), seven medium severity tactics, and six low severity tactics ($z < -.43$), as listed in Table 1. On the basis of this classification, all terrorist incidents recorded for the forty-one-month period covered by the study were coded for whether they involved low, medium, or high severity violence.

## Results

### Activity of Groups Associated with Libya

Of fifteen groups reputed to have either direct or indirect links to Libyan-sponsored radical politics,[48] nine were active during the forty-one-month period under examination. Table 2 lists the groups and the number of acts associated with each before and after the raid. With the exception of the Fatah Revolutionary Council, these groups were substantially inactive in terrorism during the period after the raid. The total number of acts attributed to groups in this category

**Table 1**
Mean severity ratings of terrorist acts

| Ranking | Type of terrorist event | $Z$ |
|---------|------------------------|-----|
| High | Nuclear | 1.58 |
| | Armed attack—missiles | 1.16 |
| | Exotic pollution | 1.13 |
| | Assassination/murder | 0.94 |
| | Armed attack—other | 0.93 |
| | Explosive | 0.70 |
| | Barricade | 0.59 |
| | Hijacking | 0.56 |
| | Car bombing | 0.51 |
| | Letter bombing | 0.45 |
| Medium | Kidnapping | 0.22 |
| | Takeover, nonaerial | 0.19 |
| | Incendiary | 0.19 |
| | Suicide car bombing | 0.14 |
| | Police shoot-out | 0.08 |
| | Sniping at a building | −0.29 |
| | Sabotage | −0.32 |
| Low | Arms smuggling | −0.74 |
| | Conspiracy | −1.19 |
| | Occupation | −1.31 |
| | Threat | −1.76 |
| | Hoax | −1.87 |
| | Theft | −1.88 |

**Table 2**
Activity of Libyan-sponsored groups before and after the raid

| Terrorist group | Activity before air raid | Activity after air raid |
|-----------------|-------------------------|-------------------------|
| RAF | 21 | 1 |
| Black September | 14 | 2 |
| Rev. Org. of Soc. Muslims | 10 | 0 |
| Arab Rev. Brigades | 6 | 0 |
| PLO | 5 | 2 |
| Ulrike Meinhof Commando | 3 | 0 |
| Black June | 1 | 1 |
| Arab Rev. Cells | 1 | 2 |
| Fatah Rev. Council | 14 | 17 |

was significantly less in the postraid period ($n = 25$) than before the raid ($n = 75$) [Chi-squared (1 df) = 13.44, $p < .001$].

### Attacks on American Targets

All acts of terrorism directed at Americans and U.S. property abroad were identified. These data are different from those above in that they include acts by all terrorists and groups targeting the United States, not just those sponsored by Libya. Figure 1 displays the number of events for each month of the forty-one-month period. It shows that there was a dramatic rise in the number of events directly after the raid[49] (18 of the 20 events of April 1986 followed the raid); with the April figures included, there were marginally more terrorist acts against U.S. targets after (37) than before the raid (33). The number dropped off the next month and continued that way until the end of December 1987. Figure 1 indicates that despite the rise in events during April 1986, the months that followed rarely recorded events at a frequency at or above the pre-April trend. It is also evident that there were more months after the raid that recorded no terrorist activity at all ($n = 8$) than for the same period before the raid ($n =3$). Taken as a whole, the findings indicate a reduced trend following an initial period of increased activity.

### Worldwide Terrorism

Figure 2 shows all terrorist events on a worldwide basis between August 1984 and December 1987, inclusive. The data show no clear seasonal or cyclical pattern. Apart from a slight increase in the number of events during the period of

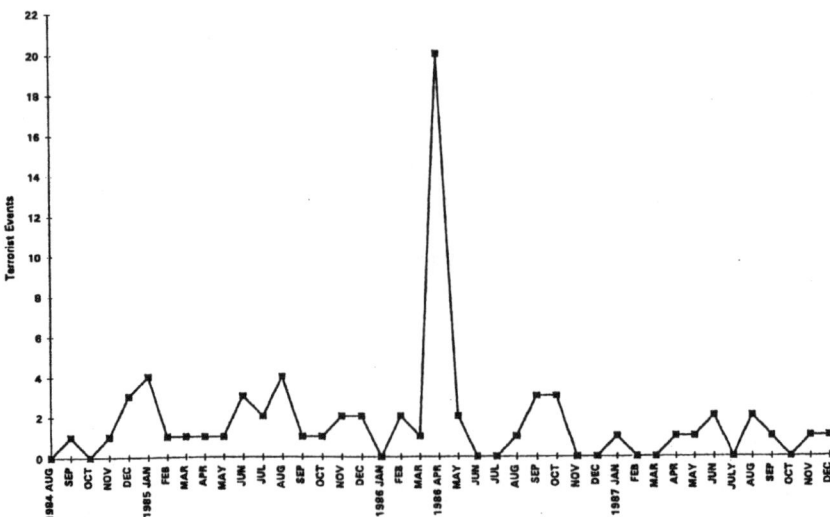

**Figure 1.** Terrorist events targeting Americans and U.S. property abroad, August 1984–December 1987.

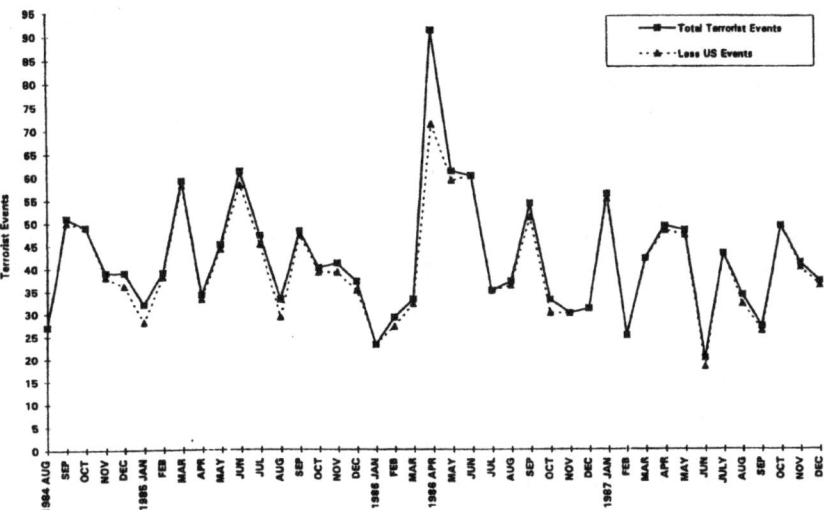

**Figure 2.** Worldwide terrorist events, August 1984–December 1987.

April to June 1986, the amount of activity appears to be fairly constant. In addition, the total number of events before the raid (838) is similar to that after the raid (871). Similar stability is evident if all acts against American targets are excluded from the worldwide data (Figure 2), with the postraid figure of 834 acts differing little from the preraid figure of 805.

Figure 3 shows the results when events are classified according to level of severity. The patterns for high-severity activities and medium-severity activities

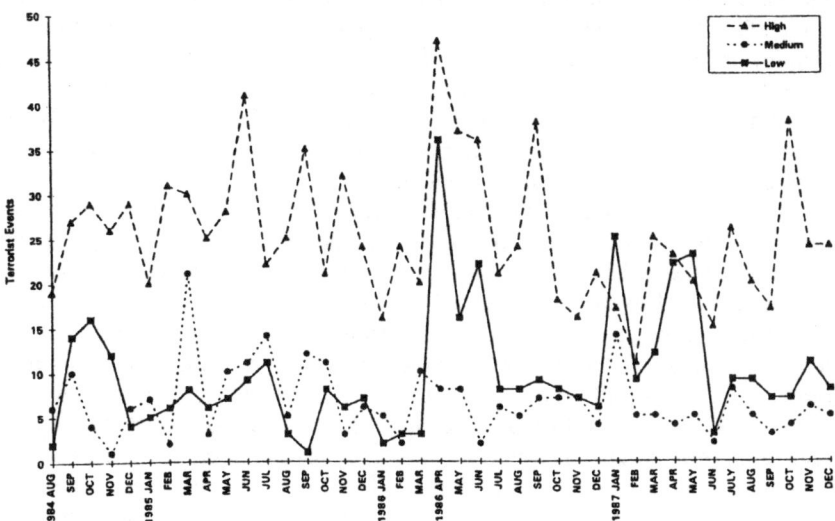

**Figure 3.** Worldwide terrorist events by severity of tactics, August 1984–December 1987.

both show an apparent decline during the period after the raid. On the other hand, the pattern for low-severity incidents shows a clear increase. Frequency counts support this impression. High-severity events show a drop of 8.1 percent, from 543 (before) to 499 (after); medium-severity events drop 21.8 percent, from 151 to 118; and low-severity events increase 43.3 percent, from 144 to 254. Chi-square analysis confirms a significant shift in the distribution of events across severity categories from before to after the raid [Chi-square $(2, N = 1,709) = 35.68, p < .0005$]. That shift is equally evident when worldwide acts involving other than American targets are considered[50] [Chi-square $(2, N = 1,639) = 33.25, p < .0005$].

## Discussion

The results presented address the consequences of the U.S. raid on Libya on three levels. Firstly, the data indicate that the immediate targets of the raid, namely, those terrorist groups supposed to be sponsored by Libya, were substantially less active in the twenty and a half months after the raid than they had been before. This applies both to the terrorist groups in question taken as a whole and to all but one of the major groups individually. The exception, the Fatah Revolutionary Council, showed little change. What is not clear is whether this apparent drop in activity of Libyan-associated groups is real or illusory—that is, whether it reflects an actual lessening of activity by these groups or simply a lesser preparedness to acknowledge responsibility for acts committed. Subsequent data suggest that the second explanation is unlikely, however.

The data at the second level of analysis indicate that the *activity* most directly targeted by the raid also showed a decline. The frequency of terrorist attacks against U.S. targets—after an initial flurry of apparently retaliatory activity—fell away after the raid, compared to preraid levels. Such a finding, considered in conjunction with the lesser recorded activity of Libyan-associated groups, renders unlikely the proposition that the apparent reduction in activity of those groups was illusory and due instead to nonacknowledgment of existing activity. Should the latter be the case, any such unacknowledged or misattributed activity was not, apparently, heavily directed at U.S. targets.

The fact that the apparent reduction in frequency of attacks against American targets followed a period of substantially heightened activity in the immediate aftermath of the raid should not pass unremarked, however. The initial upsurge in acts against the United States fostered fears that the air raid on Libya would not only fail to reduce terrorism but that it would lead to an upward spiral of violence. A dramatic rise of this kind, followed by a drop to below-baseline levels is reminiscent (graphically, though not in origin) of the *extinction burst* often observed in behavior modification techniques. It has been noted that such bursts, consisting of an immediate increase in level of the problem behavior following intervention, may mask a pattern that is otherwise in the direction of improvement.[51] Whereas an extinction burst may be regarded as an acceptable cost of the achievement of improvement in the longer term, such a cost is of a different order in the present context. In short, the United States paid dearly in the short term for the longer-term effects it sought.

The third level of analysis addresses the pattern of worldwide terrorist activity. The findings here illustrate the shortcomings of reliance on mere frequency counts of acts as an index of terrorist activity. Whereas the number of incidents in the twenty and a half months on either side of the operation was essentially unchanged, a different picture emerges when the acts are classified as being of either high, medium, or low severity, according to the ratings of independent judges. The data then reveal a significant shift away from acts of high and medium severity toward acts of low severity in violence after the raid. Removing from calculations all acts targeting Americans did not substantially alter this picture.

The reasons underlying the shift to less violent acts are unclear, and our ability to attribute them directly to the U.S. operation is constrained by the correlational nature of the data. It is apparent from Figure 3, however, that the shift does not represent the simple continuation of trends that were already in place before the raid. Nor can the shift be said to date clearly from a single point after the raid. In order to evaluate the possibility that the shift was associated with other significant political or military events, we considered the data against a chronology of global events for the period of the study.[52] This assessment revealed no other major military-political event around the time of the air raid that appeared likely to have been responsible for the changes observed. The most likely event of significance, the arms-for-hostages deal between the United States and Iran, was reportedly played out in the period from June 1985 to September 1986[53] and thus fits the data poorly.

These findings thus require us to acknowledge the possibility at least that Operation El Dorado Canyon brought about a change in the nature of international terrorism. Moreover, it is clear that this was in some degree a generalized change, extending beyond the immediate targets of the operation to acts directed against other than U.S. targets. From a deterrence theory perspective, the probable explanation is that the credibility of retaliation by target states was enhanced by a dramatic demonstration of the preparedness to retaliate by an influential target state. The effect thus suggests a degree of deterrence by proxy.

One of the implications of this finding could be that terrorists attempted to maintain their political profile, continuing to engage in terrorism as before the air raid, but were less willing to use the violent means that they had employed before. Another possibility is that the shift was due to greater caution on the part of states sponsoring terrorist groups. The choice between these (and other) possibilities is beyond the scope of this study.

## Conclusions

On the evidence of the data presented here, the immediate probable aims of the U.S. raid on Tripoli—namely, limiting the actions of Libyan-associated groups and reducing the incidence of terrorist actions against U.S. targets—were achieved.

It cannot be established with absolute certainty that these results were direct consequences of the operation. To the extent that no plausible competing explanations present themselves, the findings support the conclusion that the application of the principle of deterrence to international terrorism was at least partially successful in this instance.

The data also suggest the possibility that Operation El Dorado Canyon influenced the nature of worldwide terrorist activity. The findings from the worldwide data are consistent with the conclusion that the punitive action by the U.S. administration made clear to terrorist groups or to their sponsors the possible consequences of exceeding the tolerance of the targets of their activity, whether or not those targets were American. Whether that conclusion is warranted cannot be established—the postraid pattern may be within the bounds of normal variation or the product of other, unidentified factors. When we consider the fact that the immediate postraid period included a burst of activity, which some observers saw as indicative of an escalation of conflict, the substantial overall shift to less violent activity in the twenty-and-a-half-month period following the raid is certainly remarkable, however. Although it must remain indeterminate what the direct consequences of Operation El Dorado Canyon were, it is clear that a prolonged escalation of terrorist activity, as feared by some observers, was not among them.

### Notes

1. George Bush, *Public Report of the President's Task Force on Combating Terrorism* (Washington, D.C.: U.S. Government Printing Office, 1986).

2. Michael O'Connor, *Terrorism: Its Goals, Its Targets, Its Methods—The Solutions* (Boulder, Co.: Paladin Press, 1987).

3. Christopher Dobson and Ronald Payne, *War Without End: The Terrorists—An Intelligence Dossier* (London: Harrap, 1986).

4. See Edward F. Mickolus, *Transnational Terrorism: A Chronology of Events, 1968–1979* (Westport, Conn.: Greenwood Press, 1980), and Edward F. Mickolus, Todd Sandler, and Jean M. Murdock, *International Terrorism in the 1980s: A Chronology of Events*, vol. 2, 1984–1987 (Ames: Iowa State University Press, 1989).

5. U.S. Department of State, *Hostage Taking: Preparation, Avoidance, and Survival* (Washington, D.C.: U.S. Government Printing Office, 1984). For instance, in 1988 the United States reported that it had "over 700,000 Government military and civilian personnel, in addition to their approximately 400,000 dependents, stationed overseas." See George Bush, *Terrorist Group Profiles* (Washington, D.C.: U.S. Government Printing Office, 1988), p. 131. This figure does not include expatriates and citizens traveling and studying abroad.

6. For example, see Yonah Alexander and Allan S. Nanes, editors, *Legislative Responses to Terrorism* (International Studies on Terrorism, No. 1. Dordrecht: M. Nijhoff, 1986), and Clive Walker and Kiron Reid, "The Offence of Directing Terrorist Organisations," *The Criminal Law Review,* 1993.

7. H. H. A. Cooper, "Evaluating the Terrorist Threat: Principles of Applied Risk Assessment," in *Clandestine Tactics and Technology* (Gaithersburg, Md.: International Association of Chiefs of Police, 1979).

8. Robert Cappel, *The SWAT Team Manual* (Boulder, Co.: Paladin Press, 1979).

9. Patrick Collins, *Living in Troubled Lands: A Complete Guide to Personal Security Abroad* (Boulder, Co.: Paladin Press, 1981), and Robert D. Chapman and M. Lester Chapman, *The Crimson Web of Terror* (Boulder, Co.: Paladin Press, 1980).

10. Yonah Alexander, Yuval Ne'eman, and Ely Tavin, editors, *Terrorism: Future Trends—An Analysis of Terrorism in the World Arena* (Washington, D.C.: Global Affairs, 1991), p. 16.

11. Stephen Sloan, *Beating International Terrorism: An Action Strategy for Preemption and Punishment* (Maxwell Air Force Base, Alabama: Air University Press, 1986), p. 28.

12. Muammar al-Qaddafi, *The Green Book* (Tripoli: The World Center for Studies and Research of The Green Book, 1980).

13. Brian L. Davis, *Qaddafi, Terrorism, and the Origins of the U.S. Attack on Libya* (New York: Praeger, 1990), p. 10.

14. Ibid., p. 11.

15. Richard J. Erickson, *Legitimate Use of Military Force Against State-Sponsored International Terrorism* (Maxwell Air Force Base, Alabama: Air University Press, 1989), p. 62.

16. Grant Wardlaw, *Political Terrorism* (Cambridge: Cambridge University Press, 1982), pp. 87–102.

17. Jeffery Allen McCredie, "The April 14, 1986, Bombing of Libya: Act of Self-Defense or Reprisal?" *Case Western Reserve Journal of International Law,* vol. 19, no. 215 (1987): 215; *Time,* "Targeting Qaddafi," April 21, 1986, vol. 127, no. 16, p. 7; and *Time,* Richard Stengel, reporter, "Qaddafi: Obsessed by a Ruthless, Messianic Vision," April 21, 1986, vol. 127, no. 16, p. 17.

18. *Time,* April 21, 1986, p. 10.

19. Davis, *Qaddafi,* p. 116.

20. McCredie, "Bombing of Libya," p. 217; *Time,* April 21, 1986, p. 7.

21. *Time,* "Hitting the Source," April 28, 1986, vol. 127, no. 17, and *Time,* "In the Dead of the Night," April 28, 1986, vol. 127, no. 17, pp. 6–19.

22. Davis, *Qaddafi,* p. 120.

23. See McCredie, "Bombing of Libya."

24. Carlton C. Rodee, Totton J. Anderson, Carl Q. Christol, and Thomas H. Green, *Introduction to Political Science* (Sydney: McGraw-Hill, 1983), p. 496.

25. Ira S. Cohen, *Realpolitik: Theory and Practice* (Encino, Calif.: Dickinson Publishing, 1975), p. 149.

26. Hannan Alon, "Can Terrorism Be Deterred? Some Thoughts and Doubts," in Anat Kurz, *Contemporary Trends in World Terrorism* (London: Mansell Publishing, 1987), p. 125.

27. Bush, *Public Report,* p. 1.

28. Ibid., pp. 8–9.

29. Ibid., p. 9.

30. Cohen, *Realpolitik,* pp. 150–152.

31. The exceptions involve Israel, which faces unique threats from Middle East guerrilla armies and regional militia. See Samuel M. Katz, *Guards Without Frontiers: Israel's War Against Terrorism* (London: Arms and Armour, 1990).

32. Erickson, *Legitimate Use of Military Force,* p. 62.

33. See Davis, *Qaddafi.*

34. *Time,* April 28, 1986, p. 14.

35. Mary Kaldor and Paul Anderson, *Mad Dogs: The U.S. Raids on Libya* (London: Pluto Press, 1986).

36. David Turndorf, "The U.S. Raid on Libya: A Forceful Response to Terrorism," *Brooklyn Journal of International Law,* vol. 14, no. 1 (1986): 201–202.

37. Louis Henkin, Stanley Hoffman, Jeane J. Kirkpatrick, Allan Gerson, William D. Rogers, and David J. Scheffer, *Right v. Might: International Law and the Use of Force* (New York: Council on Foreign Relations Press, 1989), p. 46.

38. Benjamin Netanyahu, "Terrorism: An Overview," in Yonah Alexander, Yuval Ne'eman, and Ely Tavin, editors, *Terrorism: Future Trends—An Analysis of Terrorism in the World Arena* (Washington, D.C.: Global Affairs, 1991), p. 9.

39. McCredie, "Bombing of Libya," p. 241.

40. Richard Clutterbuck, *Terrorism and Guerrilla Warfare: Forecasts and Remedies* (London: Routledge, 1990), p. 158.

41. Bush, *Terrorist Group Profiles,* p. ii.

42. Thomas D. Cook and Donald T. Campbell, *Quasi-Experimentation: Design and Analysis Issues for Field Settings* (Chicago: Rand McNally, 1979).

43. See Mickolus et al., *International Terrorism,* 1989.

44. Ibid., p. xii.

45. James P. Wotton, *Terrorist Incidents Involving U.S. Citizens or Property, 1981–1991: A Chronology* (Washington, D.C.: Foreign Affairs and National Defense Division, Congressional Research Service, Library of Congress, 1991).

46. Ibid., p. 3.

47. Mickolus et al., *International Terrorism,* pp. xv–xvii.

48. See Dobson and Payne, *War Without End.* See also George Rosie, *The Directory of International Terrorism* (Edinburgh, Scotland: Mainstream Publishing, 1986).

49. In the days directly after the U.S. raid, there was a surge in attacks against Americans in retribution. Libyan radio was reported to have broadcast provocative messages to its Arab listeners, calling upon them to attack all things American (Davis, *Qaddafi*). "Several incidents of terrorism in the aftermath of the raid were attributed to Libya. One American and three British hostages were killed in Lebanon; an American working at the U.S. Embassy in Sudan was shot in the head from a passing car; and an attempt was made to bomb a U.S. Air Force officers' club in Turkey" [Jeffrey Simon, *U.S. Countermeasures Against International Terrorism* (Santa Monica, Calif.: Rand Corporation, 1990), p. 28].

50. High-severity events: 520 (before), 474 (after); medium-severity events: 141 (before), 111 (after); low-severity events: 144 (before), 249 (after).

51. M. Bloom and J. Fischer, *Evaluating Practice* (Englewood Cliffs, N.J.: Prentice-Hall, 1982), p. 447.

52. A copy is available on request to the authors.

53. Davis, *Qaddafi,* pp. 73–74.

# 28

# THE EFFECTIVENESS OF ANTITERRORISM POLICIES:
# A VECTOR-AUTOREGRESSION-INTERVENTION ANALYSIS

WALTER ENDERS and TODD SANDLER *Iowa State University*

*U*sing quarterly data from 1968 to 1988, we analyze the time series properties of the various attack modes used by transnational terrorists. Combining vector autoregression and intervention analysis, we find strong evidence of both substitutes and complements among the attack modes. We also evaluate the effectiveness of six policies designed to thwart terrorism. The existence of complements and substitutes means that policies designed to reduce one type of attack may affect other attack modes. For example, the installation of metal detectors in airports reduced skyjackings and diplomatic incidents but increased other kinds of hostage attacks (barricade missions, kidnappings) and assassinations. In the long run, embassy fortification decreased barricade missions but increased assassinations. The Reagan "get tough" policy, which resulted in the enactment of two laws in 1984 and a retaliatory raid on Libya in 1986, did not have any noticeable long-term effect on curbing terrorist attacks directed against U.S. interests.

**D**espite its recent decline, transnational terrorism still poses a real threat to nations worldwide. Transnational terrorism has followed a cyclical pattern; hence, the recent downturn is apt to be followed by an upturn (Im, Cauley, and Sandler 1987). A question of considerable importance concerns what antiterrorism policies have worked best in curbing terrorism. For example, how effective are metal detectors in airports? Do these metal detectors have unintended consequences on other types of terrorist attacks? Are U.S. diplomats safer since their embassies have been made more secure? Are U.S. antiterrorism laws effective? Did the U.S. raid on Libya in April 1986 reduce attacks against U.S. interests? We shall attempt to provide answers to these questions.

Terrorism is the premeditated use—or threatened use—of extranormal violence or force to gain a political objective through intimidation or fear. Terrorists often direct their violence and threats at a large target group, not immediately involved in the political decision-making process that they intend to influence. The larger the target group, the more difficult it is for authorities to anticipate the next attack. To bring pressures on decision makers to acquiesce to their demands, terrorists massacre innocent tourists in foreign airports, take other nations' citizens hostage, or bomb military and civilian targets. Terrorists wage their campaigns to achieve diverse political goals that may be founded on nationalistic, ideological, issue-specific, separatist, revolutionary, or nihilistic grounds. Whatever its motivation, terrorism imposes costs on governments. Terrorist groups may act independently, in a coalition with other groups (e.g., the American Battalion in South America), or as a state surrogate.[1] Targeted governments must decide how best to allocate resources to thwart terrorism, while the terrorists and their sponsors must determine what modes of attack to include in their campaigns in light of government actions. On both sides, economic decisions are required.

Both passive and active responses have been proposed by terrorist experts to thwart terrorism, e.g., Tovar 1986; Wilkinson 1986). Passive or defensive responses include erecting technology-based barriers (e.g., bomb-sniffing devices, metal detectors), hardening targets, instituting stricter laws and penalties, increasing resource commitments, and enacting international agreements. Active responses call for retaliatory raids (especially against state sponsors), preemptive strikes, group infiltration, and covert actions. In terms of U.S. antiterrorism policies, three passive and one active policy have been used since the early 1970s. Passive policies have included the installation of metal detectors in airports in January 1973 (a policy copied worldwide shortly after the U.S. lead), the fortification of U.S. embassies and military installations starting in 1976, and the passing of antiterrorism laws in 1984. The most noteworthy active response was the April 1986 U.S. retaliatory raid on Libya.

In recent years, economists have begun to assess the effectiveness of these and other policies aimed at curbing terrorism. For example, Landes (1978) used ordinary least squares regression techniques to assess the effectiveness of metal detectors, sky marshals, stiffer penalties, and intelligence profiles on skyjackings originating in the United States in the late 1960s and early 1970s. Cauley and Im (1988) applied intervention or interrupted time series analysis (see McCleary and Hay 1980) to determine the impact of metal detectors, increased expenditures to harden U.S. embassies in 1976, and the UN convention on preventing attacks against protected persons. Enders, Sandler, and Cauley (1990) refined the application of intervention analysis and focused their policy evaluation on a host of UN conventions and international responses to hijackings. Brophy-Baermann and Conybeare (n.d.) employed intervention analysis to examine the short-run and long-run effects of Israeli retaliations on the rate of terrorist attacks. Each of the previous intervention studies analyzed the effects of one or two policies on the time series of a *single mode of attack; no interactions among series were allowed.*[2]

Since terrorists must weigh the relative costs and benefits of various modes of attack when designing their campaigns, we should expect that the time series for one mode (or target) of attack may depend not only on the time series for that mode but also on those of other related modes. A primary purpose of this article is to employ vector autoregression (VAR) techniques to identify the interrelationships among the time series for different kinds of terrorist events. These interrelationships should assist us to identify modes that behave as *substitutes* or *complements* for one another. Two modes of attack are substitutes if they fulfill similar purposes (e.g., all types of hostage missions raise extortion). Modes are complements if they enhance one another's effectiveness (e.g., threats and actual events promote an atmosphere of fear; high-profile skyjackings and diplomatic attacks reinforce the public's perception of a government's vulnerabilities). A second purpose is to investigate the short-run and long-run impact of alternative policies on terrorist tactics and activity levels when the interrelationships between various modes are explicitly taken into account. To accomplish this second purpose, we engineer a procedure for combining VAR and intervention analysis. By indicating the impact of a policy on a host of terrorist attack modes, this procedure better enables us to evaluate the costs and benefits associated with a policy. If, for example, the installation of metal detectors permanently reduces skyjackings but encourages other kinds of hostage-taking missions, then the true net benefits of metal detectors must account for both effects and any other indirect impacts. The ability to identify interrelated time series would also assist in forecasting future trends in terrorism, especially if a contemplated intervention is predicted to affect one terrorist tactic or mode of attack directly.

Using quarterly data on transnational terrorist events from 1968 to 1988, we evaluate the impact of recent U.S. interventions. The most effective policies were the installation of metal detectors in January 1973 and the fortification of U.S. embassies in 1976 and thereafter. Although metal detectors decreased skyjackings, they had the unintended effect of increasing other types of hostage missions and assassinations. Significant interrelationships among series are uncovered that influence the impact of antiterrorism policies. For example, metal detectors appeared to decrease threats and hoaxes, perhaps owing to their reduced credibility. The Libyan raid led to a short-term increase in U.S. and British attacks that spilled over to other countries' interests. No long-run decrease in terrorism could be attributed to the raid. Finally, the Reagan antiterrorism laws did not inhibit terrorism directed against U.S. interests.

## CHOICE-THEORETICAL CONSIDERATIONS

Terrorists are viewed here as rational actors who attempt to maximize a *shared goal,* subject to a resource constraint. This shared goal may be denoted as utility or expected utility derived from the consumption of *basic commodities,*[3] produced from terrorist and nonterrorist activities. For example, a nihilistic group may gain utility from political instability, which is a basic commodity derived from various terrorist tactics or modes of attack (e.g., armed attack, bombings, hostage taking, threats). If the government appears ineffective in curbing these acts or if the government overreacts and appears repressive, then political instability results. Substitution possibilities among tactics arise, inasmuch as some terrorist tactic may produce the same basic commodities (e.g., extortion, media attention) but in varying amounts. Substitution is enhanced when attack modes with closely related outcomes are logistically similar. Hostage-taking events, such as skyjackings, kidnappings, and barricade missions, are logistically complex, and this augments substitution possibilities. Assassinations also require a good deal of planning, but less than hostage missions. In contrast, bombings and non-resource-using events (e.g., threats and hoaxes) are logistically simple. Complementarity results when combinations of attack modes are needed to produce one or more basic commodities. That is, combining attack modes may have greater marginal productivity in producing basic commodities than either mode individually. For example, threats when joined with actual attacks may create a greater atmosphere of fear than either alone. Skyjackings when combined with attacks against protected persons (e.g., diplomats and military officials) may make a government appear weaker than reliance on a single mode of attack. To produce these basic commodities, a terrorist group has at least three allocative decisions to make:[4] (1) a choice between terrorist and nonterrorist activities, (2) a choice between different terrorist tactics, and (3) a choice between different nonterrorist activities. The second choice involves a decision among skyjackings, bombings, and other attack modes. It also requires a choice of whom to attack— U.S. interests or those of another nation.

A resource constraint limits the terrorist group's expenditures on activities not to exceed its income or resources. The expenditures on any activity consist of the product of the activity's per-unit price and the level of the activity. Each terrorist tactic has a per-unit price that includes the value of time and resources needed to accomplish the act. Given its logistical simplicity, a bombing may well involve a lower price than the kidnapping and maintenance of a hostage. The prices faced by the terrorists for each tactic are determined, in large part, by the government's allocation of resources to thwarting various acts of terrorism. If, for example, the government were to fortify its embassies, then attacks against embassies

American Political Science Review Vol. 87, No. 4

and diplomats within the missions' grounds would become more difficult. This, in turn, means that the per-unit price of such activities has risen. Similarly, the installation of metal detectors increases the per-unit and relative price of skyjackings when compared with assassinations or other types of hostage incidents. Any government policy directed at a single type of terrorist event would change relative prices and should result in substitution between modes. If, however, the government wants to induce the terrorists to rely more on nonterrorist tactics, then the government must intervene with policies that either raise the price of all types of terrorist modes or lower the price of nonterrorist activities (e.g., easier access to elections).

By casting the terrorist group's allocation problem in a household production framework, we can state some easily derivable propositions:

PROPOSITION 1. *An increase in the relative price of one type of terrorist tactic would cause a terrorist group to substitute out of the now-more-costly mode into those terrorist and nonterrorist activities whose prices are now relatively less costly.*

PROPOSITION 2. *Terrorist events yielding similar basic commodities should display the greatest substitution possibilities. For example, more substitution is predicted between hostage-taking missions than with other types of events when one kind of hostage-taking mission's relative price has increased. If income effects are not too strong, then complementary events would respond in a similar fashion to relative price changes; that is, the increase (decrease) in the price of one complementary event causes that event and all complements to fall (rise) in number.*

PROPOSITION 3. *A decrease in all terrorist activities would result from government interventions that raised the price of all terrorist tactics relative to nonterrorist activities.*

PROPOSITION 4. *For normal goods, an increase (decrease) in its resource endowment would cause the terrorist group to increase (decrease) the level of terrorist and nonterrorist activities.*

Propositions 1–3 indicate the dilemma confronting governments. If the authorities concentrate efforts on thwarting a single terrorist tactic through, say, increased security, the terrorist will substitute into other tactics. Proposition 2 indicates the kinds of substitutions expected. Propositions 3 and 4 indicate that government policies must either raise costs to terrorist tactics across the board or limit terrorist resources if overall terrorism can be anticipated to fall. We provide evidence of substitution-and-complementarity phenomenon in our empirical results section.

## STATISTICAL METHODS AND DATA

Our basic methodology combines intervention analysis in a VAR framework.[5] The data were taken from two primary sources containing chronologies of transnational terrorist incidents (Mickolus 1980; Mickolus, Sandler, and Murdock 1989).

### Methodology

In order to explain the analytical procedure, we first consider a streamlined model in which there are only two attack modes and two policy instruments. Consider the following VAR model using only one lagged value of each attack mode:

$$y_1(t) = a_{10} + a_{11}p_1(t) + a_{12}p_2(t) + b_{11}y_1(t-1)$$
$$+ b_{12}y_2(t-1) + \epsilon_1(t) \quad (1)$$

$$y_2(t) = a_{20} + a_{21}p_1(t) + a_{22}p_2(t) + b_{21}y_1(t-1)$$
$$+ b_{22}y_2(t-1) + \epsilon_2(t) \quad (2)$$

where $y_i(t)$ is the number of type $i$ terrorist incidents occurring during time period $t$, $p_i(t)$ is an indicator of whether policy $i$ is in effect at time $t$, $\epsilon_i(t)$ is an identically and independently distributed random variable with mean equal to zero, and the $a_{ij}$s and $b_{ij}$s are parameters. Note that $\epsilon_1(t)$ and $\epsilon_2(t)$ may be correlated.

To illustrate the meaning of equations 1 and 2, recall that metal detectors were installed in U.S. airports on 5 January 1973. If policy intervention 1 represents metal detectors, the value of $p_1(t)$ can be set equal to zero for all $t <$ January 1973 and equal to unity for all $t \geq$ January 1973. Hence, the coefficients $a_{11}$ and $a_{21}$ measure the direct-impact effect of metal detectors on attack modes 1 and 2, respectively. It is important to note that even if $a_{i1}$ is found to equal zero, it is *not* possible to conclude that incident type $i$ was unaffected by policy intervention 1. As long as $b_{12}$ and/or $b_{21}$ are not zero, there are interactions among the two incident types. For example, even if $a_{11} = 0$, policy intervention 1 can have an indirect effect on incident type 1 through its effects on incident type 2. The point is that the direct effect of an intervention on a particular mode of attack may be zero even though the indirect effects may be nonzero. This observation motivates the need to study terrorist-thwarting interventions in a VAR framework as opposed to the standard univariate intervention model.

To generalize the discussion to the case of additional attack modes, policy interventions and lags, we consider:

$$y(t) = \alpha + AP(t) + \sum_{\ell=1}^{L} B_\ell y(t-\ell) + \epsilon(t), \quad (3)$$

where $y(t)$ is the $n \times 1$ vector $[y_1(t), y_2(t), \ldots, y_n(t)]'$; $y_i(t)$ is the number of type $i$ terrorist incidents occurring during time period $t$; $\alpha$ is a $1 \times 4$ matrix consisting of a constant and three seasonal dummy variables; the $B_\ell$'s are $n \times n$ coefficient matrices; and $\epsilon(t)$ is the $n \times 1$ vector $[\epsilon_1(t), \epsilon_2(t), \ldots, \epsilon_n(t)]'$, such that $\epsilon_i(t)$ is *identically and independently distributed* (i.i.d.). Note that the correlation matrix of the shocks is not necessarily diagonal. In equation 3, matrices $A$ and $P(t)$ are of particular importance for assessing the success of the alternative interventions. $P(t)$ is the $k \times 1$ vector $[p_1(t), \ldots, p_k(t)]'$, where $p_k(t)$ is an indicator of whether policy $k$ is in effect at time $t$. Each element $a_{ik}$ in the $n \times k$ coefficient matrix $A$ measures the direct-impact effect of policy intervention $p_k$ on the time series of incident type $y_i$.

As in the simple $2 \times 2$ model, even if $a_{ik}$ is equal to zero, it is *not* possible to conclude that incident type $i$ was unaffected by policy intervention $p_k$. When the off-diagonal elements of the $B_\ell$ matrices are not zero, there are interactions among the various incident types. Thus, policy intervention $p_k$ may have an indirect effect on incident type $i$ through its effects on a related incident type.

An appropriate strategy to estimate the matrices in equation system 3 is straightforward. An identical procedure is applied in each of our estimated models.

*Step 1.* Equation system 3 was estimated for lag lengths of eight quarters, four quarters, and two quarters (i.e., $L = 8, 4, 2$). Since each of the equations in equation system 3 has identical right-hand-side variables, ordinary least squares is an efficient estimation technique. Lag lengths are selected using the likelihood ratio test for the restriction that all coefficients in $B_\ell$ for $\ell > m$ (where $m = 4$ or 2) are equal to zero. The test statistic has a chi-squared distribution with degrees of freedom equal to the number of excluded parameters (i.e., $df = n(8 - m)$).

*Step 2.* As a preliminary step for ascertaining the importance of the interrelationships among the various attack modes, we obtained the variance decompositions from the moving average representation of the model estimated in step 1. The moving average representation of $y_i(t)$ expresses the number incidents as dependent on the current and past values of all the error terms and interventions.[6] Appropriately shocking the $\epsilon_1(t)$-through-$\epsilon_n(t)$ series, we can obtain the percentage of the variation attributable to each type of attack mode innovation. If two series are highly interrelated, one (or both) will explain a reasonable proportion of the forecast error variance of the other. To account for the possibility of short-term-versus-long-term interactions, we consider 4-step-, 8-step-, and 24-step-ahead forecasting horizons. When the error terms of the equations in equation system 3 are correlated with each other, there is no simple way to obtain a pure shock to any one of the series. In those instances where the estimated errors of any two series are correlated, we follow the usual practice and perform a second variance decomposition reversing the ordering of the variables involved.[7]

*Step 3.* The forecasts from an unrestricted VAR are known to suffer from "overparameterization." In order to obtain a more parsimonious model, we used the results of the variance decompositions. Many of

the series explained the preponderance of their own forecast error variance; for such variables, we used a simple two-step procedure to pare down the number of estimated coefficients. If incident type $y_j$ did not explain at least 10% of the forecast error variance of incident type $y_i$ at any of the three forecast horizons, we then considered the results of Granger-causality tests. Formally, the restriction that incident type $y_j$ does not Granger-cause incident type $y_i$ can be written as

$$b_{1ij} = b_{2ij} = \ldots = b_{Lij} = 0 \ (i \neq j), \qquad (4)$$

where $b_{\ell ij}$ is element $ij$ of matrix $B_\ell$. If we could not reject the null hypothesis that incident type $y_j$ does not Granger-cause incident $y_i$ at the .10 level of significance, we imposed the restriction given in equation 4. Thus, the restriction was imposed only in those instances in which $y_j$ explains less than 10% of the forecast error variance of $y_i$ and $y_j$ does not Granger-cause $y_i$ at the .10 level of significance.

*Step 4.* We next reestimated equation system 3, imposing the zero-restrictions implied by the causality tests. Since the right-hand-side variables were no longer identical in each regression, each was estimated using *seemingly unrelated regressions* (SUR).

*Step 5.* The SUR estimates of the $A$ and $B_\ell$ matrices can be used to show the effectiveness (or lack thereof) of the various interventions. Each element in $A$ shows only the impact effect of the intervention. The lagged impact and indirect effects are captured by the elements in the $B_\ell$ matrices. Because of the complexity of the interactions, the simplest way to demonstrate the short- and long-run policy effects is through the moving average representation.[8]

*Step 6.* Steps 1–5 were conducted for all three of our models. Our diagnostic checking included using the Ljung–Box Q-statistic to check for serial correlation in the residuals. We were also careful to look for signs of nonstationarity. In model 3, estimated coefficients and diagnostic checks led us to question the assumption that all of the series were stationary. The nonstationarity issue is difficult to address in a system of equations with multiple interventions. A variable may appear to be nonstationary owing to the effects of successive interventions. We visually inspected the time paths of each type of terrorist incident, being careful to note any evidence of nonstationary behavior. In addition, the estimated coefficients from the VAR and the forecast values from the time paths from step 5 were investigated. For reasons that we associate with the introduction of metal detectors in airports, most of the series exhibit a break immediately following the first quarter of 1973. For the post-1973 period, we formally tested each suspected series for the possibility of a unit root using the augmented Dickey–Fuller tests. If a series contains a unit root, we use its first-difference in the analysis.[9]

American Political Science Review                                                     Vol. 87, No. 4

## Data

The chronological data include the agents, victims, territories or institutions of two or more nations (Mickolus 1980; Mickolus, Sandler, and Murdock 1989). These chronologies are available as coded data sets entitled International Terrorism: Attributes of Terrorist Events (ITERATE). ITERATE 2 contains the attributes of international terrorist events from 1968 to 1977 (Mickolus 1982). ITERATE 3 contains these attributes from 1978 to 1987 (Mickolus, Sandler, Murdock, and Fleming 1989).[10] The data for 1988 were drawn from a chronology update written by Edward Mickolus and made available to us. These chronologies represent the most comprehensive data set publicly available. ITERATE draws its data from publicly available materials that have appeared in the world press. Key sources include the Associated Press, United Press International, Reuter tickers, the *Washington Post,* the *New York Times,* the *Washington Times,* and the Foreign Broadcast Information Service (FBIS). The most valuable source for ITERATE is the regional FBIS *Daily Reports,* which draws from hundreds of world print and electronic media resources and is the best single source of material on foreign coverage of terrorist incidents. The FBIS reports include important print and media sources that appear in English, Arabic, and other languages.

Germane to this study, the chronologies record the type of event, date, location, and the victims' or targets' characteristics (e.g., what nationality and whether a diplomat or not). Consistency is maintained since identical criteria for defining acts of transnational terrorism and classifying types of incidents are applied to the entire data set, which includes 84 quarters of observations from 1 January 1968 to 31 December 1988.

In total, 15 primary time series were extracted from the data. These time series consisted of the quarterly totals, or count, of events of a given type. The following basic series were constructed: (1) assassinations, (2) barricade-and-hostage-taking events, (3) kidnappings, (4) transnational skyjackings, (5) U.S. domestic skyjackings, (6) other skyjackings, (7) total terrorist incidents, (8) nonhostage crimes against diplomats and protected persons ("protected-persons events"), (9) crimes against U.S. protected persons, (10) crimes against British protected persons, (11) attacks against U.S. persons and property, (12) attacks against British persons and property, (13) all crimes against protected persons, (14) threats, and (15) hoaxes. Other time series were manufactured from these basic series. United States domestic skyjackings involved hijackings within the United States and hijackings originating in the United States in which the hijacker demanded to be flown to Cuba. Most of these hijackings were not politically based but were included to test for the effectiveness of metal detectors and screening devices. Other skyjackings involved domestic skyjackings *outside* the United States and skyjackings for political asylum and nonpolitical motives. Again, these were included to de-

termine metal detectors' effectiveness. Transnational skyjackings fit ITERATE's definition of terrorism.[11] The total terrorism series included domestic and other skyjackings along with all legitimate terrorist events. The crimes-against-protected-persons series followed the United Nations' definition for protected persons (1978, 76–77). Attacks were counted if they occurred in a country signing the UN convention on protected persons. Moreover, the attack had to involve victims from a signatory country. Threats concerned claims of future acts with no subsequent followup, while hoaxes referred to an alleged past act (e.g., a bomb planted on a plane) that never took place.

The VAR technique requires that there be no overlap among series. Hence, for the statistical models, we had to purge the overlap. In model 1, for example, the crimes-against-protected-persons series did not include any such events as occurred in the barricade, kidnapping, or skyjacking modes. This, then, permitted us to run skyjackings and other kinds of hostage events as separate series to examine interrelationships among time series. Each of the three statistical models presented have an "other events" series. In models 1 and 2, "other events" primarily included bombings and armed attacks. In model 1, "other events" excluded all hostage and protected-persons incidents. In model 2, "other events" excluded hostage events, assassinations, and threats. Finally, "other events" for model 3 concerned incidents not directed at the United States, the United Kingdom, or protected persons. For some models, we combined two or more time series of a similar nature to avoid too many zero observations and to ensure that the values of the observations were sufficiently large to justify the assumption of normally distributed disturbances (Harvey and Fernandes 1989).

## THE INTERVENTIONS

Five passive interventions and one active intervention are investigated with the VAR models. If a policy occurred during the middle of a month (e.g., the Libya retaliatory strike on 15 April 1986), the intervention date corresponds to the start of the nearest quarter (i.e., the second quarter). The first intervention concerns the installation of metal detectors in U.S. airports on 5 January 1973 and is denoted by METAL. Shortly thereafter, these devices were placed in airports worldwide to screen domestic and international flights. Screening devices represented a permanent intervention with continual updates thereafter. The next three interventions involve resource allocations to fortify and secure U.S. embassies and missions in October 1976, 1985, and 1986 and are indicated by EMBASSY76, EMBASSY85, and EMBASSY86, respectively. In 1976, spending on embassy security more than doubled. Significant additional resources were allocated to security in the 1980s as a result of the takeover of the U.S. embassy in Tehran on 4 November 1979. Security measures included the installation of metal detectors to screen visitors to

embassies. Large increases in security were authorized to start on October 1985 by Public Law 98-533.
On 12 August 1986, the U.S. Congress passed legislation authorizing an additional $2.4 billion over five
years to rebuild and fortify U.S. embassies and missions. Embassy fortification was also a permanent
intervention.

The fifth intervention concerns two U.S. laws enacted in October 1984. Public Law 98-473, signed by
President Reagan on 12 October 1984, required up to
life imprisonment for individuals taking U.S. hostages *either within or outside* the United States. Stiffer
penalities were included for destroying aircraft or
airport facilities within the United States. In addition,
penalties were raised for acts committed with a bomb
or other weapon on a U.S. aircraft. Public Law 98-533,
signed on 19 October 1984, authorized the U.S.
attorney general to pay rewards for information leading to the capture or conviction, inside or outside the
United States, of terrorists who targetted U.S. interests (Celmer 1987; Pearl 1987, 141). We refer to these
laws as part of the Reagan "get-tough" policy and
denote them as REAGAN LAWS.

The sixth intervention is the U.S. retaliatory bombing of Libya on the morning of 15 April 1986 for its
alleged involvement in the terrorist bombing of the
LaBelle Discothèque in West Berlin on 5 April 1986.
Since 18 of the F-111 fighter–bombers used in the raid
were deployed from British bases at Lakenheath and
Upper Heyford, England, the United Kingdom implicitly assisted in the raid. The grounds for retaliatory strikes were laid by National Security Decision
Directive 138, signed by President Reagan on 3 April
1984 (Celmer 1987, 3). This intervention is referred to
as LIBYA. By including REAGAN LAWS and LIBYA, we
can distinguish the relative effectiveness, if any, of
words and deeds.

## EMPIRICAL RESULTS

In constructing the three statistical models, we emphasized three criteria: (1) the included time series
must contain sufficient observations in each quarter
to permit the use of count data; (2) all overlap among
series within the same model must be purged; and (3)
the reported models must provide information not
contained in the other models. To accomplish the first
criterion, we combined time series; thus, hostage
events *not occurring* as skyjackings were added together. Kidnappings and barricade events were consequently summed in a series denoted by *hostage*. The
three types of skyjackings were combined each quarter into a series named *skyjackings*. In addition, all
non-resource-using terrorist acts (i.e., threats and
hoaxes) were summed into a time series called *threats*.
Attacks against U.S. and British interests, not involving protected persons, were denoted as *US, UK
attacks*. Finally, each model contained a time series for
other attacks that did not occur in one of the highlighted modes. The second criterion was satisfied by
systematically assigning any overlap to a single series.

## Model 1

Model 1 was designed to focus on hostage-taking
events, crimes against protected individuals, and
other types of events. Any hostage incident directed
against protected persons was included in the hostage series but purged from the protected-persons
series to avoid double counting. Since both skyjackings and hostage events were included in model
1, we tested the impact of the following interventions: METAL, EMBASSY76, EMBASSY85, EMBASSY86, and
LIBYA.

A lag length of two quarters best characterized the
four series. The chi-squared statistic for the restriction
that all coefficients on lags greater than four (greater
than two) were equal to zero had a significance level
of .675 (.667).

Table 1 reports the variance decompositions for
model 1 for three different forecasting horizons (4, 8,
and 24 quarters). The left-hand side of the table uses
the ordering consisting of skyjackings → hostage →
protected persons → other, and the right-hand, the
reverse ordering. Although each series explains the
preponderance of its own forecast error variance for
either ordering, there are important linkages between
the skyjackings and protected-persons series. With
the ordering skyjackings-prior-to-protected-persons,
innovations in skyjackings explain about 17% of the
forecast error variance in the protected-persons series, while innovations in the latter explain about 6%
of the forecast error variance in skyjackings. With the
reverse ordering, innovations in skyjackings explain
about 4% of the forecast error variance of protected
persons, while innovations in the latter explain about
15% of the forecast error variance in skyjackings. The
ordering is important, since the correlation coefficient
between the errors is .314; clearly, the two series
exhibit important comovements.

Although F-tests do not imply Granger-causality
between skyjackings and protected-persons series,
the variance decompositions imply that the two series
do tend to move together. The straightforward implication is that policy interventions affecting one of the
series have had effects on the other. Besides these
two series, we did not find any strong interrelationships among series in model 1. Imposing the zero
restriction of the causality tests, we reestimated the
equations using SUR. Specifically, we allowed each
series to depend on a constant, three seasonal dummy
variables, its own lagged values, and the four interventions. In addition, the protected-persons series was
allowed to depend on lagged values of skyjackings,
and the skyjackings series was allowed to depend on
lagged values of the protected-persons series.

In Table 2, we list the coefficients of the four
interventions resulting from the SUR model. On
impact, metal detectors decreased skyjackings by 12.2
events per quarter, a result that agrees with other
studies (e.g., Cauley and Im 1988). As predicted from
a choice-theoretic framework, raising the costs of a
skyjacking by introducing metal detectors reduced
skyjackings but increased other types of hostage

American Political Science Review

Vol. 87, No. 4

**TABLE 1**

Variance Decomposition for Model 1: Percentage of Forecast Error Variance at 4-, 8-, and 24-Quarter Forecast Horizons

| ATTACK MODES AND FORECAST HORIZONS | ORDERING FOR TIME SERIES | | | | REVERSE ORDERING FOR TIME SERIES | | | |
|---|---|---|---|---|---|---|---|---|
| | SKY-JACKINGS | HOSTAGE | PROTECTED PERSONS | OTHER | OTHER | PROTECTED PERSONS | HOSTAGE | SKY-JACKINGS |
| Skyjackings | | | | | | | | |
| 4-qu | 93.3 | 1.47 | 4.87 | .332 | 1.10 | 14.8 | 1.93 | 82.2 |
| 8-qu | 92.3 | 1.51 | 5.67 | .478 | 1.32 | 15.5 | 1.97 | 81.2 |
| 24-qu | 92.3 | 1.51 | 5.67 | .479 | 1.32 | 15.5 | 1.97 | 81.2 |
| | (.156) | (.734) | (.132) | (.911) | (.911) | (.132) | (.734) | (.156) |
| Hostage | | | | | | | | |
| 4-qu | 6.13 | 92.2 | .315 | 1.31 | 3.71 | .460 | 91.2 | 4.64 |
| 8-qu | 6.40 | 91.1 | .879 | 1.60 | 4.12 | .695 | 90.1 | 5.06 |
| 24-qu | 6.42 | 91.1 | .897 | 1.61 | 4.13 | .721 | 90.1 | 5.07 |
| | (.123) | (.028) | (.948) | (.495) | (.495) | (.948) | (.028) | (.123) |
| Protected Persons | | | | | | | | |
| 4-qu | 16.4 | 1.89 | 78.1 | 3.53 | 6.11 | 88.9 | 1.40 | 3.59 |
| 8-qu | 17.1 | 1.88 | 77.5 | 3.61 | 6.14 | 88.3 | 1.39 | 4.21 |
| 24-qu | 17.1 | 1.88 | 77.5 | 3.61 | 6.15 | 88.3 | 1.39 | 4.21 |
| | (.191) | (.439) | (.098) | (.436) | (.436) | (.098) | (.439) | (.191) |
| Other | | | | | | | | |
| 4-qu | 2.32 | 7.81 | 3.56 | 86.3 | 91.2 | 3.68 | 4.03 | 1.12 |
| 8-qu | 2.90 | 7.84 | 3.57 | 85.7 | 90.5 | 3.74 | 4.13 | 1.60 |
| 24-qu | 2.91 | 7.83 | 3.58 | 85.7 | 90.5 | 3.75 | 4.13 | 1.60 |
| | (.677) | (.307) | (.173) | (.005) | (.005) | (.173) | (.307) | (.677) |

*Note*: The numbers in parentheses are the significance levels for the joint hypothesis that all lagged coefficients of the variable in question can be set equal to zero. Quarters are denoted "qu." The underlying data are from ITERATE 2 and 3, and are quarterly observations from 1968:1 to 1988:4.

events. On impact, we estimated that installation of metal detectors led to a significant increase in other kinds of hostage incidents by 3.68 incidents per quarter.

A salient feature of our VAR approach is the finding that metal detectors affected protected persons even though the immediate impact effect of metal detectors on protected persons has a t-statistic of .015. Since the installation of metal detectors reduced skyjackings and since skyjackings affected protected persons, metal detectors indirectly affected the latter. The direct-impact effects alone do not suffice to indicate the effectiveness of the interventions; in a dynamic system, the immediate-impact and long-run effects of the policy actions can be quite different. The lower portion of Table 2 presents the long-run effects of the interventions. An interesting result is that the long-run effect of metal detectors is estimated to reduce protected persons attacks by 4.53 incidents per quarter, even though the immediate impact is .032 incidents. This enhanced long-run effect derives from the interrelationship among the series and from the eventual application of metal detectors to secure protected persons at embassies and military bases.

Three of the four series and the effects from the interventions for model 1 are displayed in Figures 1–3, with incidents per quarter on the vertical axis. The time paths labeled "predicted" are historical effects of the interventions, obtained from the moving average representation of the model. The predicted series are *not* one-step-ahead forecasts. Rather, they are the projections of the $y_i(t)$ series conditioned on the interventions alone; the one-step-ahead forecasts track the actual values quite closely. In Figure 1, the skyjacking series displays a sharp drop with the introduction of metal detectors in 1973; the drop is immediate in that the immediate-impact and long-run effects are quite close (−12.2 and −13.7 incidents per quarter, respectively). The indirect effects of metal detectors on the protected persons series can be seen in Figure 2 where it appears that the effects of metal detectors on protected persons converge to its final level in approximately four quarters. At the same time, other kinds of hostage events steadily increased until 1974 and then remained at this elevated level, as shown in Figure 3. These time paths are consistent with the hypothesis that metal detectors made it more costly for terrorist groups to execute a skyjacking successfully. In consequence, terrorist groups substituted away from skyjackings and complementary events involving protected persons and into other kinds of hostage incidents.

The other major finding in Table 2 is that the Libyan retaliatory bombing led to *increased* bombings and related incidents. Unlike the other interventions, the Libyan raid was modeled as a temporary impact. This raid significantly increased other incidents by

| TABLE 2 | | | | |
| --- | --- | --- | --- | --- |
| **Coefficients and Significance Levels of the Impacts Effects of Model 1** | | | | |
| ANTITERRORISM POLICIES | SKYJACKINGS | HOSTAGE | PROTECTED PERSONS | OTHER |
| **Temporary Effects** | | | | |
| METAL | −12.2** | 3.68* | .032 | 12.2 |
| | (2.06) | (1.62) | (2.08) | (9.91) |
| EMBASSY76 | 2.05 | −.441 | −1.53 | 1.73 |
| | (1.25) | (1.24) | (1.26) | (7.12) |
| EMBASSY85 | −1.72 | 1.39 | .935 | −1.48 |
| | (1.41) | (1.48) | (1.42) | (8.13) |
| LIBYA | −3.81 | 1.28 | 1.60 | 107.4** |
| | (4.28) | (4.27) | (4.34) | (24.84) |
| **Long-Run Impact Effects** | | | | |
| METAL | −13.7[a] | 2.51[a] | −4.53[a] | 18.2 |
| EMBASSY76 | 2.32 | −.80 | .40 | 4.1 |
| EMBASSY85 | −2.19 | 2.1 | .54 | −1.3 |
| LIBYA[b] | NA | NA | NA | NA |

*Note:* Standard errors are given in parentheses. The coefficients are unstandardized regression coefficients.
*$p \le .10$.
**$p \le .05$.
[a]Denotes a significant long-run impact effect or that the impact effect was significant through its effects on an important explanatory variable in the VAR analysis.
[b]All effects of LIBYA are temporary effects. NA Denotes not applicable.

107.4 events during the second quarter of 1986. The autoregressive nature of the system implies some persistence of this induced increase in bombings and other events. Clearly, the increase in terrorist attacks was an unintended consequence of the raid.

There appear to be only weak effects resulting from the other interventions. Neither of the embassy security measures in 1976 or 1985 had a significant influence at conventional levels. Since EMBASSY85 and

EMBASSY86 occurred so closely in time, each was included in the estimations separately. Table 2 reports results using EMBASSY85; similar results hold using EMBASSY86.

## Model 2

Model 2 included five series: skyjackings, assassinations, hostage, threats, and "other." This model was

| FIGURE 1 |
| --- |
| **Actual and Predicted Skyjackings (Model 1: 1970:1–88:4)** |

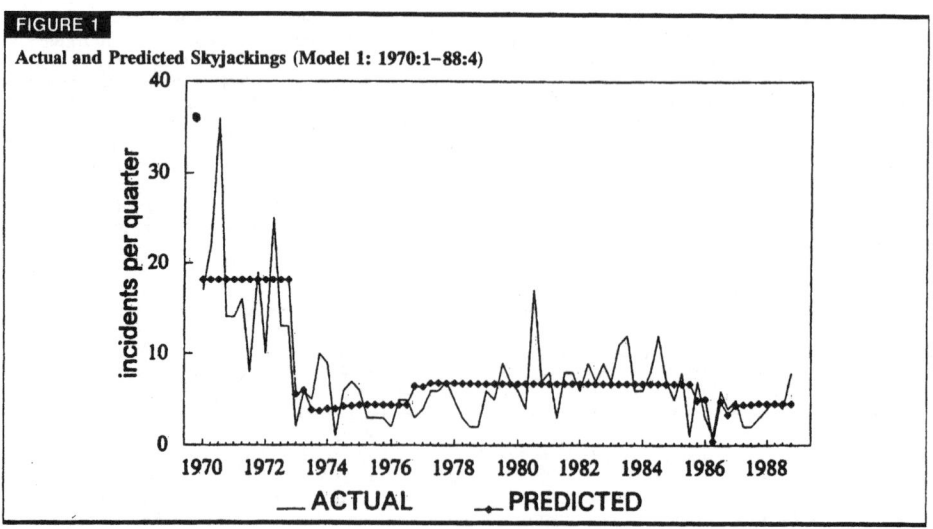

American Political Science Review                                                                Vol. 87, No. 4

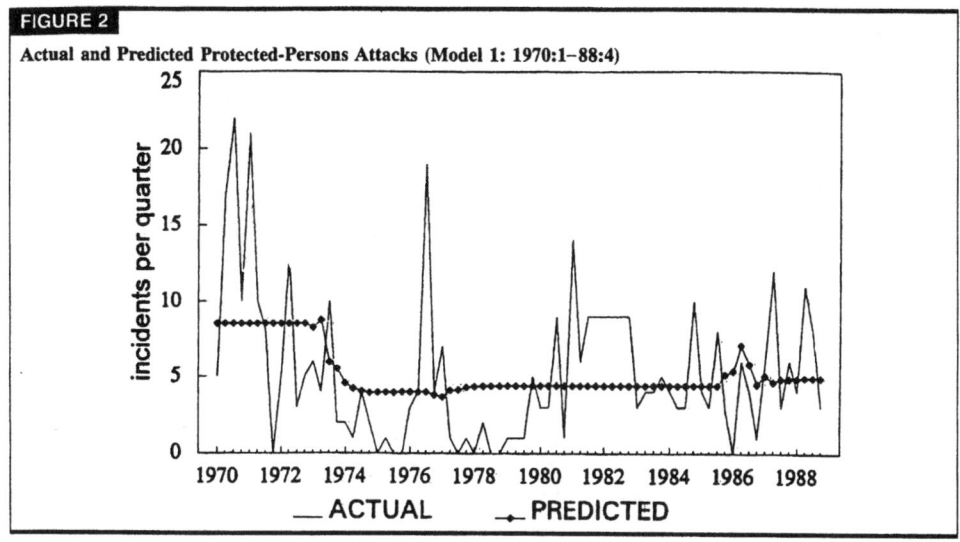

FIGURE 2

Actual and Predicted Protected-Persons Attacks (Model 1: 1970:1–88:4)

designed to consider a richer set of targets than model 1. Most important, we distinguished between non-resource-using threats and resource-using events. Although costly for governments to police, threats are relatively inexpensive incidents for terrorists to instigate. In addition, the assassination series was included to ascertain whether the hardening of targets may have led to more killings as protected individuals left more-secure grounds. This run tested the effects of the same interventions as those of model 1. As before, we estimated the model with four interventions viewing EMBASSY85 and EMBASSY86 as alternative interventions.

In contrast to model 1, the chi-squared statistic indicated that a lag length of four quarters was appropriate. The chi-squared statistic that all coefficients on lags greater than four (greater than two) were equal to zero had a significance level of .999 (.028).

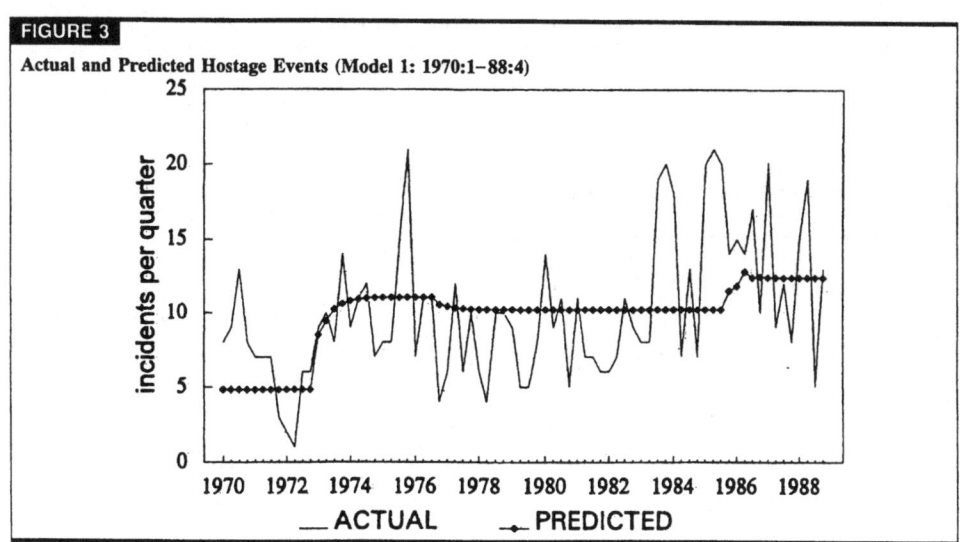

FIGURE 3

Actual and Predicted Hostage Events (Model 1: 1970:1–88:4)

### TABLE 3

**Variance Decomposition for Model 2: Percentage of Forecast Error Variance at 4-, 8-, and 24-Quarter Forecast Horizons**

| ATTACK MODES AND FORECAST HORIZONS | ORDERING FOR TIME SERIES | | | | | REVERSE ORDERING FOR TIME SERIES | | | | |
|---|---|---|---|---|---|---|---|---|---|---|
| | SKY-JACK-INGS | HOSTAGE | ASSASSI-NATIONS | THREATS | OTHER | OTHER | THREATS | ASSASSI-NATIONS | HOSTAGE | SKY-JACK-INGS |
| **Skyjackings** | | | | | | | | | | |
| 4-qu | 90.7 | 1.38 | 4.67 | 1.56 | 1.71 | 2.29 | 15.9 | 8.44 | 2.28 | 78.4 |
| 8-qu | 85.2 | 4.90 | 5.38 | 2.54 | 2.00 | 2.45 | 16.0 | 9.07 | 6.14 | 66.4 |
| 24-qu | 84.4 | 5.05 | 5.54 | 2.62 | 2.37 | 2.85 | 16.3 | 9.09 | 6.26 | 65.5 |
| | (.726) | (.305) | (.147) | (.915) | (.706) | (.706) | (.915) | (.147) | (.305) | (.725) |
| **Hostage** | | | | | | | | | | |
| 4-qu | 8.62 | 77.5 | .377 | 1.15 | 12.3 | 11.7 | 6.11 | 2.41 | 75.7 | 4.11 |
| 8-qu | 13.9 | 68.7 | .620 | 1.20 | 15.8 | 15.4 | 7.08 | 2.62 | 67.2 | 7.72 |
| 24-qu | 14.1 | 67.9 | .927 | 1.20 | 15.9 | 16.1 | 7.02 | 2.84 | 66.2 | 7.84 |
| | (.279) | (.554) | (.692) | (.259) | (.242) | (.242) | (.259) | (.692) | (.554) | (.279) |
| **Assassinations** | | | | | | | | | | |
| 4-qu | 6.00 | 8.16 | 78.5 | .502 | 6.84 | 12.9 | 5.51 | 74.1 | 7.18 | 1.67 |
| 8-qu | 13.1 | 6.85 | 61.0 | .564 | 18.5 | 27.0 | 10.4 | 52.4 | 6.39 | 3.77 |
| 24-qu | 14.1 | 6.87 | 59.8 | .761 | 18.4 | 27.2 | 10.5 | 51.5 | 6.57 | 4.15 |
| | (.809) | (.235) | (.006) | (.159) | (.207) | (.207) | (.159) | (.006) | (.235) | (.809) |
| **Threats** | | | | | | | | | | |
| 4-qu | 30.4 | 8.93 | 10.1 | 42.9 | 8.36 | 14.6 | 65.0 | 5.37 | 7.65 | 7.41 |
| 8-qu | 34.4 | 7.97 | 11.4 | 35.7 | 10.5 | 17.4 | 57.1 | 7.71 | 8.93 | 8.82 |
| 24-qu | 35.8 | 8.05 | 11.3 | 34.7 | 10.2 | 16.8 | 56.5 | 8.35 | 9.12 | 9.20 |
| | (.125) | (.049) | (.030) | (.000) | (.170) | (.170) | (.000) | (.030) | (.049) | (.125) |
| **Other** | | | | | | | | | | |
| 4-qu | 2.74 | 2.38 | 10.5 | 9.08 | 75.2 | 91.5 | 4.91 | 1.29 | 1.56 | .702 |
| 8-qu | 4.97 | 3.34 | 10.5 | 9.33 | 71.9 | 86.8 | 7.24 | 1.99 | 2.76 | 1.15 |
| 24-qu | 6.84 | 3.39 | 10.7 | 9.47 | 69.6 | 84.3 | 8.41 | 2.69 | 2.94 | 1.70 |
| | (.823) | (.731) | (.804) | (.277) | (.211) | (.211) | (.277) | (.804) | (.731) | (.823) |

*Note*: The numbers in parentheses are the significance levels for the joint hypothesis that all lagged coefficients of the variable in question can be set equal to zero. Quarters are denoted by "qu." The underlying data are ITERATE 2 and 3 and are quarterly observations from 1968:1 to 1988:4.

The variance decompositions for model 2 are reported in Table 3. The left-hand half shows the decomposition using the ordering skyjackings → hostage → assassinations → threat → other, and the right-hand half the reversed ordering. Although each incident type explains a large portion of its own forecast error variance, there is a complex set of interactions between series. The threats series is associated with all of the other series: depending on the ordering, the other four series explain as much as 65% of the forecast error variance of threat. The ordering is particularly important for the skyjackings and threat series; the correlation coefficient between the residuals of the two series in the first ordering is .382, implying that these two series move strongly together.

The information obtained from the variance decompositions was used to impose the zero restrictions and to test the impacts of the interventions. Specifically, each equation contained a constant, the three seasonal dummies, four interventions, and its own lags 1–4. The skyjackings equation also contained four lags of threats, and the threats series contained four lags of all of the other series. Using Granger-causality test results, the skyjackings and other series were allowed to affect the hostage and assassination series. Also, we allowed the other series to be affected by assassinations. The richness of the interactions is such that an intervention affecting assassinations may ultimately affect all of the other incident types.

As shown in Table 4, the results of model 2 yield several new insights. Much of the increased terrorism generated by the Libyan raid augmented non-resource-using threats: nearly half of the terrorist reaction took the form of words, not deeds. This is not to say that threats are not disruptive, since citizens and governments may feel obliged to commit real resources in response to a threat or hoax. Tourists may alter travel plans, involving sizable revenue losses for a nation's tourist industry, and firms may alter plans for direct foreign investment. Terrorists lashed back at the raid with relatively low-cost incidents (threats and bombings) in the hopes of imposing sizable costs on others. The estimated impact and long-run effects of metal detectors on skyjackings is nearly that of model 1. However, we now find a larger substitution into other hostage events and assassinations. Metal

**TABLE 4**

Coefficients and Signficance Levels of the Impact Effects of Model 2

| ANTITERRORISM POLICIES | SKYJACKINGS | HOSTAGE | ASSASSINATIONS | THREATS | OTHER |
|---|---|---|---|---|---|
| Temporary Effects | | | | | |
| METAL | −14.1** | 11.6** | 6.58* | 1.75 | 11.3 |
| | (2.52) | (3.10) | (2.96) | (3.03) | (9.74) |
| EMBASSY76 | 2.51* | −1.41 | 3.56* | 8.67** | −18.6* |
| | (1.37) | (1.26) | (1.89) | (1.98) | (9.81) |
| EMBASSY85 | .100 | 3.54* | −.967 | −5.31* | −2.81 |
| | (2.44) | (1.57) | (1.438) | (2.51) | (6.88) |
| LIBYA | −4.83 | −1.62 | 1.57 | 50.5** | 58.4* |
| | (4.56) | (4.20) | (4.39) | (4.78) | (22.51) |
| | | | | | |
| Long-Run Impact Effects | | | | | |
| METAL | −13.0[a] | 5.3[a] | 4.1[a] | −9.5[a] | 17.8[a] |
| EMBASSY76 | .98[a] | −.20[a] | 8.2[a] | 11.8[a] | −21.1[a] |
| EMBASSY85 | −.52[a] | 5.4[a] | −1.7 | 4.1[a] | −5.4 |
| LIBYA[b] | NA | NA | NA | NA | NA |

Note: Standard errors are in parentheses. The coefficients are unstandardized regression coefficients.
*$p \leq .10$.
**$p \leq .05$.
[a]Denotes a significant long-run impact effect or that the impact effect was significant through its effects on an important explanatory variable in the VAR analysis.
[b]All effects of LIBYA are temporary effects.

detectors did not have a negative impact on the hostage series, since this series included mostly kidnappings and very few barricade missions. The long-run effect on threats was estimated to decline by over nine incidents per quarter. Since many threats involved planes and embassies, which were made more secure by metal detectors, these threats may have declined as they became less credible: terrorists may have substituted deeds for words owing to metal detectors.

Model 2 is noteworthy, since the two embassy fortifications have significant impact effects. EMBASSY76 has the impact of increasing threats by over eight incidents per quarter. There is only weak evidence that EMBASSY76 affected the other series: at the .10 level for a one-tailed test, EMBASSY76 increased skyjackings and assassinations, while it decreased other events. The impact and long-run effect of EMBASSY76 on assassinations are especially interesting, since they suggest that protected individuals were more prone to assassinations when leaving secured grounds. Since threats require few inputs, these events can increase without necessitating substitution out of other events. EMBASSY85 is estimated to have increased hostage events at the expense of threats. After the late 1970s, hostage events consisted *almost entirely* of kidnappings; hence, it is not surprising that EMBASSY85 led to substitution into hostage events. On impact, hostage events rose by 3.54 incidents per quarter. In the long run, hostage events gradually increased to 5.4 additional incidents per quarter.

The predicted functions depicted in Figures 4–5 show the dynamic impacts of all of the interventions. For brevity, we reproduce the predicted functions for assassinations and threats only. In Figure 4, metal detectors in 1973 caused a rise in assassinations that was large and then permanently reinforced by EMBASSY76. In Figure 5, metal detectors induced a long-run decline in threats, while EMBASSY76 led to a short-run and long-run increase in threats. The Libyan raid in 1986 created a sharp rise in threats that declined over the next two years. Metal detectors, EMBASSY76, and the Libyan raid had some very costly unintended consequences.

## Model 3

Model 3 was designed to focus on the United States. Three series were included: attacks against protected persons, attacks against U.S. and British interests not involving protected persons *(US, UK attacks)*, and other attacks. The protected-persons series is more inclusive than that of model 1, since hostage missions were not purged. American and British attacks were combined because these countries cooperated in the Libyan raid. Moreover, both nations have maintained similar stances toward terrorism. On 17 July 1986, the U.S. Senate ratified, by a vote of 87 to 10, an extradition treaty with Britain, making it easier for British authorities to obtain custody of Irish Republican Army members seeking political asylum in the United States (Mickolus, Sandler, and Murdock 1989, vol. 2, 430). Such treaties are unusual. Five policy impacts were tested in model 3: METAL, EMBASSY76, EMBASSY86, REAGAN LAWS, and LIBYA.

Unlike the other models, one of the series in model 3 was found to be nonstationary. Using undifferenced data, the predicted function for the other series appeared nearly linear, and the sum of the coeffi-

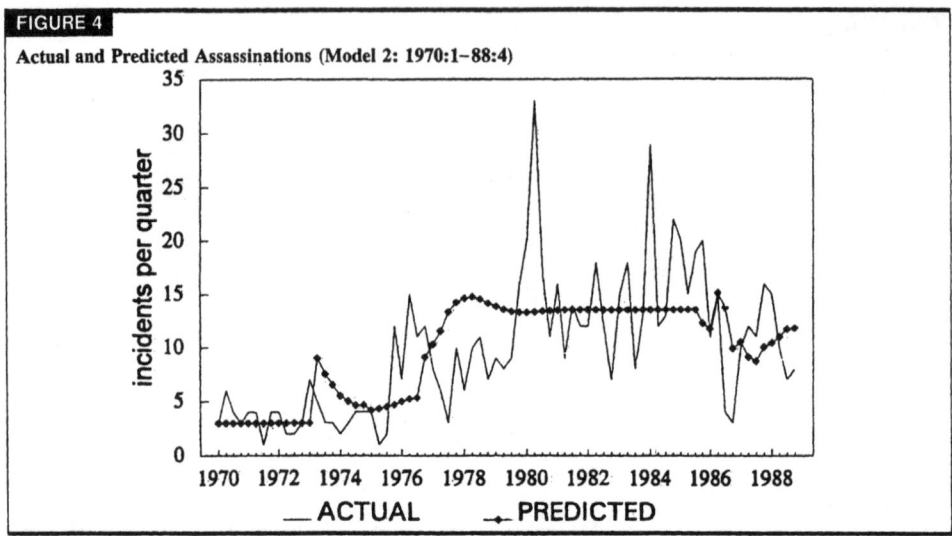

FIGURE 4

**Actual and Predicted Assassinations (Model 2: 1970:1–88:4)**

__ ACTUAL        _._ PREDICTED

cients on "own" lags was nearly unity. With an augmented Dickey–Fuller test, we were not able to reject a null of nonstationarity. We reestimated the equations using the first-difference of the other series (called *other differenced*). Based on the mean-square error, we selected the specification in which the interventions affected the level, not the slope, of the other events series.

The discussion refers to the estimation using first-differences of the other event series. A lag length of two quarters was selected, because the chi-squared statistics for lag lengths of four and two quarters were significant at the .215 and .815 levels, respectively. Decompositions are reported for the ordering consisting of *protected persons→US, UK attacks→other* and for its reverse ordering. In Table 5, attacks against the United States and the British explain about 77% of their own forecast error variance. It is particularly

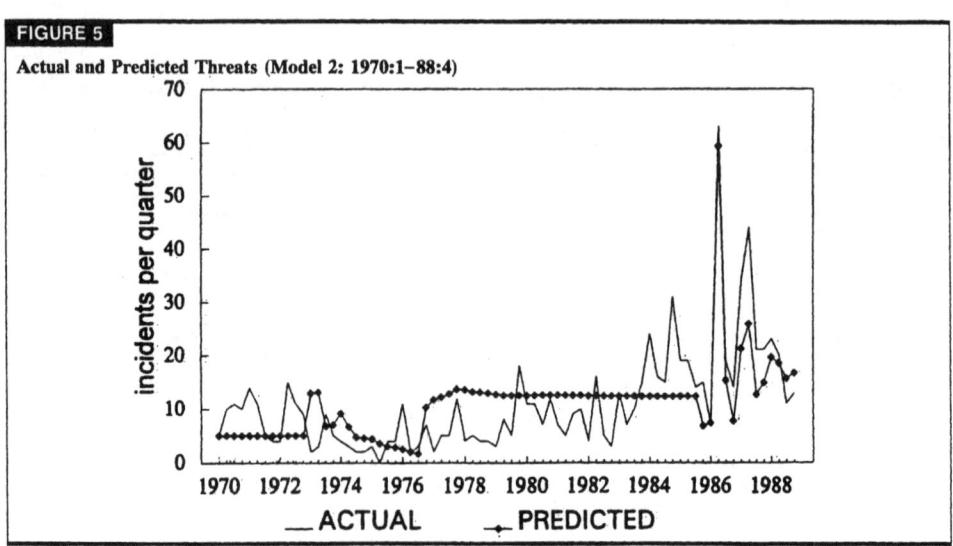

FIGURE 5

**Actual and Predicted Threats (Model 2: 1970:1–88:4)**

__ ACTUAL        _._ PREDICTED

American Political Science Review                                    Vol. 87, No. 4

**TABLE 5**

**Variance Decomposition for Model 3: Percentage of Forecast Error Variance 4-, 8-, and 24-Quarter Forecast Horizons**

| ATTACK MODES AND FORECAST HORIZONS | ORDERING FOR TIME SERIES | | | REVERSE ORDERING FOR TIME SERIES | | |
|---|---|---|---|---|---|---|
| | PROTECTED PERSONS | US, UK ATTACKS | OTHER (DIFFERENCED) | OTHER (DIFFERENCED) | US, UK ATTACKS | PROTECTED PERSONS |
| Protected Persons | | | | | | |
| 4-qu | 97.8 | 1.56 | .681 | .988 | 5.67 | 93.3 |
| 8-qu | 97.7 | 1.61 | .667 | .969 | 5.55 | 93.5 |
| 24-qu | 97.7 | 1.62 | .667 | .969 | 5.55 | 93.5 |
| | (.000) | (.564) | (.583) | (.583) | (.564) | (.000) |
| US, UK Attacks | | | | | | |
| 4-qu | 20.2 | 77.1 | 2.75 | 6.05 | 77.7 | 16.3 |
| 8-qu | 22.1 | 75.2 | 2.69 | 6.01 | 77.1 | 16.9 |
| 24-qu | 22.1 | 75.2 | 2.69 | 6.00 | 77.0 | 17.0 |
| | (.004) | (.342) | (.130) | (.130) | (.342) | (.004) |
| Other (Differenced) | | | | | | |
| 4-qu | 1.70 | 8.57 | 89.7 | 95.7 | 1.34 | 2.93 |
| 8-qu | 1.70 | 8.57 | 89.7 | 95.7 | 1.34 | 2.93 |
| 24-qu | 1.70 | 8.57 | 89.7 | 95.7 | 1.34 | 2.93 |
| | (.279) | (.248) | (.266) | (.266) | (.248) | (.279) |

*Note:* The numbers in parentheses are the significance levels for the joint hypothesis that all lagged coefficients of the variable in question can be set equal to zero. Quarters are denoted by "qu." The underlying data are from ITERATE 2 and 3 and are quarterly observations from 1968:1 to 1988:4.

noteworthy that regardless of the ordering, protected-persons attacks explain a sizable proportion of the forecast error variance of *US, UK attacks.* Since the protected-persons series included numerous attacks against U.S. and British protected persons, the interrelationship between the two series is not unexpected. Moreover, the protected-persons series Granger-causes *US, UK attacks* at the .004 level; the correlation coefficient between the residuals in the protected-persons and *US, UK attacks* equations is .269.

Using the decompositions to impose the zero-restrictions, we reestimated each equation with SUR. Each equation in the reestimation contained a constant, three seasonal dummy variables, the five interventions, and two "own-lags." The other (differenced) series used the first-differences of its own lags and the first-differences of the five interventions. Granger-causality tests indicated that the *US, UK attacks* equation contained two lags of the protected-person series.

The impacts of the five policies are reported in Table 6. In model 3, metal detectors did not appear to affect the total number of incidents directed at the United States and the United Kingdom. Given the previous significant effects of metal detectors, it is apparent that there were substitutions between the types of incidents directed at the two nations. Metal detectors did have a significant negative impact on the first-difference of other events not involving either protected persons or U.S. and British interests. The most important result from this model concerns the impact of EMBASSY76. By disaggregating attacks into those specifically directed toward the United

**TABLE 6**

**Coefficients and Significance Levels of the Impact Effects of Model 3**

| ANTI-TERRORISM POLICIES | PROTECTED PERSONS | US, UK ATTACKS | OTHER (DIFFERENCED)[a] |
|---|---|---|---|
| Temporary Effects | | | |
| METAL | −2.09 | 3.83 | −99.8** |
| | (1.80) | (4.49) | (23.01) |
| EMBASSY76 | −.934 | −12.8** | −63.4** |
| | (1.45) | (3.90) | (20.77) |
| REAGAN LAWS | .124 | −.095 | −15.8 |
| | (1.93) | (4.63) | (20.97) |
| EMBASSY86 | .897 | −5.13 | −22.5 |
| | (2.34) | (5.67) | (21.49) |
| LIBYA | 3.37 | 62.0** | 29.8* |
| | (5.08) | (12.20) | (15.40) |
| | | | |
| Long-Run Impact Effects | | | |
| METAL | −3.3 | .10 | −73[b] |
| EMBASSY76 | 2.3 | −15.7[b] | −32[b] |
| REAGAN LAWS | .13 | −.20 | −7 |
| EMBASSY86 | 1.89 | −3.8 | −11 |
| LIBYA[c] | NA | NA | NA |

*Note:* Standard errors are given in parentheses. The coefficients are unstandardized regression coefficients.
*$p \le .10$.
**$p \le .05$.
[a]All impact effects are permanent effects. The impacts shown are changes in the level of "other."
[b]Denotes a significant long-run impact effect or that the impact effect was significant through its effects on an important explanatory variable in the VAR analysis.
[c]All effects of LIBYA are temporary effects.

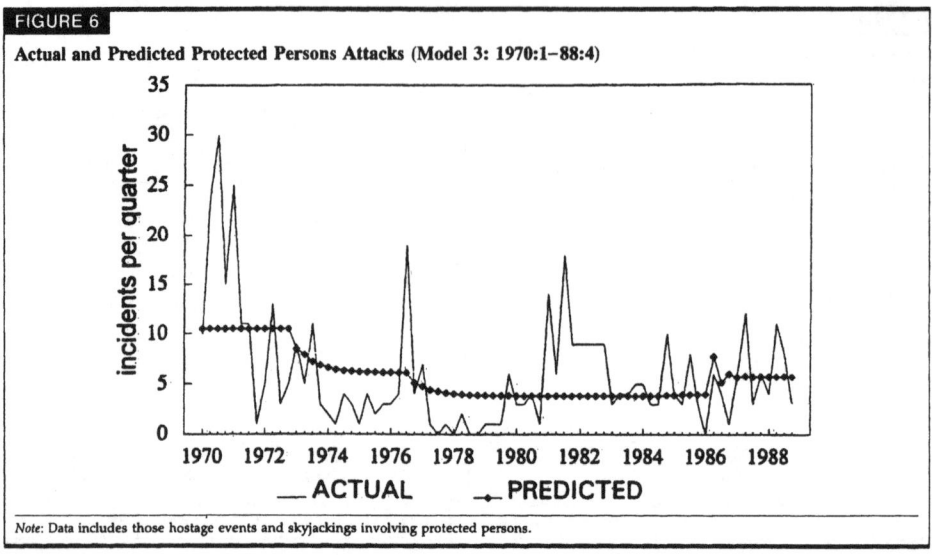

**FIGURE 6**

**Actual and Predicted Protected Persons Attacks (Model 3: 1970:1–88:4)**

*Note*: Data includes those hostage events and skyjackings involving protected persons.

States and Britain, we find that EMBASSY76 played an important role. Inasmuch as EMBASSY76 involved fortifying U.S. embassies, this disaggregation displays the impact of EMBASSY76 better than the first two runs. Previous studies (e.g., Cauley and Im 1988) never disaggregated attacks and had disappointing findings. On impact, EMBASSY76 reduced *US, UK attacks* by nearly 13 incidents per quarter; in the long run, EMBASSY76 reduced these attacks by nearly 16 incidents per quarter. This model, however, could not show the substitution into other kinds of attacks like assassinations.

The Libyan raid increased attacks on both U.S. and British interests and on other nations, but two-thirds of the increase was directed at the two nations participating directly or indirectly in the raid. Neither EMBASSY86 nor REAGAN LAWS had any significant impact. Apparently U.S. domestic laws geared to deter transnational terrorism did not work as intended. In Figure 6, the predicted function for protected persons appears to decline gradually from 1973 to the late 1970s. Both metal detectors and EMBASSY76 added to this decline, while the Libyan raid reversed the trend.

## CONCLUSION

If governments are to succeed in the efficient allocation of resources among competing means to thwart transnational terrorism, then governments must be able to calculate the impact of alternative passive and active responses. We put forth a methodology for evaluating antiterrorism policies. Our procedure

combines VAR modeling with intervention analysis and identifies each policy's quarterly impact, while accounting for the significant interrelationships among the time series for each model. These interrelationships were ignored by previous studies that examined the impact of one or more policies on a *single* time series at a time (Brophy-Baermann and Conybeare n.d.; Cauley and Im 1988; Landes 1978). In consequence, the earlier methodologies worked best in instances where little or no interaction characterized the series. The VAR–intervention procedure is best for forecasting future terrorist trends and campaigns. In particular, the technique can identify terrorist tactics that are either substitutes or complements for one another.

The following conclusions are drawn from our study:

1. The Libyan raid caused a number of different terrorist tactics to increase. A small portion of this increase spilled over to nations not involved in the retaliatory strike. Over half of the temporary increase in terrorism took the form of non-resource-using incidents.
2. Fortification of U.S. embassies and missions in 1976 reduced attacks against U.S. interests but resulted in a substitution into assassinations.
3. Metal detectors decreased skyjackings and threats but increased assassinations and other kinds of hostage incidents not protected by the detectors.
4. If governments are to evaluate a policy correctly, substitutions and complementarities must be accounted for, along with indirect effects resulting from interactions between series. For example, the

American Political Science Review                                Vol. 87, No. 4

benefits from metal detectors cannot be adequately measured by the value placed on a reduced number of skyjackings, since other events (e.g., crimes against protected persons) were affected indirectly.

5. The identification of substitutes and complements is sensitive to VAR interactions.

6. In this study, all series showed some interrelationship. The finer the disaggregation, the greater the interaction.

A number of policy insights can be drawn. First, the unintended consequences of an antiterrorism policy may be far more costly than intended consequences, and must be anticipated. In the case of metal detectors, kidnappings increased; in the case of embassy fortification, assassinations became more frequent. Protected persons may have faced more life-threatening attacks owing to security measures. By cutting down on threats, metal detectors may have induced terrorists to substitute deeds for crimes. Second, piecemeal policy, in which a single attack mode is considered when designing antiterrorism action, is inadequate. This follows because the various attack modes are interrelated through substitutability and complementarity. Third, the retaliatory raid on Libya appeared to increase terrorism in the near term, but did not have a significant long-run impact, good or bad. Fourth, U.S. domestic laws, instituted in 1984 to thwart terrorism, did not curb terrorist attacks against U.S. interests.

The methodology used here can be fruitfully employed elsewhere. In particular, it can assess the impact of significant terrorist events (e.g., the downing of Pan Am Flight 103 in December 1988) on tourism.

## Notes

The research for this study was funded by the National Science Foundation Grant SES-8907646. We wish to acknowledge the research assistance and helpful guidance of Jean Murdock, Gerry Parise, Barry Falk, and Jon Cauley.

1. State sponsorship of terrorism occurs when nations contract with terrorist groups to perform acts that impose costs on countries perceived as enemies by the sponsor and surrogate (Mickolus 1989).

2. Other econometric studies have investigated terrorist success in hostage-taking missions (Sandler and Scott 1987), the underlying factors behind the length of hostage negotiations (Atkinson, Sandler, and Tschirhart 1987), and cycles in terrorist events (Im, Cauley, and Sandler 1987). Empirical studies have also investigated whether terrorist incidents encourage or discourage further acts through a demonstration effect that gives rise to imitation diffusion (Hamilton and Hamilton 1983; Midlarsky, Crenshaw, and Yoshida 1980). Poe (1988) used elementary regression techniques to demonstrate the ineffectiveness of hardline policies. A more complete list of references can be found in Lichbach 1992.

3. A household production approach is assumed (see Ehrlich 1973).

4. These choice-theoretical problems are modeled in Islam and Shahin 1989 and Sandler, Tschirhart, and Cauley 1983. The reader should consult these articles for an explicit theoretical model.

5. Many of the ideas presented in this section are discussed

in Granger and Newbold 1986, chap. 7–8. Doan 1988, chap. 8 is particularly useful for the implementation of a VAR analysis.

6. Formally, for each incident type $j$ in equation system 3, we obtained the vector moving average (VMA) representation:

$$y_j(t) = c + \sum_{i=1}^{3} d_i D_i(t) + \sum_{i=1}^{n} \sum_{\tau=1}^{\infty} \Theta_{ji\tau} \varepsilon_i(t - \tau)$$

$$+ \sum_{i=1}^{K} \sum_{\tau=0}^{\infty} \gamma_{ji\tau} p_i(t - \tau) + \varepsilon_j(t),$$

where $D_i(t)$ is the value of each seasonal dummy in period $t$, while $c$, $d_i$, $\Theta_{ji\tau}$, and $\gamma_{ji\tau}$ are all parameters. Since we cannot estimate the VMA directly, we used the residuals of equation system 3 and the coefficients from the inverted VAR model. We decomposed the variance of each incident type $j$ into the percentages attributable to innovations in the other incident types, as well as the "own" innovation. Since the residuals in equation system 3 can be correlated across equations, we used the orthogonalized innovations obtained from a Choleski decomposition. Doan (1988) contains an excellent discussion of Choleski decomposition.

7. In terms of equations 1 and 2, if $\varepsilon_1(t)$ and $\varepsilon_2(t)$ are correlated, there are two possible ways to obtain "pure" shocks to each incident type. First, $\varepsilon_1(t)$ can be viewed a pure shock to incident type 1. This shock affects incident type 1 directly *and* $y_2(t)$ through the correlation between $\varepsilon_1(t)$ and $\varepsilon_2(t)$. The remainder of $\varepsilon_2(t)$ is deemed a "pure" shock to incident type 2. Alternatively, $\varepsilon_2(t)$ can be viewed a pure shock to incident type 2. This shock affects incident type 2 directly *and* $y_1(t)$ through the correlation between $\varepsilon_1(t)$ and $\varepsilon_2(t)$. The remainder of $\varepsilon_1(t)$ is deemed a "pure" shock to incident type 1. The first ordering of this Choleski decomposition implies $\varepsilon_1(t) \rightarrow \varepsilon_2(t)$ while the second implies $\varepsilon_2(t) \rightarrow \varepsilon_1(t)$.

When the innovations in the various series are contemporaneously correlated, the ordering of the variables used in the factorization can be important for the variance decomposition. In a VAR analysis, at the 5% level, a statistically significant correlation coefficient is usually taken to be about .2. In all models estimated, we placed correlated series adjacent to each other; reversing the ordering allows us to determine the importance of the alternative assumptions.

8. Denote the deseasonalized value of $y_j(t)$ by $\hat{y}_j(t)$. Formally, we set all of the innovations equal to zero and plot time path:

$$\hat{y}_j(t) = c + \sum_{i=1}^{K} \sum_{\tau=0}^{\infty} \gamma_{ji\tau} p_i(t - \tau).$$

9. Specifically, we estimated the equation

$$\Delta y_i(t) = r_0 + \rho y_i(t - 1) + \sum_{j=1}^{4} r_j \Delta y_i(t - j),$$

for each series $y_i$. A null nonstationarity can be rejected if the estimated value of $r_0$ is not significantly different from zero and $\rho$ is significantly less than zero, but greater than minus two. Tables compiled by Fuller (1976) contain the relevant test statistics. If a variable needs to be differenced, it is not clear whether the effects of the intervention on that variable also need to be differenced. For example, ignoring the constant and seasonals, two of the possible presentations of $y_i$ are

$$\Delta y_i(t) = \sum_{k} a_{ik} p_k(t) + \sum_{\ell} \sum_{j} b_{eij} \Delta y_i(t - \ell)$$

$$\Delta y_i(t) = \sum_{k} a_{ik} \Delta p_k(t) + \sum_{\ell} \sum_{j} b_{eij} \Delta y_i(t - \ell).$$

In the first equation, the interventions are assumed to have a permanent effect on the slope of incident type $y_i$. In the second specification, the interventions are assumed to have a permanent effect on the level. Imposing the first specification is straightforward; each value of $y_i(t)$ is replaced by its first difference in equation system 3. To impose the second specification, a near-VAR must be estimated. We estimated the system using both specifications. In model 3, the first specification yielded the best mean-square error for the "other-differenced" series.

10. ITERATE 2 is available through the Inter-University Consortium for Political and Social Research, University of Michigan, Ann Arbor. ITERATE 3 is available from Vinyard Software, 2243 Beacon Lane, Falls Church, VA 22043-1709. The working definition of *transnational terrorism* employed by ITERATE is the use—or threat of use—of anxiety-inducing, extranormal violence for political purposes by any individual or group, whether acting for or in opposition to established governmental authority, when such action is intended to influence the attitudes and behavior of a target group wider than the immediate victims and when, through the nature of its institutional or human victims, or through the mechanics of its resolution, its ramifications transcend national boundaries (Mickolus, Sandler, and Murdock 1989, xii).

11. See n. 10.

# References

Atkinson, Scott E., Todd Sandler, and John Tschirhart. 1987. "Terrorism in a Bargaining Framework." *Journal of Law and Economics* 30:1–21.

Brophy-Baermann, Bryan, and John A. C. Conybeare. N.d. "Retaliating against Terrorism: Rational Expectations and the Optimality of Rules versus Discretion." *American Journal of Political Science.* Forthcoming.

Cauley, Jon, and Eric I. Im. 1988. "Intervention Policy Analysis of Skyjackings and Other Terrorist Incidents." *American Economic Review* 78:27–31.

Celmer, Marc. 1987. *Terrorism, U.S. Strategy and Reagan.* Westport: Greenwood.

Doan, Thomas A. 1988. *Users Manual, RATS Version 3.00.* Evanston: VAR Econometrics.

Enders, Walter, Todd Sandler, and Jon Cauley. 1990. "U.N. Conventions, Technology and Retaliation in the Fight Against Terrorism: An Econometric Evaluation." *Terrorism and Political Violence* 2:83–105.

Ehrlich, Isaac. 1973. "Participation in Illegitimate Activities: A Theoretical and Empirical Investigation." *Journal of Political Economy* 81:521–65.

Fuller, Wayne. 1976. *Introduction to Statistical Time Series.* New York: John Wiley.

Granger, C. W. J., and Paul Newbold. 1986. *Forecasting Economic Time Series.* 2nd ed. Orlando, FL: Academic Press.

Hamilton, Lawrence C., and James D. Hamilton. 1983. "Dynamics of Terorism." *International Studies Quarterly* 27:39–54.

Harvey, A. C., and C. Fernandes. 1989. "Time Series Models for Count or Qualitative Observations." *Journal of Business and Economic Statistics* 7:407–17.

Im, Eric I., Jon Cauley, and Todd Sandler. 1987. "Cycles and Substitutions in Terrorist Activities: A Spectral Approach." *Kyklos* 40:238–55.

Islam, Muhammad Q., and Wassim N. Shahin. 1989. "Economic Methodology Applied to Political Hostage-Taking in Light of the Iran-Contra Affair." *Southern Economic Journal* 55:1019–24.

Landes, William. 1978. "An Economic Study of U.S. Aircraft Hijackings, 1961–1976." *Journal of Law and Economics* 21:1–31.

Lichbach, Mark I. 1992. "Nobody Cites Nobody Else: Mathematical Models of Domestic Political Conflict." *Defence Economics* 3:341–57.

McCleary, Richard, and Richard A. Hay. 1980. *Applied Time Series Analysis for the Social Sciences.* Beverly Hills: Sage.

Mickolus, Edward F. 1980. *Transnational Terrorism: A Chronology of Events 1968–1979.* Westport: Greenwood.

Mickolus, Edward F. 1982. *International Terrorism: Attributes of Terrorist Events, 1968–1977.* (ITERATE 2). Ann Arbor: Inter-University Consortium for Political and Social Research.

Mickolus, Edward F. 1989. "What Constitutes State Support to Terrorists?" *Terrorism and Political Violence* 1:287–93.

Mickolus, Edward F., Todd Sandler, and Jean Murdock. 1989. *International Terrorism in the 1980s: A Chronology of Events.* 2 vols. Ames: Iowa State University Press.

Mickolus, Edward F., Todd Sandler, Jean Murdock, and Peter Fleming. 1989. *International Terrorism: Attributes of Terrorist Events 1978–1987.* (ITERATE 3). Falls Church, VA: Vinyard Software.

Midlarsky, Manus I., Martha Crenshaw, and Fumihiko Yoshida. 1980. "Why Violence Spreads: The Contagion of International Terrorism." *International Studies Quarterly* 24:262–98.

Pearl, Marc A. 1987. "Terrorism-Historical Perspective on U.S. Congressional Action." *Terrorism: An International Journal* 10:139–43.

Poe, Steven. 1988. "Nations' Responses to Transnational Terrorist Hostage Events: An Empirical Evaluation." *International Interactions* 14:27–40.

Sandler, Todd, and John L. Scott. 1987. "Terrorist Success in Hostage-Taking Incidents." *Journal of Conflict Resolution* 31:35–53.

Sandler, Todd, John Tschirhart, and Jon Cauley. 1983. "A Theoretical Analysis of Transnational Terrorism." *American Political Science Review* 77:36–54.

Tovar, B. Hugh. 1986. "Active Response." In *Hydra of Carnage,* ed. Uri Ra'anan, Robert L. Pfaltzgraff Jr., Richard H. Schultz, Ernst Halperin, and Igor Lukes. Lexington, MA: Lexington Press.

United Nations. 1978. *Multilateral Treaties in Respect of Which the Secretary-General Performs Depositary Functions,* List of Signatures, Ratifications, Accessions, etc. as of 31 December 1977, No. E 78 V. 6. New York: United Nations.

Wilkinson, Paul. 1986. "Trends in International Terrorism and the American Response." In *Terrorism and International Order,* ed. Lawrence Freedman, Christopher Hill, Adam Roberts, R. J. Vincent, Paul Wilkinson, and Philip Windsor. London: Routledge & Kegan Paul.

Walter Enders is Professor of Economics and Todd Sandler is Professor of Economics and Political Science, Iowa State University, Ames, IA 50011-1070.

# Name Index